Government, Politics, Power and Policy in Australia

Government, Politics, Power and Policy in Australia

ANDREW PARKIN, JOHN SUMMERS AND DENNIS WOODWARD EDITION

8

AUSTRALIA

Pearson Education Australia
Unit 4, Level 3
14 Aquatic Drive
Frenchs Forest NSW 2086

www.pearsoned.com.au

Acquisitions Editor: Karen Hutchings
Senior Project Editor: Kathryn Fairfax
Editorial Coordinators: Laura Chapman and Jillian Gillies
Copy Editor: Janice Keynton
Cover and internal design by designBITE
Cover photograph from Photography E-Biz
Typeset by Midland Typesetters, Australia

Printed in Malaysia (CTP - CLP)

2 3 4 5 10 09 08 07

National Library of Australia
Cataloguing-in-Publication Data

Government, politics, power and policy in Australia.

8th ed.
Bibliography.
Includes index.
ISBN 1 74091 110 5.

1. Political parties - Australia. 2. Power (Social
sciences) - Australia. 3. Political planning - Australia.
4. Australia - Politics and government - 21st century.
I. Parkin, Andrew, 1952- . II. Summers, John. III. Woodward,
Dennis.

320.994

PEARSON
Longman   An imprint of Pearson Education Australia
(a division of Pearson Australia Group Pty Ltd)

Contents

Contributors

Geoff Anderson is a Lecturer in the School of Political and International Studies at Flinders University

Judith Brett is a Professor in the School of Social Sciences at La Trobe University

Brian Costar is a Professor in the Institute for Social Research at Swinburne University

Jennifer Curtin is a Lecturer in Politics at Monash University

Nick Economou is a Senior Lecturer in Politics at Monash University

Alan Fenna is a Senior Lecturer in the Department of Social Sciences at Curtin University

Michael Gilding is Professor in Sociology at Swinburne University of Technology

Gwen Gray is a Senior Lecturer in Political Science and International Relations at the Australian National University

Leonie Hardcastle is Deputy Registrar of the Faculty of Social Sciences and a casual Associate Lecturer in the School of Political and International Studies at Flinders University

Haydon Manning is a Senior Lecturer in the School of Political and International Studies at Flinders University

Andrew Parkin is a Professor in the School of Political and International Studies at Flinders University

Haig Patapan is a Senior Lecturer in the Department of Politics and Public Policy at Griffith University

Jane Robbins is a Senior Lecturer in the School of Political and International Studies at Flinders University

Jenny Stewart is an Associate Professor in the School of Business and Government at the University of Canberra

Jenny Tilby Stock is a Visiting Research Fellow in Politics at the University of Adelaide

John Summers is a Senior Lecturer in the School of Political and International Studies at Flinders University

James Walter is Professor of Political Science at Monash University

Ian Ward is a Reader in Political Science at the University of Queensland

John Warhurst is a Professor of Political Science at the Australian National University

Dennis Woodward is a Senior Lecturer in Politics at Monash University

The authors and publisher would like to thank the following academics for their very useful advice and feedback during the preparation of this 8th edition. These include:

- Jeff Archer, University of New England
- Beth Edmondson, Monash University
- Doug Hunt, James Cook University
- Robert Imre, Notre Dame University
- Greg McCarthy, University of Adelaide
- Gregory Melleuish, University of Wollongong
- Harry Savelsberg, University of South Australia
- Andrew Scott, RMIT
- Aredel Shamsullah, La Trobe University
- John Tate, University of Newcastle
- Rae Wear, University of Queensland.

The editors would like to thank Julie Tonkin and Sonja Beagley for their invaluable assistance.

Introduction to the eighth edition

Government, Politics, Power and Policy in Australia, a book that deals with political institutions, has become something of an institution in its own right. The appearance of an eighth edition of a book that first appeared in 1979 certainly attests to a durability of purpose and performance. The editors have enough faith in the judgment of their academic peers to suggest that it also attests to continuing quality and effectiveness.

Government, Politics, Power and Policy in Australia has always been distinctive within the pantheon of book-length political-science analyses of Australian government and politics. Although widely assigned in university-level courses, it has never been a conventional textbook. Students and teachers interested in simple outlines of the nuts-and-bolts of Australian politics have presumably met their needs mostly in other ways: via lecture delivery or via supplementary textbooks that take a more didactic approach.

The content of this book has instead always been analytical, discursive and interpretive. In other words, it has been *research*-oriented, in a broad and inclusive 'social science and humanities' sense of research as encompassing creative and systematic investigation that increases the stock of academic knowledge. The chapters in successive editions of *Government, Politics, Power and Policy in Australia* have reported on the latest interpretive theories and research findings within the context, as befits any research publication, of a portrayal of an accumulating corpus of scholarly knowledge. Contributing authors are scholars noted for their academic research publications, a feature that certainly continues here with the eighth edition. And the readership—as targeted and as quite evidently achieved—is much broader than a captive audience of students assigned the book by their academic teachers. It includes academic scholars who appreciate the window that the book provides on advances in the state of research-generated academic knowledge. Various chapters published in *Government, Politics, Power and Policy in Australia* have been widely cited as authoritative sources and as the starting point for continuing with intriguing lines of academic research inquiry.

It is interesting to peruse the successive editions of *Government, Politics, Power and Policy in Australia* as historical snapshots, changing over time, of how the Australian political system has been interpreted by leading scholars. The same exercise also reveals much about continuity and change within the political system itself. Some aspects of the political system continue to display their perennial characteristics: distinctive constitutional arrangements, a focus on political leaders, a constant interplay between Commonwealth and State governments, a bipolar party system remaining both reasonably stable and constantly under challenge, and elections that (in most cases) both major party aspirants have entered with some reasonable prospect of winning. But these continuities coexist with some interesting new features that would have been hard to anticipate in the late 1970s, such as the rise of environmentalism, the spectre of a public sector depleted by privatisation but in many ways stronger than ever in a regulatory sense, the avalanche of accessible governmental and political information facilitated by the Internet (with its impact on political campaigning a possible candidate for the next major development in politics), the strangely persistent focus of political debate on tax reform, new twists and turns in thinking about welfare policy, the rise followed by the apparent fall of republicanism as an influential movement, and so on.

This eighth edition can be distinguished from its seven predecessors in one important respect: the adoption of a (loose) overall theme. A chapter providing a liberal-democratic interpretation of politics was featured in the Power sections of several earlier editions. After discovering that several university lecturers had chosen to use that chapter as their recommended entrée into the book for student readers, the editors decided to follow their creative lead. Accordingly, in this edition, Chapter 1 offers—by way of an historical and interpretive argument—a liberal-democratic perspective on Australian government and politics. The chapter argues that this perspective provides a constructive and illuminating interpretive framework for virtually all aspects of the governmental and political system. Accordingly, Chapter 1 also provides a potential linking framework to connect together aspects of the other chapters in the book. This comes out, quite explicitly at times, in those subsequent chapters, though each of them has its own scholarly integrity and is intended to stand alone in its analysis of its own particular subject. And it should not necessarily be assumed that all contributors agree with all aspects of the argument put forward by the author of Chapter 1. In fact some later chapters critically address the issue of the plausibility or completeness of a liberal-democratic interpretation.

Another addition to this eighth iteration of *Government, Politics, Power and Policy in Australia* is a new chapter on political ideologies (Chapter 2). This has been included as a response to suggestions about the potential utility of such a chapter as a further framing resource for understanding politics, suggestions expressed not least at an academic workshop attended by most contributors held at Flinders University.

Beyond these important changes, the eighth edition retains the basic structure developed back in 1979 and then revamped a little for the fifth edition of 1994. Some chapters cover entirely new subjects that now seem to be appropriate inclusions; authors of some other retained chapters are newcomers to the team of contributors; other chapters retain the same authors and subjects (though thoroughly reviewed and updated) from the seventh edition. All chapters are focused on the Australian governmental and political system as it moves through the first decade of the 21st century. And all report on the latest research findings.

Part 1 is completely new, encompassing Chapters 1 and 2 as outlined above. Part 2 (Chapters 3 to 8) covers the institutional arrangements through which government operates in Australia. The relationship between those institutions and the citizens of Australia via the party system, the electoral system and the act of voting is the focus in Part 3 (Chapters 9 to 15). Part 4 (Chapters 16 to 21) examines various aspects of and interpretations about the distribution and exercise of power in Australia. Finally, Part 5 (Chapters 22 to 27) draws on all of the foregoing elements to discuss the impact of government and politics on Australian society within a number of key policy areas.

From the very first edition, the sequence of Parts and Chapters has a partic-ular rationale. It takes readers from the more familiar institutional aspects of Australian politics through to an appreciation of more abstract concepts such as power and to applications in the policy sphere. But readers are welcome to adopt a different approach, such as beginning with interesting policy issues and working backwards from there to uncover the institutional underpinnings and the linkages between citizens and authoritative institutions.

The editors thank their contributors, the contributors thank colleagues and assistants who have helped with the preparation of their individual chapters, and all of us thank the generation of readers who have made *Government, Politics, Power and Policy in Australia* the unexpected institution that it has become.

Andrew Parkin is a Professor in the School of Political and International Studies at Flinders University and Director of the Flinders Institute of Public Policy and Management. He has served as Editor of the *Australian Journal of Political Science* and as President of the Australasian Political Studies Association. His academic interests—in the Australian governmental system, business–government relations and liberal-democratic politics—are represented by his contributions to this book. He has also researched, published, consulted and taught extensively across various fields of public policy and management, including immigration and ethnic affairs policy, housing policy, intergovernmental relations and whole-of-government coordination strategies.

John Summers is a Senior Lecturer in the School of Political and International Studies at Flinders University. His academic interests relate to the institutions of government in Australia, with a particular interest in the role and operation of the Parliament, the Constitution, federalism and inter-governmental relations, and Indigenous policy.

Dr. Dennis Woodward is a Senior Lecturer in Politics in the School of Political and Social Inquiry at Monash University. He is the author of *Australia 'Unsettled': The legacy of 'Neo-liberalism'* and has published extensively on Australian party politics and political economy.

Conceptual and Constitutional Framework

PART 1

AUSTRALIA

Introduction

This first part of the book introduces the liberal-democratic framework that is intended to provide a theme connecting with most of the chapters which follow. It also introduces some ideological concepts that should also be useful for framing and understanding material in later chapters.

Chapter 1 explains what is meant by a liberal-democratic political system in which democratically accountable governmental institutions are held in check by constitutional arrangements and other practices designed to limit the capacity of government. In this chapter, Andrew Parkin describes how liberal democracy in this sense is a product of an evolutionary history that draws on both democratic and liberal ideas about government. He then argues that politics within liberal-democratic countries, like Australia, involves managing what he claims is a fundamental tension between the democratic and the liberal threads embedded within the political system. Parkin's position is that this framework is useful for understanding the rest of this book—the nature of Australia's governmental institutions, its political processes, the distribution of power and the directions of public policy.

In Chapter 2, Alan Fenna examines a number of ideologies which have been influential in Australian politics. He argues that political actors are often motivated, to a greater or lesser extent, by an ideology (a set of beliefs) which helps them to interpret and understand political events, to diagnose the nature and structure of society, and to shape their political goals. He discusses some of the variants of liberalism, conservatism, socialism, feminism and environmentalism. He also provides an account of what is meant by the broader ideological terms 'Left' and 'Right' which are often used in political discussion and analysis.

Understanding liberal-democratic politics

CHAPTER 1

ANDREW PARKIN

A *liberal democracy* is a political system in which democratically based institutions of government are constrained by liberal-inspired constitutional arrangements, political practices and popular expectations that limit the scope and capacity of the governmental sector. Understanding Australia as a liberal democracy reveals much about the nature and practice of its politics, its style of government, the exercise of power and the development of public policy. This chapter explains the meaning and significance of this understanding of Australia as a liberal democracy. It explores its ramifications for how the institutions of government are constituted, the kind of policies that governments promulgate and the distribution and exercise of power in society.

The chapter argues that the design and operation of liberal-democratic political systems like Australia's draw on two different sets of ideas.

Democratic ideas promote the notion that governments should be accountable to citizens: they should be elected by a majority of citizens in a free vote, and they should govern in the interests of the community. And the institutions of government should be designed to give the government the capacity to respond—through authoritative decisions, policies and services—to the expressed wishes of the majority of citizens.

Liberal ideas promote the notion that governments should be held in check by having only limited powers. They seek to ensure that governments, whether democratically elected by a majority of citizens or not, are significantly constrained in their capacity to override the interests of minorities, to stifle the rights of citizens, or to interfere with the freedom of individuals to shape their own lives.

Western political systems, as they have evolved, have drawn on ideas and practices derived from both the liberal and the democratic traditions. They feature a number of institutions, processes and understandings that are recognisably liberal in orientation and others that are recognisably democratic in orientation. It is the combination of these institutions, processes and understandings to form a functioning political system that we can label as a *liberal democracy*.

This chapter explains how the two sets of ideas—the liberal and the democratic—have shaped how liberal-democratic governmental institutions are designed and how they act. It also argues that the interrelationship between the two sets of ideas moulds the *politics* of liberal democracies. There is a fundamental tension between the liberal and the democratic dimensions of liberal-democratic political systems. Liberal-democratic politics involves, in large measure, a management of this tension, giving liberal-democratic politics a distinctive flavour and fluidity.

Democracy and government

The insistence that the government sector should be accountable to those it governs, via mechanisms such as regular elections, is a *democratic* feature that Australia shares with other developed countries around the world and increasingly with many developing countries as well. Democracy in this sense engages with people—the citizens of a democratic country—collectively. It is the citizenry as a whole that collectively chooses at elections which party or coalition should be the government.[1] Irrespective of whether it has won comfortably in an electoral landslide or holds office by just a narrow parliamentary majority, the focus of government is expected to be—rhetorically at least—on the interests of the whole community.

Prime Minister John Howard's victory speech on the election night of 10 October 2004, as he contemplated the beginning of a fourth term in government, is typical in the collectivist nature of its expression of a democratic government's responsibilities:

> I say to the Australian people in accepting their charge to lead the nation over the years ahead, the first thing I say is to rededicate myself and all of my colleagues to the service of the Australian people . . . We are happy, we are joyful that the verdict has been given by the Australian people but never forget the fact that governments are elected to govern not only for the people who voted for them, but also for the people who voted against them . . . I serve the Australian people and I commit myself to their service and their interests in the years ahead. (Howard 2004)

Broad community-oriented notions of governmental accountability are not just manifest in democratic elections. They also shape the kind of policy orientation that democratically elected governments project. The accountability of government to the broad community translates into an expectation that governments should provide or facilitate services to the broad community—and that, during election campaigns, rival political parties compete for majority support among voters by promoting particular policy and service mixes. Democratic governments typically accept responsibility to some degree for ensuring the adequate provision of a whole panoply of community services—from health systems to education systems, from police protection to environmental protection, from suburban roads to internationally connected postal services, from kindergartens to aged-care facilities. Governments employ many thousands of administrators, teachers, social workers, postal workers, soldiers, nurses, park rangers, police officers, sanitation engineers, librarians, traffic managers and a host of other people—all in the business of providing or overseeing services needed by the community. These employees, the agencies which employ them and the programs that they administer, operating under the authority of legislation passed by a democratically elected Parliament, constitute the *public sector*, and it is a characteristic of democratic politics that they encourage such public-sector-led activities and services.

These democratic practices and norms are so familiar to Australians that they seem commonplace. Yet, taking an historical view, democracy as we understand it today—with governments elected by all adult citizens, and being responsible for the provision of an extensive range of services to the community—is a fairly recent addition to the political panoply of advanced societies.

The *idea* of democracy, in the sense that governmental action should be directly accountable to citizens who enjoy an equality of political power, is not in itself recent. That sort of democracy emerged among (a minority of) Athenians in ancient Greece in the fifth to third centuries BC when the *demos* or body of citizens (defined as adult males) met in assembly to determine public policies (Maddox 2005: 4–9). But democracy in practice then disappeared for millennia. It took extended struggles for democratic government to re-emerge in Western countries, struggles that wrested power away from traditional sources (such as monarchs) and vested it instead in democratically representative institutions.

In Britain, whose historical experience has shaped Australia's arrangements, this was a relatively gradual process. The Parliament asserted increasing power over the monarch and, in turn, vested a Cabinet based on parliamentary support with effective executive power. Much later, the right to vote in parliamentary elections was granted to wider and wider proportions of adults, eventually reaching full adult franchise.

Australia was at the forefront of modern democratisation. '[T]he immigrant pioneers of the Australian continent', notes Maddox (2005: 45), 'were in some respects also pioneers of modern democracy in the eyes of the world . . . blazing a trail towards new methods of public organisation that would bring greater measures of power to the people'. The extension of the right to vote to, first, all adult male citizens and then, later, to all adult female citizens was achieved earlier in Australia than in Britain and most other Western democracies, and was accompanied by other innovations such as the secret ballot.[2]

The collectivist notion that is associated with democratic politics—with elected governments being accountable to broadly conceived constituencies or communities—is taken even further by some political groupings within democratic societies. As Fenna explains in Chapter 2, there is a democratic *socialist* strand of politics which elevates community-oriented collectivism to the highest political priority. Democratic socialists promote the idea that the democratic state, through such mechanisms as public ownership of productive enterprises and the provision of government services, should protect the collective interests of less advantaged citizens. Democracy, in the perception of some socialists, should be extended beyond a limited notion of shared political influence embodied in voting rights shared among all citizens to the idea that economic power and economic benefits should also be more widely shared.

Some historians have argued that Australia has in the past featured a particularly distinctive collectivist and egalitarian-democratic ethos, transported and nurtured here among 19th century immigrants by a 'radical fragment' of Britain.[3] It is certainly the case that elements of democratic-socialist collectivism have been nurtured within Australia through the trade union movement and the Labor Party, though—as Economou explains in Chapter 12—the extent to which the Australian labour movement's commitment to socialism was ever much more than emotional, symbolic or rhetorical is a contentious matter (see also Maddox & Battin 1991).

A different sort of 'collectivist' orientation is promoted by some conservatives.[4] A defining feature of conservatism, elaborated further by Fenna in Chapter 2, is its respect for the wisdom embodied in established procedures, customs and traditions. Sometimes this leads conservatives to be sceptical about democracy, fearing the possibility that empowered popular movements might promote dangerously radical change. But there is also a conservative appreciation and defence of democracy that values its community orientation, its potential to identify with society's norms and traditions, its honouring of the achievements of communities over time, and its ability to draw these shared traditions and perspectives together in reaching collective decisions.

Most Australians do not self-consciously describe themselves using any sort of ideological terms, let alone self-identifying as socialists or conservatives or 'collectivists'. But it would be surprising if there were many who, if asked, did not identify in some sense with democracy.[5] The idea of democracy—as expressed through practices like voting in elections and through expectations that governments ought to be responsive to community needs and aspirations—is so well embedded and so uncontentious that it is simply an accepted part of the political landscape.

But this does not mean that Australians necessarily want to entrust the government sector, however democratic its basis, with too much power or too much capacity for action. Alongside the near-universal acceptance of the need for *democratic* government, there is also a well-embedded perception that even democratic governments need to be *held in check*. And such checks are indeed a feature of the political and governmental systems of advanced Western countries. A good way to explain this is via the notion that these countries are *liberal* democracies.

Liberalism and government

The *democratic* notion—that governments should be accountable to, and serve, a broad political community—is tempered within liberal-democratic systems by a countervailing *liberal* dimension that imposes limitations on the scope and capacity of government.

As Fenna explains in more detail in Chapter 2, what we can broadly call liberalism is a set of ideas about the rights of individuals and about market-based mechanisms for economic production and distribution. These ideas arose in Western societies as a political demand for *freedom*, for release from the strictures of traditionally authoritarian governments. Whereas the democratic impulse (which arrived somewhat later in Western societies) demanded that governments be made more accountable and responsive to citizens, it was the liberal revolution that first demanded that governments be made more constrained.

Historically, what is called 'classical' liberalism was an ideology of emancipation which helped to undermine the old privileged aristocratic-feudal orders of Europe, and created in their place a society based on rights, the rule of law and liberty.[6] The rise of classical liberalism accompanied the development of the economic system known as capitalism, and liberal ideas continue to legitimise essential elements of the capitalist system: the ownership of private property, the accumulation of private wealth, and the use of the voluntary market mechanism for production and exchange.

The vocabulary and sentiments of the classical liberal tradition can be called on to defend private individuals, their rights and their markets, against 'the state'. An important political device associated with liberalism, and which attempts to serve this goal of limiting the reach of government, is a written Constitution. The specification and delimitation of the legitimate sphere of governmental activity through a formal Constitution is consistent with classical liberalism's defence of civil society and individual rights against unjustified governmental intervention.

The Constitution of the United States, which took effect in 1789, is a definitive example. Its explicit purpose was to limit the scope and capacity of government—even, perhaps especially, a democratically elected government. It divided the government sector—into a federal system and into independent legislative, executive and judicial branches—in order to limit its capacity for coherent and coordinated domination. And it specified a list of individual rights which governments may not violate no matter how popular such a violation may be.[7]

Liberal ideas and practices have shaped Australia's system of government and politics. While there have been important local adaptations and modifications to the 'classical' liberal doctrine, Maddox (2005: 249–50) points out that

> [s]uch appeals to individualism and collectivism that have been made in Australian politics have been minor variations at the extremes of a *liberal* tradition . . . [T]he Labor Party generally represents a radical-liberal point of view, while the Liberal and National Parties might be styled conservative-liberal.

Australia's major political parties have often debated what should be their basic ideological goals and indeed how they should label themselves—for example, how much should the Liberal Party be guided by classical liberal doctrine (see Chapter 11 in this book) and to what extent should the Labor Party identify itself as socialist (see Chapter 12)? But both major party groupings accept the broad reality of the predominantly private-market-oriented mixed economy within an overall economic, social and educational framework and infrastructure for which government takes responsibility. As we will see below, a compromise position, sometimes called 'social liberalism', has been influential at various times in both major parties.

A written Constitution is an important feature of the Australian governmental system, as Chapter 3 in this book discusses in detail. The Australian Constitution shares many of the features of its American predecessor. It likewise creates a federal system, the philosophical justification for which includes a dispersion of governmental authority, a limitation of the scope for concentrated and coherent government intervention, and the protection of individual rights and freedoms. As Galligan (1989: 61) explains, 'federalism is a structure that promotes liberal or pluralist democracy and restrains majoritarian, reformist democracy'. This is achieved in the Australian Constitution by a division of powers between the Commonwealth and State levels of government, by the existence of a Senate with equal representation of every State and which checks the majoritarian House of Representatives, and by the exercise of judicial review through the High Court over the constitutionality of government action.

The Australian Constitution also specifies some individual rights which prohibit the exercise of certain powers by the Commonwealth government[8] though it features nothing as extensive as the US Constitution's 'Bill of Rights'. There is a perennial debate in Australia about whether other rights should be constitutionally entrenched or legislatively recognised. The debate is usually focused, significantly, not on the question of whether the governmental system ought to give a high priority to rights-based considerations, but on whether parliamentary procedures or judicial institutions are the best way of doing this.[9]

Liberal democracy

Liberal-democratic political systems feature a number of institutions, processes and understandings that are recognisably liberal in orientation and others that are recognisably democratic in orientation. There is no single identical package common to all Western liberal democracies; there are interesting differences in detail between how (for example) Australia, the United States of America, France and Sweden are politically constituted. But these systems do have in common a number of key features, and they all exhibit a relationship between various constituent elements that can be understood as liberal aspects counterbalancing democratic aspects.

What are these key common features? From the liberal tradition, the liberal democracies all encompass:

- an insistence on the rule of law, as the only legitimate means by which government authority can be exercised, which operates as a constraint against arbitrary governmental action because the government itself must operate within the law
- judicial institutions and procedures that are sufficiently separated from the rest of the governmental sector to ensure that there is an independent check on governmental action and that governmental executives are themselves subject to the law
- a strong private market sector of the economy
- an acceptance that citizens are endowed with personal liberties and rights that no government should readily be able to remove or weaken
- the freedom of citizens to associate together within 'civil society'.
  From the democratic tradition, the liberal democracies all assert:
- the legitimacy of an extensive state sector, operating under the authority of democratically endorsed laws and policies promulgated or approved by representative institutions, accountable to and oriented towards serving the needs of the members of the political community
- the freedom of citizens, individually or in voluntarily organised groups, to engage in political activity such as seeking to influence government, seeking elected governmental office and supporting political parties (importantly including opposition political parties)[10]
- the responsibility of government to be mindful of the welfare of the citizens and communities who constitute those whom it governs, meaning in practice

that governments need to ensure the availability to citizens of at least basic welfare, educational and other benefits and services.

In combination, these are the features that have co-evolved—in various ways via complex histories in different places and times—within Western political systems over the past two or three hundred years. Liberal-democratic institutions, practices and understandings now underpin the mode of government practised throughout Western Europe, North America, Japan and New Zealand as well as Australia. A gravitation towards liberal-democratic ideals and institutions emerged in the 1990s in Eastern Europe, Russia and other parts of the former Soviet Union in the wake of the collapse of Communism and the end of the Cold War. More uncertainly, but nonetheless unequivocally, some of the same gravitation is becoming evident in many newly industrialising states as well.[11]

Historical circumstances and ideological factors have interplayed in the development of the liberal-democratic model. Events have been affected by ideas, and ideas have been affected by events. At crucial points and at crucial times in modern history—during the drafting of a national Constitution, when contemplating republican alternatives to monarchical rule, at the establishment of new institutions in a new colony, in the formation of a new political party, in devising public policies which respond to perceived problems in the local community—politicians and citizens have drawn on the historical examples of which they were aware and legitimating ideas to which they were attracted. In the process, liberal-democratic forms of politics emerged, developed and consolidated themselves.

Australia's liberal democracy, while featuring some recognisably Australian elements, is a product of this centuries-old liberal-democratic lineage with its origins in Western Europe and particularly (in Australia's case) Britain. Those who drafted Australia's Constitution in the 1890s were—at times consciously and at other times unconsciously—continuing this interplay of history and ideology in the evolution of Australia's version of liberal democracy.

The collapse in the late 1980s and early 1990s of Communism—at the time, seemingly the single most coherent alternative in the world to the Western liberal-democratic model—was such a momentous historical event that some observers portrayed the apparent triumph of liberal democracy in millennial terms. The most feted of these triumphalists was the American commentator Francis Fukuyama in a celebrated 1989 article entitled 'The End of History' (Fukuyama 1989). Three years later, he summarised his interpretation conveyed in that article:

> I argued that a remarkable consensus concerning the legitimacy of liberal democracy as a system of government had emerged throughout the world over the past few years, as it conquered rival ideologies like hereditary monarchy, fascism, and most

recently communism. More than that, I argued that liberal democracy may constitute the 'end point of mankind's ideological evolution' and the 'final form of human government' and as such constituted the 'end of history' . . . Today's stable democracies . . . were not without injustice or serious social problems. But these problems were ones of incomplete implementation of the principles of liberty and equality on which modern democracy is founded, rather than of flaws in the principles themselves . . . [T]he *ideal* of liberal democracy could not be improved on. (Fukuyama 1992: xi)

Fukuyama here portrays the apparent triumph of liberal democracy as representing the 'end of history' in the sense of being philosophically irreversible and irresistible.[12] Once people and societies grasp the awesome truth and the human potential revealed by the combination of democratic self-government and liberal individualism, he implies, there can be no going back. And something like this powerful—and, for Fukuyama here, indelible—liberal-democratic vision probably did help to inspire the remarkable events during and since this period: the removal of the Berlin Wall, the collapse from within of the Soviet Union, the astonishingly rapid adoption within some Central and Eastern European states of Western European institutions and styles of government, the (unsuccessful) rebellion centred on China's Tiananmen Square, the gradual but palpable democratisation of a number of other previously autocratic East Asian states, the liberalising of India's economy as a new adjunct to its (mostly) already robustly democratic politics, real advances in democratic reform and in the recognition of human rights in parts of Latin America and Africa.

Fukuyama's millennial triumphalism was audacious, and attracted lively criticism at the time and since.[13] Some critics were fundamentally unconvinced by his analysis. Others were sceptical that 'history'—even in Fukuyama's special philosophical sense of the word—could really be declared to have ended because no further challenge to liberal democracy was likely to be possible. In the wake of what now looks like a potentially serious challenge to 'the West' from Islamic fundamentalism, Fukuyama's brave interpretation now looks even more suspect and brazen than it did when he first promulgated it.

But one does not have to adopt Fukuyama's triumphalism to accept that the liberal-democratic form has proved remarkably adaptable and durable during its centuries of evolution and that its basic qualities—and specifically its attempted marriage of liberalism and democracy—do appear to be in the ascendancy around much of the world. The enduring coexistence, in a variety of related forms in different countries at different times, of liberal and democratic traditions to produce liberal-democratic political systems reveals what is evidently a robust, flexible and resilient model of politics and government.

Liberal-democratic politics and public policy

The liberal-democratic project is helped by the democratic and liberal traditions having some important elements or inclinations in common. They both project a respect for the rule of law, both depend on a broad recognition among citizens of the legitimacy of the political institutions and processes, both advocate that decisions be reached through consent and due process, and both imply a commitment to peaceful and evolutionary rather than violent change. They both lend support to the notion of a 'free press'—a media sector able independently to investigate and report on government and politics—because this helps with the (democratic) accountability of government to the community and with the (liberal) dispersing of power away from the government sector. Some commentators are confident that the two traditions are strongly mutually supportive or complementary (e.g. Damico 1986; Plattner 1999). It is significant that there has been no stable democracy that has not also featured a fairly robust and independent private economic sector as advocated by liberals.[14]

But, notwithstanding all of the foregoing, it would be a mistake to conclude that successful and durable liberal democracies embody a frictionless reconciliation or amalgamation of the democratic and liberal traditions. Among philosophers and political scientists, the degree to which the liberal and democratic traditions are compatible is a matter of longstanding contention. And the dramatic recent liberal-democratic advances around the world, to which Fukuyama and others have drawn attention, means that 'the relationship between liberalism and democracy has once again become a subject of intense intellectual and policy debate' (Plattner 1999: 121).

Some analysts argue that the tension between the two traditions is so serious that one side must in the end subvert the other. Hoffman (1991), for example, argues that liberalism in the end is fundamentally anti-democratic, and Levy (1994: 585), while conceding that 'democracy does have a place in liberal theory', emphasises that it is 'emphatically a subordinate one'.[15] Zakaria (2003) worries that the democratisation that has taken place in many countries around the world in recent times has been used to suppress minorities and erode liberties, creating what he fears might be better termed 'illiberal democracy'.

This chapter contends that there is a serious *tension* between key liberal and democratic assumptions and approaches to politics. It is this tension that helps to explain many features of the political arguments and political processes characteristic of liberal democracies. This tension between liberal and democratic approaches is, mostly, far from debilitating. Indeed, its existence and persistence helps to explain the success, flexibility and durability of liberal-democratic politics. But it is a tension nonetheless, and it shapes how liberal-democratic politics happen in practice.

Consider some of the key policy debates of our day, and the differing policy prescriptions that tend to emerge from alternative liberal and democratic perspectives on these debates.

Classical liberal arguments legitimise a market economy, promote 'smaller government', support lower tax levels, give a higher priority to private life than to public duties, endorse the privatisation of government-owned enterprises, and emphasise the rights of individuals and minorities vis-à-vis the interests and wishes of the broader community. A classical liberal perspective tends not to be particularly concerned about large inequalities in the distribution of economic and social power.

Democratic arguments help to legitimise collectively owned public institutions, promote the nation-building role of the state, confer esteem on service to the community through the public domain, emphasise community obligations, challenge economic and social inequality, and try to protect the egalitarian basis of the political system from distortions resulting from inequalities of economic and social power.

Liberal democracies legitimise and are responsive to *both* sets of arguments. And liberal democracies are founded upon institutions and practices—elections, representative governmental institutions, free speech, political bargaining and coalition-building, private property ownership, a robust business sector, and so on—that together reflect, promote and defend aspects of *both* sets of arguments.

This means that much of political process in a liberal democracy such as Australia involves the playing out—in debates, in decision making, in electoral contests, in political bargains and compromises, in policy prescriptions—of the tension between democratic and liberal claims. Put simply, liberal-democratic politics is how the tension between liberal and democratic values is *managed*. Structuring many political disputes and arguments—about policy directions or legislative proposals or party platforms or the acceptability of particular laws— is the much deeper phenomenon of the balance (shifting, sliding, adjusting, recorrecting, but always present) between liberal and democratic instincts, voices and embedded practices.

It is important to be clear about what is being argued here. The claim of this chapter is *not* that 'democratic' forces always line up against 'liberal' forces as the two stark sides of a political dispute over some issue or policy or preferred party. More typically, the various positions articulated in political debates represent different combinations of or compromises between liberal and democratic elements.

Consider, for example, a policy debate that has been central to Australian politics for about the last 20 years: taxation reform. (Fenna explores this policy domain in much more detail in Chapter 23.) From a classical liberal perspective, taxation is the expropriation by the state of resources owned by private individuals or private entities. Not only is such an expropriation, from this perspective, morally suspect in its own right, it also endangers the incentive structure that shapes the market sector of the economy. From a democratic perspective, however, taxes are necessary contributions made by members of the community towards the provision of public services, community facilities and social assets. These two polar positions shape and scope the political debate.[16] This does not mean that the polar positions normally produce identifiably separate political movements or policy proposals. Nearly everybody involved recognises the need for trade-offs between the two positions. They recognise the authenticity of the tension here: it would be a rare taxpayer who would not be pleased if their tax bill were smaller rather than larger, and yet it would also be a rare taxpayer who did not appreciate good government facilities and services ranging from well-maintained roads to an effective national defence force. Rather, the polar positions — embedded in the institutions and processes of politics, and in the ideas and political language that politicians and citizens reach for in shaping their thinking — structure the debate, constrain the options, and help to guide the trade-offs and bargaining. This is the distinctive quality of liberal-democratic politics.

Consider the debates about economic reform that have likewise gripped Australian politics over the past 20 years. As Woodward explains in Chapter 22, market-oriented policy prescriptions have risen to prominence within many areas of economic policy. Forms of deregulation have been introduced into financial markets, transportation, agricultural marketing and, increasingly, the labour market. Longstanding public enterprises have been privatised. The way these reforms have emerged, and have been debated, has been quintessentially liberal-democratic in character. Classical liberal ideals have been a quite explicit inspiration for the program of reform.[17] And critics of this 'economic rational-ism' often explicitly invoke concepts and lessons which are drawn from demo-cratic-communitarian discourse that is sceptical of aspects of a classically liberal orientation.[18] Part of the explanation for the success of the economic reform agenda has been that Labor governments — especially under Prime Ministers Hawke and Keating at the national level — were important for transforming many of the ideas into implemented policies. Given the natural affinity between the Liberal Party and neoliberal ideas, this situation meant that, with Labor in government, alternative perspectives were harder to mobilise. But since Labor has been in Opposition, the counterbalancing imperatives encouraged by liberal-democratic politics have reasserted themselves. Labor has become less support-ive of privatisation and labour-market deregulation, and the Howard government's ambitions have had to be negotiated (at least until mid-2005) through a Senate where the non-government majority could justify its insis-tence on compromises in the name of a more balanced position.[19]

Consider welfare policy debates, as discussed in detail by Robbins in Chapter 24. Whereas a classical liberal perspective is wary of government schemes that use funds taxed from self-reliant individuals to provide welfare support for others, a democratic perspective encourages collective social responsibility and mutual assistance. It is again the responsiveness of liberal democracies to both sets of ideas that structures the politics and policy debates around welfare reform.

Consider an issue that has resonated strongly within Australian politics in recent years: the composition of the immigration program and the arrival of undocumented asylum-seekers on Australia's shores. A classical liberal perspective, at its broadest level, is suspicious of state-imposed restrictions on the right of people to move. But a democratic perspective regards the appropriate goals of immigration policy as those which serve some conception of the community interest and which reflect the collective values and aspirations of members of the community. A democratic polity might decide to exclude immigrants altogether, or select only those with particular racial or ethnic characteristics, or select those most likely to contribute to the economic wellbeing of the community. None of those are fanciful options; elements of each have been influential, recently or in the past, in the debate shaping Australia's immigration and refugee programs (Parkin & Hardcastle 1997). How is a policy resolution to be enforced? Most Australians are likely to be profoundly uncomfortable with the mandatory detention of asylum-seekers, a discomfort that can be credited to our liberal sentiments. Yet there are also legitimate arguments, intuitively understood by many and probably most Australians, that features of their national community—from its taxpayer-funded welfare system to aspects of its intrinsic social character—depend in some measure on the maintenance of international borders which distinguish between 'insiders' and 'outsiders'.[20]

Consider another issue likely to resonate strongly within Australian politics for the immediate future: community security in the context of possible terrorist threats. Democratic governments are expected to place a high priority on protecting citizens and the public assets—the infrastructure, networks and services—upon which communities depend. But many of the powers that governments might draw upon in bolstering security—greater resourcing of police services, clandestine intelligence work, closed-circuit television monitoring systems, infiltration of worrying community groups, more rigorous checks on the identity and background of individuals, pre-emptive raids on suspect people and locations, telephone and Internet tapping, surveillance of meetings, the detention and interrogation of suspects, interconnected databases piecing together information about private individuals—are alarming, for fundamental liberal reasons, in their implications for the civil liberties of individuals and minority groups and for the enhancement of governmental power. All of these issues, along both dimensions, have been raised in Australia in recent years, and have shaped the policy responses. Typically, the policy proposals that emerge try to counterbalance increased governmental power, where thought necessary, by specifying limits to it and by building in mechanisms for oversight, scrutiny or authorisation by judicial or parliamentary bodies.[21] What is thought to be the appropriate balance is likely to change over time—for example, whereas a national identity card was proposed but became politically untenable during the 1980s, it may re-emerge as a serious option now.[22] But a healthy liberal democracy remains institutionally and philosophically attuned to the need for a balance, and its politics are characteristically the avenue for this to occur.

Many other examples could be offered to supplement these. Consider any area of domestic public policy—across the whole range from education to environmental protection, from corrections to child protection, from health care to housing, from industrial relations to immunisation, from welfare to workplace safety, from telecommunications to transport—and an underlying tension between liberal-individualist-private and democratic-collectivist-public clusters of policy prescriptions can be detected.

Sometimes, particular combinations or compromises between liberal and democratic ideas and perspectives are enduring and alluring enough to be given their own ideological labels. Some analysts argue that many aspects of Australian politics, certainly historically and to some extent today, can be understood as featuring a kind of 'social liberal' consensus position—or range of positions—that extends a liberal respect for individual rights and freedoms into an overarching recognition of a community-level responsibility for ensuring appropriate levels of equity, fairness and living standards.[23] Another notable compromise position, in many ways comparable to 'social liberalism' in practice though beginning from a democratic-collectivist rather than a liberal starting point, is the 'social democratic' approach notably prominent within the Australian Labor Party. 'Social democrats' moderate the socialist insistence on collective public ownership by conceding the value and necessity, within broad limits, of a respect for individual rights and private property.[24] The so-called 'Third Way'—a development from 'social democracy' that its advocates perceive as somehow transcending both democratic government-centric and private market-centric approaches to political and policy reform—is another of these hybrids.[25]

The policy terrain of liberal-democratic politics

As these examples illustrate, liberal-democratic politics characteristically deals with debates and disputes about governmental policies within a terrain established by the tension between liberal principles and democratic principles. Much of this politics is about attempts to resolve (always contingently and temporarily) such matters as:

- the appropriate balance between the rights of individuals and the collective interests of the wider community

- how to adjudicate between competing claims by different individuals for the recognition of their rights and liberties
- the degree to which government intervention, to supplant the market economy or redistribute resources for deployment in the market economy, is desirable
- the relationship between majority decisions and the rights of minorities
- the appropriate boundary between what should be 'public' concerns, needing government-led policy responses, and 'private' matters best left to families, communities or the business sector[26]
- the extent to which the social inequality produced or permitted by the market economy subverts the political equality assumed to underlie democratic political practices.

These matters exemplify the way in which Australian political life—the mobilisation and interplay of values and interests in the public arena—is sensitive to claims arising from *both* the liberal and the democratic traditions. They illustrate the argument of this chapter that much of the politics of a liberal democracy involves the recognition and management of the tension between the two traditions. This is a politics of debate, compromise, leadership, judgment, trial and error, and cycles of policy fashion. It is not a politics of permanent resolution; rather, as Bufacchi (2001: 27) has described, outcomes tends to be 'indeterminate and provisional'.

Liberal democracy and political power

It is important to acknowledge that liberal-democratic politics, because of the co-existence of a robust private sector encompassing interests which can be mobilised to influence government policies, necessarily falls short of achieving the kind of egalitarianism and social justice advocated by some social reformers. Welfare and social justice issues are policy matters that liberal-democratic societies argue about and resolve politically; they tend not to be regime-defining teleological goals. This is one of the ways that liberal democracy differs from some of the alternative political arrangements—such as Soviet-style state socialism or some forms of Islamic theocratic government[27]—that have been prominent elsewhere in the world in recent times.

A particularly key relationship within liberal democracies is between the government sector and the business sector, a subject so significant that it is separately analysed in Chapter 18. As elaborated there, business interests arguably occupy a specially privileged location within liberal-democratic politics. The potential power of business interests is not necessarily based on the enduring power of any particular company nor of any particular business leader. Rather, it is a systemic bias within a system that seems to need to operate—if it is to be sustainable—in the overall interests of a favourable business climate.

It is the political impact of 'private' inequality which forms the basis of the standard 'Left' critiques of liberal democracy: that the notion of a 'capitalist democracy' is an 'oxymoron' (Hoffman 1991), that it is a façade for the unjust exploitation of the economically weak by the economically powerful, and that any apparent consent given to the system by its victims is a result of the hegemonic power of private interests structured into the prevailing value system (Kuhn 2005).

Neither full justice nor a full response to this critique is possible here, though various chapters which follow in this book shed some light on the debate. A counter-argument of particular relevance to political analysts draws on the observation that there is a great variety of state institutional arrangements among different liberal democracies.[28] They also produce a great variety of public policy profiles. How Australia, for example, arranges its political life and responds to policy choices is often quite distinctive (Castles 1991). This suggests that political systems are sufficiently independent from the global capitalist economic systems to allow local democratic forces to create and sustain these variable arrangements. This observation also reminds us that there is no single liberal-democratic model of government but rather a variety of ways to achieve and maintain what seem to be workable balances between liberal and democratic forces.

The achievement of liberal democracies has been quite remarkable in world-historical terms. As Emy and Hughes (1991: 218) observe, they have 'in their relatively short life . . . achieved a degree of material prosperity and political freedom unmatched in human history'. The same authors later sensibly conclude, in what is undoubtedly an allusion to triumphant celebrants like Fukuyama, that 'arguments which claim that they are near-perfect affairs . . . must be rejected. Politics, the theory and practice of devising more viable and more desirable forms of human community, is always an unfinished business' (Emy & Hughes 1991: 524). But the notion of politics as an unfinished business itself fits comfortably within a liberal-democratic framework—a framework that can only manage, and never really resolve, the enduring and often creative tension between its liberal and its democratic constituent elements.

NOTES

1 It would be more accurate to substitute for 'the citizenry as a whole' a depiction of how particular democratic electoral systems actually work. For example, a party or coalition is elected as the government of Australia when it has won more than half of the parliamentary seats in the House of Representatives, each of these local contests being decided by a candidate winning a majority of the votes cast in that contest (after second or later preferences of voters are allocated if this is necessary to reach a majority verdict). Brian Costar in Chapter 10 of this book explains in detail how this electoral system and others used in Australia work.

2 For various perspectives on democratisation in Australia, see Oldfield (1992), Lees (1995), Sawer (2001) and Sawer & Zappalà (2001).

3 This 'radical fragment' thesis is most explicitly put forward by Rosecrance (1964), applying to the Australian case a more general perspective on 'new societies' promulgated by Hartz (1964). The historical work of Russell Ward (e.g. 1966) fits within this genre. Other commentators, in what is an interesting debate within Australian historiography, have contested the interpretation, claiming that Australian history is more dominated by individualistic and materialistic themes than the radical-collectivist thesis gives credit for (see e.g. McQueen 1970; Martin 1973; Hirst 1984; White 1981; Collins 1985; Hudson & Bolton 1997). Feminist historians have also deconstructed the masculine orientation evident in the historiographical literature (e.g. Grimshaw et al. 1994).

4 This is despite conservatism and socialism being normally regarded as ideological perspectives more in contention than in agreement.

5 Dryzek (1994) reports some interesting research uncovering four distinct 'discourses' about democracy among 'political actors and ordinary people' in Australia.

6 Liberty is understood in this classical liberal tradition in a 'negative' sense of freedom from the tyranny of coercive governments, from coerced labour and from state-controlled or guild-controlled systems of commerce. A standard criticism of liberalism is that it gives insufficient weight to 'positive' conceptions of liberty, i.e. the provision of positive supports which enable an individual to achieve his or her goals (Berlin 1969). Fenna explains this further in Chapter 2.

7 The US Bill of Rights technically encompasses the first 10 amendments to the US Constitution. But because they were definitively foreshadowed during the debate about the adoption of the Constitution, it is generally accepted that the Bill of Rights can be regarded as part of the original constitutional compact.

8 On the specification of rights within the Australian Constitution, see Williams (1999).

9 See for example Alston (1994), Moens (1994), Bailey (1995), Patapan (2000: ch. 3), Williams (2000), Carr (2001) and Williams (2004).

10 The concept of an Opposition is an interesting, crucial and under-researched aspect of liberal-democratic politics. See Dahl (1966), Dahl (1973), Blondel (1997) and Maddox (2005: 216–40).

11 For detailed analyses of the worldwide democratisation movement in recent times, peruse the academic journal *Democratization*, e.g. the December 2004 special issue on 'consolidated and defective democracy: problems of regime change' (Croissant & Merkel 2004).

12 Fukuyama adopts an Hegelian conception of 'history', conceptualising it not as a chronological series of events but as the evolution of philosophical argument about the nature and purpose of collective life towards some ultimate resolution.

13 See e.g. Cristaudo (1992), Wintrop (1993), Farrenkopf (1995) and Cumings (1999).

14 The reverse is not the case: robust private economic sectors seem to be compatible with authoritarian or autocratic forms of government.

15 For further discussion of the relationship between liberalism and democracy see, for example, Almond (1991), Graham (1992), Beetham (1997), Carter and Stokes (1998) and Vernon (1998).

16 For more on tax and liberal democracy, see Parkin (2002: 304–7) and Steinmo (2003).

17 See James, Jones & Norton (1993) and Wright (2003).

18 Among the critics of economic rationalism, there are pleas to 'restore the nation's way of life' (Carroll 1992: 191), to adopt a more 'inclusive' approach which includes 'community initiatives' (Rees 1994), to defend the traditional Australian 'nation-building state' (Pusey 1991; Dow 1999), to oppose unfettered free trade (Weekes 1992; Stewart 1994), to

reregulate financial markets (Stretton 1992), and to rely more on 'the representative system of government' as the 'one institution' that can be entrusted with key 'public good' utilities (Sheil 2000: 170). For a response to some critics, see Coleman and Hagger (2001).

19 Labor's reorientation arguably began a little earlier than its election loss of March 1996: the Keating Labor government retreated palpably from the 'economic rationalist' vanguard after its re-election in 1993.

20 For elaboration on the difficulties (and inherent liberal/democratic tensions) afflicting immigration and refugee policy, see Walzer (1983), Carens (1988), Barry & Goodin (1992), Adelman (1994), Freeman (1994), Freeman (1995), Caney, George & Jones (1996), Gibney (2004) and Birrell (2004).

21 For related analysis of criminal justice and civil liberties issues within a liberal-democratic framework, see Parkin (1998 and 2000). See also Hocking (2003) and Williams (2004).

22 On the history of the 'Australia Card' in the 1980s, see Smith (1989) and Parkin (2002: 206–7). On the recent debate about a national identity card, see Hewson (2005) and Puplick (2005).

23 Social liberalism is further elaborated in this book by Fenna in Chapter 2 and Brett in Chapter 11. See also Sawer (2003).

24 Social democracy is further elaborated in this book by Fenna in Chapter 2 and Economou in Chapter 12. See also Pierson (2001).

25 The Third Way is further elaborated in this book by Fenna in Chapter 2 and by Parkin and Hardcastle in Chapter 18. See also Giddens (1998 and 2000) and Nursey-Bray & Bacchi (2001).

26 A public/private distinction is contentious in some quarters, raising issues ranging from the plausibility of a (liberal) claim to a 'right of privacy' to feminist concerns about its gendered implications. See Okin (1991) and Steinberger (1999).

27 Defenders of liberal democracy could claim in any case that it is doubtful that Soviet-style state socialism or Islamic theocratic governments in practice have been particularly effective at enhancing citizen welfare or social justice.

28 Schmitter and Karl (1993) suggest that modern democracies (or 'liberal democracies' as understood in this chapter) display 'a matrix of potential combinations' of differing approaches to some fundamental institutional and constitutional matters, which they summarise under the headings of 'consensus', 'participation', 'access', 'responsiveness', 'majority rule', 'parliamentary sovereignty', 'party government', 'pluralism', 'federalism', 'presidentialism' and 'checks and balances'.

REFERENCES

Adelman, H. 1994, 'Justice, Immigration and Refugees', in *Immigration and Refugee Policy: Australia and Canada Compared*, eds H. Adelman *et al.*, Melbourne University Press, Melbourne.

Almond, G. 1991, 'Capitalism and Democracy', *PS: Political Science and Politics*, vol. 24, no. 3, pp. 467–74.

Alston, P. ed. 1994, *Toward an Australian Bill of Rights*, Australian National University Centre for International and Public Law, Canberra.

Bailey, P. 1995, 'Righting the Constitution Without a Bill of Rights', *Federal Law Review*, vol. 23, no. 1.

Barry, B. and Goodin, R. eds 1992, *Free Movement: Ethical Issues in the Transnational Migration of People and of Money*, Harvester Wheatsheaf, New York.

Beetham, D. 1997, 'Market Economy and Democratic Polity', *Democratization*, vol. 4, no. 1, pp. 76–93.

Berlin, I. 1969, *Four Essays on Liberty*, Oxford University Press, London.

Birrell, B. 2004, 'Managing International Population Movement: Is the Nation State Obsolete?', *People and Place*, vol. 12, no. 2, pp. 53–63.

Blondel, J. 1997, 'Political Opposition in the Contemporary World', *Government and Opposition*, vol. 32, pp. 462–84.

Bufacchi, V. 2001, 'Sceptical Democracy', *Politics*, vol. 21, no. 1, pp. 23–30.

Caney, S., George, D. & Jones, P. eds 1996, *National Rights, International Obligations*, Westview Press, Boulder.

Carens, J. 1988, 'Immigration and the Welfare State', in *Democracy and the Welfare State*, ed. A. Gutmann, Princeton University Press, Princeton, pp. 207–30.

Carr, B. 2001, 'The Rights Trap: How a Bill of Rights Could Undermine Freedom', *Policy*, vol. 17, no. 2, pp. 19–21.

Carroll, J. 1992, 'Conclusion: The Role of Government', in *Shutdown: The Failure of Economic Rationalism and How to Rescue Australia*, eds J. Carroll & R. Manne, Text Publishing Co., Melbourne.

Carter, A. & Stokes, G. 1998, 'Introduction: Liberal Democracy and its Critics', in *Liberal Democracy and its Critics*, eds A. Carter & G. Stokes, Polity Press, Cambridge, pp. 1–20.

Castles, F. ed. 1991, *Australia Compared: People, Policies and Politics*, Allen & Unwin, North Sydney.

Coleman, W. & Hagger, A. 2001, *Exasperating Calculators: The Rage over Economic Rationalism*, Macleay Press, Paddington.

Collins, H. 1985, 'Political Ideology in Australia: The Distinctiveness of a Benthamite Society', in *Australia: The Daedalus Symposium*, ed. S. Graubard, Angus & Robertson, North Ryde.

Cristaudo, W. 1992, 'The End of History?', *Current Affairs Bulletin*, vol. 69, no. 3, pp. 29–31.

Croissant, A. & Merkel, W. eds 2004, 'Democratization in the Early Twenty-First Century', special issue of *Democratization*, vol. 11, no. 5.

Cumings, B. 1999, 'The End of History of the Return of Liberal Crisis?', *Current History*, vol. 98, no. 624, pp. 9–16.

Dahl, R. 1966, *Political Oppositions in Western Democracies*, Yale University Press, New Haven.

Dahl, R. 1973, *Regimes and Oppositions*, Yale University Press, New Haven.

Damico, A. 1986, 'The Democratic Consequences of Liberalism', in *Liberals on Liberalism*, ed. A. Damico, Rowman and Littlefield, Ottawa.

Dow, G. 1999, 'Economic Rationalism Versus the Community: Reflections on Social Democracy and State Capacity', *Australian Journal of Social Issues*, vol. 34, no. 3, pp. 209–29.

Dryzek, J. 1994, 'Australian Discourses of Democracy', *Australian Journal of Political Science*, vol. 29, no. 2, pp. 221–39

Emy, H. & Hughes, O. 1991, *Australian Politics: Realities in Conflict*, 2nd edn, Macmillan, Melbourne.

Farrenkopf, J. 1995, 'Francis Fukuyama's Political Idealism', *Australian Journal of International Affairs*, vol. 49, no. 1, pp. 69–83.

Freeman, G. 1994, 'Can Liberal States Control Unwanted Migration?', *Annals of the American Academy of Political and Social Science*, no. 534, pp. 17–30.

Freeman, G. 1995, 'Modes of Immigration Politics in Liberal Democratic States', *International Migration Review*, vol. 29, no. 4, pp. 881–913.

Fukuyama, F. 1989, 'The End of History?', *Quadrant*, vol. 33, no. 8, pp. 15–25.

Fukuyama, F. 1992, *The End of History and the Last Man*, Penguin, London.

Galligan, B. 1989, 'A Political Science Perspective', in *Australian Federalism*, ed. B. Galligan, Longman Cheshire, Melbourne.

Gibney, M. 2004, *The Ethics and Politics of Asylum: Liberal Democracy and the Response to Refugees*, Cambridge University Press, Cambridge.

Giddens, A. 1998, *Third Way: The Renewal of Social Democracy*, Polity Press, Cambridge.

Giddens, A. 2000, *The Third Way and its Critics*, Polity Press, Malden MA.

Graham, G. 1992, 'Liberalism and Democracy', *Journal of Applied Philosophy*, vol. 9, no. 2, pp. 149–60.

Grimshaw, P., Lake, M., McGrath, A. & Quartly, M. 1994, *Creating a Nation*, McPhee Gribble, Melbourne.

Hartz, L. ed. 1964, *The Founding of New Societies*, Harcourt Brace and World, New York.

Hewson, J. 2005, 'Australia Card is Inevitable', *Australian Financial Review* 22 July.

Hirst, J. 1984, 'Keeping Colonial History Colonial: The Hartz Thesis Revisited', *Historical Studies*, vol. 21, no. 82, pp. 85–104.

Hocking, J. 2003, *Terror Laws: ASIO, Counter-Terrorism and the Threat to Democracy*, UNSW Press, Sydney.

Hoffman, J. 1991, 'Capitalist Democracies and Democratic States: Oxymorons or Coherent Concepts?', *Political Studies*, vol. 39, no. 2, pp. 342–9.

Howard, J. 2004, 'John Howard's Acceptance Speech', 10 October, *Sydney Morning Herald*, <http://www.smh.com.au/articles/2004/10/10/1097346684255.html#>.

Hudson, W. & Bolton, G. eds 1997, *Creating Australia: Changing Australian History*, Allen & Unwin, St Leonards.

James, C., Jones, C. & Norton A. eds 1993, *A Defence of Economic Rationalism*, Allen & Unwin, Sydney.

Kuhn, R. 2005, 'Illusions of Equality: The Capitalist State', in *Class and Struggle in Australia*, ed. R. Kuhn, Pearson Longman, Frenchs Forest, pp. 39–54.

Lees, K. 1995, *Votes for Women: The Australian Story*, Allen & Unwin, St Leonards.

Levy, J. 1994, 'The Liberal Defence of Democracy: A Critique of Pettit', *Australian Journal of Political Science*, vol. 29, no. 3, pp. 582–6.

Maddox, G. 2005, *Australian Democracy in Theory and Practice*, 5th edn, Pearson Longman, Frenchs Forest.

Maddox, G. & Battin, T. 1991, 'Australian Labor and the Socialist Tradition', *Australian Journal of Political Science*, vol. 26, no. 2, pp. 181–96.

Martin, A. 1973, 'Australia and the Hartz "Fragment" Thesis', *Australian Economic History Review*, vol. 13, no. 2, pp. 131–47.

McQueen, H. 1970, *A New Britannia*, Penguin, Ringwood.

Moens, G. 1994, 'The Wrongs of a Constitutionally Entrenched Bill of Rights', in *Republic or Monarchy? Legal and Constitutional Issues*, ed. M. Stephenson & C. Turner, University of Queensland Press, St Lucia.

Nursey-Bray, P. & C. Bacchi eds 2001, *Left Directions: Is There a Third Way?*, University of Western Australia Press, Crawley.

Okin, S.M. 1991, 'Gender, the Public and the Private', in *Political Theory Today*, ed. D. Held, Stanford University Press, Stanford.

Oldfield, A. 1992, *Woman Suffrage in Australia: A Gift or a Struggle?*, Cambridge University Press, Cambridge.

Parkin, A. 1998, 'Liberal Democracy and the Politics of Criminal Justice', *Australian Journal of Politics and History*, vol. 44, no. 3, pp. 445–69.

Parkin, A. 2000, 'Balancing Individual Rights and Community Norms', in *Drugs and Democracy: In Search of New Directions*, eds. G. Stokes, P. Chalk & K. Gillen, Melbourne University Press, Melbourne, pp. 100–13.

Parkin, A. 2002, 'Liberal Democracy', in *Government, Politics, Power and Policy in Australia*, 7th edn, Longman, Frenchs Forest, pp. 297–321.

Parkin, A. & Hardcastle, L. 1997, 'Immigration and Ethnic Affairs', in *Government, Politics, Power and Policy in Australia*, 6th edn, eds. D. Woodward, J. Summers & A. Parkin, Longman, Melbourne, pp. 486–509.

Patapan, H. 2000, *Judging Democracy: The New Politics of the High Court of Australia*, Cambridge University Press, Cambridge.

Pierson, C. 2001, *Hard Choices: Social Democracy in the Twenty-first Century*, Polity, Cambridge.

Plattner, M. 1999, 'From Liberalism to Liberal Democracy', *Journal of Democracy*, vol. 10, no. 3, pp. 121–34.

Puplick, C. 2005, 'Trouble on the Cards', *Australian* 18 July.

Pusey, M. 1991, *Economic Rationalism in Canberra: A Nation-Building State Changes its Mind*, Cambridge University Press, Cambridge.

Rees, S. 1994, 'Economic Rationalism: An Ideology of Exclusion', *Australian Journal of Social Issues*, vol. 29, no. 3, pp. 171–85.

Rosecrance, R. 1964, 'The Radical Culture of Australia', in *The Founding of New Societies*, ed. L. Hartz, Harcourt Brace and World, New York.

Sawer, M. ed. 2001, *Elections: Full, Free and Fair*, Federation Press, Annandale.

Sawer, M. 2003, *The Ethical State? Social Liberalism in Australia*, Melbourne University Press, Melbourne.

Sawer, M. & Zappalà, G. eds 2001, *Speaking for the People: Representation in Australian Politics*, Melbourne University Press, Carlton South.

Schmitter, P. & Karl, T. 1993, 'What Democracy is . . . and is not', in *The Global Resurgence of Democracy*, eds L. Diamond & M. Plattner, Johns Hopkins University Press, Baltimore, pp. 39–51.

Sheil, C. 2000, *Water's Fall: Running the Risks with Economic Rationalism*, Pluto Press, Annandale.

Smith, E. 1989, *The Australia Card: The Story of its Defeat*, Sun Macmillan, South Melbourne.

Steinberger, P. 1999, 'Public and Private', *Political Studies*, vol. 47, pp. 292–313.

Steinmo, S. 2003, 'The Evolution of Policy Ideas: Tax Policy in the 20th Century', *British Journal of Politics and International Relations*, vol. 5, no. 2, pp. 206–36.

Stewart, J. 1994, *The Lie of the Level Playing Field: Industry Policy and Australia's Future*, Text, Melbourne.

Stretton, H. 1992, 'Reconstructing the Financial System', in *Shutdown: The Failure of Economic Rationalism and How to Rescue Australia*, eds J. Carroll & R. Manne, Text Publishing Co. Melbourne.

Vernon, R. 1998, 'Liberals, Democrats and the Agenda of Politics', *Political Studies*, vol. 46, no. 2, pp. 295–308.

Walzer, M. 1983, *Spheres of Justice: A Defence of Pluralism and Equality*, Basil Blackwell, Oxford.

Ward, R. 1966, *The Australian Legend*, 2nd edn, Oxford University Press, Melbourne.

Weekes, B. 1992, 'Import Controls and the Cost of Free Trade', in *Shutdown: The Failure of Economic Rationalism and How to Rescue Australia*, eds J. Carroll & R. Manne, Text Publishing Co. Melbourne.

White, R. 1981, *Inventing Australia: Images and Identity 1688-1980*, George Allen & Unwin, Sydney.

Williams, G. 1999, *Human Rights Under the Australian Constitution*, Oxford University Press, Melbourne.

Williams, G. 2000, *A Bill of Rights for Australia*, UNSW Press, Sydney.

Williams, G. 2004, *The Case for an Australian Bill of Rights: Freedom in the War on Terror*, UNSW Press, Sydney.

Wintrop, N. 1993, 'Fukuyama: Challenge to Leftism', *Quadrant*, June, pp. 9–19.

Wright, J. 2003, *The Ethics of Economic Rationalism*, UNSW Press, Sydney.

Zakaria, F. 2003, *The Future of Freedom: Illiberal Democracy at Home and Abroad*, Norton, New York.

Understanding ideologies

In the first chapter of this book, Parkin discusses the ways in which Australian's political and governmental system is best understood as a *liberal-democratic* arrangement. He proposes that the institutions and practices of Australian political life can be usefully explained as arising from a marriage of *liberal* ideas and traditions about constitutional rule with *democratic* principles of accountability to the people.

This chapter elaborates on the meaning and significance of these liberal ideas and traditions. But it also focuses on the way that liberalism needs to be understood as an *ideological* perspective that, while generally dominant in countries like Australia, has been contested by other competing perspectives and is itself subject to competing interpretations. In order to understand Australian politics, it is important to understand liberalism—including various different strands of liberalism that offer some quite diverse political interpretations and prescriptions. But it is also important to understand the ideological challengers to liberalism, because they have also shaped Australian political ideas and practices.

What are ideologies and why do they matter?

Politics is about choices, and making choices is about using our understanding of how society functions to provide the foundation for our views about how society should function, or should be made to function. Systems of thought that build a set of prescriptions about political life from a set of interpretations of political life are known as *ideologies*.

It is in the terms provided by competing ideologies that much of our political debate is conducted. Many of political leaders and activists identify themselves with an ideological label. They regard themselves—some strictly and passionately, others more loosely and flexibly—as liberals or conservatives or social democrats or feminists or environmentalists or eco-socialists or whatever. They compete to shape what governments do and how they do it according to their own beliefs and values. And they deploy their favoured terms—freedom, security, stability, equality, justice, rights, sustainability, etc.—in pursuit of that goal. These are terms they hope will evoke an affirmative response from the public at large. Political parties—which are the principal means by which these political leaders and activists engage with the political process—typically define themselves by explicit reference to one ideology, or broad ideological cluster, or another. At the same time, a process of ideological jockeying occurs within each of those parties. Political parties thus tend to be both vehicles for the advancement of a set of ideological preferences and major sites of competition between variants of the same ideology.

For all of these reasons—because to varying degrees they have shaped the structures of our political system, shape the terms of political debate, and continue to influence our politicians and policy makers—it is important for students of politics to understand the nature of these ideologies.

For our purposes in this chapter, ideologies are usefully distinguished by their views on:

- the proper relationship between government and economy in a capitalist system
- the relationship between individual freedom and responsibility to the rest of society
- the definition of the nation
- the proper relationship between men and women
- the proper relationship between human society and the natural environment.

It might appear that the list of possible views about such matters is infinite. However, the Western political tradition has generated a very small handful of general positions on these questions. These general positions—these 'ideologies'—are relatively coherent bodies of thought that interpret the world according to a set of principles or precepts that then provide the basis for guiding decisions about how society should be organised and made to function. The most significant of these ideologies are liberalism, conservatism and socialism.

In their purest form, ideologies can be understood as complete packages of ideas that provide a coherent or consistent set of ideas about all the major dimensions of social life. From a set of premises or basic assumptions about human nature, they tell us the proper place of the individual in society, the best means of organising the economy, the appropriate role of government in society and the economy, the way one group or culture should relate to another, and much more. Moreover, they will do this such that the same set of basic principles will answer a diverse range of such questions.

Of course, this is a rather tall order, and in reality only two ideological clusters—liberalism and socialism—achieve anything like that level of comprehensiveness. While conservatism, feminism and environmentalism have quite well developed views about certain aspects of social life, they tend to have less to say about others, most notably about the very important question of how the economy should be organised. Thus their adherents tend to attach themselves to one or other of the two more complete ideologies, producing such combinations as liberal conservatism, liberal feminism or socialist environmentalism. This makes for some confusion.

Two other complicating factors further obscure the picture. The first is that liberalism and socialism are themselves fractured ideologies, with quite distinctly different variants. The second is that in the real world as represented by political party platforms, governmental policy pronouncements or the statements of political leaders, ideological positions are not anywhere near as logically coherent nor as faithfully represented as they are likely to be in the works of the key philosophers who have analysed and discussed these issues.

The liberal revolution

The dominant ideology of our time, and indeed the defining ideology of modernity, is liberalism. As Heywood (2003: 28) notes, liberalism is so defining a feature of our life that it is almost 'indistinguishable from "western civilization" in general'. Among those core Western values of liberal origin are rationalism (the principle that social and political arrangements ought to have a logical explanation and justification instead of being accepted on the grounds of tradition, belief or authority) and the principle that religious belief and practice is a personal choice, not something to be decided by the state.

A core conviction of liberalism is that human beings are of equal worth. Differences there may be, but none of those differences makes anyone fundamentally better or more deserving than any one else. Each person is first and foremost an individual, not simply a member of a social group. From this follows liberalism's defining precept: that each individual should be allowed the maximum liberty to enjoy their individual existence consistent with not infringing on the liberty of others. Likewise each individual is ultimately responsible for his or her own destiny.

CLASSICAL ORIGINS

Liberalism took shape as an ideology of liberation, seeking to free individuals from various constraints and tyrannies—most notably the tyranny of hierarchical social status and privileges and the tyranny of oppressive governments—beginning in the 17th century. In particular, early liberals sought to replace the arbitrary, autocratic rule of Europe's monarchies with constitutional government based on the rule of law and elected representation. They also sought to replace the regulated and controlled economy with one based on individual freedom of action. This was a pre-democratic age, though, and there was little suggestion that constitutional government meant democratic government. For most of these early liberals, government should be representative but not of everybody; rather it should be representative of those with a tangible 'stake' in society, those with property. Nonetheless, early liberalism did have a radical fringe of democratic thinkers and agitators such as Thomas Paine (e.g. Paine 1791–92/1995).

It was in this early constitutionalist struggle that we also find liberalism's powerful attachment to the principles of justice and individual rights. Prior to the triumph of liberalism, people were understood as enjoying privileges but rarely rights. Meanwhile, 'justice' was simply something rulers dispensed, for better or worse. Our assumption today that we have a right to a fair trial and 'natural justice', or a right to believe what we want, to say what we want or to associate as we like, is the result of that early struggle.

The pivotal thinker of early liberalism was John Locke, who lived and wrote during the period that England made the transition from monarchical rule to constitutional monarchy and parliamentarism. Locke argued three things that have ever since been fundamental to the liberal tradition. First, he asserted as axiomatic that people should be considered morally equal, free and capable of exercising reason: 'all Men by Nature are equal' and 'born Free, as we are born Rational' (1690/1988: 304, 308). Second, government must be based on the consent of the people and function through representation and the rule of law. Third, integral to an individual's freedom is the right to possess property, and the overriding purpose of individuals consenting to live in a political community is the 'mutual *Preservation* of their Lives, Liberties and Estates' (1690/1988: 350).

Locke's ideas and phraseology had a powerful influence on the development of British and American constitutionalism. They were most famously echoed in the US *Declaration of Independence* of 1776, which asserts that 'all men are created equal, that they are endowed . . . with certain unalienable [*sic*] rights, that among these are life, liberty and the pursuit of happiness'. The liberal belief in natural rights found its most famous expression in the first 10 amendments to the US Constitution, the 'Bill of Rights', ratified in 1791.

LIBERAL ECONOMICS

One of the greatest challenges for any ideology is to convince the sceptics. Because ideologies are in such large part about a distinct set of values rather than a description of facts, they are not something one can 'prove'. But the case made by the great classical economist Adam Smith for early liberalism is different and, for that reason, justly famous; it is a justification based on factual, not normative, reason. Smith laid out a powerful case for individual freedom as the most effective means of maximising the 'wealth of nations'. In his book *The Wealth of Nations* (1776/1937), Smith accepted as a starting point what seems to be the ostensibly non-liberal position that a good social arrangement is one that promotes the 'public interest'. But he then mounted a simple but powerful argument that free-market individualism was, paradoxically, serving the public interest, defined as a dynamic and productive economy, better than any other arrangement. From that moment on, liberalism was able to draw on the highly effective argument that individual freedom was not simply something that should be maximised because of some abstract philosophical or moral principles or because it helped some particular individuals to become wealthier, but rather because it promoted the tangible public welfare.

Adam Smith's argument was that the public interest is advanced when individuals are guided—as if by an 'invisible hand' to quote his famous metaphor— by their desire to maximise their own individual economic welfare. This is because a free market will reward individuals who satisfy the preferences of others, and hence create incentives for individuals to act in that way. Serving the public interest thus does not require the very visible hand of the public sector, i.e. of government. Rather, government should stand back and let the market economy function according to its own logic of the profit motive, the price mechanism and the division of labour in a 'hands off' approach that is generally referred to as *laissez faire*. Certain functions, Smith recognised, must be exercised by government, but they are specific and limited: protecting against external threat; ensuring personal security and providing a system of justice; and 'erecting and maintaining certain public works and certain public institutions which it can never be for the interest of any individual to maintain' (Smith 1776/1937: 651). Left to its own, conceded Smith, the market would not provide sufficient military protection, policing, or crucial economic and social infrastructure such as bridges and schooling (see Fenna 2004: 71–93).

The conservative reaction

Liberalism challenged the old order in many ways. It thus provoked a response among those who wanted to keep things as they were rather than change to a more dynamic, individualistic way of life—to 'conserve' rather than transform. These conservatives had trouble arguing against the market economics of liberalism and offered little by way of an alternative. But they had much less trouble contesting the social and political dimensions of liberalism. The central claim of the conservative rebuttal to liberalism was that society could not prosper with the kind of corrosive individualism, freedom and political change that liberals advocated. The choice, according to the conservatives, was between stability and chaos. Established political institutions worked, they argued, because those institutions represented long embedded practices that had been tested by time and had legitimacy, respect and authority. To unravel one part of the inherited social order would be to unravel the whole, and society would descend first into anarchy and then into tyranny.

While liberals welcomed the outbreak of the French Revolution in 1789 which threw off the old order in France, substituting instead democratic government and the 'Rights of Man', English conservative writer and parliamentarian Edmund Burke prophesied doom (Burke 1790/2003). And indeed it was not long before the 'abstract rights' that Burke scorned descended into the Jacobin regime of terror and finally the military coup of Napoleon Bonaparte. Woven through the conservative view of the world has been an organic notion of society, one that sees political communities as much more than coincidentally associated individuals but rather people whose identities arise out of their time and place and who are fortunate to have inherited the complex arrangement of rights and duties, familial and societal ties, and broader institutions that turn a group of individuals into a human *community*.

Being conservative, it must be noted is not the same as being reactionary. Burke was an outspoken defender of the rights and liberties that Englishmen had established for themselves over the centuries (see Burke 1775/1993). While 'reactionaries' regard even the status quo as unsatisfactory and seek to turn back the clock, conservatives cherish the status quo and accordingly will accept moderate change provided it does not compromise fundamental values and occurs in a very cautious manner. Indeed, the strategically minded conservative will invite those adjustments that serve to relieve pressure for more radical or threatening change.

Reform liberalism

Another 'revolution' that got underway at the same time threw up a quite different challenge to liberalism. In the first half of the 19th century Britain was transformed by the Industrial Revolution, a technological revolution that had profound economic, social and ultimately political consequences. The steam engine powered great factories, which created an industrial working class and brought about the concentration of workers in new industrial cities. Working and living conditions were appalling, with men, women and children having little alternative but to labour in oppressive and dangerous conditions at very low wages, for very long hours, while being packed into urban slums devoid of sanitation or basic amenities. Under the classical liberal regime of *laissez faire*, governments did little or nothing to intervene: no public education, no public health care, no health and safety regulations, no limits on age or hours of work, no poverty alleviation, no insurance against unemployment.

Adam Smith's 'invisible hand' was certainly powering an enormous creation of wealth, but was it serving the 'public interest'? Smith could not have envisaged how much human suffering and disadvantage the *laissez faire* system was causing. Under these circumstances, a new generation of liberals radically revised their ideas about what it took to ensure that people were granted the freedom on which liberalism was built. No longer would mere freedom *from* governmental interference or oppression suffice; according to these 'new liberals', individuals needed the material conditions that would give them a freedom *to* make something of their lives. They argued that, contrary to Adam Smith's teachings, only a more active role for government could provide those conditions for meaningful freedom. In the later 19th and early 20th centuries, this 'new' or 'reform' liberalism (also sometimes called 'social liberalism') championed factory regulation, sanitation schemes, public education, social assistance and taxation of the wealthy to provide some compensation for the great inequalities and distress brought about by industrial capitalism.

From this point on, liberalism was fractured into two quite different camps. On the one side were the classical liberals, who stuck to their principles of free markets and limited government. On the other side were the new or reform liberals, who pushed for a therapeutic use of government authority based on what they described as a 'fuller and more positive interpretation of personal liberty' (Hobson 1909: 96). Both sides believed in freedom. But for the classical liberals it was the 'negative freedom' of freedom from politically imposed constraints, while for the new liberals it was the 'positive freedom' of freedom from economically imposed constraints. The reform movement in liberalism sought an 'equality of opportunity' for individuals that went well beyond classical liberalism's emphasis on formal political equality. Both sides believed in 'justice'. But for the classical liberals it was the procedural justice of equality before the law while for the new liberals it was something closer to 'social justice' or a justice of fair shares and fair opportunities.

While the two types of freedom ('negative' and 'positive') might seem to be complementary, one building on the other, that is not how they were—or continue to be (Berlin 1969)—regarded by classical liberals. This is because providing 'positive freedom' for some, they argued, impinged on the 'negative freedom' of others. For example, providing the more disadvantaged members of society with some freedom from brute economic necessity required new laws regulating terms of employment (such as Britain's controversial *Factory Acts*) and new taxes taking some money away from the more privileged to provide services for the poor. Imposing the regulations and the taxes in the name of the positive freedom of their beneficiaries arguably abridged the negative freedom of the factory owners and of the wealthier taxpayers. At its extreme, classical liberalism's resistance to government-imposed measures promoting positive freedom for the disadvantaged culminated in 'social Darwinist' arguments that social change in human society was best left to what Herbert Spencer (1851) described as the 'survival of the fittest'. Basing policy on man's 'natural sympathy' for his fellow man, Spencer argued, would only favour 'the multiplication of those worst fitted for existence'.

Liberal pluralism

One other difference separated liberals. Classical liberalism had been a program of political and economic liberation from the arbitrary exercise of political and legal power and constraints on economic enterprise. It had not been as concerned with liberating individuals from various other constraints on their conduct and behaviour in society. But some early liberals (e.g. Locke 1689/1990) had argued strongly for religious freedom, and this aspect of the liberal tradition formed the basis for a broader strand of liberalism that emerged in the 19th century. Within this strand, the principle of individual freedom was carried to what might be regarded as its logical conclusion. These liberals argued that individuals should be able to say and do whatever they liked, regardless of how abhorrent it may seem, provided that in doing so they were not harming others.

John Stuart Mill argued this in his celebrated 1859 tract *On Liberty* (1859/1998). Mill's argument was not only that individuals had a right to be different, but that society benefited from that difference. What of the argument that somebody abusing their freedom by promulgating malicious falsehoods should be suppressed lest they poison the minds of those around them? Mill argued that such people should be free to speak. According to his optimistic view, the good ideas will eventually win out over the bad in the free market of ideas. More broadly, this strand of liberalism promotes a pluralistic view of society, regarding the good society as a healthy combination of individual and group differences.

Socialism

While the Industrial Revolution forced liberalism to develop in new directions, it also spawned an ideology that confronted liberalism in a much less compromising way. Socialism began from the opposite premise: the conviction that it was collective and not individual identities, and collective and not individual freedoms, that mattered. To regard people only as individuals, according to socialists, is to think of them in artificial isolation from their social context. And the most important social context, according to this interpretation, is the *economic* context. The economic context is the way the society is organised to produce goods and services, i.e. a society's 'system of production' or what Marx and Engels (1848/2002) referred to as the 'mode of production'.

According to Marx, individuals should be understood as members of a particular social class arising from their position in the system of production. And in a capitalist society, defined by the private ownership of the means of production, the relationship between the dominant class—the class consisting of the owners of the means of production—and the subordinate working class— the class consisting of the industrial workers whose only significant resource is their own labour—should be thought of as an inherently exploitative one. Marx described himself as a 'scientific socialist', meaning that he saw himself as laying the basis for understanding socialism as something that would emerge from great historical forces rather than as merely something for which there was a strong moral case. The driving force for this transition was the struggle between the two opposed classes of any mode of production.

Socialists looked to the replacement of the exploitative capitalist system with a system where the means of production were instead owned by the community collectively. Fierce debates took place among socialists over the choice of strategy and tactics for bringing about this transition to a new economic and political system and the movement split most significantly between those demanding revolutionary action and those proposing more evolutionary change. The choice was between somehow trying to overthrow the system in a revolutionary manner or attempting to bring about change from within.

In the Marxist revolutionary socialist tradition, it was argued that real freedom for the working class ('proletariat') would only come when the rule of the capitalist class ('bourgeoisie') was overthrown and the capitalist system replaced by a communist system of collective ownership and management. In contrast, change from within meant achieving socialism at some indefinite point in the future through socialist policies of redistribution, public ownership and public services accomplished through the ballot box.

It was the evolutionary socialists—known as social democrats—who came to prevail in the advanced societies like Australia. Importantly, the labour movement, on which the future of socialist politics depended, tended to have a pre-occupation with achieving meaningful concrete reforms for its members and hence it was unlikely to be attracted to risky revolutionary ideas. And, in these societies, as they began to manifest what are today their liberal-democratic tendencies, members of the working class won the right to vote in elections and thus workers became potentially able to use their strength of numbers to advantage in democratic systems of governance. Social democrats, then, sought to mobilise the democratic power of the working class to bring about an incremental transformation of capitalism.

What was not appreciated by the early social democrats was how difficult it would be to balance the need to manage capitalism more humanely as well as efficiently in the short term with trying simultaneously to undermine it in the long term. If a social-democratic party won office and introduced the anti-capitalist policies that their platform promised, the outcome might well be economic downturn and consequence loss of office at the next election. If, on the other hand, they won office and proceeded to implement policies that business liked, they might prove themselves economically competent but at the cost of being unfaithful to their platform and purpose as a social-democratic party. Likewise a problem for social democrats was the emerging tendency in liberal-democratic countries for the workers and their union organisations to abandon the idea of radical change in favour of a more limited and practical struggle to increase their wages and improve their working conditions. Social democrats soon gave this tendency the name 'labourism'. In Australia, where workers had been accepted into the political system with little resistance and wages were relatively high, labourism quickly became the dominant form of working-class ideology. These developments particularly affected the emerging Australian Labor Party, as Economou describes in more detail in Chapter 12 of this book.

While the core tenet of liberalism is liberty, the core tenet of social democracy is egalitarianism: the idea that to as practicable an extent as possible, the necessities and many of the amenities of life should be available to all, regardless of wealth or income. The market economy might never be transcended, but it must be tamed.

Feminism

When all these ideologies were taking shape, men and women were accorded quite different status and roles in society. Women were decidedly second-class citizens in a number of respects, most prominently in being denied, for much longer than men, the right to vote and in often having subordinate property rights and access to such key activities as education and professional employment. Feminism emerged as the ideology of the women's movement, a movement whose purpose was to eradicate those limitations on the freedom of women.

Feminism had some notable early expressions, such as the Declaration of the Rights of Women in the French Revolution (de Gouges 1791/1980) and the writings of Mary Wollstonecraft (1792/1988) in England. However, the 'first wave' of feminism was really a movement of the late 19th century, aimed at eliminating the formal inequalities that continued to be imposed on women even as democracy was finally being conceded. The 'suffragettes' demanded the right to vote for women and political equality between the sexes. Subsequent developments in feminism (a 'second wave', with ramifications ever since, is usually identified as emerging in the 1960s) focused on less formal inequalities, such as those arising from the relationship between men and women in the private sphere of family and home life, the prevalence of violence against women and economic inequalities in the workplace.

Like conservatism and unlike either liberalism or socialism, feminism is an ideology concerned mainly with social and political factors and not one that places economic relations at its core. Thus there are very different types of feminism depending on which economic system is favoured. Insofar as socialists recognised women's disadvantage, they saw the problem of gender exploitation as part of the larger system of class exploitation. Thus *socialist feminism* allies the women's cause with the workers' cause. Insofar as liberals recognised women's disadvantage, they saw it as stemming from the failure to extend rights of individual freedom and equality to both sexes. Thus *liberal feminism* is about completing the liberal project of treating all people as morally equal. And just as liberalism itself comes in different guises, so does liberal feminism. There has been a particularly strong affinity between reform liberalism and feminism, based on the shared belief that there should be an active state role in creating real equality of opportunity (Sawer 2003). Like other ideologies, feminism also varies from less radical to more radical versions. The more radical variants take a pessimistic position on the ability of males to accommodate equality of the sexes, perceiving male dominance as supported by a structurally entrenched 'patriarchy'.

Some of the main divergences in feminist thought spring from contrasting basic assumptions about human nature. Traditional society identified women as being in crucial ways different from men, a difference that justified women being assigned different, and subordinate, roles and rights. In response, the tendency in liberal feminism has been to see men and women as in essence 'born equal', with women needing to be 'liberated' from those traditional identities and constraints. Radical feminism, by contrast, tends to be predicated on a basic assumption of difference, though not the set of differences emphasised in the traditional view (rather a set that affirms the value of distinctively 'female' attributes) and certainly not that tradition's customs of gender inequality and exploitation.

Environmentalism

Environmentalism takes as its central concern what it perceives as the predatory relationship of human beings to the natural environment and the consequent threat to ecological balance and environmental sustainability. Like feminism, environmentalism comes in a variety of versions depending on the economic alliances it makes and its degree of radicalism. Moderate versions simply remind us that society needs to husband its natural resources a little more wisely, while more radical versions claim that humans are an exterminator species incompatible with nature.

Environmentalism has taken on an anti-capitalist or anti-business flavour since it frequently appears that market forces and the profit motive are to blame for damage to the environment in capitalist societies. Thus environmentalism aligns well with reform liberalism because of the latter's willingness to correct for perceived deficiencies in the market mechanism. It also aligns well with social democracy, the 'green left', for similar reasons.

But there are contrary arguments that contend that capitalism is not necessarily hostile to environmentalism. Many of the world's very worst cases of environmental damage were to be found in societies that were not capitalist at all, the societies of Soviet Eastern Europe. And liberal environmentalists seek to use market forces, particularly economic incentives, to assist with environmental protection. Free-market environmentalism goes yet one step further to claim that it can align green concerns with classical liberalism, arguing that environmental harm results from *insufficient* market forces and from an inadequate regime of property rights that gives nobody ownership responsibility for common resources like the atmosphere, the oceans, fresh water and the wilderness.

Environmentalism can be compatible with conservatism—as revealed by their common usage of the term 'conservation'—though in practice contemporary environmentalism tends to have a radical flavour. It can also be compatible with feminism.

Left and Right

Since the French Revolution, the central axis of political debate and conflict has been described as that between the 'Left' and the 'Right'. Political opinions are commonly regarded as falling somewhere on a continuum or ideological spectrum from the far Left to the far Right. The most common way of distinguishing the Left from the Right today focuses on their attitudes to equality. A defining characteristic of the Left is a stronger belief in equality—its desirability and its feasibility—as the overriding political value. A defining characteristic of the Right is a stronger belief in the acceptability and inevitability of inequality. Thus socialists are on 'the Left' because of their commitment to abolishing inequalities. Reform liberals might be described as occupying the Centre-Left because of their belief in moderating inequalities. Classical liberals are on the Right because of their strong attachment to the free market and the inequalities that it produces. Meanwhile conservatives, who may disagree with liberals on many points, are also on the Right because of their 'hostility to equality' (Gaus 2000: 174) in any domain of life—social, cultural, economic, political.

This one-dimensional Left–Right spectrum works well for this major cluster of economic and social issues but it works rather less well once the range of issues is broadened. Neither feminism nor environmentalism in their generic form can readily be located on the standard Left–Right political spectrum, though some of their variants—such as socialist feminism or liberal environmentalism—certainly can be. But the concepts of Left and Right remain central to political debate and will remain so as long as the tension between government and markets, between the collective and the individual, remains central to political life.

Ideologies in the 20th and 21st centuries

FEDERATION AND THE IDEOLOGICAL 'SETTLEMENT' IN AUSTRALIA

While the newer ideologies of feminism and environmentalism were less influential at the founding of the Australian Commonwealth, conservatism, the old and new liberalisms, and socialism were all part of the conflicts, debates and political manoeuvrings of the time. Of these it was the new liberalism that occupied the key political middle ground. Its home was in Victoria and its most obvious expression was in the movement for tariff protection of domestic manufacturing. It took political form in the protectionist Liberal Party led by Alfred Deakin. Deakin was one of the leading figures in the drafting of the Commonwealth Constitution, the most prominent 'founder' of Australia's Liberal Party tradition, and one of the country's first Prime Ministers. His influence was such that the reform liberal philosophy in Australia came to be termed 'Deakinite liberalism'. This story is elaborated by Brett in Chapter 11 of this book (also Brett 2003).

Socialism and social democracy found a home in the rapidly developing labour movement and nascent Labor Party, as explained by Economou in Chapter 12 of this book. A moderate and undoctrinaire version of social democracy has mostly predominated, sometimes disparaged by socialists as a mere 'labourist' orientation to immediate material improvements for working Australians and a disregard for any transformative socialist strategy. This moderate quality facilitated a political cooperation between Labor and the protectionist liberals that dominated the first decade of the new Australian nation after 1900, squeezing out the classical free-trade liberals and establishing the direction in which Australian policy would head. A number of accommodations were reached to produce a package that has been described by Kelly (1992) as 'the Australian Settlement' (see also Stokes 2004). The Deakinite Liberals and the Labor Party agreed on maintaining a 'white Australia' immigration policy, on protective tariffs for Australian industry, on a system of industrial arbitration for disputes between employers and employees, and on introducing old-age and invalid pensions. These were all policies that challenged the principles of classical liberalism and represented a common ground between the new liberalism and social democracy. They established the framework for Australian policy over much of the 20th century.

The big loser in this formative period of Australian political life was classical liberalism, though it always retained an influence and a strong position in New South Wales. This was most evident in the arguments about the relative merits of free trade and protective tariffs. The export-oriented rural sector in New South Wales had little to gain and much to lose from the tariffs that sheltered

Victoria's manufacturing industry. While some Australian intellectuals in these early years promoted a broader vision of limited government and free markets (Melleuish 2001), it would be some time before those ideas managed to set the political agenda.

THE KEYNESIAN EPISODE AND THE END OF IDEOLOGY

Internationally, classical liberalism was losing ground in the first decades of the 20th century to the new (reform) liberalism. But it was some time before reform liberalism could counter classical liberalism's decisive argument that nothing promoted economic growth and advance like the free market. This changed in the 1930s. With its relentless unemployment and business bankruptcies, the Great Depression called into question the market economy and free market economics. Inspired principally by the English economist John Maynard Keynes (1936), a new generation of economists, and a new generation of governments around the world, adopted the view that governments—rather than relying on a self-regulating market economy—should practise interventionist 'counter-cyclical budgeting' to temper the fluctuations in the economy. This involved governments supporting job creation, business investment and welfare spending through heavy doses of public expenditure and tax cuts when an economic downturn was threatening, to be counterbalanced by government spending cuts and tax increases during times of economic boom. Reform liberalism's belief in the *moral* imperative for government intervention was now crucially supported by this 'Keynesian revolution' through its discovery of an *economic* justification for government intervention.

Keynesian economics forced classical liberalism into ideological retreat. That retreat was so great that in the United States the connection of the word 'liberal' with market economics was lost. To this day (to the confusion of international observers and political-science students), the word 'liberal' is used in US politics to mean only Leftist reform liberalism while classical liberalism is championed by those who describe themselves as 'neo-conservatives'.

By the early 1960s it almost seemed that the ideological struggle was over. Reform liberalism and social democracy had converged around a continuously expanding welfare state and progressive taxation, tellingly administered even by conservative governments such as the long-lasting Menzies Coalition government in Australia.

OLD TRUTHS NEVER DIE: SAVING THE MARKET

But the postwar economic boom came to an end in the mid-1970s. And when Keynesian policy prescriptions only generated worrisome levels of inflation without reversing the rise in unemployment, the old debates about the role of the market were re-opened. Taxation and government spending on social services had reached historically high levels, reviving the classical liberal argument that governmental intervention was a hindrance not a help to economic performance. Faced with a sustained economic downturn that their Keynesian tools were unable to manage, reform liberals and social democrats were forced to confront the reality that, as classic liberalism had always maintained, there indeed might be a trade-off between policies (such as progressive taxation and social spending) that promoted greater equality and the goal of a productive and efficient economy. Classical liberalism—inspired by the intellectual contributions of Hayek (1944; 1960) and Friedman (1962)—suddenly put market principles back squarely into the political arena through such doctrines as 'supply side economics' and monetarism, both concerned with reducing the role of government in the economy. Since it involved a revival of an older version of the ideology it came to be termed neoliberalism, or alternatively, since it emphasised the importance of market forces, market liberalism.

In Australia a movement called 'economic rationalism' (a term seized upon by its critics and used disparagingly ever since) advocated the winding back of Keynesian-style intervention, public-sector enterprises and the remnants of the 'Australian Settlement', particularly tariff protectionism and industrial arbitration. Older notions that unemployment, poverty and disadvantage were primarily the responsibility of the affected individual, and not of the wider society, were revived (e.g. Sullivan 2000). Those Liberal Party figures who embraced this neoliberalism in the 1980s (John Howard being a prominent example) were referred to as 'dry', by contrast with their own dismissal of those who refused to abandon a gentler Deakinite version of liberalism as 'wet'.

OLD TRUTHS NEVER DIE: SAVING SOCIETY

What of conservatism? The ideological dominance of both liberal individualism and democracy in Western culture left conservatism with very little ideological purchase. The transition to democracy had mostly occurred without any of the dire consequences that conservatives had prophesied. Great institutional change had occurred without descent into anarchy or communism. Change in a range of spheres brought material, social and political improvement, not disaster. It was the future, not the past, that looked good. Arguments that retention of the monarchy was important to the integrity and stability of Australia's political system, while sufficient to defeat a divided republican movement in the constitutional referendum of 1999, nonetheless only resonated with a limited audience.

Western conservatism had always placed great emphasis on such institutions as the family and Christian churches in ordering and regulating social life. They had also been sceptical about liberalism's emphasis on universal human values, favouring a view that regarded particular communities as possessing their own local identities integral to their coherence and effectiveness. While rapid social change in the 20th century seemed to undermine many of these elements, accompanying social problems ranging from welfare dependency to ethnic conflict were held up by conservatives as vindication of their enduring preference for social homogeneity, stability and order. Some conservative-minded leaders, of whom Liberal Party figures John Howard and Tony Abbott have been conspicuous examples, have advocated—alongside support for market liberalism in the economic sphere—policies (in relation, for example, to taxation and family styles) that would slow the rate of social change. Some Australian conservatives have projected their scepticism about liberal pluralism into the advocacy of assimilationist and 'national unity' positions on issues of border security, immigration, multiculturalism and Indigenous rights.

Prime Minister John Howard has embodied a marriage of market liberalism and social conservatism—putting conservative social values ahead of individual freedom in the social sphere while having a strong attachment to individual freedom in the economic sphere. This marriage is facilitated by the way classical liberalism has little to say about social issues while conservatism has little to say about economic ones. Indeed the Liberal Party of Australia has always featured a 'curious amalgam' of liberalism and conservatism (Craven 2001: 53; also Norton 2004). There is nonetheless a tension in this marriage. Some Australian conservatives, for example, denounce 'economic rationalism' because they see society not as somehow distinct from the economy but rather as a collective entity whose interests must be served by the economy.

THE END OF SOCIAL DEMOCRACY?

If the end of the postwar boom and the crisis of Keynesianism since the early 1970s were tough on reform liberalism, they were even tougher on social democracy. By the end of the 20th century, most avenues for the political control and progressive transformation of capitalism seemed to have reached a dead end. The Left's program of 'socialisation of the means of production' through nationalisation of industry has been abandoned. Instead, many public-sector enterprises have been privatised. There is a widespread perception that the welfare state has reached its limits.

Some social democrats have responded by taking on board parts of the new thinking to produce the so-called 'Third Way', associated in Britain with the Blair Labour government, in the US with the Clinton Presidency and in Australia most notably with Mark Latham's brief and unsuccessful leadership of the Labor Party. The Third Way claims to bring together traditional Left concerns with material equality and positive freedom for all, contemporary liberal emphases on individual responsibility, negative freedom and wealth creation, and conservative concerns about the integrity of local communities (e.g. Giddens 1998). Like all attempts to adapt socialist thinking to current conditions over the past century and a half, this latest set of theoretical adjustments has proven contentious (Giddens 2000, 2001; Callinicos 2001).

Conclusion

Democratic political communities are engaged in a continuous and probably endless debate about the way they are organised and operate. A good part of that debate is empirical or factual: what approach will best get us the results we want? However, a very large part of that debate cannot be so easily settled because it is normative or value-laden: what results do we want, and what is the most desirable way of achieving those results? This is the realm of ideology.

The contest of ideologies reflects two irresolvable sets of differences. One is between different assumptions about human nature. Conservatism, for instance, combines a pessimistic and a localistic view of humanity: it is pessimistic in highlighting our universal potential for evil, and localistic in holding that we are defined by the particular culture and community in which we are based. Liberalism, by contrast, is based on much more optimistic and universalistic assumptions: we are united by our common humanity and capable of resolving our problems through the spread of freedom and enlightenment. These are primary assumptions that cannot be 'proved' or 'disproved', but from them flow a range of thoughts and conclusions about how societies ought to be governed. These different starting points are linked to a set of different end points, different sets of values about what form of political community is most desirable. Is individual freedom the highest value? Is it fairness, or stability and security, or material equality, or community and cooperation, or ecological harmony?

In a capitalist world the dominant ideology is going to be liberalism—though as we have seen, there are very different liberalisms. Classical liberalism, the original liberalism, is the central ideology of wealth *creation* in a capitalist society. It emphasises the practical and the moral value of individual freedom and responsibility, combining it with a notion of the public interest generated as the outcome of market incentives, and condones only the minimally necessary degree of government intervention in the economy. In contrast, both reform liberalism and social democracy are ideologies whose focus is the *distribution* of wealth and opportunities in a capitalist society. They promote an active role for government in rectifying social and economic inequalities. As the newer ideologies of feminism and environmentalism remind us, finally, there is more to life than just economic factors. Whether one is male or female or whether one is squandering planetary resources and wreaking ecological havoc, may be as, or even more, important.

REFERENCES

Berlin, I. 1969, 'Two Concepts of Liberty', in *Four Essays on Liberty*, Oxford University Press, Oxford.

Brett, J. 2003, *Australian Liberals and the Moral Middle Class: From Alfred Deakin to John Howard*, Cambridge University Press, Cambridge.

Burke, E. 1790/2003, *Reflections on the Revolution in France*, Yale University Press, New Haven.

Burke, E. 1775/1993, 'Conciliation with America' in *Edmund Burke: Pre-Revolutionary Writings*, ed I. Harris, Cambridge University Press, Cambridge.

Callinicos, A. 2001, *Against the Third Way: An Anticapitalist Critique*, Polity Press, Cambridge.

Craven, G. 2001, 'A Liberal Federation and a Liberal Constitution', in *Liberalism and the Australian Federation*, ed. J.R. Nethercote, Federation Press, Leichhardt, NSW.

de Gouges, O. 1791/1980, *Déclaration des Droits de la Femme et de la Citoyenne*, available as 'The Rights of Women' in *Women in Revolutionary Paris 1789–1795: Selected Documents Translated with Notes and Commentary*, ed D. Gay Levy, H. Branson Applewhite & M. Durham Johnson, University of Illinois Press, Urbana IL.

Fenna, A. 2004, *Australian Public Policy*, 2nd edn, Longman, Frenchs Forest.

Friedman, M. 1962, *Capitalism and Freedom*, University of Chicago Press, Chicago IL.

Gaus, G. F. 2000, *Political Concepts and Political Theories*, Westview Press, Boulder CO.

Giddens, A. ed 2001, *The Global Third Way Debate*, Polity Press, Cambridge.

Giddens, A. 2000, *The Third Way and its Critics*, Polity Press, Cambridge.

Giddens, A. 1998, *The Third Way: The Renewal of Social Democracy*, Polity Press, Cambridge.

Hayek, F.A. 1960, *The Constitution of Liberty*, Routledge & Kegan Paul, London.

Hayek, F.A. 1944, *The Road to Serfdom*, Routledge & Kegan Paul, London.

Heywood, A. 2003, *Political Ideologies: An Introduction*, 3rd edn, Palgrave Macmillan, Basingstoke.

Hobson, J. A. 1909, *The Crisis of Liberalism: New Issues of Democracy*, P. S. King & Son, London.

Kelly, P. 1992, *The End of Certainty*, Allen & Unwin, Sydney.

Keynes, 1936/1973, *The General Theory of Employment, Interest and Money*, Macmillan, London.

Locke, J. 1690/1988, *Two Treatises of Government*, Cambridge University Press, Cambridge.

Locke, J. 1689/1990, *A Letter Concerning Toleration*, Prometheus Books, Amherst, New York.

Marx, K. & Engels, F. 1848/2002, *The Communist Manifesto*, Penguin Classics, London.

Melleuish, G. 2001, *A Short History of Australian Liberalism*, Centre for Independent Studies, Sydney.

Mill, J.S. 1859/1998, *On Liberty and Other Essays*, Oxford University Press, Oxford.

Norton, A. 2004 'Liberalism and the Liberal Party of Australia', in *The Politics of Australian Society: Political Issues for the New Century*, eds P. Boreham, G. Stokes & R. Hall, 2nd edn, Longman, Frenchs Forest NSW.

Paine, T. 1791–92/1995, 'The Rights of Man', in *Paine: Collected Works*, ed E. Foner, Library of America, New York.

Sawer, M. 2003, *The Ethical State? Social Liberalism in Australia*, Melbourne University Press, Carlton.

Smith, A. 1776/1937, *An Inquiry into the Nature and Causes of the Wealth of Nations*, Modern Library, New York.

Spencer, H. 1851, *Social Statics: or The Conditions Essential to Happiness Specified, and the First of them Developed*, John Chapman, London.

Stokes, G. 2004, 'The "Australian Settlement" and Australian Political Thought', *Australian Journal of Political Science*, vol. 39, no 1, pp. 5–22.

Sullivan, L. 2000, *Behavioural Poverty*, Centre for Independent Studies, Sydney.

Wollstonecraft, M. 1792/1988, *The Vindication of the Rights of Women*, Norton, New York.

Government Institutions

PART 2

AUSTRALIA

Introduction

This part of the book discusses the institutional arrangements through which government operates in Australia.

The names of some of the institutions—the Parliament, the Cabinet, and so on—may be reasonably familiar to some readers, and it is easy to take their existence for granted. However, institutional arrangements are never neutral. Particular ways of setting up institutions can predispose the political system to work in certain ways, with distinctive effects on the behaviour of politicians and on the policies experienced by citizens. The object in these chapters is to understand how the purpose and structure of the institutional arrangements affect how Australia is governed.

In Chapter 3, Andrew Parkin and John Summers provide an overview of the Australian 'constitutional framework'. The chapter examines both the formal document known as 'the Constitution' and the more informal—but nonetheless absolutely vital—conventions by which the system of government operates. They describe the Australian system as a 'hybrid' with both British and American forebears, and explain the implications of this construction, particularly as it affected the 'constitutional crisis' of 1975, but also as it affects the day-to-day workings of liberal democracy in Australia. They also reflect on the debate about whether Australia should reconstitute itself as a republic independent of the British monarch.

Chapter 4 outlines the workings of Parliament and the concept of 'responsible government'. John Summers discusses the different roles of the Parliament and notes the various procedures which enable the Parliament to scrutinise the actions of government and raises questions about their effectiveness. He also notes the increasingly important role the Senate played when the 'balance of power' in that chamber was held by minor party and Independent Senators.

In Chapter 5, Geoff Anderson scrutinises the heart of the executive branch of government: the Cabinet and Prime Minister. It is at this level that the major decisions are made about government policies and strategic directions. Anderson traces the evolution of the Cabinet process over recent Australian history, and explains the political context in which it operates. He examines the role and influence of the Prime Minister, and assesses the constraints on executive government imposed by the parliamentary system.

The political management of the vast administrative apparatus for which governments and Ministers are responsible is the subject of Chapter 6. Jenny Stewart discusses recent changes in the management of the public sector, including outsourcing, privatisation, the rise of 'managerialism' and the politicisation of the public service. She evaluates the impact of these developments on the effectiveness and efficiency of the public service, and on the ways in which the public sector can be held accountable for its actions.

Federalism is a key aspect of Australia's constitutional structure and, in Chapter 7, John Summers provides a detailed analysis of how it affects the system of government. He discusses the evolution of the federal system and the relationship between the Commonwealth government and the State governments. Summers demonstrates how the legal and financial powers of Commonwealth have grown in relation to those of the States, but he also highlights features of the federal system which have restricted the capacity of the Commonwealth to be completely dominant over the States.

In Chapter 8, Haig Patapan describes the role of an important and increasingly controversial institution, the High Court. While the political significance of the High Court has, at times, been overlooked because of the judicial nature of its form and operations, Patapan explains how, through its interpretation of the Australian Constitution, its decisions have had a political impact.

The constitutional framework

ANDREW PARKIN AND JOHN SUMMERS

As Chapter One explains, liberal-democratic governmental and political systems are structured by a constitutional framework that seeks to firmly establish the rule of law, to specify and constrain the powers of government, to provide for the democratic accountability of government to the governed. The Australian system of government and politics is structured by a constitutional framework that is consistent with this liberal-democratic pattern.

One important element of the Australian constitutional framework is a formal document entitled *The Constitution of the Commonwealth of Australia*, usually known simply as 'the Constitution'. But the constitutional framework consists of more than this formal document and includes various other arrangements, understandings and conventions that are not in that document but are also central to the Australian system of government. This chapter explains how the constitutional framework—both the formal Constitution, and the informal conventions and understandings—shapes the workings of the Australian political system.

The hybrid system

The formal Constitution came into effect on 1 January 1901. Its provisions were the product of decisions made, and compromises reached, by politicians from the various Australian colonies, then independent and virtually self-governing entities, who came together during the 1890s to discuss the framework for a national Australian government. These constitutional drafters were themselves influenced by political ideas and institutions with an even older heritage.

In particular, they were familiar with the British system of government — sometimes termed the 'Westminster system' — on which the governmental institutions in each of the Australian colonies were based. They were also influenced by the system of government in the United States, a system that had been designed to address a problem similar to that facing the Australians: how to reconcile the desire for the establishment of a national government with the wish, particularly of the less populous colonies, to maintain and protect local interests and the identity of the separate colonial governments.

The compromise reached contains important elements of both the British and US systems. The result has been aptly described as 'a hybrid form of government' (Emy 1978: 181; Summers 1979: 7; Saunders 1990; Galligan 1995: 38).[1] Broadly speaking, what was retained from the British system was the notion of *responsible government*, while from the Americans was borrowed the notion of *federalism*.

Responsible government

The drafters of the Australian Constitution in the 1890s were familiar with the British parliamentary system, under which an elected Parliament was meant to represent citizens and to act as a law-making (or *legislative*) body. In Britain, the elected house of Parliament is called the House of Commons, and there is also an unelected House of Lords. This *legislative* law-making body needs to be distinguished from the *executive* branch of government. The executive branch is where, as authorised by the laws passed by Parliament, the programs and policies of government are actually carried out. In the Westminster parliamentary system, there is an important link between the legislative and the executive bodies. This is because the politicians (known as Ministers) who are responsible for leading the executive branch of government are first of all elected to the legislative body. In Britain, voters elect individual politicians to the House of Commons to represent designated local areas. The political party or coalition that, after such an election, wins a majority of seats in the House of Commons is then recognised as having won government. The Prime Minister and other Ministers who head the executive branch are drawn from the Members of Parliament that belong to this winning party or coalition. The most senior Ministers meet together in a body called the Cabinet. The overall term *the government* usually refers simply to this group of senior Cabinet Ministers, though sometimes it is used more broadly to refer to all members of the majority party or coalition in the House of Commons.

This British system evolved over centuries of constitutional development.

Originally, the British monarch—the King or Queen—monopolised executive and legislative power. But over time the Parliament became the exclusive law-maker and established its right to *authorise* the raising of taxes and the spending of money by the executive. This development established an important legislative power, separate from the power of the executive. It became a fundamental principle in the Westminster system that the government could not raise taxes or spend money unless it had been authorised by a law of the Parliament.

With the further development of the system, the British Cabinet, led by the Prime Minister, became in effect *the government*, largely usurping the monarch's executive power. While the monarch still formally embodies executive power, in practice he or she acts only as advised by the government.

In order to continue to govern, the government under the Westminster system needs to maintain the support of a majority in the House of Commons. This is because without such a majority the government would be unable to enact any new laws and, most importantly, would be unable to enact laws that authorised the raising of taxes and the spending of money for running the government. (Originally, all laws also had to be approved by the unelected House of Lords, but the power of the House of Lords to do anything more than delay legislation was removed in 1911.) If a majority in the House of Commons refuses to support the government any longer, and particularly if it denies the government 'supply' (i.e. the supply of money), then the government customarily resigns.

Because the government, in this sense, is responsible to Parliament (which is itself responsible to the citizens through elections), this Westminster system is described as a system of *responsible government* or perhaps *responsible Cabinet government*. Advocates of this system argue that the mechanisms by which it identifies and authorises the actions of the government ensure that government is kept democratic and accountable.

It is important to appreciate the relationship between the legislature (i.e. the Parliament) and the executive (i.e. the government acting through the Cabinet) under the Westminster system. Unlike the US system, where there is an explicit attempt to *separate* legislative and executive functions (through respectively a Congress and a separately elected President), they are closely *linked* under the system of responsible government. The government is drawn from the Parliament and, because it comprises the leading members of the majority party in the House of Commons, in fact 'controls' that house of Parliament. (Were such majority support to disappear on a major issue or with respect to supply, the government could no longer hold office.)

Because the executive government is drawn from, and is responsible to, the Parliament, any real separation between executive and legislature does not exist. As classically described by Walter Bagehot (1867/1963: 66, 68):

the efficient secret of the English constitution may be described as the close union, the nearly complete fusion, of the executive and legislative powers . . . The connecting link is the *Cabinet*.

. . . [The] Cabinet is a combining committee—a hyphen which joins, a *buckle* which fastens, the legislative part of the state to the executive part of the state. In its origin it belongs to the one, in its functions it belongs to the other.

The Australian system, as instituted in 1901, adopted most of these Westminster notions of *responsible government*. In Australia, an elected House of Representatives performs a function corresponding to the British House of Commons. The party or coalition that wins a majority of seats in elections for the House of Representatives forms the government. This is how, after the Australian national election held in October 2004, the coalition of the Liberal Party and the National Party—that together won 87 of the 150 seats in the House of Representatives— was confirmed as the government, and how the Liberal Party leader John Howard, who was re-elected as a Member of the House of Representatives for the Sydney electorate of Bennelong, was confirmed as Prime Minister.

The adoption of the British system of government in Australia was complicated by the fact that there is no formal British Constitution in the normal sense. There are some Acts of the British Parliament that are recognised as 'constitutional' in that they establish some elements of the governing framework (such as the *Parliamentary Act* of 1911 limiting the House of Lords' power to that of delaying legislation). However, there is no recognised supreme and authoritative document that lays down the rules about how the system will work. For this reason, it is sometimes said that Britain has an 'unwritten constitution'. The system operates largely according to informal *conventions*, comprising broadly shared understandings of how the system works. Examples of such British conventions include the notion that the government will be formed by the political party that wins a majority in the House of Commons, and that the Prime Minister will be a member of the House of Commons and not the House of Lords.

Australia, by contrast, adopted a written Constitution when it created its national governmental system with effect from 1901. This written Australian Constitution established *some* elements of the Westminster system (by, for example, creating a Parliament and by specifying that Ministers must be members of the Parliament), but it did not formally specify other elements. It was simply expected that the system would operate in the way it already had, without formal rules, in Britain and in the Australian colonies. Thus many important aspects of the Australian parliamentary system depend, as in Britain, on conventions. It was on the basis of such a convention that is not part of the written Constitution, for example, that John Howard was immediately and unambiguously recognised as the continuing Prime Minister on election night in October 2004.

The main reason why Australia, unlike Britain, has a formal written Constitution is in large part because a formal document was necessary to accommodate the second major part of Australia's hybrid system of government — federalism.

Federalism

In Britain there is a *unitary* government: the Parliament based at Westminster has absolute sovereignty over the whole country and over all matters. The founders of the United States of America, who came from what were at the time 13 separate American colonies, created a different structure — a federal system. To provide a unified approach to *some* common matters such as defence, foreign relations, international trade, immigration, currency, postal services and so on, the American founders wanted to form a new single nation. At the same time, they wanted to retain the 13 colonies with viable governments exercising sovereignty over other matters. The federal system they created achieved these objectives.

Federalism is a political solution to the problem of how to combine previously separate self-governing entities to form a new common national government. It enables the existing States to retain their identity and many of their powers at the regional, or State, level while at the same time producing a genuine national government for matters of agreed national significance.

In a federal system, governmental power is divided between separate tiers of government, each of which has a degree of authority and autonomy (or 'sovereignty') over particular governmental functions. At the national level in a federal system, a national government has the power to make and execute laws over some defined matters for the whole nation while State governments have the power to make and execute laws for their State over other defined matters. The division of power between the different tiers of government is specified by a formal written Constitution that guarantees the authority and autonomy of each tier within its area of responsibility, prevents the division of power between the tiers from being easily changed by only one of the tiers, and specifies a mechanism for resolving any disputes about which tier has responsibility over particular matters.

The USA was the first modern federation. Its national government was formally established in 1787, and the 13 former British colonies continued to exist as States with their own governments. (Since then, other States have been created and added to the federation, with the total forming the USA now being 50.)

In Australia in the 1890s, as in North America in the 1780s, the existing colonies were not prepared to give up their existence or most of their autonomy. There was also a fear in the less populous Australian colonies that any new national government could be dominated by more populous colonies and might act against their interests. There was thus insufficient political support for simply abolishing the colonies in order to create a single new national 'unitary' government. The leaders and people in the colonies would simply not have agreed to enter the new nation if it had been necessary to give up too much of their colony's autonomy.

On the other hand, the Australian colonial leaders in the 1890s were influenced by a growing Australian nationalist sentiment and by a belief, strengthened by the economic depression of the 1890s, that there would be economic advantages in creating a large single Australian common market in place of the existing 'barbarism of borderism' with its extensive system of customs and other trade barriers between the colonies. These arguments supported the idea of a national government with sovereign powers in *some* areas.

Accordingly, the federal system, pioneered in the United States, was adopted in Australia. The national government created in Australia was officially called the Commonwealth government. As in the United States, it is often also informally referred to as the federal government.

In a genuine federation—with its coexistence of different levels of 'sovereign' government—the States are not subject to direction from the national government and the national government is not subject to direction from the States. Citizens living in a federation are, in an important sense, 'dual citizens', with two direct and independent links to two formally independent levels of government. The national government obtains its mandate and legitimacy directly from the citizens: citizens elect the national government directly, and on matters within its formal powers this national government deals directly with the citizens. Likewise, citizens elect their State government directly and on matters within its formal powers this State government deals directly with the citizens (Parkin 1996).

In a federation, there is a tension or balance between two principles: a principle supporting the notion of a single nation that transcends the barriers between the component States; and, at the same time, a principle supporting the maintenance of the autonomy and sovereignty of the States. This is why there are both centralising and decentralising features in the Australian Constitution. On the one hand, there are provisions in the Constitution (sections 90, 92 and 117) that are designed to create a single nation and a common market within the new Commonwealth of Australia by removing the barriers to the movement of goods and people across State borders. On the other hand, there are provisions (sections 106, 107 and 108) that protect the integrity and independence of the constitutions, laws and powers of the States.

The Constitution also provides safeguards against hasty alteration to the compact or against unilateral amendment by either tier of government. Section 128 requires that a law to amend the Constitution must be passed by a referendum with the support of a majority of voters throughout the Commonwealth, and by a majority of voters in a majority of the States. This has indeed been an impediment to frequent alterations: only eight of the 44 attempts by referendum to change provisions of the Constitution have succeeded.

Three key features that are integral parts of the United States' federal system were adopted in Australia: a Senate, a specified division of powers between the national government and the State governments, and judicial review.

The Senate, a separate house of the national legislature in which each State, whatever its population, is represented equally, exists alongside the House of Representatives, where representation is proportional to population. The Senate has virtually the same legislative powers as the House of Representatives, and for any law to be valid it must be approved by both houses of Parliament. Some critics complain that the Senate is 'undemocratic' because of this State-related rather than population-related system of representation, and assert that Australia would be better off without the Senate or with a less powerful Senate (Watson 1977; Crisp 1983: 349). Whatever the philosophical merits of this argument, it is historically irrelevant: without the agreement to 'import' a US-style Senate, there may well have been no Australian national government at all because it was one of the crucial compromises during the debates of the 1890s that allowed federation to occur (Galligan 1995: 75–86).

The second key feature of federalism adopted in the Australian Constitution is a specified division of powers and responsibilities between the national government and the State governments. In the Constitution, specified legislative powers are granted to the Commonwealth (mostly enumerated in section 51), and the States retain whatever residual powers are not explicitly given in this way to the Commonwealth. Some powers are granted exclusively to the Commonwealth, but most are concurrent and can be exercised by both the Commonwealth and the States. Section 109 provides that, in the case of conflict between valid Commonwealth and State laws, the Commonwealth law prevails.

The powers granted to the Commonwealth are mostly those that, in the 1890s, seemed most sensibly handled at a national level: for example, 'naval and military defence', 'currency, coinage and legal tender', 'immigration and emigration' and 'external affairs'.

The residual powers left to be exercised by the States encompass most of the direct public services and regulations experienced by citizens: public schools, police and correctional services, roads, parks and recreational facilities, city planning, public housing, regulation of private housing construction and private rental housing, the regulation of retail trade, environmental protection, commuter transport services, ports, most personal welfare services, public hospitals and health centres, fire protection and other emergency services, provision or regulation of reticulated electricity and gas services, provision or regulation of water and sewerage services and so on. For Australians, their State government was intended to be, and largely remains, the government that they encounter most often.

The third feature of federalism is judicial review. Under the process of judicial review, a court (in the United States called the Supreme Court and in Australia the High Court) acts as an 'umpire' in the federal system. It determines the meaning of the Constitution where this is in dispute and, in particular, to settle disagreements about which government—national or State (or, perhaps, neither)—has power over particular matters. The High Court has the power to invalidate any laws, of either level of government, that it determines are outside the constitutional allocation of power to that government.

Each of these three features of federalism, formally incorporated in the Australian Constitution that took effect in 1901, has subsequently developed and evolved in important ways. Other chapters in this book explore some of these developments and the controversies that have arisen from them. The relationship between the Senate and the House of Representatives is further explored in Chapter 4; the changing 'constitutional balance of power' between the Commonwealth government and the State governments, including the impact of the Commonwealth's growing dominance over public finance, is discussed in Chapter 7; the impact of judicial review by the High Court is the subject of Chapter 8.

There is another aspect of federalism that has been central to the American system. This is the notion of federalism as a means of limiting the overall power of government. The US constitutional drafters, strongly influenced by the prevailing *liberal* philosophies of the day and by their experience as American colonists with the colonial regime run from Britain, were keen to institute a system of limited governmental powers. Advocates of federalism saw it as a good thing in itself because it was a means of containing government and providing a check against the potential tyranny of a powerful central government. This was a less dominant motivation in Australia but some scholars still regard it as an important feature of Australian federalism in theory and in practice (Galligan 1995; Sharman 1989; Craven 2005), and it is a feature regretted by those who would prefer stronger centralised government (Maddox 2005: ch. 3).

The US Constitution attempts to limit the overall power of government in other ways as well. The US system formally separates legislative and executive powers. The chief executive of the United States—the President—is separately elected by the people for a fixed term. Unlike the Prime Minister and Cabinet of the Westminster system, the President is not drawn from the legislature and is not dependent on the continuing support of the legislature to remain in office. The American structure was explicitly *not* adopted in Australia, with the more familiar Westminster arrangement being preferred.

Another US mechanism is the inclusion in the constitutional document of a list of citizen rights that no government—national or State—can override.[2] This was likewise not adopted in Australia, though the Australian Constitution does contain a few provisions that can be regarded as containing a statements of citizen rights,[3] and the judicial review powers of the High Court also provide a potential avenue for the judicial 'discovery' of rights, as discussed in Chapter 8 of this book.

The hybrid in practice

The combination of the principles of responsible government with a federal system, to create Australia's hybrid form of government, imposed constraints on responsible government not experienced in its original British manifestation.

FORMAL CONSTITUTION AND UNWRITTEN CONVENTIONS

The existence of a formal written Australian Constitution means that, unlike in Britain where the system operates largely by convention, there are in Australia formal constitutional specifications relating to the institutions of parliamentary government. The Constitution establishes a Governor-General (to act as the monarch's representative) and the two legislative chambers: the House of Representatives and the Senate. The Constitution specifies that there must be periodic elections (sections 28 and 32), that Ministers must be Members of Parliament (section 64), that the government cannot spend money without Parliamentary appropriation (sections 81 and 83), and that bills to raise and spend the money and amendments to money bills must originate in the House of Representatives (section 53).

However, while it was clearly understood that the Commonwealth would follow the Westminster system of responsible parliamentary government with, for example, the government formed from the majority party or coalition in the House of Representatives, most of the features of *responsible government* are not formally specified in the Constitution. They operate in Australia, as in Britain, by virtue of convention. There is no mention in the Constitution, for example, of the Prime Minister, or of the Cabinet, or of the Prime Minister needing to be a member of the House of Representatives rather than the Senate, or of the government needing to resign if its budget is rejected by the Parliament.

Indeed, in its formal written terms, the Constitution sets out several arrangements that actually appear to be contrary to Westminster procedures. For example, the Constitution specifies that all executive power 'is vested in the Queen and is exercisable by the Governor-General', who also appoints Ministers who 'hold office during the pleasure of the Governor-General' (sections 61, 62, 64). This gives the Governor-General enormous power but it was always understood that the Governor-General would exercise that power in accordance with the 'unwritten' conventions of the Westminster system, in the same way that the monarch in Britain observes Westminster's 'unwritten constitution'. This means that, in practice, the Governor-General authorises the party or coalition that wins a majority in the House of Representatives to form the government, and the Governor-General appoints the Ministers recommended by the leader of that party or coalition.

THE SENATE

The establishment of the Senate as a powerful second legislative chamber also created a tension with the principles of responsible government. Those principles assert that the executive is responsible to the legislature and, though formed on the basis only of its majority in the House of Representatives, the executive is dependent for its continued existence in office on its ability to have legislation, and particularly supply bills, enacted by the Parliament as a whole. A government without parliamentary authority to expend money would not be able to govern, and by convention it would be obliged to resign.

During the inter-colonial debates in the 1890s over the shape of the proposed Australian federation, some delegates foresaw a problem of having a system of responsible government involving *two* equally powerful legislative chambers (Galligan 1995: 75). Under section 53 of the Constitution, the Senate has 'equal power with the House of Representatives in respect of all proposed laws' except for its inability to initiate or amend money bills. There are provisions for dealing with legislative deadlocks between the two houses: section 57 allows for a double dissolution of both houses of Parliament (so that the full membership of both houses faces an election) and, if necessary, a subsequent post-election joint sitting of the two houses under certain deadlock conditions.

In practical terms, the power of the Senate would mean little if the political party that formed the government also enjoyed a majority in the Senate. However, the system of proportional representation, adopted for Senate elections in 1949, made it difficult for any major party or coalition to obtain a majority in the Senate. Between 1961 and 2004, there were only five years in which the governing party or coalition had a clear majority in the Senate, and when the Howard Coalition government won a majority in the Senate from July 2005 it was the first time for 24 years that any government had won a majority in both houses.[4]

THE MANDATE DEBATE

It is common for a party or coalition that has just won a majority of seats in the House of Representatives, and thus by convention been recognised as the government, to claim that it has received a 'mandate' from the Australian people to implement the programs and policies outlined in its election platform. After all, it is claimed, the party or coalition winning government has been chosen by the people (albeit through the indirect means of 150 separate contests for individual House of Representatives seats) after it has announced the programs and policies that it would pursue if elected. Hence, according to this 'mandate' claim, it ought to be able to implement what it undertook to do.

A good example is the 1998 pre-election commitment by the Coalition parties led by Prime Minister John Howard that, if re-elected to government, they would implement a new Goods and Services Tax (GST). Howard's government was indeed re-elected to office at the election of October 1998, and it then claimed it had a 'mandate' to implement the GST.

However, the fact that the claim needs to be made at all reveals that the notion of a 'mandate' is quite controversial within the Australian system of government (Emy 1997; Nethercote 1999; Goot 1999, 2000; Mulgan 2000), the controversy illustrating again an awkward consequence of the 'hybrid' nature of the system. In Britain, a government that controls the House of Commons can claim such a 'mandate' because the House of Lords, the second (unelected) chamber in the British system, can, at most, delay government legislation but cannot in the end defeat it. By electing a government, the British people are indeed in an important sense providing it with a mandate to implement its announced policies. But in Australia, where the hybrid constitutional framework features an elected US-style upper house (the Senate) coexisting with an elected British-style lower house (the House of Representatives), the Senate has the capacity to block government legislation. Some Senators—especially minor party or Independent Senators when they have held the 'balance of power' between the major government and Opposition parties—have met claims of a government mandate with counterclaims that they too have a 'mandate' from the Australian people: to represent the broad variety of interests among the Australian people, to act as a check on government legislation and, if necessary, to block it or negotiate improvements.[5]

This is indeed what happened with the Howard government's GST legislation after the 1998 election. The non-government majority in the Senate refused to accept the government's initial bill and, drawing on the counter-mandate argument, the leader of the Australian Democrats in the Senate regarded it as entirely appropriate for her to negotiate with the government for changes to be made as a condition for obtaining the necessary support in the Senate to enable an amended bill to pass.

Governments from both sides of politics have expressed frustration with the Senate when legislation, for which they believe they have a 'mandate', is blocked there. In 2003 the Howard Coalition government, acting on the assumption that it was unlikely to ever to win a majority in the Senate, initiated a debate about the possibility of changing the Constitution, by referendum, to reduce the power of the Senate to block or change government legislation. It ultimately abandoned the proposal because there seemed to be no public support for it and hence a referendum proposal for such a change would undoubtedly have failed.

However, as a result of the October 2004 election, the Coalition government did obtain a majority in the Senate with effect from July 2005. While that remains the case, the question of whether or not the government has a mandate to have its legislation passed, or whether the non-government Senators have a mandate to oppose the legislation, will be less relevant. Provided the Senators from the government side 'toe the line' and vote for government legislation, the government legislation will pass and the Opposition, minor party and Independent Senators will have no power to force the government to negotiate with them over the content of legislation.

CONSTITUTIONAL CRISIS 1975

The tensions embodied within the Australian 'hybrid' system of government became most visible and most acrimonious in 1975. The 'Constitutional crisis' of 1975 produced what Williams (2001) describes as 'the worst crisis to face our constitutional system' and exposed what Evans portrays as 'a gap in Australia's constitutional order' (Evans 1997: 158). The 'crisis' involved the principles and conventions of responsible government, the powers of the Senate underscored by the federal system, and the powers given to the Governor-General in the Constitution. Though it was an exceptional event in Australian history, the crisis provides an insight into the interplay and friction between the provisions of the written Constitution and the informal understandings or conventions that form a part of the constitutional framework.

The essence of the crisis was that a government with a majority in the House of Representatives (and hence entitled to govern according to the principles of responsible government) was dismissed by the Governor-General after the Senate refused to pass its budget (as the Senate was entitled to do under its formal constitutional powers). Because there were a number of other practices and conventions that this crisis put under scrutiny, it is worth relating the broad sweep of events (see also Kelly 1995).

In the double-dissolution election of May 1974, the incumbent Labor government led by Prime Minister Gough Whitlam again won a majority of seats in the House of Representatives. As a result, by undisputed convention, Mr Whitlam and his Ministers from the Labor Party were sworn into office by the Governor-General. The Labor Party did not, however, have a majority in the Senate, where the numbers were deadlocked (29 Labor, 29 Liberal-National coalition, two Independents).

Two of the Labor seats in the Senate subsequently became vacant, one through the death of a Senator and the other through a resignation. Under section 15 of the Constitution, such casual vacancies in the Senate are required to be filled by a nomination from a joint sitting of the houses of Parliament in the State from among whose Senators the vacancy has occurred. An unwritten convention had developed that, irrespective of which political party held a majority in such a joint sitting in that particular State Parliament, a replacement Senator would be chosen who was the nominee of the political party to which the departed Senator belonged. The democratic rationale for this convention was that it maintained the pattern of party representation determined by voters at previous election.

In 1975, this convention was not followed by the State Parliaments (in effect, by the State governments) of New South Wales and Queensland. The two departed Labor Senators were not replaced by the Labor Party's nominees. These State governments had become strongly opposed to the Whitlam government, which had been beset by difficulties in economic management and by allegations about inappropriate financial dealings, and which had also been attempting to increase the Commonwealth government's role in policy areas traditionally the preserve of the States. As a result of the actions of the State governments with respect to the replacement of the two Senators, the Whitlam government faced a Senate no longer with equal numbers of government and Opposition Senators plus two Independents. With the number of government Senators reduced by two, and the non-government ranks increased by two, it now faced a Senate where the Opposition could block its legislation.

In October 1975, the Leader of the Opposition in the House of Representatives, Malcolm Fraser, announced that the Senate would refuse to pass the Whitlam government's supply bills. He demanded that, in order to resolve the impasse, the Whitlam government call an election (an election that Mr Fraser was confident that the Opposition would win).

A heated debate ensued over the propriety of the foreshadowed action by the Opposition majority in the Senate and over Mr Fraser's demand. The Whitlam government and its supporters argued that a convention existed that the Senate should pass the supply bills; otherwise, given that the government held a majority in the House of Representatives, the principles of responsible government would be overturned. The Fraser-led Opposition and its supporters argued that the written Constitution gave the Senate power to reject the supply bills and that no convention existed that prevented the Senate from exercising this power. The Opposition argued that even if it had been the normal practice for the Senate to pass a government's budget, the alleged severe economic mismanagement and unorthodoxy of the Whitlam government were sufficient grounds for the Senate to use its constitutional power on this occasion. Because this meant that the government would not be able to get the Parliament to pass its budget, the Opposition claimed that, under another fundamental convention, the government should resign.

Just after 1 p.m. on Tuesday 11 November 1975, with the stand-off continuing and the looming prospect of the government running out of money if the budget was not passed, the Governor-General (Sir John Kerr) dismissed Prime

Minister Whitlam and his government. The Governor-General then saw Opposition Leader Fraser immediately, appointed him as 'caretaker' Prime Minister and announced a double dissolution of the two houses of Parliament. The formal rationale given by the Governor-General for the double dissolution, in conformity with section 57 of the Constitution, was that 21 Whitlam government bills had been twice rejected by the Senate. These extraordinary events having occurred, later that afternoon the Senate—controlled by what had been the Coalition 'Opposition' but now acting in support of the new Fraser-led Coalition caretaker government—passed the supply bills.

The double-dissolution election was held on 13 December 1975. It resulted in a resounding victory—in both houses of Parliament—for the Liberal-National coalition led by Malcolm Fraser.

These unprecedented events have been the subject of a great deal of debate and conjecture. There is a lively literature produced by both critics and defenders of the actions of the Senate and of the Governor-General, and by several of the major participants in the crisis.[6] For the purposes of this chapter, it is sufficient to draw attention to the key conflicts between formal provisions of the written Constitution, on the one hand, and unwritten constitutional conventions, on the other:[7]

- In dismissing Mr Whitlam and installing Mr Fraser as Prime Minister, the Governor-General acted within his formal powers as specified in section 64 of the Constitution, but contrary to the longstanding and fundamental convention that he should only appoint a person supported by a majority in the House of Representatives.
- In refusing to follow specific advice from Prime Minister Whitlam that he should undertake a different course of action, the Governor-General broke with the convention that the monarch or monarch's representative, whatever his or her formal powers, should use those powers only in accordance with such advice.
- The Senate's action in refusing to pass the Whitlam government's supply bills was arguably contrary to the conventions of responsible government, as those conventions rely only on the government commanding support in the House of Representatives and thus depend on the Senate passing supply, even if the Senate is not controlled by the governing party.
- In refusing to resign despite the inability of his government to get its supply bills through Parliament, Mr Whitlam—according to his critics—broke with the longstanding convention that a government must have parliamentary support for supply in order to remain in office.
- Two State governments broke with the convention about the filling of casual Senate vacancies. Ironically, the Fraser government successfully sponsored a constitutional amendment in 1977—two years after coming to office in a way directly dependent on the breaking of this convention—to change the

written Constitution (section 15) to stipulate that replacement Senators filling a casual vacancy must indeed be members of the same political party as the outgoing Senator.

The 'constitutional crisis' of 1975 raises questions about whether Australia's hybrid system of government is philosophically and practically coherent. Howard and Saunders (1977: 286) conclude on the basis of the crisis that the twin goals of the 'framers of the Australian Constitution . . . to create a federal structure [with a powerful Senate] and to preserve parliamentary government of the British kind . . . were, and are, incompatible'.

But since 1975, there appears to have been great care taken on all sides not to risk a repetition of the troubling and divisive events of the 'constitutional crisis'. Opposition and the minor parties holding the balance of power in the Senate have generally been willing to ensure the passage of the government of the day's budget, and Sir John Kerr's successors as Governor-General are perceived to have been less likely in any case to act as he did. Galligan (1995: 89–90) accordingly argues that the 'constitutional crisis' is of less enduring significance than originally feared, and that the hybrid system remains workable:

> The proof of the founders' hybrid synthesis of a federal Senate and responsible government is its durability over nearly a century of practice. After seventy-five years, when the Whitlam Government was dismissed, there was deep concern . . . that the system was contradictory and unworkable. Yet . . . the system is as vigorous as ever and pretty much universally accepted . . .

But the Senate has remained a difficult obstacle for national governments. The landslide victory to the Coalition parties in the 1975 double-dissolution election gave the Fraser government a majority in both houses and the government's legislation was thus assured of passage through the Parliament. From 1981, however, the Fraser government and then the Labor governments under Prime Ministers Bob Hawke (1983–1991) and Paul Keating (1991–1996) faced a Senate in which the Australian Democrats held or shared the balance of power. In its first three terms (1996–2004) the Coalition government under Prime Minister John Howard also faced a Senate in which non-government Senators comprised a majority.

It had been widely assumed that this situation was very unlikely to change and that the normal situation in Australian politics would be that governments would have to plan their legislative strategy carefully, and be prepared to compromise, to get their legislation through the Senate. However, as noted above, the Coalition government did obtain a majority in the Senate as a result of the election of October 2004, with effect from 1 July 2005 when Senators elected in October 2004 took their place in the Senate. This unexpected outcome has created a situation that had become unusual in Australian politics. While it maintains that majority and provided all Coalition Senators vote in support of its legislation (and this is not necessarily guaranteed), the power of the Howard government to pass laws will not be limited by the Senate any more than it is by the House of Representatives.

Monarchy or republic?

As the Australian Constitution stands, the King or Queen of the United Kingdom is also the King or Queen of Australia. Since the early 1990s, there have been prominent attempts to change this arrangement and to reconstitute Australia as a 'republic'. The question of the position of the monarch in Australia's constitutional framework, and the possibility of Australia becoming a republic, actually involve two theoretically separate issues: the role of the monarchy and a remaining legal tie between the United Kingdom and Australia. In practical terms, however, these two issues are closely connected. For Australia to become a republic and to adopt an Australian head of state would involve severing its last legal tie with the United Kingdom, and to sever the last legal ties with the United Kingdom would involve abandoning the monarchy.

The role of the monarch has rarely impinged on the daily politics of Australia. Nor has the fact that Australia's head of state is also the head of state of another nation. It is expected that the monarch will not mix the two roles and that, on all matters relating to Australia, he or she will act on the advice of the Australian government, in exactly the same way that in relation to the United Kingdom he or she acts on the advice of that country's government. Except when the monarch is actually in Australia, his or her duties are carried out by the Governor-General who is also expected to act on the advice of the Australian government. In the case of the office of Governor-General, the matter is complicated by the fact that, as discussed above in relation to the 1975 'constitutional crisis', the Constitution vests the position with very sweeping formal powers. Although the Governor-General is expected to exercise those powers in accordance with the conventions of the Westminster system, it is also understood that the Governor-General has 'reserve powers' that include the power to appoint the Prime Minister and, as happened in 1975, to dismiss the Prime Minister and his or her government (see RAC 1993: 88).

In the early 1990s, as the centenary of nationhood approached, the question of whether Australia should become a republic was raised by the Keating Labor government (see RAC 1993). The Howard Coalition government came to office in 1996 and, although Prime Minister Howard declared himself opposed to Australia becoming a republic, he honoured an election promise to establish a 'People's Convention' to consider the question. In 1998 a Convention of 152 delegates (half of whom were elected and half appointed by the government) was held to advise the government on whether or not Australia should become a republic and, if so, what sort of republic option(s) should be put to the electorate for consideration.

The lead in the political campaign in favour of Australia becoming a republic had taken by a group called the Australian Republican Movement. It advocated a model of republicanism—usually referred to as a 'minimalist republic'—that sought to sever the connection with the British monarch, but otherwise change the Australian constitutional framework as little as possible. Amongst the broader ranks of supporters of a republic, however, there was no unanimity. These ranks included many critics of the 'minimalist' model. They called for a more thoroughgoing change to the Australian system, including such proposals as the incorporation of a Bill of Rights into the Constitution, the adoption of a United States-style separation of powers, and the direct election of the head of state.

Even the limited changes to the constitutional system proposed in the 'minimalist' model raised some thorny issues that were a cause for concern to people who were suspicious that a move to a republic would lead to a shift of power in the system of government. In particular there were concerns about the powers, and the method of appointment, of a head of state.

In relation to the powers of the head of state, the minimalist position was that the formal powers of the republic's head of state should be unchanged from those of the current Governor-General. But an alternative view was that these powers were far too extensive to be left in the hands of a republican head of state and that the circumstances under which the reserve powers could be used should be codified and spelt out in written form in the Constitution. Against that argument, the advocates of a minimalist republic, and others, held that it was not possible to take account of all possible future events and that, as with the existing system, it was better not to attempt to specify in writing how the powers would be used.

In relation to the method of appointment of the head of state, some change would be unavoidable under any form of Australian republic. Under the existing procedures, the Prime Minister, in effect, appoints the Governor-General, but he or she does so through the formal mechanism of making a recommendation to the monarch. The minimalist preference was to leave the power of appointment of the head of state with the Prime Minister. Although this would not have changed what were, in effect, the existing arrangements, the suggestion that the head of state should be simply appointed by the Prime Minister of the day raised many concerns.

Some advocates for a republic argued for an elected head of state. They were not necessarily advocating that this elected head of state should have any more powers, or play any more prominent role in practice, than the current Governor-General. But they wanted an election to choose the head of state for what they regarded as democratic reasons: to give the Australian people an enhanced role in the process and to facilitate a greater popular identification with the change to the new system. For some of these advocates, the Irish system of government, which operates along these lines, seemed to be a good model to follow.

But it was argued by some commentators that to introduce an elected head of state would unavoidably be a fundamental change to the constitutional system. The election of the head of state would politicise the role, and an elected head of state could be seen to have a mandate to play some sort of executive role and might be much more likely to use the wide-ranging constitutional powers of the head of state independently of the government.

After deliberations lasting a fortnight, a majority of the delegates to the People's Convention supported a modified minimalist model. They recommended that Australia should become a republic in which the selection of the head of state would be by a process that required the nominee to be endorsed by a two-thirds majority of a joint sitting of both houses of the Parliament. Although it did not support the proposed change, the Howard government agreed to put this proposal to the electorate in a constitutional referendum.

The campaign against the proposal for Australia to become a republic was led by a group calling itself Australians for a Constitutional Monarchy. These defenders of the existing monarchical arrangements argued that the existing system should be maintained because it had proven itself as consistently able to produce sound, stable and democratic government. They maintained that there was a dangerous uncertainty about the role and behaviour of a future republican head of state—an argument often summarised in the saying 'if it isn't broken, don't fix it'. It was not worth taking the risk, they argued, of making the change because Australia was in any case already a *de facto* republic; the monarch in practice exercised no power. Further, they argued, it was precisely because the monarchy was not involved in the politics of the nation that allowed it, in times of crisis or deep political division, to perform a valuable role as a non-political unifying symbol.

The referendum to amend the Constitution to make Australia a republic was held in November 1999. The proposal was decisively defeated. Less than 46 per cent of the electorate voted in favour of it and it did not obtain a majority in any State.

It is possible that, in part, the lack of sufficient public support for the proposal was due to the particular model of a republic that was offered to the electorate. Public opinion polls suggested that a majority of electors actually supported the idea of Australia becoming a republic, but they did not support the particular model that was proposed in the referendum. In particular, a model in which the head of state was selected by politicians and not directly elected by the people was unpopular.

However, it must also be remembered that the Australian electorate has always shown great caution in relation to changing the Constitution. As stated above, only eight of the 44 referendum questions put to the electorate have passed. It is possible that any referendum proposal on the question of Australia becoming a republic would be treated very cautiously by the electorate, and especially if it did not have strong bipartisan support.

The evolving constitutional framework

This chapter has analysed Australia's 'hybrid' system of government. It has argued that there is a persistent tension, displayed most dramatically in the 1975 'constitutional crisis', between the Westminster-derived 'responsible government' elements and the US-inspired federalist elements of the system. The chapter has described how the written Australian Constitution coexists with unwritten conventions that usually determine how the system actually operates.

As the debates about the 'constitutional crisis' and the possibility of an Australian republic reveal, some commentators believe that the Australian constitutional framework has served Australia well and that no further changes are necessary, but others regret its flaws and inconsistencies and hope for change. All, however, would agree that a thorough understanding and appreciation of the constitutional framework—as manifest both in the Constitution and in the unwritten conventions—is a necessary precursor to an effective and productive debate about future directions.

NOTES

1   A similar concept is intended by Thompson's notion of 'the "Washminster" mutation' (Thompson 1980), with 'Washminster' being a contraction of 'Westminster' (in reference to the British system) and 'Washington' (in reference to the US system).

2   The Bill of Rights is technically not included within the original Constitution of the United States but constitutes instead the first 10 amendments to it. These were, however, foreshadowed during the debates about the ratification of the Constitution in the 1780s, and it is not unreasonable to regard them as a de facto part of the original Constitution.

3   The sections of the Constitution usually recognised as inviting a rights-based interpretation are as follows, though note that there is a complex legal history attending to each of them (Coper 1987: ch. 8; Coper 1992; Hancks 1992; Williams 2000: ch. 2):

   • Section 41 mentions 'a right to vote' but this in practice is generally regarded as an obsolete provision without practical force.

   • Section 51(ii), with section 99, stipulates that Commonwealth tax laws cannot 'discriminate between States or parts of States'.

   • Section 51(xxxi) requires that the 'acquisition of property' from 'any State or person' must be 'on just terms'.

   • Section 80, which specifies 'trial . . . by jury', has little substantive effect because it is limited to 'trial on indictment'.

   • Section 92, which stipulates that 'customs, trade, commerce, and intercourse among the States . . . shall be absolutely free', has until quite recently been interpreted by the High Court as, in effect, 'a substantial guarantee of individual liberty against collective controls' (Hancks 1992: 94). The Court has, however, now moved to a much narrower interpretation which sees section 92 simply as guaranteeing free trade between the States and precluding protectionist measures which discriminated against interstate trade or products in favour of local producers (McEvoy & Summers 1996).

- Section 116 prohibits the Commonwealth from 'establishing any religion . . . imposing any religious observance . . . prohibiting the free exercise of any religion' and imposing any 'religious test' on any Commonwealth office.
- Section 117 prohibits any State from discriminating against a person resident in another State.

4   The term of State Senators elected in October 2004 commenced on 1 July 2005 and the Coalition Government did not have a majority in the Senate until that date.

5   There is evidence presented in Chapters 4, 10 and 14 of this book that voters are more inclined to vote for minor parties and Independent candidates in Senate than in House of Representatives elections, perhaps giving some credence to this counter-mandate claim.

6   The critics include Archer and Maddox (1976), Howard (1976), Horne (1976), Emy (1978: ch. 4), Mayer (1980), Browning (1985) and Coper (1987: ch. 6). The defenders include O'Connell (1976), West (1976), St John (1982), Barwick (1983), Markwell (1984) and Gibbs (1997). The participants' accounts are Kerr (1979), Whitlam (1979, 1997), Smith (1995) and Fraser (1997). Good journalistic accounts include Kelly (1995) and Oakes (1976).

7   There are further matters of debate and dispute beyond those discussed in this chapter. These include the propriety of the Governor-General receiving confidential advice from the Chief Justice of the High Court and of the use of the 21 Whitlam government bills as the formal trigger for the double dissolution of Parliament.

REFERENCES

Archer, J. & Maddox, G. 1976, 'The 1975 Constitutional Crisis in Australia', *Journal of Commonwealth and Comparative Politics*, vol. 14.

Bagehot, W. 1867/1963, *The English Constitution*, Fontana, London.

Barwick, G. 1983, *Sir John Did his Duty*, Serendip, Sydney.

Browning, H. 1985, *1975 Crisis: An Historical View*, Hale & Iremonger, Sydney.

Coper, M. 1987, *Encounters with the Australian Constitution*, CCH, Sydney.

Coper, M. 1992, 'Section 92 of the Australian Constitution Since *Cole v. Whitfield*', in *Australian Constitutional Perspectives*, ed. P. Lee & G. Winterton, Law Book Company, Sydney.

Craven, G. 2005, 'Federalism and the States of Reality', *Policy*, vol. 21, no. 2, pp. 3–9.

Crisp, L. 1983, *Australian National Government*, 5th edn, Longman Cheshire, Melbourne.

Emy, H. 1978, *The Politics of Australian Democracy*, 2nd edn, Macmillan, Melbourne.

Emy, H. 1997, 'The Mandate and Responsible Government', *Australian Journal of Political Science*, vol. 32, no. 1, pp. 65–78.

Evans, H. 1997, 'Lost Causes and Lost Remedies', in *Power, Parliament and the People*, eds M. Coper & G. Williams, Federation Press, Sydney.

Fraser, M. 1997, 'Lessons from 1975', in *Power, Parliament and the People*, eds M. Coper & G. Williams, Federation Press, Sydney.

Galligan, B. 1995, *A Federal Republic: Australia's Constitutional System of Government*, Cambridge University Press, Cambridge.

Gibbs, H. 1997, 'The Dismissal and the Constitution', in *Power, Parliament and the People*, eds M. Coper & G. Williams, Federation Press, Sydney.

Goot, M. 1999, 'Whose Mandate? Policy Promises, Strong Bicameralism and Polled Opinion', *Australian Journal of Political Science*, vol. 34, no. 3, pp. 327–52.

Goot, M. 2000, 'Mulgan on Mandates', *Australian Journal of Political Science*, vol. 35, no. 2, pp. 323–5.

Hancks, P. 1992, 'Constitutional Guarantees', in *Australian Constitutional Perspectives*, eds P. Lee & G. Winterton, Law Book Company, Sydney.

Horne, D. 1976, *Death of the Lucky Country*, Penguin, Harmondsworth.

Howard, C. 1976, 'The Constitutional Crisis of 1975', *Australian Quarterly*, vol. 48, no. 1, pp. 5–25.

Howard, C. & Saunders, C. 1977, 'The Blocking of the Budget and the Dismissal of the Government', in *Labor and the Constitution, 1972–75*, ed. G. Evans, Heinemann, Richmond.

Kelly, P. 1995, *November 1975: The Inside Story of Australia's Greatest Political Crisis*, Allen & Unwin, Sydney.

Kerr, J. 1979, *Matters for Judgment*, Macmillan, London.

Maddox, G. 2005, *Australian Democracy in Theory and Practice*, 5th edn, Pearson Education, Sydney.

Markwell, D. 1984, 'The Dismissal: Why Whitlam was to blame', *Quadrant*, vol. 23, no. 3, pp. 11–21.

Mayer, D. 1980, 'Sir John Kerr and Responsible Government', in *Responsible Government in Australia*, eds P. Weller & D. Jaensch, Drummond, Richmond.

McEvoy, K. & Summers, J. 1996, 'South Australia and the High Court', in *South Australia, Federalism and Public Policy*, ed. A. Parkin, Federalism Research Centre, Australian National University, Canberra.

Mulgan, R. 2000, 'The "Mandate": A Response to Goot', *Australian Journal of Political Science*, vol. 35, no. 5, pp. 317–22.

Nethercote, J. 1999, 'Mandate: Australia's Current Debate in Context', Parliamentary Library Information and Research Services, Research Paper no. 19, 1998–99 series, Canberra, <http://www.aph.gov.au/library/>.

Oakes, L. 1976, *Crash Through or Crash: The Unmaking of a Prime Minister*, Drummond, Richmond.

O'Connell, D. 1976, 'The Dissolution of the Australian Parliament: 11 November 1975', *The Parliamentarian*, vol. 57, no. 1, pp. 1–14.

Parkin, A. 1996, 'The Significance of Federalism: A South Australian Perspective', in *South Australia, Federalism and Public Policy*, ed. A. Parkin, Federalism Research Centre, Australian National University, Canberra.

RAC [Republic Advisory Committee] 1993, *An Australian Republic: The Options. Volume 1 — The Report*, AGPS, Canberra.

Saunders, C. 1990, 'The Constitutional Framework: Hybrid, Derivative but Eventually Australian', in *Public Administration in Australia: A Watershed*, ed. J. Power, Hale & Iremonger, Sydney.

Sharman, C. 1989, 'Governing Federations', in *Governing Federations: Constitution, Politics, Resources*, eds M. Wood, C. Williams & C. Sharman, Hale & Iremonger, Sydney.

Smith, D. 1995, 'The 1975 Dismissal: Setting the Record Straight', in Proceedings of the 5th Conference of the Samuel Griffith Society, Sydney, 21 March–2 April, <http://www.exhibit.com.au/~griffith/v5chap7.htm>.

St John, E. 1982, 'The Dismissal of the Whitlam Government', in *The New Conservatism in Australia*, ed. R. Manne, Oxford University Press, Melbourne.

Summers, J. 1979, 'Parliament and Responsible Government in Australia', in *Government, Politics and Power in Australia*, eds J. Summers, D. Woodward & A. Parkin, Flinders University Relations Unit, Adelaide.

Thompson, E. 1980, 'The "Washminster" Mutation', in *Responsible Government in Australia*, eds P. Weller & D. Jaensch, Drummond, Richmond.

Watson, L. 1977, 'Upper Houses: Do They Belong in Democracies?', in *Change the Rules! Towards a Democratic Constitution*, eds S. Encel, D. Horne & E. Thompson, Penguin, Harmondsworth.

West, F. 1976, 'Constitutional Crisis 1975—An Historian's View', *Australian Quarterly*, vol. 48, no. 2, pp. 48–58.

Whitlam, G. 1979, *The Truth of the Matter*, Penguin, Harmondsworth.

Whitlam, G. 1997, 'The Coup 20 Years After', in *Power, Parliament and the People*, eds M. Coper & G. Williams, Federation Press, Sydney.

Williams, G. 2000, *A Bill of Rights for Australia*, UNSW Press, Sydney.

Williams, G. 2001, 'Constitution Remains a Dud Vehicle', *Australian*, 1 January.

CHAPTER 4

Parliament and responsible government

JOHN SUMMERS

Parliament is a representative and a law-making body. It is composed of representatives of the people, elected at periodic elections, and it is vested with the power to enact laws. Parliament has a number of roles, some of which are absolutely central to the system of responsible Cabinet government that operates in Australia and to the *liberal* and *democratic* values which are said to be entrenched within it.[1]

First, the institution of Parliament plays a part in the *election of the government*—the *democratic* element in the system of government. The Australian people do not *directly* elect the government but, rather, vote to choose Members of Parliament. It is only through the process of electing the Parliament that voters have a role in the selection of the government. Following the British system (or 'Westminster model'), the government (in the form of the Cabinet—the Prime Minister and other Ministers) is drawn from Parliament. The political party that wins a majority in the lower house of the Parliament forms the government.

Second, Parliament is central to the whole rationale of the system of *responsible government* and to the *liberal* ideals that the system is said to embody. It is through Parliament that, between elections, the government is said to be held accountable to the people over whom it governs. According to the theory of 'responsible Cabinet government', it is to the Parliament that the government is responsible.

The government is notionally responsible to Parliament not only for its own actions but for those of the government's administrative arm (the public service). There is a chain of responsibility that indirectly renders the government and its bureaucracy accountable to the electorate: the bureaucracy is responsible to the government, the government to Parliament, and Parliament, in turn, to the voters. If the government loses the 'confidence' of Parliament (i.e. if it loses the support of a majority of members in the House of Representatives), it loses office. Regular elections provide the electorate with the opportunity to change their representatives and thereby change the government. Governments are therefore checked in the exercise of their power and are deterred from being contemptuous of the people over whom they govern.

The accountability of government to the voters through periodic elections is supposed to be reinforced by procedures of Parliament, which again provide checks on the executive branch of government and its bureaucracy. The Standing Orders of the Parliament contain a number of provisions that allow Members of Parliament to question and inquire into the government's actions and to speak, if they wish to, in opposition to the government. On each day that the Parliament sits, during Question Time, members can ask 'questions without notice' of Ministers about their actions and those of their departments. The procedures of the Parliament allow Members to move and debate motions of 'no confidence' against the government or against a particular Minister, and to raise matters of national importance. Through these mechanisms, Members of Parliament can debate matters on which they think the government is vulnerable and can highlight or expose what they consider to be its shortcomings.

Important aspects of this role of the Parliament are the doctrines of *individual ministerial responsibility* and *collective ministerial responsibility*. Simply stated, the doctrine of individual ministerial responsibility is that Ministers are responsible to Parliament for their own actions, and for those of their departments. In the event of maladministration or improprieties, a Minister should resign. The essence of the doctrine of collective ministerial responsibility is that all Ministers must take responsibility for Cabinet decisions, and that in public a Minister must not disagree with those decisions. A Minister wishing to disagree publicly with a Cabinet decision should first resign from the Ministry. The rationale for both doctrines is that, if followed, they should prevent irresponsible executive action. The doctrines provide that, for all actions of government, there should be some person (such as a Minister) or some body (such as a Cabinet) that can be held responsible: it should not be possible for Ministers or governments to deny responsibility for their own actions or for those of the government bureaucracy.

All this, however, is an ideal picture. How it applies in practice in Australia needs to be understood in the context of two additional factors, which this chapter now analyses in detail. First, the 'Westminster model' on which it is based has been significantly modified in Australia by being grafted onto a federal system. The most important modification made to the system by the drafters of the federal Constitution of the Commonwealth of Australia was the establishment of the Senate, an elected second chamber of the Parliament in which each State is equally represented. Second, the ideal picture of the 'Westminster model' is based on a description of the Parliament's formal procedures and the outward appearance, which in many ways obscures an understanding of the exercise of power within the Parliament. An analysis of the actual workings of the Parliament is needed to fully understand its functioning and its role in relation to the government's exercise of executive power.

The Australian Parliament and the Constitution

Although it was clearly understood by the drafters of the Constitution that there would be a system of responsible government—that is, there was (and still is) an expectation that Parliament would exercise control over the executive, and would play a restraining and checking role, both on the government's use of its executive power and on government finances—this was not spelt out in the Constitution (cf. Bach 2003: 338–9). Indeed, because the conventions and principles of this system are so ill-defined, it is doubtful that they could have been spelt out in such a document. The Australian Constitution does, however, create a Westminster type of government to the extent that the Ministers must be drawn from the legislature (section 64). It establishes a Parliament of two houses, the House of Representatives and the Senate, and gives to it considerable powers. Parliament is vested with the legislative power of the Commonwealth (section 1), including power over financial legislation (sections 81 and 83).

Seats in the House of Representatives are apportioned between the States in proportion to their population, with a minimum of five seats for each of the States. In the Senate, each of the States is represented equally. Section 24 requires that the House of Representatives be, 'as nearly as practicable', twice the size of the Senate. There are now 76 Senators, 12 from each of the States and two from each of the Territories, and 150 members in the House of Representatives. The term of each House of Representatives between elections can be no more than three years from its first day of sitting (section 28), but it can be less if the government chooses.[2] Senators are elected for a fixed period of six years but with staggered terms, so that half the Senators are elected every three years (section 13). Each proposed law must be passed by a majority in both the Senate and the House of Representatives, and the Senate's powers are identical to those of the House of Representatives except in relation to financial legislation: the Senate cannot initiate or amend financial legislation but it can request that the House of Representatives amend the legislation and, most importantly, the Senate can reject the bill.

In the event of a deadlock between the two houses of Parliament—when legislation passed by the House of Representatives and rejected by the Senate is again, after an interval of three months, passed by the House of Representatives and rejected by the Senate—the government can force (via advice to the Governor-General) a 'double-dissolution' election in which the House of Representatives and the *whole* Senate face election simultaneously. In the event that following the double-dissolution election the same legislation is again passed by the House of Representatives and rejected by the Senate, the legislation can be put to a 'joint sitting' of the Parliament in which the members of both chambers sit as one body (section 57).

'Party government' and the 'executive state'

Although some of Parliament's ascribed functions rest only on conventions and expectations, its formal constitutional powers are, as noted above, considerable. Despite this, it is commonly observed that in Australia, as in many other countries, Parliament falls short of fulfilling the role ascribed to it by the theory of responsible government (Reid & Forest 1989; Blewett 1993; Evans 1993; Lovell 1994; Sharman 1994). According to this argument, Parliament is unable effectively to scrutinise legislation or adequately to check and restrain the government's use of executive power. The inadequacies of Parliament are attributed to a number of factors, as sketched in the analysis that follows.

PARTY DOMINATION OF THE LEGISLATURE

Within a decade of Australian federation, as both houses of the legislature became dominated by political parties with highly disciplined parliamentary membership, the executive had gained firm control of the legislative process and of the conduct of Parliament. The leaders of the major political parties are able to maintain strict control over their membership, especially when they form the 'governing party'. Members of the government party have only very rarely 'crossed the floor' of the house to vote with the Opposition. Labor Party members pledge themselves to vote in Parliament in accordance with the majority decision of the Labor Caucus (i.e. of the Labor Party's Members of Parliament). While the Liberal and National Party members have no formal pledge, they have not broken ranks any more than Labor members. Election to Parliament depends on party endorsement, and it is a rare Parliamentarian who risks his or her endorsement by voting against a party decision.

The role of political parties within the Parliament has led some authors to argue that 'responsible Cabinet government' disguises a reality that would better be described as 'responsible *party* government' (Stewart & Ward 1996: 100–2; Lucy 1985: 6–10). The theory of responsible *Cabinet* government presents the main conflict in the Parliament as being between the Parliament and the executive: the government is held accountable to, or is responsible to, the Parliament. According to the 'responsible *party* government' argument, however, the *real* political battle in the Parliament is between the government and opposition parties. As long as the governing party holds its majority, the government and its Ministers are more accountable to their party than to the Parliament (Lovell 1994: 49). Between elections it is the majority party that will make or break a Minister or Prime Minister. Unless there are defections from the governing party, the government will be able to defeat any censure or no-confidence motion in the House of Representatives. Faced with accusations of wrongdoing or mismanagement, the most important consideration for the members of the governing party will be the effect on the electorate. If a Minister has support within the party, and if, on balance, it appears that the electoral consequences of keeping a Minister in the government are less damaging than removing him or her, the party is unlikely to insist that the Minister resign.

One other feature of the Parliament in which political parties have played a role relates to the preselection of women as parliamentary candidates. Although women won the right to stand for election to the Commonwealth Parliament with the passage of the *Commonwealth Franchise Act* in 1902, it was not until 41 years later that the first woman was elected. In 1943 Enid Lyons was elected as an United Australia Party candidate to the House of Representatives and Dorothy Tangney, for the ALP, was elected to the Senate (Millar 1994: 53–64). It was not until much later that women were preselected in any significant numbers to safe seats by either of the major political parties. As recently as 1980 there were no women in the House of Representatives. In the last two decades of the 20th century there was a small but steady increase in the numbers of women in both chambers but proportionally in greater numbers in the Senate. Following the 2004 election women comprised 24.7 per cent of the members of the House of Representatives and 36.8 per cent of the Senators.

The presence of women in the Parliament has had an impact on the position that the parliamentary parties have adopted on some questions and ultimately on the way some matters have been resolved by the Parliament (see Chapter 21 of this book). However, the presence of women in the Parliament does not appear to have led to any change in the role that highly disciplined political parties play within the legislature. On the question of 'toeing the party line' and voting in the Parliament in accordance with the dictates of the party, women in the major parties have been as compliant as the men.

PARLIAMENTARY PROCEDURES

Parliamentary procedures are supposed to provide the Parliament with the tools to scrutinise legislation and to hold the government and its agencies account-able. The domination of the legislature by political parties, however, allows the government to use the Parliament's rules and procedures to its own advantage. Parliamentary procedures and safeguards have been eroded and conventions of responsible government have been devalued. The legislative process has been considerably modified, allowing shortcuts and the hasty enactment of even the most important legislation.

For a Bill to become an Act of Parliament it must, in both houses, go through three 'readings' and be considered by each house in a 'committee stage'. The first and third 'readings' of any Bill are largely a formality. It is only in the 'second reading' that any real debate takes place, and it is only in the less formal committee stage that there is a detailed discussion of a Bill's individual clauses. The three readings and committee stage, if spread over a number of days or even weeks, should allow members to examine the evidence and mount their arguments about a Bill. However, practices have been adopted that allow the government to speed Bills through all stages (Reid & Forest 1989: 149–55, 160–1, 178):

1. By use of the closure motion or 'the gag', the government, through its majority, is able to end debate on any question.
2. The so-called 'guillotine' allows the government to break up a Bill into sections and set a timetable for discussion of that Bill.
3. The Australian Parliament has also adopted measures that allow the committee stage to be bypassed and the whole process of legislative enactment to be condensed. The expectation was once that legislation would not pass through both the second and third readings on the same day. Standing orders have been adopted that allow this to happen.

Further, the 'committee stage', as it exists in the Australian Parliament, is a cumbersome and ineffective way of giving close attention to detailed or complex legislation. The use of freestanding committees, outside of the normal sequence by which a house of Parliament considers a Bill, to give careful and detailed consideration to proposed legislation, is often suggested as a means of restoring some of Parliament's legislative competence. To this end, two joint standing committees of both houses of Parliament—one on Public Works and one on Public Accounts—were established in 1913, and in 1932 the Senate created a Standing Committee on Regulations and Ordinances.

In 1970 the Senate expanded the committee system with the creation of 12 standing committees. This committee structure has provided the Senate with a mechanism to give much more detailed consideration to legislation and the budget. The committee system has been further developed in recent years in the Senate and the House of Representatives and there have been a number of Senate and joint select committees established to report to the Parliament on specific issues (Evans 1995a: 359–400; Commonwealth of Australia 2004).

The development of the committee system has been seen as a measure that has strengthened the Parliament in relation to the executive:

> By some accounts, committees are places where parliamentarians can try to come to grips with technical submissions, where they can admit to uncertainty, and where

their opinions can be influenced and shaped by argument. These characteristics are present by virtue of committee deliberations being undertaken largely outside the glare of the public spotlight, which targets and encourages adversarial behaviour. Committees are valuable, therefore, because (in whichever chamber they operate more effectively) they deepen parliamentary scrutiny of legislation, and increase the chances of informed and improving amendments. (Lovell 1994: 50)

While committees have the potential to improve the capacity of the Parliament to examine legislation and check the executive, and have in some cases clearly done so, it is also a fact that when one party has a majority on a committee, or there is political advantage to be had, there is a capacity for committees to become forums in which parties seek political advantage in exactly the same way as they do in the Parliament.

It is very rare for an individual 'backbench' parliamentarian of either the government or Opposition party to be able to play any significant role in initiating legislation. The government determines the parliamentary timetable and normally little time is allocated for so-called 'private members' business'. There are also limits on the scope of legislation that can be introduced by private members. The ancient convention of the 'financial initiative of the crown', which is written into the Australian Constitution (section 56), requires that all financial legislation be initiated by the government. Private members are therefore restricted to initiating non-money bills.

Another way in which the Parliament has lost legislative competence is through 'subordinate' or 'delegated' legislation. Many Acts of Parliament delegate to the Minister or some public body the authority to make the detailed regulations and ordinances that give operational effect to the legislation. While such regulations and ordinances must be tabled in Parliament and may be disallowed by a simple majority in either house, only in the Senate has there been any attempt to methodically examine delegated legislation through its Standing Committee on Regulations and Ordinances. This committee has at times performed its auditing function with zeal, and appears more bipartisan in its workings than many other parliamentary committees.

With respect to financial legislation, Parliament has fared no better. The Constitution (under sections 81 and 83) requires government expenditure to be authorised by legislation, but Parliament's power over financial matters is no greater than its power over any other matter. Both houses have established committees in an attempt to improve their capacity to audit government expenditure. The Public Accounts Committee, a joint committee of both houses, examines government expenditure to ensure that money has been spent in accordance with parliamentary appropriations. Its investigations are largely confined to matters raised in the Auditor-General's Report. The Expenditure Committee of the House of Representatives, established in 1976, performs a similar auditing function, checking against waste in government expenditure. To examine proposed expenditure more closely, the Senate established five (later six) Estimates Committees in 1970. Since 1980, the House of Representatives has also referred expenditure proposals to Estimates Committees.

Established parliamentary procedures—Question Time, censure motions, urgency debates—are important to the checking and restraining role that is ascribed to the legislature. Of these, Question Time routinely attracts the most media attention and receives the most publicity (it has been telecast on the ABC television network since 1990), and is generally regarded as the most important procedure the Parliament has for checking the executive.

In the afternoon of each day's sitting (for about 45 minutes in the House of Representatives and for unlimited time in the Senate), Members can ask Ministers questions without notice about the conduct of the government. Question Time potentially provides Parliament with a means of testing the government and probing into the actions of the government's administrative arm. As it actually operates, however, there are limits on the usefulness of Question Time for getting information that a government wishes to conceal. Ministers are able to evade questions or to give verbose or irrelevant answers. Questions are taken alternately from government and non-government members, allowing friendly or prearranged questions to take up half the time for questions and to lessen the pressure on Ministers (House of Representatives 1993: 21–5). Nevertheless, parliamentary questions can elicit important information and in some cases can force the government to act. One important example relates to the case of Cornelia Rau, an Australian resident who was wrongly held in detention for 10 months. A series of very specific questions in Parliament in February and March 2005 forced the Minister of Immigration and Multicultural Affairs to provide detailed answers about the actions of the Department of Immigration and Multiculturalism and Indigenous Affairs in detaining Cornelia Rau and led to the revelation that a number of other people, who were legally in Australia, had been wrongly held in detention (Kirk 2005). The forum provided an important platform for revealing maladministration by the Department.

Because of the media prominence given to Question Time, it can be very telling for a government. Its combative nature, and the attention that the media gives it, makes Question Time a very testing time for the Prime Minister and other Ministers (and also for the Opposition Leader). It is one of the forums in which the party leaders, and aspiring leaders, are able to perform before their party colleagues and attempt to win their support or confidence. A poor performance in Question Time can weaken the reputation of a Minister or Leader of the Opposition.

However, the media publicity about Question Time is a double-edged sword, and the impact of the media interest in Question Time is illustrative of problems that exist with the conduct of all parliamentary business. Because Question Time is a good forum for the Opposition to get maximum publicity for attacks on the government, it has become very adversarial in nature and, as in most other parliamentary activities, the contest revolves around the battle between the parties. Question Time is often presented by the media as a contest between the government and the Opposition, and as much attention is given to how the 'combatants' perform as to the substance of the questions and answers. Some questions, and some answers, appear to be aimed more at the press and the electorate than at the issue before the Parliament. In reality, some of the best work done by the Parliament, in terms of detailed consideration of government proposals, is probably conducted away from the spotlight, where parliamentarians from both sides of politics can be less concerned with the competition between the parties (Lovell 1994: 50).

Questions *with* notice can also be addressed to the government. They are normally used where detailed information is being sought. Answers are given in writing and are printed in *Hansard* (the official written record of the proceedings of the Parliament). Although these 'questions on notice' can sometimes be used effectively to probe into the actions of the government, the practice lacks immediate political impact.

A censure motion against the government in the House of Representatives, if successful, would force the resignation of the government. However, the outcomes of censure motions in the House of Representatives, where the government has a majority of votes, are a foregone conclusion. Nevertheless, Opposition parties use the device of moving and speaking to a censure motion to publicise their criticisms of the government. The procedures of a discussion of 'a matter of public importance' or an 'urgency debate' also provide the Opposition with parliamentary time during which it can focus attention on issues on which it thinks the government is vulnerable. In using these procedures the Opposition will, as with Question Time, be aiming to gain maximum publicity outside Parliament.

The same is true of other parliamentary activities—grievance debates, 'address in reply' debates and 'adjournment' debates—which allow wide-ranging discussion but have little or no impact in Parliament. They are used not just to address Parliament, but in the hope that the message will reach the media and the electorate. The government, too, uses Parliament in this way. Ministerial statements and other important speeches are often much more for the benefit of the press gallery than the Parliament.

MINISTERIAL RESPONSIBILITY

Parliament's capacity to restrain the exercise of executive power rests heavily on the doctrines of individual and collective ministerial responsibility. However, it has been widely accepted that these crucial doctrines have never operated as a means of ensuring that Ministers are held responsible for their actions or that governments are held accountable for the actions taken in their name in any 'Westminster' type of Parliament.

One problem is that the doctrines are far from precise: exactly who is meant to be responsible for what, and to whom, is not clear (Blunt 2004). More importantly, it is argued that Ministers and governments are largely immune from *parliamentary* sanctions because the government holds a majority of the seats in the House of Representatives. Here, as elsewhere, political parties have intervened. In the face of accusation of scandal or maladministration, Ministers have been able to deny responsibility for actions of their departments, and governments have been able to discount the importance of the matter. When a Minister is under attack in Parliament, the government parties will usually close ranks and attempt to 'tough it out'. Only when political expediency or tactics require it will a transgressing Minister be asked by the Prime Minister to resign (Thompson & Tillotsen 1999: 48–54; Davis *et al.* 1993: 79–83). Even so, questions and urgency motions in the Parliament have played a decisive role in bringing to light aspects of ministerial behaviour that have ultimately led to the resignation of the Minister. In the case of the Commonwealth Parliament, the Senate—where in recent decades the government has not had control—has played an important role in pressing questions about ministerial conduct (see below). Not all cases of apparent ministerial misconduct or maladministration result in ministerial resignation. In some cases the Minister and the government are able to weather the parliamentary attack (Thompson & Tillotsen 1999: 50–4). However, there have been in recent years a number of cases where Ministers have been forced to resign after persistent questioning in the Parliament.

In 1994 Ros Kelly, the Minister for Environment, Sport and Territories in the Keating Labor government, was forced to resign after persistent questioning in the Parliament over her role in the administration of Commonwealth grants to sporting bodies (Uhr 1998: 152–4). Under the Howard government, five Ministers and one 'Parliamentary Secretary' (a Member of Parliament who, while not technically a Minister, is appointed to assist a Minister) were forced to resign from their Ministerial positions and return to the 'backbenches' of Parliament (Thompson & Tillotsen 1999: 52–3). While it is usually the case that it is the continuing political damage to the government caused by media reports which forces the ministerial resignation, it is the Parliament which provides the forum in which the questions can be pursued and the information about ministerial conduct sought out.

THE GROWTH OF THE EXECUTIVE BRANCH OF GOVERNMENT

In the 20th century, and especially after World War II, there was an enormous growth in the scope and scale of government. Governmental activity expanded in the fields of education, public health, transportation, the regulation of commerce and industry, social welfare, and service industries such as energy supply, public transport, and postal and telecommunication services. Government's role as economic manager has expanded, both through budgetary policy and regulation of banking and other financial institutions. More recently, governments have undertaken even more regulatory activities: equal opportunities for various social groups, race relations, corporate affairs and consumer protection.

Each government department has at its head a Minister and, depending on their size and importance, a Minister may be responsible for one or several departments. In theory it is the Ministers and the Cabinet that direct this public bureaucracy and determine the policy that the public service puts into effect, and it is the Ministers and Cabinet that are accountable to the Parliament for their actions and those of the public service. However, the scale of governmental activity presents difficulties for this notion of government responsibility. The antiquated procedures of the Parliament are not well suited to provide a check on the extensive activities of government. Although opposition parliamentarians are sometimes politically very effective in attacking the actions of Ministers or the public service, through focusing on some particular government activity or on a particular Ministry, the Parliament is limited in its capacity to audit and vet the very extensive range of government activities.

There is little dispute that the development of political parties and the expanded role of government have contributed to the growth of the executive's power in relation to the Parliament. However, some authors have argued that the dominance of the legislature by the executive, as they see it, has a simpler and more fundamental explanation (Sharman 1994; Reid & Forest 1989: 16–18, 469–71; Evans 1992). Sharman, for example, argues that there is an essential imbalance of power between the Parliament and the executive which is basic to the system of government itself:

> By definition, a parliamentary system is one in which the executive is chosen from the membership of the legislature and remains in office only so long as it retains the support of a majority of members in the popular house . . . As a consequence of the dependence of a parliamentary executive for its very existence on maintaining a supporting majority in the legislature, there is a powerful incentive for the executive to contrive stable majorities in Parliament. Once established, these stable majorities can be used to regulate the conduct of parliamentary business to suit the government of the day. In other words, the present dominance of the executive over the parliamentary process in the lower house is not just an artefact of a disciplined party system, but the logical consequences of a parliamentary derived executive. The bias of a parliamentary system is inherently towards executive control of Parliament. (Sharman 1994: 116)

Unlike a presidential system, in which the executive is elected directly and is not dependent for its existence on the support of a majority in the legislature, the government in the Westminster system must have control of the legislature to be secure in office. There is an overwhelming impetus in a system of responsible government for governments to seek to control the legislature.

The Senate

The argument made here about the weakness of the Parliament in relation to the government focuses on the House of Representatives, where the government holds a majority. To make a full assessment of the role and performance of the Parliament, however, it is necessary to look in more detail at the role of the Senate.

A strong Senate, with powers almost equal to those of the House of Representatives, was originally seen as a guardian of States' rights. It was not, however, a simple matter to get agreement on the constitutional provisions which would combine responsible government and a powerful second legislative chamber. Galligan (1995: 75) argues that the 'single most contentious issue for the Australian founders, and the one that took up the most space in the convention debates . . . was the design of the Senate and its accommodation with responsible government'. On the one hand, there was the problem of having a system of responsible government and two equally powerful legislative chambers. To which chamber would the government be responsible? And what would happen when the two chambers disagreed? On the other hand, a powerful Senate, in which each State was equally represented, was seen to be a protector of States' rights, and without it some of the States would have held out against joining the federation.

As noted above, the Constitution contains provisions for dealing with disagreements between the two houses of Parliament through 'double dissolutions'. These provisions, however, do not necessarily resolve the conflict between the two chambers. It is quite possible that the double-dissolution election will return houses that are still deadlocked. Of the six double-dissolution elections held since 1901, only three have given the incoming government a majority in the Senate, and the one joint sitting, in 1974, enacted some of the legislation which had provided the grounds for the double dissolution but did nothing to overcome the conflict between the two chambers.

The picture, drawn above, of members of the House of Representatives being directed by political parties applies equally to Senators. For much of the first half of the 20th century, the majority party in the House of Representatives also had a majority in the Senate. When the government party commanded a majority in the Senate, the Senate's substantial powers were never used to embarrass the government, even less to block its legislation or to force it from office.

However, when the governing party does not have a majority in the Senate, the party loyalties of Senators can have a quite different effect on government.

PROPORTIONAL REPRESENTATION AND THE 'REVIVAL' OF THE SENATE

The introduction of proportional representation for Senate elections in 1949 greatly increased the likelihood that the majority party in the House of Representatives would not control the Senate. Proportional representation made it easier for Independent or minority party candidates to win places in the Senate. In the case of the single-member electoral system that operates in the House of Representatives, a candidate requires 50 per cent of the vote (plus one vote) in an electorate to win a seat. In contrast, to win a seat at an ordinary Senate election (when half the Senate is being elected—that is, six from each State), a candidate needs to win only 14.3 per cent of the vote over the whole State. At a double dissolution, when 12 Senators are being elected from each State, a candidate needs to win only 7.7 per cent of the vote to be elected.[3]

When the system of proportional representation was first used for the Senate in 1949, the major parties shared between them 95.3 per cent of the first-preference vote with only 4.7 per cent going to the minor parties. Since that time, the share of the first-preference vote won by minor parties and by Independent candidates in Senate elections has increased significantly, as demonstrated in Figure 4.1. Their representation in the Senate has also increased significantly. In

FIGURE 4.1 | **Share of first-preference votes won by minor parties and Independent candidates in Senate elections, 1949–2004**

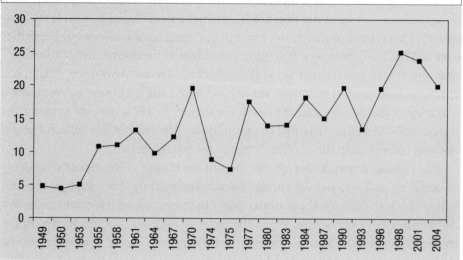

the 1999 election, a high point for the minor parties and Independents, they received 25 per cent of the Senate first-preference vote and won six of the 40 positions being contested.

In the mid-1950s, the Menzies Liberal–Country Party Coalition government lost control of the Senate. The immediate impact of the increased representation of minor parties in the Senate was not dramatic, but it did result in a 'revival' of the Senate through the development by the Senate of new procedures for scrutinising legislation. Between 1965 and 1972, the Coalition government was faced with a Senate in which the Democratic Labor Party (DLP) held the balance of power. The DLP was not prepared to side with the Labor Party Opposition to defeat the government on any major issue but it was prepared to participate in moves by Labor Senators to assert the Senate's power through the extensive expansion of its committee system.

This role the Senate has continued to develop. The Senate has held inquiries, with public hearings, on a number of issues. Rules designed to prevent legislation being rushed through the Senate at the end of a parliamentary session have also been adopted. A new committee structure, adopted in 1994, included eight Legislative Committees, each with a government majority and a government Senator as chair, and eight Reference Committees, each with a non-government Senator as chair.

The 'revival' of the Senate has been regarded by some commentators as a welcome strengthening of the legislature in relation to the executive (Reid 1968; Solomon 1973; Reid & Forest 1989: 29–33; Sharman 1990). These commentators have portrayed the Senate as asserting itself and enhancing its own ability to provide some checks on the legislative process and governmental finances, and to make the government more accountable.

However, the role that the Senate plays in relation to the government of the day depends on its party composition. The 'revival' of the upper house has not liberated Senators from the dictates of their parties. It is true that some major party Senators have displayed a greater measure of independence from their party than their counterparts in the House of Representatives, and that some of the debates in the Senate and Senate Committees are more bipartisan and questioning of the executive than in the House of Representatives. However, in matters that are crucial to the major parties, the parties have exercised the same control over their members in the Senate as they have over members of the House of Representatives (cf. Reid & Forest 1989: 29–33).

The 'revival' of the Senate which commenced in the 1960s was the product of the party composition of the Senate. The government parties lost control of the Senate as Independent and minority party Senators gained the balance of power. However, whenever a major political party gains a majority in the Senate, the Senate's so-called 'revival' weakens because Independent and minor party Senators can hope to play a significant role only when they hold the balance of power. The Senate has demonstrated that it has enormous power, but it will not be exercised against governments that have a majority in that house. On the other hand, governments facing an Opposition majority in the Senate can expect that the Senate's power will be used against them when it is to the Opposition's political advantage.

The Whitlam Labor government, elected in 1972, faced a hostile Senate, which blocked a large amount of the government's legislative program. In 1974 the Liberal–Country Party Opposition in the Senate forced a double dissolution, and then in 1975 brought down the Labor government. As a result of a very large swing against the Labor Party in the 1975 election, the Fraser Coalition government obtained a majority in the Senate between 1976 and 1981. In that period some government legislation was amended but at no stage was there any question of the Senate's powers being used to challenge the government's legislative program. After 1981 the Fraser government lost its majority in the Senate and once again the Senate began to amend and reject government legislation. In February 1983 Fraser obtained a double dissolution on the grounds that government legislation, including nine sales-tax bills, had been rejected by the Senate.

The Hawke and Keating Labor governments, for the whole of their period in office (1983 to 1996), faced a Senate in which one Independent and minor party Senators held the balance of power. The Senate rejected a number of government bills, and other significant legislation was abandoned by the government before its introduction in the Senate after minor party Senators announced that they would vote with the Opposition and prevent its passage. In addition the minor parties and the Independent, when negotiating with the government about legislation before the Senate, were able to insist on amendments to include their own priorities in the legislation.

The Howard Coalition government in its first three terms (1996–2004) also faced a Senate in which it did not have a majority and had the same sorts of problems as the Labor government in having some of its legislation passed by the Senate. For example, when it came to office in 1996 an important plank in its policy involved changes to the industrial relations system. The legislation was passed by the Senate only after protracted negotiations with the Democrats and significant amendment.

In the 1998 election the Coalition government was re-elected having campaigned on a policy of introducing a Goods and Services Tax (GST), the most controversial aspect of which was that the new tax would apply to food and other 'essentials'. The legislation to implement the tax was rejected by the Senate, and initially the government indicated that it was not prepared to compromise on the legislation. However, after protracted negotiations with the Democrats, who held the balance of power, the legislation was passed (despite not all of the Democrat Senators agreeing to support the compromise) with basic foods excluded from the tax.

In its first three terms the Coalition had legislation blocked or modified in a number of areas which it said were central to its program, including the privatisation of Telstra, industrial relations legislation, the terms under which disability pensions were paid, anti-terrorist and security legislation and the US free trade agreement.

The significance of the Senate for governments goes beyond its legislative powers. A Senate Committee on which the government does not have a majority can pursue inquiries which, in the House of Representatives, the government could block. Such a committee can call witnesses, and can seek information and documents that the government would rather went unnoticed. In 2002, for example, a Senate Committee into a Certain Maritime Incident received a great deal of publicity. The inquiry related to a claim which had been made by the Coalition Government prior to the 2001 federal election that asylum-seekers, whose vessel had been intercepted by the navy, had thrown their children overboard in an attempt to gain access to Australian territory. The claim was later shown to be false, and the inquiry found that the Defence Minister, Peter Reith, 'had deceived the Australian people during the 2001 Federal Election campaign concerning the state of evidence for the claim that children had been thrown overboard' (SSCICMI 2002: xxiv). In 2004, following a public statement by Mike Scrafton, a former ministerial staffer, that raised questions about the extent to which the Prime Minister had knowingly made false claims that children had been thrown overboard, another Senate inquiry was established. The non-government majority on the Committee concluded that the 'clear implication' of Scrafton's evidence was 'that the Prime Minister misled the Australian public in the lead-up to the 2001 federal election' (SSCSE 2004: 45). Although the inquiry did not have any immediate impact on the Coalition's electoral fortunes, as with many other Senate inquiries, it was able to bring to light information about the operation of government which would otherwise have remained undisclosed.

Senate Estimates Committees have come to play an important role in scrutinising the actions of the government. Twice a year—when the Budget and the supplementary estimates are presented to the Parliament—the eight Senate Legislative Committees sit as Estimates Committees. These Committees have six members each; three from the government party, two from the Opposition and one from the minor parties or Independents. Committee hearings are open to the public and the press. Importantly, in terms of parliamentary scrutiny and the examination of the action of the government, Committee members are able to question public servants from the relevant agency directly, and well as the responsible Minister (Commonwealth of Australia 2005).

In recent years, as the Senate has become politically more important and the media have paid greater attention to the hearings and reports of Senate Committees, the activities of the committees have become more partisan. Anne Lynch, the Deputy Clerk of the Senate (a senior Senate administrative office), observes that in the 1970s committee hearings, even on controversial matters, were characterised by bipartisanship, deliberation and cooperation across party lines, and that committee reports were largely unanimous. By the late 1990s, however, debates in the committee hearings were much more likely to split on party lines and reports of the Legislative Committees were more likely to contain a dissenting report, with the government and non-government Senators simply restating their respective party's policy. The same development has taken place with the Reference Committees. Although it was intended that the Legislative Committees would examine legislation, appropriation bills and government reports referred to them by the Senate, and that the Reference Committees would deal with policy and other general matters, the non-government majority in the Senate has, on a number of occasions, referred legislation to Reference Committees where the government was unable to control the content of the committee's majority report (Lynch 1999: 180–1; Uhr 1998: 148). Lynch explains that:

> the active nature of Senate committees and the unpredictability of outcomes in the Senate have kept the media's attention firmly focused on the work of Senate committees. It is possible that some senators have found the temptation irresistible to play to the media gallery in order to obtain greater coverage of their immediate party position or agenda. (Lynch 1999: 180–4; see also Grattan 1999: 166; Costar 2000: 11)

The importance of the Senate, however, does not lie in its members being less influenced by party politics. The 'revival' of the Senate has not necessarily made its members or their deliberations, or the reports of the various committee inquiries, any less partisan than those in the House of Representatives. The importance of the Senate is that it has constitutional powers almost equal to those of the House of Representatives, and that for most of the period since the introduction of proportional representation the political party that controlled the House of Representatives and formed government did not control the Senate. It was widely believed that that situation was likely to continue (see DPM&C 2003: 6, 27–30). Against those expectations the Coalition government won a majority of Senate places at the 2004 election (see below). It is yet to be seen whether this outcome will be a brief interruption to what had become the usual pattern or whether it signals a more permanent change.

The Senate and responsible government

The 'revival' of the Senate was welcomed by some commentators, who emphasised the importance of the *liberal* aspects of the Australian system of government. They saw the Senate as enhancing the powers of the Parliament against the executive. The notion of 'responsible Cabinet government' which underpins this view and which underpins much of the argument made in this chapter about the performance of the Parliament—that a fundamental role of the legislature must be to check and restrain the power of the executive and to make it account-able — is influenced by a *liberal* view which sees government (even governments that are democratically elected) largely as something that must never be trusted. The potential for the abuse of power, according to this view, is such that the executive must be constantly scrutinised, restrained, checked and held account-able. It is not sufficient simply that there be periodic elections. In this view, checks and balances against the government must be maximised. A governmen-tal system without ongoing safeguards against the exercise of executive power would be little more than an 'elected dictatorship', in which citizens would have the opportunity of choosing which (potentially) autocratic government would rule for the next term. This ideal of responsible government, which judges the Parliament overwhelmingly in terms of its capacity to limit the executive, emphasises *liberal* values at the expense of *democratic* ones.

According to this view, the Senate increases the Parliament's ability to perform the role ascribed to it by the theory of responsible government, by more adequately scrutinising legislation, by questioning the government and in this way holding it accountable. The Senate is seen as a valuable institutional safeguard (Thompson 1994: 105–7; Evans 1995b; Reid & Forest 1989: 358–60, 362–3, 477–84; Sharman 1990). From an alternative viewpoint, however, the Senate has the potential to produce unstable and ineffective government. Writing after the 'constitutional crisis', in which an opposition-controlled Senate even-tually brought down the Whitlam Labor government, Sawer argued that:

> [w]e live in an age when governments are expected to be active, and even the most 'conservative' are committed to economic management and a multitude of welfare services. This is not possible if the initiatives of a government based on a House of Representatives majority are to be constantly 'checked' by a hostile majority in the Senate. (Sawer 1977: 140)

Likewise, Maddox argues that the Senate's powers are used inconsistently and, when linked to a system of responsible government, can produce instability. Maddox asks whether bicameralism 'is an appropriate superimposition on Australian responsible government':

> The Australian founders may have followed the Americans by creating a Senate in the quest for government *stability* but, ironically, nothing has been more influential in creating uncertainty and *instability* in our central institutions in recent years than the misapplication of Senate powers. We have seen that the Senate performs its various functions as a presumed 'states' House' and as a house of review but poorly, and its alternative periods of acquiescence and obstructionism raise further cause for doubt. (Maddox 2005: 193; emphasis in original)

Whereas the first perspective sketched above regards government as a necessary evil that must be subject to the maximum institutional restraints in order that its power is restricted to an absolute minimum, this alternative view represented by Sawer and Maddox sees government as a means for carrying out the wishes of the community and as an instrument for reform. This requires that there is some stability in the system and that governments that have been democratically elected have sufficient power to carry out their mandate. This view of the role of government and the Parliament emphasises what it argues is the *democratic* element in responsible government. A crucial feature of the Parliamentary system, from this viewpoint, is the convention that the government must be formed by the party that commands a majority in the House of Representatives. The government has the *responsibility* to carry out the collective wishes of the electorate and it is through the House of Representatives that the electors select the government. The Parliament provides a forum for the Opposition to oppose the government, to speak against its programs and to publicise what it regards as the government's weaknesses. The government is then held account-able for its actions to the electorate at election time.

According to this view, the democratic process and popular reforms can be undermined if the checks and restraints in the Parliamentary system are such that the government can be prevented from carrying out its mandate. A system of strong parliamentary checks and balances may produce *limited* government but it will not necessarily be *responsible* government. If executive power is shared between the government and the legislature, and if every governmental measure is the product of compromise with the legislature, who then can the electorate hold responsible? In a system of extreme checks and balances, in which the government is constantly curtailed, there will, according to this viewpoint, not be effective government and there will be less, not more, accountability.

In this vein, Maddox argues that an evaluation of the Australian Senate should take account of the conservative role that it plays. The Senate has undermined the legislative programs of popularly elected governments and has, in one case, had a hand in forcing a government with a majority in the House of Representatives from office. The argument for strong checks and balances and review of legisla-tion, he says, is often used spuriously when the real purpose is to limit and frus-trate legitimate reforms which are part of the program on which a government was elected through the House of Representatives (Maddox 2005: 181–93).

Major parties and the Senate

The position taken on the Senate by the major political parties appears to be simply opportunist. Both, when in Opposition, have combined with the minor parties and Independents and used their numbers in the Senate to frustrate the government; but, when in government themselves, both have argued that the Senate should not stand in the way of a democratically elected government. The Hawke and Keating Labor governments argued that it was improper for the Senate to force changes in the government's budget and to stand in the way of its initiatives. Famously Paul Keating, when Prime Minister, referred to the Senate as 'unrepresentative swill' (CPDHR 4/11/1992: 2547). The Coalition, whose Senators often played a hand in amending and defeating the Labor government's budget measures and amending its legislation, has in government denounced the 'obstructionist' Senate. In making this argument, the Howard government has raised the notion of a *mandate*, arguing that in a system of responsible government the elected government has a mandate to put its explicit election promises into effect.

In 1980s and 1990s it appeared that it would always be difficult for either of the major parties to win a majority in the Senate. When there is sufficient electoral support for several Independent or minority party candidates to be elected, it was difficult for the government formed in the House of Representatives to win a majority in the Senate.

Faced with this situation Ministers in the Howard government called for 'reform' of the Senate to limit its capacity to frustrate the plans of the elected government. Liberal spokesperson Senator Helen Coonan, in a number of articles and speeches, argued that the Senate was a 'handbrake on democracy' and that the use of the Senate's powers to reject government legislation, and to delay and force compromises, prevents the government from responding urgently and decisively to rapidly changing national and international situations (Coonan 1999a, 1999b, 2000). Coonan argued that 'steps should be taken'—either constitutional change or amendment to the electoral laws—'to ensure that there is at least a prospect of the government of the day obtaining a majority in the Senate' (Coonan 2000: 22).

In 2003 the Prime Minister, John Howard, issued a discussion paper in which he canvassed the idea of changing section 57 of the Constitution to make it easier to break deadlocks between the House of Representatives and the Senate. He argued that under the existing electoral laws it was almost impossible for the government to win a majority in the Senate and that the non-government majority in the Senate held 'control over the legislative and policy agenda upon which the government of the day had been elected'. (DPM&C 2003: 6. Reproduced with permission.)

The provisions in section 57 of the Constitution for breaking a deadlock between the House of Representatives and the Senate, the Prime Minister argued, were too cumbersome and time consuming.

As stated above, section 57 provides that a government may seek a double dissolution if legislation which is passed by the House of Representatives is rejected by the Senate and is, after an interval of three months, again passed by the House of Representatives and rejected by the Senate. If the government is re-elected at the double-dissolution election and the legislation is again passed by the House of Representatives and rejected by the Senate the government can put the legislation to a joint sitting of both houses of the Parliament.

In the discussion paper the Prime Minister argued that:

> constitutional reform is needed to rebalance the relationship between the two houses
> and to ensure that where the houses are deadlocked, the Parliament as a whole may
> reconcile the difference as expeditiously as possible.
>
> Without such reform, governments will be unable to implement policies which
> have both a popular mandate and are essential to promoting good government.
> (DPM&C 2003: 7. Reproduced with permission.)

The Prime Minister proposed two options for changing the deadlock provisions, both of which provided for a joint sitting of the two chambers without the requirement for a double-dissolution election. Under the first option, section 57 would be amended to allow for a bill which had been twice passed by the House of Representatives and twice rejected by the Senate (with an interval of three months) to be put to a joint sitting of both houses of the Parliament. The second option was to allow for legislation which was twice blocked by the Senate during the term of one Parliament, and was again blocked by the Senate after a normal general election, to be put to a joint sitting (DPM&C 2003: 38–44).

The Prime Minister's proposals were attacked by the minor parties and Independents, and commentators who believed that a Senate in which neither of the major parties held a majority provided valuable safeguards. Both of the proposals it was argued would allow a government to use the device of the joint sitting without the need to face the electorate in a double dissolution. The first proposal, however, would allow governments which held a majority of the combined numbers in the House of Representatives and the Senate (which is almost always the case) to pass whatever legislation it wished (Evans 2004: 13–4).

Given the history of referendums in Australia, any such proposal for constitutional change was unlikely to succeed even with the support of both major political parties. When the Labor Party indicated that it would only support a proposal to amend section 57 of the Constitution if it included the removal of the Senate's power to block a government's budget—a proposal which was unacceptable to the Coalition—it appeared that there was no chance that either of the proposals would be passed at a referendum. In June 2004 the Prime Minister announced that although he believed that 'the Senate was preventing good government' he would not proceed with the proposals because there was not sufficient public support for a change (*The Age*, 2 June 2004).

Whatever the arguments for or against the Senate, the fact is that it is a potent weapon and governments in Australia which do not also have a majority in the Senate cannot assume that their legislation or budgets will automatically be passed by the Parliament. Until 2004 it had appeared unlikely that either of the major political parties could hope easily to win a majority in the Senate. With the expectation that no government could win a majority in the Senate, the

Senate was often portrayed as a feature of the Australian Constitution which provided a permanent check on the executive branch of government (see for example Crossin 2004: 146).

In 2004, however, the Coalition government did obtain a majority of places in the Senate, having won exactly half the places at the 2001 election and a bare majority at the 2004 election.[4] As discussed above, when the government does hold a majority in both chambers the Senate plays a very different role. At the time of writing the Senators elected in 2004 had not taken their place. It has been assumed by many commentators that the Coalition government will be able to enact most, if not all, of the measures which had previously been blocked by the Senate. Whether any Coalition Senators will defy the government and vote against any of the government's proposals, and if so on what issues, will be a matter of intense political interest during the Coalition's fourth term. In the longer term, a matter of importance to the nature of the political system in Australia is whether the Coalition's achievement of a majority in the Senate is a temporary change or whether it signals a more permanent change to the pattern of the last decade and a half.

Conclusion

The traditional theory of 'responsible government' attributes to the Parliament a number of roles: it is the law-making body, it has a role in restraining the use of executive power, and it has a role in the democratic process whereby voters elect the government. Two developments have very significantly affected the way the Parliament performs the first two of these functions.

First, the development of modern disciplined political parties early in the 20th century changed the relationship between the executive and the legislature. When the government party has a majority in *both* chambers of the Parliament, the outcome of parliamentary deliberations is almost a foregone conclusion.

However, the second development—the 'revival' of the Senate—has significantly altered this portrayal of a parliament dominated by the executive. By necessity the government party (or coalition) controls the House of Representatives, but the introduction of proportional representation for Senate elections has facilitated the election of Independent and minor party Senators. When minor parties hold the balance of power in the Senate (or when the Opposition has a majority), the nature of the government's relationship with the Parliament is changed. Governments have had to negotiate the passage of legislation, including revenue measures, through the Senate and have had their actions subject to Senate inquiries. When the government does not have a majority in the Senate, the outcome of Parliamentary deliberations is not a foregone conclusion.

NOTES

1   For a discussion and explanation of 'liberal' and 'democratic' values, see Chapters 1 and 2 of this book.

2   The power to recommend the early dissolution of the House of Representatives has enabled Prime Ministers to call elections at a time they believe will be to their electoral advantage. The legal responsibility for dissolving the Parliament rests with the Governor-General (see sections 5 and 28 of the Constitution), but no request for an early election has so far been refused.

3   For further details on the electoral system, see Chapter 10 of this book.

4   In the 2004 election for the Senate, with 45.9 per cent of the national primary vote and in excess of 44 per cent in all States, the Coalition won sufficient preferences from other parties to win 21 of the 40 places being contested (i.e. four of the six in Queensland, three of the six in each other State and one of the two in both the Northern Territory and the ACT). The incoming Senators from the 2004 election, whose terms began on 1 July 2005, joined the continuing Senators who had been elected at the 2001 election in which the Coalition had obtained 41.8 per cent of the national primary vote and sufficient preferences from other parties to win exactly half the Senate places.

Having won a majority of positions at the 2004 election the Coalition should be well placed to hold its majority beyond the next election. Unless there is a double dissolution the term of the Senators elected in 2004 will run from 1 July 2005 to 30 June 2011. At the next Senate election after 2005 the Coalition need only win 50 per cent of the places to maintain its majority in the Senate.

REFERENCES

Bach, S. 2003, *Platypus and Parliament: The Australian Senate in Theory and Practice*, Department of the Senate, Canberra.

Blewett, N. 1993, 'Parliamentary Reform: Challenges for the House of Representatives', *Australian Quarterly*, vol. 65, no. 3, Spring, pp. 1–14.

Blunt, D. 2004, 'Responsible Government: Ministerial Responsibility and Motions of "Censure"/"No Confidence"', *Australian Parliamentary Review*, vol. 19, no. 1.

Commonwealth of Australia 2004, *Senate Brief No 4: Senate Committees: Why Committees*, Parliament of Australia, Canberra.

Commonwealth of Australia 2005, *Senate Brief No 5: Consideration of Estimates by the Senate's Legislation Committees*, Parliament of Australia, Canberra.

Coonan, H. 1999a, 'The Senate—Safeguard or Handbrake on Democracy?', *The Sydney Papers*, vol. 11, no. 1.

Coonan, H. 1999b, '"Survival of the Fittest": Future Directions for the Senate', in *Representation and Institutional Change: 50 Years of Proportional Representation in the Senate*, eds M. Sawer & S. Miskin, Department of the Senate, Canberra.

Coonan, H. 2000, 'Safeguard or Handbrake on Democracy?', in *Deadlock of Democracy? The Future of the Senate*, ed. B. Costar, University of New South Wales Press, Sydney.

Costar, B. 2000, 'Introduction', in *Deadlock of Democracy? The Future of the Senate*, ed. B. Costar, University of New South Wales Press, Sydney.

Crossin, T. 2004 'Polls Apart: Reforming the Senate—Who Wants it and Why?', *Australian Parliamentary Review*, vol. 19, no. 1.

CPDHR, Commonwealth Parliamentary Debates (House of Representatives), Canberra.

Davis, G. Wanna, J. Warhurst, J. & Weller, P. 1993, *Public Policy in Australia*, 2nd edn, Allen & Unwin, Sydney.

DPM&C [Department of the Prime Minister and Cabinet] 2003, *Resolving Deadlocks: A Discussion Paper on Section 57 of the Australian Constitution*, Commonwealth of Australia, Canberra.

Evans, H. 1992, 'Parliament: An Unreformable Institution?', *Papers on Parliament*, no. 18, pp. 21–36.

Evans, H. 1993, 'Party Government: The Australian Disease and the Australian Cure', *Legislative Studies*, vol. 7, no. 2, pp. 17–23.

Evans, H. 1995a, *Odger's Australian Senate Practice*, 7th edn, AGPS, Canberra.

Evans, H. 1995b, 'Can Parliament Be Reformed?', in *The Australian Political System*, eds D. Lovell, I. McAllister, W. Maley & C. Kukathas, Longman, Melbourne, pp. 52–3.

Evans, H. 2004, 'Why the Prime Minister's Proposals Would Dismantle the Constitution', in *Upholding the Australian Constitution, Proceedings the Sixteenth Conference of The Samuel Griffith Society*, Perth, <http://www.samuelgriffith.org.au/paperspdf/vol16.pdf>, accessed 5/1/05.

Galligan, B. 1995, *A Federal Republic: Australia's Constitutional System of Government*, Cambridge University Press, Melbourne.

Grattan, M. 1999, 'Reporting the Senate: Three Perspectives', in *Representation and Institutional Change: 50 Years of Proportional Representation in the Senate*, eds M. Sawer & S. Miskin, Department of the Senate, Canberra.

House of Representatives 1993, *About Time: Bills, Questions and Working Hours: Report of the House of Representatives Standing Committee on Procedures of the Inquiry into the House of Representatives*, AGPS, Canberra.

Kirk, A. 2005, 'Government Keeps Quiet on Mistaken Deportation', ABC Online, <http://www.abc.net.au/pm/contents/2005/s1358125.htm>, accessed 10/5/2005.

Lovell, D. 1994, 'Parliamentarians as Legislators', *Legislative Studies*, vol. 9, no. 1.

Lucy, R. 1985, *The Australian Form of Government*, Macmillan, Melbourne.

Lynch, A. 1999, 'Personalities versus Structure: The Fragmentation of the Senate System', in *Representation and Institutional Change: 50 Years of Proportional Representation in the Senate*, eds M. Sawer & S. Miskin, Department of the Senate, Canberra.

Maddox, G. 2005, *Australian Democracy in Practice*, 5th edn, Pearson, Sydney.

Millar, A. 1994, *Trust the Women: Women in Federal Parliament*, Department of the Senate, Canberra.

Reid, G. 1968, 'Australia's Commonwealth Parliament and the "Westminster Model"', in *Readings in Australian Government*, ed. C. Hughes, University of Queensland Press, Brisbane, pp. 109–22.

Reid, G. & Forest, M. 1989, *Australia's Commonwealth Parliament 1901–1988*, Melbourne University Press, Melbourne.

Sawer, G. 1977, *Federation Under Strain*, Melbourne University Press, Melbourne.

Sharman, C. 1990, 'Australia as a Compound Republic', *Politics*, vol. 25, no. 1, pp. 1–5.

Sharman, C. 1994, 'Reforming Executive Power', in *We, the People: Australian Republican Government*, ed. G. Winterton, Allen & Unwin, Sydney, pp. 113–24.

Solomon, D. 1973, 'The Senate', in *Australian Politics: A Third Reader*, ed. H. Mayer, Cheshire, Melbourne, pp. 527–36.

SSCSE [Senate Select Committee on the Scrafton Evidence] 2004, Report, Commonwealth of Australia, Canberra, <http://www.aph.gov.au/Senate/committee/scrafton_ctte/report/report.pdf>, accessed 26/4/05.

SSCICMI [Senate Select Committee for an Inquiry into a Certain Maritime Incident]

2002, Report, Commonwealth of Australia, Canberra, <http://www.aph.gov.au/Senate/committee/maritime_incident_ctte/report/contents.htm>, accessed 26/4/05.

Stewart, G. & Ward, I. 1996, *Politics One*, 2nd edn, Macmillan, Melbourne.

Thompson, E. 1994, 'A Washminster Republic', in *We, the People: Australian Republican Government*, ed. G. Winterton, Allen & Unwin, Sydney, pp. 97–112.

Thompson, E. & Tillotsen, G. 1999, 'Caught in the Act: The Smoking Gun View of Ministerial Responsibility', *Australian Journal of Public Administration*, vol. 58, no. 1, March.

Uhr, J. 1998, *Deliberative Democracy in Australia: The Changing Place of Parliament*, Cambridge University Press, Melbourne.

CHAPTER 5

Executive government

GEOFF ANDERSON

Introduction: Why were these people smiling?

On a Tuesday morning, 26 October 2004, a group of politicians took part in a ceremony with the Governor-General in the drawing room of his residence at Yarralumla in Canberra. Later, their faces beaming satisfaction and pride, they emerged to pose with him so that newspaper photographers and television camera teams might record the event. But what had they been doing, why were they so satisfied, why the beaming smiles?

The answer is that they had just been confirmed as winners of the ultimate prize in our system of politics, government and public administration. By reason of their party's election victory two weeks earlier, they had been sworn in as Ministers of the Crown with the more senior among them to become members of the Cabinet. Years of struggle, perhaps even a lifetime, had been invested in gaining the right to be part of that photo opportunity: hours of grinding work, of high risks and low compromises, of cajoling colleagues for support, of representing their party at hundreds of inconsequential functions and finally surviving an exhausting and tense election campaign.

Now they could smile because they knew that they stood at the centre of political and administrative power; the 'repository of legitimate political authority', able and empowered to take the initiative in government, and to control and direct the administrative apparatus of the state (Page 1997: 124).

Yet, as important and as powerful as this group might be, the Australian Constitution makes no real reference to their central role, nor does it even mention 'the Cabinet'. Instead section 61 provides that executive authority is vested in the Crown and exercised by the Governor-General. Section 62 establishes the Federal Executive Council, which is chosen by the Governor-General, to provide advice on how to exercise that authority. Under section 64, the Governor-General may appoint members of that Executive Council as the 'Queen's Ministers' to administer 'departments of state', that is, to run the country.

Even more significantly, there is no reference in the Constitution to the Prime Minister who occupies pride of place in this smiling group, having led his colleagues through the political campaigns that gained them the right to be part of the photo. But we all understand and accept that the Prime Minister will be the face of the government once it gets down to business. Through media reports on national affairs and the major decisions that affect our lives, we see 'the PM' at the centre of events, announcing initiatives and explaining the government's actions. Much is expected of this office and the person who occupies it (Davis 2002: 49) and more than anything else the Prime Minister's performance will determine the success of the government and shape the legacy that it will leave. The range of issues that might form the criteria for this judgment is extraordinarily diverse. It may be the explanation of complex economic conditions, new policies to manage social change, or justification for the behaviour of colleagues. Then at times of national tragedy and exultation alike the PM will be looked to for leadership and for the expression of the national mood. In moments of uncertainty that might lead to fear, such as terrorist attacks on Australian citizens abroad, the PM will be expected to provide a reassuring response.

But the Prime Minister is also a political figure and the leader of a political party, another institution on which the Constitution is mostly silent. The Prime Minister is responsible for advancing the party's policies, defending its members and maximising its support among voters to win more seats at the next election.

For all practical purposes, regardless of the precise words of the Constitution, it is the Prime Minister and the Cabinet who sit at the apex of the 'executive' branch within our system of parliamentary democracy. This is sometimes a source of confusion to new students of Australian politics as well as to visitors familiar with other systems of government. The explanation for the apparent anomaly can be found in the history of the Westminster system of parliamentary democracy, the way in which it was transferred to Australia at the time of federation and its development since that time. As discussed in Chapters 3 and 4 of this book, its explanation requires an understanding of the conventions that give form and practical substance to our system of government and their interplay with the formal provisions of the Constitution:

- Government is formed by the party, or coalition of parties, that holds the most seats in the House of Representatives.
- Following an election, the leader of the majority party is called on by the Governor-General to form a government and to lead it as the Prime Minister.
- The Prime Minister recommends to the Governor-General the people who are to be appointed as Ministers. The Governor-General acts on that advice and makes the appointments in line with section 64 of the Constitution, which also provides that those appointed shall be members of the Executive Council.
- Section 63 provides that the Governor-General, in exercising the constitutional powers of the office, acts on the advice of the Executive Council. In effect, this means on the advice of the Prime Minister and the Cabinet.

Together these conventions and provisions place the Prime Minister and Cabinet in a central position within our system. The primary focus of this chapter is the role of Cabinet and how it works. However, Cabinet cannot be understood simply as a static administrative mechanism. Rather it is a living institution within our political and administrative system that develops and changes in line with the pressures of managing a growing nation, as well as the political events that will shape the nation's future.

The origins of the Cabinet

The origins of the institution that we now call the Cabinet are to be found in the steady transfer of power from the Crown to Parliament that took place in Britain during the 18th century. The development of Cabinet's central role in directing and governing the state, while also providing a means of linking this executive power with the legislature, has been seen as the means by which the 'perennial power struggle between the sovereign and parliament' was resolved in an orderly manner (Hennessey 1986: 2). English monarchs had governed through a Privy Council of Ministers chosen for their loyalty as much as their competence. However, over time this became unwieldy, and decision making increasingly passed to a smaller 'council of cabinet' (the name 'cabinet' deriving from the small room or chamber in which these ministers would meet to resolve any disagreements so that they could present unanimous advice to the King. By the time George I came to the throne in 1714, the growth in the power of Parliament had seen this inner group comprise Ministers who 'enjoyed the trust of the monarch *and* carried clout in parliament' (Hennessey 1986: 2). Their power to direct the affairs of state grew when the new monarch, who came from the German branch of the royal line and was not comfortable speaking in English, chose to no longer attend its meetings. So, 'for all practical purposes after 1717 "cabinet" ceased to be a body meeting in the presence of the King' (Hennessey 1986: 2) and began to consolidate its central role as the executive of government.

Almost three centuries on, the Privy Council remains as the formal body through which the legal power of the Crown (or the state) is exercised in the United Kingdom. In Australia, the Federal Executive Council mirrors its role and provides a historical link to the origins of our system of government. But, as in the UK, the Cabinet is the body that exercises executive power, even if its decisions require formal approval by the Governor-General and the Executive Council to give them full legal standing.

Cabinet and the (Australian) Westminster system[1]

The distinguishing feature of the Westminster system is the location of Cabinet—the apex of the system of executive government—within the Parliament. This is a central concept of representative or parliamentary democracy in that it provides the crucial link in the chain of accountability between those we elect to represent us, and the administrative power of the state. In theory, the Parliament chooses members of the Cabinet from among its own members; they then hold office for only so long as they individually or collectively retain the confidence of Parliament, and their very presence among those who have 'chosen' them provides an immediate and constant means for all members of the Parliament to hold the Cabinet to account. This formal model of parliamentary sovereignty and accountability assumes that Parliament is composed of members who are independent of each other, having been chosen by voters in local constituencies on the basis of a judgment as to their overall beliefs and likely attitude to matters that will come before the Parliament (Davis 2002: 50). In practice, a number of factors cut across this apparently simple and direct process to make it more complex.

The most overt of these is the role of political parties. With the exception of a small handful of Independents, members of Parliament today owe their primary allegiance to the party that selected them to stand for election under its banner. When it comes to the Cabinet and its accountability to Parliament, individual Ministers in fact owe their continued existence in the job to how well they maintain support within their party, either indirectly through the judgment of the party leader and Prime Minister (as in the case of the Coalition) or directly (as in the case of the Labor Party).

Moreover, they might depend on a particular group or faction within that party for continuing support. This is particularly so in the Labor Party, where the system of factions has become both formalised and extremely rigid, acting as parties within a party with the primary objective of organising support to win both party and parliamentary positions (Weller 2004: 638). In a Labor government, the parliamentary party (known as the 'Caucus') elects the members of the Ministry, with a Labor Prime Minister retaining only the right to allocate responsibilities. The process of election means that the factional balances within the party are transferred into the Ministry, with negotiations between factional leaders dealing with any need to balance State and gender representation.

In contrast, a Prime Minister leading a Liberal and National Party Coalition government has the right to choose who shall be in the Ministry and to allocate the portfolios or departments for which they will be responsible. But while the freedom given to a Coalition Prime Minister might fit more readily into the 'expectations' of Westminster tradition (Weller 2004: 638), the leader will have no less a need to balance internal party rivalries, take account of the demands of States and regions, and recognise the need to represent the increasing proportion of female members of Parliament.

The politics associated with the need of the National Party to differentiate itself from the Liberal Party on policies that affect rural areas can also create special problems for a Coalition Cabinet, as the debate on the full privatisation of Telstra during 2005 demonstrated. Nevertheless, it remains unusual for a vote in either house of the Australian Parliament to be decided on other than 'party lines'. Examples of government members 'crossing the floor' to defeat legislation introduced by the executive are very rare and in the case of the Labor Party would lead to suspension or expulsion from the party. The disciplined party vote in the Parliament is in any case cast on the basis of decisions made within their party room where 'the Ministry' represents a large group of votes. Moreover, it is a bloc that is bound tightly together by the conventions of collective ministerial responsibility (see below) combined with the politics of mutual self-interest.[2]

Critics such as the outspoken Clerk of the Senate Harry Evans decry the impact of party politics on Parliament as the imposition of a 'modern autocracy', with government MPs little more than a 'cheer squad' for the Prime Minister and the executive (Evans 2005). However, we need to be careful not to place all responsibility for change at the feet of political parties. The breakdown in the traditional concept of the Westminster 'chain of accountability' (Ward 1999: 32) can also be attributed to the role of the media in shaping attitudes and controlling information, or the growth of non-government organisations and other lobby groups who influence Ministers and parliamentarians. A modern view of parliamentary democracy might also suggest that rising demands for citizen participation have raised questions about the role of legislatures and Ministers alike (Bishop & Davis 2002: 14). Similarly, concepts of 'governance' may suggest that the state no longer has a monopoly over the institutions necessary to govern (Pierre & Peters 2000: 68). This in turn may broaden and extend lines of accountability into different dimensions, rather than simply fracture them.

The key point is that Parliament, while part of our constitutional machinery, is also a political institution. Cabinet, being part of it, is also driven by, and at other times shapes and directs, the political currents that ebb and flow through its chambers. Given its fundamentally political character we should not be surprised that political parties play a central role.

What does Cabinet do, and how does it work?

The functions of Cabinet are wide-ranging. Essentially it is part of the constitutional machinery of government, but it also constitutes the highest administrative body within government. It both sets broad policy settings and determines the detail of implementation, and it stands at the apex of the political and party system. It is inside the Cabinet room that the often competing priorities and sometimes contradictory objectives of policy, politics and administration intersect and find resolution.

Patrick Weller (1990: 32ff) and later Glyn Davis (2002: 53) have sought to describe these broad-ranging functions in terms of the major roles that Cabinet plays. For Weller, there are six roles:

- a clearing house, endorsing routine business, making authoritative choices about new policy issues, legitimising the activities of the public sector
- an information exchange, letting ministers know what is happening across government
- an arbiter, resolving disputes between agencies and between ministers
- a political decision maker, applying political judgments to bureaucratic nominations
- a coordinator, preventing overlap, duplication or inconsistencies across the range of government activity
- the 'guardian of the strategy', keeping the 'big picture' in front of government, so that long-term strategic interests are not lost amid disputes over policy detail.

Davis adds a further three roles:

- an allocator of resources, developing and monitoring a budget strategy, making major expenditure choices
- a crisis manager, handling difficulties from internal party disputes to major world events, even wars
- a watchdog, ensuring that individual ministers and agencies are not making unilateral decisions without government consideration.

This is a conceptual schema: these roles are not separated out to correspond to any particular arrangement of Cabinet's agenda; rather elements of each might be found in the way Cabinet deals with the issues that come before it. Cabinet is also more than just a meeting; it makes more sense to see it as 'system' (Page 1997: 109) that brings together the work of a network of officials and advisers, which it then considers within the context of a wide range of views, opinions and demands from business, the community, trade unions, the media and, of course, its political colleagues and opponents.

Cabinet also provides the motive power or engine for administrative government. The fuel is the process of setting the Cabinet agenda, gathering the information required so that issues are properly considered, and recording and monitoring the implementation of decisions. These tasks, and the deliberations of Cabinet on which they are centred, set the work program for the public service and in turn establish 'a rhythm' for the business of government (Davis 2002: 54) which ultimately plays a significant part in determining whether the political machine is also running smoothly.

The key components of this rhythmic system of Cabinet are the regularity of Cabinet meetings and the strict protocols for how information is prepared for consideration and programmed for presentation. This process not only allows Cabinet to manage large quantities of information but also provides an orderly process to bring together and reconcile differing viewpoints (Keating 1996: 23).

Cabinet meetings are programmed to take place at least once a week, regardless of whether the Parliament is sitting, but not every Minister takes part. Participation is limited to Cabinet Ministers, who are in overall charge of each portfolio or department. As of 2005, there were 17 Cabinet Ministers including the Prime Minister. There were 13 non-Cabinet or 'junior' Ministers and a further 12 Parliamentary Secretaries who only attend if they are required in relation to particular issues that are relevant to their responsibilities, and then only for that agenda item. This means that meetings of the whole Ministry of 42 Ministers are rare. Under John Howard's leadership, a meeting of the whole Ministry is held at the beginning of each session of Parliament, that is at least three times a year, although he may also hold additional meetings if he wishes to take broader soundings on a particular issue or discuss the strategic issues facing the government.[3]

All matters that come before the Cabinet do so by way of a written submission from the responsible Minister, except for special circumstances in which the Prime Minister has agreed that an issue requires urgent consideration. These submissions must follow a common format. They must be concise (no more than 10 pages) and must include a cover sheet containing an Executive Summary that 'should enable Ministers to grasp the essentials on which they are being asked to make a decision'. (DPMC 2004: 15. Reproduced with permission.) Submissions are accompanied by standardised 'impact statements', which generally focus on technical issues. Following the rise of the Family First Party to both prominence and political influence following the 2004 election, a 'Family Impact Statement' may also soon feature in Cabinet deliberations. Aside from the politics of this particular issue, the aim of standardising the presentation of information is both to limit the amount of material that comes before Ministers, and to ensure that it is focused on the absolute essentials: why Cabinet needs to consider the proposal, what are the critical matters for decision and the political sensitivities or possible criticisms, and whether there are any timing constraints that need to be taken into account (DPMC 2004: 16). The rules also aim to prevent Cabinet from becoming a debating forum on questions of fact by setting out procedures for consultation among Ministers and their officials so that there is agreement on the factual matters that form the basis for Cabinet discussion (DPMC 2004: 21).

While the range of issues that comes before Cabinet is diverse, some effort is made to limit what actually needs to be considered so that the first option for Ministers is to attempt to settle matters through correspondence and consultation. Again the aim is to reduce the workload of Cabinet and to maintain a more strategic focus rather than get caught up in administrative detail. Subject to these provisos, the *Cabinet Handbook* sets out a list of the sort of matters that would normally come before Cabinet: (DPMC 2004: 13. Reproduced with permission.)

- new policy proposals and significant variations to existing policies
- proposals likely to have a significant effect on employment in either the public or private sector
- expenditure proposals (normally considered only in the budget context)
- proposals requiring legislation
- proposals likely to have a significant impact upon relations between the Commonwealth and foreign, State, Territory or local government
- proposed responses to recommendations made in parliamentary committee reports
- government negotiation of, and agreement to, international treaties
- requests from parliamentary committees for references that have significant policy or administrative implications.

A great deal of the work of the Cabinet is dealt with by committees comprising just a subset of its members, either because the matters are routine, such as the government's parliamentary program, or because they involve intensive and detailed work, such as the expenditure review process leading to the budget, or because they are highly sensitive, for example matters involving national security. There are both permanent and standing committees of Cabinet as well as ad hoc committees to deal with specific issues from time to time (DPMC 2004: 1).

Alongside the rules that determine the form of submissions and their subject matter, there is also a strict timetable for their consideration. The basic unit of that timetable is the 'Five Day Rule' which simply means that submissions must be lodged at least five days before the Cabinet meeting at which they are to be considered. The objective is to provide adequate opportunity for Ministers to consider the proposal and for the Cabinet Secretariat to obtain and collate the 'coordination comments' of the various departments that have been consulted about the impact of the proposal for their area of responsibility.

In April 2002, Prime Minister Howard introduced an additional process described as the 'ten day ministerial consideration period'. His objective was to provide a more strategic focus for Cabinet discussions while also streamlining the handling of matters of a more routine nature. Under these arrangements, the Prime Minister identifies submissions that do not require detailed discussion in Cabinet. These are made available to Ministers for a period of 10 days after which, and providing that any matters raised by Ministers have been resolved, the recommendations of the submission are endorsed at the next meeting of Cabinet (DPMC 2002: 53).

A further change was made in March 2004 to implement the recommendations of the Defence Procurement Review (Kinnaird, Early & Schofield 2003), which called for a two-stage or 'two-pass' process to be part of Cabinet consideration of proposals for the procurement of defence equipment, which invariably involves very large expenditures over a long time-frame. The objective of this change was to ensure that Cabinet had the opportunity at the 'first pass' to determine the strategic necessity of acquiring additional defence capability before deciding on the actual equipment and technology at the 'second pass' (DPMC 2004: 36–9).

All of these deliberations and discussions—whether they are held in Cabinet, in one of its committees, or as part of a meeting of the whole Ministry—are secret, with the records only being made publicly available after 30 years. This principle of confidentiality is a cornerstone of the convention of collective responsibility of Ministers; that is, decisions reflect collective conclusions and are binding on Ministers as government policy both outside and within the party room. This principle allows for open and frank discussion while Ministers work toward a collective position and offers a degree of protection for Ministers once the decision is made.

The Cabinet system: a work in progress

The precise procedures and structures that make up the Cabinet system today are of relatively recent invention in terms of the whole span of Commonwealth administration since federation. Essentially this is because Cabinet is a product of convention and practice. There are no formal constitutional provisions that describe how it must be structured or how it must operate, nor is there any legislative framework except for the provisions of the *Ministers of State Act*, which sets an upper limit on the number of Ministers. Instead it is a matter for the government of the day, and particularly the Prime Minister, to determine the shape and structure of the system they want (DPMC 2004: 1). Consequently the 'Cabinet system' that operates today is one that has evolved over time and it is continuing to change and develop in response to administrative pressures and political events.

An obvious change has been the steady growth on the number of Ministers. In 1901, section 65 of the Constitution allowed for seven Ministers 'until the Parliament otherwise provides'. A century later, the expansion of the role of government, and the growth in the size and complexity of public administration, has seen the number of Ministers more than quadruple to 30, with a further 12 Parliamentary Secretaries providing them with support. However, not all Ministers enjoy the distinction of 'Cabinet rank'.

The practice whereby Cabinet comprises some but not all members of the Ministry was first introduced with the Menzies Ministry of 1956 and, except for the period of the Whitlam Labor Government (1972–75), it has been continued by all subsequent governments (Parliament 2002). Labor's egalitarian principles required that all members of the Ministry deliberate together, thus ensuring, in the sardonic words of Whitlam's biographer, that 'a Labor Cabinet would be unwieldy as possible' (Freudenberg 1978: 252). But, by September 1975, Prime Minister Whitlam had had enough and took a proposal to the Labor Caucus that an inner Cabinet of 12 be established to streamline decision making. The Caucus committee had not reported before the Governor-General, John Kerr, dismissed the government in November. When Labor returned to office under Bob Hawke in 1983, the new Prime Minister was determined to put efficiency before sentiment and was able to win Caucus agreement to an inner Cabinet (Blewett 2003: 74–5), making it the norm for both sides of politics.

By establishing the first committee of Cabinet in 1950, Prime Minister Menzies was also responsible for an earlier innovation to improve the efficiency of decision making and relieve Cabinet of dealing with business of lesser importance (NAA 2005). Successive governments have further developed this initiative, to manage the critical issues of the time or the changing strategic directions of government. For example, in 1973 as his government struggled to control expenditure, Prime Minister Whitlam established the Expenditure Review Committee, which is now a permanent part of the Cabinet system and central to the budget process. In 2001, Prime Minister John Howard established a Sustainable Environment Committee to reflect new government priority on issues such as 'greenhouse' policy, salinity and water quality, land clearing and biodiversity (Howard 2001).

The re-election of the Hawke Labor government in July 1987 saw the introduction of a far more fundamental change. Hawke created a two-tier ministerial structure with a senior and junior Minister sharing the administration of departments. This reform was accompanied by a significant reduction in the number of departments, so that each Cabinet Minister could take overall charge of a 'portfolio' represented by the department's area of responsibility (Nethercote 1999). The change was expected to provide for better coordination of decision making and greater coherence in the policy advice coming to Cabinet. It also meant that for the first time since Menzies split the Ministry 'all portfolios would be represented in a workable-sized cabinet' (Codd 1990).

To make these changes the government had to test the conventional legal understanding that section 64 required each Minister to administer a separate department of state. The Federal Court subsequently upheld the government's changes when it agreed that the Constitution did not prevent the executive from a 'proper opportunity' to introduce administrative arrangements which are appropriate in particular circumstances (Nethercote 1999).

The development of the position of Parliamentary Secretary during the period of the fourth Hawke government (1990–91) also saw the evolution of a new 'third tier' of Ministers within the Cabinet system. This role had existed during the Fraser government but it had been limited to one of assisting a Minister; it did not attract extra pay or involve any parliamentary duties and those who held the positions were not sworn in as members of the Executive Council (Healy 1993: 56). However, under every successive government, the position has grown in numbers, status and responsibility. After 1990 Parliamentary Secretaries were sworn in as members of the Executive Council and in that year the House of Representatives resolved that, with some exceptions, procedures that referred to Ministers would be taken to include Parliamentary Secretaries, with the Senate following suit soon after (Healy 1993: 57). Finally in 2000 an amendment to the *Ministers of State Act* saw Parliamentary Secretaries recognised as Ministers and entitled to an additional salary (AGS 2004).

The last episode in this evolution of the modern Cabinet system came with an unsuccessful challenge in the High Court to the constitutional validity of the appointment of Parliamentary Secretaries as Ministers. The Court not only judged that these appointments were valid, but also confirmed there was nothing in sections 64 or 65 of the Constitution that precluded the appointment of more than one Minister to administer a department (AGS 2004).

The evolution of the Cabinet system, both in terms of procedures and structure, is the story of Ministers responding to the growing pressures of modern government. Keating and Weller (2000: 50–2) suggest that these pressures arise in seven areas:

- the increasing span and complexity of government
- the interrelationships between issues that cross portfolios traditionally organised on functional lines
- the tendency for expectations on government to exceed its capacity to deal with an increasing range of 'seemingly intractable problems'
- improvements in technology leading to the increased availability of information and analysis which can in fact 'constrain' proper consideration of issues
- the increasing proliferation of interest groups outside of the traditional framework of political parties
- the shortening time-frame for decision making
- media pressures encouraging a shift to a 'presidential' style of executive.

The response of the political executive to this environment has been to assert greater control over the decision-making process. This has led to structures or procedures that reduce their workload, so that time and space are available for planning and strategy, and to more fundamental changes such as that initiated by Prime Minister Hawke in 1987, the aim of which, he told Parliament, was to 'enhance ministerial control over the Public Service' and to increase the 'responsiveness of the bureaucracy to the Government's wishes' (Hawke 1987).

Core principles: collective and individual ministerial responsibility

Since federation, there have been inevitably been some changes to the Cabinet structure and process, including some changes to the core principles of collective responsibility and ministerial accountability which underpin the Cabinet system. For example, Davis and his colleagues (1993: 81) point out that the original need for collective responsibility in governments that were not exclusively based on party has been largely removed as the party system has strengthened its hold over Parliament, making it now 'less a constitutional principle than a tactical necessity'.

The development of a two-tiered and later a three-tiered Cabinet system has also challenged the collective concept, given that on most occasions a majority of the Ministry would not have been present when the Cabinet made a decision that then became 'government policy'. Prime Minister Hawke's solution was to insist on strict adherence to the agreed collective position among members of the Cabinet, but allow non-Cabinet Ministers to pursue issues within the Labor Caucus.[4]

The bipartisan acceptance of this approach is demonstrated by its incorporation into the Howard government's *Cabinet Handbook,* which applies the strict interpretation of the principle of collective responsibility to non-Cabinet Ministers and Parliamentary Secretaries only if they take part in a particular decision by being present at the relevant Cabinet meeting. Nevertheless, all Ministers are expected to give their support in public debate to decisions of the Cabinet and of course are bound by any decisions of full Ministry meetings both in public statements and in internal party meetings (DPMC 2004: 4). In theory this gives some freedom to Ministers and Parliamentary Secretaries to take up issues on which they wish to propose a view different to that of their colleagues in the Cabinet, particularly within the party room. In reality, party discipline and hope of further advancement (a natural trait of the politician) tempers such freedom to the point that it is rarely if ever witnessed. If a formal policy is yet to be determined, then debate can be more willing. This was the case in July 2005 when the Prime Minister, in the wake of the London Tube bombings, suggested that a national identity card might be part of the government's response to the possibility of terrorist acts in this country. The suggestion led to a number of Ministers, from all three tiers of the Cabinet system, expressing their concern and in some cases their opposition.

Collective responsibility, however, is still a meaningful tradition, despite concessions to take account of a more complex structure between the Cabinet and the Ministry (Davis 2002: 57). This cannot be said of the principle of individual ministerial responsibility, the convention that Ministers take personal responsibility for maladministration within the department for which they are responsible. Hardly a parliamentary session passes without strident demands by the Opposition for a Minister to resign because he or she has breached this 'Westminster principle', yet resignations on these grounds are rare. This says more about the cut-and-thrust of politics than the behaviour of Ministers and is not evidence that successive governments have thrown aside an important principle. Rather, the complexity and size of government departments, the impact of 'managerialism' on their administration (see Chapter 6 in this book), and the development of administrative law have moved the concept of ministerial responsibility some distance from a time when a government department was in effect an administrative extension of the Minister, with no independent existence in terms of accountability (Thompson & Tilotsen 1999: 57).

Individual ministerial responsibility is also made more complex by the fact that Ministers play many different roles simultaneously, roles relating not only to their departments, but also to their colleagues in the Ministry and, most importantly, to the Prime Minister for the overall accountability and credibility of the government (Weller 1999: 62). Disentangling these concepts means that the older and narrower notion of responsibility can be better defined (Weller 1999; Thompson & Tilotsen 1999). Essentially, the circumstances today in which Ministers might face resignation are:

- inappropriate personal or ethical behaviour, financial impropriety or conflicts of interest
- inability to support a decision of Cabinet, the general policy direction of the government, or the leadership of the Prime Minister
- direct personal responsibility for policy or administrative failures, particularly if these have been ignored or 'covered up'.

The Howard government sought to codify the principles that apply in a published *Guide on Key Elements of Ministerial Responsibility* (Howard 1998). However, these are never applied independently of the judgment of the Prime Minister and a political assessment of the potential damage to the government and to the Prime Minister's authority of a resignation being demanded or accepted. For example, the release in July 2005 of the report into a case of wrongful detention highlighted serious systemic failings within the Department of Immigration, Multicultural and Indigenous Affairs (Palmer 2005). Not surprisingly, the publication of the report brought demands from the Opposition and sections of the media for the resignation of the Minister for Immigration. In rejecting these demands Prime Minister Howard replied:

If there is a failure for which the Minister is not directly responsible, it's not fair to say that the Minister should lose his or her head—that's a fair principle. I think ministers should go when plainly they have been directly responsible, and I think ministers should be in difficulty if their continued presence is an embarrassment to the government. (ABC 2005)

In doing so, the Prime Minister made clear the modern basis for individual ministerial responsibility: the need for direct personal responsibility, described as the need to find a 'smoking gun' (Thompson & Tilotsen 1999). But he also appears to have enshrined as a principle what most commentators assumed, that in reality it is a question of the degree of embarrassment that a Prime Minister, and the government, can tolerate.

Role and power of the Prime Minister

The discussion of the part a Prime Minister plays in determining a Minister's future leads naturally to considering the role and power of the Prime Minister in the Cabinet system as a whole. By any measure it is considerable, such that it has been suggested that rather than a 'Westminster system', or even a Cabinet system of government, there has been a shift to 'Prime Ministerial government' (Hart 1992: 191).

There can be no doubt that in terms of directing and controlling government the Prime Minister has a significant array of 'great advantages'. Patrick Weller (1990: 37) lists seven:

- the power to hire and fire ministers
- the power to set the agenda, structure and process of Cabinet
- control over machinery of government
- leadership of a disciplined party, and thus control of Parliament
- centralised control of access to the media
- extensive personal patronage
- the development of a large bureaucratic machine of which the Prime Minister is the head.

But Cabinet is a group of politicians as well as a constitutional and administrative institution, acutely sensitive to the tidal movements of opinion within the community and the party room. A Prime Minister is always constrained by the need to govern with the support of colleagues, and they in turn feel the constraint of electoral opinion and their party's requirements. In any political environment, an individual's authority and the power to enforce his will depends on shifting alliances, the cooperation of colleagues, and above all success in convincing those being led that the incumbent remains their best option as the leader who can guarantee their continued survival. As Bob Hawke found when he was deposed by his party colleagues in 1991, a record of four successful elections is no defence against a fractured Cabinet, a nervous Caucus, and above all an aggressive alternative leader.

In short, each of Weller's seven advantages have to placed within the context of politics, and where they intersect with the political environment the advantage may be far from absolute. Further, authority and power that flows from administrative and structural advantage within the Cabinet system can be quickly reduced to insignificance if the politics turn sour. The subtleties for a Labor Prime Minister are more obvious, given the limitations imposed by Caucus on his right to hire and fire, the general Labor Party principle of the supremacy of the party room, and beyond that the formal party rules that give power to an extra-parliamentary National Executive and Conference. But a non-Labor Prime Minister cannot afford to be any less sensitive to the party room and the organisation beyond Parliament.

That said, in many respects the advantages identified by Weller that relate to the constitutional and administrative role of the Prime Minister as the leader of Cabinet have increased in potency since he listed them a decade and a half ago. This is particularly so as regards the Prime Minister's control of Cabinet, his ability to manage the media, and his role as head of the wider bureaucratic machine.

The advantage that accrues to a Prime Minister by reason of control over the Cabinet process has increased with the creation of new policy and implementation units designed to service the Cabinet. For example, the Cabinet Policy Unit is staffed by contracted personnel from outside the public service and its head, who is also the Cabinet Secretary, is directly responsible to the Prime Minister (DPMC 2004: 2). The Cabinet Implementation Unit has also extended the Prime Minister's reach with its broad mission working across all agencies to 'assist in ensuring the committed and effective delivery of key government decisions' (DPMC 2005).

Over the past decade, the advantages that arise from the centralised control of access to the media have been matched by a significant increase in the internal media resources that can be mobilised by a Prime Minister. Public relations have become institutionalised within government in what Ward (2003) describes as 'an Australian PR State'. The 'topographical features' of this new political landscape are media minders as an institutionalised feature of the personal staff of the Prime Minister and his Ministers, media units composed of professional journalists hired to coordinate government media relations and monitor news coverage of the government, public affairs sections within departments, and the whole-of-government coordination of promotional activities (Ward 2003: 25, 28). If the marketing of government activity has truly become 'a central activity of modern statecraft' (Deacon & Golding 1994, cited by Ward 2003: 25), then the Prime Minister is now far better placed to practise the art.

Changes to the manner of appointing and terminating the appointments of Departmental Secretaries (i.e. the public servants appointed as the heads of government departments) also provide potential for the Prime Minister to be more than a titular head of the 'large bureaucratic machine' which is the public service. Since 1993 a series of legislative changes have seen the position of Departmental Secretaries change from a permanent appointment by the Governor-General, to one of limited tenure (Weller & Wanna 1997). These changes culminated with the *Public Service Act 1999* which effectively gave the Prime Minister alone the right to hire and fire.[5] Prime Minister Howard has given formal assurances that the termination powers 'would not be undertaken lightly', and more generally has expressed a commitment a 'non-partisan and professional' public service while rejecting any move towards a US-style system (quoted by Mulgan 1998: 7; see also Howard 1998: 14). However, Departmental Secretaries are only human and it would be a surprise if they were not now more responsive to the requirements of the Prime Minister and his government; such responsiveness was after all the motivation for reform.

Finally, changes in the nature of the issues with which government has to deal have tended to promote the role and importance of the Prime Minister. Peters and his colleagues (2000: 7) make the point that the 'exigencies of security, defence and diplomacy' have traditionally been a reason for strengthening the role of the leader. So too have been the growth of the state and increased complexity of modern administration and the demand for coordination from the centre, which in turn reinforce the Prime Minister's role.

Is this any way to run a country?

The focus of this chapter has been the Cabinet and its executive role in our system of government. However, in many respects the Cabinet is only the politically visible peak of a much broader and deeper executive apparatus. Davis (1997: 85) uses the concept of a 'core executive' to describe 'a complex, collective enterprise which extends beyond the parliamentary arena to embrace interlocking networks of advisers and bureaucrats . . . a powerful configuration of ideas, players and structures'.

This highlights a key theme of this chapter: Cabinet and the Ministry do not exist in a vacuum. Understanding the way in which Cabinet operates, and the decisions it makes, requires an appreciation also of how these wider networks outside of the Cabinet room function and relate to each other.

Another theme has been change. As governments have reacted to the demands and pressures of running a modern nation increasingly integrated with its region and the global economy, they have reshaped the Cabinet system. That process will continue and will be influenced by new pressures, for example the demands for more open government (Keating & Weller 2000: 71), or the need to balance traditional accountability with the threat posed by global terrorism.

The question remains as to whether a system which traces its origins to the arcane protocols determining relations between a monarch and the Parliament in Britain in the 18th century remains relevant to 21st century Australia. Is this the best way to run a country? Certainly it is unlikely that any major corporation would consider organising its management along the lines of the Cabinet system; indeed the requirements of corporations law for continuous disclosure to external stakeholders would forbid them from doing so.

The answer is that administration and management is only one part of the function and purpose of Cabinet. Most importantly, it is also a political institution in which the political issues and conflicts are resolved and political power confirmed, and by most measures has been successful as a means to bring together politics, policy and administration. As an institution based on convention and practice, it has the flexibility to adapt without facing the constraints of the Constitution. Indeed it has changed significantly over the past 20 years, but there are signs that it remains an 'institution under stress' (Keating & Weller 2000: 71). The relatively long period of economic growth that Australia has experienced, and the growing revenues that have accompanied such growth, may have masked some of the pressures that government, and hence Cabinet, will need to resolve; for example the intergenerational and financial stress of an ageing population.

But, as Australia moves further into this new century, the ability of the Cabinet system to continue to adapt may not only determine our collective future and wellbeing, but also the relevance of our political system, the respect and deference it is given by its citizens, and their preparedness to continue to accept its authority.

NOTES

1 Academic commentators and politicians alike usually refer to our system of government as the Westminster system, by which they mean it is based on political institutions and conventions that reflect the procedures and practices of the Houses of Parliament at Westminster in London. However, there is also an unstated assumption that we have developed an Australian version that is far from an exact copy, for example, more a 'Westminster syndrome' than a system (Parker 1976 cited by Davis 2002: 50). See Chapter 3 of this book for a more detailed discussion.

2 This power is not absolute. Party discipline may provide security for the executive in the House of Representatives, but over the past two decades the Senate has been a different story as minor parties combined with the Opposition to use the committee system to investigate and review government decisions and proposals. Nor is the backbench always quiescent. For example, in 2005 a small group of Liberal Party backbenchers moved to introduce a Private Members Bill to change the harsher aspects of the government's mandatory detention policy for illegal immigrants. They also made it clear that they were prepared to 'cross the floor' and vote against the government if their proposals were not accepted, but after negotiations with the Prime Minister they gained a number of concessions and did not proceed with their legislation. While the incident provides an

example of the backbench influencing the actions of the executive, that the matter was resolved in the context of the party room and not the Parliament is typical.

3 The rules establishing Cabinet's program of meetings, the attendance of Ministers and officials, the conduct of its business, the handling of its documents and the recording of its decisions are set out in a *Cabinet Handbook* which is publicly available through the Department of the Prime Minister and Cabinet's website (DPMC 2004). The responsibility for managing this process resides with the Cabinet Secretariat, which is part of the Department of the Prime Minister and Cabinet.

4 In November 1983, Stewart West, a Cabinet Minister in the first Hawke government, refused to be bound by the Cabinet decision to support uranium mining at Roxby Downs in South Australia. As a result, he was demoted to the outer ministry, to return five months later after agreeing to observe Cabinet solidarity (Blewett 2003: 76).

5 Section 58 concerning the appointment process, and section 59 which deals with termination, both provide that the Prime Minister must first receive reports from the Public Service Commissioner and the Secretary of his Department before exercising his powers. The Act also refers to the *Barratt v Howard* case of 1999 in which the Federal Court of Australia described the basic requirements of procedural fairness.

REFERENCES

ABC 2005, 'PM defends Vanstone in Wake of Dept Head Resignation', *ABC News Online*, 10 July, <http://www.abc.net.au/news/newsitems/200507/s1410860.htm>, accessed September 2005.

AGS [Australian Government Solicitor] 2004, *Legal Briefing Number 72*, Commonwealth of Australia, 29 October 2004, <http://www.ags.gov.au/publications/agspubs/legalpubs/legalbriefings/br72.pdf>, accessed September 2005.

Bishop, P & Davis, G. 2002, 'Mapping Public Participation in Policy Choices', *Australian Journal of Public Administration*, vol. 61, no. 1, pp. 14–29.

Blewett, N. 2003, 'The Hawke Cabinets', in *The Hawke Government. A Critical Retrospective*, eds Susan Ryan & Troy Bramston, Pluto Press, North Melbourne.

Codd, M. 1990, 'Cabinet Operations of the Australian Government', in *Decision Making in Australian Government: The Cabinet & Budget Processes*, eds B. Galligan, J.R. Nethercote & C. Walsh, Centre for Research on Federal Financial Relations, Canberra.

Davis, G. 1997, 'The Core Executive', in *New Developments in Australian Politics*, eds B. Galligan, I. McAllister & J. Ravenhill, Macmillan, South Melbourne.

Davis, G. 2002, 'Executive Government: Cabinet and the Prime Minister', in *Government, Politics, Power and Policy in Australia*, 7th edn, eds J. Summers, D. Woodward & A. Parkin, Longman, Frenchs Forest.

Davis, G., Wanna, J., Warhurst, J. & Weller, P. 1993, *Public Policy in Australia*, 2nd edn, Allen and Unwin, St Leonards.

Deacon, D. & Golding, P. 1994, *Taxation and Representation*, John Libbey, London.

DPMC [Department of the Prime Minister and Cabinet] 2002, *Annual Report 2001-02*, Commonwealth of Australia, Canberra, <http://www.dpmc.gov.au/annual_reports/index.cfm>, accessed September 2005.

DPMC [Department of the Prime Minister and Cabinet] 2004, *Cabinet Handbook*, Commonwealth of Australia, Canberra, <http://www.dpmc.gov.au/guidelines/docs/cabinet_handbook.pdf>, accessed September 2005.

DPMC [Department of the Prime Minister and Cabinet] 2005, Website, Cabinet Implementation Unit, <http://www.dpmc.gov.au/implementation/index.cfm>, accessed September 2005.

Evans, H. 2005, 'A Day Spent in the Gallery Would Shock the Founding Fathers', *Sydney Morning Herald* 21 June.

Freudenberg, G. 1978, *A Certain Grandeur. Gough Whitlam in Politics,* Sun Books, Melbourne.

Hart, J. 1992, 'An Australian President? A Comparative Perspective', in *Menzies to Keating*, ed. P. Weller, Melbourne University Press, Melbourne.

Hawke, R.J.L. 1987, 'Ministerial Statement: Changes to Administrative Arrangements', House of Representatives Hansard, 15 September, <http://parlinfoweb.aph.gov.au/piweb/view_document.aspx?id=264222&table=HANSARDR>, accessed September 2005.

Healy, M. 1993, 'The Role of Parliamentary Secretaries', *Legislative Studies,* vol. 8, no. 1, pp. 46–60.

Hennessy, P. 1986, *Cabinet,* Basil Blackwell, Oxford.

Howard, J. 1998, 'A Guide on the Key Elements of Ministerial Responsibility', Canberra, <http://www.dpmc.gov.au/guidelines/docs/ministerial_responsibility.pdf>, accessed September 2005.

Howard, J. 2001, 'Cabinet Committees', Media Release, 13 December, <http://www.pm.gov.au/news/media_releases/2001/media_release1462.htm>, accessed September 2005.

Keating, M. 1996, 'Defining the Policy Advising Function', in *Evaluating Policy Advice,* eds J. Uhr & K. Mackay, Federalism Research Centre/Department of Finance, Canberra.

Keating, M. & Weller, P. 2000, 'Cabinet Government: An Institution Under Pressure', in *Institutions on the Edge? Capacity for Governance,* eds M. Keating, J. Wanna & P. Weller, Allen & Unwin, St Leonards.

Kinnaird, M., Early, L. & Schofield, B. 2003, *Report of the Defence Procurement Review,* Canberra, 15 August, <http://www.defence.gov.au/publications/dpr180903.pdf>, accessed September 2005.

Mulgan, R. 1998, 'Politicisation of Senior Appointments in the Australian Public Service', *Australian Journal of Public Administration,* vol. 57, no. 3, pp. 3–14.

NAA [National Archives of Australia] 2005, *Cabinet Committee Papers,* 1950 Cabinet Records, <http://www.naa.gov.au/the_collection/Cabinet/1950_cabinet_notebooks/abbreviations.htm>, accessed September 2005.

Nethercote, J. 1999, 'Departmental Machinery of Government since 1987', *Research Paper* no. 24, 1998–99, Parliament of Australia Parliamentary Library, Canberra, <http://www.aph.gov.au/library/pubs/rp/1998-99/99rp24.htm#Cabinet>, accessed September 2005.

Page, B. 1997, 'Cabinet', in *Politics in Australia,* 3rd edn, ed. Rodney Smith, Allan and Unwin, Sydney.

Palmer, M. 2005, *Report of the Inquiry into the Circumstances of the Immigration Detention of Cornelia Rau,* Commonwealth of Australia, Canberra, 6 July, <http://www.minister.immi.gov.au/media_releases/media05/palmer-report.pdf>, accessed September 2005.

Parliament [Parliament of Australia Parliamentary Library] 2002, 'Cabinets', *Parliamentary Handbook*, 31 August, <http://www.aph.gov.au/library/handbook/historical/cabinets.htm>, accessed September 2005.

Parker, R.S. 1976, 'The Meaning of Responsible Government', *Politics,* vol. 11, no. 2, pp. 178–84.

Peters, B.G., Rhodes, R.A.W. & Wright, V. 2000, 'Staffing the Summit – The Administration of the Core Executive: Convergent Trends and National Specificities', in *Administering the Summit Administration of the Core Executive in Developed Countries,* eds B.G. Peters, R.A.W. Rhodes & V. Wright, Macmillan, Basingstoke.

Pierre, J. & Peters, B.G. 2000, *Governance, Politics and the State*, Macmillan, Basingstoke.

Thomson, E. & Tilotsen, G. 1999, 'Caught in the Act: The Smoking Gun View of Ministerial Responsibility', *Australian Journal of Public Administration*, vol. 58 no. 1, March, pp. 48–54.

Ward, I. 1999, 'Federal Government', in *Institutions in Australian Society*, ed. J. Henningham, Oxford University Press, Melbourne.

Ward, I. 2003, 'An Australian PR state?', *Australian Journal of Communication*, vol. 30, no.1, pp. 25–42.

Weller, P. 1990, 'Cabinet and the Prime Minister', in *Government, Politics and Power in Australia*, 4th edn, eds J. Summers, D. Woodward & A. Parkin, Longman Cheshire, Melbourne.

Weller, P. 1999, 'Disentangling Concepts of Ministerial Responsibility', *Australian Journal of Public Administration*, vol. 58, no.1, pp. 62–4.

Weller, P. 2004, 'Parliamentary Democracy in Australia', *Parliamentary Affairs*, vol. 57, no. 3, pp. 630–45.

Weller, P. & Wanna, J. 1997, 'Departmental Secretaries: Appointment, Termination and their Impact', *Australian Journal of Public Administration*, vol. 56, no. 3, pp. 13–25.

Managing and restructuring the public sector

CHAPTER 6

JENNY STEWART

Governments deploy substantial resources in order to meet their objectives and to carry out the basic functions of the state. People employed in (or contracted to) the public sector are needed to collect taxes, pay pensions, run health and education systems, administer regulation and to advise on policy. *Public sector management* is the broad term used to describe how these activities are organised and controlled, and the principles and values which make managing in the public sector a distinctive activity—similar to, yet different in fundamental respects from, its private sector counterparts.

It is important to remember that, like any form of management, public sector management is supposed to be a means to an end, not an end in itself. The purpose of the departments, statutory authorities and other bodies which constitute the public sector is to carry out the business of government—the policies and actions through which governments both rule and serve us.

This is the continuing thread in all public sector management, whenever and wherever it is carried out. What has changed over recent decades in Australia is our understanding of where the boundary between the public and the private sectors can most productively be drawn, and a growing realisation that administration need not, indeed should not, rest on public sector bureaucracy alone. There is plenty of scope, much of it still unexplored, for new forms of engagement with clients, customers and stakeholders.

To understand public sector management in Australia, you need the following tools:

- an appreciation of the Australian state, its structure, and the role of the executive within that structure
- an understanding of the general problem of accountability and in particular of the relationship between elected and non-elected members of the executive (i.e. between politicians and public servants)
- an understanding of the differences between administration and management, and the implications of those differences for accountability and efficiency.

This chapter seeks to illuminate the problems and prospects of public sector management through the lens of *accountability*. Such an approach gives a useful guide for understanding the concerns of the vast literature, both Australian and international, that has accumulated around the idea of 'new public management' (NPM).

The state

A *state* is a political entity through which authority is exercised over a given territory.[1] Governments that control states are empowered to tax citizens, to regulate their activities and, when they fail to comply, to penalise or even imprison them. Unless public authority has collapsed or been eroded, no other organisation has these powers. This is the principal reason why, in a democracy, the exercise of state power must be carefully controlled and public officials held accountable for their actions.

While states differ greatly in their detailed structure, they have certain common design features. They are commonly divided into three parts—legislature, executive and judiciary. Put simply, the legislature (in Australia, the Parliament) makes the laws, the executive (the appointed component of which is the focus of this chapter) carries them out, and the judiciary (the courts) interprets them. Tensions between these three branches of government are inevitable, as each has a tendency to exert its own type of power without reference to the others.

The United States' (Presidential) system of government attempts to make a virtue of these tensions by using the legislature (Congress) as a counterweight to the power of the executive (the President). In Westminster-type systems like Australia, where the political executive must be drawn directly from the membership of the legislature, the drama is more muted but is nevertheless real. From the point of view of the executive, negotiating and managing relationships with Parliament, the courts and the apparatus of administrative law involves considerable effort, but is necessary if the business of the state is to be carried out effectively.

The executive has two components—an elected component and an appointed component. In Westminster-type systems, the elected executive comprises the Ministry—politicians from the governing party who are commissioned by the head of state to be responsible for the executive functions of the state. These functions involve administering the vast body of statute law by means of which governments run the many organisations that define our lives. Ministers are assisted in this task by the appointed executive: that is, by public servants (those employed under *Public Service Acts* or their equivalents) and by others employed by, or contracted to, the government.

Parliament has one key weapon in its battle with the executive: it controls access to revenues generated by taxation. Governments must present their taxing and spending plans to Parliament in the form of a budget, which must be debated and passed by the Parliament. While in Westminster systems party control of the lower house means that passing the budget is little more than a formality, and debate can be somewhat ritualistic, in systems with an upper house or Senate, scrutiny of the budget, and in particular of departmental performance, can be both detailed and hard-edged.

In addition to the oversight role performed by parliamentary public accounts committees, parliaments employ a powerful Auditor-General to audit the financial statements produced by agencies.[2] Auditors-General have widened the scope of their regular activities to include performance audits which critically assess the implementation of policy from a wide range of perspectives.

One of the key arguments in favour of the 'new public management' described later in this chapter is that it simplifies relations between the Parliament and the executive by enhancing the quality of information going to Parliament and making clearer the activities of public officials (see Keating 1990). On the other hand, by giving officials greater responsibility for making management decisions, the new techniques arguably muddy the waters of accountability. This is a difficult area to analyse clearly (see Mulgan 1997 for a useful overview) but remains crucial to understanding the claims and counter-claims made about the benefits of change.

Accountability

From a narrow efficiency perspective, accountability is a tiresome overhead adding appreciably to the costs of making decisions. But accountability of public officials is the cornerstone of an effective democracy. Accountability is not a 'thing' in itself; it is a set of relationships through which political and bureaucratic actors must account for their integrity and their performance. There is a framework, partly based on conventions and partly based on statutory requirements, which sets out these relationships and which has changed and evolved as problems have occurred and new opportunities have arisen.

In democracies, the basic accountability relationship is between politicians and the electorate. Free and fair elections are the cornerstone of this relationship. Without the certainty that they will face the electorate at regular intervals, governments are likely soon to become secretive, unresponsive and dictatorial. However, this fundamental form of accountability is a blunt one. Voters can return or reject a government on the basis of their perception of its performance over a specified period of time. They cannot effectively hold governments accountable for particular policies when they are enacted, or for specific misdeeds when they occur.

Of the institutions of the state, it is Parliament which has the primary responsibility for holding government accountable between elections. In Westminster systems, Ministers provide the nexus between government and Parliament, and must answer to Parliament for their actions, both individually and collectively.[3]

The traditional model of Ministerial responsibility, sometimes called 'upwards' accountability (Corbett 1996: ch. 11), implies that public servants are covered by Ministers' accountability to Parliament because every decision is authorised by a superior officer in a chain which goes all the way up to the Minister. But in reality Ministers cannot be held personally accountable for decisions which they do not know about and over which they have little control. In any case, Ministers show a singular lack of enthusiasm for resigning even when misdeeds can be laid fairly directly at their door. This leaves a rather large gap in at least one respect: how can public servants be held accountable for the many decisions they make that are based on delegated powers and subject to legislation but which nevertheless involve the exercise of considerable discretion?

Judicial review (i.e. the review of government decisions through the courts) has always been available to citizens where the basis for court action can be found. However, the complexity and cost of court proceedings are prohibitive for all but the richest or most aggrieved litigants.

Beginning in the mid-1970s, the Commonwealth government, followed by the governments of most Australian States, enacted measures to extend the ambit of judicial review, also providing for administrative review through bodies such as the Administrative Appeals Tribunal (AAT). The office of the Ombudsman, established at the Commonwealth level in 1976, provided a first point of contact for many citizens dissatisfied with, or confused by, a decision made by a government agency. Although the Ombudsman's powers did not extend to overturning particular decisions, recommendations for change were usually accepted by the relevant agency.

Critics could still argue, however, that public servants got off far too lightly. Few were ever dismissed for incompetence, nor was there any practical way for the users of government services to exercise any direct influence on the way they were set up or delivered. For one thing, there was little information available. People knew if the trains were frequently late, or if it took weeks to have a new phone installed, or if it seemed that their child was failing to learn to read, but in general measuring and acting on these things was not part of the culture of most public organisations.

Moreover, up until the mid-1980s, when government business enterprises were established on a quasi-commercial footing, there was little financial information available on which to base an assessment of performance. The question increasingly on politicians' lips — 'Are we getting value for money?' — was difficult, if not impossible, to answer in relation to most agencies.

Staff performance was another difficult area. Relations between public servants and government were governed by *Public Service Acts* which, together with relevant awards, set out the terms and conditions under which public servants were employed. Until the mid-1980s, *Public Service Acts* were administered by Public Service Boards. These, at their best, defined and protected the traditions of a public service independent of direct political control by the government of the day. While a public servant's work performance was the basis for decisions about promotion (seniority came into it, at the Commonwealth level at least, only when two equally meritorious candidates were competing for one promotional vacancy), there was little provision for regular performance review. What was euphemistically called 'underperformance' was often ignored, because public servants were protected by tenure.

The Australian public services of the 1980s, while they got the job done, are now regarded as having been too bureaucratic to respond flexibly to change, too large for the work they were required to perform, and not sufficiently accountable for the resources they used. In both political and practitioner circles, there was considerable dissatisfaction with both the performance and, to some extent, the ethos of traditional public administration.

From administration to management

According to Hughes, there is a quantum difference between administration and management (Hughes 1998: ch.1). *Administration* refers to the carrying out of prescribed functions, with little regard being paid to the costs of doing so. *Management* means using resources to their best effect, given a set of departmental objectives. It also, according to Hughes, comprehends the idea of 'strategy' — that is, aligning the purposes of the organisation with the demands of its environment. Management has become the preferred term for describing how public servants should do their job.

'New public management' (NPM) is the term coined by Hood (1991) to describe the broad rationale for the changes that have overtaken the public sector. While appearing in its different guises in different countries, NPM gave expression to particular political values about the size ('too big') and role ('too dominant') of government. But NPM was more than just an ideology. It was also clearly influenced by a theory. The proponents of NPM argued for the superiority of their new techniques compared with the centralised control and adherence to process of 'old' public administration. The claimed superiority derived from particular rationales, drawn from both the economics literature and from management theory, for improved organisational performance.

Underlying the managerialist thrust was the perception that government is inherently vulnerable to being 'captured' by the self-interests of 'producers' (e.g. public servants) and to being insufficiently responsive to the needs of 'consumers' (i.e. citizens and taxpayers). The mechanisms of accountability to Parliament were too vague, too slow and too indirect to deal with these problems. The agenda of NPM was to install a consumer voice in the delivery of services by introducing a number of new mechanisms—the outsourcing of services to the private sector (which would introduce competition into what had previously been monopoly provision by the state) and the empowerment of consumers through performance measurement and citizens' charters.

As a paradigm, NPM tended to focus on the individual agency and its performance. The overall pattern of reform, however, needs to be seen in the context of changes in conceptions of the role of the state, and of the pattern of desirable relationships between the public, private and not-for-profit sectors.

The 1960s and 1970s saw the beginning of the end of the belief, widely held by political elites since World War II, that the state should play the dominant role in both economic management and social welfare. In the English-speaking countries, in Scandinavia and to a lesser extent in the nations of Western Europe, the free-spending public budgets of the past came to be seen as a drain on the economy and a constraint on growth. The use of public budgets to counteract downturns in private sector activity (so-called Keynesian demand management) also fell into disfavour. There was a move away from big, to smaller, government. As a consequence, resource constraints began to affect every area of the public sector. In political terms, the Left, having been in the ascendancy in the 1960s, was rapidly eclipsed by the Right. Indeed the entire political spectrum shifted to the Right to such an extent that social-democratic and Labor parties also had to espouse the cause of smaller government if they wished to win or to retain office.

Every country, however, had its own variations on this theme. In New Zealand, for example, a conviction among the political elite that the old ways gave the country no future led to a virtual revolution in the way the state worked (Boston *et al.* 1996). State-run industries were privatised or shut down, and purchaser–provider arrangements became the norm for those services which remained the responsibility of government.

The pattern in Australia was more pragmatic. Here in the 1980s, when NPM came to prominence, that prudent economic management required a smaller public sector because, in a country with large current account deficits (i.e. deficient net export performance and/or insufficient savings), the call of the public sector on national savings had to be reduced. The plunge in the value of the Australian dollar in 1986 was taken to be compelling evidence of the need for drastic surgery to trim the public sector. Within the Australian government, the Expenditure Review Committee of Cabinet became prominent as a result of this process, annually as part of the budget process—and repeated over many years—searching for ways to reduce the rate of growth in budgetary outlays. The effect was particularly severe on the level of Commonwealth funding transferred to the States.

Within the public service, the rhetorical case for change stressed improved efficiency and effectiveness, but these budget reductions meant that in practice agency resources were cut whether managerial reforms worked or not. Typically in Australia it has been the central finance-related agencies—i.e. Treasuries and Departments of Finance—that have been promoting and enforcing change (Wanna, Kelly & Forster 1996).

Implementing change

Because Australia's State and Territory governments were under more financial pressure than the Commonwealth, they moved sooner than the Commonwealth to refashion the statutory basis of their public services through new *Public Sector Management Acts* and new *Financial Management Acts* (Stewart 1996). But the political demise of two of the most ardent reforming governments, the Liberal governments led by Premiers Nick Greiner in New South Wales and Jeff Kennett in Victoria, seem to reveal that, sooner or later, voters have their revenge on governments that acknowledge only the benefits and not the costs of change.

The Commonwealth's approach has been more cautious. At the beginning of this process, Labor was in government and felt it necessary to secure the acquiescence of the public-sector unions in public service reform. Some significant progress was achieved: the more fluid pattern of public service employment that now prevails owes much to the agreements reached then after negotiation with the unions about freeing up the many restrictions that had previously made it difficult to move employees around between positions and agencies, and about the circumstances under which staff numbers could be reduced via attrition.

The Hawke government's *Public Service Legislation (Streamlining Act) 1986* made it possible for staff to be declared as 'excess' to requirements and in consequence made redundant. Generous redundancy provisions were negotiated with the unions, and public service superannuation, particularly the Public Service Superannuation Scheme (PSS) introduced from 1990, made redundancy followed by retirement an attractive financial option for many public servants. Retirement 'packages' were keenly sought by a very wide range of employees.

In this way, what might have been powerful resistance to change was cleverly overcome. At the same time, in the context of a gradual shift to productivity-based wage bargaining under the Accord then in place between the Labor government and the trade union movement, the multi-layered classification structure of the Australian (i.e. Commonwealth) Public Service was reduced in complexity, and 'multi-skilling' became the norm.

In at least some cases, so-called 'voluntary' redundancies were in fact disguised sackings of staff who were seen as too set in their ways to adapt to the new order. But, one way or the other, most redundant public servants went quietly. In this way (and in others), the number of public servants was considerably reduced.

The Howard Coalition government, through the application of its *Workplace Relations Act* to the public sector, and its decisions on the outsourcing of information technology and of employment services, has shown that it is determined to maintain the pressure for change.

The overall effects have been particularly pronounced for employees of the Commonwealth government. Let us look first of all at a very crude gauge—the numbers of government employees as recorded by the Australian Bureau of Statistics. (These numbers include wage and salary earners working in any type of organisation created by, and accountable to, Parliament.) Between May 1993 and November 2004 (covering the last three years of the Keating Labor government followed by the advent of the Howard Coalition government), the number of Commonwealth government employees fell by 35 per cent, from 378 000 to 247 000, reflecting over a decade of retrenchments, privatisations and outsourcing. Within that total, however, the numbers employed specifically under the *Public Service Act* (i.e. public servants working in government agencies rather than statutory bodies) began to increase after 1999 (from 113 268 in that year to 131 522 in June 2004), reflecting the impact of new functions, and the need to rebuild lost capacity (ABS 2000, 2005; APSC 2004a).

Implications of change

Because Australia is a federation with many different governments, it is difficult to generalise about the evolution of public sector management. But it can be useful to see change as a working out of the effects of two competing logics: on the one hand, an understandable desire (on the part of both politicians and many public servants) to improve the efficiency of the public sector; on the other, the imperative (for politicians and their advisers) to use the public sector to carry out ever-expanding political and policy agendas. We can trace these effects in four key arenas:

- privatisation and the public–private boundary
- relations between politicians and public servants

- financial management
- human resource management.

PRIVATISATION AND THE PUBLIC–PRIVATE BOUNDARY

One of the key ideas driving change has been the perception that government had become too big, and that its boundaries required redefinition through a process of privatisation. In assessing the overall implications of privatisation, it is important to appreciate the different but related senses in which the term is used:

1. *Asset sales*: selling to the private sector assets that were previously publicly owned (e.g. the sale in 1997–99 of just under 50 per cent of Telstra, the government-owned provider of telecommunications services).
2. *User-charging*: making services that were previously provided free to users subject to fees (e.g. the charging of fees to university students through the Higher Education Contribution Scheme).
3. *Outsourcing* (sometimes referred to as *contracting out*): engaging providers — usually for-profit firms or not-for-profit agencies — to deliver services previously delivered by public employees (e.g. the engaging of private-sector firms to operate public transport routes).
4. *Public–private partnerships*: forming complementary relationships in order to undertake tasks such as building infrastructure, establishing new kinds of schools, and involving business more closely in planning-related tasks such as regional development.

Privatisation remains controversial because it redefines the role of the state, because it changes relationships between the public, private and not-for-profit sectors, and because it re-allocates power and resources between consumers, producers and owners. Those in favour of public ownership argue that 'natural monopolies' (such as the provision of water, power and telecommunications) are managed more effectively in the public interest if they are kept in public hands. Where these activities are profitable, governments as owners can ensure that the 'dividends' are used for the collective benefit of the community. Those against public ownership point to what they claim is the greater flexibility and efficiency of the private sector, especially in rapidly changing business environments such as telecommunications. They argue that, in selling their assets, governments get a better return because private buyers, anticipating being able to install more innovative management and being more adept at responding to market opportunities, will offer a good sale price. Arguments for outsourcing stress the greater efficiency of the private sector in providing services, with resulting cost savings for government. In addition, outsourcing enables public agencies to access skills that are difficult to retain in the public sector, or that are not needed on a continuing basis. Those opposed to outsourcing point to a variable performance in practice in terms of cost savings: careful empirical research studies have shown that sometimes outsourcing results in significant savings but sometimes it results in cost increases instead (Hodge 2000). Some commentators have argued that, even when apparent savings are demonstrated, they may occur at the expense of service quality, and/or reflect poorer wages and working conditions in the new provider organisations, rather than greater efficiency or even effectiveness (Quiggin 1996). One salutary example is the unsuccessful attempt by the Commonwealth government in the late 1990s to outsource its entire information technology requirements (ANAO 2000; Humphry 2000). Overall, it seems that outsourcing (and ongoing contracting) works best where pragmatic rather than ideological choices can be made about what to outsource, and where purchaser organisations (that is, the public agencies) have the knowledge and experience to craft appropriate contracts and to monitor them closely.

The outcomes of asset sales have been similarly mixed. Some (such as the sale of Qantas) have by most accounts been successful (although the Qantas success has arguably more to do with a dominant market position than with privatisation as such). Privatisations of public utilities (such as electricity) have proved much more problematic, although in the case of the electricity industry, it is difficult to separate ownership changes from the effects of the massive restructuring and re-regulation that occurred as a result of National Competition Policy reforms adopted in 1995.

In the Australian case, with the probable exception of Telstra, the wave of privatisations that began in the 1990s has now subsided. The agenda in the 21st century will revolve around finding the best ways to manage the vast panoply of activities that governments continue to undertake. Involving the private sector in these activities solves some problems, but creates others. Government must shift towards forms of *governance*, that is, exercising its authority in situations where many different kinds of organisations—public, private or non-profit—are involved. Indeed if we were to define the 'core business' of government, we would have to say that it is, precisely, *governance*. As Osborne and Gaebler (1992: 45) put it,

> services can be contracted out or turned over to the private sector. But governance cannot. We can privatize discrete steering functions, but not the overall process of governance. If we did we would have no mechanism by which to make collective decisions, no way to set the rules of the marketplace, no means to enforce rules of behaviour.

RELATIONS BETWEEN POLITICIANS AND PUBLIC SERVANTS

It is understandable that politicians can feel overwhelmed, and in some cases intimidated, by the public service. Agencies employing hundreds, sometimes thousands, of people are responsible to a single Minister, in whose name count-less decisions are made. Ministers are not necessarily expert in their portfolio responsibilities, and as Prime Ministers, for a variety of political and other reasons, are in the habit of reshuffling their Cabinets at regular intervals, many Ministers are obliged to change jobs just as they are beginning to learn the ropes.

Ministers are assisted by their own advisory staff, political appointees who are employed under an Act separate from that of public servants. Under the Keating and Howard governments, adviser numbers grew to more than 400 (Maley 2000). Very often it is these Ministerial advisers who form the bridge between public servants and politicians. They act as the 'eyes and ears' of the Minister and advise him or her on a wide variety of issues. There is some evidence that, as a result of their control over access to the Minister, Ministerial advisers exercise a significant, if variable, influence over the policy agenda (Ryan 1995).

While public servants have a good deal of competition when it comes to attracting the Minister's attention, they stand alone when it comes to responsi-bility for implementing policy. When Ministers are intelligent, decisive and well informed, they are able to make good use both of the public service and of their political advisers. When they are not, advisers—whether they want to or not—are obliged to fill the vacuum.

Politicians and public servants inhabit different worlds. This is true even in the geographic sense as, unlike their British counterparts, Australian Ministers do not have offices within their departments but instead work from premises in the Parliamentary building itself. We know, from a number of memoirs by Labor government Ministers of the 1990s, that what looms largest for politicians is not the public service but the party-political world, populated by their party colleagues, closest advisers and to some degree by the media (e.g. see Button 1994; Hawke 1994; Blewett 1999).

We know rather less about the way Departmental Secretaries (i.e. the public service department heads) and other senior public servants perceive their relationship with Ministers. Weller and Grattan's now dated but still insightful book *Can Ministers Cope?* (1981) recorded a high degree of frustration on the part of senior public servants with what they perceived to be the lack of competence of many Ministers. For their part, many Ministers were likewise unimpressed by public servants, who seemed unresponsive to their needs (Weller & Grattan 1981: chs. 3–4). A large part of the impetus for reforming the public service came from a sense (on the part of politicians) that the balance of power between themselves and their senior public servants had shifted too far in favour of the latter.

The incoming Labor government of 1983, led by Prime Minister Hawke, was full of reforming zeal. A White Paper, *Reforming the Australian Public Service,* produced in 1983, proposed a more flexible system for the appointment of Department heads and the creation of a Senior Executive Service (SES) covering the most senior public servants below the rank of department head. Although the White Paper's proposals seemed quite modest, they represented a deliberate shift (towards politicians) in the power relations between Ministers and Departmental Secretaries. The proposals were given legislative effect in 1984 and, in 1993, further legislation enabled the appointment of Departmental Secretaries on the basis of limited-term contracts. An additional salary loading was given to compensate for this loss of tenure.

These changes addressed what was for many politicians the key reason for change—the problem of obtaining full cooperation from senior public servants in planning and implementing the government's program. Unless, politicians reasoned, they had more power to choose their agency heads and could dispense with those who did not meet their needs, their effectiveness as Ministers would be undermined.

Under the Howard Coalition government, the *Public Service Act* of 1999 made it quite plain that the appointment of Departmental Secretaries can be terminated at any time by the Prime Minister, subject only to a report from the Secretary of the Department of the Prime Minister and Cabinet. SES officers can be 'compulsorily retired' (i.e. sacked) by their Departmental Secretary, and have no recourse to the unfair dismissal provisions of the *Workplace Relations Act*. The new Act has cemented the powers of the Departmental Secretary who has 'all the rights, duties and powers of an employer in respect of APS [i.e. Australian Public Service] employees in the Agency'. Moreover, the Act states that a Departmental Secretary cannot be directed by a Minister to engage particular individuals.

As former Departmental Secretary Sir Lennox Hewitt (Hewitt 1997) has pointed out, the new Act effectively placed the last nails in the coffin of what used to be a 'career service'. Appointments can now be made by any agency at any time, and there are no longer strictly defined points of entry (e.g. post-school or at graduate level). The role of the Public Service Commissioner is no longer to oversee the framework of the public service but rather to advise on, and to promote, what it calls 'APS values'. For the first time, the *Public Service Act 1999* specified these values, which included the statement that 'the APS is apolitical, performing its functions in an impartial and professional manner'. However, it could be argued that by making the crucial position, that of Departmental Secretary, subject to the incumbent retaining the favour of the Minister, it would be very difficult for the service to remain 'apolitical'.

The record of many State government SESs has not been an encouraging one in this respect. A number of States established an SES well before the Commonwealth, and were in a position to review a decade's experience by the end of the 1990s. The NSW SES, established by the Greiner Liberal government in 1989, was a case in point. The NSW Auditor-General, the independent-minded Tony Harris, found that there were 'several features of the current SES model, or its application, which hinder the capacity of the SES to operate effectively in line with the Government's stated objectives' (Harris 1999: 21). Interviews with serving SES officers indicated that 'there is an acknowledgement of the inevitability of an increasing shift towards a formalised Washington model of public sector politicisation'. What this meant was that informal, often highly political, criteria were used to evaluate performance. There was also evidence of apparently partisan political appointments to Departmental Secretary and to SES positions. The Auditor-General recommended that steps be taken to remove the employment of SES personnel from direct political control and to ensure that fair and open assessment criteria, which should include 'political acumen', be used (Harris 1999).

Back at the national level, difficulties have emerged in the relationships between Ministers, ministerial advisers and public servants. The so-called 'children overboard' affair—in which the Prime Minister and other senior Ministers in the Howard government claimed, incorrectly as it was soon demonstrated, that asylum-seekers intercepted by the Australian navy in late 2001 had threatened to throw their children into the sea unless rescued and taken to Australia—was particularly troubling. Later investigation by a Senate Committee revealed the extent to which ministerial advisers were able to manage the flow of information between public servants, the military and Ministers (particularly the Prime Minister), so that the Ministers could retain a political advantage by continuing to use information they should by then have known to be false but whose inaccuracy had not formally been drawn to their attention by their advisers. Despite the pivotal role of ministerial advisers, they could not be brought before Senate Estimates Committees to report on their actions, and many commentators considered that there was a lack of accountability in relation to key players (Weller 2002).

A later survey of Commonwealth public servants, undertaken in 2004 for the Public Service Commission, confirmed the existence of a grey area of largely unstructured contact between Ministers, their advisers and public servants. The survey found that 20 per cent of public servant respondents reported direct contact over the previous two months with Ministers or their advisers (an astonishingly high figure). Further, 80 per cent of respondents reported that they were given no guidance by their department (or were not sure what guidance there was) as to how to handle concerns they might have regarding requests from ministerial advisers (APSC 2004b). No equivalent survey has been undertaken of ministerial advisers, but it seems reasonable to assume that they, too, lack guidance when it comes to their roles and responsibilities.

The real test of change is whether or not better public policy and more effective management are emerging from the current arrangements, as compared to those which preceded them. This is not an easy question to answer, as so much depends on the personalities involved. Nevertheless, there are strong reasons to doubt whether the theory and practice of new public management (NPM) have adequately dealt with the unique relationship between political and bureaucratic agency heads. Some protection of the position of Departmental Secretaries may be necessary.

FINANCIAL MANAGEMENT

Financial management has been at the heart of developments in public sector management. It is also one of the most difficult areas in which to make an assessment of the real, as opposed to the rhetorical, impact of change.

The key question is the extent to which the devolution of functions from central agencies has been accompanied by a genuine devolution of control and accountability. On the one hand, agencies are encouraged to believe that, like the private sector, they have considerable freedom in the way they manage their resources in order to achieve their corporate objectives. On the other, their budgets are subject to rigorous control by Cabinet and by the Department of Finance, and may be cut at any time regardless of their performance. In addition, agencies are required to report in detail on their activities to Parliament, which means, in effect, that any aspect of their use of resources may come in for hostile, or at least critical, attention from the Opposition.

These conflicting demands reflect underlying differences between the public and the private sectors. In the private sector, the 'bottom line' and associated returns to shareholders take precedence over other objectives. Unless a corporation can earn sufficient returns to keep itself in business, it will fail to survive. In contrast, the public sector obtains its funds not from the marketplace but from government savings, borrowings or tax revenues. While some have argued that this means government is to be regarded as a surrogate owner of the enterprise, government is clearly not a shareholder in the same way as an individual or even an institution might have shares in a private sector company like BHP Billiton. Government itself is acting on behalf of millions of taxpayers and citizens who are compulsorily, rather than voluntarily, engaged in the enterprise. In these circumstances, the venue in which accountability must ultimately be exercised is Parliament, not the marketplace.

One of the main arguments for NPM is that it makes it much easier for politicians to review governmental performance. This is done through statements provided at budget time (known as Portfolio Budget Statements) which give each agency's past and projected expenditure on an 'accruals' basis (i.e. taking into account asset depreciation and commitments rather than cash alone) and which relate agency activity (measured by 'outputs') to government policy objectives ('outcomes'). With this information, it is possible (at least in theory) to appreciate the full cost of achieving particular outcomes.

The transition to the new form of budgeting and reporting took place over a number of years. In the 1970s, departments used line item budgets, where every type of resource was separately classified. Each classification was a component of the relevant Appropriation Bill, so that it was possible to see a precise connection between the official parliamentary authorisation of the expenditure, and the uses to which it was put. Clearly, though, these kinds of data are not particularly relevant for management purposes, because they are solely related to 'inputs'. Managers need to know and to understand the relationships achieved between these inputs and the products or services the enterprise produces—its 'outputs'.

By the early to mid-1980s, agencies had moved to program budgets, which were intended to group expenditures by the program or purpose which they were designed to serve.

The next step was to require departments to classify their activities into 'output' groups (e.g. reports produced, or claims of a particular type assessed). In turn, these outputs were related to broad 'outcomes' (e.g. the particular results which the output was supposed to affect). Each output was purchased by the government for a particular price. In practice, finding the right level of detail with which to classify outputs has proved elusive. Too broad, and the reader of the budget statement finds it difficult to relate the information to the agency's programs and activities. Too narrow, and the same problem results. Evaluating this information remains difficult. For the previous financial year, the reader can compare the 'actual' amount expended with the budgeted amount. This gives some idea of the agency's budgeting accuracy. For information on performance outcomes, it is necessary to turn to the agency's annual report, which records the agency's achievements against nominated performance indicators.

It is a moot point as to whether the new budgetary and reporting formats give users a clearer understanding of what agencies are achieving with the resources given to them. Because of the novelty of the approach, formats have changed frequently, making year-on-year comparisons extremely problematic. An examination of the *Hansards* of Senate Estimates Committees shows that, at least as far as the Commonwealth Parliament is concerned, it is political priorities which determine the range and point of questions.

As far as internal management is concerned, it is difficult to determine whether performance and other information is really being used to allocate and, where necessary, to ration resources. While the Commonwealth's Management Advisory Board (1997) painted an exciting future picture of fully benchmarked financial performance based on activity-based costing, the reality is that financial management can never be divorced from its political and budgetary context.

HUMAN RESOURCE MANAGEMENT

Australian public sector management has been criticised for a lack of attention to human resource management (O'Faircheallaigh, Wanna & Weller 1999: ch. 9; Martin & Coventry 1995). It is probably true to say that few, if any, agencies have been able to integrate the way they recruit, develop and deploy their people with their professed 'corporate objectives'. In part, this is a consequence of the bureaucratic form. In any task-dominated environment, whether public or private, it is less expensive, certainly in the short run, to treat employees as replaceable cogs in a machine rather than as individuals to be developed and retained.

On the other hand, there has been considerable progress towards devolving human resource management to the agency level (while keeping firm central control on running costs). The *Public Service Act 1999* makes it plain that agency heads, and not the Public Service Commission, are responsible for the overall 'shape' of their organisation, and for hiring, firing and remunerating employees. Faced with looming skills shortages as 'baby boomers' retire, many agencies are giving increased attention to workforce planning, employee satisfaction and flexible employment conditions. As the outgoing Public Service Commissioner put it in 2004, one of the major challenges for the service was the need to match capabilities with 'the context in which the APS will be operating over the next few years (including the impact of demography and new technology, and changing community expectations)' (APSC 2004c).

Undoubtedly the acid test for any human resource management regime, particularly in the public sector, is the extent to which it allows underperformance to be managed. One of the safeguards of the traditional public service was that public servants had tenure. Tenure supposedly made it possible for public servants to exercise the prerogatives of an apolitical public service without the fear that they would lose their jobs. But tenure also came to stand for the cosy certainties of a 'job for life'. In theory, provided the appropriate processes have been followed, it is now possible to dismiss public sector employees on the same grounds as those in the private sector. But in practice, only a handful of public servants have their appointments terminated (i.e. are sacked) each year. Retrenchment, although more costly to the taxpayer, requires much less courage on the part of managers.

Nevertheless, the spread of performance management does, at least, focus some attention on the problem. At the most basic level, most if not all public servants will have some kind of understanding with their supervisor (known as a performance agreement) about what tasks they will accomplish in a given period of time. Staff employed under individualised contracts (such as Australian Workplace Agreements) may have specified 'outputs' associated with their employment. Where collective arrangements (i.e. certified agreements negotiated with public-sector unions) are in place, improvements in pay and conditions are specifically related to trade-offs designed to bring about greater productivity.

There has been a general trend away from pyramid-shaped agencies towards diamond-shaped agencies, where the bulk of employees are not at the bottom end of the classification structure but in the middle. Have public servants been giving themselves pay rises by inflating the classification level for a given type of work, or does this reflect the effects of multi-skilling, technological change, and changes in the character of public service work? The answer is that we are probably looking at a combination of all these factors.

Have we reached the point at which to work for a particular agency is analogous to working for a company in the private sector? Just as there are forces pushing agencies further apart, there are others which tend to bind them together. As employers, governments are keen to see 'their' public service embodying principles and practices which they hold dear. Under the Hawke and Keating Labor governments, Labor's commitment to equal employment opportunity saw concerted efforts to increase the proportion of women in senior management positions, to improve Aboriginal employment, and to make the APS more representative of the ethnic diversity of Australian society in general. The Howard Coalition government has since sought to implement more flexible and 'family-friendly' workplaces. As employers, governments (and by extension agency heads) have far more complex responsibilities than their private sector counterparts.

Expectations of senior executives remain somewhat clouded. It seems clear that they are expected to be leaders as well as managers (or at least some will be leaders and some managers), but most are still feeling their way forward when it comes to building a practical context for these roles. Some take refuge in highly risk-averse behaviour (Gregory 1997: 96); others opt for the protection of professional specialisation. Few have the confidence to chart a course of their own while bringing the 'troops' with them.

But the problem of 'politics' remains. Governments continue to redesign portfolios on the basis of their political priorities, rather than management logic, making longer-run strategic planning a possibly redundant undertaking. The Commonwealth government's decision following the 2004 election to move five agencies from the Family and Community Services portfolio to the Finance portfolio, in order to create a new Department of Human Services that would be subject to more direct ministerial control, seemed to fly in the face of the NPM dictum to 'let the managers manage'.

Issues and problems

ACCOUNTABILITY AND OUTSOURCING

Political keenness for outsourcing may have diminished. But the basic conceptual problems inherent in all purchaser–provider relations remain. As we noted earlier, outsourcing brings a different type of accountability to bear—that of the marketplace. Proponents of NPM would argue that, where the resources of competition have been well used, traditional modes of accountability that rely on disclosure are unnecessary. If a provider fails to perform, the contract itself will act as a sanction.

It could, however, be argued that contracts should involve the same level of disclosure as would occur if the work had been done departmentally—that is, a purchase 'price' for the output should be reported to Parliament. This implies that contracts should be open to parliamentary and to public scrutiny, but in practice most are protected by commercial-in-confidence provisions. There is some evidence that the recourse to confidentiality derives not from the firms themselves but from governments' habitual desire for secrecy (Harris 1999).

The accountability of purchasers remains something of a grey area. Peter Boxall, former head of the Federal Department of Finance, has stated that 'the bottom line is that you cannot outsource accountability. A department or agency remains accountable to its minister—and its minister to parliament—for any outsourced activity' (Boxall 1997: 7). Yet in large, complex contracts, there will be many decisions made by contractors for which public servants—and, by implication, Ministers—cannot be held accountable. As a number of Auditor-General reports have made clear, it is the process of contract management, and the expertise that is brought to bear on it, which is most clearly the domain of public servants. This is ironic, given that NPM was supposed to transcend the preoccupation with process which characterised old-style public administration. But some of the older virtues, such as a regard for due process and the maintenance of careful records, undoubtedly have a place in the new order.

POLITICISATION AND THE ETHOS OF PUBLIC SERVICE

Commentators are somewhat divided on the extent to which 'politicisation' is a problem in public sector management. In any case, it is important to distinguish the sense in which the term 'politicisation' is used. In the classical sense, politicisation means that political allegiance to the party in power is necessary for high-level appointments to the public bureaucracy; or, in a more diffuse interpretation, it can mean that bureaucrats feel constrained about being too critical in the advice they give Ministers, lest their jobs or career prospects be placed at risk.

Practitioners have been quick to assert that their value to Ministers lies in their being forthright in the advice they give, whether or not they are employed under contract. On the other hand, where there has been an opportunity for empirical research to investigate this claim, the results are not so reassuring. On the basis of a survey of the New South Wales SES, sponsored by the Audit Office, Judy Johnston (1999: 15) observed that political–bureaucratic relations had become politicised to the point where 'on the balance of probabilities . . . it would appear that the public interest is often secondary to the self-interest of the relevant actors'.

It is difficult to see any change in current practice unless politicians become convinced that it is in their interests for officials to feel free to speak their minds when giving advice. Further movement towards the American model, where the appointments of senior officials are clearly 'politicised' but are also subject to review by Congress, may be inevitable.

Yet procedural and structural changes can only achieve so much. How to define and develop public service ethics in a complex and ambiguous managerialist age is a problem of some difficulty. The *Public Service Act 1999* specifies three kinds of values to be observed by public servants: they must be apolitical, openly accountable for their actions, and responsive to the needs of government. While most public servants surveyed in 2004 reported that, in their current job, they were confident of their ability to balance these values, we have little information on how they were doing it, or the practical meaning of the balance point (APSC 2004b). Managing by means of values, when structures and incentives have changed so much, places considerable pressure on the professionalism of public servants.

PUBLIC–PRIVATE PARTNERSHIPS

In the early 1990s, Osborne and Gaebler's book *Reinventing Government* swept through the public sector management community in Australia (Osborne & Gaebler 1992). Their idea that governments should 'steer not row' (decide on directions, but not implement them) became accepted doctrine.

In the years since then, governments have clearly not abandoned the idea of direct bureaucratic provision of services, but increasingly this is not the model of first choice. Where policy implementation involves complex relations with the private sector, such as in regional development, health, employment and community services, the formation of networks—sometimes involving formal contracts, sometimes not—has been gaining ground. The idea of forging partnerships between business and government has proved attractive to governments of diverse political persuasions, as they search for new forms of low-cost policy capacity (Domberger, Farago & Fernandez 1997).

As already noted earlier in this chapter, these new ways of exercising authority have been described as *governance* to distinguish them from the more traditional 'government'. How far governance will prove compatible with the traditional Westminster-derived structures of accountability is an open question. Will political executives be comfortable with ways of working which, at least potentially, involve bureaucrats interacting directly with communities in the formation and execution of policy? Or will they continue to equate accountability with control, never quite trusting 'accountability for results' (Stewart 2001)?

The future of the public sector

In 1996, Gary Sturgess canvassed the possibility of a 'virtual state' in which only core activities remained within the public sector (Sturgess 1996). The reality has proved rather more complex. Citizen demands on the state have probably grown, rather than abated. Governments are busier than ever, if the parade of legislation through State, Territory and federal Parliaments is any guide.

Nor is it clear that developments in public sector management will necessarily shrink the sphere of public action. The emphasis on customer service is a case in point. If governments are serious about treating citizens as customers with individual needs, they must inevitably face the fact that doing so is far more costly than the traditional 'one size fits all' approach. This will apply whether the services are delivered by government employees or by providers in the private or not-for-profit sectors.

In retrospect, the idea that the state might be reduced to a small cluster of purchasers surrounded by a galaxy of contracted providers seems simplistic. What seems to be happening is that the borders between public and private, and between public and not-for-profit, are growing more blurred, as governments seek to combine the benefits of outsourcing with the continuity and interchange that sensible policy demands. As we have seen, these relationships are still evolving, with future developments strongly subject to political change.

It seems likely that more fundamental (and irrevocable) changes have occurred in the culture of Australian public services. For obvious reasons, the proponents of change have talked up the benefits of the demise of a career public service and downplayed or ignored the costs.

The benefits are clear—a sharpened focus on performance and on individual accountability. The costs are more difficult to specify, let alone to quantify. In the lower to middle echelons of the public service, where the cold draughts of politics do not reach, it is possible simply to 'get on with the job' in some kind of security. At the higher levels, the waters are more treacherous than ever. One is reminded of the fate of top courtiers in the courts of Renaissance monarchs. The higher you go, the more dangerous it gets. Its failure to devise a model of management that accounts for the realities of politics may yet prove the Achilles heel of public sector reform. The questions to be resolved are as much ethical as they are technical.

NOTES

1   The term 'state' is a generic description; hence Australia can be understood as a 'state' in this sense. The word is also used in Australia to describe the component States (e.g. the State of Queensland) that make up the Australian federation. Confusingly, this means that the Australian state (using the term in the generic sense) features six States (using the term in the federalist sense). Normally the context makes the intended meaning clear. This

book follows the convention of—where possible—using the lower-case 'state' for a generic entity and the upper-case 'State' for a component province of a federal system.

2 In keeping with convention, the term 'agency' is used here to encompass any government department, bureau or authority within the public sector.

3 See Chapters 4 and 5 of this volume for discussion of the limitations of this process.

REFERENCES

ABS [Australian Bureau of Statistics] 2000, 2005, *Wage and Salary Earners, Australia*, ABS catalogue no. 6248.0 and 6248.0.55.001, Canberra.

ANAO [Australian National Audit Office] 2000, *Implementation of Whole of Government IT Infrastructure Consolidation and Outsourcing Initiative*, Commonwealth of Australia, Canberra, <http://www.anao.gov.au>, accessed 4/4/05.

APSC [Australian Public Service Commission] 2004a, *APS Statistical Bulletin 2003–04*, Canberra, <http://www.apsc.gov.au>, accessed 4/4/05.

APSC [Australian Public Service Commission] 2004b, *State of the Service Report 2003–2004*, Canberra, <http://www.apsc.gov.au>, accessed 31/3/05.

APSC [Australian Public Service Commission] 2004c, Commissioner's Overview, *Annual Report 2003–04*, Commonwealth of Australia, Canberra.

Blewett, N. 1999, *A Cabinet Diary: A Personal Record of the First Keating Government*, Wakefield Press, Kent Town.

Boston, J., Martin, J., Pallot, J. & Walsh, P. eds 1996, *Public Management: The New Zealand Model*, Oxford University Press, Auckland.

Boxall, P. 1997, 'Competitive Tendering and Contracting', *Canberra Bulletin of Public Administration*, no. 86, pp. 6–9.

Button, J. 1994, *Flying the Kite: Travels of an Australian Politician*, Random House, Sydney.

Corbett, D. 1996, *Australian Public Sector Management*, 2nd edn, Allen & Unwin, Sydney.

Domberger, S., Farago, S. & Fernandez, P. 1997, 'Public and Private Sector Partnering: A Reappraisal', *Public Administration*, vol. 75, no. 4, pp. 777–87.

Gregory, R. 1997, 'After the Rhetoric: Some Patterns of Attitudinal Change', *Australian Journal of Public Administration*, vol. 56, no. 1, pp. 82–99.

Harris, T. 1999, 'The Auditor-General's Last Stand', *Canberra Bulletin of Public Administration*, no. 93, pp. 1–3.

Hawke, R. 1994, *The Hawke Memoirs*, William Heinemann, Australia, Melbourne.

Hewitt, L. 1997, JCPA Hansard, 9 September 1997, pp. 283–4.

Hodge, G. 2000, *Privatisation: An International Review of Performance*, Westview Press, Boulder.

Hood, C. 1991, 'A Public Management for All Seasons?', *Public Administration*, vol. 69, no. 1, pp. 3–19.

Hughes, O. 1998, *Public Management and Administration: An Introduction*, Macmillan, Melbourne.

Humphry, R. 2000, *Review of the Whole of Government IT Outsourcing Initiative*, Commonwealth of Australia, Canberra, <http://www.dofa.gov.au/humphryreview/>, accessed 4/4/05.

Johnston, J. 1999, 'Serving the Public Interest: The Future of Independent Advice?', *Canberra Bulletin of Public Administration*, no. 91, pp. 9–18.

Keating, M. 1990, 'Managing for Results in the Public Interest', *Australian Journal of Public Administration*, vol. 49, no. 4, pp. 387–98.

Maley, M. 2000, 'Too Many or Too Few? The Increase in Federal Ministerial Advisers', *Australian Journal of Public Administration*, vol. 59, no. 4, pp. 48–53.

Management Advisory Board 1997, *Beyond Bean Counting: Effective Financial Management in the APS—1998 and Beyond*, PSMPC, Canberra.

Martin, J. & Coventry, H. 1995, 'Human Resource Management', in *From Hawke to Keating: Australian Commonwealth Administration 1990–1993*, ed. J. Stewart, CRPSM & RIPAA, Canberra.

Mulgan, R. 1997, 'The Processes of Accountability', *Australian Journal of Public Administration*, vol. 56, no. 1, pp. 25–36.

O'Faircheallaigh, C., Wanna, J. & Weller, P. 1999, *Public Sector Management in Australia: New Challenges, New Directions*, 2nd edn, Macmillan, Melbourne.

Osborne, D. & Gaebler, T. 1992, *Reinventing Government: How the Entrepreneurial Spirit is Transforming the Public Sector*, Addison Wesley, Reading, MA.

Quiggin, J. 1996, 'Competitive Tendering and Contracting in the Australian Public Sector', *Australian Journal of Public Administration*, vol. 55, no. 3 pp. 49–58.

Ryan, N. 1995, 'Ministerial Advisers and Policy-Making', in *From Hawke to Keating: Australian Commonwealth Administration 1990–1993*, ed. J. Stewart, CRPSM & RIPAA, Canberra.

Stewart, J. 1996, 'Public Management in 1995: The Year that Was', *Australian Journal of Public Administration*, vol. 55, no. 1, pp. 118–26.

Stewart, J. 2001, 'Networks and the New Public Policy', *Canberra Bulletin of Public Administration*, vol. 102, pp. 1–4.

Sturgess, G. 1996, 'Virtual Government: What Will Remain Inside the Public Sector?', *Australian Journal of Public Administration*, vol. 55, no. 3, pp. 59–73.

Wanna, J. Kelly, J. & Forster, J. 1996, 'The Rise and Rise of the Department of Finance', *Canberra Bulletin of Public Administration*, no. 82, pp. 53–62.

Weller, P. & Grattan, M. 1981, *Can Ministers Cope? Australian Federal Ministers at Work*, Hutchinson, Richmond.

Weller, P. 2002, *Don't Tell the Prime Minister*, Scribe Publications, Melbourne.

The federal system

JOHN SUMMERS

The Commonwealth was created in 1901 when six self-governing colonies agreed to come together under a federal constitution. This federal compact, embodied in the Constitution, gave some governmental powers to the Commonwealth but also preserved the colonies (as States), with their governments and most of their governmental powers intact. As is explained further in Chapter 3 of this book it is this constitutional division of power between different levels of government, neither constitutionally subordinate to the other, that defines a federal system.

The words of the Constitution have changed very little in the 100 or so years of its existence. Out of 44 attempts to change the Constitution by referendum, only eight have been successful, and only two or three of these have been significant in terms of the balance of power between the States and the Commonwealth. However, this stability in the written Constitution conceals great changes at the political, social and economic levels. The power of the States in relation to the Commonwealth—the 'federal balance of power'—is constantly changing, and is the product of a complex interrelationship between the legal, economic and *political* capacities of the two tiers of government. The formal constitutional framework provides restraints and broad outlines within which the relations between the Commonwealth and the States take place, but it is not the whole picture.

This chapter examines the changing relationship between the Commonwealth and State governments since the creation of the Commonwealth of Australia and examines the political significance of the relationship.

Judicial review and the federal balance

Judicial review is a crucial element in the federal system. The High Court has power to review Commonwealth or State legislation and to determine whether it is within the powers granted in the Constitution to the relevant tier of government. The High Court can invalidate any legislation that it finds to be unconstitutional. In the process of acting as umpire in the federal system and ruling on the constitutionality of legislation, the High Court has, over the years of federation, had a great effect on the federal balance of power. Changing interpretations of the Constitution by the High Court have, in effect, resulted in constitutional change without any significant change in the written Constitution itself (Crisp 1983: 58–82; Galligan 1987; Bradsen 1990; Solomon 1992).

In the early years of the federation, the High Court was dominated by judges who took a very narrow view of the Commonwealth's powers. The Court adopted two 'implied' doctrines that guided its decisions: a doctrine of 'intergovernmental immunities' prevented the legislation of one tier of government applying to the instrumentalities of the other; while a doctrine of 'reserve power' held that the powers of the Commonwealth, as spelt out in the Constitution, were regarded as being limited by powers *assumed* to be reserved to the States.

By 1920, the composition of the High Court bench had changed and, in an important turning point, the Court moved in the *Engineers* case to abandon the assumptions that had underpinned the previous period. The Court overturned a previous judgment, the *Railway Servant's* case of 1906, in which it had been found that the Commonwealth's industrial relations power did not apply to the employees of State governments. The judgment in the *Engineers* case rejected the doctrines of 'implied immunities' and 'reserve powers' and marks the beginning of a period during which the Court took a broad view of Commonwealth powers. In terms of the federal balance, an important case of this period was the *Uniform Tax* case (1942), which resulted in an effective Commonwealth monopoly of income tax (and is discussed further below).

In the immediate post-World War II period, a number of interventionist initiatives of the Chifley Labor government, aimed at achieving planned economic growth and at instituting broad national welfare measures, were thwarted by High Court decisions based on this interpretation of section 92. The most notable of these was the *Bank Nationalisation* case (1948), in which the Court adopted a 'free enterprise' interpretation of section 92 and held that the Labor government's attempt to nationalise the banks was thereby invalid. Sawer (1963: 216) characterises the late 1940s as a 'period of intense judicial activity during which government policy was frustrated by judge-made doctrine rather than clear constitutional restriction'.

During the period of the Liberal and Country Party Coalition government at the Commonwealth level in the 1950s and 1960s, many fewer initiatives tested the boundaries of Commonwealth powers. However, at the end of that period, in the *Concrete Pipes* case (1971), the Court cleared the way for the Commonwealth government to make much greater use of section 51(xx) (the 'corporations' power) to regulate corporate and economic activity in Australia.

The election of the Whitlam Labor government in 1972 was followed by a flood of Commonwealth activity which was very directly aimed at changing the federal balance. Commonwealth programs were initiated relating to such areas of State responsibility as urban development, housing, education and health, by means of offering specific purpose payments (or conditional grants) to the States (as authorised by section 96, which declares that a Commonwealth law 'may grant financial assistance to any State on such terms and conditions as the [Commonwealth] Parliament thinks fit'). The use of conditional grants in this way by the Commonwealth had been upheld by the Court since the *Federal Roads* case in 1926, and the Whitlam government's programs did not suffer at the hands of the High Court in the same way as the Chifley government legislation had (Sawer 1977: 2–24). (The significance of conditional grants is discussed in more detail below.)

A number of High Court decisions in the 1980s appear to have greatly expanded the scope for Commonwealth legislation. The most significant cases have been ones in which the Court has held that, within certain limits, the Commonwealth's power over 'external affairs' in section 51(xxix) can provide it with power to legislate on matters that would otherwise be State responsibilities if this gives effect to international agreements. In the *Koowarta* case (1982), the Court upheld antidiscrimination legislation, which the Commonwealth argued was giving effect to an international convention, to which Australia was a signatory, on the elimination of racial discrimination. In the *Dam* case (1983), starkly different policy alternatives rested on the Court's decision. The Tasmanian government planned to build a hydro-electric dam on the Franklin River in south-west Tasmania and it regarded the matter as being purely a State responsibility. The site for the dam, however, was in an area nominated for World Heritage listing, which made it the subject of an international agreement, and the Commonwealth argued that the conservation of the natural heritage of the area was a Commonwealth responsibility. The Court held that section 51(xxix) did give the Commonwealth power to legislate to prevent the building of the dam. The Court adopted the same position in the *Lemonthyme and Southern Forests* case (1987–8) and upheld a Commonwealth law which had the effect of preventing logging in Tasmanian forests being considered for World Heritage listing.

The Court's decisions to uphold the legislation on the basis of the external affairs power have been criticised because they have the potential to completely shift the federal balance. There are now an enormous number of international agreements on a vast range of topics. The concern is that the extent of Commonwealth power is potentially determined by the treaties it enters into, not by the enumerated powers in the Constitution, and the Commonwealth could obtain power over almost every area of government which had previously been regarded as a State responsibility.

However, the Court has placed limitations on the use of section 51(xxix) in terms of the type of international agreement that would provide the basis for Commonwealth action and on the scope of a power that an international agreement can sustain. The agreement must be genuine and not entered into simply as a contrivance to gain power over the States, and the legislation cannot extend beyond the implementation of the treaty (Galligan 1987: 240–8; Solomon 1992: 27–8, 140–5).

In *Ha* v *New South Wales* (1997), the High Court struck down a New South Wales business licensing law and put the validity of all business licence fees in doubt. Previous High Court decisions on section 90 had adopted increasingly broad interpretations of the meaning of 'excise tax' and had made it more and more difficult for the States to design taxes that were not open to constitutional challenge. Any State tax that could possibly be interpreted as a sales or consumption tax, or a levy on production or turnover, was not available to the States. The States had been forced to adopt elaborate and complex business licensing laws to raise fees from businesses licensed to sell petrol, tobacco or alcohol (McEvoy & Summers 1996: 159–64). Revenue from these business licence fees was an indispensable component of State budgets. In 1996/97 business licence fees raised revenue for the States of about $5.2 billion (CGC 1999: 25).

In summary, the effect of judicial review has been to increase the power of the Commonwealth at the expense of the States. This shift in the legal balance of power in favour of the Commonwealth, however, has not been a simple or linear process. There have been setbacks for the Commonwealth, and sometimes the Commonwealth has gained power in one area but lost it in another. It must also be understood that, although the legal balance has moved in favour of the Commonwealth, the States have largely retained the power to make laws in those areas of government which most directly affect peoples lives—health services and hospitals, the criminal law and the police, primary and secondary education, public transport, local government etc.

The structure of Commonwealth–State financial relations

One crucial component of the shift in the legal balance of power relates to ability of the two tiers of government to raise taxes and to Commonwealth–State financial relations. In the drafting of the Constitution, it was intended that the States and the Commonwealth would be financially independent. Thus each tier of government has constitutional power to raise its own revenue independently of the other. With the exception of customs and excise taxes, all taxes are available to both tiers of government. There is provision for tax sharing, because (as noted above) the Commonwealth has power under section 96 to 'grant financial assistance to any State on such terms and conditions as the Parliament thinks fit', but beyond the first 10 years of federation there was no constitutional requirement on how that tax sharing should take place.

An essential feature of the federation agreement was the abolition of interstate tariffs and the adoption of uniform national tariffs: only the Commonwealth would have the power to impose 'duties of customs and of excise' (section 90). In the 1890s customs duties were a major source of government revenue and after federation this revenue would go to the Commonwealth. Ever since, despite their taxing powers, the States have never been in a position to raise all their own revenue. Over the years since federation, the States have become increasingly reliant on the Commonwealth for their revenue and increasingly subject to its dictates about how that revenue will be spent.

The erosion of the financial autonomy of the States is, in part, the result of economic developments. Some of the sources of revenue that were an important part of State budgets at the time of federation—income from public utilities, public transport and the sale of Crown land—have diminished in economic importance and, in the case of public transport, have often become a large drain on State budgets.

By far the most important factors in the growth of financial dominance by the Commonwealth came from two other developments:

- the limitations on the range of taxes available to the States—the States' loss of access to income tax in 1942, and the restrictions on the types of other taxes available to the States due to the High Court's interpretation of section 90 of the Constitution (the prohibition on the States levying 'duties of custom and excise')
- the use of 'specific purpose payments' (SPPs)—also refered to as conditional or tied grants—made under section 96 of the Constitution by the Commonwealth to the States.

These two factors dominate the history of Commonwealth–State financial relations.

HISTORICAL BACKGROUND

As the Commonwealth's financial commitments expanded with the payments of pensions and then with the costs of World War I, demands on its revenue began to outstrip the yield from existing taxes and the Commonwealth began to exercise its concurrent powers to raise taxes in areas that had previously been the preserve of the States. In 1910 the Commonwealth introduced a land tax, in 1914 estate duties, in 1915 income tax and in 1916 an entertainment tax.

In 1910/11, the Commonwealth provided 'special assistance grants' under section 96 to Western Australia and then, in 1912/13, to Tasmania, the two least populous and poorest States. The onset of the depression in 1929 was a severe blow to the finances of all governments, but the States, especially the smaller-population ones, were hit hardest. The Commonwealth was now paying special grants to three States—Western Australia, Tasmania and South Australia—and, in the process of determining the amounts and purpose of the grants, was in a position to investigate the finances and budgets of these States.

In 1933, in order to regularise the criteria for making the payments and to insulate itself from the inevitable political controversy, the Commonwealth government established a permanent specialised commission: the Commonwealth Grants Commission. The Grants Commission's task was to determine what assistance was necessary to enable a State which, despite making reasonable efforts at revenue-raising, had financial difficulties in operating at a level 'not appreciably below' that of the other States. This process of attempting to compensate for the differing capacities of the States to raise revenue from their own sources and differing costs in providing the same public services through the payment of special assistance grants to some States is often referred to as *horizontal fiscal equalisation*, a concept explored in greater detail below.

THE UNIFORM TAX SCHEME

Australia entered World War II with a multiplicity of taxes being collected concurrently by Commonwealth and State governments, but income tax had become the most important source of government revenue. The Commonwealth Labor government asked the States to abandon their direct taxes for the duration of the war (in return for reimbursement grants) in order that the Commonwealth could impose uniform taxes throughout Australia. The Commonwealth argued that all Australians should contribute on an equal basis, according to their income, to support the war effort. The Premiers would not agree and, in 1941, the Commonwealth passed a package of four Acts to impose the scheme on the States.

This legislative scheme was challenged by the States, but the High Court upheld the laws. In 1946 the Commonwealth legislated again to maintain the uniform tax scheme in peacetime. The Commonwealth did *not* have the *legal* power to stop the States from continuing to collect income tax, but the practical effect of these laws was the same. The States were in no position to resist, because to have continued State income tax would have entailed both a loss of the Commonwealth grant and 'double taxation' within that State. The scheme, and its continuation in peacetime, further moved the federal financial balance in favour of the Commonwealth and left the States with less room to move. In 1957 the Victorian government again challenged the scheme in the High Court, but its essential provisions were upheld.

The extent and distribution of Commonwealth reimbursements to the States became a matter of continuing dispute between the States and the Commonwealth and, at times, between the States themselves. There are a number of dimensions to this intergovernmental conflict: the total amount of money made available by the Commonwealth in grants, the distribution of the grants among the States, and the extent to which the Commonwealth has attempted to direct State spending through the use of conditions authorised under section 96.

SPECIFIC PURPOSE PAYMENTS (SPPs)

Starting in the 1950s, the Commonwealth government has made increasing use of 'specific purpose' (or 'tied') grants to the States. Unlike 'general purpose' (or 'untied') payments, which the States received as their share of income tax and which could be allocated by the States as they wished, specific purpose payments (SPPs) are made on 'terms and conditions' set by the Commonwealth, as permitted under the authority of section 96. Through these SPPs the Commonwealth has been able effectively to influence policy and priorities in areas of State constitutional responsibility. Some of the conditions attached to the payments have been very broad and have left the States considerable flexibility. Even so, by use of SPPs the Commonwealth has not only been able to decide how much of the tax revenue the States would get but increasingly on what and how the money would be spent.

VERTICAL FISCAL IMBALANCE

The situation in which there is a disparity between the taxing capacity and the revenue needs of the two tiers of government—the Commonwealth raises more revenue than it needs for its own purposes, and the States who raise less than they spend, obtain the balance of their revenue from transfers from the Commonwealth—is referred to as *vertical fiscal imbalance*. In 2002, for example, the Commonwealth was raising more than 70 per cent of the total government revenue in Australia but spending only about 57 per cent on its own purposes. To put it another way, the Commonwealth was raising about 20 per cent more revenue than it used for its own purposes and the States were raising, from their own sources, less than 60 per cent of the money they spent. The imbalance has been increased by the new tax system, under which the States have abandoned some of their own indirect taxes and most States, if not all, will remove more of their indirect taxes after 2006.

At one level, this financial dominance by the Commonwealth has a positive outcome. The national government's capacity to influence the total level of government expenditure gives it much greater capacity in the overall management of the economy. There are, however, also problems with this lopsided financial relationship between the two tiers of government.

One matter that has concerned many commentators has been the extent to which the fiscal imbalance separates decisions on government spending from the responsibility for raising the revenue. States continue to have constitutional responsibility for the provision of the majority of government services but are limited in their capacity to collect revenue. This imbalance, it is argued, obscures responsibility. There is no clear nexus between decisions about expenditure on services and the responsibility for raising the revenue.

More importantly, from a federalist point of view, the financial dominance of the Commonwealth is a fundamental weakness in the system. The centralisation of financial power has the potential to undermine the federal division of power. Not only does the Commonwealth direct the level of spending by the States but, through the use of specific purpose grants, the Commonwealth can set priorities in policy areas that are the constitutional responsibility of the States. As the financial balance of power moves more and more in favour of the Commonwealth, the autonomy of the States is threatened.

Fiscal federalism since the 1970s

FROM WHITLAM TO KEATING 1972–1996

By 1972 SPPs had become 30 per cent of total grants to the States and 18 per cent of State budgets. The Whitlam Labor government assumed national office in 1972 with a 'new federalism' policy that explicitly called for the use of Commonwealth financial powers to implement programs in areas of State responsibility. Whitlam argued that many of the problems facing Australian society could be solved only at a national level with Commonwealth finance. Labor Party policy called for a massive expansion by the Commonwealth of tied grants to the States, particularly in education, urban development and urban planning, transport, hospitals, community health and legal aid—areas that were the constitutional responsibility of the States. In the three years, from 1972/73 to 1975/76, SPPs rose from 30 to 49 per cent of total grants, and from 18 to 33 per cent of State budgets.

By the end of 1975, when the Whitlam government was dismissed, there had been a strong political reaction against Labor's centralism. Non-Labor State Premiers were successful in mobilising political opinion against what they described as 'financial blackmail' by Canberra.

Despite promising to institute tax-sharing arrangements and scale down the use of SPPs, the Coalition government under Prime Minister Malcolm Fraser, which replaced the Whitlam government in December 1975, produced little or no increase in the financial autonomy of the States. For the States, however, the real problem in the late 1970s and into the 1980s became one of obtaining sufficient revenue, whether tied or untied, to relieve the pressure on their budgets (Groenewegen 1983: 123–58).

After the advent of the Hawke Labor government in 1983, the financial position of the States did not improve. As the Commonwealth, responding to Australia's international balance of payments crisis of the mid-1980s, attempted to reduce the total level of public-sector expenditure, further pressure fell on the States. Commonwealth grants to the States were cut, both as a proportion of Commonwealth outlays and of Gross Domestic Product. Also, the proportion of SPPs rose: from 26 per cent of total payments in 1982/83 to 35 per cent in 1992/93 (James 1992: 103).

In August 1993, the Report of the Committee of Inquiry on National Competition Policy—the 'Hilmer Report'—recommended that state-owned instrumentalities such as water and electricity utilities, which had previously operated as protected monopolies within the States, should compete on equal terms with private business (Hilmer 1993). Such reforms, it was argued, would reduce costs for businesses and make Australia more internationally competitive. State governments, however, were wary of changes under which they would lose control of these utilities. Even if it were true that the nation and the States would gain financially from the initiative, there were risks that investment and employment could be lost from some States to other States. For the States there were political difficulties in giving up control of the utilities, and the Commonwealth stood to gain much more financially than did the States.

In April 1995, after protracted negotiations, it was agreed that the Commonwealth would make additional payments—National Competition Payments—to the States in three stages *and* maintain a guaranteed real level of per-capita general-purpose grants, on condition that the States progressively implement the National Competition Policy.

THE HOWARD GOVERNMENT SINCE 1996

The Howard Coalition government came to office in March 1996 promising to maintain the States' funding, to 'breathe new life into federalism' through addressing the problem of the disparity between the States' responsibilities and their tax revenue, and to reduce the use of tied grants. Within a very short time, however, there was friction between the Commonwealth and State governments over what the States saw as an attempt by the Commonwealth to devolve responsibility to the States for various programs, which were growing in cost, without any greater access to taxing powers to pay for them.

The Howard government has made no move away from the use of tied grants, which by 2000/01 had become 42 per cent of total Commonwealth grants to the States (Commonwealth of Australia, 2000: 11).

In August 1997, as noted above, a High Court decision in *Ha v New South Wales* in relation to the constitutional prohibition on the States collecting excise taxes (section 90) created a potentially critical financial problem for the States.

The possible financial crisis for the States was averted by the adoption of a plan jointly devised by the Commonwealth and State governments. The Commonwealth increased its own taxes on tobacco, alcohol and petrol and reimbursed the States for the amount their business licence fees would have raised. While the taxes collected under the 'safety net' scheme were regarded as State revenue, collected on their behalf by the Commonwealth, the effect of the High Court decision was to make the States even more financially dependent on the Commonwealth.

In the Howard government's second term there was, as part of the extensive reforms to the whole tax system, a radical change to Commonwealth–State financial relations. In June 1999 the Commonwealth and State governments signed an agreement under which the Commonwealth agreed to transfer the revenue from the new Goods and Services Tax (GST) to the States to replace the Commonwealth Financial Assistance Grants, and the States agreed to abolish or reduce a number of their own indirect taxes and to review their taxes again after five years. A Ministerial Council, made up of the Commonwealth and State Treasurers, was established to oversee the operation of the agreement, and to replace the annual Premiers' Conference.

This change was seen as a turning point in Commonwealth–State financial relations because, it was said, for the first time the States would receive a guaranteed revenue from the Commonwealth and access to a 'growth tax'. Instead of the annual wrangle between the Commonwealth Treasurer and the State Premiers about the size of the Commonwealth grant, the revenue from the GST would automatically be paid to the States. On the other hand, although the States agreed to this change and welcomed the immediate prospect of having greater certainty about their income, the change increased even further the extent to which State budgets relied on taxes collected by the Commonwealth.

In its first five years the GST has yielded much more revenue than had been expected, easing the pressure on State budgets. However, the implications of the States' increased dependence on the Commonwealth became clear when, following the 2004 election, the Commonwealth Treasurer, Peter Costello, called on the States to abolish some additional direct taxes. The Treasurer argued that under the 1999 Intergovernmental Agreement relating to transfer of GST revenue to the States, the States were obliged to review their own taxes in 2005, and that as the States had received much more from the GST than anticipated they were now in a position to abolish some of their remaining direct taxes. The States argued that they could not afford to abolish the taxes and that they were not legally obliged to do so under the Intergovernmental Agreement. The Commonwealth Treasurer warned that if the States failed to abolish the direct taxes the Commonwealth Government would review the payment of GST revenue to the States. Some States noted that, with a majority in the Senate after July 2005, the Coalition government would be free to pass legislation on the matter, and agreed to review their direct taxes and to phase some out over a number of years.

As of mid-2005, New South Wales was holding out against the demands of the Commonwealth, and it is yet to be determined how the matter would be resolved. However, the issue demonstrated that, with the States so reliant on revenue collected by the Commonwealth, a Commonwealth government with a majority in the Senate has great potential to dictate to the States on a matter—taxing power—that was completely within the jurisdiction the States. Further, to the extent that the States do reduce their own direct taxes, it will make them even more reliant on the Commonwealth for funds.

As noted above, an aspect of the financial dominance of the Commonwealth is its ability, through SPPs, to influence matters which are State responsibilities. As the use of SPPs by the Commonwealth has increased over the last 50 years the conditions attached to the funds were variable—some have been narrow and restrictive but others have been quite open and allowed the States considerable discretion about exactly how the funds were used and about the policy objectives they pursued. Under the Howard government SPPs have increased to over 50 per cent of the total Commonwealth payments to the States and more restrictive conditions have been attached to the use of the funds (WADF&T 2005). In 2004 the Commonwealth government stated that it was 'seeking greater accountability in SPP agreements' and that future SPP agreements would include 'key objectives' and 'detailed performance indicators' and that to 'encourage increased accountability', an amount of the payment would be 'contingent on the states' timely reporting of the agreed financial and performance information *to the satisfaction of the responsible [Commonwealth] Government Minister*' (Commonwealth of Australia, 2003: 19, emphasis added)

The imposition of greater control has been rationalised by the Coalition government in terms of efficiency and effectiveness, but the effect is that the Commonwealth has greater capacity to pursue its own policy objectives on matters which are the constitutional responsibility of the States. Although in many cases the Commonwealth only provides a proportion of the funds for State programs, it is potentially able to impose its conditions on the whole program. To the extent that the Commonwealth is able to do this it is able to dictate to the States how *their* funds will be spent and on the policy goals of programs. Also, the added reporting requirement forces the States to spend more of their own funds on compliance—planning, gathering the information, monitoring programs and preparing timely reports 'to the satisfaction of the responsible [Commonwealth] Government Minister'.

One use of SPPs by the Coalition government which has been very controversial relates to jointly funded construction projects. In order to receive the Commonwealth funds for jointly funded construction projects, a State must agree that the Commonwealth's Construction Code, which places a number of limitations on the operation of trade unions, will apply to the project. In some instances this requirement was of particular concern to States because the Commonwealth announced the imposition of the conditions only after the joint funding had been negotiated

Another cause for complaint by the States was the Commonwealth's announcement during the 2004 election campaign that it would pay for its share of a joint State–Commonwealth National Water Initiative (NWI) (see below) from funds that the States had expected to receive as National Competition payments. From the point of view of the States this was, in effect, a unilateral decision by the Commonwealth to discontinue the National Competition payments, which amounted to approximately $800 million per annum (NCC 2004: 8). The Commonwealth government argued that under the National Competition Agreement it was not obliged to continue the payments beyond 2005. On the other hand, the States, who had suffered a permanent loss of income as a result of implementing the National Competition Policy (because, for example, privatised utilities were now paying Commonwealth tax rather than dividends to the State), believed that the payments would be a continuing component of the transfer of funds from the Commonwealth to the States.

The role of the States

In theory the States have the option of increasing their own taxation and charges and, during the Fraser Coalition government in 1979, were even invited to levy an income tax surcharge. Some State charges and taxes have certainly been increased. However, other taxes have been reduced and several abandoned: in all States death duties have been abolished, in most States land tax exemptions have been granted, and no State government took up the 1979 option of the income tax surcharge.

At that time Mathews has argued that the States had done little to assert their financial autonomy and had acquiesced in centralised financing:

> [I]t can be explained very easily in political terms, since State leaders not only avoid the responsibility of having to make unpopular taxing and other revenue decisions but gain positive political advantages as champions of State interests against what they claim is a remote and parsimonious Federal government in Canberra. (Mathews 1983: 48)

According to this argument, the squabbles over finances, in which Premiers denounced the stinginess of the Commonwealth, was largely for local publicity purposes.

While it may be true that the States found it convenient to have been able to escape the responsibility for taxation and revenue decisions, the problem remains that it is extremely difficult for any single State government to win the political battle that would be entailed in the introduction of additional taxation (or indeed in the reduction of services). The intensive political campaigns in each of the States for the abolition of death duties is an indication of the problem that State governments face. Abandoning that source of revenue was a move that the States could ill-afford to make, but the political fight to retain the tax (or to reimpose it) was one they could not win. The reintroduction of succession duties or the removal of land tax exemptions would meet now with bitter opposition. Once succession duties had been abolished in Queensland in 1976, the political pressure within each of the other States to do the same intensified. The same is true of State land taxes, payroll tax concessions, charges and royalties.

Since 2000, the GST has yielded much more revenue for the States than had originally been estimated and has significantly improved their budgetary situation. Even so, the High Court's interpretation of section 90 of the Constitution has left the States with only a limited range of taxes, many of which (e.g. payroll tax, land tax and stamp duty on transactions) are politically sensitive because they are seen to be an additional cost to employers and therefore a 'tax on employment'. There is pressure on the States to minimise these taxes because of increasing competition between the States to provide an economically attractive environment for business and commerce and investment.

One consequence of the pressure is that (with the exception of Western Australia) State finances have become more reliant on income from gambling which is one area of expanding revenue. In 2002/03 income from gambling made up approximately 12 per cent of State government own-source revenue (ANU Centre for Gambling Research 2004). State governments (except Western Australia) now appear to have a financial interest in promoting gambling, despite what is claimed to be the adverse impact on other economic areas and the undesirable and costly social consequences of the expansion of the gambling industry.

COMPETITION BETWEEN THE STATES

One feature of the Australian federal system, which is related to State finances, is the economic rivalry and competition between States. State governments are under political pressure to attract investment and industry to their State.

From one point of view, this competition can be seen to be a good feature of the federal system because it creates an incentive for States to provide appropriate infrastructure and public services efficiently. A State with relatively high taxes and government charges, or without the necessary infrastructure, will not be attractive to potential investors.

There are, however, features of the competition between State governments that have a much more negative effect. Large employers can play States off against one another to get concessions, in the form of reduced government charges and taxes or in direct financial assistance, in order to locate their business in a particular State. States are forced into bidding wars against one another to attract or retain businesses. The former Industry Commission argued that State governments often face a dilemma. Although they can ill afford to make concessions, and can do so only to the detriment of other employers and taxpayers in the State, they cannot afford to do nothing while businesses in the State are being induced to relocate, and new business investment is being attracted, to other States (Industry Commission 1996).

HORIZONTAL FISCAL EQUALISATION

A longstanding aspect of intergovernmental financial relations is the distribution of Commonwealth grants *among* the States on an equalising basis. Until the early 1980s, the process of horizontal fiscal equalisation involved the payment by the Commonwealth of additional funds as special assistance grants to those States which were assessed by the Commonwealth Grants Commission (CGC) as being financially disadvantaged (as explained above). Since 1982, equalisation has been sought not through making extra payments to some States: rather, the Grants Commission calculates per-capita 'relativities for distributing among the States the pool of general revenue assistance made by the Commonwealth' (CGC 1996: 6). Under the 1999 Intergovernmental Agreement the same fiscal equalisation principle is now applied to the distribution of the GST revenue among the States. Table 7.1 shows the per-capita relativities determined

TABLE 7.1	Per-capita relativities for the distribution of GST and health care grants to the States, estimated distribution to the States and the impact of fiscal equalisation, 2005–06			
	Per-capita relativities	Distribution using relativities ($ million)	Distribution on equal per-capita basis ($ million)	Difference due to equalisation[1] ($ million)
NSW	0.86846	13 090	15 069	−1 979
VIC	0.87552	9 783	11 171	−1 388
QLD	1.04389	9 240	8 850	+390
WA	1.02500	4 603	4 490	+113
SA	1.20325	4 107	3 413	+694
TAS	1.55299	1 672	1 076	+596
ACT	1.14300	822	720	+103
NT	4.26682	1 921	450	+1 471

1. The difference is the amount each State 'gains' or 'loses' as a result of fiscal equalisation on the basis of the CGC relativities as opposed to an equal per-capita distribution.

Source: Commonwealth of Australia (2005: 1, 3 & 12); CGC (2005: xi).

by the CGC for 2005/06 and the resultant per-capita distribution of GST revenue and health care grants among the States, and the effect of the fiscal equalisation relativities as compared with an equal per-capita distribution.

Fiscal equalisation has always been controversial, especially in New South Wales and Victoria. Its purpose is to create some equity between the residents of all States in terms of their access to government services, such that the apportionment of Commonwealth grants between the States should enable each State to provide a similar level of services with similar levels of taxation. It is defended on the grounds that it is an important aspect of the maintenance of one Australian community in which all citizens have roughly equal access to the services that governments provide.

Critics of fiscal equalisation argue that it produces and maintains inefficiencies in the allocation of resources. The States that lose by the transfer of funds have always objected, but in recent years their complaints have also become more strident. Since the late 1980s, as State budgets came under more pressure, the Victorian and New South Wales governments have joined forces to campaign for the abolition or reduction of the differentials. The taxpayers of their States, they have argued, are subsidising the rest of Australia, and their budget situation would be greatly improved if all States received an equal per-capita share. This pressure from the two most populous States is certain to continue, and the competition between the States over the share of Commonwealth grants will remain an important feature of the federal system.

STRENGTHS OF THE STATES?

The legal and financial balance in the federation has moved in favour of the Commonwealth at the expense of the States. Despite this, the States have often been able to exercise considerable bargaining power in their dealing with the Commonwealth. There are several reasons for this.

First, notwithstanding the constitutional shift of power, the States retain the power to make laws over an enormously wide range of issues, and the areas in which the States have clear constitutional responsibility relate to government services that are close to the everyday concerns of voters: education, hospitals, law and order, housing, urban planning, local government, and urban transport.

To bypass that law-making power, the Commonwealth has had to resort to complex and indirect legal devices or financial leverage. For example, the use of the external affairs power by the Commonwealth to legislate on State matters has been very controversial, and in each case there have been political costs to the Commonwealth. Commonwealth governments have been reluctant to use the power, and have only done so when, on balance, there was political support for the move.

The States, in providing the bulk of government services, remain the largest public sector employer, accounting for nearly three-quarters of all civilian public employees. State budgets account for almost 43 per cent of total government spending, and the States are responsible for the building and maintenance of most public infrastructure (ABS 2005a, 2005b). The microeconomic reform programs of the Hawke and Keating governments—to renew public infrastructure and reform the operation of the energy and transport services—could not have been be carried out without the cooperation of the States.

Second, the power exercised by the Commonwealth through its financial dominance and its use of tied grants has not always translated into policy control. The conditions attached to some tied grants are very detailed and restrictive, but other grants are quite general and leave the States with wide discretion in the spending of the funds. In addition, SPPs, though they can be seen as an intrusion by the Commonwealth into State policy areas, have not always worked against the interest of State governments in terms of relations with the electorate and winning political support. State politicians have been very skilful at taking credit for Commonwealth-funded projects and at directing blame onto the Commonwealth for deficiencies or cutbacks in the programs.

Third, in the conflict between the two tiers of government there is a political dimension which has often worked in favour of the States and against the Commonwealth. In some open conflicts the States have been able to out-manoeuvre the Commonwealth and win support for their cause in the name of 'States' rights'. In the past local loyalties and suspicion of Canberra has played an important role in maintaining the strength of the States. Sharman (1990: 108) argues that in Queensland, Tasmania and Western Australia, for example, there are longstanding 'feelings of vague hostility to Canberra'. Regional loyalties are 'reinforced by the differing needs and patterns of development of the various States and by the existence of distinct state political cultures'. In a battle for political support, the Commonwealth has often been restricted in its ability to appeal to regional identification. Premiers can pursue the particular concerns of their constituency but the Commonwealth has needed to give the appearance of being above sectional interests and of acting in the interests of the whole nation.

Intergovernmental conflict and collaboration

In the conflict between the two tiers of government there have been some initiatives by the Commonwealth that have not been resisted by the States. Through its funding of tertiary education, for example, the Commonwealth now effectively controls university education, even though it has no direct constitutional powers in the area, and there has been little or no resistance from the States.

In other areas, the Commonwealth has been able to win political support nationally for intervention in areas of State responsibility against the wishes of a State government. In 1978 the Coalition government, under Malcolm Fraser, used the Commonwealth's power to regulate exports to prevent sand mining on Fraser Island in defiance of the Queensland government. The Hawke Labor government alienated voters in Tasmania, but won support nationally, when in 1983 it used the Commonwealth's external affairs power to prevent the construction of the Franklin Dam. It also intervened to prevent logging of the Daintree rainforest in Queensland, and in 1988 to prevent woodchipping in the Lemonthyme and Southern Forests of Tasmania. In each case, the Commonwealth government made the calculation that the electoral backlash within the State was outweighed by nationwide electoral support.

One matter that was seen as a 'win' for the Commonwealth was the Howard government's success in forcing apparently reluctant States to pass uniform firearms legislation following the Port Arthur massacre in April 1996. The Commonwealth had no clear constitutional powers in the area but was able to persuade all States to agree to national uniform gun laws. The Commonwealth's persistence in this matter, and the eventual agreement by all State governments, despite well-organised resistance from the 'gun lobby', was due to overwhelming public support for the measures across Australia.

In other cases, however, Commonwealth governments have been much less successful, and the States appeared to be anything but powerless and irrelevant. The political power of the States was strikingly demonstrated under the Whitlam government. As already described, Whitlam came to office in 1972 with a policy for direct Commonwealth involvement in areas of State responsibility using SPPs to the States, and for bypassing the States with direct payments to local government and other regional groups. As Whitlam's 'new federalism' policy was put into effect, the government faced increasing political opposition from the States. The capacity of the States to mobilise 'anti-Canberra' forces and to become a rallying point for opposition to the Commonwealth played a significant role in the electoral reaction against the 'power-hungry' Whitlam government. Ironically the centralist policy of Whitlam politicised federal relations and appeared to give strength to the 'States' rights' sentiment in the electorate.

In its early years the Hawke Labor government attempted to avoid the sort of political difficulties Whitlam had experienced with the States. With the exception of the intervention in Tasmania to prevent the construction of the Franklin Dam, the Hawke government tried to avoid conflict with the States. By the end of the 1980s, however, there were a growing number of policy areas in which intergovernmental friction came to the surface and, as the Hawke government cut back on its grants to the States, the Premiers became increasingly combative. In 1990, following a particularly acrimonious Premiers' Conference, Hawke proposed a review of the whole federal system in Australia. By the second half of 1991 progress was made in achieving intergovernmental cooperation and coordination on a range of microeconomic reform areas: interstate road and rail transport, ports, energy, uniform food and labelling standards. When Keating, a strong centralist, succeeded Hawke as Prime Minister in 1991 the process of reform of the federal system broke down. In 1992, however, Keating did agree to the establishment of the Council of Australian Governments (COAG), comprising the Prime Minister, the Premiers and Chief Ministers and the President of the Australian Local Government Association, which would meet twice a year to discuss intergovernmental matters.

The outcome of these initiatives have been described as *collaborative federalism*. Although cooperative arrangements between the States and the Commonwealth were not new, Martin Painter (1998) argues that the changes instigated by Hawke and Keating in the early 1990s marked a 'fundamental reshaping' of Australian federalism.

> State and Commonwealth governments [cooperated] ever more closely on joint schemes of policy and administration. As a consequence there has been a shift in the rules of the game of federal politics towards collaborative, as distinct from arm's length, patterns of intergovernmental relations. While conflict and political sparring remain commonplace, state and Commonwealth ministers and officials are more and more … devising joint schemes of policy and administration that emphasis national uniformity and the removal of interstate barriers and differences. (Painter 1998:1)

The Howard Coalition government came to office in 1996 with a stated policy which rejected what it claimed was the centralism of the defeated Labor government. From the outset, however, the Coalition government clashed with the States and throughout its first three terms it was often in conflict with the States over finances. During its third term, the Coalition government appeared to be adopting a more centralist position, making a number of proposals to take greater control in areas of State responsibility, such as vocational training, schools, industrial relations and hospitals.

In July 2004 intergovernmental relations appeared in a more positive light when all States (except Western Australia and Tasmania) came to an agreement with the Commonwealth to jointly fund the National Water Initiative (NWI); a scheme designed to improve the management of surface and ground water in Australia and to increase the amount and quality of water in the rivers of the Murray–Darling Basin. The Agreement was welcomed by political leaders from the States and the Commonwealth, and by commentators, as an important achievement in federal cooperation which would provide a solution to what had been an intractable problem caused by divided sovereignty. The goodwill, however, was short lived due to the Commonwealth's unilateral changes to the financial arrangements as described on page 146.

The October 2004 federal election, at which the Howard government won a majority in both chambers of the Parliament, appears to have been a turning point, after which the Coalition adopted a more uncompromising centralist position and a more combative approach to the States. Following the election there was an ongoing battle of words between the Commonwealth and the States, with each blaming the other for problems with the health system (including a shortage of doctors and medical specialists and long waiting lists in public hospitals) and adequacy of Australia's infrastructure (the ports and transport systems). The Commonwealth became increasingly assertive, demanding that the States repeal some direct taxes (see above) and indicated that it intended to press ahead with a number of measures relating to areas of State responsibility including industrial relations, public hospitals, vocational training, the ports and education.

The NWI became the cause of further intergovernmental dispute when the Commonwealth announced that its payments would be conditional on the States agreeing to comply with a range of Commonwealth policies and practices, including the industrial relations provisions in the Commonwealth's constructions code. A Queensland Minister said that his State had signed up to the NWI in the belief that it was a partnership; the Commonwealth had imposed the conditions only after the States had agreed to participate in the scheme. He said '[n]o business would sign up to a contract like this . . . [T]his isn't an agreement, this is extortion. This is the federal government at its meanest and trickiest best, and it's certainly no way to conduct a partnership about how to manage the nation's most precious resource' (*Australian Financial Review*, 18 May 2005).

With a backdrop of intense intergovernmental disputes, it was anticipated that the COAG meeting in June 2005 would simply result in more confrontation between the Prime Minister and the Premiers. Against these predictions, however, the Premiers said that they were satisfied with the spirit in which the meeting was conducted and with the outcome, and the Prime Minister said that it was 'the most productive COAG meeting he had been to in his nine years as Prime Minister' (*Australian Financial Review*, 4–5 June 2005). Although the States did not agree to one of the Commonwealth's prime requests—the transfer of their industrial relations powers to the Commonwealth—and indicated that they would challenge the constitutional validity of any Commonwealth industrial relations legislation in the High Court, there was agreement to cooperate on most other potentially divisive issues that came before the meeting. COAG agreed to:
- establish a working party on restructuring the federal arrangements to improve the health system
- create a national approach to vocational education and training
- establish a national approach to the planning for and regulation of ports and export-related infrastructure
- investigate ways of extending the National Competition Policy
- retain the National Water Initiative (COAG 2005).

The cooperative arrangements that emerged from the COAG meeting, although unexpected in the context of the heated disagreement that had preceded the meeting, are not an unusual feature of the workings of the Australian federal system. As argued above, collaborative arrangements became a common feature of intergovernmental relations in the early 1990s. Increasingly intergovernmental agreements, in which the Commonwealth was able to use its financial power to dictate, or at least influence, policy outcomes related to important areas of State responsibility. The 2005 COAG meeting appears to have extended even further the process by which the Commonwealth has become involved in matters for which it has no direct constitutional responsibility.

The politics of federalism

Because federalism by its nature divides power and is a check on government, the federalist ideal is associated with a *liberal* belief that government should be limited and decentralised. On the other hand, for those who see the need for strong effective government that is capable of carrying out a mandate for social and economic change, federal structures are an encumbrance. Even with overwhelming public support, the government of the whole nation may be impeded in pursuing a range of policies. According to this view, federalism frustrates government and 'inhibits change' (Maddox 2005: 184).

For most of the history of the Australian federation the two major political party groupings were portrayed as being clearly divided on the question of federalism, with the Labor Party perceived as anti-federalist and the Liberal and National parties as pro-federalist. Labor's traditional concern for the nation-wide regulation of industry, commerce and industrial relations were seen to require strong central government. The non-Labor side of politics has been concerned to maintain constitutional limitations on government in support of liberal values and 'small government' policies, and hence has tended to support the federal division of power. However, this was only ever a rough generalisation. The major political parties are themselves federal in structure and have often been internally divided on the issue of federalism. While Commonwealth Labor governments have often been frustrated by federalism, State Labor governments have used State jurisdictions to pursue Labor policies and have often held out to protect the powers of the States against the Commonwealth.

Liberal–National Coalition governments at the Commonwealth level have been reluctant to give up power, and some past Liberal Prime Ministers — notably John Gorton in the late 1960s and Malcolm Fraser in the late 1970s — clashed with State governments, and Liberal State branches, over their use of Commonwealth power. Even so, the Liberal Party has presented itself as a champion of federalism. The Howard government came to office in 1996 with the promise that it would reverse the centralism of the previous Labor government. In its third and fourth terms, however, it dropped any pretence of respecting the constitutional powers of the States. As described above, in the period following the 2004 federal election the Coalition government embarked on a concerted attack on the States and appeared to see some political advantage in being in conflict with the States.

To some extent the willingness of Coalition Ministers to 'take on' the States and Territories, all of which have had Labor governments since 2002, could be explained by partisan politics. John Howard, rejecting the proposition that he had abandoned the traditional Liberal Party commitment to federalism, argued that his position was that of a 'nationalist' not a centralist. His government's actions in relation to the States, he argued, were necessary because the States were failing 'to deliver what the nation needs' (Howard 2005). There is no doubt, however, that the statements and actions of the Coalition government represented a clear reversal of the traditional Liberal Party position and of its stated policy in the party platform.

As of mid-2005, the federal system appears to be in a state of flux. From one point of view the changes in the system—the more dominant role being taken by the Commonwealth and the increased intergovernmental collaboration—are welcome developments. For those who see the Constitution as outdated, and the divided sovereignty as a cause of inefficiency, and States' rights as an impediment to democratically elected national governments, the agreements and cooperation between the two tiers of government, and the development of joint programs, are a way of overcoming the 'problems' caused by federalism and of making government more effective.

From the point of view of some supporters of a federalist structure, however, the essential features, and the benefits, of a federal system are being undermined. The federal division of governmental powers in the written Constitution no longer describes the reality of Australian government. The demarcation of government responsibilities between the two tiers of government has become blurred and power has become too concentrated at the centre. Decisions of the High Court have too greatly expanded the law making power of the Commonwealth at the expense of the States and the States have become too financially dependant on the Commonwealth. From this federalist point of view intergovernmental agreements further undermine the federal structure. The joint programs, in which the Commonwealth's financial power allows it to dictate the terms, can transform the States into agents of Commonwealth policy. The States are no longer independent political entities which are sovereign in their own areas of constitutional responsibility. To the extent that the constitutional division of power is eroded, the benefits of federalism—diversity, the accommodation of regional difference, protections against the concentration of power—are diminished.

According to one observer,

[t]he most likely scenario is one where the States continue to slide, none too gracefully and with occasional rallies, into a position of increasing subservience . . . The

same forces which have driven the federation over the past half-century will presumably continue to drive it . . . The Senate will never give allegiance to the States. The High Court will continue to interpret the enumerated powers of the Commonwealth broadly and, if anything, more broadly than before. (Craven 1992: 68–9, and see Craven 2005)

It is certainly true that the Australian federal system no longer conforms (if it ever did) to the federal model in which each tier of government operates within the limits of its discrete constitutionally defined powers. However, it is not the case that the States have become completely powerless or irrelevant. The Commonwealth must still operate within the Constitution and, while it can, in some areas, completely bypass the States, in many policy areas relating to service delivery, it must negotiate with, and work through, the States. One matter which affects the bargaining strength of the States is the level of political support for them and for States' rights. As argued above there have been periods when the States have been able to outmanoeuvre the Commonwealth and counteract its jurisdictional and financial supremacy with their political strength.

It is possible that with developments in communications and the mass media regional loyalties and States' rights are becoming politically less significant. At the time of writing, despite the best efforts of Labor Premiers in all States, there had not been the same political reaction against the centralism of the Coalition government as there was against the Whitlam government in the 1970s. It is yet to be seen whether the Howard government's initiatives will ultimately engender a political reaction in support of States' rights or whether other changes in Australian society have lessened the importance of regional loyalties.

An example of a State government successfully using regional loyalties as a political weapon against the Howard government arose out of Commonwealth plans to establish a low-level nuclear waste repository near Woomera in outback South Australia. The South Australian government campaigned against the establishment of the repository and in July 2004 won a case in the Federal Court in which the Court found that the Commonwealth had not satisfied the requirements of its own legislation in compulsorily acquiring the land for the facility. It was open to the Commonwealth to persist in its plans but to have done so could have been electorally costly for the Coalition. With an election only several months away, the Coalition government decided against a further disputation with the State government and abandoned the proposal. In this case the Commonwealth did have the constitutional power to carry out its plans and the objections of South Australian voters were as much about not wanting the nuclear waste 'in their backyard' as it was about defending States' rights, but it does demonstrate the potential of political opinion to be mobilised within a State against the Commonwealth. It is not yet evident whether the States will be able to rally opinion against the Commonwealth on a wider range of issues or whether the States' rights has lost some of its effectiveness as a weapon for the States.

Conclusion

There have been strong centralising forces working within the Australian federation over the century or so of its existence. Since 1901 the role of the Commonwealth as national government has become increasingly important, both domestically and in Australia's relations with the rest of the world, and to a large extent this has been at the expense of the States. The Commonwealth has become financially dominant and is able to use SPPs to influence policy in areas of State responsibility. The federal division of governmental power has been further eroded by the development of collaborative arrangements between the two tiers of government. From one point of view these development have completely undermined the federal nature of the Australian political system.

While it is the case that the Australian system does not fit the ideal model of a federal system it is not the case that States have become completely irrelevant or powerless. The Commonwealth cannot completely circumvent the States; it must still act within constitutional limitations and, in many policy areas, it must deal with the States. In those dealings with the States its financial strength gives the Commonwealth great leverage but does not give it a free hand.

One of the States' strengths has been their political leverage. At the beginning of its fourth term the Howard Coalition government appeared to win a number of political battles against the States. However, it is not yet clear whether that signals a permanent shift in the political balance in intergovernmental relations or whether, as has happened before, there will be a political reaction against the centralist policies of the Commonwealth. Whatever the case, developments in this area in coming years will be vital in shaping intergovernmental relations, and more broadly, the nature of government in Australia.

REFERENCES

ABS [Australian Bureau of Statistics] 2005a, 'Wages and Salary Earners, Public Sector, Australia', Canberra, <http://www.abs.gov.au/Ausstats/>.

ABS 2005b, 'Government Finance: Total Public Sector, All Australian Governments Combined', Table 27.1, Canberra, <http://www.abs.gov.au/Ausstats/>.

ANU Centre for Gambling Research 2004, *Gambling Government Revenue: All Australian States and Territories*, ANU Centre for Gambling Research, Canberra.

Bradsen, J. 1990, 'Judicial Review and the Changing Federal Balance of Power', in *Government, Politics and Power in Australia*, eds J. Summers, D. Woodward & A. Parkin, 4th edn, Longman Cheshire, Melbourne.

CGC [Commonwealth Grants Commission] 1993, *Report on General Revenue Grant Relativities, Volume I Main Report*, AGPS, Canberra.

CGC 1996, *Report on General Revenue Grant Relativities: 1996 Update*, AGPS, Canberra.

CGC 1999, *Report on General Revenue Grant Relativities, Volume I Main Report*, Commonwealth Grants Commission, Canberra.

CGC 2005, *Report on State Revenue Sharing Relativities: 2005 Update*, Commonwealth Grants Commission, Canberra.

COAG [Council of Australian Governments] 2005, *Communiqué*, Canberra, 3 June, <http://www.coag.gov.au/meeting/030605coag030605.pdf>, accessed 24/6/05.

Commonwealth of Australia 1996, *Budget Paper no. 3: Commonwealth Financial Relations with Other Levels of Government 1996–97*, AGPS, Canberra.

Commonwealth of Australia 2000, *Budget Paper no. 3: Commonwealth Financial Relations with Other Levels of Government 2000–01*, AGPS, Canberra.

Commonwealth of Australia 2003, *2003–04 Budget Paper no. 3: Federal Financial Relations 2003–04*, Commonwealth of Australia, Canberra.

Commonwealth of Australia 2005, *2005–06 Budget Paper no. 3: Federal Financial Relations 2005–06*, Commonwealth of Australia, Canberra.

Craven, G. 1992, 'The States—Decline, Fall or What?', in *Australian Federation: Towards the Second Century*, ed. G. Craven, Melbourne University Press, Melbourne.

Craven, G. 2005, 'Federalism', *Policy*, vol. 21, no. 2, Winter.

Crisp, L. F. 1983, *Australian National Government*, 5th edn, Longman Cheshire, Melbourne.

Galligan, B. 1987, *The Politics of the High Court*, University of Queensland Press, Brisbane.

Groenewegen, P. 1983, 'The Fiscal Crisis of Australian Federalism', in *Australian Federalism: Future Tense*, eds A. Patience & J. Scott, Oxford University Press, Melbourne.

Hilmer, F. (chair) 1993, *National Competition Policy: Report of the Independent Committee of Inquiry*, AGPS, Canberra.

Howard, J. 2005, 'Reflections on Australian Federalism', Transcript of speech given to the Menzies Research Centre, Melbourne, 11 April.

Industry Commission 1996, *State, Territory and Local Government Assistance to Industry: Draft Report*, Industry Commission, Canberra.

James, D. 1992, *Intergovernmental Financial Relations in Australia*, Australia Tax Research Foundation, Sydney.

Maddox, G. 2005, *Australian Democracy in Theory and Practice*, 4th edn, Pearson Education, Sydney.

Mathews, R. 1983, 'The Commonwealth–State Financial Contract', in *A Fractured Federation?*, eds J. Aldred & J. Wilkes, Allen & Unwin, Sydney.

McEvoy, K. & Summers, J. 1996, 'South Australia and the High Court', in *South Australia, Federalism and Public Policy*, ed. A. Parkin, Federalism Research Centre, ANU, Canberra.

NCC [National Competition Council] 2004, *Annual Report 2003–2004*, AusInfo, Canberra.

Painter, M. 1998, *Collaborative Federalism: Economic Reform in Australia in the 1990s*, Cambridge, Melbourne.

Sawer, G. 1963, *Australian Federal Politics and the Law, 1929–1945*, Melbourne University Press, Melbourne.

Sawer, G. 1977, *Federation Under Strain: Australia 1972–1975*, Melbourne University Press, Melbourne.

Sharman, C. 1990, 'The Commonwealth, the States and Federalism', in *Government, Politics and Power in Australia*, eds J. Summers, D. Woodward & A. Parkin, 4th edn, Longman Cheshire, Melbourne.

Solomon, D. 1992, *The Political Impact of the High Court*, Allen & Unwin, Sydney.

WADT&F [Western Australia Department of Treasurery and Finance] 2005, *Common-*

wealth-State Finance, Perth, <http://www.dtf.wa.gov.au/cms/tre_content.asp?ID=775>, accessed 27/5/05.

LEGAL CASES

Amalgamated Society of Engineers v *Adelaide Steamship Co. Ltd* ('Engineers case') (1920) 28 CLR 129.

Bank Nationalisation case, see *Bank of New South Wales* v *Commonwealth* (1948) 76 CLR 1.

Bank of New South Wales v *Commonwealth* (1948) 76 CLR 1.

Commonwealth v *Tasmania* (1983) 158 CLR 1.

Concrete Pipes case, see *Strickland* v *Rocla Concrete Pipes Ltd* (1971) 124 CLR 468.

Dam case, see *Commonwealth* v *Tasmania* (1983) 158 CLR 1.

Engineers case, see *Amalgamated Society of Engineers* v *Adelaide Steamship Co. Ltd* (1920) 28 CLR 129.

Federal Roads case, see *Victoria* v *Commonwealth* (1926) 38 CLR 399.

Federated Amalgamated Government Railway and Tramway Service Association v *New South Wales Railway Traffic Employees Association* (Railway Servant's case) (1906) 4 CLR 488.

Ha v *New South Wales* (1997) 189 CLR 465.

James v *Commonwealth* (1936) 55 CLR 1.

Koowarta v *Bjelke-Petersen* (1982) 153 CLR 168.

Lemonthyme and Southern Forests case, see *Richardson* v *Forestry Commission* (1987–88) 164 CLR 261.

Railway Servant's case, see *Federated Amalgamated Government Railway and Tramway Service Association* v *New South Wales Railway Traffic Employers Association* (1906) 4 CLR 488.

Richardson v *Forestry Commission* (1987–88) 164 CLR 261.

South Australia v *Commonwealth* (1942) 55 CLR 373.

Strickland v *Rocla Concrete Pipes Ltd* (1971) 124 CLR 468.

Uniform Tax case, see *South Australia* v *Commonwealth* (1942) 55 CLR 373.

Victoria v *Commonwealth* (1926) 38 CLR 399.

CLR = Commonwealth Law Reports

The High Court

HAIG PATAPAN

An independent judiciary, separate from the executive and legislative arms of the state, is an indispensable feature of a liberal-democratic system of government. It is the independence and separation from the other organs of the state that enables the judiciary to serve the 'liberal' function of protecting against untrammelled governmental power.

The High Court is at the apex of Australia's judicial system. Because it is an institution that adjudicates constitutional disputes and decides major common law questions that fundamentally influence the nature of the polity, it is also a profoundly political institution. This chapter examines the political significance of the High Court by exploring the way it has changed as an institution, assumed an increasingly pivotal role in the determination of political questions, and thereby helped to delineate the character of Australian democracy.

These changes are most evident in the nature of the decisions that the Court has handed down and in their implications for Australia's other political institutions. Accordingly, this chapter evaluates some of the Court's most important recent judgments, especially its decisions on implied constitutional rights and native title, to see how it is shaping politics. The chapter concludes by contemplating the practical and theoretical limitations on the Court's ability to influence Australian democracy, and its future role as an institution of governance in Australia.

The High Court as a political institution

The High Court is made up of seven judges (formally entitled Justices), appointed by federal Cabinet on the recommendation of the Attorney-General, who is required to consult the States. Once appointed, judges cannot be removed except for misbehaviour or incapacity; they have security of tenure until they turn 70, when they must retire.

The High Court of Australia is entrenched in Chapter III of the Australian Constitution, which specifies the judicial power, jurisdiction and independence of the Court. The Court interprets and applies the law of Australia, including Australian common law (the unwritten law derived from the traditional law of England as developed by judicial interpretation). It also decides cases of special federal significance, including challenges to the constitutional validity of laws, and hears appeals, by special leave, from federal, State and Territory courts.

The framers of the Australian Constitution sought to establish a US-style judiciary that would exercise federal judicial review, whereby the laws passed by the Parliaments of the Commonwealth or of the States are examined to determine whether they are in accordance with the allocation and demarcation of powers set down in the Constitution (Thomson 1986). Such a role for the High Court was thought necessary in a federal system because it was considered essential to have an impartial and disinterested party to negotiate the disputes that would inevitably arise between States and the Commonwealth. As the Constitution was seen primarily as a legal document, the judiciary was the natural choice for such an interpretive and adjudicative role. Thus the founders envisaged the Court to be an arbitrator of federalism and a defender of the Constitution.

It took some time for the High Court to cement its place at the apex of Australia's legal system. This is because Australia's transformation into an independent, sovereign state was a gradual, evolutionary process, finally recognised by the enactment of the *Australia Acts* in Australia and the UK in 1986, which formally terminated the power of the UK Parliament to legislate for Australia. These gradual changes were mirrored in the increasing authority of the High Court within the Australian legal system, most importantly in its gradual transformation into the final court of appeal in Australia with the freedom to determine its own legal direction (Galligan 1986; Bennett 1980; Sawer 1956, 1963). Though the majority of founders intended the High Court to be Australia's supreme court of appeal, the Constitution retained appeals to the Imperial Privy Council in London as a result of compromises made when the Constitution was formally enacted at Westminster (La Nauze 1972). As a result the High Court was not the final court of appeal until 1986, when the final avenue of appeal to the Privy Council was abolished.

The constitutional decisions by the Court have had major political consequences. For example, by upholding the Commonwealth's wartime income tax legislation in 1942, the Court's decision allowed the Commonwealth to implement nationally uniform taxation, making it politically difficult for the States to impose income tax. Later decisions expanding the meaning of 'excise' (an exclusive taxation power given to the Commonwealth by section 90 of the Constitution) completed the fiscal dominance of the Commonwealth.[1] In a series of decisions between 1945 and 1949 on the interpretation of section 92 of the Constitution—which requires that 'trade, commerce and intercourse among the States . . . shall be absolutely free'—the Court blocked Labor's postwar reconstruction program that had envisaged national ownership of airlines and banking and a comprehensive system of social services.[2] In 1982, as this chapter describes below, a judgment concerning the validity of a contract entered into by the Aboriginal Development Commission upheld the Commonwealth *Racial Discrimination Act 1975*, establishing a new basis for the recognition of the rights and claims of Indigenous Australians.[3] The Court's rejection the following year of Tasmania's challenge to the Commonwealth's *National Parks and Wildlife Act 1975* (which prohibited the construction of a dam in a World Heritage-listed area) was based on a broad interpretation of the Commonwealth's external affairs power (section 51(xxix)), reconfiguring environmental politics in Australia and more fundamentally altering the legal foundations of Australian federalism.[4]

In these cases major political issues, principally concerning the federal division of powers, were resolved by the Court in the course of it determining the validity of often-obscure legislation. In the view of the majority of Justices, they were decided as *legal* questions, not taking into account the *political* implications of the case. It is not surprising that the Court understood its role to be essentially legal given the primacy of Parliament and representative democracy in shaping what is conventionally regarded as the political sphere. In the words of Sir Owen Dixon, former Chief Justice of the High Court and one of Australia's most eminent jurists, 'strict and complete legalism' was necessary for the Court's independence (Dixon 1965; Craven 1992).

This 'legalist' view of the Court's proper role was, however, challenged by changes that gave it a much greater prominence in Australian public life. Its entrenchment as the final court of appeal in 1986, as noted above, was one of these changes. Other changes emphasised the High Court's role as a national court. A federal Court of Appeal was established in 1976 specifically to free the High Court to decide constitutional issues and appeals of national importance. In 1979 Commonwealth legislation gave the Court maximum independence to manage its building, staff and finances. This increasing importance was symbolised by the construction of a new High Court building in 1980, close to Parliament House in Canberra. The Court's procedures also reflected its growing stature. By 1984 most non-constitutional appeals to the Court required special leave, which was granted only when they raised important public issues or questions of law (O'Brien 1996).

These institutional changes coincided with important international legal developments to which Australia—as a sovereign independent nation now taking a greater role in international affairs—was exposing itself. One of the most significant of these developments was the increasing importance of human rights in international law. Unlike some other courts of final jurisdiction (e.g. the US and Canadian Supreme Courts), the Australian High Court has not been in a position to draw upon a Bill of Rights, various attempts to enact a constitutional or statutory Bill of Rights in Australia having proven unsuccessful (Williams 1999a; Charlesworth 1993; Galligan 1990; Bailey 1990). However, the Australian government began committing itself to a growing number of international human rights covenants and conventions, raising questions about the High Court's ability to play some sort of mediation role with respect to the recognition of rights. Moreover, there were increasing challenges to the assumption that notions of responsible government and parliamentary democracy, which prescribed a limited role for the judiciary, were sufficient to protect fundamental rights. To those advocates who sought to use the judiciary to protect rights, the reality of party discipline, executive dominance over Parliament and the increasing power of the administrative state represented an insufficiently checked and insufficiently accountable power in Australian politics. In short, responsible government and parliamentary democracy represented an arena where—legitimised by 'democratic' principles such as majority rule—executive government could threaten the liberal principles enshrining individual rights and freedoms.

It was in this context that the Court turned to a recognition of individual rights and freedoms, premised on a new view of the Constitution as a 'social contract' rather than merely an Imperial statute (Mason 1989; Toohey 1993).

The new politics of the High Court

It was especially during the tenure of Sir Anthony Mason as Chief Justice of the High Court, referred to as the Mason Court (1987–1995), that the High Court augmented its traditional federal judicial review with a new politics that engaged with these fundamental liberal-democratic issues. Since then, subsequent decisions by the Brennan Court (1995–1998) and the Gleeson Court (1999 to the time of writing) have tended to show greater restraint in the extension and elaboration of these issues. An insight into these changes can be gained by examining the claim made during this period by a majority of Justices that the Court 'makes' the law, by considering its decisions on rights and freedoms, and by analysing its groundbreaking decisions on native title (e.g. Galligan 1986; Zines 1997; Solomon 1999; Patapan 2000).

INTERPRETATION OF LAWS

The traditional view that judges interpret and declare the law, not make it, has been rejected by a majority of the Court in recent years in favour of a new approach to interpretation, described variously as a 'dynamic' or 'policy' approach (Mason 1996a, 1996b; Gleeson 1999; Lindell 1994). This new method, which requires judges to take into account community values in interpreting legislation, is said to acknowledge openly those values that were previously only implicit in the Court's judgments, exposing them to general debate and thereby making judicial decision making more open and accountable.

But admitting that the Court in some sense 'makes' the law raises a number of difficulties. The main objection is that, in a democracy, law-making should be undertaken by the people or their representatives; judges, who are unelected, should not usurp this legislative role. The retort to this objection has been that the Court has a proper and legitimate role in repairing and keeping the law up to date with changing community values (Brennan 1993; Mason 1995; Preston & Sampford 1996; Gleeson 1997). If community values shape, guide and constrain the judiciary, then it is possible through such arguments to justify judicial law-making as another form of representative governance. By construing the community to include practitioners, scholars and the larger deliberative community, so this argument goes, it may be possible to have more representative and therefore authoritative decisions by the Court. Clear judgments that are a consequence of public debate are more likely to reach an outcome in accord with the principles of the polity; at the very least they will gain wider support and acceptance in the community. Yet there are major questions about this argument, such as the nature of such a community, and the judiciary's ability to discern (while perhaps shaping) community values. Perhaps aware of these concerns, more recent statements by Chief Justice Gleeson indicate a return to 'legalism' as the proper basis for judicial interpretation by the High Court. According to Gleeson, the judicial task is one of interpretation, not creativity (Gleeson 2000; 2001).

This continuing debate regarding approaches to interpretation reveals the changing role of the Court and its willingness to make its judgments clearer and more accessible to the general public and in doing so, expose itself to what it considers informed criticism.

RIGHTS AND FREEDOMS

The Constitution has few explicit rights guarantees.[5] The move by a majority of the Mason Court in the 1990s to discern rights and freedoms as implications from the Constitution has been described by its critics as 'judicial activism' (Craven 1999).

The Court indicated its new approach in two decisions handed down on the same day in 1992, the *Nationwide News* and the *Australian Capital Television* cases.[6] In these cases, the Court declared that there was implicit in the Constitution a 'right of political communication' that limited the laws Parliament could make, for example, in enacting legislation regulating political advertising.[7] Subsequently, in *Theophanous* (1994), the Court held that such a constitutional right of political communication could be relied on as a defence in a defamation action.[8]

These cases suggested that the Court's implied rights decisions could, in time, build up to an extensive judicially created Bill of Rights (e.g. see Symposium on Rights 1994). But this possibility was then checked by the Court's decision in *McGinty* (1996), where it held that the principle of 'one vote one value' was not an essential aspect of representative government and therefore could not be invoked as a constitutional principle to overturn Western Australia's malapportioned electoral system.[9]

McGinty was followed by two decisions which reconsidered *Theophanous*. In *Lange*, a defamation action by former New Zealand Prime Minister David Lange, the Court by a unanimous judgment confirmed the implied constitutional right of political speech but rejected the view that such constitutional entitlements could be used as a defence in a private legal action.[10] *Levy* (1997) concerned attempts by a Mr Laurence Levy to protest against duck hunting in Victoria by entering without a permit areas designated as accessible only with a permit.[11] He argued that Victorian legislation limiting access to such areas was unconstitutional because it infringed this new constitutional principle of free political speech. Though the Court agreed that actions as well as speech were protected by the implied constitutional right, it rejected Levy's particular claim on the grounds that the right was not absolute, that the Victorian legislation aimed at securing public safety and that it did so in an appropriate way.

Finally, in *Kruger* (1997), a case dealing with the so-called Aboriginal 'stolen generations', the Court indicated its reluctance further to extend its implied rights decisions into new areas.[12] Mr Kruger and others were Aborigines who had been taken from their families when they were young, under the authority of the Northern Territory *Aboriginals Ordinance* which made the Chief Protector of Aboriginals legal guardian of any Aborigine. They claimed that the Ordinance and various related Acts were contrary to implied constitutional rights and guarantees of legal due process, legal equality, and freedom of movement, association and religion. They also argued that the relevant legislation and the actions of the Northern Territory's Chief Protector amounted to genocide and hence were unconstitutional. But a majority of the Court held that the relevant provisions were not invalid by reason of any rights, guarantees, immunities or freedoms contained in the Constitution. The Court also confirmed that such implied rights could not be relied on to commence ordinary legal actions. Thus the *Kruger* case appeared to mark the limits, at least for the present, of the Court's implied rights decisions.

SEPARATION OF POWERS

In addition to its decisions on freedom of political communication, the Court has interpreted the constitutional separation of powers between the judicial and the other arms of the state as an important source for the protection of liberty and thereby a limitation on the scope of parliamentary legislation (Winterton 1994; Zines 1997; Parker 1994). For example, the Court has held that the legislature may not interfere with the judicial process, particularly with the requirements of natural justice.[13] In *Dietrich* (1992), the Court extended the common-law right to a fair trial to recognise a limited notion of a right to legal counsel.[14] The issue in *Dietrich* was whether an accused person charged with a serious crime punishable by imprisonment, but who could not afford to pay for a lawyer, has a right to be provided one at public expense. The majority of the Court held that in such cases a judge should adjourn or stay the trial until legal representation is available. Justices Deane and Gaudron went further by claiming that a fair trial was not just a common-law right; rather, it was entrenched in the Constitution's requirement of the observance of judicial process and fairness, an implicit consequence of the separation of judicial power.[15]

In the *War Crimes* (*Polyukhovich* v *Commonwealth* 1991) case, the High Court decided that the Constitutional separation of judicial power prevented the Commonwealth Parliament from enacting a Bill of Attainder (an enactment that punishes a specified person or group) because it would amount to an invalid usurpation by Parliament of judicial power.[16] A Court majority accepted that Parliament could enact retrospective legislation. But Justices Deane and Gaudron, relying on the separation of judicial powers, again went further in their minority opinion, claiming that Parliament could not make retroactive criminal laws as these would usurp judicial power.[17]

ADMINISTRATION AND *TEOH*

The *Teoh* case (*Minister of State for Immigration and Ethnic Affairs v Ah Hin Teoh* 1995) is important because it shows how the Court, relying on international treaties and conventions, was able to influence the Commonwealth government's administrative decision making. A treaty entered into by the executive arm of government was previously thought to have no legal effect until validly incorporated into Australian law by Parliament (Alston & Chiam 1995; Opeskin & Rothwell 1997). The High Court's *Teoh* decision—which held that mere ratification by the executive government was enough for a 'legitimate expectation' that administrative decision makers would act consistently with a treaty—appeared to undermine this principle.[18]

The case concerned a Malaysian citizen, Mr Teoh, whose application for a permanent entry permit into Australia was refused on the ground of bad character because he had been convicted of drug offences. The government had considered the compassionate argument that Teoh's wife and family faced a bleak future if resident status was refused but it did not find this compelling enough to waive the character requirement. Teoh successfully challenged this decision in the Federal Court. The government then appealed to the High Court to overturn the Federal Court ruling. A majority of the High Court held that, unless Parliament or the executive declared otherwise, the signing by the executive government of an international convention (in this case the *United Nations Convention on the Rights of the Child*) gave rise to a legitimate expectation that the Minister would act in conformity with it by treating the best interest of the applicant's children as a primary consideration.[19] As the Minister had not done so in this case, and the applicant had been denied a fair opportunity to persuade the Minister, the appeal by the government was dismissed.

The *Teoh* decision was praised by some commentators for resolving Australia's 'split personality' on human rights: Australia projects an impressive international commitment to human rights but this, according to these commentators, coexists with an inadequate domestic implementation of multilateral human rights instruments (Charlesworth 1995; Walker 1996). But other commentators condemned the decision for its implied diminution of Australia's political sovereignty: it meant that administrative and policy decisions reached as a result of Australia's democratic political debate and deliberation were now made subject to unaccountable internationally determined principles.

The political response from the Keating Labor government was unfavourable. The Minister for Foreign Affairs called *Teoh* a 'plainly bad decision', creating 'a decision-making environment that is unworkable in practice', upsetting the balance between executive, legislature and judiciary (Evans 1996; Lavarch 1995). The government announced that henceforth a treaty would no longer raise expectations that governmental decision makers would act in accordance with it, nor would it form the basis for challenging administrative decisions if not incorporated into law. It also attempted to pass legislation to displace formally the contrary expectations found by the Court. This legislation, however, had not passed by the time of the 1996 election and then lapsed when the Howard Coalition government took office. In due course, the Howard government affirmed the same position that unincorporated treaties did not give rise to legitimate expectations in administrative law, and it likewise attempted to enact clarifying legislation almost identical to Labor's. But Labor, now in Opposition, decided to oppose this legislation on the grounds that the *Teoh* decision had not caused the problems initially feared.

NATIVE TITLE

Perhaps the most contentious aspect of the new politics of the High Court in the 1990s arose from its decisions on 'native title'. In 1982 a group of Torres Strait Islanders, including Mr Eddie Mabo, commenced legal action against the State of Queensland on behalf of the Meriam people, asking the courts to declare that the Meriam people held native title to the three Murray Islands (Mer, Dauar and Waier). To pre-empt this legal action, the Queensland Parliament in 1985 enacted legislation intended to extinguish any native title rights if they existed. In its *Mabo (No. 1)* decision of 1988, the High Court held that this Queensland legislation was inconsistent with the Commonwealth *Racial Discrimination Act 1975* and therefore was invalid.[20] This allowed the litigation to proceed. The High Court then handed down its judgment on *Mabo (No. 2)* in June 1992.[21] By a 6 to 1 majority, the Court upheld, under certain stringent conditions, the plaintiffs' claim that the common law of Australia recognised native title, rejecting the notion that Australia had been *terra nullius* (literally 'empty land') when it was settled by the British. According to the Court, the content and nature of the rights that may be enjoyed by the owners of native title are determined by the traditional laws and customs observed by those owners.

While this decision raised important issues concerning Indigenous rights, the *Mabo* case revealed the great limitations of addressing such issues as if they were simply legal problems. Though the case succeeded in establishing a vital moral and legal foundation for the claims of Indigenous Australians, it did this within the legal framework of property, using language that had the effect of constricting the terms of debate and consequently the reach of any future political settlement. Here was a case that could have benefited from public deliberation and political compromise rather than legal adjudication.

But perhaps this was what the Court sought to initiate in handing down its decision for, as Chief Justice Mason claimed, native title was one of those controversial questions on which the political community seemed happy to defer to the judiciary (Virtue 1993).

Though the immediate effect of the decision on the litigants was clear — recognising the native title rights of the Meriam people to the Murray Islands — its implications for land use elsewhere in Australia were far from certain. Indigenous people claiming native title would have to justify their claims through the courts by demonstrating that their claims satisfied stringent conditions (such as continuing traditional connection with the land and non-extinguishment of native title by lawful means). The validity of land dealings since the enactment of the *Racial Discrimination Act in* 1975 was in question, and compensation would have to be paid for extinguishment of native title after the date of enactment. Though the Court's decision and even the Court itself were subjected to criticism (for example, some State governments and some mining and pastoral groups claimed that the decision created intolerable uncertainty), it is arguable that the case made possible a political resolution that would not have been possible otherwise (see generally Goot & Rowse 1994; McRae, Nettheim & Beacroft 1997).

After a series of extensive, complex and unpredictable negotiations and compromises—involving a diverse range of interests, problems with determining how to represent Indigenous communities, and the vagaries of federalism—a political resolution emerged in the form of the Commonwealth *Native Title Act 1993* (Brennan 1995; Attwood 1996; Stephenson 1995). This *Native Title Act* was thus the outcome of a subtle interplay of the legal and political, where the action was initiated by the courts, implemented by Parliament, and subsequently endorsed by the judiciary. It offered the potential for a new settlement between Indigenous and non-Indigenous Australians.

But could the judiciary consistently take the lead in the formulation of native title and rely on Parliament to support and take up its initiatives? This became a crucial question in the *Wik* case.[22] In June 1993, prior to the operation of the *Native Title Act*, the Wik Peoples commenced proceedings in the Federal Court against the State of Queensland, the Commonwealth and others, claiming native title and possessory title rights over an area of land and waters in far north Queensland. At issue was whether the granting to graziers many years previously of pastoral leases over the same land had extinguished native title. If it had not, then extensive areas of Crown leasehold land all around Australia could be subject to native title claims.

The members of the High Court were divided on this question. The majority held that the grant of pastoral leases did not necessarily extinguish native title rights although, to the extent that native title was inconsistent with leasehold interests, leasehold interests would prevail. For the minority, the right of exclusive possession granted by the leases was inconsistent with native title; therefore native title could not coexist with leasehold estate and was necessarily extinguished.

The majority decision in *Wik* proved to have serious and far-reaching political consequences. The Court's decision was strongly criticised by some graziers, farmers and miners for the uncertainty and decline in the value of pastoral properties that they claimed it produced. Because of the uncertainty, the Queensland government refused to issue further leasehold and mining tenements and placed restrictions on development work on pastoral properties (Hiley 1997; Hunter 1997; Horrigan & Young 1997). The High Court itself came under political attack. Queensland Premier Rob Borbidge described the Court as 'an embarrassment' (*Australian* 19 February 1997). Prime Minister Howard entered the debate, emphatically rejecting a law-making role for the Court, while Deputy Prime Minister Tim Fischer criticised the judgment as an example of undesirable 'judicial activism' which should be overcome by appointing a new High Court judge who was 'conservative with a capital C' (*Courier-Mail* 5 March 1997).

After discussions with Premiers and Chief Ministers, pastoralists, mining and resource groups and the National Indigenous Working Group, the Howard government responded to the *Wik* decision with a 'Ten-Point Plan' to amend the *Native Title Act 1993*. This *Wik* Bill passed the House of Representatives. But in the Senate, where the government was in a minority, it was opposed by Labor, the Democrats, the Greens and Tasmanian Independent Brian Harradine, and after numerous proposed amendments it was initially rejected. Following further extensive debate and negotiations, especially with Senator Harradine, who held the balance of power and wanted to avoid a double dissolution which he feared would be followed by a racially divisive election, an amended Bill finally passed the Senate on 8 July 1998.

The *Wik* decision confirmed that judicial politics were now an essential aspect of the wider political struggles of Indigenous Australians. However, the *Wik* case also indicated that there were significant limitations to judicial politics. This became even clearer in subsequent decisions of the Court. Two cases—the *Yarmirr* case (*Commonwealth* v *Yarmirr* 2001) in which the High Court recognised the existence of native title in relation to the sea, and in *Yanner* (*Yanner* v *Eaton* 1999) in which it held that the *Native Title Act* preserved the rights of Murrandoo Yanner to hunt crocodiles in a traditional manner—appeared to advance and clarify Indigenous rights. But in two other cases—*Ward* (*Western Australia* v *Ward* 2002) and the *Yorta Yorta* case (*Yorta Yorta* v *Victoria* 2002)—the Court's strict reading of the provisions of the *Native Title Act* raised significant hurdles for future claimants of native title.

Limits to new politics

This review of recent Court decisions, in the context of the claim by a majority of Justices on the Court that in some sense it 'makes' the law, reveals a number of significant features of the new politics of the High Court. Foremost is the fact that, on a range of fundamental issues, the Court has taken an active part (in some cases the lead) in policy formulation. In pursuing this role, the Court has relied on the notions of representative democracy and responsible government claimed to be secured in the Constitution, as well as on the common law and the notion of popular sovereignty. It has also turned to international sources, especially international law and the decisions of Canadian, US and UK courts, to shape and guide its decisions. Importantly, this active policy-making role of the Court has affected other institutions of governance, in particular by imposing limits on the legislative capacity of both Commonwealth and State Parliaments.

But there are significant limits on the Court itself in its attempt to shape Australian politics. To start with, the foundational principles of the rule of law and the separation of powers remain firmly entrenched. There are also important questions of legitimacy: should an unelected bench of judges override the will and judgment of the people's representatives, and to what extent is this form of judicial review consistent with parliamentary democracy? The immediate focus of such questions has been the way judges are selected and appointed, prompting calls to make the Court more representative by accommodating and promoting geographical balance, minority representation and gender equality. Thus the appointment in 2003 of Justice Dyson Heydon of the NSW Court of Appeal to replace retiring Justice Mary Gaudron, who had been the first and only woman on the Court, attracted criticism because it meant a complete absence of female representation and also meant that only the east coast States were represented on the bench.

There are a number of practical limits to how far the Court can redefine aspects of Australian liberal democracy. The incremental nature of the Court's decisions, the retrospective nature of its judgments, the changing membership of the Court and the limits imposed by the specific issues in dispute in each case are the most obvious. But perhaps the most significant difficulty, in the context of the new politics of the High Court, is the problem of communication. The Court has sought to make its decisions more open to deliberative democratic politics by writing clearer and more accessible explanations of the decisions, by stating its policy presuppositions and by acknowledging its law-making role. In doing so, the Court has encouraged and welcomed what it considers to be informed criticism of its decisions. The Court has appointed a public relations officer, it has set up a website and it now provides quick access to its decisions (Williams 1999b). Nevertheless, major obstacles remain. The perceived independence and impartiality of the Court are crucial for its authority, and a Court that is seen as political, that enters the everyday political fray, risks its authority. The sustained and personal attacks on the Court, especially after *Wik*, reveal how vulnerable the judiciary is to such political criticism.

The 'Kirby incident' in 2002 confirmed the extent to which individual judges, despite the protection of the Constitution, have limited resources in countering a concerted political attack. In March 2002, under the protection of parliamentary privilege, Liberal Senator Bill Heffernan made certain allegations of a personal nature against Justice Michael Kirby. Kirby issued a statement from the High Court denying the claims. Within a week, following the discrediting of his claimed documentary evidence, Heffernan tendered with deep regret his apology to Kirby, unreservedly withdrawing his allegations. Kirby accepted the apology, noting that the wrong he had suffered was 'insignificant in comparison to the wrong done to Parliament, the High Court and the people' (High Court 2002).

The decision of the then Commonwealth Attorney-General Daryl Williams not to 'speak for' the courts has exacerbated the problem, leaving the Court without its traditional public defender. Traditionally, judges refrain from commenting on cases before the courts and are especially careful to abstain from comments on governmental policy, relying instead on the Attorney-General to defend their reputation and independence (Thomas 1997; Mason 1990; Edwards 1984). Williams decided to abandon this tradition on the grounds that the Attorney-General is a politician (chosen like any other Minister from the parliamentary ranks of the governing party) and therefore may come into conflict with the interests of the judiciary, and that, given the demands on a modern Attorney-General, his or her response on behalf of the judiciary may not be adequate or timely (Williams 1995). Williams nominated instead the Judicial Conference of Australia (made up of judges and magistrates, other judicial officers and former members of superior and intermediate courts) as the appropriate representative body to speak for and on behalf of the judiciary, especially in the political sphere. In doing so, Williams acknowledged the increasing possibility of tension between a law-making judiciary, on the one hand, and the executive and Parliament, on the other. But the establishment of institutions such as the Judicial Conference may have the unintended consequence of encouraging greater political and partisan attacks on the judiciary because it is now a publicly accountable institution with the means to defend itself politically.

Conclusion

This chapter has argued that the High Court has augmented its traditional judicial review with a new politics that has engaged fundamental liberal-democratic concerns such as rights and freedoms, citizenship, separation of powers and native title. The Court has reshaped the contours of Australian democracy by facilitating significant political changes and by imposing major limits on the authority and discretion of the executive and Parliaments. This increased judicial involvement in Australian politics has challenged other political institutions, and has presented far-reaching theoretical and practical questions concerning the role of the Court in Australian democracy.

In many respects, the Court's decisions have been consistent with international trends towards greater judicialisation of politics and potentially the politicisation of the judiciary (Holland 1991; Jacob et al. 1996; Neal Tate & Vallinder 1995; for criticism of American developments see Tucker 1995; Rosenberg 1991; Horowitz 1977). A subtle aspect of these changes is the way courts of final jurisdiction are increasingly relying on each other's decisions, borrowing and adopting judgments and ideas across a number of jurisdictions. This sustained dialogue suggests an evolving international constitutionalism that transcends conventional political boundaries (e.g. see Saunders 1996). In this light, the High Court of Australia represents an increasingly powerful judiciary, which in its deliberations and judgments is shaping and mediating international developments and redefining the future of liberal-democratic governance.

NOTES

1 *South Australia* v *Commonwealth* (1942) 65 CLR 373; *Victoria v Commonwealth* (1957) 99 CLR 575; *Capital Duplicators Pty Ltd* v *Australian Capital Territory* (1992) 177 CLR 248; *Ha* v *New South Wales* (1997) 189 CLR 465.

2 See Galligan (1986: ch. 4); *Australian National Airways Pty Ltd* v *Commonwealth* (1945) 71 CLR 29; *Bank of New South Wales* v *Commonwealth* (1948) 76 CLR 1; *A-G (Victoria)* v *Commonwealth* (1945) 71 CLR 237; *British Medical Association* v *Commonwealth* (1949) 79 CLR 201.

3 *Koowarta* v *Bjelke-Petersen* (1982) 153 CLR 168.

4 *Commonwealth* v *Tasmania* (1983) 158 CLR 1.

5 See for example the requirement that acquisition of property by the Commonwealth from any state or person be on just terms (s. 51(xxxi)), that a trial on indictment of any offence against the law of the Commonwealth shall be by jury (s. 80), that the Commonwealth shall not make any law for establishing any religion or prohibit the free exercise of any religion (s. 116), and the right not to be subjected to discrimination on the basis of State residence (s. 117) (Williams 1999a).

6 *Nationwide News Pty Ltd* v *Wills* (1992) 177 CLR 1; *Australian Capital Television Pty Ltd* v *Commonwealth* (1992) 177 CLR 106.

7 See *Nationwide News Pty Ltd* v *Wills* (1992) 177 CLR 1; *Australian Capital Television Pty Ltd* v *Commonwealth* (1992) 177 CLR 106.

8 *Theophanous* v *Herald & Weekly Times Ltd* (1994) 182 CLR 104; *Stephens* v *West Australian Newspapers Ltd* (1994) 182 CLR 211.

9 *McGinty* v *Western Australia* (1996) 186 CLR 140.

10 *Lange* v *Australian Broadcasting Corporation* (1997) 189 CLR 520.

11 *Levy* v *Victoria* (1997) 189 CLR 579.

12 *Kruger* v *Commonwealth* (1997) 190 CLR 1.

13 *Leeth* v *Commonwealth* (1992) 174 CLR 455 at 470 per Mason CJ, Dawson and McHugh JJ.

14 *Dietrich* v *The Queen* (1992) 177 CLR 293; per Mason CJ, Deane, Toohey, Gaudron and McHugh JJ; Brennan and Dawson JJ dissenting.

15 *Dietrich* v *The Queen* (1992) 177 CLR 293, Deane J at 326; Gaudron J at 362; see generally Hope (1996).

16 *Polyukhovich* v *Commonwealth* (1991) 172 CLR 501.

17 *Polyukhovich* v *Commonwealth* (1991) 172 CLR 501 at 606–29 per Deane J; 703–8 per Gaudron J.

18 *Minister of State for Immigration and Ethnic Affairs* v *Ah Hin Teoh* (1995) 183 CLR 273. For a discussion of the previous case law, see Walker (1996: 209–11).

19 Per Mason CJ, Deane, Toohey and Gaudron JJ; McHugh J dissenting.

20 *Mabo* v *Queensland (No 1)* (1988) 166 CLR 186.

21 *Mabo* v *Queensland (No 2)* (1992) 175 CLR 1. Eddie Mabo died on 21 January 1992, not knowing the outcome of the case.

22 *Wik Peoples* v *State of Queensland* (1996) ALR 129.

REFERENCES

Alston, P. & Chiam, M. eds 1995, *Treaty-Making and Australia: Globalisation versus Sovereignty*, Federation Press, Sydney.

Attwood, B. ed. 1996, *In the Age of Mabo*, Allen & Unwin, Sydney.

Bailey, P. 1990, *Human Rights: Australia in an International Context*, Butterworths, Sydney.

Bennett, J. 1980, *Keystone of the Federal Arch: A Historical Memoir of the High Court of Australia to 1980*, AGPS, Canberra.

Brennan, F. 1995, *One Land, One Nation*, University of Queensland Press, Brisbane.

Brennan, G. 1993, 'A Critique of Criticism', *Monash University Law Review*, vol. 19, no. 2, pp. 123–6.

Charlesworth, H. 1993, 'The Australian Reluctance About Rights', *Osgoode Hall Law Journal*, vol. 31, pp. 196–232.

Charlesworth, H. 1995, 'Australia's Split Personality: Implementation of Human Rights Treaty Obligations in Australia', in *Treaty-Making and Australia: Globalisation versus Sovereignty*, eds P. Alston & M. Chiam, Federation Press, Sydney, pp. 129–40.

Craven, G. 1992, 'Cracks in the Facade of Literalism: Is there an Engineer in the House?', *Melbourne University Law Review*, vol. 18, no. 3, pp. 540–64.

Craven, G. 1999, 'The High Court of Australia: A Study in the Abuse of Power', *University of New South Wales Law Journal*, vol. 22, no. 1, pp. 216–42.

Dixon, O. 1965, *Jesting Pilate: And Other Papers and Addresses by Sir Owen Dixon*, Law Book Co., Melbourne.

Edwards, J. 1984, *The Attorney General, Politics and the Public Interest*, Sweet & Maxwell, London.

Evans, G. 1996, 'The Impact of Internationalisation on Australian Law: A Commentary', in *Courts of Final Jurisdiction: The Mason Court in Australia*, ed. C. Saunders, Federation Press, Sydney.

Galligan, B. 1986, *Politics of the High Court*, University of Queensland Press, Brisbane.

Galligan, B. 1990, 'Australia's Rejection of a Bill of Rights', *Journal of Commonwealth and Comparative Politics*, vol. 28, no. 3, pp. 344–68.

Gleeson, M. 1997, 'The Role of the Judiciary in a Modern Democracy', paper presented to Judicial Conference of Australia Annual Symposium, Sydney, 8 November.

Gleeson, M. 1999, 'Legal Oil and Political Vinegar', paper presented to Sydney Institute, Sydney, 16 March.

Gleeson, M. 2000, *The Rule of Law and the Constitution*, Boyer Lectures 2000, ABC Books, Sydney.

Gleeson, M. 2001, 'Occasional Address', Griffith University, Brisbane, 20 April.

Goot, M. & Rowse, T. eds 1994, *Make a Better Offer: The Politics of Mabo*, Pluto Press, Sydney.

High Court of Australia 2002, 'Media Releases', Canberra, <http://www.hcourt.gov.au/publications_04.html>.

Hiley, G. ed. 1997, *The Wik Case: Issues and Implications*, Butterworths, Sydney.

Holland, K. ed. 1991, *Judicial Activism in Comparative Perspective*, Macmillan, London.

Hope, J. 1996, 'A Constitutional Right to a Fair Trial? Implications for the Reform of the Australian Criminal Justice System', *Federal Law Review*, vol. 24, no. 1, pp. 173–99.

Horowitz, D. 1977, *The Courts and Social Policy*, Brookings Institution, Washington, DC.

Horrigan, B. & Young, S. eds 1997, *Commercial Implications of Native Title*, Federation Press, Sydney.

Hunter, P. 1997, 'The Wik Decision: Unnecessary Extinguishment', in *The Wik Case: Issues and Implications*, ed. G. Hiley, Butterworths, Sydney.

Jacob, H., Blankenburg, E., Krittzer, H., Provene, D. & Sanders, J. 1996, *Courts, Law, and Politics in Comparative Perspective*, Yale University Press, New Haven, CT.

La Nauze, J. 1972, *The Making of the Australian Constitution*, Melbourne University Press, Melbourne.

Lavarch, M. 1995, 'The Role of International Law-Making in the Globalisation Process', in *Treaty-Making and Australia: Globalisation Versus Sovereignty*, eds P. Alston & M. Chiam, Federation Press, Sydney, pp. 177–84.

Lindell, G. 1994, 'Recent Developments in the Judicial Interpretation of the Australian Constitution', in *Future Directions in Australian Constitutional Law*, ed. G. Lindell, Federation Press, Sydney, pp. 1–46.

Mason, A. 1989, 'A Bill of Rights for Australia?', *Australian Bar Review*, vol. 5, pp. 79–90.

Mason, A. 1990, 'Judicial Independence and the Separation of Powers—Some Problems Old and New', *University of New South Wales Law Journal*, vol. 13, no. 2, pp. 173–211.

Mason, A. 1995, 'Trends in Constitutional Interpretation', *University of New South Wales Law Journal*, vol. 18, no. 2, pp. 237–49.

Mason, A. 1996a, 'Courts and Community Values', *Eureka Street*, vol. 6, no. 9, pp. 32–3.

Mason, A. 1996b, 'The Judge as Law-Maker', *James Cook University Law Review*, vol. 3, no. 1, pp. 1–15.

McRae, H., Nettheim, G. & Beacroft, L. 1997, *Indigenous Legal Issues: Commentary and Materials*, Law Book Co., Sydney.

Neal Tate, C. & Vallinder, T. eds 1995, *The Global Expansion of Judicial Power*, New York University Press, New York.

O'Brien, D. 1996, *Special Leave to Appeal: The Law and Practice of Application for Special Leave to Appeal to the High Court of Australia*, Law Book Co., Sydney.

Opeskin, B. & Rothwell, D. eds 1997, *International Law and Australian Federalism*, Melbourne University Press, Melbourne.

Parker, C. 1994, 'Protection of Judicial Process as an Implied Constitutional Principle', *Adelaide Law Review*, no. 16, pp. 341–57.

Patapan, H. 2000, *Judging Democracy: The New Politics of the High Court of Australia*, Cambridge University Press, Melbourne.

Preston, K. & Sampford, C. eds 1996, *Interpreting Constitutions: Theories, Principles and Institutions*, Federation Press, Sydney.

Rosenberg, G. 1991, *The Hollow Hope: Can Court Bring About Social Change?*, University of Chicago Press, Chicago, IL.

Saunders, C. ed. 1996, *Courts of Final Jurisdiction: The Mason Court in Australia*, Federation Press, Sydney.

Sawer, G. 1956, *Australian Federal Politics and Law, 1901–1929*, Melbourne University Press, Melbourne.

Sawer, G. 1963, *Australian Federal Politics and Law, 1929–1949*, Melbourne University Press, Melbourne.

Solomon, D. 1999, *The Political High Court: How the High Court Shapes Politics*, Allen & Unwin, Sydney.

Stephenson, M. ed. 1995, *Mabo: The Native Title Legislation*, University of Queensland Press, Brisbane.

Symposium on Rights 1994, Symposium on Constitutional Rights for Australia, *Sydney Law Review*, vol. 16, no. 2, pp. 141–305.

Thomas, J. 1997, *Judicial Ethics in Australia*, Law Book Co., Sydney.

Thomson, J. 1986, 'Constitutional Authority for Judicial Review: A Contribution from the Framers of the Australian Constitution', in *Official Record of the Debates of the Australasian Federal Convention*, vol. 6, ed. G. Craven, Legal Books, Sydney.

Toohey, J. 1993, 'A Government of Laws, and Not of Men?', *Public Law Review*, vol. 4, no. 3, pp. 158–74.

Tucker, D. 1995, *The Rehnquist Court and Civil Rights*, Dartmouth, Aldershot.

Virtue, B. 1993, 'Putting Mabo in Perspective', *Australian Lawyer*, July, p. 23.

Walker, K. 1996, 'Treaties and the Internationalization of Australian Law', in *Courts of Final Jurisdiction: The Mason Court in Australia*, ed. C. Saunders, Federation Press, Sydney.

Williams, D. 1995, 'Who Speaks for the Courts', in *Courts in a Representative Democracy*, Australian Institute of Judicial Administration, Melbourne.

Williams, G. 1999a, *Human Rights Under the Australian Constitution*, Oxford University Press, Melbourne.

Williams, G. 1999b, 'The High Court and the Media', *University of Technology of Sydney Law Review*, no. 1, pp. 136–47.

Winterton, G. 1994, 'The Separation of Judicial Power as an Implied Bill of Rights', in *Future Directions in Australian Constitutional Law*, ed. G. Lindell, Federation Press, Sydney, pp. 185–208.

Zines, L. 1997, *The High Court and the Constitution*, Butterworths, Sydney.

LEGAL CASES

A-G (Victoria) v *Commonwealth* (1945) 71 CLR 237.

Australian Capital Television Pty Ltd v *Commonwealth* (1992) 177 CLR 106.

Australian National Airways Pty Ltd v *Commonwealth* (1945) 71 CLR 29.

Bank of New South Wales v *Commonwealth* (1948) 76 CLR 1.

British Medical Association v *Commonwealth* (1949) 79 CLR 201.

Capital Duplicators Pty Ltd v *Australian Capital Territory* (1992) 177 CLR 248.

Commonwealth v *Tasmania* (1983) 158 CLR 1.

Commonwealth v *Yarmirr* (2001–2002) 208 CLR 1.

Dietrich v *The Queen* (1992) 177 CLR 293.

Ha v *New South Wales* (1997) 189 CLR 465.

Koowarta v *Bjelke-Petersen* (1982) 153 CLR 168.

Kruger v *Commonwealth* (1997) 190 CLR 1.

Lange v *Australian Broadcasting Tribunal* (1997) 189 CLR 520.

Leeth v *Commonwealth* (1992) 174 CLR 455.

Levy v *Victoria* (1997) 189 CLR 579.

Mabo v *Queensland (No. 1)* (1988) 166 CLR 186.

Mabo v *Queensland (No. 2)* (1992) 175 CLR 1.

McGinty v *Western Australia* (1996) 186 CLR 140.

Minister of State for Immigration and Ethnic Affairs v *Ah Hin Teoh* (1995) 183 CLR 273.

Nationwide News Pty Ltd v *Wills* (1992) 177 CLR 1.

Polyukhovich v *Commonwealth* (1991) 172 CLR 501.

South Australia v *Commonwealth* (1942) 65 CLR 373.

Stephens v *West Australian Newspapers Ltd* (1994) 182 CLR 211.

Theophanous v *Herald & Weekly Times Ltd* (1994) 182 CLR 104.

Victoria v *Commonwealth* (1957) 99 CLR 575.

Western Australia v *Ward* (2002) 213 CLR 1.

Wik Peoples v *State of Queensland* (1996) ALR 129.

Yanner v *Eaton* (1999) 201 CLR 351.

Yorta Yorta v *Victoria* (2002) 214 CLR 422

ALR = Australian Law Reports

CLR = Commonwealth Law Reports

Party and Electoral Politics

Introduction

Part 2 of this book examined governmental institutions. Now Part 3 looks at the relationship between those institutions and the citizens of Australia. The key intermediaries linking governments and citizens are the party system and the electoral system.

A political party is an organised group of people which presents candidates at elections and, if successful, provides its parliamentary representatives with organisational support. Political parties are a central feature of liberal democracies, and provide a means of organising the potentially chaotic relationships between citizens and governments by packaging and coordinating candidates for election, usually by presenting distinctive sets of policies.

The role that political parties play in liberal democracies in structuring electoral choice and as a link between citizens and the government is examined by Dennis Woodward in Chapter 9. He provides an account of the different types of parties that have been important in liberal democracies generally and in Australia in particular. Woodward discusses how the parties and the party system have developed in Australia and analyses recent changes in key features of party system.

In Chapter 10, Brian Costar explains how electoral systems translate citizens' votes into election winners and losers. This is not simply a technical or arithmetical exercise. As Costar explains, different electoral systems produce different results and have a profound effect on the nature of the contest and on its outcome.

The next four chapters examine the political parties that have been particularly influential in recent Australian politics.

In Chapter 11, Judith Brett scrutinises the Liberal Party. Its recent sustained period in national government, beginning in March 1996, followed a lengthy period in Opposition that began in the early 1980s. Brett's analysis goes even further back. She examines the important role of Robert Menzies in helping to found the party in the mid-1940s and in establishing its appeal to a wide spectrum of voters. She also places the party firmly as the ideological heir of earlier non-Labor parties. Brett comments on the reasons for the Liberal Party's national electoral success from 1996. She highlights the potential conflict between the party's radical economic program and its more conservative social and moral agenda, and raises questions about the extent to which the actions of the Liberal Party in office conform to the principles of liberalism.

The Labor Party is Australia's oldest surviving party, currently relegated to the role of national Opposition. In Chapter 12, Nick Economou dissects the Labor Party. He examines the changes in the party's social base, its leadership, its organisational structure, and its relationship with the trade unions. He analyses the perennial debate about what the Labor Party should stand for and whether it has maintained the essential character of its earlier years.

In Chapter 13, Dennis Woodward examines the National Party—its history, organisation, ideology and support base—and looks at how it has survived name changes and the erosion of its rural voting base and unfavourable electoral redistributions to remain a key element on the non-Labor side of politics. He describes its coalition relationship with the Liberal Party, and examines the question of the National Party's long-term viability.

Chapter 14 focuses on the most visible minor parties—the Australian Democrats, the Greens, One Nation and Family First—and on Independents. Although minor parties do not usually play a central role in the competition between the major parties to win government, they have been an important force in the Senate. In this chapter, Jenny Tilby Stock discusses the organisational structure, support base and policies of the most successful of the minor parties, and the role that they have played in shaping political outcomes in Australia. With the Coalition government's success at obtaining a majority in the Senate in 2005, it appeared that the minor parties lost much of their significance. But Tilby Stock argues that minor parties and Independents will continue to play an important role in the political process.

The focus for Chapter 15 shifts from parties to voters. Haydon Manning provides an insight into the factors that influence the way Australians vote. He uses survey data to analyse the patterns of party preferences among voters and to explain the origins of these patterns. He begins with some explanations that have been prevalent in recent journalistic interpretations of Australian election outcomes, then continues on within an explanatory framework more typical of academic analyses of the subject. A particular focus here is the social dimension of voting behaviour, including the extent to which party preferences are an expression of the class, gender or religious background of voters. Manning also critically examines the proposition that voting behaviour has become more volatile over recent years.

Political parties and the party system

DENNIS WOODWARD

Political parties seem to be essential elements in a liberal democracy. They perform a number of roles without which a functional liberal democracy would be hard to imagine. They structure electoral choices for voters between competing alternatives, they help formulate policy choices and they provide a link between citizens and government. They are certainly ubiquitous: every functional liberal democracy has always featured political parties, and Australia's pattern of party politics—while necessarily having its own local idiosyncrasies—would be broadly familiar to academic analysts from around the Western world.

The Australian party system: two-party dominance

The basic pattern of Australia's party system started to develop in the 1880s and was essentially set in place by 1910 (Loveday, Martin & Parker 1977). Thereafter it has been characterised by a notable degree of stability (Aitkin 1982: 1). Since 1910 the party system has been dominated by two party groupings—the Australian Labor Party (ALP) and a major non-Labor or anti-Labor party grouping (generally a Liberal Party or its equivalent joined, at least since the 1920s, in coalition with the Country/National Party). These two groupings win the overwhelming share of votes cast and seats won in the Parliament. Despite party splits in the ALP, several reorganisations of the major non-Labor party and the emergence of new parties, this 'two-party dominant' type of party system has always reasserted itself.

This is not to overlook that there are currently (and have been in the past) a number of other political parties that attract sufficient support to gain representation in the Senate and whose preferences in contests for the House of Representatives can be significant. Rather, it is to highlight the fact that, at the federal level, governments are always formed by one of the two dominant party blocs.

A party typology

The particular circumstances of Australian political history have shaped the details of how Australia's political parties have evolved. Other chapters in this book explore these circumstances and details in relation to today's main parties in Australia. As a helpful background to those particular histories, it is useful to sketch out a somewhat more conceptual framework—applicable in almost any liberal-democratic system—for understanding the evolution of parties over the past century or so.

In the 19th century, within Western countries where there had been some expansion of voting rights, political parties first emerged as rather loose groupings, formed within legislatures, of like-minded people coalescing around prominent individuals. Now, in the early 21st century, the typical major political party is a tightly disciplined, professionalised body employing sophisticated techniques in their quest to win and hold power.

Thus parties have changed. In this process of change, parties have changed their roles, their relationship to civil society and the state apparatus, and their nature. These transformations have been responses to changes in the electorate, in other parties, and in the nature of society (such as shifting social, cultural, religious or class divisions). In many cases, party names have altered little, but what they stand for, what they inspire in voters, how they are organised and how they operate often bear scant resemblance to their original form.

A way of understanding the changing nature of political parties is through some 'ideal types' originally devised to explain the dynamics of party politics in Western Europe over the last century or so. These 'ideal types' are the *cadre party*, the *mass party*, the *catch-all party*, the *electoral-professional party* and the *cartel party*. The notion of 'ideal types' means that, for the sake of clarity, the main features of each type are highlighted and their differences accentuated even though, in reality, actual parties are unlikely to exactly match these ideal characterisations. As they evolve, actual parties are liable to have residual features from earlier types or to display tendencies that have yet to be fully established.

CADRE PARTY TYPE

The first in this typology has been labelled a *cadre* (or *elite*) party type (Duverger 1964: 63–7). Typically, such a party existed at a time of limited franchise (such as in colonial Australia) before the right to vote was extended to all adult men. It had virtually no party organisation beyond its parliamentary membership and depended for its finances on the support of wealthy individuals. Its electoral appeal was based on the innate qualities of its candidates who were generally prominent citizens. Without much party organisation outside of the Parliament to dictate policy to them, elected candidates enjoyed largely unfettered parliamentary freedom; this means that the parliamentarians in these cadre parties were very much 'trustees' (Pitkin 1967). Cadre parties typically had no detailed policy program, and portrayed their actions in terms of furthering the broad 'public interest'. In the Australian context, the forerunners in the late 19th century and early 20th century of today's Liberal Party came closest to representing this type (see Brett's Chapter 11 in this book). Some local councils in Australia today feature groupings of elected council members which bear some of the hallmarks of cadre parties.

MASS PARTY TYPE

Cadre parties were mostly supplanted by *mass* parties (Duverger 1964: 63–70). Their rise was associated with the introduction of the full (or at least full male) franchise. As their name implies, they had a large mass membership whose individual small contributions provided the necessary party finances. Their mass membership, formed into numerous electorate-level local party branches, provided a link between their parliamentary candidates and the electorate at large, and was seen as an active source of policy development. Such parties were typically Leftist in their ideological tendencies, i.e. they were typically Labour, social democratic or socialist parties. Their mass membership formed the base of a strong, even dominant, extra-parliamentary organisation to which the parliamentary wing of the party was expected to be subservient. Such parties had a highly developed programmatic set of policies—the 'party platform'— that their parliamentary leaders were pledged to implement. Mass party leaders, therefore, were very much 'delegates' (Pitkin 1967) of a wider movement and their electoral appeal was to a section of the electorate on the basis of proposed policies.

From its formation, as Economou shows in Chapter 12 of this book, the Australian Labor Party (ALP) was clearly a mass party in this sense. When the Liberal Party was established in the mid-1940s it also adopted many of the trappings of a mass party, although the dominance of the parliamentary wing over the party's organisational wing and mass membership reflected the party's cadre-type predecessors.

CATCH-ALL PARTY TYPE

In the post-World War Two era, mass parties tended to evolve into a different party type—the *'catch-all'* party (Kirchheimer 1969). The rise to dominance of catch-all parties was a product of a number of factors. Social change, in particular rising affluence, dampened the class divisions that had been a driving force behind mass parties. Sectional appeals to the working class no longer provided a winning electoral formula. At the same time, the emergence of radio and then television undercut part of the rationale for mass parties. Politicians, especially party leaders, could more easily talk directly to the electorate and were less reliant on party members to act as intermediaries with the broader electorate in spreading the party message.

The catch-all party, therefore, witnessed a decline in the importance of the extra-parliamentary organisation, notably the mass membership, in favour of the parliamentary wing of the party. Members were less crucial for the party's finances that increasingly relied on corporate donations and professional fundraising activities. Similarly, members played a more limited role in determining party policy as the parliamentary leaders came to dominate this process. As a consequence, the party's platform was de-emphasised, more pragmatic policies with broader electoral appeal were adopted and the party moved away from its sectional focus. Instead, it sought to appeal to all sections of the community—hence the term, invented by Kirchheimer (1969), 'catch-all'. This appeal was on the basis of the personal qualities of the party leaders and specific policy issues that would have universal support.

In Australia, the Liberal Party can be seen as having first moved in this direction and its remarkable electoral success from 1949 to 1972 can, in part, be attributed to its successful catch-all appeal. It was not until the late 1960s that the ALP, led by Gough Whitlam, began the difficult transition to the catch-all type that was to eventually give it electoral victory. Chapters 10 and 11 in this book document these changes.

ELECTORAL-PROFESSIONAL PARTY TYPE

According to Panebianco (1988), the catch-all party has evolved sufficiently to create a qualitatively different party type: the *electoral-professional* party. In many respects, this new party type is simply a refinement or further development of its catch-all predecessor. A characteristic feature of the electoral-professional party type is the decline in the level of mass membership. Its extra-parliamentary party organisation is generally bypassed except for a small band of professional party officials. This type of party is financed by corporate donations, direct marketing fundraising by professional fundraisers and by government funding. To all intents and purposes, the party platform has been replaced by sophisticated market research/opinion polling to shape policies that will have maximum electoral appeal. This appeal is very much based on the media image of the party leader and market-research-driven issues. Appearance often triumphs over substance. The leader communicates directly with the public via carefully staged television appearances and by means of talkback radio. Media monitoring and attempts to manipulate the media feature prominently as does the use of paid advertising. Parties and their leaders are marketed by experts in much the same way as supermarket chains market their products.

It could be argued that the ALP under Prime Minister Hawke from the early 1980s became the first Australian political party to resemble this electoral-professional type. The Hawke-led Labor Party enjoyed a string of electoral successes despite declining overall electoral support, an outcome arguably attributable to the professionalism of its electoral strategies and campaigns. By 1996, however, the Liberal Party had eclipsed the ALP in the electoral-professional stakes (Williams 1997) and seems to have retained the advantage ever since at the national level in Australia.

CARTEL PARTY TYPE

Katz and Mair have argued that the 'electoral-professional' type of party has developed into a new type: the *cartel* party (Katz & Mair 1995). Such a claim is far from accepted within the discipline of political science and its applicability outside Western Europe is contentious. In particular, whether Australian parties display cartel party features is a matter of debate (see e.g. Goot 2003).

Cartel-type parties are distinguished by the limited competition between them and by their location in an important sense *within* the state apparatus. The existing, established, major parties are said to have become 'cartelised' by contriving to share power and state patronage among themselves to the exclusion of new rivals and to behave in the same manner as business cartels. In this view, politics has become a self-protecting profession, with political actors aware of their mutual interest in protecting their livelihood and thus less likely to pursue a 'winner takes all' approach. Party competition is seen to be contained and managed, with a de-emphasis on particular policy differences in favour of rivalry being based on claims to being more efficient and effective managers. Political campaigns for cartel parties become even more capital-intensive than for 'electoral-professional' parties, with greater centralisation and professionalism. Increasingly, according to the European proponents of this interpretation, cartel parties become reliant on the state for a major part of their funding and their operations. For example, the dominant parties anticipate a substantial amount of government-provided election funding based on their electoral support; government-funded free media spots; and government employment for a vast retinue of staff who are essentially party advisors.

Ordinary party members are relegated to playing little more than the role of 'cheer leaders'.

It could be argued that the major Australian political parties today display some of the features of 'cartel' parties. On occasion, they seem to have colluded to exclude a new competitor, for example in their actions against the Pauline Hanson's One Nation party. There has been public funding of party election expenses in Australia since 1984. There is an increasing incidence of party sympathisers being employed, on the public purse, as parliamentary and political advisers. And governments seem increasingly inclined to spend public funds on expensive media campaigns to explain policy initiatives that are arguably partisan in nature. But perhaps of all the ideal types, the cartel type most reflects developments in Europe and it is a little premature to suggest that Australia's major parties—which are still highly competitive within a strong 'winner take all' electoral culture—have become fully fledged 'cartel' parties.

The future of the Australian party system

At the beginning of this chapter, it was observed that Australia has long featured a 'two-party dominant' party system. There is some evidence to suggest that the traditional hold over the electorate enjoyed by the two major party groupings is under challenge. An increasing proportion of electors have no or little party loyalty, Independents have been able to gain seats in the House of Representatives where previously the major parties had a monopoly, and the primary votes of the major parties have fallen somewhat since the 1980s.

But this trend should not be exaggerated. Whereas the major parties' combined lower house primary vote in 1987 was 92 per cent of all votes cast, and it later fell to 83 per cent in 1990 and just 80 per cent in 1998, the most recent elections of 2001 and 2004 have seen recoveries from these particularly low levels of support. It seems that any apparent dissatisfaction with the major parties and strong 'protest votes' for minor parties did not lead to permanent shifts in voter sympathy, and the favoured recipients at various times during the 1990s (Democrats and Pauline Hanson's One Nation respectively) have failed to consolidate their gains. While the 84 per cent of lower house primary votes gained by the major parties in the November 2004 election is below the highest historic levels of support, it implies that the major parties have at least arrested any trend of declining support.

A parallel trend is evident in the Senate. Major party dominance in voting for that chamber was already less pronounced by the 1980s and subsequent falls in support have been minor. For example, in 1987 the major parties attracted 85 per cent of the vote but only 80 per cent in 1990. Their share of the vote increased to 86 per cent in 1993 but fell to 80 per cent in 1996. It fell further in 1998 to 75 per cent, recovered marginally in 2001 to 76 per cent and then rose in 2004 to again be 80 per cent.

These results are far from signalling the death knell of Australia's 'two-party dominant' type of party system. Whether or not the Liberal–National Coalition, under John Howard and his successors, continues to dominate in federal elections, and whether or not the Labor Party, under Kim Beazley and his successors, manages to win government in the near future, it seems safe to conclude that it will be these two groupings that continue to shape the Australian political landscape.

REFERENCES

Aitkin, D. 1982, *Stability and Change in Australian Politics*, 2nd edn, Australian National University Press, Canberra.

Duverger, M. 1964, *Political Parties*, University Paperbacks, London.

Goot, M. 2003, 'Helped or Hindered? Pauline Hanson's One Nation and the Party Cartelisation Thesis', paper presented to Annual Conference of the Australasian Political Studies Association, Hobart, 29 September–1 October, <http://www.utas.edu.au/government/APSA/MGootfinal.pdf>.

Kirchheimer, O. 1969, *Politics, Law and Social Change: Selected Essays of Otto Kirchheimer*, ed. F. Burin & K. Shell, Columbia University Press, New York.

Katz, R. & Mair, P. 1995, 'Changing Models of Party Organization and Party Democracy: The Emergence of the Cartel Party', *Party Politics*, vol. 1, no. 1, pp. 5–28.

Loveday, P., Martin, A. & Parker, R. 1977, *The Emergence of the Australian Party System*, Hale & Iremonger, Sydney.

Panebianco, A. 1988, *Political Parties: Organization and Power*, translated by M. Silver, Cambridge University Press, Cambridge.

Pitkin, H. 1967, *The Concept of Representation*, University of California Press, Berkeley.

Williams, P. 1997, *The Victory: The Inside Story of the Takeover of Australia*, Allen & Unwin, St Leonards.

The electoral system

CHAPTER 10

BRIAN COSTAR

An electoral system is a device for translating the votes won by candidates in elections into an authoritative outcome, such as seats in a Parliament. Free, fair and frequent elections are essential conditions for any functioning democracy. Determining the best way of translating votes into an election outcome is an exercise fraught with difficulty. Notwithstanding widespread agreement that elections should be free, fair and frequent, there can be disagreement over what fairness means and over other fundamental goals. Should, for example, the prime consideration in an electoral system be achieving an outcome that mirrors the opinion of voters? Or is putting into place a stable and 'strong' government of greater importance?

Votes are not natural phenomena. They are convenient contrivances which try to simplify the complex political attitudes and preferences held by people into a series of marks on a ballot paper. Different ways of doing this—i.e. different ways of organising elections, setting up ballots and counting the votes—may produce different outcomes. For example, in political systems such as Australia's, governments are formed according to the number of seats won in the lower house of Parliament rather than according to the sum total of votes obtained. This highlights the critical role of the electoral system that happens to be in place for determining the winning candidates in these House of Representative seats.

Different electoral systems can be explained and defended by recourse to different conceptions of democracy. Advocates of *majoritarian* democracy, a conception which gives a high priority to producing clear election winners and producing governments which can enjoy clear-cut parliamentary dominance, are inclined to favour the single-member electoral systems which (for reasons that this chapter explains later) tend to produce that outcome. However, advocates of *consociational* democracy, a conception which envisages democracy as a form of power-sharing among groups, generally endorse proportional representation methods (Hague & Harrop 1987: 50–2). As it happens, Australia uses both of these electoral systems and hence both of these varieties of democracy: Australians elect their House of Representatives using the (majoritarian) single-member system and elect their Senate using (consociational) proportional representation.

When the new Commonwealth of Australia legislated its electoral procedures in 1902 (the first 1901 election having been conducted on rules drawn up by the six colonies), they mirrored the British and American procedures in two major respects. First, voting and enrolment were voluntary. Second, the electoral system was based on a simple *plurality* system where the candidate in each electorate who won the most votes (even if not a majority of all votes cast) was declared the winner of that seat.

Over the next quarter of a century, the Commonwealth Parliament legislated changes that have made Australia's electoral system unique in the world. The first major change was the 1911 requirement that compelled eligible electors to enrol to vote, extended in 1924 to a compulsory vote. In 1918 the plurality system was replaced by the *preferential* method. It is the combination of these two practices in elections for the House of Representatives which continues to make Australia's electoral system unique.

Who votes?

An inclusive franchise encompassing all adult citizens is widely regarded as a necessary condition for representative democracy. Yet most of the countries recognised as Western democracies have fulfilled this important condition only relatively recently. Great Britain, for example, did not achieve universal adult male suffrage until 1918, denied full voting rights to women until 1928, and retained forms of 'plural voting' (more than one vote per citizen) until 1948. By contrast Australia, together with New Zealand, was a world leader in extending the right to vote beyond the narrow confines of male property owners. The enfranchisement of women was first achieved in South Australia in 1894, and was implemented for national elections by the first Commonwealth Parliament in 1902. By 1907, all the impediments to a full adult franchise had been expunged from Australia's seven lower house voting systems in the six States and at the Commonwealth level (Butler 1981: 12-19; Crisp 1984: 137).

Compared with the other democracies this was an impressive achievement, tainted by two deficiencies. The first deficiency was that Indigenous Australians were largely excluded. 'Aboriginal natives', except for those already entitled to vote in State elections, were excluded from the franchise, were only granted the right to enrol to vote in 1962, and it was not until 1983 that the same electoral provisions applied to Indigenous as to non-Indigenous Australians (Summers 2000: 5–8). The second deficiency was that pre-democratic practices, typically a property-based franchise, were retained for some State upper house and local government elections, and the instillation of full representative democracy in these arenas was not achieved until many decades later.

Today's *Electoral Act* provides that all persons who are entered on the appropriate electoral roll are entitled to vote. The restrictions pertaining to enrolment are that a person must be an Australian citizen and have attained the age of 18 years (reduced from 21 in 1973), must be 'of sound mind', must not be 'convicted of unpardoned treason', must not be serving a prison sentence of three years or longer, and must have lived for at least one month at his or her current residence. While about 94 per cent of all those enrolled on the electoral roll actually vote in any given election, we can be less certain about how close the level of enrolment is to the goal of universal enrolment. The Australian Electoral Commission (AEC) estimates that about 600 000 eligible citizens were not enrolled prior to the 2001 election (*Australian* 6 October 2004).

An interesting restriction relates to the voting rights of prisoners. The United States excludes from voting large numbers of people convicted of a felony, whether they are in prison or not. Perhaps reflective of our partial convict heritage, Australia has adopted more liberal policies. An attempt in the 1890s to insert a clause into the draft Constitution, which would have denied convicted felons of the right to vote for all time, was soundly defeated. Until 1983, only convicted criminals serving prison sentences of at least one year were liable to be removed from the electoral roll. In 1983, this was liberalised to require a sentence of five years or more. But recently the Federal Parliament has moved back in a more restrictive direction: in late 2004, it legislated to reduce the five-year disbarring sentence to three years and then, after the Coalition gained control of the Senate on 1 July 2005, it legislated to disenfranchise all convicted prisoners.

The strongest argument for denying criminals the vote, an argument that seems particularly persuasive in the USA, is that by their criminal behaviour they have broken their 'contract' with society and should be regarded as being 'civilly dead' (Costar 2003: 95). But societies like Australia—at least until its recent reversals of earlier liberalisation—have seemed more inclined to regard being sent to jail for relatively short sentences as punishment enough. Excluding shorter-term prisoners from the franchise seems to undermine the potential rehabilitative function of the penal system. It is also arguably dangerous, on the classic liberal grounds of holding governments accountable and in check, for the state to be exercising a power to disenfranchise a group of citizens who are likely to be particularly dissatisfied with state actions. Because Australia's rate of imprisonment is comparatively low, denying longer-term inmates the vote has had negligible electoral impact in practice, though it is hard to disagree with Orr's argument that it is 'unsupportable on political equality grounds' (Orr 2004: 9)

Other democracies are far more protective of prisoners' voting rights. The Canadian Supreme Court invalidated a prisoner exclusion law in 2001 and in March 2004 the European Court of Human Rights ruled that the British law which denies all prisoners voting rights is in breach of the European Convention on Human Rights (Costar 2004: 10).

Another interesting restriction on citizen access to voting rights is revealed by Parliament's 2005 decision to close the electoral roll on the day the writs are issued for an election (i.e. the day that an election is officially announced). This change adversely affects a potentially substantial number of citizens. Previously, people had seven days after the issue of the writs to initiate an enrolment or to update their enrolment details. An average of 300 000 people have taken advantage of this period of grace at each election since 1983, about 80 000 of them being first-time young voters who had turned 18 since the previous election.

These amendments to the scope of and access to the franchise reveal that aspects of the right to vote are governed by parliamentary legislation rather than being fully and unequivocally enshrined in the Constitution. Most Australians would be surprised to learn this. Rubenstein is among the analysts who argue that it is not desirable to leave such democratic fundamentals to partisan parliamentary politics and that we instead need a constitutional Bill of Rights to secure them (Rubenstein 2003: 109).

Compulsory voting

While Australia's long history of generally inclusive franchises has been applauded by liberal democrats, the decision to go one step further and *compel* eligible persons both to enrol and to vote has been more controversial. All Commonwealth and State elections now involve compulsory voting, and the practice is becoming increasingly prevalent at the local government level in some States.

Compulsory voting has its supporters and its detractors. One set of opponents argues that compulsion drives to the polls the apathetic and ill-informed, with consequent dangers for the quality of their decision. In response, it has been contended that the obligation to vote encourages the otherwise apathetic to take some interest in politics, thereby contributing to the health of the democracy. The empirical evidence has been sufficiently inconclusive on this point to allow both camps to hold their views with equal fervour. Another, more sophisticated, critique of compulsion is that it deprives the citizen of the political right to abstain from voting as a positive protest against all parties or candidates or against 'the system' as a whole.

Perhaps the undoubted denial of political liberty associated with compulsion is compensated for by the high turnout of voters and the increased legitimacy thereby conferred on the elected government. There are also strong practical arguments sustaining compulsory voting. To be blunt, compulsion works. At the 1922 Senate election, the last conducted under voluntary provisions, the voter turnout was just under 58 per cent. This rose dramatically to 91.3 per cent in 1925 at the first election held under the compulsory provisions. The turnout at national elections now rarely falls below 94 per cent of the enrolled voters. Both major political parties in Australia have usually supported compulsion for practical rather than philosophical reasons, because it relieves them of the expensive and time-consuming task of encouraging their supporters to go to the polls. But there are periodic moves to abolish it. In 1994 a Bill abolishing compulsory voting sponsored by the Liberal government in South Australia passed its Legislative Assembly but was rejected by the Legislative Council.

According to opinion polls, most Australians are strongly supportive of compulsory voting. Two polls in early 2005 put the level of support at 74 per cent of respondents (*Sydney Morning Herald* 29 March 2005). But this did not discourage the Howard Coalition government from issuing a Discussion Paper in 2005 canvassing the virtues of voluntary voting but not voluntary enrolment.

Because compulsion has been part of the electoral landscape for so long, it is difficult to assess the partisan impact of a reversion to voluntarism. But it is generally accepted that levels of voluntary political participation tend to be correlate directly with socioeconomic status (Hague & Harrop 1987: 91ff). This implies that, if compulsion were removed, the non-voters would most likely be concentrated among the less well off. Over time the major parties might well be tempted to pitch their electoral messages only to the regular voters, disadvantaging those in the lower socioeconomic strata and the parties they currently support.

Preferential voting

In 1918, in response to the emergence of the Country Party which threatened to split the non-Labor vote to Labor's advantage, the Nationalist government introduced *preferential* voting.

Under this system, voters are required to rank *all* candidates in order of preference. In order to be elected, a candidate must secure an absolute majority (i.e. more than 50 per cent) of all valid votes cast. If no candidate receives such a majority after the count of first preferences, then the candidate with the smallest number of first-preference votes is eliminated, and his or her ballots are distributed among the remaining candidates according to the second preference indicated. This process of elimination and distribution of preferences continues until a candidate achieves an absolute majority.

The major advantage of preferential voting is that it minimises the possibility of a candidate being elected despite being disapproved of by a majority of voters. However, the compulsory requirement means that voters *must* express second and subsequent preferences in order to cast a valid vote even if they strongly support only one candidate and equally dislike all the rest. As Emy (1978: 599) has observed, the system thus makes some dubious assumptions about the 'intensity of like and dislike which candidates arouse in electors'. There exists a nagging doubt about whether voters are expressing real political preferences or merely completing the ballot paper to ensure that they cast a valid vote for the candidate of their first choice. If the latter is the case, then it is possible that the preferential system at times manufactures majorities that may distort the real intention of voters.

These objections should not be lightly dismissed, and they may help to explain why Australia's voting system remains unattractive to the rest of the world (a 1992 New Zealand plebiscite that canvassed several alternative voting methods saw only 6 per cent support it). But neither should the impact of the preferential method at the national level be exaggerated. Most House of Representative contests are decided without the need to distribute preferences to identify a winner, because one of the candidates wins an absolute majority on first-preference votes. Even when preferences need to be distributed in the other contests, their effect is usually to confirm as victor the candidate who led on the first count. At the 1987 federal election, preferences were distributed in 36 per cent of House seats but they overturned first-count leaders in only four seats. First-count leaders were defeated in 10 seats in 1990, in 12 in 1993, in seven in both 1996 and 1998, six in 2001 and eight (representing just 5.3 per cent of all seats) in 2004.

This is not to imply that the preferential system cannot have an impact on the outcome of elections. Victoria's longest-serving Premier, Henry Bolte, won six consecutive State elections between 1959 and 1970 without his Liberal Party ever polling more than 39 per cent of the primary vote. The second preferences of the right-wing Democratic Labor Party's (DLP) voters secured his victories.

An analysis of the 1998 Queensland and federal elections illustrates how preference allocation by parties can affect the capacity to translate votes into seats. In Queensland, Pauline Hanson's One Nation party burst on to the State electoral scene in the June 1998 State election by winning 22.7 per cent of the primary vote and 11 of the 89 seats in the Queensland Parliament. One Nation also performed fairly well in the subsequent October 1998 federal election, winning 14.4 per cent of the vote in Queensland and 8.4 per cent of the vote nationally. But One Nation won no seats in the House of Representatives. The National Party, in contrast, won just 10 per cent of the vote in Queensland and

7.9 per cent nationally, and yet won five House of Representatives seats in Queensland and 16 seats nationally.

The different outcomes for One Nation at the Queensland State election and the federal election cannot be attributed wholly to its lower level of primary voting support. It is also partly explained by the fact that, at the State election, the Coalition parties recommended that their supporters direct preferences to One Nation, but they reversed this at the federal poll, in effect preferring the Labor Party to One Nation. Starved of preference votes, no One Nation candidate was able to achieve an absolute majority. Had a system of plurality voting been in place, Pauline Hanson would have retained the seat of Blair which she had won in 1996. The explanation for the National Party's success, despite its overall lower level of voting support, is both that its vote was more concentrated in specific electorates and that it benefited from a consistent flow of Liberal Party preferences.

This example shows that preferential voting is not necessarily friendly to minor parties in terms of election outcomes, though it does give them a potential capacity to affect the outcome through negotiating conditions for recommending the distribution of the preference votes of their supporters.

A variant of preferential voting is *optional preferential* voting. Under this method, an elector is required to number only as many candidates as there are vacancies to be filled. Thus where the election is for a single member, such as for a House of Representatives seat, only one candidate needs to be supported. Voters may, if they wish, offer rankings for some, or all, of the other names on the ballot paper but they are not required to. In an optional preferential system, it is thus possible for a candidate to be elected without obtaining an absolute majority. The major arguments in favour of optional preferential voting are that it reduces the distortion of 'real' preferences by not requiring voters to distinguish between equally unwelcome candidates, and that it reduces the level of invalid ('informal') votes by minimising the number of correct numbers required on the ballot paper.

Optional preferential voting is employed in State elections in New South Wales, Queensland and the ACT. Despite being recommended by a 1983 Joint Select Committee on Electoral Reform, the federal Parliament has not adopted optional preferential voting for federal elections.

The preferential voting system is neither inherently anti-Labor nor anti-Coalition. Its partisan impact depends on the political persuasion of the minor parties and Independents whose preferences are distributed. Because the DLP was closer in its policy orientation to the Coalition parties than to the Labor Party, especially in its crucial foreign policy stance, the Coalition parties rather than Labor received the bulk of DLP voters' second preferences. More recently, because the Democrats and Greens have been closer in their policy orientation to Labor, Labor has benefited more from preferential voting than the Coalition.

Independent candidates can sometimes benefit by attracting the second preferences of both the major parties.

Despite the differences between the plurality and preferential systems, they share one important feature: they operate on the basis of single-member, geographically delineated units called (variously) electorates, seats, constituencies, districts or divisions. Single-member systems determine an overall winner by simply adding up the number of seats that each party wins. They do not set out to allocate parliamentary seats in proportion to the overall total number of votes obtained by the parties across all the electorates.

In practice, these systems often produce an exaggerated overall majority in the legislature for the winning party or coalition compared with the actual proportion of overall votes won by that party or coalition. A quite small advantage in total votes can sometimes deliver a comfortable parliamentary majority to a party or coalition. For example, at the 2004 federal election the Coalition polled 52.7 per cent of the House of Representatives 'two-party preferred' vote (i.e. the effective vote for their two major party blocs—the Liberal–National Coalition and Labor—after the distribution of preferences from minor-party and Independent voters). But the Coalition won 58.0 per cent of the seats.

It is quite possible for a party or coalition with a *minority* of the overall two-party preferred vote to win a majority of seats. To illustrate how this can happen, it would be mathematically possible for a party to win an election with just over a quarter of the total overall vote—by winning just over half the votes in each of just over half the seats. Or, more realistically, if a party wins by narrow majorities in a majority of seats and another party wins the remaining seats by large majorities, then it is possible for the winning party to have less votes than the losing party. Something like this occurred in the federal elections of 1954, 1961, 1969, 1990 and 1998. The lack of symmetry between votes and seats in single-member electoral systems occurs because not all votes that go to make a party's system-wide tally contribute to the election of winning candidates, and are thus 'wasted'. There can (by definition) be only one winner in each single-member constituency contest. This means that some votes will be cast for the winner in excess of the bare majority needed for victory, while others will be cast for losing candidates.

The Senate and proportional representation

Australia has a bicameral legislature with the upper house, the Senate, virtually equal in power with the House of Representatives. Until 1948 the Senate's electoral procedures mirrored those of the House: a plurality system operated from 1901 to 1918 and a preferential system from 1919 to 1948. These procedures generally resulted in the government (i.e. the party that won a majority in the House of Representatives) also controlling the Senate. The reasons why the Chifley Labor government chose in 1948 to implement a proportional system are complex (Uhr 1999), but a desire to protect Labor's large Senate majority at the 1949 election was prominent. Labor's decision was to have important but unintended consequences for Australia's system of government.

Because proportional representation (PR) utilises multi-member districts and does not require candidates to win a majority of the vote in order to win seats, it determines seats in much better overall proportion to votes won.

There are two main types of PR.

Under the *list system*, which was briefly used in the South Australian upper house in the 1970s, voters are restricted to endorsing lists of candidates put forward by the parties. Parties are then allocated seats in proportion to the vote obtained by their lists, with particular candidates being elected if they are ranked (by the party) sufficiently high on the list.

The *single transferable vote* (STV) method (sometimes termed *quota preferential*) has been used in Tasmanian House of Assembly elections since 1907 (where it is known as the Hare-Clark system) and for the Commonwealth Senate since 1949. A simplified explanation of the Senate voting procedure illustrates the main feature of the STV system. Each State constitutes one multi-member division (i.e. electing a number of Senators to represent the same geographical area). A quota is calculated by dividing the total number of valid votes by one more than the number ('n') of Senators to be elected and adding one vote. In percentage terms, the quota is this: 100 per cent divided by (n + 1), plus one vote. In Senate elections since 1984 (when the representation for each State was raised to 12), this formula produces a quota of about 7.7 per cent for a full Senate election (with 12 seats to fill) and about 14.3 per cent for a half-Senate poll (when there are six seats to fill). Each party's candidates are grouped together on the ballot paper but, in contrast to the list system, voters must express preferences for all of them as in the preferential system. The Senate ballot paper now simplifies this task, by giving voters the option of voting 'below the line' to indicate their preferences for all candidates as in the preferential system or voting 'above the line' by simply indicating support for the one party's registered distribution of preferences.

Note that, while the system is designed to produce an outcome proportional to the overall pattern of votes for each party, it is not mathematically precise. This is due both to the elimination of low-scoring candidates as part of the process of counting votes until all the quotas are filled (which has the effect of inflating the support for the remaining candidates), and to the final nationwide Senate result being obtained by adding together of the separate outcomes from each of the eight State and Territory electorates. At the 2004 election, for example, the Coalition polled 45.1 per cent of the Senate vote but received 52.5 per cent of the Senate places. In order to get closer to 'perfect' proportionality, all of the 76 Senators would have to be chosen from a single, nationwide electorate. This is not allowed under the Constitution.

PR is not without its detractors. A major criticism is that it can encourage a proliferation of political parties and consequently, because this can make it more difficult for a single party to win a majority, encourage instability of government. PR certainly gives minor parties a greater chance of winning seats, and minor parties such as the Democratic Labor Party, the Australian Democrats, the Greens and, recently, Family First have taken advantage of it to be elected to the Senate. It is also true that a probable effect of extending PR to the House of Representatives would be to greatly increase the likelihood of producing a Parliament in which neither of the two major party groups hold an absolute majority of seats, leaving members of minor political parties and/or Independents holding the so-called 'balance of power'. It would be thus possible for more than 90 per cent of the electorate to vote for one of the two major parties yet for the composition of any parliamentary majority effectively to be 'controlled' by a group supported by less than 10 per cent of the voters. Thus, proportionality of representation at the electoral level may be translated into disproportionate legislative influence.

On the other hand, political systems are influenced by factors other than voting methods. Tasmania, for example, despite having adopted PR as long ago as 1907, has not experienced any serious or prolonged splintering of the party system and has generally been characterised by governmental stability. The election of 'Green' Independent candidates at the 1989 State election was aided by the PR voting method, but their emergence was the result of political factors unrelated to the electoral system.

Many PR proponents assert that elections should be 'for the benefit of electors, not political parties' (Lakeman 1970: 354). But this claim is open to question: it assumes that the ultimate goal is to achieve the broadest possible representation of political opinion in Parliament, without an overriding concern for the nature of the government that such a Parliament might produce. It could be argued, to the contrary, that elections in liberal democracies should produce a government capable of implementing and being judged on its declared program, unencumbered by the need to strike compromising deals with other, often minority, parties. If this is the primary objective, then a PR system has significant drawbacks.

Ultimately, the controversy (Wright 1980; Ray 1982; Lijphart & Groffman 1984) reduces to a choice between a system that provides for a wide representation of political opinion but which probably gives undue legislative influence to minorities, or a system that under-represents minority opinions in favour of clear-cut majorities of seats to one or other of the major party groupings.

Australia's federal electoral procedures are a constructive compromise. They consist of a single-member preferential system in the House of Representatives, from which the government is drawn, and a PR system for the Senate.

Neither of the major parties had a majority in the Senate between June 1981 and July 2005. Major-party frustration with the increasing activism of (sometimes) unpredictable minor parties and Independent Senators during that period brought forth a number of proposals to change the electoral system to make it more difficult for minor parties to win Senate seats. In 1994 the Keating Labor government floated the idea of dividing each State into 12 single-member electorates with each choosing a Senator by the preferential method, but did not proceed with the proposal. A more complex, but equally contentious, proposal was advanced by Liberal Senator Helen Coonan in 1999: it would require Senate candidates to achieve a minimum threshold of primary votes to proceed to the next stage of the count (Costar 2000). Again the suggestion has not been acted on. But it remains possible that the major party pikes will 'gang up' on the political minnows (as happened in Tasmania prior to the 1998 State election).

A largely unanticipated result of the 2004 election was that the Coalition won a majority of Senate places, the first time a party had achieved this since the election of December 1977. The reason for the victory was the unusually high Coalition primary vote, and a fall in the Democrats' vote, which snared the Coalition three places in five States and four in Queensland.

The result in the 2004 election produced new criticism of the Senate voting procedures. As noted above, the Senate employs the single-transferable vote method of PR which theoretically gives the power to the voter to choose among the candidates. However, since the introduction of 'above the line' voting in 1983, about 95 per cent of voters choose that option because of its convenience and because it reduces the chance of recording an accidental informal vote. Yet it also effectively converts the STV PR system into a de-facto closed list system. This is because the political parties register their how-to-vote cards containing their preference allocations with the Australian Electoral Commission (AEC) and, when an elector chooses to vote above the line, she accepts her party's registered preference allocation as her own without necessarily being aware of its detail. For example, the recently formed Family First Party, despite beginning the vote count with only 1.88 per cent of the primary vote, won the final Senate place in Victoria in the 2004 election because it was the major recipient of other parties' registered preference allocations.

Current controversies

For many decades the most controversial federal electoral issue was malapportionment, whereby some electorates (usually rural) contained significantly fewer enrolled voters than others (usually urban). The alleged party bias inherent in this system was much debated, but the issue was finally laid to rest by electoral reforms in 1983. The Commonwealth and all States bar Western Australia now operate systems that require a reasonable equality of enrolment across constituencies. In terms of efficiency and effectiveness, and adherence to modern democratic principles, the Australian electoral procedures approach world's best practice, but this is not to say that contentious issues do not remain.

MONEY

Electoral law specialist Graeme Orr (2004: vii) has observed that 'the single greatest issue confronting elections in the developed world is the influence of private money'. In Australia the Commonwealth implemented a method of public funding in 1983 whereby parties and candidates who obtained a required threshold of the primary vote (4 per cent) receive an indexed payment for every vote won (currently $3.92 per elector). Three of the States (New South Wales, Victoria, Queensland) and the Northern Territory also publicly fund election campaigns.

When the idea of public funding was debated in the early 1980s, one of its anticipated benefits was to lessen the parties' reliance on private donations. This has not happened: as well as receiving $40 million from the public purse for the 2004 federal election the parties received a further $80 million in private dona-tions in the year 2003–04. Over the three years 2000–03, the ALP received $132 million in funding of which only 18.8 per cent came from public sources; the figures for the Liberal Party over the same period were $120 million and 17.5 per cent (Jaensch, Brent & Bowden 2004: 32). There are laws which require the public disclosure of the source of private donations but their transparency is limited by the money often reaching the party coffers via so-called 'associated entities' (such as Canberra Labor Club Ltd and Cormack Foundation Pty Ltd), no fewer than 81 of which submitted returns to the AEC in early 2005.

Public funding is often defended as lubricating the democratic process by allowing a multitude of voices to be heard. In reality the current system aids the major parties because, by definition, they receive most of the funds. These funds are then typically transferred to commercial media networks and public relations firms to pay for the ever-increasing costs of political advertising.

Two other issues involving political money involve the blurring of public and private interests.

The first involves the fine line between, on the one hand, a government legit-imately spending funds to advertise the existence and availability of services to citizens and, on the other hand, illegitimately using public money to boost the electoral stocks of the political party which happens to be the government. In the last six months of 2004 (and note that an election was held, in the midst of this period, on 9 October), the federal government spent $95 million on official advertising. The figure for the first half of 2005 (with no election imminent) is estimated to be less than $12 million (*The Age* 24 March 2005).

A second problem is the increasing practice of 'buying time with a minister' (Van Onselen & Errington 2004: 4). This involves government ministers making themselves available—at formal breakfasts, dinners and even when jogging—to those able to afford fees of often thousands of dollars which then go into the minister's party's coffers to be used for electoral campaigns. The bait is the opportunity to lobby the minister. As Van Onselen and Errington (2004: 6) ask: 'Is it legal? Technically. Is it ethical and proper? Absolutely not'.

The lack of regulation of political money is the most serious shortcoming of Australia's electoral procedure. Few would disagree that reform of the electoral funding regime is 'long overdue' (Mercurio & Williams 2004: 31), but why should the parties want to tamper with a system that so favours them?

ELECTORAL FRAUD

A regular feature of testimony before inquiries by the Australian Parliament's Joint Standing Committee on Electoral Matters (JSCEM) into the conduct of elections are complaints of widespread fraudulent enrolment and multiple voting (Copeman & McGrath 1997). As the *Electoral Act* requires compulsory enrolment of eligible voters, few impediments are placed in the path of those wishing to enrol. For example, minimal formal identification is required to enrol. While it is an offence to do so and is liable to be prosecuted, it is possible to vote more than once in an electoral division with little chance of detection on polling day and for the multiple votes to be undetectable during the vote count.

While critics are loud in their claims that the system is open to fraud, this is quite different from showing that the system is actually defrauded to such an extent as to undermine its integrity and/or to alter actual results. While the notorious 1990 enrolment of Curacao Fischer Catt—a feline whose occupation was listed as 'pest exterminator' (*Sydney Morning Herald* 16 November 2000)—has entered electoral folklore, former Electoral Commissioner Colin Hughes (1998) has taken to task those who, for apparent political purposes, make extravagant allegations of corruption based on flimsy evidence. To take but one example: the JSCEM review of the 1987 federal election noted that the AEC had identified 11 525 instances of apparent multiple voting across Australia. Checking of the electoral roll identified only 266 electors who admitted to having voted more than once, of whom just 45—out of the 9.7 million Australians who voted in the election—were referred for prosecution (JSCEM 1989: 80).

One of the major flaws in the conspiracy theory of electoral rorting is that, in order to rig an election result, a very large number of fraudulent voters would need to be concentrated in those key seats which determined the result, and the conspirators would need to be able to predict in advance which those seats would be.

PARTY CORRUPTION

Australian political parties are essentially voluntary organisations, subject to very few external controls beyond certain minimal requirements to qualify for public funding. While this may be slowly changing—for example, the Queensland *Electoral Act* now requires standards on internal democracy as a precondition of party registration (Jaensch, Brent & Bowden 2004: 24)—parties are generally at liberty to conduct their own internal affairs, including how they preselect parliamentary candidates, as they please. Because political parties have relatively few members (less than 2 per cent of the electorate belongs to a political party), it can be relatively easy, where parties determine candidate preselection by means of a ballot of local branch members, to influence the outcome by engaging in the practice known as 'branch stacking'. This involves the signing up of large numbers of new members into party branches with the sole intention of their voting for a particular candidate in an internal contest. These new 'members' typically have their membership fee paid for them by faction leaders, and most of them are inactive in the branch after casting their vote. As about 60 per cent of the House of Representatives seats are classified as 'safe' for one party or the other, winning the preselection ballot virtually guarantees a seat in Parliament. Hence, the unregulated informal party ballot effectively determines the outcome, later simply confirmed by the regulated formal electoral process.

Throughout 1999 and 2000 it was revealed that factional chieftains within the Queensland branch of the Labor Party were corrupting the Commonwealth electoral roll by deliberately falsifying the addresses of enrolees to permit them to vote in party preselection ballots for electorates in which they did not reside. This device remained undetected for a time because of the very small number of bogus voters involved, yet it is a serious offence against the *Electoral Act* and one offender was subsequently jailed for nine months. (It is important to distinguish this case from any suggestion of seeking to influence general election outcomes, as it appears that those fraudulently enrolled voted in internal party ballot but not at any general election.)

One suggestion for minimising the rorting of internal party ballots is to make it a condition of the receipt of public funding for parties to have their candidate selection ballots conducted by the Australian Electoral Commission, as has been the case for some time in relation to internal trade union elections. The AEC is not enthusiastic about the idea on resource grounds and because it might embroil it in perceived partisanship (AEC 2000).

DISQUALIFICATION OF MEMBERS

Largely because the Australian Constitution is not prescriptive about the details of voting procedures, the High Court has only intermittently determined cases relevant to the electoral system. One function of the High Court, however, is to sit as a 'court of disputed returns' to adjudicate certain types of disputes arising from elections to the Commonwealth Parliament. It was in this capacity that the court delivered judgment in the case of *Sykes* v *Cleary* on 25 November 1992.

Phillip Cleary had won the House of Representatives seat of Wills as an Independent at a by-election on 11 April 1992. At the time of his election, Cleary was on leave without pay from his position as a teacher employed by the Victorian Ministry of Education. It was on this point that a defeated candidate petitioned the High Court to invalidate Cleary's election on the grounds of section 44(iv) of the Constitution, which states *inter alia* that 'any person who . . . holds any office of profit under the Crown . . . shall be incapable of being chosen or of sitting as a senator or a member of the House of Representatives'. By a 6 to 1 majority, the High Court ruled that Cleary did hold such an 'office of profit under the Crown' — because he had not actually resigned from being a Victorian public sector employee — and declared his election void.

The Court also ruled, by a 5 to 2 majority, that two other candidacies, those of Bill Kardimitsis (Labor) and John Delacretaz (Liberal), were also invalid, because section 44(i) disqualifies for election to Parliament any person who is 'under any acknowledgement of allegiance, obedience, or adherence to a foreign power, or is a subject or a citizen or entitled to the rights or privileges of a subject or a citizen of a foreign power'. Kardimitsis and Delacretaz had been born in Greece and Switzerland respectively and the Court ruled that, although they were naturalised Australian citizens, they had not taken 'reasonable steps to divest' themselves of their original citizenship 'and the rights and privileges of such a citizen'. The entire by-election was thus voided and the electors of Wills were left without representation until the 13 March 1993 general election, when Cleary (having by then resigned his teaching position) again won the seat.

Not surprisingly the High Court's decisions caused controversy, but they should have caused no surprise. Two earlier reports — a Senate committee report in 1981 (SSCCLA 1981) and a Constitutional Commission report in 1988 (Constitutional Commission 1988) — substantially anticipated the High Court ruling in Cleary's case. But successive governments have chosen not to address the issues by way of seeking a constitutional amendment despite the conclusions of the House of Representatives committee report in July 1997 that parts of s. 44 were discriminatory (HRSCLCA 1997).

Those dual citizens at risk under the 'foreign power' clause may avoid disqualification by writing to the relevant authorities in their former homelands, clearly revoking their citizenship. This, under the High Court ruling, would suffice even for those nations which do not permit the revocation of their citizenship.

In the case of the 'office of profit' clause, what is required is that any prospective candidate holding such an office must resign from it prior to nominating for election. This discriminates against certain groups of public-sector employees in two ways. First, not all public servants affected by section 44(iv) have statutory rights of automatic reinstatement to their job should they fail to be elected to Parliament. Second, with specific reference to Senate elections, Senators-elect (unlike successful House of Representatives candidates, who are paid from polling day) do not receive payment until 1 July of the relevant year in which their Senatorial term begins. Section 13 of the Constitution permits Senate elections to be held up to 'one year before the places are to become vacant', and it is not uncommon for Senate elections to be held some months in advance of when newly elected Senators may take their places. For example, new Senators elected on 9 October 2004 could not sit in the Senate until 1 July 2005. Public servants, but not private-sector employees, wishing to contest Senate elections must resign their jobs before nomination and may be rewarded for victory by prolonged unemployment until they actually take up their places. Three of the High Court judges in the Cleary case drew attention to the effect of section 44(iv) discouraging public servants from seeking parliamentary office, and commented that 'there is force in the view that the field of potential candidates for election should be as wide as possible' (Saunders 1992).

Despite the publicity that attended the Cleary case, several candidates since then have encountered similar problems. Elected at the March 1996 election as the member for the NSW House of Representatives seat of Lindsay, Liberal Jackie Kelly was deemed by the High Court to be ineligible to sit because she held an office of profit at the time of her nomination. She won the subsequent by-election on 19 October 1996. In anticipation of a similar challenge, newly elected Liberal Senator Jeannie Ferris from South Australia resigned from the Senate in July 1996 and was then appointed by the South Australian Parliament, under the terms of section 15 of the Constitution, to the casual vacancy so created. Later, Senator Heather Hill (Pauline Hanson's One Nation party) was successfully challenged on the grounds that she was ineligible to contest the 1998 election because she held British as well as Australian citizenship. The High Court ruled that Britain is 'a foreign power' for the purposes of section 44.

EXPAND THE FRANCHISE?

As noted earlier, Australia has a comparatively open franchise, but should it be expanded to include, say, permanent residents of Australia who are not citizens? At first glance, the case looks weak, on the grounds that the right to vote should reasonably be the preserve only of citizens. Yet the word 'citizen' was consciously omitted when the Commonwealth Constitution was drafted in the 1890s and only became operational after the passage of the *Citizenship Act 1949*. Between 1902 and 1983 all 'British subjects' who fulfilled the residency requirements could be enrolled to vote.

A group of citizens which some claim is effectively excluded from the franchise are the one million members of the so-called 'Australian diaspora', i.e. Australian citizens living abroad. The current law provides that any person who leaves Australia with the intention of returning may remain on the electoral roll for six years, after which they are required to apply each year to retain the right to vote. It has been recently argued (Duncan *et al.* 2004: 45) that, in a globalised world, these provisions are anachronistic and inadequate and that citizens resident overseas should be accorded political representation via an 'Australian International Senator'. This idea is yet to gain significant political support.

ELECTRONIC VOTING

Since the adoption of the 'secret ballot' in the 19th century, Australia has always employed paper ballots which electors are required to mark in pencil. The USA, by contrast, has long employed various types of voting machines, some of which are electronic. The different technologies have been produced by different electoral methods: the US conducts genuine *general* elections at which a multitude of contests (from national President down to, in some jurisdictions, local officials) appear on a single ballot paper making it very difficult to complete by hand. In contrast, the most complicated task an Australian federal elector currently faces is to rank order a number of House of Representatives candidates, place a single mark above the line on a Senate ballot paper and, occasionally, indicate YES or NO on a referendum paper.

Nevertheless, there has been some recent Australian interest in electronic voting. Two types of 'electronic voting' need to be distinguished: voting via the Internet and voting by way of electronic machines such as, for example, touch screens at polling places. Interest in Australia has centred on the latter option and a limited, successful trial of touch screens was conducted at the 2001 Australian Capital Territory Legislative Assembly (Elections ACT 2004). Supporters of electronic voting machines point out that they would speed up the counting of votes and protect the secrecy of the ballot for sight-impaired and other citizens with disabilities who currently have to reveal their voting intentions to third parties to cast a ballot. Problems with electronic machines are that some types do not leave a paper trail to allow ballot rechecking and that their initial installation would be expensive ($30 million according to one official estimate (Barry *et al.* 2001: 11)).

Conclusion

Fair electoral procedures are essential to the operation of modern representative democracy. This chapter has argued that there is no perfect electoral system, but some procedures are clearly fairer than others. Electoral procedures remain susceptible to manipulation and distortion. The independence of the Australian Electoral Commission, supported by all political parties, is a significant protection in relation to the actual conduct of elections, but there remains a danger that political parties will where possible attempt to design or reform the procedures to their own competitive advantage. We therefore need to be constantly vigilant in understanding the significance of electoral systems and in improving them where appropriate in ways that preserve and advance the democratic accountability of our parties and politicians.

REFERENCES

AEC [Australian Electoral Commission] 2000, 'Submission to the Joint Standing Committee on Electoral Matters Inquiry into the Integrity of the Electoral Roll', Submission no. 26, 17 October, Canberra, <http://www.aec.gov.au/_content/Why/committee/jscem/electoral_roll/sub26/js_sub26.pdf>.

Barry, C., Dacey, P., Pickering, T. & Byrne, D. 2001, *Electronic Voting and Electronic Counting of Votes: A Status Report*, Australian Electoral Commission, Canberra.

Butler, D. 1981, 'Electoral Systems', in *Democracy at the Polls*, eds D. Butler, H. Penniman & A. Ranney, American Enterprise Institute, Washington.

Constitutional Commission 1988, *Final Report*, AGPS, Canberra.

Copeman, C. & McGrath, A. eds 1997, *Corrupt Elections: Recent Australian Studies and Experiences of Ballot Rigging*, Towerhouse Publications, Kensington.

Costar, B. 2000, *Deadlock or Democracy? The Future of the Senate*, UNSW Press, Sydney.

Costar, B. 2003, 'Odious and Outmoded? Race and S 25 of the Constitution', in eds J. Chesterman & D. Phillips, *Selective Democracy: Race, Gender and the Australian Vote*, Circa, Melbourne.

Costar, B. 2004, 'Inside but Outside the System: Eroding the Right of Prisoners to Vote', *Human Rights Defender*, vol. 13, no. 2, October, pp. 9–11.

Crisp, L.F. 1984, *Australian National Government*, 5th edn, Longman Cheshire, Melbourne.

Duncan, M., Leigh, A., Madden, D. & Tynan, P. 2004, *Imagining Australia: Ideas for Our Future*, Sydney, Allen & Unwin.

Elections ACT 2004, 'Electronic Voting and Counting', Australian Capital Territory Electoral Commission, Canberra, <http://www.elections.act.gov.au/elecvote.html>.

Emy, H. 1978, *The Politics of Australian Democracy: Fundamentals in Dispute*, 2nd edn, Macmillan, Melbourne.

Hague, R. & Harrop, M. 1987, *Comparative Government and Politics: An Introduction*, 2nd edn, Macmillan, London.

HRSCLCA [House of Representatives Standing Committee on Legal and Constitutional Affairs] 1997, 'Aspects of Section 44 of the Australian Constitution: Subsections 44(i) and (iv)', Parliament of Australia, Canberra, <http://www.aph.gov.au/house/committee/laca/Inquiryinsec44.htm>.

Hughes, C. 1998, 'The Illusive Phenomenon of Fraudulent Voting Practices: A Review Article', *Australian Journal of Politics and History*, vol. 44, no. 3, pp. 471–91.

Jaensch, D., Brent, P. & Bowden, B. 2004, *Australian Political Parties in the Spotlight*, Democratic Audit of Australia, ANU, Canberra, <http://democratic.audit.anu.edu.au/PartyAudit.pdf>.

JSCEM [Joint Standing Committee on Electoral Matters] 1989, *Inquiring into the Conduct of the 1987 Federal Election and the 1988 Referendums*, Report no. 3, AGPS, Canberra.

Lakeman, E. 1970, *How Democracies Vote*, Faber & Faber, London.

Lijphart, A. & Groffman, B. 1984, *Choosing an Electoral System: Issues and Alternatives*, Praeger, New York.

Mercurio, B. & Williams, G. 2004, *Australian Electoral Law: 'Free and Fair'*, Federal Law Review, vol. 32, pp. 1–31.

Orr, G. 2004, *Australian Electoral Systems—How Well Do They Serve Political Equality?*, Australian National University, Canberra.

Ray, R. 1982, 'Rethink the Electoral System', in *Labor Essays*, eds G. Evans and J. Reeves, Drummond, Melbourne.

Rubenstein, K. 2003, 'Can the Right to Vote Be Taken Away? The Constitution, Citizenship and Voting Rights in 1902 and 2002', in eds J. Chesterman & D. Phillips, *Selective Democracy: Race, Gender and the Australian Vote*, Circa, Melbourne.

Saunders, G. 1992, 'The Cleary Case: Who Should be Eligible to Stand for Parliament?', *Constitutional Centenary*, vol. 1, no. 3.

SSCCLA [Senate Standing Committee on Constitutional and Legal Affairs] 1981, *Report: The Constitutional Qualifications of Members of Parliament*, Parliament of the Commonwealth of Australia, Canberra, <http://www.aph.gov.au/Senate/committee/legcon_ctte/completed_inquiries/pre1996/constitutional/report.pdf>.

Summers, J. 2000, 'The Parliament of the Commonwealth of Australia and Indigenous Peoples 1901–1967', *Research Paper* no. 10, 2000–01, Department of the Parliamentary Library, Canberra, <http://www.aph.gov.au/library/pubs/rp/2000-01/01RP10.htm>.

Uhr, J. 1999, 'Why We Chose Proportional Representation', in *Representation and Institutional Change*, eds M. Sawer & S. Miskin, Australian National University, Canberra.

Van Onselen, P. & Errington, W. 2004, 'Political Donations and Party Fundraising: Buying Time With a Minister?', *AQ*, vol. 76, issue 6, November–December.

Wright, J. 1980, *Mirror of the Nation's Mind: Australia's Electoral Experiments*, Hale & Iremonger, Sydney.

The Liberal Party

JUDITH BRETT

The re-election of the Howard government in October 2004 confirmed the Liberal Party of Australia's domination of Australian national politics since its defeat of the Labor government in March 1996. This chapter analyses the Liberal Party's historical development, its organisational principles, the role of its leaders and its main policy trajectories. The chapter pays particular attention to the meaning and significance within the Liberal Party of the 'liberal' notion that is the source of its name and which continues to shape—in complex and sometimes contradictory ways—the party's activities and its policies.

Origins: non-Labor parties 1901–1945

The Liberal Party of Australia was formed in December 1944, with the formal announcement occurring in February 1945. Although this represented a new beginning, it was also the continuation of a political tradition that has been central to Australian politics since 1901. Throughout the 20th century, Australian party politics were organised around the opposition between Labor and 'non-Labor'.[1] In the 1920s the Country Party was formed on the non-Labor side to represent the small rural farmers. This changed the dynamics of the party electoral competition and led to the formation of coalition non-Labor governments, but it did not alter the fundamental opposition at the heart of the party system, which remained Labor versus non-Labor. To understand the interests and ideas that have shaped today's Liberal Party we need to go back to the first decade of the 20th century, when the party system as we know it today was taking shape.

THE FIRST DECADE

The catalyst for the emergence of the Australian party system that we know today was the decision by the labour movement to build a political party. This decision radically changed Australian parliamentary and electoral politics. In 1901, when the first Commonwealth Parliament met, the 24 members elected by various State-based labour parties came together to form the Federal Parliamentary Labor Party. Electoral support for Labor rose steadily all through the first decade of the 20th century until, at the 1910 federal election, Labor won almost 50 per cent of the vote and formed a majority government. For a political organisation that had begun less than 20 years previously, this was a remarkable result.[2]

Labor's success precipitated a crisis among the non-Labor groupings, forcing them to think hard about the differences among them and about what it was that distinguished them from Labor and its supporters. In the 1890s trade had been the most contentious issue in non-Labor circles, and there were fierce divisions between those who supported free trade and those who thought that Australia's young manufacturing industries should be protected from imports. Support for free trade was strongest in New South Wales, where the economy was based on commodities like wool and coal; and support for protection strongest in Victoria, where manufacturing had been developed to provide employment for the migrants who had come in the goldrush. By 1908 supporters of protection in alliance with Labor had triumphed, and the protection of domestic markets for manufactured goods was entrenched in legislation. The trade question was settled and did not re-emerge as a controversial political issue until the 1970s.

George Reid, the leader of the NSW-based free traders, conceded defeat and turned his attention to opposing Labor's socialist ambitions, by which he meant Labor's support for the extension of government-owned enterprises and for government regulation of living and working conditions. Employers' groups increased their level of organisation to meet the challenge of organised labour in Parliament. The first non-Labor party was called, briefly, the Fusion Party, as it was formed from the coming together of erstwhile bitter enemies, and then the Liberal Party from 1910 to 1917.

POLITICAL, ECONOMIC AND SOCIAL LIBERALISM

The choice of the word 'Liberal' to describe the new party needs some explanation. It is also the word chosen in 1944 by the successor Liberal Party of

Australia, and points to the importance of the political tradition of liberalism in non-Labor's political thinking. As Chapter 1 of this book describes, liberalism is a tradition of political thought which places the rights and interests of the individual at the centre of its political thinking, and is suspicious of the state's power.[3] Liberals maintain that, wherever possible, individuals should be left to make their own choices, free from state direction or control.

To appreciate the development of the Liberal Party in Australia, it helps to differentiate between political, economic and social dimensions of liberalism. In the development of liberalism in Western thought, *political liberalism* came first as a struggle to limit the power of the monarchic state in order to achieve civil rights and liberties for the individual: trial by jury, freedom of movement, freedom of religion, freedom of expression and of the press, freedom of assembly, and the rights of individuals to their property. These were the basis for the development of constitutional politics in which the coercive power of the state was limited and constrained by law and by public opinion, and in which political opposition was both possible and legal. This political liberalism supported the claims of Parliament against the monarchy for a greater say in the government of the country. The Westminster system of responsible Parliamentary government, with its limited role for the monarch, its division of powers between the different arms of government, and its institutionalisation of a legal opposition to the government of the day, is very much a product of liberal political thought.

Liberalism also fought for the economic rights of the individual, the right to buy and sell land, labour and goods without the interference of the state. This version of liberalism, often called *economic liberalism* or laissez-faire liberalism, was developed in the 18th century. The state's proper role was to defend the country from invasion and to provide a strong framework of law and order to protect life and property. Economic activity would take place within this, driven by self-interest and regulated by the laws of the market.

As the 19th century progressed, with its glaring inequalities and widespread misery, a new version of liberalism developed, often called *social liberalism*. It also began with the individual, but instead of focusing only on the individual's economic role and legal status, it asked how society could be organised so that each individual had the opportunity to develop his or her full human potential. It thus had a very different view of the role of the state from earlier versions of liberalism, and looked to the state to eliminate the various obstacles, such as poverty or lack of education, which prevent people from leading fulfilling human lives. Social liberalism drew inspiration from Christianity's concern with the moral and spiritual wellbeing of all people, and was much less suspicious than economic liberalism of the role of the state.

The first Australian Liberal Party was formed out of adherents of both economic and social liberalism. Throughout the 20th century both strands have contributed to non-Labor political thinking and policy, although there have always been tensions between them. In the Australian context, economic liberals, who support the importance of the market in the regulation of the economy and in particular in setting wage levels and working conditions, and who generally oppose the regulation of economic activity by the state, are often called conservatives. The tensions between social and economic liberalism within the Liberal Party became acute during the 1980s as economic liberal ideas gained many supporters within the party. We look at the recent conflict in the party over economic liberalism later in this chapter.

The Labor Party was also deeply influenced by social liberalism, and by the belief that the power of the state should be used to reform society and make it more just. Before the fusion of Alfred Deakin's Liberals and George Reid's conservatives, the Labor Party and Alfred Deakin's Liberals had cooperated to introduce legislation, such as the old-age pension and tariff legislation, to help protect workers' living standards. However, despite many shared social-liberal ideas, Liberals like Deakin were deeply opposed to the way the new Labor Party was organised. The different values embodied in the different organisations divided non-Labor from Labor as decisively as did different attitudes to the role of the state.

ORGANISATION

Modern political parties are made up of two parts, sometimes referred to as 'wings': a parliamentary wing, composed of those from the party elected to Parliament, and an extra-parliamentary wing, composed of the organisations outside Parliament which canvass votes, raise money for elections, and may also participate in policy formation. Until the formation of the Liberal Party in 1944, Australian non-Labor parties had fairly loose organisational links between the parliamentary members and the outside electoral organisations, whose role was generally confined to campaigning at elections and tended to lapse into inactivity between elections. The extra-parliamentary organisation was there to support the parliamentary wing and to work for the re-election of its members. The direction of policy of the party was entirely a matter for the parliamentarians, who would exercise their independent judgement according to the debates and deliberations in the parliamentary wing of the party.

By contrast, the new Labor Party had a quite different understanding of the proper relationship between the two wings. The pledge which Labor candidates had to sign, promising that they would support the party's policy, was fundamentally at odds with the Liberals' belief in the importance of each individual's freedom of judgement. As well, the control of the party organisation over policy challenged the position of Parliament as the supreme deliberative body in the land. Liberals saw themselves as part of a tradition which had fought for the sovereignty of Parliament against the interference of the monarch, and were opposed to this sovereignty now being compromised by interference from party bodies outside Parliament. The lines of division between Labor and non-Labor as they developed in this formative period before the outbreak of World War I were mainly formed around a different emphasis on the role of the state and a different form of party organisation. These lines of division had a clear class dimension. Those with substantial property as well as the home-owning middle class on the whole supported a less interventionist state; the working classes on the whole placed their faith in government programs to improve their living and working conditions. In this period the term 'socialist' started to be used to describe Labor's more expansive vision of the state's role, although before the 1917 Bolshevik Revolution in Russia it did not have quite the power to frighten that it acquired later.

BETWEEN THE WARS

Between World War I and the formation of the Liberal Party of Australia at the end of World War II, the main non-Labor party went through two reformations. The first was in 1917, when the Labor Prime Minister Billy Hughes and some Labor Party members left the Labor Party to join with its opponents to form a National government. The issue that led to this dramatic defection was conscription to fight in World War I. Many in the Labor Party were deeply opposed to conscription, particularly many Catholics of Irish descent who saw Britain not as the mother of Empire but as the oppressor of Ireland. This led to another layer of difference between Labor and non-Labor. Henceforth the Labor Party was more identified with Australian national independence and non-Labor with imperial loyalty and deference to Britain. As well, a sectarian division was imported into the differences between Labor and non-Labor which lasted till the 1960s. The Nationalists became identified with Protestants, Labor with the Catholics. This was particularly evident in the parliamentary representatives. When Philip Lynch became a Minister in Prime Minister Fraser's Cabinet in 1975, his Catholicism was a matter for remark. Today, however, the prominence of Catholics like Tony Abbott in John Howard's Cabinets show that Catholicism is no longer a barrier to advancement in the Liberal Party. Abbott himself remarked in 2002 that 'of the third Howard Government's 42 frontbenchers, 13 are Catholic (which makes Catholics perhaps slightly over-represented)—and in NSW the party's last five leaders have been Catholic—which is a remarkable transformation for a party once run (at least in Catholic eyes) by the Protestant ascendancy' (Abbott 2002).

The second reformation of non-Labor was in 1931. The Nationalists had been defeated by the Labor Party in 1929, on the eve of the Great Depression. Dissension within the Labor Party over how to deal with the financial, economic and social crisis of the early 1930s led to Labor Federal Treasurer, Joseph Lyons, leaving the party over what he saw as unorthodox financial policies. He became leader of a new party, the United Australia Party (UAP), which won the 1932 election and remained in power till 1941 when it was defeated on the floor of the House of Representatives. Labor formed a government under John Curtin as Prime Minister. The subsequent election in 1943 was the lowest point for non-Labor in federal politics. Labor triumphed at the polls, with the United Australia Party winning only 14 seats, the Country Party nine, and a big vote for non-Labor Independents and candidates from rival non-Labor parties (Bolton 1996: 28–9). Many on the non-Labor side, including Menzies, decided something had to be done and began discussions on the formation of yet another non-Labor party—this time one that would avoid the problems which had plagued the previous non-Labor parties. The outcome was the formation, two years later, of the Liberal Party of Australia. Now well past its 60th anniversary, when none of its predecessors made even their 15th, its longevity is a testament to the success of its founders' work.

Liberal Party of Australia 1944–1983

ORGANISATION

The new party needed to provide an effective opposition to the Labor Party and to be a credible representative of non-Labor interests and values. Its formation required both organisational and ideological work. The previous non-Labor parties had a number of recurring organisational problems, which were a consequence of the organisational primacy of their parliamentary wing. They had fragile branch structures which tended to disappear between elections, were heavily dependent on business and financial organisations for their funds, suffered from poor communication between parliamentarians and the organisations in the electorate, and had weak national organisation and coordination, with a great many differences among the State-based non-Labor organisations. Here the tight, national organisation of the Australian Labor Party provided a model.[4] The aim, as Ian Hancock (2000) put it in a recent study, was to become 'national and permanent'.

The new party was based on six State divisions, with local branches, and various regional and State-based committees, culminating in the State Councils as the key representative body within each State division. All the various non-Labor organisations were required to dissolve themselves into the new party. Because of the desperation of the situation most did, with the notable exception of the Country Party, which has repeatedly resisted pressure to give up its separate identity. It was hoped that a vigorous branch structure would give the new party a sound financial basis, independent of the need to seek funds from various interest groups. And where such funds were sought, they were to be kept strictly in the hands of the extra-parliamentary organisation, to avoid the perception which had been so damaging to the UAP that the parliamentarians' independence was compromised by the party's dependence on a few large donors. A federal division was established, with a Federal Council made up of representatives from the State divisions and the federal parliamentary leadership, and a Federal Secretariat to provide coordination, research, publicity and assistance to the federal parliamentarians.[5] With the development of modern techniques of campaigning, the importance of the Federal Secretariat has since grown enormously.

However, although the new party had a much more coherent and centralised organisation than its predecessors, it retained three essential features of the previous non-Labor party organisations. First, it retained a strong federal structure, with the six State divisions having a great deal of autonomy, for example in their preselection procedures. This feature has persisted until recently, with the federal (national) division lacking the power to intervene in the affairs of a State division, even if they were damaging the Liberal Party's cause at a national level. Following the disastrous 1993 federal election result (when the Party's confidence about unseating the Keating Labor government was unexpectedly dashed), the Federal Conference significantly increased the power of the Federal Executive, giving it reserve powers to overturn preselections, discipline Members of Parliament and intervene in State divisions in cases of financial mismanagement (*Australian* 31 October 1994). However, these powers have been little used.

The second central organising principle it retained was the control of the parliamentary party over the formation of party policy. Extra-parliamentary bodies, such as the State and Federal Conferences, have a consultative role in policy formation, but if the leader of the parliamentary party chooses not to consult, he or she cannot be made to do so. In practice this means that the degree of involvement of the extra-parliamentary bodies in policy has fluctuated a great deal. It was vigorous in the party's early years, but fell away somewhat as the Menzies government's hold on office became more secure. After the Labor Party victory under Gough Whitlam in 1972, the Liberal Party organisation reasserted itself and the platform was overhauled from the first time since 1944. Again in the 1980s and first half of the 1990s, the extra-parliamentary organisation argued for the advantages of close consultation and the need for the parliamentarians to be open and sensitive to the views of party members.[6] The pattern is clear: the organisational wing is most assertive when the party is in opposition; once back in government organisational issues tend to fade into the background.

The primacy of the parliamentary party is closely related to the Liberal Party's third organising principle: the power of the leader of the parliamentary party. Within the parliamentary party, it is the leader who has ultimate responsibility for the formation of party policy. For example, *Fightback!*, the policy document on which Liberal leader John Hewson based his 1993 election campaign, was produced with almost no consultation with either the party room or the party organisation, including its Joint Standing Committee on Federal Policy (Puplick 1994: 40).

The concentration of formal power in the office of the parliamentary leader shows the importance of strong leadership for the Liberal Party. The Liberal Party has been politically successful when it has had an electorally successful leader who has been able to give cohesion and direction to the party. The first leader, Robert Menzies, remains the pre-eminent example of this. The party's periods of political difficulty have been marked by destructive conflicts over leadership, for example after Harold Holt (Menzies' immediate successor) drowned in 1966, and again in the period from the defeat of Malcolm Fraser in 1983, when the Liberal leadership changed hands six times until John Howard finally defeated Labor in 1996. Since then, Howard has led the party to three more election victories (1998, 2001, 2004). In each of these elections—in 1998, when he campaigned on the unpopular introduction of a consumption tax, in 2001 over asylum-seekers and in 2004 over Australia's involvement in the Iraq conflict—Howard has presented himself as a strong, conviction-based leader who would not be swayed by public opinion or by criticism from elites (Simms & Warhurst 2000; Warhurst & Simms 2002). As Howard has consolidated his leadership, so the Liberal Party has tightened its grip on national government. By contrast, in the States, where strong Liberal leaders are lacking, electoral success eludes the party.

One other organisational feature of the party needs to be mentioned: the place given to women in the extra-parliamentary organisation. A women's section was established, with guaranteed representation on the party's key decision-making bodies. The Victorian division instituted equality of representation between men and women throughout the organisation. This was a reflection of the central place which the Australian Women's National League had played in non-Labor politics since its formation in 1903 (Sydenham 1996). It has not, however, translated itself into equal numbers of women gaining preselection for winnable seats, although the significant increase in the number of successful women Liberal candidates at the 1996 federal election has been largely maintained ever since.

REVIVAL OF SOCIAL LIBERALISM

When the new Liberal Party of Australia was formed in 1944, the choice of the name Liberal was a deliberate assertion of the links between the new party and the social-liberal traditions of Deakin's party. Menzies in particular was adamant that the new party must be seen as progressive and not reactionary. During

World War II there had been a general shift in people's expectations of the role that the state should play in ensuring both economic stability and the welfare of all citizens. The British economist John Maynard Keynes had developed radical new ideas about how governments could manage demand in order to avoid destructive periods of both inflation and depression, and these were rapidly taking hold among economists. As well, Australians had become used during the war to a high degree of government planning and control. The philosophy and policies of the new Liberal Party took these changes into account, stressing the important role of government planning in shaping postwar Australia, the need for partnership between the state and private enterprise in the development of Australia's resources, and the state's responsibility for full employment and the social welfare of all its citizens. From the perspective of today, there was a clear postwar consensus between the Liberal Party and the Labor Party over an active role for the state in the development of the economy and in the provision of security of employment and minimum levels of welfare. Where the new party's philosophy differed from that of the Labor Party was in the greater place it saw for private enterprise and for individual effort and initiative, and in its more general suspicion of government planning and regulation, which it described as socialist (see Menzies 1944).

Once formed, the new party had to convince the electorate that it really did represent a new beginning and a credible opponent to the popular and successful Labor government. Here Menzies proved himself to be a consummate public politician. From his 1942 speech 'The Forgotten People' onwards, he pitched his appeal to people's hopes for quiet, home-centred lives after the war, an appeal with particular resonance for women. (For a detailed analysis of the values to which Menzies appealed in 'The Forgotten People', see Brett 1992.) Although he used symbols and arguments of particular appeal to the middle class, he rejected the language of class and challenged Labor's appeal to the working class as divisive and sectional. The new Liberal Party, he said, would govern in the national interest on behalf of all Australians. The Liberal Party won the 1949 election and by the mid-1950s had established a clear electoral ascendancy over the Labor Party. Menzies and the Liberal Party were greatly aided in this by the Cold War, which led to an association in the minds of many people between the ALP's commitment to government planning and the Communist regimes of the Soviet Union and Eastern Europe, by the bitter split in the ALP in 1954, and by the long postwar boom which delivered to Australians the prosperity and stability that Menzies had promised.

THE PRAGMATISM OF OFFICE

As the Liberal Party settled securely into government, it had little need to worry about its philosophy. In office, it approached the problems of government pragmatically, often deviating from various of the principles enshrined in the party's philosophy if this made electoral sense or seemed the most sensible option. The Liberal Party's hold on national office was repeated at the State level, with Liberal leaders like Henry Bolte in Victoria (1955–1972), Thomas Playford in South Australia (1938–1965) and Robert Askin in New South Wales (1965–1975) dominating their States' politics in much the same way as Menzies dominated federal politics. By the time Menzies retired, the Liberal Party's association with strong leadership, political experience and good government were more important both to it and the public than its philosophy, and it had generally become associated with social and political conservatism (see Jaensch 1992: 270–3, for a discussion of the problems of determining the party's philosophy).

Menzies' resignation in January 1966 heralded a period of leadership instability in the federal party. It also marked the beginning of a difficult period of adjustment to social change within Australia. Australia had changed a great deal since 1949 and new social groups were starting to make political demands which challenged many of the assumptions of conservative Australians. Second-wave feminism was demanding a range of changes to women's position in Australian society; an emerging Aboriginal leadership with growing mainstream support was protesting about a lack of civil rights and appalling living conditions for Indigenous Australians; new thinking about the virtues of multiculturalism and pressure from an emerging (mostly southern European-origin) immigrant leadership was challenging the assimilationist assumptions of the 1950s; and pressure was building on the White Australia Policy. The Liberal Party was ill-placed to deal with these changes, particularly when faced with a resurgent ALP under the leadership of Gough Whitlam and with widespread protest about Australia's involvement in the Vietnam War (Bolton 1996: ch.8).

Labor was elected triumphantly in 1972, to be defeated again after the 'constitutional crisis' of late 1975. The Liberal Party had found the role of Opposition difficult but, after a turbulent three years, was returned to power under the leadership of Malcolm Fraser. This confirmed to the party its idea of itself as the natural party of national government, the one with the experience, particularly the economic experience, to govern responsibly for the good of all. However, the long postwar boom had ended and with it the postwar consensus on the relationship between the state and the economy. Along with other industrialised economies, Australia started to experience the twin economic evils of high inflation and rising unemployment, a situation outside the Keynesian models which had guided postwar economic policy. Economists and political theorists started looking for new economic and political theories to explain this. The role which government should play in the economy, settled for the past 20 years, became a matter of fierce debate, and this debate on the whole took place on the non-Labor side of politics among the members and supporters of the Liberal Party.

The Liberal Party since 1983

IN OPPOSITION: 1983–1996

From the mid-1970s onwards, some political theorists and economists, mainly in the United States and Britain, started to argue that the reasons for the economic difficulties facing all Western economies lay in the enormous expansion in the size of government and the role of the state in the postwar period. The solution was a radical reduction of the public sector and an increase in the role of the market to replace public provision in the distribution of goods and services in society. Various measures were recommended to achieve these aims: public expenditure reduction, privatisation (i.e. the transfer of government enterprises and resources to the private sector), and the deregulation of various activities—such as banking, foreign exchange and industrial relations—under state regulation. Market solutions were promoted as leading to greater efficiency through competition and offering individuals greater choice than the bureaucratic rigidity of state-provided services allowed.

These ideas involved a revival of economic liberalism at the expense of social liberalism. The new economic liberal ideas, known in Australia as 'economic rationalism', were spread through a network of publications and informal contacts, and started to influence some members of the Liberal Party (see Kemp 1988). They involved a substantial break with the settled assumptions of Australian politics, not only with the social-liberal assumptions of the postwar consensus but also with the policies put in place in the first decades of the Commonwealth: the policies of protection for Australian manufacturing, of subsidies for rural industries and cross-subsidies for regional areas, and of centralised arbitration in industrial relations. Prime Minister Malcolm Fraser, although he spoke a great deal about the need to reduce people's reliance on the government and to reduce government expenditure, in practice supported the continuation of these settled policies, as did many other members of the party. This is the context of the debilitating conflict within the Liberal Party throughout the 1980s between what became known (following the description of similar divisions within the British Cabinet led by Prime Minister Margaret Thatcher) as the 'dries' and the 'wets'.

Throughout the 1980s, the social liberals were gradually defeated and driven out of the Liberal Party. At the same time, Labor governments successfully implemented many of the reforms—such as financial deregulation, privatisation of government enterprises, substantial reductions in producer subsidies and tariff protection—for which Liberal Party economic liberals had been arguing. This pushed the Liberals further to the Right in order to maintain their electoral distinctiveness: if Labor planned to reduce average levels of protection to 5 per cent, a Liberal government would reduce them to zero. It also removed from the party people with experience in areas of social and cultural policy, and until Howard became leader in 1995 the Liberal Party was outpoliticked by Labor on a number of key social and cultural issues: multiculturalism, Indigenous policy and the republic.

The meaning of the term 'individual', the central value of Liberal Party philosophy, has changed significantly over the century. At the time of Deakin's Liberal Party, and still in 1944 when the current Liberal Party was formed, the term 'individual' was closely associated with the values of independence, self-reliance and enterprise, and with a sense of duty and obligation to contribute to society. In the consumerist and permissive 1980s, the term 'individual' had become more associated with choice and self-indulgence, and a party promoting individualism was likely to arouse fears about the basis of society's cohesion. Might not giving individuals more freedom to choose and compete lead to increased inequality? Is not freedom of choice leading to a dangerous moral relativism which is undermining society's shared moral framework (Brett 1994, 2003)?

One response to this shift within the Liberal Party has been a moral and social conservatism, most strongly associated with John Howard, which stresses the central social and moral role of the traditional family. In 1988 during his first period as party leader, Howard launched *Future Directions* to set out the Liberal and National Party's vision for Australia's future. *Future Directions* combined economic liberal ideas about the urgent need for smaller government, a conservative affirmation of the role of the family, and traditional nationalism under the banner of 'One Australia'. The document's cover portrayed a married couple and their two children standing in front of the picket fence of a solid brick home with a wide verandah and a newish-looking car. As an image it harked back to the home and family-centred 1950s, to the perceived prosperity of that decade, and to the simple nationalism of an era when Australia thought of itself as a white British country. *Future Directions* argued for renewed emphasis on the values and experiences which bind Australians together in contrast to the Labor government's support for a multiculturalism centred on difference. And it contrasted its more assimilationist approach to Indigenous affairs with one based on self-determination and reparative justice (Brett 1989, 2003; Kelly 1994: ch. 22). Similarly when Prime Minister Keating began the process which led to a referendum on the question of Australia becoming a republic, the Liberal Party took the conservative position of support for the status quo, despite support for the republic on the part of some prominent Liberal politicians, such as Nick Greiner and Peter Costello.

BACK IN GOVERNMENT

In March 1996 the Liberal Party, under John Howard's leadership, won its first federal election in 13 years, and it won with a landslide. The 1996 victory had been preceded by convincing electoral wins in the States and, by the time of the federal election, there were Liberal or National Party governments in all States except NSW. How was Howard able to solve the problems the Liberals faced since the defeat of Fraser and in the first part of the 1990s?

Elections are both won and lost, and much of the reason for the Liberal's 1996 win was the electorate's accumulated disaffection with Labor after its 13 years of government. However, Howard and the Liberals had learnt from the 1993 election. Although Howard has been an economic liberal since the early 1980s, he played down the economic liberal aspects of his vision during the campaign, and was generally hard to draw on specific policies. The electorate had been scared in 1993 by the ideological radicalism of Hewson's free-market policies, and Howard's apparent return to the Liberals' generally pragmatic approach to policy was reassuring. Once in office, the extent of Howard's commitment to economic liberal ideas became more evident—for example, in the areas of industrial relations reform and changes to higher education. However, he moved slowly in the first term of his government.

The Liberal's 1996 campaign slogan—'For all of us'—was pitched to appeal to 'mainstream Australia'. In the words of campaign director Andrew Robb (1997: 37), 'we would not just consider the wellbeing of a select few, but we would consider the broad national interest'. This strategy gave new life to a recurring theme in Liberal Party philosophy: that it stands for the national interest and the good of all, against those who press vested sectional interests. This theme was stressed by Menzies and can regularly be heard in Howard's speeches (Johnson 2000; Brett 2003). The most obvious and historically important sectional interest which the Liberal Party opposes is the trade union movement, but it is a view that is easily extended to other groups—the feminist lobby, the multicultural lobby, the Aboriginal lobby—any of which can easily be marginalised as selfish groups pursuing sectional agendas. In 1996 the strategy was designed to capitalise on the widely held perception that Labor had abandoned its core constituency, the 'battlers' and working-class outer-suburban families, while it pandered to the values of tertiary-educated cosmopolitan, urban elites, in particular their support for multiculturalism.

In the short term, the strategy was successful: post-election analysis of the vote revealed a significant swing of blue-collar voters to the Liberal Party (Robb 1997: 40–1; Singleton, Martyn & Ward 1998). Some of these voters swung back to Labor in 1998, and some went to the new One Nation party led by Pauline Hanson (Bean & McAllister 2000: 179–80). The slogan 'For all of us' conveyed a stronger sense of what the Liberals opposed than what they stood for. The contrast was between a vaguely defined 'us' and whatever minority most aggrieved you. The consensual space filled up with grievances about various 'Them' who were preventing a self-declared mainstream 'Us' from receiving their fair share of resources and recognition. During the first term many more grievances flooded into the empty centre than Howard had bargained for, and for his first term he struggled to regain control of the political agenda from Pauline Hanson (Brett 2003: ch. 9).

The Howard government won a second term in 1998. The election was very close, with Labor in fact winning the primary vote. Howard campaigned on the introduction of a consumption tax, the GST, and presented himself as a conviction politician (Simms & Warhurst 2000). Howard was much more confident in the second term. As well as tax reform, he engaged in what have been described as the Culture Wars in which he promoted conservative cultural positions on questions like the republic and the understanding of settler–Indigenous history against those supporting the need for radical revision of traditional historical understandings of Australia's settlement. The recurring theme was that Australia had more to be proud than ashamed of in its history, and in particular that accusations of racism against earlier generations of Australians were unwarranted (Macintyre & Clarke 2003; Manne 2004). During the second term the referendum on the republic was held and defeated. The defeat was the result of division amongst supporters of the republic on the method of electing the head of state rather than the strength of support for the constitutional monarchy, however, it was a political win for Howard and the Coalition government which had officially opposed any change (Warhurst & Mackerras 2002).

Even so the Liberal Party's second term was rocky. The introduction of the GST and accompanying changes to the way businesses paid their taxes caused widespread resentment, particularly amongst small businesspeople who faced massive increases in paperwork. At the beginning of 2001, with an election due at the end of the year it looked as if Labor had to do little except wait for government to fall into its lap. The Howard government responded to its falling popularity with some energetic and targeted pump-priming, aimed particularly at groups which had shown high support for One Nation at the 1998 election—the elderly and people in the country. The political atmosphere began to change in August 2001 when a Norwegian ship called the *Tampa* picked up Afghan and Iraqi asylum-seekers from a sinking Indonesian fishing boat. The Howard government refused the *Tampa*'s captain permission to land the asylum-seekers on Australian territory and they were finally sent to Nauru for processing. The *Tampa* incident was followed by the September 11 attacks on the twin towers of the World Trade Center in New York and on the Pentagon by Muslim terrorists. These two events pushed the economy and the GST from voters' minds (Manne 2004).

The Howard government centred its campaign for re-election in November 2001 on the need for strong, decisive government in a turbulent and unsafe world and for a tough policy of border protection in the face of organised people smuggling. It said little about other areas of policy. Labor was caught unprepared and was easily defeated. The vote for One Nation halved, its leader Pauline Hanson failed in her bid to win a Senate seat, and the party virtually collapsed as a political force after the election. Howard's critics argue that this is because he was exploiting the racist fears that One Nation represented. His supporters point out that the issue is one of asserting the government's control over immigration and that in fact the Howard government increased the migrant intake (Solomon 2002; Warhurst & Simms 2002). The third term was a political triumph for the Liberals as the federal Labor Opposition struggled with the unconvincing leadership of Simon Crean. Demoralised and confused, Labor changed leadership to Mark Latham in early 2004, and at the end of that year the Coalition government won again.

Throughout the four terms, the government's policy priorities have been those that Howard has focused on for the past 20 years: tax reform, family policy and industrial relations reform (Singleton 2000; Manne 2004). As well, the government's approach to multiculturalism and Indigenous issues has been framed by Howard's commitment to a traditional Australian nationalism that values unity and shared experience above the celebration of difference. And, since the November 2001 election, Howard's tough and unbending stance on border protection and the detention of asylum-seekers has strengthened the government's popularity.

That it is Howard himself and his style of leadership that most explains the Liberals' recent success at the national level is confirmed by the Liberal Party's problems at the State level. When Robert Menzies dominated the federal Liberal government in the 1950s and 1960s, there were also powerful Liberal State Premiers, such as Henry Bolte in Victoria and Robert Askin in New South Wales. By mid-2005 there had been no State or Territory Liberal government anywhere in Australia for more than three years and none in which a strong and effective Liberal Opposition leader was putting real pressure on the incumbent governments. Of the nine elected governments in Australia at national, State and Territory levels, only one—the national government led by Prime Minister Howard—included the Liberal Party. At the federal level, the ALP is floundering and directionless in a way that is reminiscent of the Liberals during the 1980s, even though it has strong State Premiers; but at the State level Labor premiers face weak, directionless oppositions. This confirms the perception of a process of de-alignment in the Australian electorate, in which party identifications are weakening and in which leadership and incumbency deliver the cohesion and direction once found in the strength of the party organisation.

HOW LIBERAL IS THE LIBERAL PARTY?

At the beginning of this chapter, a distinction was drawn between political, economic and social liberalism. Critics of the Liberal Party often distinguish between what they call ' "small l" liberalism'—in other words, philosophically liberal positions such as political, economic and social liberalism—and what they refer to as 'the "large L" Liberal Party'. These critics accuse the Liberal Party (i.e. the 'large L' Liberals) of ignoring or damaging what they see as core values of liberal (i.e. 'small l' liberal) political thought. This terminology can be very confusing but it does raise the interesting and important question of how 'liberal' the 'Liberal' Party really is.

The Howard government clearly identifies more with economic liberalism's confidence in the market than with social liberalism's faith in the state. The Howard government's record in terms of political liberalism is less easily identified. Political liberalism is the tradition of thought which focuses on the civil and political rights of individuals and is suspicious of the state's desires to weaken or ignore those rights in the exercise of its power. A key liberal maxim, attributed to Lord Acton in 1887, is that 'power corrupts and absolute power corrupts absolutely'. Political liberalism advocates all sorts of institutional ways of preventing those who exercise state power from abusing it: for example, civil liberties protected either by common law and the courts or by a Bill of Rights; an independent judiciary to ensure that the government of the day cannot use the legal system to suppress political opposition; two-chamber parliaments to prevent hasty legislation which may deprive some citizens of their rights; federalism which divides power between levels of government and so ensures that each will watch the other lest it encroach on its power; and so on. These are discussed in other chapters of this book.

A key question to be asked about the Liberal Party then is the strength and nature of its political liberalism when it is in government, when it faces the demands and the temptations of holding state power, when it can claim a democratic mandate for pursuing policies which may breach some of liberalism's core values. And, at both State and federal levels the experience of the Liberal Party in government reveals that, despite its name, Liberal governments are not immune from the temptations of power. In fact the Liberal Party's tradition of strong leadership means that Liberal governments are often as impatient with the constraints on the power of the executive as they accuse Labor governments of being.

For example, Jeff Kennett, Liberal Premier of Victoria in the 1990s was severely criticised for his breach of principles of political liberalism as he used his executive power to pursue an agenda of economic liberal reform, and to silence government critics (Costar & Economou 1999). Similarly, the Howard government has been criticised for breaching core values of political liberalism.

To give some examples: the mandatory detention of asylum-seekers, while their applications for refugee status are being processed, breaches many liberal principles. The idea of human rights embodies the core liberal commitment to individual rights which exist prior to the state and which the state should not alienate, and it can be argued that the practices of mandatory detention in what for all intents and purposes are prisons breach the human rights of the men, women and children detained. Similarly, the failure of the Howard government to protest strongly to the government of the United States about the detention of Australian citizens, David Hicks and Mamdouh Habib, in the prison at Guantanamo Bay without formal charges seems to put protection of the civil rights of Australian citizens second to the need not to offend a powerful ally.

Some liberal (i.e. 'small l' liberal) critics have focused on what they see as the Howard government's damage to the institutional conventions of political liberalism as they are embodied in Australia's federal Constitution and Parliament. For example various Ministers in the Howard government have publicly criticised decisions of the High Court, seemingly showing little respect for the key liberal principle of the independence of the judiciary (Irving 2004: 105–7). Changes to the practice of the relationship between Ministers, their advisers, the Parliament and the public have also been criticised as blurring lines of government accountability to both Parliament and the public. In what has become known as the 'children overboard affair' asylum-seekers were accused by the Prime Minister during an election campaign of throwing their children into the sea, and the incident was cited as evidence of the undesirability of such people coming to Australia. Although government officials soon knew that these accusations were false, definitive, formal advice was slow to reach the Ministers concerned and the Prime Minister. How had this happened, and what did it show about the way the Liberal Party in government pursued the truth and the public's right to know (Weller 2002)?

The Howard government's approach to federalism and the rights of the States is another area where the Liberal government is departing from long-established liberal positions. The liberal defence of federalism is that it divides power between levels of government and so protects against the potential abuses of concentrated power, and the Liberal Party has always championed States' rights against the centralising ambitions of federal Labor governments. It was one of the sources of political opposition to the Whitlam Labor governments. In its third and fourth terms, however, the Howard government has been attempting to increase the role of the federal government in areas of State jurisdiction, in particular in health, secondary education and industrial relations. Federal–State relations in Australia have always had a party political dimension. In the third term, and at the time of writing (mid-2005), all the State and Territory governments were Labor, and this has obviously given momentum to the Howard government's desire to move power from the States to the federal level, as has the absence of strong Liberal premiers to argue for States' rights. Nevertheless it is a marked departure from the tradition of constitutional liberalism the party has represented in the past (Craven 2005).

We can also ask of the Liberal Party in government, how liberal are its internal practices? That is, how much freedom is there inside the party for individuals to express their views and in particular to disagree with those who hold the power? Does the Liberal Party exercise any less discipline over its parliamentary members than the Labor Party, which has always been overt in its demands for party discipline? The answer is no, and again the evidence points to low commitment in practice to the liberal values of freedom of expression and the value of dissent. This is particularly the case when the party is in government. Malcolm Fraser's authoritarian propensity to treat differences from his views as indications of disloyalty was one of the reasons Don Chipp left the party to form the Australian Democrats (Warhurst 1997). More recently, in 2002 Tasmanian candidate Greg Barns lost his endorsement after he openly criticised the government's policy on asylum-seekers. He has since become an outspoken, dissident 'small l' liberal, criticising his former party for its failure to uphold the liberal value of freedom of speech for its own members (Barns 2003).

In all of these cases the government and/or the leadership of the party is arguably breaching principles of political liberalism in order to achieve some other goal: to protect the sovereignty of the territory; to prosecute the war against terrorism; to achieve certain policy outcomes for which they claim they have a democratic mandate; to pursue policy reforms they regard as in the national interest; to maintain the discipline and unity necessary for effective government and for re-election, and so on. Liberal values are being weighed against other goals and values, and political judgments are being made. The party's name is thus only an imperfect guide as to its history, to its policies and to how it will behave in government.

NOTES

1   A note on spelling: under the influence of enthusiasm for spelling reform, the Australian Labor Party dropped the 'u' from its name early in the 20th century (McMullin 1991: ix). In reflection of this, the parties opposed to Labor are hereby termed non-Labor. The older spelling for 'labour' is retained elsewhere, as in labour movement.

2   The complicated politics of the first decade after federation are told as clearly and concisely as anywhere in Macintyre (1986: ch. 4). For a much more detailed account of the emergence of the Australian parties in the last decade of the 19th century, see Loveday, Martin & Parker (1977).

3   See also the discussion by Andrew Parkin in Chapter 1 of this book.

4   Robert Menzies outlined these problems in his opening address to the conference in Canberra in October 1944, one of the two conferences which hammered out the

organisation and philosophy of the new party. His address is reprinted in Starr (1980: 73–6). See also Menzies (1967).

5 See Jaensch (1992: 257–70) for a much more detailed discussion of the organisation of the Liberal Party of Australia.

6 See, for example, the Liberal Party's 'Valder Report' (named after the Chair of the Committee, John Valder) of 1983 (LPA 1983).

REFERENCES

Abbott, T. 2002, 'Operators versus Representatives: The story of Political Parties in the Modern Era', Presentation to Melbourne Media Club, 8 August, <http://www.tonyabbott.com.au/speech/parties.html>.

Barns, G. 2003, *What's Wrong with the Liberal Party?*, Cambridge University Press, Cambridge.

Bean, C. & McAllister, I. 2000, 'Voting Behaviour', in *Howard's Agenda: The 1998 Australian Election*, eds M. Simms & J. Warhurst, University of Queensland Press, Brisbane.

Bolton, G. 1996, *The Middle Way. The Oxford History of Australia, Volume 5, 1942–1995*, 2nd edn, Oxford University Press, Melbourne.

Brett, J. 1989, 'Future Directions: New Conservatism's Manifesto', *Current Affairs Bulletin*, vol. 66, no. 1, pp. 11–17.

Brett, J. 1992, *Robert Menzies' Forgotten People*, Macmillan, Sydney.

Brett, J. 1994, 'Liberal Philosophy from Fraser to Hewson', in *For Better or Worse: The Federal Coalition*, ed. B. Costar, Melbourne University Press, Melbourne.

Brett, J. 2003, *Australian Liberals and the Moral Middle Class: From Alfred Deakin to John Howard*, Cambridge University Press, Cambridge.

Craven, G. 2005, 'Betrayal of Menzies', *Australian*, 1 March.

Costar, B. & Economou, N. 1999, 'The Victorian Liberal Model—A "Kennett Revolution"', in *The Kennett Revolution: Victorian Politics in the 1990's*, eds. B. Costar & N. Economou, UNSW Press, Sydney.

Hancock, I. 2000, *National and Permanent?: The Federal Organisation of the Liberal Party of Australia 1944–1965*, Melbourne University Press, Melbourne.

Irving, H. 2004, 'A True Conservative?', in R. Manne ed., *The Howard Years*, Black Inc. Agenda, Melbourne.

Jaensch, D. 1992, *The Politics of Australia*, Macmillan, Melbourne.

Johnson, C. 2000, 'Howard and the Mainstream', in *Howard's Agenda: The 1998 Australian Election*, eds M. Simms & J. Warhurst, University of Queensland Press, Brisbane.

Kelly, P. 1994, *The End of Certainty: Power, Politics and Business in Australia*, revised edn, Allen & Unwin, Sydney.

Kemp, D. 1988, 'Liberalism and Conservatism in Australia since 1944', in *Intellectual Movements and Australian Society*, eds J. Walter & B. Head, Oxford University Press, Melbourne.

Loveday, P., Martin, A.W. & Parker, R.S. eds 1977, *The Emergence of the Australian Party System*, Hale & Iremonger, Sydney.

LPA [Liberal Party of Australia] 1983, *Report of the Committee of Review, Facing the Fact*, chair J. Valder, Canberra.

Macintyre, S. 1986, *The Succeeding Age. The Oxford History of Australia, Volume 4, 1901–1942*, Oxford University Press, Melbourne.

Macintyre, S. & Clarke, A. 2003, *The History Wars*, Melbourne University Press, Melbourne.

McMullin, R. 1991, *The Light on the Hill: The Australian Labor Party 1891–1991*, Oxford University Press, Oxford.

Manne, R. ed. 2004, *The Howard Years,* Black Inc. Agenda, Melbourne.

Menzies, R. 1944, *Address to the Canberra Conference*, 14 October, cited in Starr 1980, pp. 90–4.

Menzies, R. 1967, 'The Revival of Liberalism in Australia', in *Afternoon Light: Some Memories of Men and Events,* Cassell, Melbourne.

Puplick, C. 1994, *Is the Party Over?*, Text Publishing, Melbourne.

Robb, A. 1997, 'The Liberal Campaign', in *The Politics of Retribution: The 1996 Federal Election*, eds C. Bean, S. Bennett, M. Simms & J. Warhurst, Allen & Unwin, Sydney.

Simms, M. & Warhurst, J. eds 2000, *Howard's Agenda: The 1998 Australian Election*, University of Queensland Press, St Lucia. Queensland.

Singleton, G. ed. 2000, *The Howard Government: Australian Commonwealth Administration 1996–1998*, University of New South Wales Press, Sydney.

Singleton, J., Martyn, P. & Ward, I. 1998, 'Did the 1996 Federal Election See a Blue-collar Revolt Against Labor?', *Australian Journal of Political Science*, vol. 33, no. 1, pp. 117–30.

Solomon, D. 2002, *Howard's Race: Winning the Unwinnable Election*, Harper Collins, Sydney.

Starr, G. 1980, *The Liberal Party of Australia: A Documentary History*, Drummond/ Heinemann, Melbourne.

Sydenham, D. 1996, *Women of Influence: The First Fifty Years of Women in the Liberal Party*, Women's Section, Liberal Party of Australia, Victorian Division, Melbourne.

Warhurst, J. ed. 1997, *Keeping the Bastards Honest: The Australian Democrats First Twenty Years*, Allen & Unwin, St Lucia, Queensland.

Warhurst, J. & Mackerras, M. eds 2002, *Constitutional Politics: The Republic Referendum and the Future*, University of Queensland Press, St Lucia, Queensland.

Warhurst, J. & Simms, M. eds 2002, *2001: The Centenary Election*, University of Queensland Press, St Lucia, Queensland.

Weller, P. 2002, *Don't Tell the Prime Minister*, Scribe Publications, Melbourne.

The Labor Party

NICK ECONOMOU

The Australian Labor Party (ALP) is the oldest of Australia's political parties. Indeed, it is one of the oldest trade union-based political parties in the world and its brief term in government in 1904 was the first time that a trade union-based party had governed any nation. Its formation became the catalyst for the emergence of Australia's modern party system (Loveday 1977). Labor has held national government a number of times, the most sustained period being the 13 successive years of the Hawke and Keating Labor governments between 1983 and 1996. But it has also experienced some very long periods in Opposition, where it now languishes since the electoral defeat of the Keating Labor government in March 1996. Labor has been noticeably more successful in many of the States.

This chapter analyses the character and significance of the ALP. It discusses two themes particularly relevant to understanding the role of political parties—especially parties which see themselves on the reformist Left side of politics—within liberal-democratic political systems. The first of these themes is the ALP's evolving ideological and policy profile: how does a party that has embodied, at least in its early period, significant scepticism about aspects of a liberal political perspective (especially the liberal support for individualism and for a private-enterprise economy) cope within the parameters of a liberal democracy? The second theme is the ALP's own organisational politics: why have the party's internal machinations been so prominent in its history, sometimes arguably at the cost of electoral success?

Policy debates complicated by internal machinations have characterised the ALP throughout its history, ensuring that drama and pathos are never far from the surface. The problem of trying to link policy goals with organisational means helps to explain why the ALP is arguably the most disciplined of the Australian parties and has the most explicit expectations of loyalty from its members. The party requires those who join to sign a pledge of loyalty. There are explicit rules about the obligation of Labor Members of Parliament to reach decisions collectively through the 'Caucus' (i.e. the meeting of all Labor MPs) and to abide by such collective decisions on the threat of expulsion from the party. In the operational culture of the Labor Party, defying the collective will or breaking the pledge is one of the most heinous transgressions—referred to colloquially in the party as 'ratting'—that a party member may commit (see Iremonger 2001). There is also a sense of Labor activists being loyal to notions of a Labor 'tradition' although just exactly what this entails is, as this chapter explains, a source of controversy.

History

The Australian Labor Party's origins go back to the formation of skill-based trade unions in the 1850s and 1860s. These led to 'labour leagues' (the colonial terminology for what would today be thought of as peak interest group organisations) formed to lobby colonial Parliaments on labour laws. In the early 1890s, a series of strikes occurred in the maritime, transport, agriculture and mining sectors in defence of wages and conditions that were being threatened by the onset of a major economic recession (Buxton 1974). This industrial action—coordinated across the mainland colonies—was defeated by employers with the assistance of the various colonial governments, some of whom used troops to break up strikes. It was in the aftermath of defeat in this industrial action that the union movement decided to pursue its political agenda through the parliamentary process. In order to do this, a party organisation was created for the express intention of putting up 'Labour' candidates at any future election, for these candidates to win seats and, if possible, form a 'Labour' government.

The formation of the Australian Labor Party during the 1890s (the original spelling 'Labour' was dropped in 1912 in favour of the American-style 'Labor') roughly coincided with Australia's federation movement. But the trade unions had little interest in federation beyond seeing the creation of a national policy-making system as one way of protecting the value of local labour by affirming race-based immigration restrictions. Thus the creation of the Australian federation occurred with little labour movement input. Ironically, when the first federal election was held, the Australian Labor Party was sufficiently organised to field candidates and win enough seats in the new Parliament to play an important role in the subsequent formation of Australia's first national governments.

The Labor Party's record in national elections since then has been patchy. Labor formed its first administration as a minority government in 1904 under the Prime Ministership of JC Watson. Labor won national government in its own right in 1910 under Andrew Fisher's leadership although, somewhat enigmatically, Fisher resigned the leadership and Prime Ministership upon declaring that Australia was to assist the British Empire in the Great War. The leadership passed to WM (Billy) Hughes who, in 1916, through his advocacy of conscription for service in the war, precipitated a cataclysmic split in the party. Hughes, defeated by his parliamentary Labor colleagues, defected to the non-Labor side of politics to create and lead the Nationalist Party and he then continued as Prime Minister until 1923. Labor remained in Opposition until 1929 when, on the eve of the economic upheaval caused by the onset of the Great Depression, it was returned to government with James Scullin as Prime Minister. The Scullin government lasted only three years before collapsing amidst division and rancour over the direction economic policy should take. The party split for a second time, with a number of Labor MPs defecting to 'Lang Labor' in support of NSW Labor Premier Jack Lang and his opposition to Scullin's 'Premiers' Plan' proposal to reduce government expenditure in response to the Depression.

Labor was soundly defeated in the 1931 election by the United Australia Party (UAP) led by a former Scullin Labor government Minister (and former Labor Premier of Tasmania), Joe Lyons. Ten further years in Opposition followed until, in 1941, the minority UAP–Country coalition government disintegrated due to internal strife and Labor's John Curtin was given the chance to form a government. In the 1943 election, in the midst of the Second World War, the Curtin Labor government was easily returned. Curtin died in 1945, and was succeeded as leader by Ben Chifley who led the party to another electoral victory in 1946.

The Chifley government cast itself as the government of postwar reconstruction and this sometimes put it in conflict with both the union movement (especially when it used troops to break a coal strike) and business (especially when it tried to nationalise the privately owned banks only to have its legislation invalidated by the High Court) (Crisp 1961). These issues contributed to Labor's electoral loss in 1949 to the recently formed Liberal Party under the leadership of Robert Menzies.

The subsequent period was to be very difficult for Labor, though this was not immediately evident. Under Chifley's continuing leadership, the party came close to winning the 1951 election. Then, after Chifley's death, Dr HV (Bert) Evatt became party leader and in 1954, although not winning government because it did not win a majority of House of Representatives seats, Labor succeeded in winning a majority of the national two-party preferred vote. Within a few years, however, Evatt and the entire ALP were to be rocked by the third and arguably the most destructive of the splits to afflict the party.

The circumstances of the split of 1955 were complicated and had much to do with the broader ideological divisions between the Western democracies and the Communist bloc in world politics (Crisp 1973: 206–7; Costar, Love & Strangio 2005). As in the United States, an anti-communist impulse became prominent in the Australian political debate, fuelled in part by the control exercised by the Communist Party of Australia (CPA) over a small but strategically significant number of trade unions. The ALP had been aware of this growing Communist influence within certain unions and a number of party members had formed so-called 'Industrial Groups' in a bid to wrest back control of these unions to the ALP cause.

Dr Evatt was initially a supporter of the Industrial Groups, but by the time he became party leader the evolution of political events had changed his perspective. The Menzies Coalition government made two attempts (one by legislation and one by constitutional referendum) to outlaw the CPA. Acting in his professional capacity as a barrister and constitutional lawyer (before ascending to the Labor leadership), Evatt successfully argued in the High Court for the legislation—the *Communist Party Dissolution Act*—to be disallowed. Then later, in his capacity as Labor leader, Evatt opposed the Menzies government's proposal to outlaw the CPA via constitutional amendment. Evatt's motivation reflected his values as a lawyer and a civil libertarian. But politically both Evatt and the party that he led became easy targets for the Menzies government's campaign of vilifying Labor as 'soft on communism', a campaign given impetus by the publicity surrounding the defection in 1954 of a Soviet diplomat, Vladimir Petrov.

Meanwhile the 'Industrial Groups' were continuing to work within the branches of the ALP and its affiliated unions. Concerns began to be expressed within other sections of the party about the motivations behind and the growing influence of the Industrial Groups. Sectarian factors also came into play: support for the Industrial Groups appeared to be coming from organisations associated with the Catholic Church, especially in Victoria where the Church was headed by Archbishop Daniel Mannix who as a much younger man had played a prominent role in the Labor Party's 1916 conscription-induced split (Murray 1970).

In 1955, matters came to a head at the ALP National Conference. Dr Evatt denounced the Industrial Groups as vehicles for unwelcome outside influence on the party, and he moved for the expulsion of those associated with them. The meeting literally split into separate conferences held in separate halls. Eventually many pro-Group members (including some prominent MPs, party officials and trade unions) left the party and formed their own rival political party: the Democratic Labor Party (DLP). They left behind a weakened ALP and the collapse of State Labor governments in Queensland and Victoria.

Federal Labor proceeded to suffer serious electoral defeats under Evatt in elections in 1955 and 1958, three defeats in 1961, 1963 and 1966 under Evatt's successor Arthur Calwell, and then one further defeat in 1969 under a new young leader EG (Gough) Whitlam. By 1972, Labor had endured 23 successive years of federal Opposition.

In December 1972, the Labor Party returned to national government under Whitlam's leadership and proceeded to experience three extraordinary years of 'crash through or crash' politics (Oakes 1976). In November 1975, the Governor–General dismissed the Whitlam government because of its inability to get its supply bill through the Senate and the party suffered a landslide defeat at the election a month later (see Emy 1978; Sexton 1979; Kelly 1994). Another period of opposition ensued until 1983 when Bob Hawke, former Rhodes scholar and former President of the Australian Council of Trade Unions (ACTU), led Labor to election victory (Kelly 1984).

This was the beginning of an unprecedented period of sustained Labor government at the national level, marked by a leadership transition from Hawke to Paul Keating in 1991. Labor remained in government until it was defeated in 1996, having experienced 13 unbroken and largely stable years of federal Labor dominance, brought to an end not by splits, divisions or the intervention of the Head of State but by the voters indicating that they had had enough.

Some commentators had previously surmised that Labor is only ever called upon by the people to be the party of national government during times of emergency (Jennett & Stewart 1990; Jaensch 1989). The longevity and stability of the Hawke–Keating governments countered that claim. However, it remains true that Labor has spent considerably more time as the federal Opposition than as the national government. This contrasts with the performance of the Labor Party in some of the States. Labor has been in government more often than not in New South Wales and Tasmania. It has dominated Queensland except for the period from the mid-1950s split until 1989. Labor has also enjoyed long periods of government in South Australia (Moon & Sharman 2003) where the advent of the Rann Labor government in 2002 meant that—despite its lack of success in federal elections—Labor was in office in every State and Territory.

Policies and traditions

Two broad ideological concepts—*democratic socialism* and *social democracy* (roughly coinciding with a factional division within the party between the Left and the Right that this chapter describes below)—can be helpful in understanding the policy profile of, and the debates within, the Labor Party. As we shall see, both are sceptical of some of the liberal ideas embedded within a liberal-democratic political system.

Whereas a liberal perspective begins with respecting the aspirations of individuals, a socialist perspective begins with a social understanding and respect for the role of communities. Broadly described, *socialism* envisages common community (i.e. public-sector) ownership of economic resources. It regards capitalism as exploitative of workers and responsible for the undesirable concentration of wealth. It regards public-sector control of economic resources as a panacea to this exploitation and inequality. Public-sector control, taken to its most extreme, can include enforced government ownership of privately owned resources or activities, a process known as nationalisation (invoked when the Chifley Labor government attempted in the late 1940s to nationalise Australia's private banks). *Democratic* socialism refers to the legitimisation of this kind of public-sector economic control by the democratic election of a party advocating such policies.

Social democracy also starts from the premise that capitalism is exploitative and that its inequalities ought to be addressed through government policy intervention. But social democracy is more accommodating of private property ownership and the capitalist system. Social democrats shy away from the notion that state ownership and control of the economy is the only way forward. Rather, social democrats see the state's ability to regulate and its ability to redistribute resources through various policies as a means to 'civilise' capitalism. Social democracy is commonly associated with the so-called 'welfare state' with its array of taxation measures directed particularly at higher income earners and its welfare support intended to assist the less affluent (Sandercock 1982; Emy 1974: 374–6).

There is some overlap between aspects of social democracy and more socially aware forms of liberalism. But social democrats are normally regarded (unlike liberals) as part of the Left because they are share the Leftist perspective that society should be respected as a collective phenomenon within which collective politics are a legitimate means for seeking policy reform. In particular, social democrats tend to be more comfortable than liberals with trade unionism, with the public ownership of some enterprises such as utilities, and with the idea of disciplined party politics.

This mutual recognition of the legitimacy of collective approaches to politics is the cohesive element that can align social democrats with democratic socialists in the formation and operation of a trade union-based left-of-centre party like the ALP. Labor has accommodated both sets of ideas, or rather the broad spectrum of ideas across the ideological terrain defined by these two sets of ideas.

This common ground helps to explain what Beilharz (1994) describes as the consistent 'labourist' theme throughout the ALP's history. From its formation at the end of the 19th century, Labor's approach to the political debate was dominated by the pursuit of industrial objectives such as the award of decent wages, the improvement of working conditions (such as job security, sick pay, etc.), support for the idea of wage arbitration and, by extension, a defence of the legitimacy of trade unions (Childe 1923; Crisp 1973; Beilharz 1994). While now less predominant, this 'labourist' approach has remained a constant theme in Labor Party thinking ever since. For example, the national Labor governments of 1973–1996 under Prime Ministers Hawke and Keating entered into an Accord with the Australian Council of Trade Unions ensuring the active participation of the ACTU leadership in the development of the government's industrial and economic policies (Emy & Hughes 1991: 172–9; Gruen & Grattan 1993).

But the relationship between the ALP and the union movement can be fraught, especially during periods of Labor government. Some critics viewed the Hawke government's Accord with the ACTU as antithetical to the material interests of the broader labour movement (McEachern 1991; Stilwell 1986) because it gave the ACTU only a limited power-sharing role but required it to trade away wage and award benefits. Earlier, under Gough Whitlam's 1972–1975 Labor government, there had been massive disagreements between the union movement and the government over wages policies (where the government urged restraint) and tariffs (where, spectacularly in 1973, the government suddenly cut industry protection by 25 per cent and presided over a leap in unemployment rates) (Glezer 1982: 117–124).

The Labor Party itself has at various times sought to place in its official platform a definitive declaration of what the party stands for. The early Labor Party was publicly committed to a state-ownership-oriented socialism, and declarations of such socialist aspirations were prominent in the party's official platform. During the 1921 National Conference, a major dispute arose over this 'Socialist Objective', and a compromise was reached between the democratic socialist and the social-democratic positions. Party delegates endorsed a socialist declaration that the party sought 'the socialisation of industry, production, distribution and exchange' and 'the nationalisation of banking'. But they also added a qualification (known as the Blackburn Declaration) that, consistent with a social-democratic approach, limited the application of the Socialist Objective. It stated that the Objective would only be applied 'to the extent necessary to eliminate exploitation and other anti-social features' and that the party was not committed to the seizure or abolition of private property (see Crisp 1973).

Occasional debate on this issue continued thereafter. Eventually the Socialist Objective was removed by a Special Conference in 1982. By that stage, most Labor leaders perceived that a reference to socialism might alienate voters, and in any case the party had moved on from any notion that it was committed to nationalisation. Federal Labor's one significant attempt at nationalisation — the Chifley government's bank initiative of 1946 — had been nullified by the High Court in a landmark legal case and the party had then lost the 1949 election and suffered 23 years in Opposition.

Federal Labor governments have nonetheless created some significant government-owned corporations, often to provide some form of competition to privately owned monopolies or to ensure that important services (education, communication, transport and broadcasting) were available to Australians living outside the major population centres. Thus the Labor Party is associated with the creation of the (later privatised) Commonwealth Bank from the ashes of the bank nationalisation attempt, the Australian National Line, Commonwealth Railways and the Trans-Australia Airlines corporation. From this history has emerged the notion that the ALP is the party most strongly committed to defence of the public sector. Yet it was the national Hawke Labor government during the 1980s that either privatised or commenced the process of privatising a number of these public corporations.

The Hawke government's approach to economic policy became the catalyst for a vigorous debate about whether it was betraying Labor's true policy tradition (Maddox 1989; Maddox & Battin 1991; Jaensch 1989; Johnson 1989). The Hawke government's commitment to pro-market economic reform led not just to the sale of publicly owned corporations but also to extensive economic deregulation, the opening up of formerly protected industry sectors to international competition, and the floating of the Australian dollar's exchange rate on the international currency market. Some analysts (e.g. Jaensch 1989) argued that Labor under Hawke had become so pragmatic in its bid to maximise its appeal to the voters as a 'catch-all' party that it could no longer be regarded as fitting within the social-democrat/democratic-socialist spectrum. But other observers, less convinced in any case about the relevance of debates about ideology, maintained that the Hawke government's electoral pragmatism was consistent with the party's history (Emy & Hughes 1991; Johnson 1989). Some in the Hawke government itself—most notably its then Treasurer Paul Keating (Keating 1987: 172–86)—rejected these critiques, insisting that the government was pursuing reforms appropriate to the times in complete accordance with an authentic Labor tradition.

These sorts of interpretive disputes—especially about the extent to which Labor in government really offers a substantially reformist alternative to its non-Labor adversaries—have occurred throughout the ALP's history. In the 1970s, at the height of the Whitlam government, Catley and McFarlane (1974) described the alleged similarities of the two major parties in Australia in terms of the Lewis Carroll twins Tweedledum and Tweedledee. Back in the 1920s, Childe (1923) had put forward a much-celebrated critical analysis along similar lines.

Different perceptions about the legacy of the 1972–1975 Whitlam government have loomed large in recent debates about the 'Labor tradition'. Atypically for Labor leaders at that time, Gough Whitlam did not come from the trade union movement. Rather, his origins were in the professional middle class. As Opposition Leader in the late 1960s and early 1970s, Whitlam became an advocate for radical reform in areas outside the traditional 'labourist' agenda.

He had particular passions for policy reform in relation to urban planning, equal opportunity, multiculturalism, Australian cultural identity, pay equality for women, and economic autonomy for Indigenous people based on land rights (Hocking & Lewis 2003; Warhurst 1996). The Whitlam-led ALP also opposed the Vietnam War with one of its prominent MPs—the MHR for Yarra and sometimes leadership rival Dr Jim Cairns—emerging as something of a leader of Australia's anti-war protest movement (see Strangio 2002).

From December 1972, Whitlam led Australia's first postwar Labor government since the defeat of the Chifley government in 1949. For all its many faults and failures, the Whitlam government could not be accused of shying away from its reform agenda. Immediately upon its election, the Whitlam government declared that Australia's involvement in the Vietnam War was officially over. This began a period of scepticism about Australia's relationship with the United States, an element of the Labor approach to foreign policy that still reverberates in (mainly the Left) sections of the party to this day. The Whitlam government abolished tuition fees for university students and introduced a universal health insurance scheme called Medibank (the precursor of today's Medicare). It established a Department of Ethnic Affairs, and 'multiculturalism' became official government policy. Under Whitlam, the Commonwealth government involved itself in a host of urban policy and planning matters mainly through the extensive use of Specific Purpose grants to the States, to the chagrin of the non-Labor State Premiers (Patience & Head 1979). The Whitlam government signed a range of international treaties with the United Nations that established the basis for greater Commonwealth powers over human rights, equal opportunity, the environment and Indigenous affairs. And it legislated in several notable instances to transfer ownership of parcels of Crown land to local Indigenous peoples, thus ensuring that the politics of 'land rights' would become an important item on the national agenda.

This resumé of major reform (achieved notwithstanding an Opposition-controlled Senate) has given the Whitlam legacy a strong influence on popular perceptions of the Labor tradition. The Whitlam government's extensive use of welfare programs has meant that Labor tends to be viewed as the party more likely to preside over an expanding welfare state. Whitlam's commitment to Indigenous rights, women's rights, to the arts, to urban renewal and to the environment has meant that these issues tend to also be viewed as part of Labor's traditional policy agenda. Even the bombastic style of governing adopted by Whitlam—the so-called 'crash through or crash' approach—is sometimes seized upon by Labor activists as part of the party tradition as well.

The Whitlam years and the way in which the Whitlam government was brought to an end facilitated some important socioeconomic changes within the Labor Party itself. It inspired an influx of branch members with university qualifications, employed in human services (such as lawyers, teachers and social workers) and holding cosmopolitan outlooks. This influx in turn later changed the profile of Labor Members of Parliament in a similar direction.

Concomitant changes are also discernible in the patterns of Labor's electoral support (Bean 2000). The strongest Labor-voting electorates in the country still tend to be those with a 'traditional' Labor profile, with relatively large numbers of blue-collar, overseas-born, non-English-speaking and lower-income voters clustered in the industrial suburbs of the State capitals and some provincial cities. Some of these electorates, however, now feature substantial numbers of human-services-employed, tertiary-educated higher-income earners, 'gentrifying' their social profile. While members of this social group have 'middle class' character-istics, a status traditionally associated with Liberal Party support, their more cosmopolitan 'post-materialist' outlook tends to link them to the post-Whitlam Labor Party and to distinguish them from the small business or technocratic professionals usually identified as continuing strong supporters of the Liberal Party (Scott 1991; 2000). This explains why election results show that these (typically inner-city) electorates continue to display strong Labor support notwithstanding their socioeconomic transformation. Clearly the post-Whitlam Labor Party has acquired a new core voter constituency in addition to the blue-collar constituency that has historically sustained it.

Organisation

The prominence of splits and divisions in the Labor Party's history reveals the degree to which internal affairs impact upon it. Some of the battles that have gone on within the Labor Party have been as momentous as those conducted by the party against its adversaries in the party system.

The Labor Party's organisational arrangements assume a strong normative commitment to the decentralisation of power within the party away from the parliamentary wing and towards the rank-and-file branch membership and affiliated trade unions. This reflects the party's origins as a parliamentary vehicle for the broader labour movement. The party's rules treat each level of the party as a delegate of the level below, with the higher levels given power to enforce unity, discipline and loyalty in exchange for an expectation that they will in turn be bound by general policy decisions made at the lower levels. How this works out in practice—whether, for example, national Labor Prime Ministers and Labor governments are significantly bound by decisions made within the party organisation—is an interesting and sometimes controversial matter.

In each of the State and Territory branches, the supreme policy-making body is the regular State/Territory Conference comprising delegates from local branches and from affiliated trades unions. While the rules governing election of delegates, the ratio of affiliated union delegates to branch membership delegates, and the frequency with which conferences meet have varied over the years, the basic role of the conference has remained constant. The conference determines a policy platform that is supposed to be binding on the State parliamentary members of the party (referred to as the Labor Caucus). It can also perform other important functions, such as determining the process for preselecting parliamentary candidates and choosing the members of the State Executive which runs the party at the State level between conference meetings. The conference elects the State President and the State Secretary, both of whom are key members of the State Executive.

State and Territory Conferences elect delegates to the Labor Party's supreme national policy-making body, known as the National Conference. Like its State counterparts, the National Conference endorses a policy platform that is supposed to be binding on the Labor Members of Parliament, including national Labor governments. It likewise deals with administrative and organisational affairs that are referred to it, and it elects a National President, a National Secretary and a National Executive. Like its State equivalents, the National Executive runs the party between meetings of the National Conference. The hierarchical nature of the party's organisational structure means that both the National Conference and the National Executive have the power to intervene in the affairs of the State and Territory branches, though this is always a controversial action to contemplate and happens relatively rarely.

There is a general organisational pattern here that fits Labor's historical origins: power may be delegated to particular bodies or to individual leaders, but in turn those leaders are expected to carry out decisions arrived at collectively. This same pattern characterises the operations of the parliamentary Caucus at both State and national levels. Labor MPs meet together in Caucus and agree on a collective position on which they will vote as a unified block in the Parliament itself. Any dispute over policy or tactics is supposed to be thrashed out in Caucus, and not in public or on the floor of the parliamentary chambers. Caucus in turn is expected to be guided, if not bound, by the policy platform formulated by the relevant party conference. The parliamentary party leader is likewise supposed to be bound by the party's policy platform. And it is Caucus, rather than the party leader, which decides who shall be in a Labor Ministry (or Shadow Ministry when in Opposition); the leader can only allocate portfolios. In short, the party leader is assumed — at least as envisaged under party rules and traditions — to be just another of the delegates operating on behalf of the broader labour movement. This is an assumption that is probably at odds with the broader electorate's perception of a party leader as being the head of the party for which they vote and primarily accountable to the voters rather than to the party organisation. The tension between these two different notions of leadership accountability explains some of the organisational conflict that the ALP has experienced.

An array of political struggles can occur within this organisational framework. As already noted, some of these struggles have been so profound they have precipitated major crises and splits. There have been other less catastrophic battles that have nonetheless resulted in organisational reform.

A particularly notorious incident arose from the announcement in March 1963 that the Menzies Coalition government proposed to allow the establishment of a United States military base in Australia. A special session of Labor's National Conference was convened at which, in accordance with its rules, the Labor Party's policy would be determined. At this time the National Conference comprised 36 delegates—six each from the six State branches. There was no representation from the federal parliamentary Caucus or leadership. The parliamentary leaders—in this instance, leader Arthur Calwell and his deputy Gough Whitlam—waited in the foyer of Canberra's Kingston Hotel to be told the outcome of the Conference's deliberations. The spectacle of the Labor parliamentary leadership waiting to be told party policy by a group of delegates about whom the public knew very little—aptly described by senior press gallery journalist Alan Reid as the '36 faceless men'—became a matter of public controversy and embarrassment for Labor (Scalmer 2001: 100–102). Labor's National Conference looked more like a sinister semi-secret cabal than a party organ designed to decentralise decision-making power.

Gough Whitlam certainly perceived the situation in this way, and reform of the National Conference was an important part of his agenda when he became Labor's national parliamentary leader in early 1967. Whitlam pressured the National Conference into accepting the inclusion of Labor's parliamentary leaders—the four federal parliamentary leaders (i.e. the leaders and deputy leaders from the House of Representatives and the Senate) and a single parliamentary leader from each State (i.e. the Premier or Leader of the Opposition)—as delegates. This, for the first time, gave Labor's parliamentary wing representation within the extra-parliamentary party structure. The four federal parliamentary leaders were also given voting rights on the National Executive (Crisp 1973: 1998–9). In the context of the way the party had been previously organised, this represented a major change in normative outlook as well as a structural change.

In 1970, Whitlam survived a challenge to his leadership originating in the party's Victorian branch that arose from opposition to this organisational change. In the following year, Whitlam exacted revenge when, at his behest, the National Executive agreed to intervene in and reorganise the Victorian branch which had been underperforming electorally because (at least according to Whitlam and his supporters) its dominant figures appeared to be more intent on internal party power struggles than on winning elections. All of these reforms— giving greater prominence to the parliamentary wing of the party and showing a willingness to intervene in underperforming State branches—are often cited as events that helped Labor achieve national electoral success under Whitlam's leadership in 1972.

Between 1972 and 1975, the party then grappled with the difficulties of national government. The Whitlam Labor government was dismissed by the Governor-General in November 1975, and Labor then suffered landslide electoral defeats, with Whitlam still in the leadership, in December 1975 and December 1977. Following the 1977 defeat, Whitlam finally made way for Bill Hayden as parliamentary leader.

Hayden convened a Committee of Inquiry chaired by the National President, Bob Hawke, to investigate the party's organisation. The Committee argued that further organisational reform needed to occur. It recommended an expansion of the number of delegates to National Conference and the abandonment of the federalist principle, under which each State had equal representation, in favour of a greater degree of proportional representation, where the number of delegates from each State and Territory branch would bear some relationship to their respective party memberships. These recommendations were debated at the 1981 National Conference, which eventually agreed to reform itself as a body made up of 100 (later reduced to 99) delegates in proportion to the number of House of Representatives electorates in each State (see Lloyd 1983). The party leaders continued to be members, along with a single delegate from the Young Labor organisation. Meanwhile the size of the National Executive was expanded to 20 delegates.

It was this reformed organisational structure that then underpinned the party during what became the longest continuous period of national Labor government, under Prime Ministers Bob Hawke (1983–1991) and Paul Keating (1991–1996). Hawke in particular appeared to be very cognisant of the importance of the biennial National Conference, and debate on nearly every major policy decision made by his government would commence as a debate leading to a National Conference vote. This, in turn, made the conference an important political event worthy of media coverage—a far cry from the days of the '36 faceless men'. There were occasional colourful incidents—such as a branch member storming on to the floor of a 1984 conference session to symbolically burn his Labor membership card in protest against the direction that uranium policy was taking. But mostly National Conferences became (and have remained ever since) closely managed events almost devoid of passion or division despite the controversial nature of many of the policy matters on the agenda. The orderly conduct of National Conferences during the years of the Hawke–Keating Labor governments depended in no small way on the emergence of a formal and highly disciplined factional system (see below) (Emy & Hughes 1991: 134–43).

Since the Keating Labor government's electoral defeat in 1996, the issue of organisational reform has arisen again. Kim Beazley became Labor's national leader but handed over to Simon Crean after losing the 1998 and 2001 elections. In 2001, Crean commissioned former Prime Minister Bob Hawke and former NSW Labor Premier Neville Wran to undertake another organisational review.

Their investigation reported growing rank-and-file dissatisfaction with the operation of the party's organisation (Hawke & Wran 2002). In response to this report, State branches were required to review the ratio of affiliated trade union delegates to branch delegates at State Conferences, the rationale being that effective internal party democracy depended on the voice of rank-and-file party members, who belonged to local branches, not being overwhelmed by party delegates representing trade unions. There has been haphazard adoption of this proposal: for example, by 2005 Victoria had complied but New South Wales and Queensland had resisted.

Crean was replaced by Mark Latham as parliamentary leader in December 2003. Invoking the memory of Gough Whitlam's approach in the 1960s, Latham set about sponsoring quite dramatic organisational reform particularly of the National Conference. The National Conference continues to be described in the party rules as the supreme policy-making body. But under Latham's reforms it now meets only once every three years and comprises 400 delegates (up from 99) (ALP 2004).

This reconstituted National Conference met for the first time just ahead of the what was, for Labor, the ultimately unsuccessful 2004 federal election. With an election looming, the delegates at the meeting were careful to behave moderately and to be seen to be supporting the leader. Critics suggested that the increase in delegate numbers had resulted in an increase in delegates with union connections and the continuing dominance of factional alignments (Crikey 2004). The Latham-inspired reforms to the National Conference remain in place, though Latham himself resigned as parliamentary leader in January 2005 to be replaced by Kim Beazley.

Factionalism

Factions, the political scientist Giovanni Sartori once observed, can act like 'sub-parties' operating within the greater organisational whole of a political party (Sartori 1976: 71). Factions are commonly described using the terms Left, Right and Centre, implying some sort of ideological, issue-based or strategic (radical versus pragmatic) spectrum (Emy & Hughes 1991: 137, Lloyd & Swan 1987). To some critics, however, such terms can overstate the importance of differing political ideals. Lloyd and Swan (1987), for example, have argued that, at least with respect to its operation in the Australian Labor Party, factional politics are more often about the struggle to exercise power within the party's organisation.

Factional politics have been an integral part of the ALP since its inception. As a broad left-of-centre party encompassing a variety of philosophical outlooks, Labor has always had discernible Left and Right blocs within the party organisation and within the Caucus. Factional behaviour is arguably also encouraged within a party that claims, like Labor, to be disciplined, within which various organs claim power over policy making and the election of office bearers, and in which there is formal 'caucusing' (i.e. the practice of reaching a collective decision binding on all members). Factional divisions do not exhaust the internal tensions that can emerge within the ALP—tensions have also arisen historically between the parliamentary and extra-parliamentary wings, between the parliamentary leaders and the rest of the party, between different groupings of affiliated trade unions and between different State branches. But factions have become the most enduring divisions and tend also to shape the way that the others are managed.

The expansion of the National Conference in 1981 set the stage for the contemporary factional system. Most of the delegates sent to the enlarged National Conference were elected on factional tickets and they voted during the conference in factional blocks. The convenors of the major factions emerged as major power-brokers or 'machine men' (see Lloyd 1983: 253). The division of the ALP into three broad factional groups—the Right, the Left and the Centre-left—underpinned the formal factional system that emerged then and which continues to influence the operation of the party to this day.

The Right faction is an alliance of three important groups: the Centre Unity group that is based in New South Wales and dominates Labor politics in that State, the Labour Unity group drawn from other States and particularly strong in Victoria, and a Queensland-based group dominated by officers from the Australian Workers Union (Wanna 2000).

The party's Left faction used to be a single entity known as the Socialist Left. It had a formal organisation (complete with membership lists, official caucusing and even its own newsletter) in every State. It was strongest in Victoria, although it also had a large (minority) presence in New South Wales where it maintained a colourful rivalry with the Centre Unity group. But the Socialist Left has now fragmented into a series of subgroups. These include the Pledge Left (formed in Victoria to oppose the privatisation of public corporations), a 'moderate Left' formed around Federal MP Martin Ferguson, and a so-called 'hard Left' grouping led by Victorian Senator Kim Carr (Hudson 2000).

The Centre-left existed as a prominent third faction during the years of 1983–1996 federal Labor government. Its leadership comprised primarily of sitting Labor MPs, it emerged as a group of Hayden sympathisers in the aftermath of the parliamentary leadership transition in 1983 from Bill Hayden to Bob Hawke. Later the faction broadened out to encompass some delegates to National Conference and some affiliated unions. The Centre-left was influential for much of the 1980s and 1990s because it typically held the balance of power between the Right and the Left, and exercised this power in Caucus, the National Executive and the National Conference, usually to support policy positions initiated by the Right (Emy & Hughes 1991: 139). The Centre-left went into a decline after Labor's federal election defeat in 1996 although, thanks to the continuing careers of some of its MPs, a group of parliamentarians without formal alignment to either the Right or Left remains. This Centre group is under pressure, however, and the future direction in Labor factionalism appears to be heading towards a clear two-way factional divide between Left and Right.

The public tends to be most aware of Labor's factional politics during moments of stress or crisis such as disputes over policy or over the parliamentary candidate preselection process. This tends to reinforce a negative perception of the phenomenon. Factional politics can indeed be destructive. But formal factionalism can also be a source of order and stability. The party's factional system since the 1980s has mostly engendered a relatively orderly power-sharing between the three major factional blocks, and most of the disputes that have arisen have involved temporary breakdowns of previous agreements.

Factional politics have become ubiquitous within the modern Labor Party. Members of the party who seek to hold positions in the organisation or who wish to win preselection normally must do so through the factional system. Very few factionally unaligned 'independents' progress through the party's structure. The two remaining major factional blocks—the Right and the Left— are pivotal to the functioning of the party, and the rivalry between the two can sometimes be as intense and bitter as the combat conducted between Labor and the Liberal and National parties.

The future

Despite past speculation that the decline of the traditional working class could lead to its fragmentation and weakening (see Kemp 1978: 358), the ALP has endured as one of the two primary participants in the Australian party system. As of 2005, it governs in every Australian State and Territory. Labor Party activists would doubtlessly see winning the next federal election, due in 2007, as the critical challenge for the party.

Periods of Opposition, such as the one Labor has been experiencing at the federal level since March 1996, provide space for the party to reflect on its future directions and its organisational structures. An emerging debate about the nature of Labor's relationship with the trade union movement is a recent example. The ability of unions to affiliate with the Labor Party (in the process making a substantial financial contribution to the party) has been a feature since the party's inception. Questions have been raised about the future appropriateness of this relationship. The concerns are partly tactical, reflecting a fear that being seen to be too close to the unions may alienate voters. But they also reflect the significant decline in the relevance of unions within the workforce. The proportion of Australian workers who belong to trade unions has fallen dramatically, from nearly 60 per cent in the 1980s to only slightly more than 20 per cent in

2005. Are union interests now over-represented within the Labor Party's organisational structure? (See Manning 1996.)

The rise of the so-called 'post-materialist' agenda (see Gow 1990) has been an important influence in the reconceptualisation of Labor's policy tradition, but with this has come the challenge of how Labor relates to some of the post-materialist social movements. Women's politics, for example, is important within the contemporary ALP, in contrast to previous eras in which the macho world of the trade union politics at the time tended to make Labor Party politics very masculine as well. The so-called EMILY's List group within the Labor Party now actively seeks to achieve gender equality among party office-holders and to assist women to gain preselection as endorsed Labor candidates in winnable seats (Sawer 2000). Its campaign has succeeded in producing rule changes, which now require that not less than 40 per cent of Labor's 'party positions' and parliamentary candidatures be held by women (ALP 2004). This aspect of Labor Party politics is further discussed in Chapter 21 of this book.

The ALP has also needed to manage its relationship with the environmental movement. The Whitlam and especially the Hawke governments placed environmental protection to the forefront of their policy agendas. From Hawke's time onwards, Labor leaders, Ministers and Shadow Ministers have tried to recruit environmental leaders as advisory staff (Economou 2000). Former Australian Conservation Foundation President Peter Garrett, enticed to seek preselection as a Labor parliamentary candidate, was elected to the House of Representatives at the 2004 election. Similar dynamics have been at work with regards to Labor's relationship with the Indigenous community although Labor has yet to find a parliamentary position for an Indigenous leader commensurate with Garrett's stature within the environmental movement.

It is not easy for Labor to balance its traditional trade union connection with the agenda of the new social movements. Modern Labor now has these two major constituent blocks which tend to have quite different sociocultural dispositions. On some issues—like support for social programs and recognising the importance of education—these constituencies can find common ground. But there is disagreement on other matters such as environmental policy, Australian–US relations, immigration and refugee policy, and international human rights issues.

Whenever Labor does find itself in national government, it faces additional stresses, such as the needs to manage its relationship with union interests while also being responsible for managing the national economy.

Whether the Labor Party can win back national government in the near future, or whether alternatively it is destined to a long Opposition period akin to its 1949–1972 experience, is likely to depend to a considerable degree on its management of these ongoing tensions.

REFERENCES

ALP 2004, *National Constitution of the ALP. As Amended at the 43rd National Conference 2004*, <http://www.alp.org.au/download/now/national_constitution_2004.pdf>.

Bean, C. 2000, 'Who Now Votes for Labor?', in J. Warhurst & A. Parkin eds, *The Machine: Labor Confronts the Future*, Allen & Unwin, Sydney.

Beilharz, P. 1994, *Transforming Labor: Labor Tradition and the Labor Decade in Australia*, Cambridge University Press, Melbourne.

Buxton, G. 1974, '1870–1890', in ed. F. Crowley, *A New History of Australia*, Heinemann, Melbourne.

Catley, R. & McFarlane, B. 1974, *From Tweedledum to Tweedledee: The New Labor Government in Australia*, ANZ Books, Sydney.

Childe, V.G. 1923, *How Labor Governs*, 2nd edn (1964), Melbourne University Press, Melbourne.

Costar, B., Love, P. & Strangio, P. eds 2005, *The Great Labor Schism: A Retrospective*, Scribe, Melbourne.

Crikey, 2004, 'The Who's Who of National Conference', *Crikey Daily*, Website, 29 January, <http://www.crikey.com.au/politics/2004/01/29-0001.html>.

Crisp, L. 1973, *Australian National Government*, 3rd edn, Longman Cheshire, Melbourne.

Crisp, L. 1961, *Ben Chifley*, Angus and Robertson, Sydney.

Economou, N. 2000, 'Labor and the Environment: Greening the Workers' Party', in eds J. Warhurst & A. Parkin, *The Machine: Labor Confronts the Future*, Allen & Unwin, Sydney.

Emy, H. 1978, *The Politics of Australian Democracy: Fundamentals in Dispute*, 2nd edn, Macmillan, Melbourne.

Emy, H. 1974, *The Politics of Australian Democracy*, 1st edn, Macmillan, Melbourne.

Emy, H. & Hughes, O. 1991, *Australian Politics: Realities in Conflict*, 2nd edn, Macmillan, Melbourne.

Epstein, L. 1967, *Political Parties in Western Democracies*, Pall Mall, London.

Glezer, L. 1982, *Tariff Politics: Australian Policy-Making 1960–1980*, Melbourne University Press, Melbourne.

Gow, D. 1990, 'Economic Voting and Post-Materialist Values', in eds C. Bean, I. McAllister & J. Warhurst, *The Greening of Australian Politics*, Longman, Melbourne.

Gruen, F. & Grattan, M. 1993, *Managing Government: Labor's Achievements and Failures*, Longman, Melbourne.

Hawke, R. & Wran, N. 2002, *National Committee of Review*, ALP, Canberra.

Hocking, J. & Lewis, C. eds 2003, *It's Time Again: Whitlam and Modern Labor*, Circa, Melbourne.

Hudson, G. 2000, 'Victoria: Factional Battles, Realignments and Renewal', in eds J. Warhurst & A. Parkin, *The Machine: Labor Confronts the Future*, Allen & Unwin, Sydney.

Iremonger, J. 2001, 'Rats', in eds J. Faulkner & S. MacIntyre, *True Believers*, Allen & Unwin, Sydney.

Jaensch, D. 1989, *The Hawke Keating Hijack*, Allen & Unwin, Sydney.

Jennett, C. & Stewart, R. eds 1990, *Hawke and Australian Public Policy*, Macmillan, Melbourne.

Johnson, C. 1989, *The Labor Legacy: Curtin, Chifley, Whitlam and Hawke*, Allen & Unwin, Sydney.

Keating, P. 1987, 'Traditions of Labor in Power: Whitlam and Hawke in the Continuum', in *Traditions of Reform in New South Wales*, Pluto Press, Sydney.

Kelly, P. 1994, *The Unmaking of Gough*, Allen & Unwin, Sydney.

Kelly, P. 1984, *The Hawke Ascendancy*, Angus and Robertson, Sydney.

Kemp, D. 1978, *Society and Electoral Behaviour in Australia*, University of Queensland Press, Brisbane.

Lloyd, C. 1983, 'The Federal ALP: Supreme or Secondary?', in eds A. Parkin & J. Warhurst, *Machine Politics in the Australian Labor Party*, Allen & Unwin, Sydney.

Lloyd, C. & Swan, W. 1987, 'National Factions and the ALP', *Politics*, vol. 22, no. 1, pp. 100–10.

Loveday, P. 1977, 'The Federal Parties', in eds P. Loveday, A. Martin & R. Parker, *The - Emergence of the Australian Party System*, Hale & Iremonger, Sydney.

Maddox, G. 1989, *The Hawke Government and the Labor Tradition*, Penguin, Melbourne.

Maddox, G. & Battin, T. 1991, 'Australian Labor and the Socialist Tradition', *Australian Journal of Political Science*, vol. 26, no. 2, pp. 181–96.

Manning, H. 1996, 'The Labor Party and the Unions: Organisation and Ideology During the Labor Decade', in ed. M. Simms, *The Paradox of Parties*, Allen & Unwin, Sydney.

McEachern, D. 1991, *Business Mates: The Power and Politics of the Hawke Era*, Prentice Hall, Melbourne.

Moon, J. & Sharman, C. eds 2003, *Australian Politics and Government: The Commonwealth, the States and the Territories*, Cambridge University Press, Melbourne.

Murray, R. 1970, *The Split: Labor in the Fifties*, Cheshire, Melbourne.

Oakes, L. 1976, *Crash Through or Crash: The Unmaking of a Prime Minister*, Drummond, Melbourne.

Patience, A. & Head, B. 1979, *From Whitlam to Fraser: Reform and Reaction in Australian Politics*, Melbourne University Press, Melbourne.

Sandercock, L. 1982, 'Democratic Socialism and the Challenge of Social Democracy', in eds G. Evans & J. Reeves, *Labor Essays 1982*, Drummond, Carlton.

Sartori, G. 1976, *Parties and Party Systems*, Cambridge University Press, London.

Sawer, M. 2000, 'Women and Labor: A Question of Heartland?', in eds J. Warhurst & A. Parkin, *The Machine: Labor Confronts the Future*, Allen & Unwin, Sydney.

Scalmer, S. 2001, 'Crisis to Crisis: 1950–1961', in eds J. Faulkner & S. MacIntyre, *True Believers: The Story of the Federal Parliamentary Labor Party*, Allen & Unwin, Sydney.

Scott, A. 2000, *Running on Empty: Modernising the British and Australian Labor Parties*, Pluto Press, Sydney.

Scott, A. 1991, *Fading Loyalties: The Australian Labor Party and the Working Class*, Pluto Press, Sydney.

Sexton, M. 1979, *Illusions of Power: The Fate of a Reform Government*, Allen & Unwin, Sydney.

Stilwell, F. 1986, *The Accord and Beyond: The Political Economy of the Labor Government*, Pluto Press, Sydney.

Strangio, P. 2002, *Keeper of the Faith: A Biography of Jim Cairns*, Melbourne University Press, Melbourne.

Wanna, J. 2000, 'Queensland: Consociational Factionalism or Ignoble Cabal?', in eds J. Warhurst & A. Parkin, *The Machine: Labor Confronts the Future*, Allen & Unwin, Sydney.

Warhurst, J. 1996, 'Traditional Hero: Gough Whitlam and the Australian Labor Party', *Australian Journal of Political Science*, vol. 31, no. 2, pp. 243–53.

The National Party

Almost from the time that it burst on to the federal scene in the December 1919 election, the National Party of Australia (then called the Country Party)[1] has played a role disproportionate to its electoral support. This has certainly been the case since 1922 when the party first found itself holding the 'balance of power' in the House of Representatives and secured substantial concessions from the major conservative party before agreeing to join a coalition government. Despite occasional breaks in the coalition pattern established at that time, it has generally been followed at the federal level ever since. This has enabled the National Party, when in government with its coalition partner, to control the ministerial portfolios of most concern to its rural constituents (such as trade and primary industries) and to deliver considerable largesse to them.

The National Party, however, now appears to be in a state of inexorable decline. Its twin roles as the champion of rural producer groups and defender of rural and regional dwellers have been undermined by the long-term shrinkage of agricultural employment and deleterious demographic changes. Its attempts to expand its support base beyond its traditional non-metropolitan clientele, symbolised by its name changes,[2] have failed dismally and it has subsequently been challenged in its non-metropolitan heartland. While the National Party appears to have successfully dispelled the late 1990s' threat from Pauline Hanson's One Nation party, dissatisfaction from erstwhile supporters has seen it lose seats to Independents. Its coalition with the Liberal Party, moreover, is proving to be a mixed blessing. The material benefits that it brings are offset by political costs arising from close association with unpopular policies, and the electoral alliance has not prevented the loss of National seats to the Liberals.[3] With its representation in the House now at record lows, the National Party faces the prospect of a gradual decline into insignificance unless it can miraculously reverse its fortunes.

Electoral support

The National Party's representatives in the federal Parliament are drawn from only three States: Queensland, New South Wales and Victoria. The party's base of support has remained geographically confined to certain rural and regional electorates in those States, reflecting its origins as a sectional party for primary producers and as a voice for those living beyond the metropolitan capitals. Unfortunately for the National Party, this constituency has diminished in absolute and relative terms over time.

Despite a long history of calls to 'unlock the land' and for 'closer settlement', Australia never became a land of yeoman farmers. Small farms progressively gave way to more viable larger ones, and technological change enabled the consolidation of, for example, dairy farms into massive operations. Agribusiness has increasingly displaced the 'family farm'. While this has been a long-term trend, it accelerated towards the end of the 20th century. For example, between 1971 and 1991, the number of farms declined by 127 441 (Dawson 1994). By June 2002 there were only 133 868 farms (in which the main activity was agricultural) left in the whole of Australia. Of these, the main types were beef farming (34 110), grain growing (15 911), mixed farming (15 610), sheep farming (13 911) and dairy farming (11 135) (ABS 2004: 419).

At the same time as the number of farms has been falling, mechanisation has also reduced the demand for farm labour. For example, the total number of persons employed in agriculture in 2004 was 345 700, representing only a little above 4 per cent of the Australian workforce (ABS 2005). Yet farm employment had accounted for 28 per cent of the workforce in 1933 and 15 per cent in 1954 (Nixon 1988). Clearly, to the extent that the National Party sought to represent farmers, it has largely lost the mainstay of its support base.

The National Party's support from the outset, however, was not restricted to primary producers. It fed off rural resentment—feelings that people 'in the bush' were grossly neglected compared with those 'in the city', especially in regard to the provision of government services. This even fuelled abortive moves to establish new States; for example, in the New England area of New South Wales. Observers have long ago noted that the National Party's appeal was as much regionally based as it was sectionally based (Aitkin 1973), with almost half of its votes coming from businesspeople, professionals, retirees and public servants in rural towns (Barbalet 1975; Richmond 1978). Yet, here again, demographic changes have also reduced (or diluted) this former base of support. Put simply, a number of trends have conspired to depopulate, relatively diminish or alter the composition of rural and regional electorates to the detriment of the National Party.

Most obviously, as the number of farms has diminished and as agricultural employment has disappeared, it has triggered a drift in the rural population to the major cities. Smaller country towns, whose prosperity was dependent on the farm sector and rural population, have declined and this process has been accelerated by bank closures and the rationalisation of government services (such as school and hospital closures) that followed in the 1990s. Australia's fastest population declines have occurred in rural areas (ABS 2004: 90). At the same time as (mostly younger) rural folk have been heading for the cities (and for some regional towns), the vast bulk of postwar immigrants into Australia have taken up residence in the capital cities, increasing the relative disparity between Australia's urban and rural population.

The starkness of the demographic change that has taken place during the life-time of the National Party can be seen by the fact that whereas in 1901 64 per cent of Australians had lived outside the capital cities, this figure had fallen to 40 per cent by 1962 and to 35 per cent by 2002 (ABS 2004: 92). Moreover, most of those living outside the major cities have now become concentrated in regional centres (accounting for 31.1 per cent of the population), leaving just 2.6 per cent of Australians living in 'remote' or 'very remote' areas (ABS 2004: 94).

This long-term (and accelerating) demographic trend has long threatened the existence of rural parliamentary seats, the bastion of the National Party, through electoral redistributions. An example was the abolition of the Victorian House of Representatives seat of Wimmera in 1977 (Mackerras 1978). As a result, the National Party has fought rearguard campaigns to stave off redistributions and to maintain a degree of malapportionment allowing rural electorates to have substantially fewer voters than urban seats. (In this respect, the National Party has shown that it has not supported the standard conceptualisation of representative democracy as embracing a vote of equal value for all adult citizens.) The last vestiges of any rural bias in the federal electoral system was finally removed under the Hawke Labor government in the 1980s, but the National Party succeeded in its push for this to be implemented via a expansion of the total number of seats in Parliament rather than by a reduction in the number of rural electorates.[4] As Table 13.1 shows, this enabled the National Party to actually increase its House of Representatives seats (from 17 to 21) in 1984 in an enlarged House of Representatives, but it was to prove only a temporary stay of inexorable decline.

One reason for the National Party's respite proving only temporary was another twist in the demographic tale. In recent decades there has developed a

TABLE 13.1	National Party performance in the House of Representatives elections, 1983–2004			
Year	Seats won	Total seats	% of seats won	% of votes
1983	17	125	13.6	9.0
1984	21	148	14.2	10.6
1987	19	148	12.8	11.5
1990	14	148	9.5	8.4
1993	16	147	10.9	7.4
1996	18	148	12.1	8.2
1998	16	148	10.8	5.3
2001	13	150	8.7	5.6
2004	12	150	8.0	5.9

trend of people moving from the metropolitan capitals to settle on the Queensland and New South Wales coast. These people have predominantly been retirees but have also included so-called 'sea changers'[5] and younger people seeking alternative lifestyles. This movement into National Party electorates has changed their social composition and made them less safe for the party because the new arrivals come with established party loyalties that do not typically include an attachment to the National Party. While former Liberal voters are probably prepared to vote for National Party sitting members, given the option they are liable to prefer a Liberal candidate to a National one. Incoming Labor supporters pose an immediate direct threat in National Party-held seats, as do Green supporters whose preferences favour the ALP.

This has been most apparent in the northern New South Wales House of Representatives coastal seats of Richmond and Page. They fell to the ALP in 1990, were regained by the National Party in 1996 and have been marginal seats ever since. The Green vote in 2004 was 12.4 per cent and 10.8 per cent respectively in these two seats (Curtin & Woodward 2005) and, in the case of Richmond, was a key factor in bringing about the defeat of the sitting National member (and Minister) Larry Anthony. Similarly, the Nationals' loss of the Queensland seat of Fairfax (encompassing the Noosa Heads and Sunshine Coast precincts) to the Liberal Party in 1990 might be attributable to a 'sea-change' effect.

Too much weight, however, should not be placed on these demographic changes in explaining the decline of the National Party in recent decades. It is true that the party has been conscious of the threat posed by the shrinkage of its support base and has variously explored the possibility of an alliance with the Democratic Labor Party (DLP) in 1974 (Woodward 1985), changed its name in an attempt to shake off its sectional and regional image, and even broke the coalition relationship in 1987 and campaigned more widely in an ill-fated quest to supplant the Liberal Party.[6] The failure of these approaches led to a major internal review of the National Party (Nixon 1988) that recommended a return to focusing on its traditional rural and regional electorates. And it has indeed been the party's inability to hold these traditional seats that has most significantly contributed to its decline.

As Table 13.1 shows, 1984 stands out as a high point in the National Party's electoral fortunes. In the election held in that year, it increased to 21 the number of House of Representative seats that it held in the expanded Parliament, constituting a marginal increase in the percentage of seats that it held in that chamber. Since that time, however, the National Party has seen its lower house seats reduced to only 12—its lowest proportion of seats in the post-1983 expanded Parliament—and its percentage of the vote slump to historic lows. This has not been a straight linear decline, but the trend is unmistakeable.

The National Party's representation slumped the most between 1987 and 1990. It lost the Queensland seat of Groom in a by-election in 1988 and a further four seats in the 1990 election. This loss of support might be attributable in part to the taint of corruption associated with the National Party State government in Queensland as a result of revelations by the Fitzgerald Inquiry in that State (Prasser, Wear & Nethercote 1990). The party recovered from this low point to hold 18 House of Representatives seats after the 1996 election, with a respectable 8.2 per cent of the vote. But it has since seen its House of Representative numbers fall in each subsequent election and its proportion of the vote decline to its lowest level ever (in 1998) and fail to recover much thereafter. This needs some explanation, especially since it has occurred while in government when the party could be expected to be in a position to deliver benefits to its constituents.

Essentially, the National Party appears to have lost support because it has failed to protect its traditional supporters from unpopular 'economic rationalist' policies that have been continued or extended under the Howard Coalition government. The introduction of a Goods and Services Tax, the privatisation of Telstra and the pursuit of 'competition policy' have come to symbolise a policy direction that is perceived as detrimental by many rural dwellers. It has come on top of financial deregulation that is widely perceived to have led (in the early to mid-1990s at least) to high interest rates and to farm foreclosures, the reduction of government subsidies and the shift to 'user pays' principles for the delivery of some public services, the removal of import protection for some rural produce despite other countries maintaining their restrictions on Australian agricultural exports, the move away from regulated marketing boards that guaranteed uniform higher prices to farmers for agricultural goods, and the closure of many rural schools, hospitals and train services. Rural discontent has also arisen over gun-control reform, native title legislation and fuel prices. When the impact of these policies has coincided with extended drought and/or with falls in commodity prices, rural discontent has threatened an electoral backlash. The National Party seems to have been blamed for acquiescing with its coalition partner's preference for policies seen as detrimental to many of its erstwhile supporters.

This growing rural resentment underpinned a sharp fall in the National Party's vote (to 5.3 per cent) in the 1998 election. This share of the vote was substantially less than the 8.4 per cent secured by Pauline Hanson's One Nation party which garnered considerable numbers of 'protest votes' in rural electorates (Davey 2000). By the time of the 2001 election, the threat from One Nation had been contained (its support falling to 4.3 per cent of the vote) but support for the National Party barely increased. Disillusionment with the party found expression in the election of Independents (campaigning on a platform of looking after their constituents) in some of its safest seats. The National Party failed to dislodge these Independents despite a concerted campaign in 2004.

A closer inspection of the seats that the National Party has lost in the two decades since 1984 reveals some interesting patterns. It no longer holds nine of the 21 House of Representative seats that it held then. It has lost four seats in each of Queensland and New South Wales and one in Victoria. Of these nine losses, five have been lost directly to the Liberal Party (Farrer, Hume, Fairfax, Groom and Murray). It has lost two (Fisher and Richmond) to the ALP, Fisher later being won in turn by the Liberal Party. It has lost two to Independents (New England and Kennedy). In addition, the National Party currently holds two seats that it has regained after temporarily losing them to the ALP: Hinkler (lost in 1987 but regained in 1993) and Page (lost in 1990 but regained in 1996). Two of the seats held in 1984 were lost, regained and then lost again: Richmond (lost 1990; regained 1996; lost 2004) and Kennedy (lost 1990; regained 1993; lost 2001) and it also managed to win a seat (Capricornia) in 1996 that it subsequently lost in 1998.

What these results reveal is that it is the Liberal Party that has constituted the greatest threat to the Nationals and that (apart from Richmond) the seats lost since 1984 have been relatively 'safe' (in the broad Labor versus non-Labor sense) and mostly inland rather than coastal. Moreover, while it has evidently been possible for the party to win back seats lost to the ALP, seats lost to the Liberals appear to be permanently lost.

Incumbency is crucial. When sitting National Party members have retired and the vacancy has opened up contests with a Liberal Party candidate, formerly very safe National seats can be lost to their coalition partner. (The Liberal Party now holds twice as many non-metropolitan seats as the National Party.) Incumbency has also played a part in the case of those seats lost to Independents. In Kennedy, the sitting National Party member defected and successfully ran as an Independent, while in New England the incumbent National had only occupied the seat for one term, having replaced a former party leader (Ian Sinclair) who had held the seat for 35 years.

A few other factors should be considered in explaining the decline in the National Party's support. First, there has been a reduction in both the proportion of Australian voters who identify with any particular party and in the intensity of any such identification. There is no reason to assume that National Party voters have been immune from this trend. Second, since the establishment of the National Farmers' Federation (NFF) in 1979,[7] there has been a major body representing rural interests that has supplanted some of the role previously performed by the National Party. This was particularly the case during the long period of Labor governments (1983–1996) during which the local National Party member became largely irrelevant for many rural constituents. They came to rely instead on the NFF to lobby the Labor government on their behalf. Third, improved communications (such as satellite TV) has meant that rural Australia is less isolated, more liable to have access to nationally focused rather than parochially focused media, and more likely to see electoral contests in two-party terms, making it harder for National Party candidates to distinguish themselves from the Liberals. Indeed, there is some evidence to suggest that even during the most recent (October 2004) election, rural candidates found it difficult to gain local media coverage (O'Loughlin 2004). All this bodes ill for the National Party.

Ideology and policy

National Party politicians have a reputation as 'horse traders'—shrewd, tough, pragmatic negotiators who openly seek benefits for their clients. In the past, National Party leaders proved adept at 'getting their way' in disputes with their coalition partner and showed themselves to be verbally aggressive against their opponents. The National Party has on occasions been prepared to make self-interested deals that its critics could label as unprincipled. At the State level, for example, it has at times entered into alliances with the ALP, forsaking its conservative coalition partner. In the most recent instance of this phenomenon, the South Australian Labor government was given an absolute majority government in July 2004 when the sole National member in that State's lower house accepted a ministerial position (Parkin 2005).

Despite this ruthless pragmatism, however, it has been suggested that there is an ideological basis that underlays the National Party's policy stance. Aitkin (1988) popularised the expression 'countrymindedness' to depict the set of values that he found common amongst those living in rural northern New South Wales.[8] In this view, farming is an ennobling activity undertaken by rugged individualists who struggle against capricious weather and uncertain markets to play a central role in the nation's economy. Government support for those suffering from the privations of rural living is consequently seen as justified, especially when rural virtue is contrasted against the perceived immorality of the cities. The wholesome, healthy rural lifestyle (according to this perception) ought to be encouraged and government assistance serving this purpose should not be seen as in any way resembling 'socialism'. An echo of this view was apparent in a statement made by the President of the NFF, Peter Corish, in the lead-up to the 2004 election: 'If it's not in the interest of Australian agriculture, then it's not in the national interest' (Breusch 2004).

It is these sentiments that the National Party has sought to placate, encourage and represent. In particular, the National Party has sought to claim credit for the delivery of rural health packages, family and community services for regional Australia, and petrol and diesel subsidies for rural areas (McGauran 2000). It has also sought electoral credit in recent years for rural and regional grants delivered through the Howard government's Regional Partnerships and Sustainable Regions Programs, for compensation to sugar growers who failed to gain additional access to the US market through the US–Australia Free Trade Agreement, for better rural communications, for the government's $2 billion water policy package, for 'regional export hubs', and for more funding for rural roads (Curtin & Woodward 2005).

The National Party reflects its constituents on a range of political, social and moral issues, making it the most conservative of Australia's significant parties. Its political conservatism was most apparent in the Cold War era when it was the staunchest opponent of communism. It also has a long history of fierce opposition to trade unions, reflecting a widespread view in rural Australia. While this stance can be traced back to the shearers' strike of the 1890s, it was manifested as recently as 1998 with the involvement of National Party Transport Minister, John Sharp, in the unsuccessful attempt to have all maritime union workers removed from Australia's docks in the 'waterfront dispute' (Elias 1998). The National Party (and rural Australia) has consistently demonstrated the strongest attachment to the monarchy and national symbols such as the flag. This attachment was again demonstrated by the opposition mounted by the leaders of the National Party to Australia becoming a republic (*The Age* 19 January 1999) and the resounding rejection of the republic referendum proposal in rural Australia in 1999 (Jackson 1999).

The National Party is a strong repository of 'traditional family values' and is often informed by the strong Christian beliefs held by its members, who have often been outspoken in their opposition to legalising homosexuality or liberalising drug laws (e.g. *Sydney Morning Herald* 19 June 1999). They have opposed affirmative action for women, taken conservative stances on immigration policies and multiculturalism, and been accused of racism (e.g. *Sydney Morning Herald* 17 February 1996). National Party members have also shown a 'pro-life' position on the abortion issue and have sought to restrict abortions by proposing the removal of Medicare benefits for the procedure (e.g. *Courier-Mail* 8 February 2005).

Coalition relations

As already noted, the National Party spent only a brief period in the national Parliament before joining a coalition with a predecessor of the Liberal Party. It has subsequently been in coalition with the major non-Labor party throughout most of its existence, even including periods when both parties found themselves in Opposition. This relationship, however, has not always been fully harmonious and has included periods when it has totally broken down at the national level.[9] It has also quite often been acrimonious at the State level, leading to long periods of rupture in some States even while the Coalition continued to function at the federal level.

The coalition relationship has been a complex one. As well as the differing situations that sometimes arise between the State and federal representatives of the two parties involved, there is often a different view of the coalition relationship held by the Nationals' parliamentary members and by the party's extra-parliamentary organisation. Generally, National Party politicians in the federal Parliament tend to be closer to their Coalition counterparts than they are to their own party's organisational members. This is reflected in the propensity of former to be more sympathetic than the latter to the periodic calls for an amalgamation of the two coalition parties.

There can be significant policy differences between the two Coalition parties at the parliamentary, organisational and broad membership level. When this occurs, National Party parliamentarians face some complicated choices. Should they threaten to break with their Coalition partner unless the Liberals agree to concede their preferred policy? This is a tactic that needs to be credible to be effective and is thus one that cannot be employed too often. It is also something that loses its bargaining power if National Party support is not required to form government. Moreover, it carries definite risks. It raises the prospect of exchanging the benefits of being a part of government and having some leverage, however limited these might appear, for the powerlessness and uncertainty of Opposition or sitting on the cross benches.

There are even dangers attached to any signs of public disagreement between the Coalition partners. Such divisions are liable to have electoral repercussions to the detriment of both parties because voters appear reluctant to support parties that show signs of disunity. (To avoid this prospect, the Nationals and Liberals shared a campaign headquarters and ran a wholly joint campaign for the first time in the 2004 federal election campaign.) On the other hand, however, there are also risks in appearing supinely to endorse, for the sake of Coalition unity, policies that are unpopular with the National Party's constituents. As noted earlier, the Nationals have suffered from precisely this since 1996. It requires considerable skill on the part of National Party leaders to stand up for their constituents' interests, influence their larger Coalition partner in an era when their own electoral support (and bargaining power) is waning, and yet maintain Coalition unity.

An alternative to trying to walk this tightrope is the prospect of the National Party amalgamating with the Liberal Party. Calls for such an action were made in the wake of electoral defeats in the 1980s and early 1990s (Costar 1996) but they were bitterly resisted by the National Party organisational wing. A more recent call for the merger of the two parties at the federal level that was to form part of a speech by Liberal Senator Nick Minchin was so swiftly rejected by the then National Party leader, John Anderson, that it was withdrawn from the speech (Emerson 2002). Proposals for a merger of the Coalition partners at the State level in Queensland, however, were being openly debated in late 2004 (Ludlow 2004).

While the option of the National Party amalgamating with the Liberal Party has some attractions, it is not without its drawbacks. Those in favour of a merger argue that it would avoid divisive electoral contests between the Coalition partners and enable a totally united (and more effective) opposition to the Labor Party. They also argue that it would avoid the duplication of efforts and the consequent waste of resources.

It would, however, mean the death of the National Party's separate identity, something that the party has fought tenaciously to maintain throughout its history. Moreover, there is no evidence to suggest that the non-Labor vote would be increased by a merger. Rather, it is most likely that the non-Labor vote is maximised under current electoral arrangements. Additionally, there is the danger that, were a merger to take place, a new or breakaway party would form to represent those rural interests that feel that they are ignored by the major parties.[10]

Conclusion

The National Party currently finds itself at an electoral low point, with its representation in the House at its lowest level and its proportion of the vote close to its lowest ever. The days when it was able to dictate to its larger Coalition partner—'the tail wagging the dog' (Richmond 1978)—appear to be over. Not that the National Party ever commanded a great percentage of the vote. Rather its disproportionate influence was a result of its (limited) electoral support being concentrated in specific rural seats that it (unlike other minor parties with similar but less concentrated overall voting support) was able to win, and these seats often proved crucial for the formation of a non-Labor government. Increasingly, both of these factors are under threat.

Long-term and more recent economic and demographic changes have undermined the National Party's base of support. These processes appear to be
irreversible. However, the party has long managed to maintain itself despite
these inexorable changes. Its more recent electoral decline can mostly be
attributed to its inability to defend its territory from its Coalition partner. It is
ironic that the party has alienated some of its traditional supporters as a result of
supporting the policy directions of the Liberal Party and yet it has been the
Liberal Party that has been the ultimate beneficiary of this disgruntlement.

There still appears to be some scope for a party that is prepared to champion
local rural interests and to act as a voice for those unhappy with some of the
government's policies, judging by the success of Independents who have
pursued this course. Whether the National Party can regain this role is yet to be
seen. There is also the possibility that the National Party may gain greater
bargaining power over its Coalition partner as a result of its Senate representatives being crucial (as a result of the 2004 election) for the government to control
the Senate. How the National Party handles this situation might well determine
the party's future. It would be interesting if in the short term the National
Party's influence was increasingly derived from its role in the Senate; if so, it
would be following the past pattern set by other minor parties represented in
the Senate.

Failing this, it is hard to see the National Party avoiding electoral eclipse. It
seems to find it difficult to differentiate itself from the Liberal Party. If its
electoral appeal is limited to the government benefits it can deliver to rural and
regional electorates, the Liberal Party has shown that it can fulfil this role just as
well.

NOTES

1 Country Party candidates and candidates endorsed by rural organisations had been
elected to State parliaments even earlier than the 15 candidates (endorsed by the Australian
Farmers Federal Organisation) elected in 1919 that were to form the federal Country
Party in early 1920. On the origins of the Country Party, see Ellis (1963) and Graham
(1966).

2 The party changed its name from Country Party to National Country Party in May 1975
and to National Party in October 1982. For the sake of convenience, National Party is
used throughout this chapter to include its earlier names.

3 At the federal level, there is an agreement that neither the National Party nor the Liberal
Party will field a candidate against a sitting member of the other party. Once a member of
either party retires, however, the other party is entitled to contest the vacant seat. In recent
times, these 'three-cornered contests' (National, Liberal and Labor) have tended to be
won by the Liberal Party so that each time a National Party member retires, the seat is
lost to the Liberal Party.

4 Prior to changes in the electoral law enacted by the Whitlam Labor government in the
1970s, there had been a 20 per cent tolerance (from the average) in the number of voters in

each electorate. As rural seats were losing voters, they tended to have fewer voters than the average (and substantially less than those growing suburban seats that were above average), especially if there had not been a recent redistribution. The Whitlam government reduced the variation permitted to 10 per cent. Despite National Party pressure to reverse this change when the Coalition returned to government under Prime Minister Fraser, the 10 per cent tolerance remained. The only concession won by the National Party was a change to the electoral law to take into account the geographical size of electorates. This ensured that sparsely populated, large (rural) electorates were those that consistently had fewer voters than average. The Hawke Labor government legislated to remove this concession and set the requirement that boundaries should be drawn to anticipate demographic changes such that (while maintaining the 10 per cent tolerance), the difference in numbers of voters in each electorate should be only 2 per cent above or below the average half way through the life of a redistribution. This meant that rural seats typically had *more* voters than average immediately after a redistribution.

5 So named after the ABC television series *Sea Change*, in which the main protagonist escapes the big city 'rat race' for a quieter and friendlier seaside life.

6 This ill-fated strategy had its origins in Queensland where the National Party first changed its name and where, under the Premiership of Joh Bjelke-Petersen, it had been the senior partner of the State Coalition government. 'Joh' broke with the Liberal Party and the National Party governed alone in Queensland, securing government in its own right at the 1986 State election. Bjelke-Petersen was encouraged to launch a 'Joh for PM' campaign with the goal that he would lead the Nationals (who severed coalition ties with the Liberal Party in 1987) to repeat at the federal level what he had accomplished at the State level. In the event, Bjelke-Petersen failed to stand, the rupturing of the Coalition helped the Hawke Labor government to be re-elected, and the National Party lost two seats despite increasing its share of the vote as a result of contesting many more seats (Woodward & Costar 1988; Coaldrake 1987).

7 The NFF was formed by bringing together 12 federal commodity councils and 10 State-based organisations to give it a near monopoly in representing Australia's farmers (Mathews 1994: 206).

8 Whether this also applied in other rural areas is a moot point.

9 The Coalition formed in 1922 was broken (after electoral defeat) in 1929. It was reformed in 1934 and lasted until 1941. It was again reformed after the 1949 election, lasting until electoral defeat in 1972. It was reformed in 1974, briefly broken just prior to the 1987 election, re-established after that electoral defeat and maintained ever since.

10 This has already happened with the formation of the New Country Party in Queensland prior to the 2004 election. Its platform claimed dissatisfaction with the Coalition's lack of support for regional Australia but it failed to gain any significant electoral support (New Country Party 2005).

REFERENCES

ABS [Australian Bureau of Statistics] 2004, *2004 Year Book Australia* no. 86, Australian Bureau of Statistics, Canberra.

ABS [Australian Bureau of Statistics] 2005, *2005 Year Book Australia* no. 87, Australian Bureau of Statistics, Canberra.

Aitkin, D. 1973, 'The Australian Country Party', in *Australian Politics: A Third Reader*, eds H. Mayer & H. Nelson, Cheshire, Melbourne.

Aitkin, D. 1988, ' "Countrymindedness": The Spread of an Idea', in *Australian Cultural History*, eds S. Goldberg & F. Smith, Cambridge University Press, Cambridge, pp. 50–7.

Barbalet, J. 1975, 'Tri-Partism in Australia: The Role of the Australian Country Party', *Politics*, vol. 10, no. 1, pp. 1–14.

Breusch, J. 2004, 'Farmers Plough Own Furrow', *Australian Financial Review*, 9 September.

Coaldrake, P. 1987, 'The Nationals: Where to From Here?', *Current Affairs Bulletin*, vol. 64, no. 7, pp. 12–17.

Costar, B. 1996, 'The Future of the National Party of Australia', in *The Paradox of Parties: Australian Political Parties in the 1990s*, ed. M. Simms, Allen & Unwin, Sydney.

Curtin, J. & Woodward, D. 2005, 'Rural and Regional Voters Return Home', in *Mortgage Nation: The 2004 Federal Election*, eds M. Simms & J. Warhurst, Curtin University of Technology, Perth. (forthcoming)

Davey, P. 2000, 'The National Party', in *Howard's Agenda: The 1998 Australian Election*, eds M. Simms & J. Warhurst, University of Queensland Press, Brisbane.

Dawson, B. 1994, 'Rural Employment in Australia', *Rural Society*, vol. 4, no. 2, pp. 14–21.

Elias, D. 1998, 'The Docks: War and Peace: The Full, Dramatic Account of the Battle to Break Australia's Waterfront Union', *The Age*, 17 June.

Ellis, U. 1963, *A History of the Australian Country Party*, Melbourne University Press, Melbourne.

Emerson, S. 2002, 'Merger Call Splits Parties', *Australian*, 24 May.

Graham, B. 1966, *The Formation of the Australian Country Parties*, ANU Press, Canberra.

Jackson, M. 1999, 'Rural "No" Loud and Clear', *Weekly Times*, 10 November.

Ludlow, M. 2004, 'Qld Nats-Lib Merger Gains Momentum', *Australian Financial Review*, 19 November.

Mackerras, M. 1978, 'No Change: Analysis of the 1977 Election', *Politics*, vol. 13, no. 1, pp. 131–8.

Mathews, T. 1994, 'Employers' Associations, Corporatism and the Accord: The Politics of Industrial Relations', in eds S. Bell & B. Head, *State, Economy and Public Policy in Australia*, Oxford University Press, Oxford.

McGauran, J. 2000, 'The National Party in Government—Budget 2000: Rural and Regional Australia', Press Release, Melbourne.

New Country Party 2005, 'New Country Party: Australia's Voice', website, Brisbane, <http://www.newcountryparty.org.au/> accessed 16 February 2005.

Nixon, P. 1988, *National Party of Australia: The Future*, Committee of Review into the Future Direction of the National Party of Australia, Canberra.

O'Loughlin, T. 2004, 'Getting Front Page is Hard', *Australian Financial Review*, 8 October.

Parkin, A. 2005, 'South Australia: July to December 2004', *Australian Journal of Politics and History*, vol. 51, no. 2, pp. 303–9.

Prasser, S., Wear, R. & Nethercote, J. eds 1990, *Corruption and Reform: The Fitzgerald Vision*, Queensland University Press, Brisbane.

Richmond, K. 1978, 'The National Country Party', in *Political Parties in Australia*, eds G. Starr, K. Richmond & G. Maddox, Heinemann, Richmond.

Woodward, D. 1985, 'The Federal National Party of Australia', in *Country to National: Australian Rural Politics and Beyond*, eds B. Costar & D. Woodward, Allen & Unwin, Sydney.

Woodward, D. & Costar, B. 1988, 'The National Party Campaign', in *Australia Votes: The 1987 Federal Election*, eds I. McAllister & J. Warhurst, Longman Cheshire, Melbourne.

The Greens, Democrats, minor parties and Independents

JENNY TILBY STOCK

In a system dominated by the Labor Party and the non-Labor Coalition, minor parties are destined to play a lesser, though occasionally strategic, role. They are usually effectively excluded from the lower houses of Parliament at the Commonwealth and State levels where governments are formed, and the most they can realistically hope for is to be part of a strategic 'balance of power' between the two major party blocs. Since 1949 only the Democratic Labor Party (1955–74) and the Australian Democrats (since 1977) have lasted a generation and only those two parties have ever achieved so-called 'party status' in the Senate (a designation conferred, under Parliament's own internal rules, when a group holds at least five seats and which entitles the group to resources like additional support staff and office space). Even at the height of their numbers and influence, the parliamentary tenure of such parties is fragile; the DLP disappeared overnight in the double dissolution of 1974, and the Democrats are now likely to vanish in the space of two half-Senate elections.

The federal election of October 2004 was significant for the minor players because it brought to an end two-and-a-half decades in which the Senate had been a 'hung' chamber and one in which they had, in various combinations, used their numbers to moderate the power of executive government and improve accountability (Thompson 1999). When—and perhaps whether—minor parties will again play a pivotal role in the national Parliament is in some doubt, but they have a continuing presence and potential there, as they do and have had in other Parliaments around the country.

Whether founded by breakaways from an established party, or coming in from outside, minor players face the established electoral bases, resources and ideological breadth of the mass Labor and Liberal/National parties. To survive, they must raise funds, harness the enthusiasts they attract and develop ways of managing the inevitable clashes within the ranks over principle, procedure and parliamentary ambition. Some new parties burst on to the scene and disappear just as rapidly, like One Nation; others rise more slowly and, fitfully or surely, fill their niche for longer. Most are dangerously dependent on leaders who have 'charisma' or can generate favourable media attention. Sooner or later they succumb, and to date no small party has come close to supplanting Labor or the Coalition or to becoming a third major party.

Whatever their relative strength in the nation's legislatures, minor parties are important because they cater to emerging new constituencies, voicing concerns the bigger parties have overlooked or would rather ignore. By keeping the parties of government responsive, they stimulate change. For periods, when their elected members hold the balance of power in hung chambers, they are the focus of intense lobbying and of pressure to do deals. Out of the spotlight, their members may also do valuable and generally under-recognised work on parliamentary committees and inquiries.

But any aspirations they harbour about supplanting the old parties founder on the single-member seat system. While they can and do win by-elections, especially when one of the major parties fails to contest, and when there is some local protest vote, their tenure is often brief. So is that of anyone who jumps ship from a major party during their term of office. It is a 'Catch-22' situation. Voters, however disenchanted with Labor or the Coalition, are unlikely to desert them in sufficient numbers unless and until the alternatives look like winning lower house seats.[1] Aspirants nonetheless contest such seats in order to keep their party in the public mind, to boost their chances of gaining upper house seats and to negotiate preference deals.

To reach even the modest quotas required for election to the Senate and to those State and Territory houses using the proportional representation method of election, minor party candidates need their primary vote topped up by surplus votes from the major parties and/or those passed on from excluded candidates with even fewer primary votes. For years the Democrats, as a centrist party, got preferences from both Labor and the Coalition. But as minor and micro parties have proliferated on the fringes in recent years, the allocation of preferences has assumed greater importance, especially since 1984 when the introduction of a simplified 'above the line' Senate ballot option forced all parties to nominate where their surplus or discarded votes shall go. The temptation to offer and succumb to dubious inducements—as highlighted in Queensland's 2001 Shepherdson Inquiry (QCJC 2001)—point to the need for some oversight and regularisation of the inter-party preference deal process. This has not happened, and each election sees a flurry of negotiations to stitch up deals. Major parties try to secure preferences from all sorts of fringe groups in order to shore up marginal lower house seats, and in return allocate their own surplus votes to either help or exclude such groups where it counts. The results can be bizarre, with popular minor party candidates failing and those with tiny primary votes scraping in.

This chapter examines four minor parties, all currently at different phases of their existence. The 'major minor party', the Australian Democrats, may be in terminal decline, the Greens are a promising work in progress, One Nation's party is over and Family First is an untried new phenomenon. The chapter also analyses those hardy individuals, the 'Independents'.

The Australian Democrats

For a good quarter century, the Democrats were significant players on the Australian political landscape (Warhurst 1997; Stock 2002). Formed in the aftermath of the cataclysmic constitutional crisis period of 1974–75, disillusioned moderates on both sides responded to former Liberal Minister Don Chipp's call for the 'emergence of a third political force, representing middle-of-the-road - policies which would owe allegiance to no outside pressure group' (Chipp 1977: 577). The party was formally launched in mid-1977, personnel coming largely from the remnants of earlier dissident Liberal groupings, especially the Australia Party and breakaway Liberal-origin parties in South Australia and Western Australia.

That the new party so quickly (1980–81) got a total of five Senators elected, party status and the balance of power is remarkable. Much of the credit goes to the personality and total dedication of Chipp himself, and the novelty of much of what the Democrats had to offer at the time. That the party endured for so long and achieved so much is no less remarkable. For over two decades until 2002 they were the third force, with some inspiring leaders, attractive policies and a democratic way of operating. They drew votes in their own right and were also the most obvious place for the fluctuating 'protest' vote.

In the Senate, where their numbers peaked at nine in the period July 1999 to June 2002, the Democrats held sole balance of power from 1983 to 1993, and shared the balance of power between 1981 and 1993 and between 2002 and 2005. As believers in open and accountable democratic processes, the Democrats Senators contributed enthusiastically to the expansion and reinvigoration of the Senate and joint Senate–House committee systems, and were vital participants in the Senate's more rigorous scrutiny of bills from the House of Representatives. To them goes much of the credit for refashioning the Senate as a genuine house of review. The Democrats' hard work and expertise in their chosen fields earned them legitimacy, although most their quieter parliamentary achievements went unnoticed in the wider community.[2] Their own private members' bills receive short shrift; even if passed in the Senate with Opposition assistance, they usually failed in the lower house. Janet Powell's doggedly pursued 1989 Bill to end tobacco advertising in the print media was one of the few Democrat bills to succeed. Some of their best and most carefully worked out ideas, rejected as naive and impractical when first put forward, later appear, sometimes virtually unchanged, in government bills—Sugita (1995: 313) cites the Hawke Labor government's 'lifting' of a Democrat Bill in legislation to save the Franklin River—while the Democrats claim as the most blatant example Vicki Bourne's World Heritage legislation, renamed and adopted intact by the same government (Democrats 2005a).

Most of the early period of Democrat 'power'—nationally and in South Australia—was under Labor governments. The Democrats helped these Labor governments implement reform in areas which accorded with their principles and policies, but later proved helpless when the big parties united on issues they opposed, like deregulation and privatisation. The election of the Howard Coalition government in 1996 led the Democrats' then national leader Cheryl Kernot to claim that the electorate had 'deliberately provided two competing mandates: one for the government to be changed and one for a balance of power check on that new government in the Senate' (*Australian* 21 March 1996, cited in Goot 1999). After his re-election in 1998, however, Prime Minister Howard could claim a 'mandate' even for the still widely unpopular Goods and Services Tax (GST) proposal, something that Labor opposed outright as did a majority of the Democrat membership. Five of the seven Democrat Senators, including Meg Lees, Kernot's successor as national leader, chose to exercise real power by agreeing, after protracted negotiations forcing some concessions from the government, to pass the Bills. But the result was that Labor kept to its opposition pledge, the Coalition got its promised new tax, and the Democrats wore the blame for letting the GST happen at all and for the defects of the equity compromises they had hammered out. Much of the goodwill earned over the years by their skilled mediations, notably on native title, workplace relations and the environment was lost. To younger voters, the Democrats had evidently become part of the political mainstream, with the relatively untried Greens now appearing to better fulfil the outsider role of a fresh new idealistic party.

LEADERSHIP

All parties depend on leaders, none more so than new parties that may initially be little more than the 'leader'. As the party's public face, the leader must attract favourable media attention and clearly articulate what the party stands for. Within the organisation they must also travel about, inspire the faithful, help sort out State problems and be a source of energy and ideas. If like the Democrats the party survives and grows, leaders must also run a party room composed of a collection of Senators from a variety of States whose branches operate in virtual isolation and may also feel little connection with their Senators' activities in Canberra. (Only in South Australia long term, sporadically in New South Wales, and for a period in Western Australia have Democrat State branches enjoyed a meaningful role in State politics and the fillip that provides.) From a small and sometimes inexperienced pool, leadership talent has to be nurtured, and leaders replaced at the right time. This has posed real problems for a party like the Democrats whose leaders are elected by the membership at large. When caught out by electoral defeat or resignation, an already cumbersome postal ballot process has to crank into gear while, until recently, as few as 100 members in a State could bring on a leadership challenge any time.

For the most part the Democrats have had leaders who managed these multiple tasks well, and the party flourished best in the earlier Chipp years, and under skilled and popular leaders Janine Haines (1987–90) and Cheryl Kernot (1994–97). So highly was Kernot regarded (and so keen was she to play more than a mediating role against the Howard government) that she was enticed to join Labor in 1997. Her shock defection, immediately after the Democrats' best-ever results in the South Australian State election of October 1997, may have marked the end of the time when strong, popular leaders could carry the party, and what has happened since helps to explain the Democrats' decline.

Seasoned deputy Meg Lees took over, with the young and ambitious Natasha Stott Despoja, a fellow South Australian, as her deputy. Lees rallied the party and continued the Democrat's respected parliamentary role. But her willingness to work closely with the Howard government and her perceived capitulation on aspects of the GST and on environmental law exposed a party now divided on its role—between those wanting the party to be an honest broker between two increasingly convergent (and rightward moving) major parties and those wanting to champion the constituency (on the Left) seemingly abandoned by both major parties.

Stott Despoja, apparently attractive to a younger and especially female demographic, came under pressure to mount a leadership challenge (Rogers 2004). Duly elected leader in early April 2002, with Aden Ridgeway as her deputy, this 'dream team' could not save a party in disarray. The party managed to win back four of its five contested Senate positions in the October 2001 federal election, but Lees resigned hurt to form her own party in July 2002, reducing party ranks in the Senate to eight, while her ally Andrew Murray sulked 'in exile'. To the dismay of many party members, the 'gang of four' Senators, including Ridgeway, then forced Stott Despoja to resign in August 2002. Two of her allies contested the leadership, the committed but low-key Queenslander Andrew Bartlett being elected in October. Extensive media coverage throughout these events exposed a dysfunctional party apparently riven by personal feuds, destructive power struggles and loss of direction. Then in December 2003, Bartlett misbehaved in a drunken altercation with Liberal Senator Jeannie Ferris on the floor of the Senate. This embarrassing incident (for which Bartlett apologised and which he attributed in part to a health condition) was for many Democrats supporters the last straw. A year later, after the party's worst poll results ever, Bartlett's hapless deputy, Victorian Senator Lyn Allison, took the leadership reins.

PRINCIPLES AND POLICIES

The Democrats were born in the era when post-materialist values began to take hold. Their policies correspondingly espouse the values of fairness, honesty and integrity, and a concern for environmental and economic sustainability, peace, human rights and social justice. Keen to throw off the 'fairies at the bottom of the garden' tag once attached to them by the then Labor government's Finance Minister Peter Walsh, the Democrats produced for the 1993 election a detailed and costed proposal for economic recovery and job creation, *Getting to Work*, a blueprint supplemented by a host of policy papers prepared for subsequent budgets and elections. A more pragmatic attention to the detail of matters like small-business assistance and reform of the taxation system has informed Democrat thinking, to the extent that they became the preferred group with whom the major parties could 'do business', rather than the more radical Greens.

For years the Democrats were able to advance these causes in and out of Parliament, and built up a credible record, an example being Kernot's significant role in mediating the contending forces and finally brokering the historic native title legislation in 1994 (Stock 2002). The current disillusion with the Democrats stems less from a loss of faith in these causes, or in the need for a party devoted primarily to them, but rather from the failure of the Democrats to behave like a party of principle above the dirty realities of party politics.

EQUALITY AND PARTICIPATORY DEMOCRACY

When they began, one of the Democrats' most attractive and novel features was that they offered the widest possible participation in decision making to ordinary members wishing to make a genuine contribution to the evolution of a new and different political force. The consultative processes worked well while the party was small and while decisions did not require quick resolution. The party's *National Journal* and website (Democrats 2005b) have assisted in keeping members informed and trying to develop some coherence of approach, but only a small proportion of the membership has actually participated actively. In retrospect, the Democrats may have invested far too much energy devising and finding agreement on policies they would never have to implement and upon which they would rarely be called to adjudicate.

Democrats' candidates, once elected to the Senate, are free to operate there and on committees according to their collective interpretation of Democrat principles and agreed policy. Conscience voting is allowed (a notable example being Stott Despoja's and Bartlett's vote against the final GST legislation in June 1999), but may prove very divisive. 'Dissidents' must still answer to their State Executives and to a national 'compliance' body which claim to be in closer touch with the mood of members than is the party room. Each Senator, with a parliamentary salary and allowances, staff and facilities, inevitably develops new power bases which may separate him or her from the ordinary membership, while onerous parliamentary and committee duties keep Senators in Canberra for long periods.

Unsurprisingly, the disconnection between the ideals of participatory democracy and the realities of a party required to act decisively and in a coherent, focused way has been a major cause of internal instability (Gauja 2004). The Democrats have been learning the hard way, and possibly too late, what older bigger parties know, and the Greens are starting to appreciate: the limits of grassroots democracy, and the need for a higher degree of delegation, trust and discipline.

A WOMAN-FRIENDLY PARTY

Born during the second wave of feminism and espousing inclusiveness, the Democrats' women have not had to fight entrenched patriarchy to the same extent as the older parties. After a slow start, women became prominent at all levels. The Democrats' second leader, Janine Haines, became in 1986 the first woman to lead an Australian political party. As many women as men have been elected as Democrat Members of Parliament. Six of the party's nine national leaders have been women, most emerging from the community sector. A side-effect has been the disproportionate impact on the Democrats of the media's propensity to build up and later tear down women leaders and aspirants (Henderson 1999; van Acker 2003, Rogers 2004). Since the mid-1980s, the Democrats have been the party most consistently responsive to women's issues (Hill 2003) and arguably their example has prompted the other parties to increase their numbers of women in parliament and in ministries. A concern to ensure that the Democrats sustained their good record led to a decision at their 2000 National Conference to form a Democrat women's network to encourage more talented women to come forward and be sustained (VIDA 2005).

ELECTORAL PREFERENCES

Unwilling to compromise their independence or alienate part of their following, the Democrats did not originally recommend to their supporters any particular preference distribution. Typically they issued two-sided how-to-vote cards, one side in effect distributing preferences to Labor and the other to the Coalition. However, the mid-1980s saw State branches start to do preference-exchange deals with Labor in the cause of electoral reform, to the dismay of some members and achieving no obvious electoral benefits. Since then, the practice has become common, although South Australia, the Democrats' most consistently successful State (and in whose upper house the Democrats have been firmly ensconced since the introduction of proportional representation in the 1970s), was the last branch to compromise, still largely adhering to two-sided how-to-vote cards.

Forced at the federal level in 1984 (due to the new above-the-line voting option) to specify where preferences should flow in the Senate, the Democrats initially went for an even-handed 50/50 split between Labor and the Coalition. Under pressure from a resurgent Green movement and an increased reliance on major party preferences, the party reluctantly decided instead to attempt to maximise electoral leverage in the lead-up to the 1996 federal election (*Australian* 24 July 1995). Except in Western Australia, where the Greens got in first, most deals were with Labor (Macklin 2000). A fair proportion of regular Democrat voters continue to exercise their independence by choosing the tedious below-the-line option.

In lower house seats, where voters can choose freely, the *actual* direction of Democrat preferences varies according to the character of the seat and the relative popularity of the parties and leaders in any contest, but tends to favour Labor by margins ranging from slight to significant.

CORE SUPPORT AND ELECTORAL APPEAL

Given its origins and small-l liberal leanings, the party has performed best, if sporadically, in the comfortable, established suburbs of the capital cities and the ACT. Significant support in Adelaide's southern suburbs and eastern hills has made South Australia the most consistently strong Democrat State. The party has not resonated in rural or traditional working-class electorates despite its championing of the small-business sector, including the family farm, its opposition to the Howard government's most draconian workplace reforms and its continued defence of the rights of workers to organise and to access arbitration tribunals. Nor have the Democrats had much impact in the less affluent outer suburbs or among non-Anglo ethnic communities.

In 1991, the leader referred to the party's 'traditional base of upper middle-class, middle-aged, predominantly female voters' (*Australian* 4 October 1991). And Bean (1997: 79) concluded that, even after 20 years, the Democrats had 'no more than a hint of a distinctive social base'. Even sympathisers admit that, however egalitarian their policies, their 'image . . . as middle-class teachers or members of the "chattering classes" has posed a barrier to their being seen as representatives of blue-collar workers or of "battlers" ' (Sawer 1999: 102), while critics dismiss them as 'a collection of ersatz Liberals', who 'do not have a core constituency to represent' (Lohrey 2002, 69).

The Democrats' ability to maintain an adequate level of support has depended until recently largely on any protest vote and on Labor's fluctuating appeal to the middle ground. But in the 2001 federal election, many of the voters alienated by the Howard government's treatment of asylum-seekers and Labor's vacillations, began turning to the Greens. Likewise in the 2004 federal election, such voters either turned back to Howard, the man they trusted to keep them equally safe from dangerous aliens and rising interest rates, or again went to the Greens. Although the Democrats had opposed the Iraq war and vigorously championed the cause of asylum-seekers (including visits by leaders to the detention centres), most of the protest vote now seemed directed to the Greens. Deprived of their usual public funding due to their declining share of the vote, and deprived of party status in the Senate by now having only four Senators, the party cut staff and relocated its national office to Adelaide in December 2004.

The Greens

Ascendant in the polls, the Greens did not, as widely forecast, end up with more Senators than the Democrats after the October 2004 federal election. At four Senators each, neither the Greens nor the Democrats nor the newest Senate party, Family First, hold the balance of power, and any drift away from the major parties towards the minor parties seems to have been arrested.

Entering Parliament has never been the first choice of environmental activists. They have tended to prefer to deal with local, State and even national issues by community education, direct grassroots actions and lobbying. It has taken decades for discrete green groups to find the coherence and discipline necessary to form themselves into several State Green parties and into a national political party in 1992; WA, having followed a different trajectory, was the last to join a decade later.

This late development may give Green parliamentarians, as 'the authentic representatives of this developing constituency', 'a sense of tradition, their own potent history and folklore' perhaps not available to the Democrats (Lohrey 2002: 69). Part of a worldwide green movement, the Australian Greens also reflect that movement's deep divisions (variously described as purists versus pragmatists, and resource ecologists versus radical ecologists), and are further divided on how best to make the compromises necessary to operate in the formal political system.

GREENS IN THE SENATE

Joining the Democrats in the Senate in 1990, and sharing the balance of power with them between 1993 and 1998, were members of two Greens parties originating on opposite sides of the continent. The protest movement in the early 1980s against the visits to Fremantle of nuclear-powered US warships propelled charismatic Quaker activist Jo Vallentine into the Senate in 1984 for the newly formed Nuclear Disarmament Party. She was re-elected in her own right in 1987. Then, in March 1990, the Western Australia Green Party (WAGs) were officially launched as an amalgamation of Vallentine's Peace Group, the Alternative Coalition and two Greens groups. Re-elected as a Green Senator in 1990, Vallentine retired in March 1992. She was replaced by fellow WAG Christabel Chamarette, who was joined after the 1993 election by Dee Margetts.

The two WAG Senators sprang to prominence after 1993 as the Keating Labor government required two votes in addition to the Democrats' seven in order to get contentious legislation through the Senate. Negotiations over the government's 1993–94 budget between hardened Labor number-crunchers like Gareth Evans and Robert Ray and 'the gumnut twins', as they disparagingly described the two Green women Senators, exposed an irreconcilable clash of expectations between the traditional power-wielders doing 'whatever it took' and community-based idealists catapulted into the big league. The two Greens learned fast, however (Young 1999), and on parliamentary reform were instrumental in forcing the government to stop flooding the Senate with legislation at the end of parliamentary sessions (Mulgan 1996; Uhr 1999).

Chamarette lost her seat at the 1996 election, and the Greens might have slid into oblivion but for the fact that the incoming Howard Coalition government was still two votes short of a majority and Margetts was joined by another Green, albeit a very different one with whom she worked less closely (Bach 2003: 164). The arrival in Canberra of Senator Bob Brown, a veteran of Tasmania's Lake Pedder, Franklin River and Wesley Vale paper mill environmental battles and of 10 years in the Tasmanian lower house, can be seen as a turning point for the formation of a national Green political movement. A conviction politician of palpable sincerity and openness, who had learned to give the media what it wants, Brown was 'somebody in parliament that you can organise around, that gives you a national profile, a vital bit of political capital that you can move to other states' (Ben Oquist, quoted in Norman 2004: 177). Margetts lost her seat in the 1998 election, and Brown became for three years the sole voice for what was still really no more than 'a confederation of like-minded groups in various States, the branches of which are autonomous' (Australian Greens 2000).

From its original focus on the environment, the Green agenda broadened as their Senate record shows, in line with the vision spelt out by Brown and Singer

(1996). They rejected outright the Howard government's Workplace Reform Bill first submitted to the Senate in 1996, and were as steadfast as the Democrats against the one-third sale of Telstra, labelling the one billion dollar environmental package promised from the Telstra proceeds as a bribe and not a serious commitment (although much later in June 2002, the membership had to bring Brown into line over trade-offs he seemed to be contemplating in return for agreeing to the sale of the remaining government share of Telstra). As Howard cranked up his attacks on trade unions, elements in the union movement began to turn to the Greens, reviving in some memories of earlier such alliances in the Sydney 'green bans' of the 1970s.

Brown was re-elected to the Senate in 2001, along with the candidate of the newly united NSW green movement, Kerry Nettle, and the pair distinguished themselves particularly by their unequivocal stance on a number of 'Left' issues, notably human rights. They earned notoriety and cemented their anti-war credentials by their verbal challenge to US President George W. Bush as he addressed the Australian Parliament in October 2003.

But despite the Greens fielding more lower house candidates and nearly doubling their Senate vote to 7.7 per cent, their gains in the October 2004 election were limited to new seats in WA (Rachael Siewert) and Tasmania (Christine Milne). As expected, they failed to retain the House of Representatives seat of Cunningham, which had been picked up by Green candidate Michael Organ in an October 2002 by-election when Wollongong locals with environmental concerns had rejected the Labor candidate imposed on them.

The expectation that the Greens were poised to take the Democrats' place as a Senate powerbroker was enough to set alarm bells ringing in some quarters in the lead-up to the 2004 election. Previously considered weird but relatively harmless fringe players, they now had to be taken seriously. Labor wanted their preferences, aware of the high Green support already showing up in State elections and by-elections in some of its inner-city electorates with high ethnic-minority populations (especially in Melbourne). The Greens' natural enemies, instead of largely ignoring their wish list of policies, trawled through them and mounted scare campaigns, a technique already used to some effect in the NSW election following the Cunningham loss (ABC 2003). Business warned predictably of threats to future growth, and Liberals claimed that an incoming Labor government, elected on Green preferences, would have to pass some of the Greens' 'loopy laws' on drugs, taxes, etc. (*Australian* 3 September 2004 and 7 October 2004). Such over-the-top advertising gave the Greens more publicity than they needed, and a *Melbourne Herald Sun* article was later censured for its inaccuracy by the Press Council (*Australian* 10 March 2005). The Christian Right also attacked the Greens' liberal social attitudes, prompting a measured counter-ad from Senator Brown (*Australian* 7 October 2004). At the same time the Greens were being criticised by elements in their own constituency for being diverted from their core responsibilities to the environment (Lohrey 2002; *Australian* 2–3 October 2004).

In the end, the Greens were cruelly denied the final Senate seat in Victoria, when Green candidate David Risstrom's impressive 8.8 per cent of the primary vote was finally surpassed on preferences by a Family First candidate starting from a mere 1.88 per cent primary vote. In Queensland, serious dissension within the Greens (*Australian* 22 December 2003) had dashed veteran activist Drew Hutton's chances of taking the Democrat place in the Senate.

GREENS IN STATE AND TERRITORY PARLIAMENTS

At the State level, adept leadership and the cooperative spirit possible in small communities was able to turn popular energies into Green parliamentary representation first in Tasmania and later in Western Australia.

In the island State, the powerful Hydro-Electric Commission's right to dam pristine alpine lakes and wild rivers began to be challenged in the 1970s, the destruction of Lake Pedder and the campaign to save the Franklin River galvanising a green vote on the mainland as well, notably helping the Labor Party under Bob Hawke to win the 1983 federal election. The dependence of the Tasmanian economy on its water and forests, and the number of jobs and revenues involved, has always made Tasmanian governments of all persuasions wary of conservationists. It was only the Hare–Clark system that allowed first 'Independents', later identifying themselves as Greens, to win seats in the Tasmanian lower house, first Bob Brown replacing Democrat Norm Sanders who moved to the Senate, and then Gerry Bates in 1986. Their influence peaked when five Greens members formed an Accord with a minority Labor government from 1989 until 1992 (Brown & Singer 1996; Norman 2004). But the Accord ultimately failed and the Greens were reduced to a lone member after Labor and Liberal cynically combined in 1998 to raise the quota necessary for election (from 12.5 to 16.7 per cent in each of the five multi-member seats) by cutting the size of the chamber from 35 to 25. A comeback in the 2002 Tasmanian election saw four Greens elected, along with just six Liberals ranged against Jim Bacon's majority Labor government of 15.

The Greens in Tasmania have helped save numerous pristine wilderness areas and have spurred reform in areas as diverse as gay law and the banning of genetically modified crops. But their uncompromising stand on old-growth forest protection, in particular, led the major parties to swear never again to go into partnership with them. Premier Bacon skilfully accommodated Green concerns. His successor Premier Paul Lennon is noticeably less willing to do so when jobs in forestry and pulp-milling are at stake. But Tasmania remains the State where Greens have the best parliamentary record and most future potential.

In Western Australia, reform of the upper house (the Legislative Council) saw the first Green elected in 1993, and the 1996 WA election gave three Greens and two Democrats the balance of power in that house during the final term of the conservative Court Coalition government and raised the profile of issues around water, salinity and the milling of jarrah and karri forests. The 2001 WA election, which brought narrow victory to the Labor Party led by Geoff Gallop, with the help of a group of 'Liberals for Forests' candidates, saw the five Greens assume sole balance of power in the 34-seat Legislative Council. The Gallop Labor government consolidated its hold in the February 2005 WA election and, although the Greens retained their share of the vote (7–8 per cent) they lost their three rural representatives. In a finely balanced Legislative Council, however, they retain their pivotal positioning.

The only other places where Greens have been successful, although a lot less influential, have been in NSW and the ACT. The large Legislative Council in NSW means a quota so low that a wide variety of small parties has found a place, including one or two Greens at a time for the last decade. Three Greens now form the largest single party in the grouping of 11 on the cross-benches between 18 ALP and 13 Coalition MLCs. In the ACT's 17-seat single chamber, proportional representation (PR) has always given small parties and Independents a key role, and minority governments commonly depend on a variety of them. Two Greens were elected in 1995, and one in each of the 1998, 2001 and 2004 (when Labor's Jon Stanhope was able to form the ACT's first majority government) elections.

Despite bouts of strong polling and concerted campaigning, no Green (or Democrat) has ever been elected in the three places lacking PR—either house in Victoria or the single-chamber parliaments of Queensland and the Northern Territory. In South Australia, where the environment vote has traditionally elected Democrats to the Legislative Council, the Greens gained a seat in the House of Assembly when Labor's Kris Hanna changed parties in January 2003.

THE FUTURE?

Currently the most promising minor party, Green candidates are likely to go on being elected to the Senate and to other quota-based chambers. If and when their votes become vital in those chambers, they will again be wooed and their willingness to compromise (and even deny supply to a government under exceptional circumstances) tested. Fracture lines have already rent the Green movement, and electoral success will almost certainly bring similar problems to those suffered by the Democrats. Bob Brown's ability to unite his party's constituency will also be tested, and much will depend on a successor when he leaves the scene. Perhaps fortunately for a party less structured and amenable to compromise than the Democrats, the parliamentary route is not the only one open to its followers.

Due to the similarities in stated aims and core principles of Greens and Democrats, the idea of their merging has periodically arisen. Tentative approaches have been made but usually rebuffed (Lohrey 2002). The willingness of the two parties to preference each other with their registered above-the-line preference distribution in the Senate, to maximise the chances of one or other getting the sixth seat in any State, worked well until 1996. In that year a damaging public contest between the two parties over the one winnable Senate seat in both Western Australia and Tasmania, resulted in the Democrats' Andrew Murray beating the Greens' Christabel Chamarette in WA and the popular Democrat Robert Bell losing to the Greens' Brown in Tasmania. Personal differences of style and operation between former Democrats' leader Cheryl Kernot and Greens leader Bob Brown exacerbated tensions during that campaign. Despite Kernot's subsequent departure, the relatively poor showing of the Greens in relation to the Democrats in 1996 and 1998 reduced the latter's interest in such moves. The position is now reversed. But so long as a core constituency in both the Democrats membership base and the Green movement remains resolutely opposed to a merger, the parties are unlikely in the short term to go beyond efforts at parliamentary and electoral cooperation.

One Nation

Pauline Hanson's irruption onto the political scene at the March 1996 federal election was a seismic trigger whose effects are only now dying down. Though disendorsed by the Liberal Party late in the 1996 campaign for remarks denounced as racist, Hanson, a small-business owner, appeared on the ballot paper as the Liberal candidate in the normally safe Labor seat of Oxley. She was swept into the House of Representatives by a combination of anti-Labor voters and those who agreed with her strong views. Her controversial maiden parliamentary speech—penned like most of her earlier speeches by John Pasquarelli (1998)—on 10 September 1996 attracted both adulation and hostility for its voicing of the grievances of those who saw themselves as the forgotten victims of the 'politically correct' social policies of the Hawke–Keating era and the economic rationalism of both major parties. Irresistible to the media in a way similarly outspoken MPs like Graeme Campbell could only envy, the redhead attracted devotees, donations and the Liberal carpetbaggers Pasquarelli, and later David Oldfield and David Ettridge, sufficient to launch her own party, One Nation, in April 1997.

Prime Minister Howard responded feebly and too late to her factual inaccuracies and crude views on Asian immigration, multiculturalism and Aboriginal welfare. By then, Australia's trade, tourism and the higher education business with Asia was damaged, and fissures opened up in both Coalition parties. The Nationals led by Deputy Prime Minister Tim Fischer had the most to lose, but

Labor leader Kim Beazley also soon discovered that blue-collar workers in particular were susceptible to Hanson's anti-globalisation views on jobs, tariff protection and national sovereignty.

The Queensland State election of June 1998 turned this disquiet into panic, after One Nation candidates won 23 per cent of the vote and took 11 seats from both Labor and the Nationals, thanks to preferences from Coalition voters. The minority Liberals in particular took a beating, losing votes from their conservative supporters to One Nation and from their liberal supporters to Labor (Brennan & Mitchell 1998), which was then able to form government. The subsequent implosion of One Nation's parliamentary party in Queensland, its members united only in their determination to differentiate themselves from 'normal' politicians, still left the Nationals vulnerable to the simplistic rhetoric of the offshoot Country–City Alliance.

Following a surreal campaign (Kingston 1999), the federal election of 1998 showed both the limits of One Nation's popularity and the ability of the other parties to minimise its parliamentary representation. Hanson's seat had disappeared in a redistribution but, although she topped the poll in the adjacent seat of Blair, she got too few preferences to win. Despite being the choice of 1 in 12 voters nationwide, outpolling both the Nationals and the Democrats, One Nation managed to get only one Senate seat, effectively wrested from the Nationals in Queensland. Hanson then struggled to raise the money to repay public funding debts incurred when her party's registration in Queensland was ruled fraudulent. Public brawling with erstwhile colleagues, including Oldfield (who won a seat in the NSW Legislative Council in 1999, but was then expelled from the party), did little to restore One Nation's standing.

Meanwhile, with very little campaigning in Western Australia's February 2001 election, the 'Pauline Hanson's One Nation' name was sufficient to secure nearly 10 per cent of the vote and three non-metropolitan upper house seats, although their votes were not needed by the incoming Gallop Labor government. A week later, when the Beattie Labor government's 'crimson tide' swept across Queensland, One Nation fielded candidates in only 39 seats and saw its vote halved from the 1998 level, but with novice candidates won back two seats and captured another. Six of the 10 surviving former One Nation MPs ran for re-election as the Country–City Alliance but all lost their seats. Of the remaining four, who ran as Independents, only one held his seat. Three years later, in the February 2004 Queensland State election, Rosa Lee Long became the first One Nation member ever to be re-elected, but she admitted that One Nation 'was a spent political force' and that she expected to become Independent (*Australian* 31 January 2005). In the February 2005 Western Australian State election, all three One Nation Legislative Councillors, by then running as Independents, lost their seats.

Prime Minister John Howard's handling of the *Tampa* incident from late August 2001, his development of a set of border security policies and his strong response to the international threats thrown up by the September 11, 2001, terrorist attacks were such that Hanson could boast of being his 'adviser' on race and immigration (Hanson 2001). In the 'security' federal election held so soon after, One Nation's vote halved compared with its 1988 level, having lost more credibility during the brawl in WA over its preselection of Labor renegade Graeme Campbell. The Nationals' Ron Boswell, long a fighter against right-wing infiltration of his party, campaigned aggressively and effectively against One Nation in Queensland. Hanson herself topped the Senate minor party polling in Queensland with 10 per cent of the primary vote, but preferences instead returned Boswell and the Democrats' Andrew Bartlett. Hanson quit the One Nation presidency in January 2002, triggering a succession fight. Then her attempt to enter the NSW Legislative Council in March 2003 failed when she just missed gaining the final (21st) position.

In August 2003, Hanson and Ettridge were found guilty by a Brisbane jury of gaining registration for the One Nation party by claiming as 'members' a list of names signed up to a parallel 'support movement' with no voting rights. This was another dimension to the alleged fraud that had earlier resulted in One Nation losing its claim for public election funding. Hanson and Ettridge were each sentenced to three years' jail. But in November they were released when the conviction was quashed by a Queensland Court of Appeal that strongly criticised her prosecution. These events temporarily revived the party, with former adviser Pasquarelli declaring that a sympathy vote would get Hanson elected to the Senate, if only she kept her 'airy-fairy rubbish' policies to herself (*Australian* 8–9 November 2003). But she did not contest the Senate election of October 2004. One Nation's Senator Len Harris, who did stand again for re-election in 2004, was not successful, with the Nationals' Barnaby Joyce winning the vital sixth Queensland seat in a contest with the Greens.

Family First

A surprise newcomer in the October 2004 federal election was Family First, formed in South Australia by former senior Assemblies of God pastor Andrew Evans in June 2001 and launched in September. It was built around the politics developed to counter 'the gay lobby, the drug lobby and other groups perceived as undermining family values' (*Advertiser* 6 November 2004), and was inspired by the success of No Pokies candidate Nick Xenophon in winning an SA Legislative Council seat in 1997. The new party contested the SA elections of February 2002, with the help of 1400 members/partners. Swapping preferences with the Liberals in most seats, Evans won a seat in the Legislative Council after gaining a primary vote of 4 per cent, nearly half a quota. Evans attributed this success to sustained grassroots targeting of like-minded community groups, but played down the church connections. Evans' most positive subsequent parliamentary achievement has been the successful passage in June 2003 of his Bill to get the statute of limitations on pre-1982 sex offences lifted.

Emboldened to form itself into a national body in March 2004, Family First launched its federal campaign in August, selecting as leader its Senate candidate for SA, 37-year-old Indigenous lawyer and sportswoman Andrea Mason. Targeting mortgage-belt voters in the 26–55 age group who were raising families and trying to get ahead (*Sunday Mail* 8 August 2004), Family First raised $1.3m for a media blitz, promoting its conservative family policies and attacking the Greens, their main rivals for the minor party vote. Results in the October 2004 election for the Senate and in the 126 House of Representatives seats contested showed that, at around 2 per cent of the vote, the Family First message failed to resonate much beyond its Pentecostal, aspirational base. But Family First did assist the Coalition in certain seats by reducing the flow of preferences from Democrats and Greens to Labor.

The major upset, Family First's capture of the sixth Senate seat in Victoria for candidate Steve Fielding, was the pay-off from a particularly astute preference strategy, devised on advice from an unnamed Adelaide academic (*Australian* 24 September 2004). Before the election, Family First secured agreement from Prime Minister Howard that a re-elected Coalition government would 'assess the family impact of all legislation before it goes to cabinet', and the first meeting of the PM with Senator-elect Steve Fielding and party chairperson Peter Harris took place in March 2005 (*Australian* 11 October 2004 and 3 March 2005). Access at such high level is remarkable, and some observers see a pattern in Howard's accommodation of the so-called 'Religious Right' (Maddox 2004).

Family First is unlikely again to be able to 'creep under the radar' of its main competitors at election time. Nevertheless, analysis of its vote shows a potential to further erode Labor's blue-collar base (*Australian* 29 November 2004), and the Nationals worry about its wooing of the residual One Nation vote in Queensland and WA. Although Senator Fielding's vote is not yet vital to the Howard government's legislative program, there are enough points of potential difference—over Telstra, industrial relations, treatment of refugees and tax policies, for example—to ensure that he will be yet another factor in a possibly unstable Senate mix.

Independents

There have often been Independents in Australian parliaments and they have, on occasions, decided the fate of governments (Costar & Curtin 2004). Most enter Parliament as representatives of one of the major parties, and then resign or are expelled. Those with a strong following in their local communities have a better chance of surviving the next election, as do high-profile upper house

Independents in proportional-representation systems. But most do not, as the major parties do their best to get the seat back.

Genuine Independents, elected as such and then re-elected from an established local base, are rare. Ted Mack and Peter Andren are two examples who have recently served in the House of Representatives, the former representing North Sydney for two terms from 1990 to 1996 and the latter winning the rural New South Wales seat of Calare in 1996 and being returned at every election since (Costar & Curtin 2004: 57–71).

In recent years, more Independents have begun appearing and making life difficult for the governing parties. Major party elected members seem readier to leave their party during their terms while insisting on retaining their parliamentary seats, giving themselves perhaps several years as an Independent before needing to face re-election. Voters, too, seem more prepared to return a renegade who has stood up to or defied the party, especially if that party is itself out of favour or voters wish to 'send a message' to those in power. When neither major party bloc emerges from an election with a healthy majority of seats, there is not only greater scope for Independents to extract concessions but an increased temptation for others to take the step of leaving the party fold when denied some preferment or on a point of principle.

All States in recent years have seen minority governments kept in office by Independents of various descriptions, resulting in some instability, but with increasing gains in accountability (Jackson 1995; Moon 1995; Sharman 2002; Stone 2003). The power of an Independent to make or break governments has been graphically illustrated in Queensland, Victoria and South Australia, with the fall of the Goss government mid-term following the Mundingburra by-election in February 1996, and the formation of the Beattie, Bracks and Rann minority Labor governments in 1998, 1999 and 2002 respectively.

The 1996–1998 House of Representatives contained five non-Labor and non-Coalition members, although they could not affect the operations of a house in which the Coalition's majority was so great. With greater disciplining in the major parties' State branches and refining of preselection processes, four of them vanished in 1998, leaving Andren as the only genuine Independent. The rural turmoil of the Hanson years was reflected in the defection from the National Party of two popular local members, Bob Katter in Kennedy (Queensland) and Tony Windsor in New England (NSW). Both held their seats in 2001 and in 2004, and continue to represent significant attitudes and interests that the major parties cannot.

In the Senate, where majorities are absent or much more finely balanced, the most significant Independent of recent times has been Senator Brian Harradine of Tasmania. Expelled from the ALP by its Federal Executive in 1975, the long-serving and conservative former Trades and Labor Council Secretary was elected to the Senate in the December 1975 double dissolution, and kept his seat thereafter until deciding not to contest the October 2004 election. So secure was he that the only chance for a Tasmanian Democrat or Green to win a Senate seat (the Democrats' Bell in 1990, and the Greens' Brown in 1996 and 2001) was in the alternate elections when Harradine himself was not up for re-election.

With the further erosion of the Labor government's position in the Senate after the 1993 election, Harradine's Senate vote became more crucial to both sides. The defection from Labor of its Queensland Senator Mal Colston on budget night in August 1996 changed the Senate's complexion even more in the Howard government's favour, and gave the two Independents unprecedented leverage. Harradine's attitudes on moral issues were consistent with his Catholicism, but some felt let down by his allowing through, because he feared precipitating a race-based double dissolution fuelled by 'blind intolerance, hatred and bitterness', of the 1998 watering down of the *Native Title Act* (quoted in Costar & Curtin 2004: 54). On issues like the Telstra partial sale, for example, on which both the Democrats and Greens were uncompromising, the government finally won over Harradine and Colston in a fashion that could be seen as blatant pork-barrelling. Harradine continued to wring concessions for his vulnerable island State, but Colston, seen as a Labor 'rat' who deserted his party for venal reasons, retired at the 1999 election.

After the Democrats lost the sole balance of power with Meg Lees' defection in 2003, she, Harradine, One Nation's Len Harris and Labor defector Shayne Murphy became a loose independent grouping from whom the Howard government could hope to pick up the two vital votes lacking on contentious issues. But the new Senate formed as a result of the October 2004 election, which came into effect in July 2005, includes none of these four and there are no Independents.

Conclusion

Minor parties and Independents are unlikely to disappear. Although the major parties consider them an annoying distraction from the main game, and some major party tacticians favour 'reforms' aimed at removing them from the system, their value is generally understood.

When respected long-serving Liberal Senator Chaney left Parliament in 1993, it was his 'firm conviction that good government was served by the government of the day not having control of the Senate', and he referred nostalgically to 'the 1970s, when senators on the conservative side were less bound by party discipline' (Chaney 1999: 135). We may well be entering another such era as a result of the Coalition government gaining a majority in the Senate with effect from July 2005.

But it is likely that subsequent elections will see minor party members and Independents resuming the balance of power in the Senate and in an increasing number of State and Territory chambers. The 'canary in the mineshaft' role that they perform is a valuable one. And the concerns driving them—environmental sustainability, the impact of rapid economic change, human rights and individual freedoms in an age of global terror—will not go away.

NOTES

1 One reason for One Nation's brief success in Queensland was that it was breaking into a three- rather than two-party system, with the (atypically) dominant Nationals at odds with the Liberals.

2 For their own view of their record and role in the Senate, see *inter alia* Kernot (1997), Democrats (1998) and Bartlett (2000).

REFERENCES

ABC [Australian Broadcasting Corporation] 2003, 'Background Briefing', Radio National, 1 June.

Australian Greens 2000, web page, Canberra, <http://www.greens.org.au/>.

Bach, S. 2003, *Platypus and Parliament: The Australian Senate in Theory and Practice*, Department of the Senate, Canberra.

Bartlett, A. 2000, 'The Role of the Senate', Australian Democrats website, Black Forest SA, <http://www.democrats.org.au/campaigns/senate>.

Bean, C. 1997, 'The Australian Democrats after Twenty Years: Electoral Performance and Voting Support', in *Keeping the Bastards Honest*, ed. J. Warhurst, Allen & Unwin, Sydney.

Brennan, G. & Mitchell, N. 1998, 'The Logic of Spatial Politics: The 1998 Queensland Election', *Australian Journal of Political Science*, vol. 34, no. 3, pp. 379–90.

Brown, B. & Singer, P. 1996, *The Greens*, Text Publishing Co., Melbourne.

Chaney, F. 1999, 'Should Parliament be Abolished?', in *Representation and Institutional Change: 50 Years of Representation in the Senate*, eds M. Simms & S. Miskin, *Papers on Parliament*, vol. 34, pp. 131–41.

Chipp, D. 1977, Parliamentary speech, *Commonwealth Parliamentary Debates: House of Representatives*, 24 March.

Costar, B. & Curtin, J. 2004, *Rebels with a Cause: Independents in Australian Politics*, UNSW Press, Sydney.

Democrats 1998, 'Issue Sheet '98: Parliamentary Matters—Mandate', Australian Democrats website, Canberra, <http://www.democrats.org.au/issue/pmmandate.htm>.

Democrats 2005a, 'Final Report', Australian Democrats Future Directions Project.

Democrats 2005b, Website, Black Forest SA, <http://www.democrats.org.au/>.

Gauja, A. 2004, 'The Internal Organisation of the Australian Democrats: Lessons for Participatory Parties', Paper presented to APSA Conference, Adelaide University, 29 September.

Goot, M. 1999, 'Whose Mandate? Policy Promises, Strong Bicameralism and Polled Opinion', *Australian Journal of Political Science*, vol. 34, no. 3, pp. 327–52.

Hanson, P. 2001, Interviewed by L. Oakes, Nine Network *Sunday* show, 14 October, <http://sunday.ninemsn.com.au/sunday/political_transcripts/article_944.asp?s=1>.

Henderson, A. 1999, *Getting Even: Women MPs on Life, Power and Politics*, HarperCollins, Sydney.

Hill, L. 2003, 'The Political Gender Gap: Australia, Britain and the United States', *Policy, Organisation & Society*, vol. 22, no. 1, pp. 69–96.

Jackson, R. 1995, 'Foreign Models and Aussie Rules: Executive-Legislative Relations in Australia', *Political Theory Newsletter*, vol. 7, no. 1, pp. 1–18.

Kernot, C. 1997, 'Balancing Acts—Wielding the Balance of Power', *Australian Journal of Public Administration*, vol. 56, no. 2, pp. 32–9.

Kingston, M. 1999, *Off the Rails: The Pauline Hanson Trip*, Allen & Unwin, Sydney.

Lohrey, A. 2002, *Groundswell: The Rise of the Greens*, Quarterly Essay no. 8, Black Inc., Melbourne.

Macklin, M. 2000, 'Preference Process for the 1996 Election', press release, Canberra, 28 November.

Maddox, M. 2004, *God under Howard: The Rise of the Religious Right in Australian Politics*, Allen & Unwin, Sydney.

Moon, J. 1995, 'Minority Government in the Australian States: From Ersatz Majoritarianism to Minoritarianism', *Australian Journal of Political Science*, vol. 30, Special Issue, pp. 142–63.

Mulgan, R. 1996, 'The Australian Senate as a "House of Review"', *Australian Journal of Political Science*, vol. 31, no. 2, pp. 191–204.

Norman, J. 2004, *Bob Brown: Gentle Revolutionary*, Allen & Unwin, Sydney.

Pasquarelli, J. 1998, *The Pauline Hanson Story . . . by the Man Who Knows*, New Holland Publishers, Sydney.

QCJC [Queensland Criminal Justice Commission] 2001, *The Shepherdson Inquiry: An Investigation into Electoral Fraud*, Brisbane, <http://www.cmc.qld.gov.au/library/CMCWEBSITE/finalreport.pdf>.

Rogers, A. 2004, *The Natasha Factor: Politics, Media and Betrayal*, Lothian, Melbourne.

Sawer, M. 1999, 'Dilemmas of Representation', in *Representation and Institutional Change: 50 Years of Representation in the Senate*, eds M. Simms & S. Miskin, *Papers on Parliament*, vol. 34, pp. 95–108.

Sharman, C. 2002, 'Politics at the Margin: Independents and the Australian Political System', in *Papers on Parliament*, vol. 39, pp. 53–69.

Stock, J.M.T. 2002, 'The Australian Democrats and Minor Parties', in *Government, Politics, Power and Policy in Australia*, 7th edn, eds J. Summers, D. Woodward & A. Parkin, Longman Pearson, Sydney.

Stone, B. 2003, 'Australian Bicameralism: Potential and Performance in State Upper Houses', *Papers on Parliament*, vol. 40, pp. 19–37.

Sugita, H. 1995, 'Challenging "Twopartism": The Contribution of the Australian Democrats to the Australian Party System', PhD thesis, Flinders University of South Australia, Adelaide.

Sugita, H. 1997. 'Parliamentary Performance in the Senate', in *Keeping the Bastards Honest*, ed. J. Warhurst, Allen & Unwin, Sydney.

Swift, S. 1996, 'An Outline of Issues Relating to the Party's Preferences Decision', *National Journal*, July, pp. 8–10.

Thompson, E. 1999, 'The Senate and Representative Democracy', in *Representation and Institutional Change: 50 Years of Representation in the Senate*, eds M. Simms & S. Miskin, *Papers on Parliament*, vol. 34, pp. 41–54.

Uhr, J. 1999, *Deliberative Democracy in Australia: The Changing Place of Parliament*, Cambridge University Press, Cambridge.

van Acker, E. 2003, 'Media Representations of Women Politicians in Australia and New Zealand: High Expectations, Hostility or Stardom', *Policy, Organisation & Society*, vol. 22, no. 1, pp. 116–36.

VIDA 2005, 'Australian Democrats VIDA Network', Webpage, <http://www.vida.democrats.org.au/html/index.php>.

Warhurst, J. ed. 1997, *Keeping the Bastards Honest*, Allen & Unwin, Sydney.

Young, L. 1999, 'Minor Parties and the Legislative Process in the Australian Senate', *Australian Journal of Political Science*, vol. 34, no. 1, pp. 7–27.

Voters and voting

HAYDON MANNING

This chapter reviews what we know, from political-science research, about the way that Australians vote at national elections. It focuses initially on the way that media commentators and party strategists conceptualise the behaviour of voters. It then reviews some of the academic research on some classic questions about the extent to which particular social characteristics of voters—such as their social class, their religious affiliation and their gender—seem to impact on their voting preferences.

Political-science survey research confirms that most voters seem to know their party preference well before an election campaign commences. Most voters seem, in effect, to be loyal partisans of one or another of the rival political camps—mainly Labor or Liberal, but in some cases National, Green or whatever. On closer examination, these loyalties can often be quite long term, and indeed sometimes represent a continuation of the voting habits of a voter's parents.

Such loyalty and predictability could possibly be interpreted as an indication of an unthinking, habitual lack of engagement with politics. But alternatively, it might instead reflect an informed and engaged commitment to the ongoing political values embodied in a particular party. It might thus be no more mysterious than the way in which most people seem to maintain their basic outlook on life over time and indeed the way in which families can share personal values across generations. This kind of continuity of party loyalty may also reflect a consistent judgment that the particular party in question, on balance, best represents the voter's social and economic interests. Continuity across generations would likewise follow from the not uncommon situation that social and economic circumstances can remain fairly similar across a family from one generation to another.

But some voters do change their vote from election to election, and the number of these 'switchers' seems to be increasing. Much is now written about the increased 'electoral volatility' and about the idea that the proportion of so-called 'rusted-on voters' — the party loyalists — is declining. This chapter later reviews some of the evidence on this matter.

With the aid of large-scale national scientific surveys of political opinion, political scientists are able not only to map electoral trends but also to investigate some of the ways the trends might be explained. Until relatively recent times, political scientists have concluded that the most predictable aspect of voting patterns related to the association between a person's party preference and their socioeconomic class and, for younger voters at least, the party preference of parents. Both factors are linked with ongoing patterns of advantage and disadvantage within society, with party preferences being forged by experiences within the family and the workplace, the latter often reinforcing the former. In effect, analysts have mostly concluded, at least until recently, that a person's 'life chances' have depended greatly upon the type of paid work undertaken, and the career and income opportunities that this presents during a working life, and that political preferences have mostly followed from this.

The basic structures of Australian party politics have been more or less built on this foundation. The Australian Labor Party was originally formed by trade unions in the 1890s with the explicit aim of protecting wage-earners considered to be members of the 'working classes'. Today's Liberal Party was reborn in 1944 under the leadership of Robert Menzies as a party with a particular attraction for the 'middle classes', defined broadly in occupation-related terms. (Menzies referred to this social grouping as the 'forgotten people' that he intended particularly to represent (Brett 1992)). Two prominent political scientists observed in 1974 that occupational class remained 'the rock on which the [Australian] party system rests and a major influence on electoral behaviour' (Aitkin and Kahan 1974: 477). The great electoral contest between Labor and Non-Labor seemed indeed to rest upon the foundation stone of class.

Notwithstanding the adversarial rhetoric and social antagonism that this class-based foundation may have generated, it was a structure that has forged a remarkable degree of political stability in Australia. The contest between Labor and non-Labor that it supported was established by 1910 and has largely remained in place since that time. The only slight nuance is that by 1920 the Country Party (during the 1970s renamed the National Party) had emerged, though it has proved, for the most part, a loyal coalition ally for the anti-Labor cause. Of all the possible social or economic divisions which might conceivably have become politicised, it was the class division (tempered by the urban–rural divide embodied in the National Party) that seemed to matter in Australia in terms of how people voted. To the extent, for example, that ethnicity and religion were important factors in society (in creating, for example, a potential divide between Australians of Anglo Protestant and Irish Catholic background), they largely reinforced and were subsumed under the class division (though see Brett 2002 for a sceptical view of this orthodox interpretation).

Looking back over the 20th century from the vantage point of early 21st century however, it is clear that the 'class contest' was never actually all-encompassing. Both Labor and the Liberals were compelled, if they wanted to be electorally competitive, to appeal to less loyal ('swinging') voters. This is because winning office has always been difficult without drawing considerable support from groups beyond each party's core support base. Here the art of political leadership, campaigning skills, party discipline, the perceived character and quality of policies—most notably in recent years, economic policy—and, finally, good political luck could all help immensely. Nevertheless, the class-based appeal, rhetoric and policies of the parties, bolstered by the background ideological contrast between Labor's ostensible commitment to social reform (on behalf of the more disadvantaged) and the Liberal and National parties' relative conservatism (representing the interests of more advantaged people less attracted to social change and redistribution), did make for clarity of party differentiation.

In more recent times, the steady increase in the 'primary vote' (i.e. first-preference vote under the preferential voting system) won by minor parties has suggested a longer-term shift in loyalty by more voters away from the major parties. This is an important trend but it should not be overstated. At the 2001 and 2004 national elections, the combined major parties' primary vote actually increased slightly. And some degree of election-to-election volatility in voting support is not new, notwithstanding the overall stability of the party system (Goot 1994: 175–9). In recent times voters have been confronted, sometimes quite suddenly, with the rise of new parties, such as Pauline Hanson's One Nation party in 1998 and the Family First party in 2004. Some instability and change is to be expected in these circumstances.

The new lexicon: battlers, aspirationals and 'doctors' wives'

After every national or State election, debate invariably follows over why the voters voted the way they did and how the outcome this time compares to previous outcomes. In recent times, a popular theme has been whether or not a party or leader has 'captured' part of their opponent's supposed 'constituency' or 'support base' among voters. During the period of the Howard government, three particular 'constituencies'—colourfully referred to by journalists and party strategists as the *battlers*, the *aspirationals* and the *doctors' wives* — have entered the language of Australian politics.

After the March 1996 federal election, the term 'Howard's battlers' emerged to help explain how the Liberal Party, led by John Howard, had apparently attracted substantial voting support from within the Labor Party's traditional support base, and specifically from many blue-collar and lower-income white-collar households. It was the Liberal Party's then Director and chief campaign strategist, Andrew Robb, who most prominently attributed his party's success to 'Howard's battlers' when addressing the National Press Club as part of a traditional post-election review (Robb 1997). According to Robb, many of Australia's blue-collar wage-earners and their families ('the battlers') had become unhappy with the Keating (and Hawke) Labor governments because they had been affected and made insecure by economic reforms whose benefits they did not see as flowing their way. He also thought that these 'battlers' perceived Labor as being unduly influenced by various 'special interest' groups to focus on matters not directly relevant to mainstream 'battling' families. Labor had for too long, according to Robb, concentrated on pleasing the 'affluent end of middle Australia' and had targeted the 'socially progressive' and 'highly educated' at the expense of the crucial group that he now dubbed 'Howard's battlers'.

Robb's analysis was not simply based on intuition or abstract judgment. He drew upon Liberal Party surveys of a sample of voters questioned on election day as they left polling places in marginal seats. Rodney Cavalier, a former Labor member of the NSW Parliament, largely concurred with Robb's analysis at the time. He argued that, once the Liberal Party had identified this mood among members of Labor's traditional electoral heartland, John Howard managed to strike 'deep into the soft underbelly of Labor's constituency which the party had been holding by a thread in three successive [previous] elections' (Cavalier 1997: 32).

The term 'Howard's battlers' has indeed been frequently used ever since in commentary dealing with the Howard-led coalition's succession of electoral victories. Its precise meaning may be slightly fluid — later versions seem to add 'lower white-collar workers' to the original blue-collar notion of 'battlers' (Crosby 2000: 65) — but it is an explanation that seems to satisfy many observers (e.g. Singleton, Martyn and Ward 1998; Brett 2003: 188).

The term 'the aspirationals' seems to have come into the political lexicon a bit later. During his brief tenure as Labor's federal leader from December 2003 to January 2005, Mark Latham often referred to the idea that Labor needed to win support from so-called 'aspirational voters'. These were the voters likely, he surmised, to be attracted by his metaphorical emphasis on a 'ladder of opportunity' for Australians. Latham seemed to conceive of these 'aspirationals' as members of middle-class (or aspiring middle-class) households — relatively well off, or hoping soon to be so, though perhaps indebted via substantial home mortgages—living in the outer suburbs of Australia's big cities. This was a constituency, whose attraction was no doubt bolstered by the marginal nature of many outer suburban seats, that Latham hoped, on Labor's behalf, to capture. Yet Latham seemed to fear that without the hard electoral work and policy repositioning by Labor that he was advocating their 'aspirational' qualities might instead push them towards the Liberals because that party was more associated with material advancement and reward.

Another apparently new categorisation of voters also entered journalistic jargon during the 2004 campaign: the so-called 'doctors' wives'. It was postulated by some analysts that many financially well-off voters—typically living in inner metropolitan electorates and normally expected to be Liberal Party supporters—were disenchanted with the Howard government's policies on non-economic issues like the war in Iraq, the treatment of asylum-seekers and environmental protection. They might therefore be inclined to vote for Labor or the Greens instead of the Liberals. Exactly why the journalists and analysts homed in on a phrase like 'doctors' wives' that invokes a particular occupation (medical doctors or, more precisely, married male medical doctors) and on a gendered role (their wives) is an interesting issue of social interpretation in itself. But the intention of the metaphor was clear: it identified a group of well-off and relatively secure voters who might potentially deviate from their immediate material economic interests (presumed to dictate a Liberal Party vote) to cast a vote instead on the basis of non-material values and policy preferences.

'Battlers', 'aspirationals' and 'doctors' wives': is there any evidence to support any of these interesting and provocative but sweeping interpretations? This is where political-science research might be able to help.

BATTLERS

The idea of 'the battler' has a rich resonance in Australian vernacular language. It depicts a recognisable (and perhaps somewhat mythical) caricature of a male breadwinner who, mainly through manual labour, works to advance his family. In recent discussion (e.g. Scalmer 1999), the picture seems to be slightly more inclusive: 'battlers' are wage-earners of both genders who regard themselves as hard-working and self-reliant, are critical of welfare 'handouts', are disinclined to be members of a trade union and indeed have a tendency to prefer to be self-employed contractors. What unites them is a perception that they and their families are 'doing it tough', inasmuch as their household financial circumstances are not improving. Have such people indeed been attracted away from Labor and towards the Coalition parties in recent years?

We can try to test such an imagined notion against firm evidence drawn from political-science surveys of voters, the most helpful of which are the series of

Australian Election Study (AES) surveys. These are surveys of a scientifically selected sample of Australians conducted to coincide with each of our recent national election campaigns. The scientific sample gives us some confidence that we can infer from the pattern of information generated by AES respondents what might be the situation characterising all Australian voters.

But some interpretive care is required. First, even the best surveys cannot guarantee that their sample of respondents is exactly representative of the whole population. For this reason, their results need to be interpreted cautiously (within a margin of error that most interpreters estimate might be plus or minus 3 percentage points for any particular result). Second, anecdotal and imprecise terms like 'the battlers' need to be pinned down to fit the precise questions and categories necessarily used to generate useful data from survey responses.

From among the many questions canvassed in successive AES surveys, the analysis which follows opts for a broad occupation characteristic and an attitude-related question to demarcate the survey respondents who could be described as 'battlers'. For the purposes of this analysis, a survey respondent is a 'battler' if (1) he or she is employed in a blue-collar or lower-paid white-collar occupation *and* (2) if he or she opts, in response to the survey question 'How does the financial situation of your household now compare with what it was 12 months ago?', for the answer 'about the same', 'a little worse' and 'a lot worse'. Table 15.1 provides some AES data to contemplate.

Table 15.1 suggests that many 'battlers'—at least as measured among those AES respondents selected here according to our definition—indeed turned

TABLE 15.1	The 'battler' vote
	House of Representatives party preference for AES respondents classified as 'battlers', 1990 to 2004 (percentages)

	1990		1993		1996		1998		2001		2004	
	AES battlers	Actual election	AES battlers	Actual election	AES battlers	Actual election	AES battlers	Actual election	AES battlers	Actual election	AES battlers	Actual election
Coalition	44	43	55	44	63	47	26	39	25	43	31	46
Labor	51	39	38	45	24	39	53	40	56	38	59	38
Other	5	17	6	11	13	14	21	21	20	19	10	16
Total	100	100	100	100	100	100	100	100	100	100	100	100
No. respondents considered battlers	573		725		304		266		394		192	
Total no. AES respondents	2037		3023		1797		1897		2010		1769	

Source: AES (2005).

against the Labor Party in 1996, the year that John Howard led the Coalition to electoral victory. But Table 15.1 also suggests that the process had commenced at the previous election. It then indicates that, at the 1998 election, Labor regained more support from this group (perhaps, an interpreter might speculate, due to the distaste of some of these 'battlers' for the Coalition government's proposal at that election to introduce a goods and services tax). The 1998 data also show a significant increase of support among our AES 'battlers' for 'Other' parties, i.e. for a party other than Labor or the Coalition. About one-fifth (21 per cent) of the 'battlers' were in this category, and more detailed AES evidence (not shown in Table 15.1) reveals that this included 11 per cent who reported that they supported Pauline Hanson's One Nation party. By 2004, the support among the AES 'battlers' for Labor was back up to 59 per cent, the highest level in any of the AES surveys reported in Table 15.1, well in excess of their support for the Coalition parties and well in excess of Labor's actual level of support among all voters at the election.

This all implies that that the shift of the 'battlers' towards the Coalition parties in 1993 and in 1996 seems to have been something of a 'protest vote' against the Keating Labor government, rather than a manifestation of a longer-term sustained shift as argued by various strategists and commentators.

ASPIRATIONALS

Two influential observers—the journalist Paul Kelly and the social commentator Hugh MacKay—used troubling metaphors to describe Australian society in the early 1990s. Kelly (1992) wrote of the 'end of certainty' while MacKay (1993: 17) referred to the 'age of anxiety'. This was a period where a degree of insecurity—a product of several economic recessions over the previous 20 years interspersed by some radical policy-driven economic restructuring—seemed to characterise the mood of the nation. But 10 years later, the 2001 and 2004 national elections occurred against the backdrop of an Australian economy enjoying sustained growth and hence a society in which the majority were benefiting from steadily improving living standards. There is evidence (Harding 2005) that a new sense of confidence had emerged to replace the more sombre mood of the early 1990s. Many people experienced steady improvements in their disposable incomes, home owners found that the market value of their houses had appreciated, and relatively low interest rates meant that financial institutions were able to encourage their customers to borrow even more funds to buy property. In this more confident environment, despite it resting on high levels of personal debt, the idea emerged that some of the people seeking economic advancement, and making the investments designed to promote their advancement, were likely to have their voting preferences shaped by their aspirations for advancement. These were, according to some interpreters, the 'aspirational voters' (Henderson: 2001).

As noted above, Mark Latham during his brief period as Labor leader sought to reorient his party's focus towards attracting or maintaining the support of these 'aspirationals'. For Latham, this meant that the Labor Party ought to shift its focus away from its traditional social-democratic politics and towards a so-called 'Third Way' approach. Latham (1998 and 2001) had written books advocating this approach, which was also associated with the British Labour Party under Prime Minister Tony Blair. The 'Third Way' places more stress on the citizen self-reliance and less on an interventionist role for government, and this seemed to fit with what 'aspirational voters' wanted. Latham accordingly fashioned his rhetoric to appeal to individual incentive. When accepting his party's leadership in December 2003, he told the gathered journalists that 'I stand for things I've been doing all my life—working hard to climb that ladder of opportunity, working hard, studying hard. I believe in an upwardly mobile society where people can climb the rungs of opportunity . . . to a better life for themselves and their family' (*Sydney Morning Herald* 2 December 2003). The 'ladder of opportunity' represented Labor's new focus on individuals' aspirations for upward mobility. It was viewed by Latham in particular as a way of undercutting the Liberal Party's potential support base in the outer suburbs.

Much debate surrounded the virtues, or otherwise, of this shift in Labor's thinking. Some critics argued Labor was mistaken to pitch for voters who 'aspire to wealthy lifestyles characterised by trophy homes, private schooling, flash cars, home theatres and whatever marks them out as having "made it" ' (Hamilton 2003). For renowned author Thomas Kenneally, 'aspirational is an ugly adjective which countenances an idea uglier still; it countenances the end of egalitarianism' (cited in Stephens 2001).

Our task here is to assess the electoral implications. This means that we must first be clear about who might constitute these 'aspirational voters'. A host of demographic, social and economic factors are bandied around by commentators to describe this group. They seem to have in mind middle-income earners who are, or who hope to be, 'upwardly mobile' (i.e. moving to a higher level on the socioeconomic ladder). They do not seem to be envisaged as confined to either just blue-collar or just white-collar occupations. A more speculative view (Hewett 2004) is that the 'aspirationals' are defined in part by their vulnerability to interest rate rises due to the high levels of personal debt that they are paying off. In terms of their social attitudes and outlook, the commentators tend to associate the 'aspirationals' with entrepreneurial, individualistic, 'conservative Right' values. The 'aspirationals' are supposed to be anti-egalitarian, anti-trade union, and in favour of tax cuts. Some commentators envisage them as driving new cars and sending their children to fee-charging private schools. (For some of the commentary from which this picture is constructed, see Carney 2001; Green 2001; Stephens 2001; MacKay 2001; Davidson 2001; Burchell 2003; Glover 2004 and Manne 2004.)

As with the 'battlers' above, we need to decide upon a set of measures to define 'aspirational voters' in a way that fits with the characteristics of respondents measured during the Australian Election Study surveys. For our purposes here, the 'aspirationals' among AES respondents are defined as those (1) whose household income is in the middle ranges[1] *and* (2) who favour tax cuts rather than increased government spending.[2] Using this simplified definition, 253 respondents to the 2004 AES survey—16 per cent of all respondents—can be classified as 'aspirational'. Table 15.2 reports their voting preferences.

Table 15.2 reveals that 51 per cent of all of the 2004 AES respondents favoured the Coalition parties. (The actual 2004 election result produced a 46 per cent share of the vote for the Coalition parties, revealing how even the most careful sampling techniques can produce a group of respondents not quite a precise cross-section of the whole voting population.) But the support among the AES 'aspirationals' for the Coalition is 63 per cent compared with just 28 per cent for Labor. This all suggests that there is a strong affinity between 'aspirational' status and Coalition support. Whether or not the Latham-led Labor campaign rescued this result from being even worse for Labor, whether Latham had a negative effect or whether Latham's strategy made no difference at all is not something that the data can reveal.

A closer examination of the data not reported in Table 15.2 shows that among AES 'aspirationals' living in outer suburbs support for the Coalition party was even higher, at 70 per cent of these respondents. Because the number of respondents in such a subsample of a survey is fairly small, and hence the effect of any sampling error would be relatively greater, this figure needs to be treated with particular caution. But it does suggest that Labor might indeed face a problem in marginal outer-suburban seats with the 'aspirational' voters. The actual number of 'aspirationals' living in the outer suburbs might not seem to be very large (on the basis of the AES sample, around 14 per cent of outer-suburban

TABLE 15.2	The 'aspirational' vote House of Representatives preferences for AES respondents, 2004		
	Coalition %	Labor %	Other %
'Aspirational' AES respondents (n = 253)	63	28	9
All AES respondents (n = 1625)	51	37	12
Actual 2004 result	46	38	16

Source: AES (2005).

residents seem to be 'aspirational' using the definition that we have constructed), but this might be large enough to play an important part in determining the outcome of marginal seat contests if their support for the Coalition parties is indeed so pronounced. The winning margin in some of these seats is so close that the shift of a relatively small number of votes might make a difference between winning and losing.[3]

So the identification of the so-called 'aspirationals' does seem to usefully highlight a category of voters, albeit perhaps part of a broader middle-class grouping, that is electorally significant. The five most marginal Coalition-held seats as of 2005 are located in Australia's metropolitan outer suburbs. Labor needs to win these seats to win government. Understanding the needs of the 'aspirationals' does seem to be important for a winning Labor strategy.

DOCTORS' WIVES

As already noted above, the 2004 election campaign produced commentary speculating that Liberal candidates contesting inner urban seats might suffer a backlash from a group described as the 'doctors' wives' (eg. Suich 2004; Farr 2004; Brett 2004). Liberal Party focus-group research had apparently identified a potential danger of a backlash from higher-income voters who were normally Liberal supporters but who had become disgruntled with the Howard government's position on matters such as the treatment of asylum-seekers, environmental policy and the war in Iraq. Dubbed the 'doctors' wives' group, it is better understood as a metaphor for inner-urban Liberal voters, both women and men, whose 'moral consciences' were thought to potentially sway them to vote on this occasion for Labor or the Greens. At least some Labor campaign strategists took the notion seriously enough to develop a set of environmental policies aimed at either attracting such voters directly to Labor or at least gaining the second preferences of what they expected to be a higher Green vote than usual.

To test the validity of the supposed 'doctors' wives' phenomenon using 2004 AES data, we can begin by identifying solid Liberal supporters by looking at the survey question that asks respondents for their 'party identification'.[4] As Table 15.3 indicates, about 41 per cent of AES respondents reported a Liberal Party identification. Of these, 87 per cent reported that they voted for a Liberal candidate in the House of Representatives. Only 4 per cent of them reported voting for a Labor or a Green candidate. Table 15.3 then examines those Liberal identifiers who also indicated a policy preference, in response to specific survey questions, that seemed to conflict with the Howard government's position on either the Iraq war or asylum-seekers or the environment.[5] This subgroup accounts for nearly half of all Liberal identifiers (and 19 per cent of AES respondents), but reveals virtually no difference in its voting preference for the 2004 election (taking into account the possible ±3 per cent margin of error in these

TABLE 15.3	'Doctors' Wives'? House of Representatives preferences for AES respondents, 2004 (percentages)				
		Liberal	Labor/Green	Other	Total
Identifies as Liberal (n = 668, 41% of AES respondents)		87	4	9	100
Identifies as Liberal + policy difference (n = 339, 19% of AES respondents)		86	5	9	100
Identifies as Liberal + policy difference + high income (n = 93, 5% of AES respondents)		88	8	5	100

Source: AES (2005).

numbers). Table 15.3 finally looks at the subset of this subgroup identified by having a household income in the top 20 per cent of respondents. Again there is no noteworthy change in voting behaviour in this group compared with the earlier constructions.

This all suggests that, whereas the notion of 'the aspirationals' did seem to provide a useful explanation for some voting patterns at the 2004 election, the notion of 'the doctors' wives' in practice seems to explain very little.[6]

Key characteristics of voters and their party choice in 2004

What other social, demographic or attitudinal characteristics might help to explain voting preference in the 2004 election? Table 15.4 facilitates some contemplation of this question. It presents a series of snapshots of the characteristics (such as age, household income, educational qualifications, employment, religious affiliation and self-perceived social class) of AES respondents in 2004 organised according to the party for they voted at the 2004 election.[7] Comparing any particular party column with the final column, showing the overall pattern that applies to all the respondents together, reveals the extent to which that party's supporters differ from the overall population. Note again that the validity of this exercise depends a lot on how representative the AES sample is of all Australian voters, and note also that these data do not allow us to say that the particular pattern of characteristics causes or even influences the respondents to vote for their preferred party. All that these data can reveal is a pattern of *association*; causality is a much more difficult thing to demonstrate.

Consider, for example, the AES respondents who reported voting for a Green candidate. They seem stand out in a number of respects from the whole group of AES respondents: they are more likely to be female, to be younger, to earn a

TABLE 15.4	Social characteristics and party preference House of Representatives preferences for AES respondents, 2004 (%, unless otherwise stated)				
	Liberal (n=750)	Labor (n=596)	National (n=73)	Green (n=133)	All (n=1660)
Average age (years)	50	50	57	43	50
Gender					
Male	50	48.5	47	41	48
Female	50	51.5	53	59	52
Gross household income					
Low income	16	26	31	24	23
Middle income	51	47	56	41	49
High income	33	27	13	35	29
Post-school qualifications					
University degree	22	24	12	55	25
Other post-school qualification	45	39	40	29	41
No post-school qualification	33	38	48	16	34
Employment sector					
Self-employed	22	11	37	13	17
Public-sector employee	22	34	18	30	27
Private-sector employee	57	54	46	57	56
Workplace authority					
Middle or upper management	39	25	30	31	32
Supervisor or lower management	26	30	30	31	28
Non-supervisor	35	46	39	39	40
Religious affiliation					
Catholic	25	29	32	16	26
Protestant	47	35	55	26	40
Other	12	12	6	11	12
No religion	16	24	7	47	21
Self-assessed social class					
'Upper class'	2	1	3	1	1½
'Middle class'	55	41	49	60	49
'Working class'	37	48	39	28	40
'None'	6	10	9	12	9
Geographical location					
Inner metropolitan	28	33	4	39	29
Outer metropolitan	33	27	9	26	29
Provincial urban	12	13	10	15	13
Rural	28	28	77	20	30
Housing tenure					
Home owner	47	43	64	35	45
Home buyer with mortgage	32	27	17	28	29
Renting or boarding	21	30	19	38	26

Source: AES (2005).

high income, to be a university graduate, to profess no religious affiliation, and to self-classify as a member of the 'middle class'. (Remember that 'more likely' is a comparative statement of tendency and should not be used to create a one-dimensional caricature of a 'typical' party voter. Even though, for example, Green-supporting respondents are *more likely* to profess no religious affiliation, it remains true that a majority of them still *do* profess some religious affiliation.) Some other interesting findings from Table 15.4 are that Green-voting and Labor-voting respondents are less likely to be self-employed, and that National Party voters are less likely to have acquired a post-school educational qualification and are more likely to be older.

Social class

The analysis so far illustrates how political-science research, especially research based on surveys of representative samples of voters, can shed some light on the relationship between social characteristics and voting behaviour. The three examples used—the battlers, the aspirationals and the so-called doctors' wives—are fairly recent and unconventional attempts to classify and possibly explain voting behaviour. We can now turn to some longer established and more academically conventional classifications and explanations.

As we have already seen, the history and structure of the Australian party system presupposes a division based mainly on social class. The notion of 'social class' refers to a pattern of entrenched differences between the less privileged and more privileged sectors of society. Historically, the common assumption was that blue-collar 'manual workers' could be broadly identified as constituting a less privileged 'working class' and white-collar 'non-manual workers' as a more privileged 'middle class'. This seemed to fit the mutually reinforcing aspects of most Australians' lives: where they worked, where they lived, how much they were paid, job security and promotion prospects, their recreational tastes—and who they voted for.

Figure 15.1 provides some evidence about the relationship between class and voting behaviour over the past 40 years, defining class by using the traditional blue-collar/manual-work versus white-collar/non-manual-work conceptualisation. Drawing on nine surveys of representative samples of voting-age Australians undertaken between 1967 and 2004, it charts the level of support for the Labor Party among respondents whose occupations were either mainly manual or non-manual in character.

The top two lines in Figure 15.1 shows that, consistently over time, respondents from manual-worker circumstances were more likely than those from non-manual worker circumstances to vote for the Labor Party. This is consistent with the traditional party divide. But each survey also reveals a substantial minority of manual-worker respondents voting against Labor. And it also seems to show a

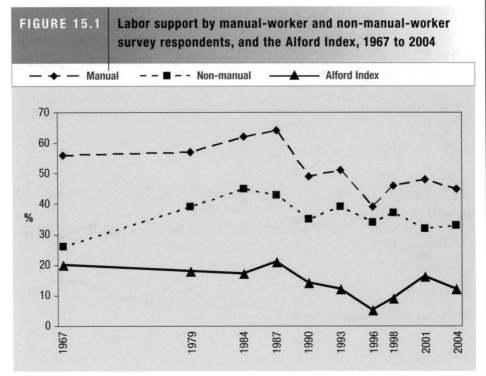

FIGURE 15.1 Labor support by manual-worker and non-manual-worker survey respondents, and the Alford Index, 1967 to 2004

Sources: ANPA (1975); APAS (1982); NSSS (1987); AES (1987); AES (1990); AES (1993); AES (1996); AES (1998); AES (2002); AES (2005).

convergence: whereas in the late 1960s the proportion of manual-worker respondents supporting Labor was more than double the proportion of non-manual-worker respondents, the gap closed over the next 30 years. The convergence was caused by both a decline in the proportion of manual workers supporting Labor and an increase in support for Labor from among non-manuals.

Another way of charting this same convergence is via the so-called 'Alford Index', reported via the bottom line in Figure 15.1. The Alford Index (first adopted by Alford 1963) is calculated by subtracting the middle line in Figure 15.1 from the top line, i.e. by subtracting the proportion of non-manual-worker survey respondents voting Labor from the proportion of manual-worker survey respondents voting Labor. It is a measure of the degree of 'class voting'. The bottom line in Figure 15.1 shows the trajectory of the Alford Index. It declines steadily from 1967 until 1996, followed by some increase since (though not back to the 1967 level). It indicates clearly the decline in 'class voting' as measured by the traditional notions of social class.

Figure 15.2 provides another perspective on the relationship between social class defined in traditional way (as blue-collar/manual worker versus white-collar/non-manual worker) and voting. It charts the shift in voting preference among the survey respondents from a non-manual (i.e. white-collar) workforce background. The Labor line in this figure is identical to the middle line in

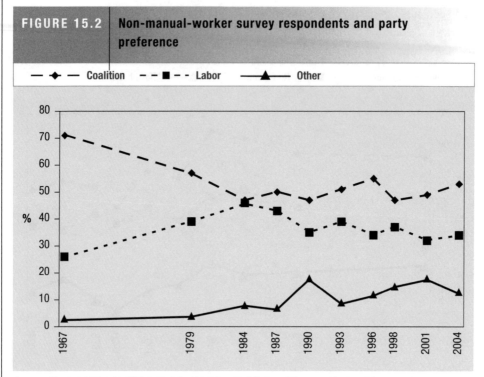

FIGURE 15.2 Non-manual-worker survey respondents and party preference

Sources: ANPA (1975); APAS (1982); NSSS (1987); AES (1987); AES (1990); AES (1993); AES (1996); AES (1998); AES (2002); AES (2005).

Figure 15.1, but also seen here is the level of non-manual support for the Coalition and, importantly, for other parties (e.g. the Australian Democrats). 'Middle class' (i.e. non-manual-worker) support for the Coalition parties fell rapidly between the 1967 and 1984 surveys, and since then has remained a fairly steady fluctuation around 50 per cent of middle-class respondents. Based on this evidence, it can no longer can it be said that the Australian 'middle class'—if this is defined as Australians associated with white-collar 'non-manual' occupations—comprises unequivocally strong supporters of the Coalition.

In 1978, the academic David Kemp (later to enter national politics as a Liberal and ultimately serve as a Cabinet Minister in the Howard government) anticipated and interpreted these trends. He argued that the working class—the Labor Party's traditional support base—was in numerical decline due to the economic changes that were reducing the traditional blue-collar 'manual' jobs in old labour-intensive industries like mining, manufacturing, the waterfront and the railways (Kemp 1978). Moreover, he argued, the political attitudes and aspirations of the remaining blue-collar households were in any case becoming more akin to those of the 'white-collar' middle class (a process termed, in social-science jargon, *embourgeoisement*). In these circumstances, according to Kemp, the Labor Party's links to the trade union movement and its old-fashioned appeal to working-class symbols were becoming a liability. The 1950s and 1960s had seen aspects of 'middle-class' life—such as buying a home on a quarter-acre block in the suburbs and enjoying rising levels of real wages—become available to many blue-collar breadwinners and their households. By the 1970s, according to Kemp, the traditional link between, on the one hand, a voting preference for a particular party and, on the other hand, a voter's social class—as traditionally defined in blue-collar/manual occupations versus white-collar/non-manual occupations—was weakening. Kemp predicted that the Labor Party would struggle to represent the new social reality.

This kind of analysis is important and convincing as far as it goes. It clearly demonstrates that the traditional conceptualisation of social class now has a much weaker association with voting behaviour. But does this really demonstrate that social class is having less influence? Or is it, alternatively, that 'social class'—the claim that there are important differences between the less privileged and more privileged sectors of society—may still be a useful predictor of voting behaviour, but that its social basis has changed away from the traditional form? In other words, maybe the manual/non-manual distinction is simply no longer a good proxy for the distribution of relative economic privilege and security.

Social change has accelerated in Australia, and economic change has swept through the job market and workplaces during the 1980s and 1990s, making the assumption of a strong association between blue-collar/white-collar and less-advantaged/more-advantaged increasingly doubtful (Manning 2002). Many white-collar workers today are not particularly advantaged; and conversely a number of blue-collar workers today are not particularly disadvantaged.

Consider voters who earn their livelihoods from modestly paid and relatively insecure white-collar jobs. These people do not fit comfortably within a 'middle-class' classification. Relatively low-paid white-collar service jobs (in sales, banking, insurance, administration, hospitality and elsewhere) have expanded in number significantly over recent decades. These jobs have been a particularly key source of employment for many women, often as casual or part-time employees. Many of these 'non-manual' wage-earners (for example, those working in clerical, hospitality or retail jobs) find their working life experiences more akin (in terms of job security, relative pay levels, and so on) to those experienced traditionally by the old blue-collar working class.

This is not to suggest that these lower-paid white-collar employees and their families experience the same type of political socialisation found historically among blue-collar workers. Today's wage-earners—whether blue collar or modestly paid white collar—are unlikely to have a strong sense of 'workers' solidarity' against 'the bosses'. Nor do they live in the close-knit type of communities (in inner cities, around ports, in factory districts, in old mining communities) which once acted to forge a sense of working-class identity. The decline in trade union membership rates, which have halved over the last

20 years to below 20 per cent of employees, and the fact that union membership is now more prevalent among public-sector employees than among those working for a private-sector 'boss', are good indications of this decline in working-class identity and solidarity.

Likewise, the idea that manual workers can today be characterised as disadvantaged members of a 'working class' is becoming a less convincing generalisation. There has always been the complication that some manual workers are self-employed tradespeople, in effect small-business owners. The proportion of blue-collar workers in this category has increased in recent decades, as more big employers in the private sector outsource work to independent contractors. There are perceived taxation advantages in skilled manual workers setting themselves up, if they can, as small independent businesses rather than being taxed as employees. Whatever the causes and motivations, a 'small business' mentality—even among manual workers—is likely to be more hostile toward the Labor Party. This is borne out by survey findings: for example, according to the 2004 AES study, 60 per cent of self-employed respondents working in manual occupations supported the Coalition parties (see also Roskam 2005).

No matter what definition of class is employed, occupational class seems to have a weaker association with voting behaviour than it did in the past. Bearing this in mind, it is worthwhile to look at a number of aspects of voters' experience of employment and how, over time, they have changed. Table 15.5 reports some findings. It categorises AES survey respondents according to the sector of the economy in which they are employed, the type of work that they do, whether or not they belong to a trade union, and (as a proxy measure of their authority and rank in the workplace) their managerial or supervisory role as an employee. To allow some assessment of change over time, data are presented from the 1987 and the 2004 AES surveys.

Table 15.5 reveals a number of interesting things. It suggests, for example, that the Labor Party tends to be supported more strongly among public-sector employees than among private-sector employees or the self-employed. This is an advantage to the Coalition parties, and its significance is heightened by structural economic change: whereas in 1987, private-sector employees and the self-employed constituted 62 per cent of the employees among AES respondents, by 2004 this had increased to 68 per cent. Table 15.5 also reports that, in the 2004 AES survey, the Coalition had a very substantial lead over Labor (by a 20 percentage-point margin) among full-time employee respondents, whereas back in 1987 Labor had a clear lead in this category. Unemployed respondents continue to show a disproportionately high level of support for Labor but the Coalition seems to have built a new majority among students and retirees (a growing portion of the population). (Bear in mind that the subsamples among AES respondents for some of these categories is quite small, meaning that the

TABLE 15.5	Occupational characteristics and party preference, AES survey respondents, 1987 and 2004			
	1987		2004	
	% vote for Coalition	% vote for Labor	% vote for Coalition	% vote for Labor
Employment sector				
Government	32	60	40	44
Private	42	51	49	35
Self-employed	65	33	66	23
Family business or farm	65	30	66	23
Occupation/hours				
Full-time job	43	50	54	34
Part-time job	46	47	48	36
Unemployed	24	69	32	53
Student	34	58	40	29
Keep house	45	48	46	42
Retired	41	55	52	39
Trade union membership				
Union member	30	64	34	50
Not a union member	53	40	55	31
Authority in workplace				
Upper-level manager			65	25
Low/middle-level manager			53	34
Supervisor			47	40
Non-supervisor			45	42

Sources: AES (1987); AES (2005).

possibility of sampling error is correspondingly much larger and hence these findings should be treated with particular caution.)

Some evidence of a continuing social class influence, though not necessarily of the classic white-collar versus blue-collar type, comes from considering the data reported in Table 15.5 under 'authority in the workplace'. AES respondents in the 'non-supervisor' category could be white-collar or blue-collar workers, and the data do show substantially stronger relative support for Labor among this group than among, for example, the 'upper manager' group. Labor still seems to attract disproportionate support from trade union members, but here again social change favours the Coalition: the proportion of employees who are union members has declined dramatically.

Gender

An established finding from past voting studies has been the so-called 'gender gap': the apparent tendency (slight but significant and enduring) for women to be more likely than men to vote for the Coalition parties. Writing in the mid-1990s, the political scientist Leithner (1997a) argued (based on some complex statistical evidence and inferences) that this 'gender gap' is apparent at every Australian national election since 1910 (with the interesting exception of the 1917 election[8]), with the Coalition parties enjoying an average of about a 4 percentage-point greater level of support among women than among men. Note carefully (because it can easily be misunderstood) that the so-called 'gender gap' is *not* a claim that women are more likely to vote for the Coalition than they are for Labor. The overall balance of party preference among women voters can fluctuate from election to election just as it does, of course, among men. In some elections, the Coalition wins a majority of the female vote, in others Labor does. The 'gender gap' claim is rather that, *relative* to men, there has been a slight but consistent tendency for more women to support the Coalition parties at any given election.

This is an interesting and potentially significant feature of voting behaviour. For Coalition party strategists, it had been an advantage to cherish and if possible enhance. For Labor Party strategists, the 'gender gap' has been seen as requiring attention (leading in part to the adoption of various 'affirmative action' strategies to pre-select more women candidates in the belief that this might help to close or reverse the gap).

Why might women, as a group, be more likely than men, as a group, to be supportive of a conservative party? Two sorts of explanations have been put forward (Norris 2000; Hill 2003).

The first explanation looks at the possible effect of purported differences in the values tending to be associated with women and men. If women were traditionally regarded as being more nurturing, budget conscious and 'risk averse', this might make enough women more amenable to 'conservative' appeals to cause the gender gap (Curtin 1997). The second explanation focuses on differential life experiences. Because, especially in the past, men were more involved in the workforce and more likely to have different work experiences (such as in heavy industry, as members of trade unions and so on), more men than women were thereby exposed, according to this argument, to pro-Labor influences.

Both explanations would be susceptible to change over time. Rigid gender-linked social roles and values have been changing, in part as a result of the feminist movement. And gender-linked workforce differences have also been changing and probably converging. These trends would suggest that the 'gender gap' should probably narrow over time.

We can assess these propositions by comparing survey trends over time. Figure 15.3 does this by drawing not only on the regular election-linked AES surveys but several other comparable surveys as well. In interpreting Figure 15.3, remember that the *overall* patterns and trends of party preferences trends among women respondents and among men respondents are generally very similar. In the last two AES surveys (2001 and 2004), for example, the Coalition parties enjoyed a clear margin of support over Labor among both women and men AES respondents. Conversely, a majority among both women and men AES respondents supported Labor in the 1984 and 1987 surveys undertaken during the period of dominance of the Hawke Labor government. But, as explained earlier, the 'gender gap' puzzle does not focus on these trends. Rather it focuses on the *relative* support for each party among women and men.

Figure 15.3 traces this 'gender gap' by measuring the *difference* between the support for the Labor Party among male AES respondents and the support for the Labor Party among female AES respondents. (It would be equally valid to measure the 'gap' by using Coalition party support instead.)

Figure 15.3 reveals a fascinating pattern. This evidence suggests that there has

FIGURE 15.3	Labor's gender gap Percentage-point difference between male and female survey respondents voting Labor, House of Representatives, 1967–2004

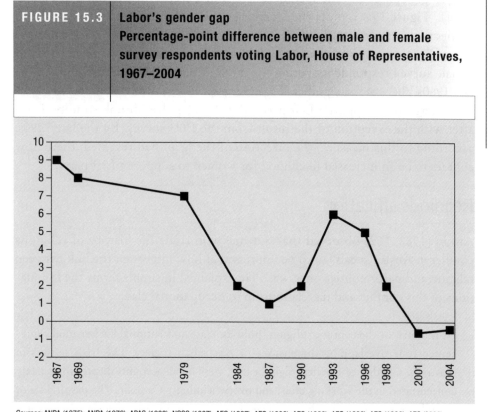

Sources: ANPA (1975); ANPA (1976); APAS (1982); NSSS (1987); AES (1987); AES (1990); AES (1993); AES (1996); AES (1998); AES (2002); AES (2005).

indeed been a 'gender gap' in the past. But it has diminished rapidly over the (nearly) 40 years covered by these surveys to the point where it now seems practically non-existent. The most recent AES data, as Figure 15.3 reports, actually show a very slight tendency in 2001 and 2004 for female respondents to be *more* likely than male respondents to support Labor. Remember that a solid majority within *both* gender groups supported the Coalition parties in both 2001 and 2004, but this majority was slightly bigger among male than among female AES respondents. But a word of caution: the measured 'gap' here is so small as to be within the margin of possible statistical error due to sampling, so it would not be prudent to trumpet this finding as a solid gender-gap 'reversal'.

A more complete insight into the 'gender gap' claim needs to take into account the role of minor parties. In recent decades, Australian politics has seen a number of minor parties gain parliamentary representation. There is some evidence to suggest, for example, that supporters of the Australian Democrats and the Greens are more likely to be female than male, and this needs to be taken into account. To make sense of the effect of minor parties using the limited survey data at hand, it helps to aggregate them into a 'Left' grouping (e.g. the Australian Democrats, the Nuclear Disarmament Party and the Greens) and a 'Right' grouping (e.g. the Democratic Labor Party, One Nation and Family First).[9] Figure 15.4 replots the 'gender gap' by adding support for the 'Left' parties to the support for Labor. It shows the difference between the proportion of male survey respondents voting for the Left parties and the proportion of female survey respondents voting for the Left parties. It indicates that, in the late 1960s, there was a significant 'gender gap' in terms of the increased likelihood for men to support a Left party. But this 'gap' has shrunk steadily thereafter with the exception of the result from the 1993 survey. By the late 1990s, according to this measure, the direction of the 'gap' had reversed: there now appears to be an increased likelihood for women to support a Left party.

Religious affiliation

Aitkin (1982: 162) observed that 'no-one who reads the history of religious conflict in Australia can fail to be impressed at how important the link between religion and party politics once was'. He explained in simple terms the foundations of this conflict and its relationship to occupational class:

> At the turn of the century religion, politics, class and national background represented four overlapping dimensions of Australian society. The Irish settlers in Australia, whether of convict origin or free, were on all accounts disproportionately concentrated in the working class, and overwhelmingly Catholic. The pastoralists of the inland and the urban bourgeoisie dominated the governmental and political structures of the colonies, and were overwhelmingly Protestant (Aitkin 1982: 162).

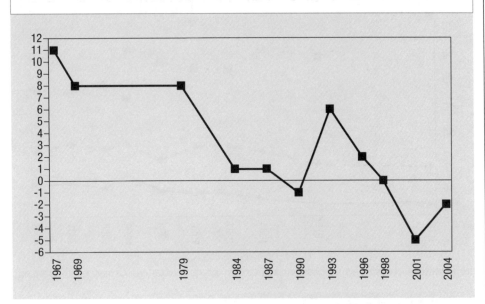

FIGURE 15.4 Left parties' gender gap
Percentage-point difference between male and female
survey respondents voting for Left parties, House of
Representatives, 1967–2004

Sources: ANPA (1975); ANPA (1976); APAS (1982); NSSS (1987); AES (1987); AES (1990); AES (1993); AES (1996); AES (1998); AES (2002); AES (2005).

The Australian party system evolved in parallel with this, with Catholics associated strongly with the Labor Party and Protestants with the Liberal Party or its precursors. Within the Liberal and National parties, it was rare ever to find a Catholic preselected as a candidate for a parliamentary seat, whereas Labor has always featured many Catholic politicians. However this association, as Aitkin makes clear, was largely a surrogate for social class, and it then persisted over time. But this pattern then changed. A major catalyst for change was the advent in the 1950s and 1960s of the Democratic Labor Party which saw a weakening of the long-term habitual association between some Catholics and the ALP. By the 1970s, the historic sectarian divide eroded as the social differences between Australian Catholics and Protestants began to converge in terms of socio-economic profile while the combination of consumerism and higher education attainment saw more voters (though still a minority) prepared to declare that they had no religious affiliation.

Figures 15.5 and 15.6 plot, by religious affiliation, the proportion of survey respondents over an almost 40-year period who have reported they voted respectively for the Coalition parties and for Labor in the House of Representatives. Several features stand out. First, the Coalition-voting support base used to

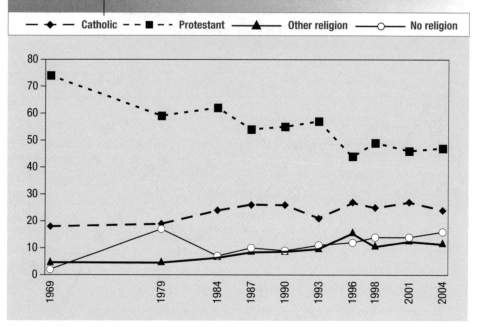

FIGURE 15.5 | **Religious affiliation of Coalition-voting survey respondents, 1969 to 2004**

— ◆ — Catholic – – ■ – – Protestant —▲— Other religion —○— No religion

Sources: ANPA (1975); ANPA (1976); APAS (1982); NSSS (1987); AES (1987); AES (1990); AES (1993); AES (1996); AES (1998); AES (2002); AES (2005).

FIGURE 15.6 | **Religious affiliation of Labor-voting survey respondents, 1969 to 2004**

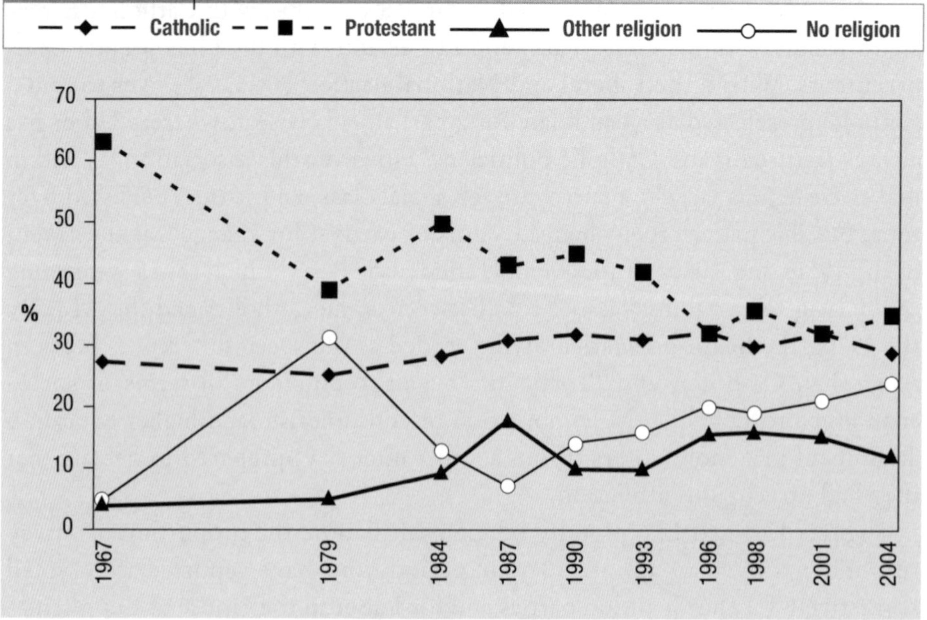

— ◆ — Catholic – – ■ – – Protestant —▲— Other religion —○— No religion

Sources: ANPA (1975); ANPA (1976); APAS (1982); NSSS (1987); AES (1987); AES (1990); AES (1993); AES (1996); AES (1998); AES (2002); AES (2005).

be overwhelmingly dominated by those who nominated a religious affiliation with a Protestant church, but the proportion has fallen steadily ever since. This decline must be caused either by some shift of Protestant-affiliated voters to other parties, or by an overall decline in the proportion of Protestant voters as a whole, or by a combination of both. A similar decline is observable among Labor voters, although with a lower initial starting point. Second, the proportion of Coalition-supporting respondents nominating a Catholic affiliation has increased over the period, from less than 20 per cent to around 25 per cent of Coalition supporters, and has remained steady at around 30 per cent of Labor-supporting respondents.[10]

Religious affiliation may be merely nominal, and a better sense of real religious engagement is probably to ask respondents how frequently they attend church. The 2004 AES found that just 15 per cent of respondents attended church on a frequent (i.e. weekly) basis, and that this was associated with some variation depending on party support. Comparing party supporters, 21 per cent of National Party-supporting respondents were frequent attenders, compared with 16 per cent of Liberal supporters, 12 per cent of Labor supporters and just 8 per cent of Green supporters (see also Bean 1999; Smith 1998).

A 'volatile' electorate?

Federal and State election results during the 1990s saw the major parties' share of the primary vote steadily erode. This fuelled much commentary about growing public cynicism and the decline of the so-called 'rusted on' voter (e.g. Burchell and Leigh 2002). But the trend can be exaggerated: the vast majority (80 per cent or more) of Australians continue to support the major parties. While the figure used to be 90 per cent or more, 80 per cent is still a large proportion. It seems that a longer-term 'identification' with a major political party remains a stronger feature of voting in Australia than in, for example, Europe or North America (Bean and McAllister 2002; Leithner 1997b).

Another way of looking at trends over time is through the notion of electoral volatility, which refers to the degree of vote shifting between parties from one election to the next. The greater the shift of support between parties from election to election, the greater the degree of volatility. Political scientists can measure this volatility mathematically, using a so-called 'volatility index'.[11] The 2004 poll produced one of the more 'volatile' results of recent times (due to a decline in Labor's vote and a collapse of support for the Democrats compared with the 2001 election). But, at the same time, overall support for the major parties increased to more than 84 per cent (having reached a low point of 79.6 per cent at the One Nation-influenced 1998 election), suggesting that overall the party system remains fairly stable. Calculations by Goot (1994: 178) using the mathematical measure of volatility reveal that electoral volatility was far more pronounced at various elections from the 1920s to the 1940s than it has been since the 1980s, notwithstanding the attention paid in recent times to claims about volatility.

Whenever an election day approaches, there is usually much discussion among journalists and party strategists about 'undecided' voters. Party election campaigns are predicated on the existence of a sizable proportion of 'undecided' voters who might be swayed by all the campaign events, launches, media advertisements, direct-mail contacts and other persuasive inducements. The AES surveys associated with each federal election ask respondents when they decided on which party they were going to vote for. In the 2004 AES, about two-thirds of respondents reported that they had already decided on their vote before the election campaign was officially launched. About a quarter made their mind up during the campaign, and 8 per cent on election day itself. These proportions seem to have changed only marginally from election to election. They mean that election campaigns are, in effect, pitched at the minority of voters (about 30 to 40 per cent of the total) who have not already decided their voting intention.

Conclusion

Over the last three decades a broad ideological consensus between the major parties, at least among their national-level leaders, has evolved around neoliberal economics, known widely in Australia as 'economic rationalism'. While some differences between the parties have existed, they have been mainly over the pace of reform rather than its content. This convergence has probably contributed to some weakening of long-held voter perceptions of the major parties. Most voters continue to identify with a major party but fewer than before are 'rusted on' supporters. And the traditional 'blue collar versus white collar' class basis of the major parties' core electoral constituencies now seems less relevant to the parties as they shape policy and promises during election campaigns.

But this does not necessarily mean that social class—in the sense of enduring structures of advantage and disadvantage in society—is no longer an influence on voting. The evidence in this chapter suggests that the typical 'Aussie battler' seems as loyal to Labor as ever, notwithstanding a brief flirtation by some disgruntled 'battlers' with the Coalition parties in 1993 and 1996. And the chapter also finds some evidence to support the notion that the 'aspirationals' are attracted to the Coalition parties. With social and economic change probably shrinking the number of battlers and expanding the number of aspirationals, this may help to explain the national electoral dominance of the Coalition parties since the first election of the Howard government in 1996.

But even successful parties should never feel too comfortable. The Coalition may be dominating recent national elections, but Labor has dominated recent

State and Territory elections. All it may take is an economic downturn and an invigorated Opposition for an electoral equation to change quickly.

Voters are subject to a complex web of influences as they approach the polls. Habits of loyalty to a particular party probably remain important for most. But many voters will shift party preferences if they feel the shadow of tough economic times and if they assess the other party as being fitter to govern. So much rests now on these shorter-term assessments by voters that the traditionally strong predictors of voting, like traditional class location, have diminished in significance. It is interesting to ponder how a party system originally forged on traditional class (and reinforcing religious) foundations may change in ensuing years now that both factors seem so much weaker.

NOTES

1 More precisely, AES respondents in the 2004 survey who reported a gross household income of between $30 000 and $70 000, a range encompassing approximately the middle 40 per cent of respondents. It should be noted, by comparing AES responses with Australian Bureau of Statistics data on the household income range in Australia, it appears that the AES respondents have overall tended to under-report their income in answering the AES question.

2 The precise AES question is: 'If the government had a choice between reducing taxes or spending more on social services, which do you think it should do? Strongly favour reducing taxes; Mildly favour reducing taxes; Depends; Mildly favour spending more on social services; Strongly favour spending more on social services'.

3 Consider the outer Adelaide electorate of Kingston. In 2004, the Liberal candidate defeated the incumbent Labor member by just 119 votes after the distribution of preferences. The evidence presented in this chapter gives us reasonable grounds for supposing that the 'aspirational voter' factor helped the Liberal candidate to win this seat.

4 Respondents are asked the question: 'Generally speaking, do you usually think of yourself as Liberal, Labor, National or what?'

5 The three AES survey questions were specifically whether they 'disagreed' with government's position on Iraq (q. F6), 'disagreed' with 'turning back asylum seekers' (q. E4) or considered the 'environment' as an 'important' factor in considering how to vote (q. D1).

6 It transpired that Labor did wrest three inner urban seats from the Liberal Party at the October 2004 election. In each instance (the seats of Adelaide and Hindmarsh in SA and Parramatta in NSW), local issues surrounding the Liberal candidates probably explain the outcome. There might be stronger, but still anecdotal, evidence for a 'doctors' wives' phenomenon in the case of the rural NSW seat of Richmond, centred around Byron Bay. There are suggestions that a growing migration of ex-urban retirees, many with the kind of economic security allied with an interest in non-material issues that is said to define the 'doctor's wives' phenomenon, contributed to the electoral tide ebbing away for the sitting National Party member, who lost his seat.

7 See Leigh (2005) for similar, but more detailed, findings.

8 The 1917 aberration seems to be explained by unusually strong support among women for Labor's anti-conscription stance: Leithner's data suggest that three in four women supported Labor whereas three in four men supported Hughes' pro-conscription Nation-

alist Party. If this is true—and Leithner's statistical reconstruction of these elections before the days of national surveys is somewhat complex and possibly contentious—it is a remarkable instance of a very deep gender divide.

9 This sort of aggregation is fraught with difficulties. For example, while it is likely that the Australian Democrats have attracted some voters with a 'Left' orientation, it has also campaigned on government accountability, balance of power and small business issues that have also attracted some voters from the Centre-Right. Likewise, the Democratic Labor Party's policies on social welfare and industrial relations were firmly on the Left, whereas its foreign policy stance (which tended to dominate its political alliances and tactics) were firmly on the Right.

10 The reason why the 1979 response rate nominating 'no religion' is markedly higher than adjacent surveys derives from the questionnaire first asking respondents whether they thought of themselves as having a religion before asking for religious affiliation.

11 The 'volatility index', devised by Pedersen (1979), is calculated by first determining shifts in support (positive and negative) received by each party (including minor parties and independents) in consecutive elections, adding each result and dividing it by two (see also Goot 1994). For the mathematically inclined, the equation for this calculation is $V = \frac{1}{2}\Sigma\,[P_{i,\,t}]$, where $P_{i,\,t}$ is the percentage of the vote obtained by party i at election t.

REFERENCES

AES [Australian Election Study] 1987, computer file, McAllister, I., Mughan, A., Ascui, A. & Jones, R. compilers, SSDA no. 445, Social Sciences Data Archives, Australian National University, Canberra.

AES [Australian Election Study] 1990, computer file, Jones, R., McAllister, I. & Gow, D. compilers, SSDA no. 570, Social Sciences Data Archives, Australian National University, Canberra.

AES [Australian Election Study] 1993, computer file, Jones, R., McAllister, I. & Denemark, D. compilers, SSDA no. 763, Social Sciences Data Archives, Australian National University, Canberra.

AES [Australian Election Study] 1996, computer file, Jones, R., McAllister, I. & Gow, D. compilers, SSDA no. 943, Social Sciences Data Archives, Australian National University, Canberra.

AES [Australian Election Study] 1998, computer file, Bean, C., Gow, D. & McAllister, I. compilers, SSDA no. 1001, Social Sciences Data Archives, Australian National University, Canberra.

AES [Australian Election Study] 2002, computer file, Bean, C., Gow, D. & McAllister, I. compilers, SSDA no. 1048, Social Sciences Data Archives, Australian National University, Canberra.

AES [Australian Election Study] 2005, computer file, Bean, C., McAllister, I., Gibson, R. & Gow, D. compilers, SSDA no. 1079, Social Sciences Data Archives, Australian National University, Canberra.

Aitkin, D. & Kahan, M. 1974, 'Australia: Class Politics in the New World', in *Electoral Behaviour: A Comparative Handbook*, ed. D. Rose, Free Press, New York.

Aitkin, D. 1982, *Stability and Change in Australian Politics*, 2nd edn, Australian National University Press, Canberra.

Alford, R. 1963, *Party and Society*, Rand-McNally, Chicago.

ANPA [Australian National Political Attitudes Wave I] 1975, computer file, Aitkin, D.,

Kahan, M. & Stokes, D. compilers, ICPSR no. 7282, Inter-University Consortium for Political Research, Michigan.

ANPA [Australian National Political Attitudes Wave II] 1976, computer file, Aitkin, D., Kahan, M. & Stokes, D. compilers, ICPSR no. 7393, Inter-University Consortium for Political Research, Michigan.

APAS [Australian Political Attitudes Survey] 1982, computer file, Aitkin, D. compiler, SSDA no. 9, Social Sciences Data Archives, Australian National University, Canberra.

Bean, C. 1999, 'The Forgotten Cleavage? Religion and Politics in Australia', *Canadian Journal of Political Science*, vol. 32, no. 3, pp. 551–68.

Bean, C. & McAllister, I. 2002, 'From Impossibility to Certainty: Explaining the Coalition's Victory in 2001', in *2001: The Centenary Election*, eds J. Warhurst & M. Simms, University of Queensland Press, St Lucia.

Brett, J. 1992, *Robert Menzies' Forgotten People*, Macmillan, Sydney.

Brett, J. 2002, 'Class, Religion and the Foundation of the Australian Party System: A Revisionist Interpretation', *Australian Journal of Political Science*, vol. 37, no. 1, March, pp. 39–56.

Brett, J. 2003, *Australian Liberals and the Moral Middle Class*, Cambridge University Press, Melbourne.

Brett, J. 2004, 'Patronising Women Voters', *The Age*, 24 September.

Burchell, D. 2003, *Western Horizon: Sydney's Heartland and the Future of Australian Politics*, Scribe, Sydney.

Burchell, D. & Leigh, A. eds 2002, *The Prince's New Clothes: Why Do Australians Dislike their Politicians?*, UNSW Press, Sydney.

Carney, S. 2001, 'A Landslide that Never Was', *The Age*, 9 March.

Cavalier, R. 1997, 'An Insider on the Outside', in *The Politics of Retribution: The 1996 Federal Election*, eds C. Bean, M. Simms, S. Bennett & J. Warhurst, Allen & Unwin, Sydney, pp. 23–33.

Crosby, L. 2000, 'The Liberal Party', in *Howard's Agenda: The 1998 Federal Election*, eds. M. Simms & J. Warhurst, University of Queensland Press, St Lucia.

Curtin, J. 1997, 'The Gender Gap in Australian Elections', *Research Paper 3, 1997–98*, Parliamentary Library, Canberra, <http://www.aph.gov.au/library/pubs/rp/1997-98/98rp03.htm>.

Davidson, K. 2001, 'Good Schools Become A Private Benefit', *The Age*, 26 April.

Farr, M. 2004, 'Why the PM Fears Doctors' Wives', *Daily Telegraph*, 21 May.

Glover, D. 2004, 'Don't Ditch the "Elites"', *Australian*, 29 November.

Goot, M. 1994, 'Class Voting, Issue Voting and Electoral Volatility', in *Developments in Australian Politics*, eds J. Brett, J. Gillespie & M. Goot, Macmillan, Melbourne, pp. 153–81.

Green, A. 2001, 'Outer Suburbs Will Decide Who Rules', *The Age*, 13 January.

Hamilton, C. 2003, 'Work Less, Earn Less, Live a Little: Tracking the Anti-Aspirational Voter', *Online Opinion*, <http://www.onlineopinion.com.au>, 22 January, accessed 15 November 2004.

Harding, A. 2005, 'Recent Trends in Income Inequality in Australia', Presentation to the Conference on 'Sustaining Prosperity: New Reform Opportunities for Australia', Melbourne 31 March. National Centre for Social and Economic Modelling, University of Canberra, <http://www.natsem.canberra.edu.au/>, accessed 8 April 2005.

Henderson, G. 2001, 'Just a Fancy Word for the Up and Coming', *Sydney Morning Herald*, 11 December.

Hewett, J. 2004, 'Carr is Labor's Albatross in Lathamland', *Australian Financial Review*, 15 September.

Hill, L. 2003, 'The Gender Gap: Australia, Britain and the United States', *Policy, Organisation and Society*, vol. 22, no. 1, pp. 73–100.

Kelly, P. 1992, *The End of Certainty: The Story of the 1980s*, Allen & Unwin, Sydney.

Kemp, D. 1978, *Society and Electoral Behaviour in Australia*, University of Queensland Press, St Lucia.

Latham, M. 1998, *Civilising Global Capital: New Thinking for Australian Labor*, Allen & Unwin, Sydney.

Latham, M. 2001, *What Did You Learn Today?: Creating an Education Revolution*, Allen & Unwin, Sydney.

Leigh, A. 2005, 'Economic Voting and Electoral Behavior: How do Individual, Local and National Factors Affect Partisan Choice', *Economics and Politics*, vol. 17, no. 2, pp. 265–96.

Leithner, C. 1997a, 'A Gender Gap in Australia? Commonwealth Elections 1910–96', *Australian Journal of Political Science*, vol. 32, no. 1.

Leithner, C. 1997b, 'Electoral Nationalisation, Dealignment and Realignment: Australia and the US, 1900–88', *Australian Journal of Political Science*, vol. 32, no. 2.

Mackay, H. 1993, *Reinventing Australia: the Mind and Mood of Australia in the 90s*, Angus and Robertson, Sydney.

MacKay, H. 2001, 'Hands Up, All You Aspirational Weirdos', *The Age*, 8 December.

Manne, R. 2004, 'How Trying to Please is a Trap for Latham', *Sydney Morning Herald*, 9 August.

Manning, H. 2002, 'Voting Behaviour', in *Government, Politics, Power and Public Policy in Australia*, eds A. Parkin, J. Summers & D. Woodward, 7th edn, Longman, Melbourne.

Norris, P. 2000, 'Gender: A Gender-Generation Gap', in *Critical Elections: British Parties and Voters in Long-Term Perspective*, eds G. Evans & P. Norris, Sage, London, pp. 148–64.

NSSS [National Social Science Survey] 1987, computer file, Kelley, J., Cushing, R. & Headey, B. compilers, SSDA no. 423, Social Sciences Data Archives, Australian National University, Canberra.

Pedersen, M. 1979, 'The Dynamics of European Party Systems: Changing Patterns of Electoral Volatility', *European Journal of Political Research*, vol. 7, pp. 7–26.

Robb, A. 1997, 'The Liberal Party Campaign', in *The Politics of Retribution: The 1996 Federal Election*, eds C. Bean, M. Simms, S. Bennett & J. Warhurst, Allen & Unwin, Sydney, pp. 23–33.

Roskam, J. 2005, 'Self Reliance and the Employment Revolution', *IPA Review*, vol. 57, no. 1, pp. 3–5.

Scalmer, S. 1999, 'The Battlers Versus the Elites: The Australian Right's Language of Class', *Overland*, no. 154, Autumn, pp. 9–13.

Singleton, J., Martyn, P. & Ward, I. 1998, 'Did the 1996 Federal Election See a Blue Collar Revolt Against Labor? A Queensland Case Study', *Australian Journal of Political Science*, vol. 33, no. 1, pp. 117–30.

Smith, R. 1998, 'Religion and Electoral Behaviour in Australia: Searching for Meaning', *Australian Religion Studies Review*, vol. 11, no. 2, pp. 16–37.

Stephens, T. 2001, 'Kenneally Laments "Ugly" Way of Being', *The Age*, 7 December.

Suich, M. 2004, 'Debating the "Doctors' Wives" Phenomenon', *The Age*, 17 September.

Governance, Power and Society

AUSTRALIA

Introduction

The previous parts of this book focused on the formal institutional structures of government and on their connection with citizens through the party and electoral systems. Underlying those sections was an implicit assumption that governments possess and exercise political power, and that the Australian people, in their role as citizens and voters, are affected by political power through the formal avenues of government.

Those assumptions are directly scrutinised in this fourth part of the book. This part looks at a variety of alternative perspectives on the distribution and exercise of power in Australia. These theories and interpretations all recognise that, while Australian citizens may enjoy identical political resources in the strict sense of an equal right to vote and to run for office, they are in social and economic terms quite heterogeneous with different levels of resources and opportunities.

In Chapter 16, James Walter discusses leadership in Australia and more broadly in liberal democracies. He argues that inevitably there are leaders who, through the formal powers of their position or by other informal means, exercise more power than other citizens. This is a challenge to the liberal and to the democratic ideals embodied within liberal-democratic political systems, both of which are concerned to limit and hold accountable the power of leaders. He discusses the leadership style of Australian political leaders and examines the means by which they have been able to maintain and exercise political power.

Chapter 17's focus is on the role of interest groups in organising and representing a diverse range of interests within the political system. John Warhurst examines the different types of interest groups, their operation and influence within the political system, and their relationship with government. He discusses the concern that some well-resourced interest groups representing particular interests wield undue influence and thereby distort the process of liberal-democratic politics.

The business sector is a particularly important interest group within a liberal-democratic system. In Chapter 18, Andrew Parkin and Leonie Hardcastle examine the business sector and the various ways in which it interrelates with the government sector. They scrutinise several influential, though contrasting, interpretations of the balance of influence in government-business relations, and examine the implications of the business sector appearing to occupy a privileged position within liberal democracies.

In Chapter 19, Ian Ward discusses the role of mass media and the crucial role that they play in liberal-democratic politics. He examines the extent to which the media influence public opinion. Ward looks at the effect of the concentration of private ownership and control of the major media organisations, the relationship between governments and the media, the role of talk-back radio in everyday politics, and how developments in the media have affected the political process.

Two theoretical perspectives—Marxist and elitist—that are particularly critical of a liberal-democratic interpretation of politics and political power in Western countries are examined by Michael Gilding in Chapter 20. Both the Marxist and the elite schools of thought argue that, contrary to the more benign assumptions of liberal-democratic theories, political power in societies like Australia is concentrated in the hands of a relatively small group of people. Marxist theories stress the importance of economic power, as a dominant force in its own right and in determining outcomes in the political process. Elite theories focus on the role of entrenched elites who, it is argued, exercise political power, in their own interest, independently of the democratic process.

In Chapter 21, Jennifer Curtin explains feminist approaches to the understanding of politics and feminist critiques of liberal democracy. She examines the role of women in the formal processes of Australian politics, and reports on the recent outcomes for women in terms of political participation and the representation of women's interests in the decision-making process.

JAMES WALTER

16 Political leadership

Leadership is a particularly interesting and problematic concept within liberal-democratic politics. This is because the idea of leadership can operate in considerable tension with both the liberal and the democratic strands that contribute to liberal democracy. A liberal perspective values the rights and freedoms of individuals, while a democratic perspective values collective decision-making processes such as majority rule. Strong leadership does not seem to be a strong theme in either perspective.

Consistent with this, liberal-democratic systems mainly address the issue of leadership by trying to constrain it. They impose checks and balances (recognition of rights, separation of powers, political pluralism, constitutionally defined limits on government) that, at least in the arena of governmental power, are intended to constrain collusive groups and powerful individuals. This chapter examines how leadership operates within liberal-democratic systems like Australia, drawing on a range of academic research, and assesses the effectiveness of these constraints.

The significance of political leadership

Leadership—like death and taxes—is one of the certainties in our lives. Every group or association in which you are involved will produce a leader or a subgroup who will be given authority as a means of achieving the group's aims. Someone has to do the leader's work—clarifying objectives, organising, focusing, suggesting strategies, acting for us, taking responsibility. The rest of us sacrifice some of our autonomy in giving the leader licence to undertake these tasks. Wherever we look, we have to acknowledge 'the indispensability of *leadership* in all social life, and in every major form of social organisation' (Hook 1943). Analysts of group processes (e.g. Bion 1961) have shown that, even within an egalitarian group, purposely coming together with the principle of determining its actions collectively, leaders will emerge. Such dynamics are evident in every group, at every level.

When we talk of political leadership, however, we refer to groups that have broad impacts upon all of us: political leadership concerns those who play the decisive roles in institutions that determine 'who gets what, when, how' (Lasswell 1936).

Despite its familiarity, leadership is mysterious. Even in a small group, and even where leader roles are conscientiously rotated, not all will take a turn at the helm—indeed, some would resist even if pressed to do so. Who, then, aspires to leadership, and why? And leadership involves risks, not only for the incumbent (think of election aftermaths and the obloquy usually directed at the losing leader), but also for followers (power can be misused, derailing the group's intentions; power might even be turned against us).

The quandary can be expressed this way: we need leaders, since without their drive and ambition, nothing might be done and society would atrophy; yet, though there have been wise leaders, a proportion of the people who aspire to leadership might be driven less by the social good than by the desire for power and deference (see Lasswell 1948). How then can we ensure the benefits of leadership, and—as demanded by liberal-democratic principles—defend against the misuse of power?

The cautionary case of Mark Latham

Sometimes a leader comes along whose actions pointedly illustrate the nature of this quandary. Take, for instance, the case of the ill-fated former leader of the Australian Labor Party (ALP), Mark Latham.

After three successive federal election defeats in 1996, 1998 and 2001, Labor's Federal Caucus evidently preferred to opt for a potential saviour, rather than for a process of working towards a distinctive and attractive policy profile, in electing Latham as its parliamentary leader in 2003. An intelligent and forceful man—he had once resigned from Labor's Shadow Ministry when his ideas were not accepted—it was thought that Latham could short-circuit the party stalemate and shake up the incumbent Coalition government led by John Howard. A man of ideas—Latham had written several books (e.g. Latham 1998, 2001 & 2003)—surely, a majority of his colleagues evidently hoped, he could generate policy change.

At first, this leadership accession seemed successful. Latham refused to debate issues on Howard's terms, cleverly shifting debate to his own stronger ground. He was unconventional and gained much attention. Given considerable licence by his colleagues, he was able to appear decisive, promoting unexpected, and hence refreshing, ideas.

Despite promising beginnings, however, the Labor Party was to learn the cost of surrendering to a dominant and wilful leader. Though Latham was given to bold policy initiatives, when it came to campaigning he was to prove unable to show how they connected together into a vision for Australia. He relied instead on vacuous and tiresomely repetitive slogans (he would provide 'the ladder of opportunity'; he would 'ease the squeeze' on middle Australia). Despite tactical gains on some issues, this approach—lacking a long-term vision—did not add up to a strategy. Latham was careless in exhibiting his disdain for some groups (e.g. business) and his impatience with others (e.g. liberal intellectuals), and he seemed unable to empathise with the aspirations of many (e.g. those who chose private education for their children). Latham came to be a divisive figure rather than one who could rally diverse constituencies behind the ALP.

Apparently supremely confident of his own intellectual ability, Latham evidently would not listen to advice from others. He came to rely on a small, insulated inner circle given to 'groupthink' (a concept discussed further below). There was little reflection, and the pros and cons of ideas endorsed by the leader were not debated. During the 2004 election campaign, the Labor Shadow Ministry, rather than working as a team, was simply told what the leader had decided to do. Significant policy statements emanated from his office rather than from the relevant Shadow Minister (sometimes without adequate airing with that Shadow Minister).

The Labor Party had, in effect, surrendered everything to Latham—to his ability, instincts and political judgment. It was a gamble that comprehensively failed, illuminating starkly the likely outcome of vesting too much in singular leadership without ensuring reciprocity and the means of marrying the leader's ambitions with the group's needs.

What can we learn from this? We learn that it pays to be attentive to the character of a leader, and that there must be restraint imposed on a leader's proclivities by the aims and values of the group. If risk is to be managed, reciprocity between leadership initiatives and group objectives must be achieved.

Social scientists have long sought to understand the risk potential in the social dynamics of leadership, and the characteristics that might be expected of certain types of leadership aspirant. The next two sections of this chapter draw on some of their efforts.

Leadership behaviour: academic research and typologies

There are now many varieties of leadership research undertaken by academic social scientists. Here we can take up just a few illustrative examples.

An influential early exponent of the psychological analysis of leadership was Harold Lasswell at the University of Chicago. He was interested in why some people seem motivated to seek power, and proposed that the core of the political personality was a tendency to use power to overcome actual or threatened loss of values, including self-esteem (Lasswell 1948). Lasswell's successors went into more detail, proposing that particular constellations of power-related traits were characteristic of different leader types (Stogdill 1974), and elaborating on the motives driving an investment in power (Winter 1973).

Lasswell pioneered the use of leadership typologies. Whether their aim was the acquisition of power to satisfy some personal deficit or to pre-empt a potential threat, leaders would nonetheless fall into different *types* according to the skills they relied on in gaining access to and then shaping decision making. Lasswell identified three types: the *agitator*, who works on mobilising people, seeking a response from the crowd; the *administrator*, who is more comfortable with direct interpersonal relations and with working through systems and organisation to shape outcomes; and the *theorist*, who seeks to change the world though changing the ways in which we think (Lasswell 1930).

Lasswell cautioned that few political actors will turn out to be 'pure' types— most will fall on a spectrum from the most people-oriented (agitators) to the most abstract (theorists). But there has been success in utilising Lasswell's approach in understanding, for instance, the agitator aspects of revolutionary leaders (Wolfenstein 1967). And his typology has the advantage of alerting us to the nature of politics as work, and the skill preferences that political leaders develop in such work.

Typologies have since become a staple in the comparative study of US Presidential leadership. The aim has been to identify the qualities that enhance or diminish performance in particular aspects of the role of being President of the United States, while addressing sociological and historical features of the context in which a President acts (Barber 1972; Burns 1978; Greenstein 2000; Neustadt 1990). Such approaches have since been extended to leaders in Westminster-type polities (Kaarbo 1997; Elcock 2001).

A good example is the work of David Barber on Presidential *character* as a likely indicator of performance (Barber 1972). It is useful, too, because he also focuses upon how leaders approach their political work. Barber's typology depends upon two dimensions, the level of application to political work (*active* or *passive*), and the nature of emotional engagement with the work (*positive* or *negative*). The rubric is easily applied: what does a leader do, and how does he or she feel about it?

On the basis of Presidential case studies, using these dimensions, Barber generates four types: the *active–positive* (hard working, positively oriented, this leader is the ideal, the adaptive personality, for example, President Franklin Roosevelt); the *active–negative* (closer to Lasswell's 'power' oriented personality, this leader is compulsive, hard-working but defensive, prone to provoke crises and then to persist in a failing policy position, for example President Richard Nixon); the *passive–positive* (compliant and other-directed, seeking rewards for being cooperative rather than assertive, for example President William H. Taft); and the *passive–negative* (withdrawn, often drafted into position and driven to serve by a sense of duty, for example President Dwight Eisenhower).

Barber's message was that active–positive leaders and active–negative leaders tend to dominate—and that somehow political systems should try to prevent the accession to power of conflict-prone, rigid, compulsive active–negative leaders.

Barber's characterisations have been challenged—for instance, Fred Greenstein's study of President Eisenhower (Greenstein 1982) presented a much more wily and effective operator than could be expected of a withdrawn, passive–negative type. Nonetheless, Barber's typology gained credence because his analysis of President Nixon—at the time engulfed in the Watergate crisis—appeared to account so well for Nixon's dysfunctional behaviour.

Barber's typology has since been explored in relation to Australian leaders. Was Prime Minister Gough Whitlam, for instance, an active–positive leader (see Walter 1980: 181–3)? Is Prime Minister John Howard, who calls himself 'the one who wins the battles', an active–negative type (see further below, and Walter 2004: 20)?

Graham Little, an Australian political scientist with expertise in psychology, has illuminated mainstream politics with a sophisticated model of what he called 'political ensembles' linked to 'political climates' that favour the success of one type of political ensemble rather than another (Little 1985). Little's typology of 'political ensembles' crystallises around '*strong*', '*group*' or '*inspiring*' leaders. Each leader, and each ensemble, has a characteristic way of addressing relations between 'self' and 'others'—indeed, ensembles are formed because they share a common assumption about how to address this relationship, and recognise a leader who expresses their common project.

The '*strong*' leader sees self–other relations as competitive, favouring structure and firm direction as a way of managing this dilemma, but will identify threats and battles that must be fought. This shares aspects of Barber's active–negative type. Little's example of a 'strong leader' was Prime Minister Malcolm Fraser. The '*group*' leader sees relations as 'self-in-other' (the sense of self is only achieved in relation to other people) and emphasises shared needs and interdependence, valuing loyalty and collective solutions (with some similarities to Barber's passive–positive type). Little's example of a 'group leader' was Jim Cairns in his role as an anti-Vietnam War campaigner in the late 1960s and early 1970s prior to becoming Deputy Prime Minister in the Whitlam Labor government. The '*inspiring*' leader believes that self and other can be held together in mutual rapport, different and equal, capable of engaging together in mutual adventure, perhaps chiming with Barber's adaptive, active–positive leader. Little's example of an 'inspiring leader' was Prime Minister Gough Whitlam. Again, pure types will be rare; most of us (and most leaders) will mix these inclinations.

Where Lasswell and Barber looked, in different ways, at political work, Little's contributions remind us that leadership success depends on a resonance with followers' needs, and that we should focus our attention on the way shared world views (the world as competitive, needing structure; or the world as a collective where belonging should be valued; or the world as a platform for exploring individual potentials) are at the heart of what makes a group coherent. Further, political climates will tend to favour particular leaders (and the dominance of particular ensembles) at particular times. For instance, in hard times or times of challenge, where aggression seems an appropriate measure, 'strong' directive leaders may be favoured (e.g. Fraser after the oil crisis and economic dislocations of the mid-1970s and Howard more recently in relation to concerns about terrorism and border security). Where the mood is more expansive, the tenor up-beat, an 'inspiring' leader' may gain the lead (e.g. Whitlam during the last years of the postwar boom). But can the truly gifted leader change the political climate (as with President Roosevelt 'inspiring' Americans to adopt his radical 'New Deal' package of policy reforms in the face of the 1930s Depression)?

Yet another academic approach has been to look at group processes as they relate to decision making in leadership groups themselves. An influential and hotly contested example is Irving Janis's theory of *groupthink* (Janis 1972). Seeking to understand the sources of various 'policy' mistakes, Janis came to the conclusion that high cohesiveness and a concurrence-seeking tendency within a decision-making group (such as a Cabinet) can interfere with critical thinking and produce the syndrome that he dubbed groupthink.

Typical indicators of groupthink are: the group's commitment to consensus or compliance with directive leadership, which preclude the open examination of alternative or dissenting views; selective utilisation of confirming information; a drive for quick and painless unanimity on issues the group has to confront; the suppression of personal doubts; a belief in the inherent morality of the group; the emergence of 'mindguards' who police group orthodoxies; and a view of opponents as evil.

Some critics have been unconvinced by Janis's theory (Aldag & Fuller 1993; Turner & Pratkanis 1998). But it has recently come to public prominence again in relation to government decisions in Britain and the United States in 2002 to promulgate the Iraq war. Inquiries in each country came to the conclusion that 'groupthink' had played a role in the acceptance by leadership groups of manifestly inadequate evidence.

Australia's political leaders: academic analyses

There have been several attempts to sketch Australian typologies of political leadership. An early example was Sol Encel's characterisation of Australia's Prime Ministers as either *'larrikins'* or *'prima donnas'* (Encel 1974: 170–1). The *larrikins*—tough, independent, irreverent, aggressively masculine—have a talent for down-to-earth speaking, contempt for ideas or ideals, but love the cut and thrust of politics. Prime Ministers Reid, Fadden, Hughes and Gorton were Encel's exemplars in this category. *Prima donnas*, in contrast, evince an air of superiority that is odd in a community said to be 'self-consciously egalitarian'. Encel was unsure whether Australians' characteristic suspicion of authority drove these men to assert their right to wield it, or if it was relative lack of competition that induced a sense of 'absolute superiority'. He assigned Prime Ministers Deakin, Bruce, Curtin, Menzies and Whitlam to this category.

Encel's typology does no more than describe patterns. It does little to help us understand which of these types is effective and in what circumstances, though it is interesting to ponder how our political leaders since 1974 (when Encel wrote) might be assigned to his categories.

Graham Maddox (2000: 490–1) has posited an alternative typology of *'initiators'* (conquerors, entrepreneurs and/or lawgivers, such as Prime Ministers Deakin and Chifley); *'protectors'* (those who guarantee our security under threat, like Prime Minister Curtin); and *'maintainers'* (whose role has been to preserve an enduring stability, like Prime Minister Menzies). The maintainers, he argues, have been Australia's most successful leaders.

While Encel and Maddox illuminate character projection and associated working patterns, neither attempts to account for the drive underlying such leadership preferences. Maddox attempts to link the ascendance of types with the political climates, but neither analyses the strengths and weaknesses of their types nor attempts to predict performance, and they make few connections with debates about leadership typologies in, for instance, the US tradition (see Lasswell 1930 above, Barber 1972 above).

There is more sophistication evident in recent biographies of individual leaders, drawing on leadership studies and on psychoanalytic theory.

James Walter's exploration of the strengths and the weaknesses of Gough Whitlam as a leader who simply never learned to be small, and who thus could inspire others but would eventually be brought down by his failure to recognise realistic limitations, is one example (Walter 1980). Drawing on contemporary developments in theories of narcissism, Walter attempted explicitly to engage the reader in the debate about interpretation.

Judith Brett's influential psychoanalytic study of our longest-serving prime minister, Sir Robert Menzies (Brett 1992), broke new ground in concentrating on his message—what it meant (psychologically) for him, and why it appealed to a postwar constituency that Menzies characterised as 'the forgotten people'. Brett's analyses of Menzies and of John Howard (Brett 2003: ch. 9) are among the most innovative studies of effective leadership through the creative use of language, with these leaders mobilising support by articulating what certain followers implicitly 'recognise' but have not heretofore expressed.

Don Watson's perceptive insider account of Paul Keating's Prime Minister-ship (Watson 2002) makes use of psychoanalytic insights into depression. He delineates not only how Keating's decisions were made (and fudged) but also how his leadership style illuminates the political climate in which he acted.

Australian contributions to theoretical studies of leadership have been limited. John Kane (2001) has demonstrated that a leader's legitimacy will depend upon a capacity to generate and maintain 'moral capital' that is acknowl-edged by followers, but none of his examples are Australian. John Uhr (2002 & 2003) has shown how indispensable an appreciation of a leader's rhetoric is in understanding leadership, though he acknowledges that it is 'not the only element' in a satisfactory account. Graham Little's revelatory analysis of 'strong', 'group' and 'inspiring' leaders and their 'political ensembles' has been discussed above (Little 1985). His later study of British Prime Minister Margaret Thatcher, US President Ronald Reagan and Australian Prime Minister Malcolm Fraser as exemplars of the 'strong leader' in action illuminated the political tran-sitions of the 1980s (Little 1988). Little's trenchant portrait of Thatcher as the strong leader *par excellence,* adapting the conventional traits to her own ends, indicated that women could dominate by beating men at their own game. Alan Davies (1980), in an encyclopaedic study, showed how leaders drew on the skills defined by Lasswell (as agitators, administrators or theorists); capitalised on shared outlooks; and 'sculpted' with emotion; his book is peppered with Australian examples throughout.

Good leadership and effective institutions

Everything reviewed above indicates that good political leadership—that is, leadership that utilises power to achieve what is perceived as the public good (rather than simply satisfying a leader's ambitions); leadership that not only responds to democratic expectations but is also properly communicative, facili-tating informed citizen judgment—depends on effective institutions. Indeed, institutional deficiency so marked as to give a leader unlimited licence is a defining feature of dangerous regimes such as that of the ill-starred Saddam Hussein in Iraq (Glad 2002).

Social complexity and the need for organisational efficiency *will* produce elites even in democratic polities (Weber 1922, and see also Gilding's Chapter 20 in this book). But if elites can be held to account, if transparency can be maintained, and if citizen judgment can be exercised, the risk of elite dominance can be contained. Leaders may not always be wise or principled, and some proportion of them may be driven by an investment in power for its own sake, but we can profit from their ambition as long as they are constrained to work with others. For example, political parties, parliamentary scrutiny, and Cabinets negotiating collective decisions and committed to Ministerial responsibility all serve to curb leadership excess. Processes like groupthink might capture even wise leaders, committed to good ends, if policy debate is not vigorous and competitive, if multiple options are not examined, and if inner-circle assumptions are not challenged. The checks and balances of liberal democracy, and the accompanying conventions of party, public service, Cabinet and parliamentary processes, are intended to encourage good leadership and to hedge against leadership caprice.

This brings us back to the question raised in the introduction to this chapter: how effective are they?

Until the 1970s, the general attitudes of members of the public to leaders were benign; people seemed to accept that they knew what they were doing (Aitkin 1977; Kemp 1978). That relatively benign view no longer prevails. By the late 1990s, 74 per cent of survey respondents had little confidence in the federal government; 84 per cent distrusted both major parties; and there had been a 30 per cent drop in confidence in government over the preceding 13 years (Papadakis 1999; Marsh & Yencken 2004: 28–30). A survey of 'middle Australia' (Pusey 2003) showed that there is more consistent support for old economic institutions than for the new market-based and deregulated institutional arrangements advocated by political elites; and that, overall, reformers have not won consensus for 'the new consensus'. Peter Saunders (2002: 264) has summarised an extensive survey of social attitudes by remarking on 'a sense of alienation and powerlessness in which a gulf has opened up between the values and priorities of ordinary Australians and those in positions of political power and influence'. Elite opinion and public opinion have diverged.

Arguably, institutional developments that have made leaders more dominant, and the institutions that ensured that they acted in 'our' interests less effective, impel this diminution in confidence. Parliament, parties, the public policy process and the role of the Prime Minister are at the heart of this disquiet.

In the past 30 years, according to various studies of political parties (Jaensch 1994; Marsh 1995: Ward 1991; Katz & Mair 1995), our major political parties have changed in structure, style and character. They used to be characterised as so-called *mass parties* which had clear programmatic ideologies and an extensive membership. But they changed to become *catch-all parties* (attempting to net a broad constituency by matching policy to public mood) and later *electoral professional parties* (relying on communications professionals and expert advisers rather than party activists) and perhaps *cartel parties* ('part of the state apparatus itself' (Katz & Mair 1995: 14)). There is contestation over the extent to which such descriptions apply (see, for instance, Goot 2003), but all analysts agree that the dominant parties are now capital intensive, professional, centralised and dependent on the projection of leader effectiveness. Party branches, conferences, policy committees and the like have been supplanted, and the capacity for ordinary members to feel they can be heard has withered away. The networks of advice and support, capital generation and communication centre on the leader rather than the party at large. This gives the leader a licence and impact unmatched in former party structures.

Party transitions have been complemented by changes in the role of the Prime Minister. Ian McAllister (2004: 2) remarks 'that prime ministers and opposition leaders have replaced many of the roles historically played by political parties in ensuring the efficient operation of the parliamentary system'. Weaker voter attachments enhance the role of the leader. With partisan dealignment, party leaders 'stand in' for the role that parties used to play in representing issues, integrating interests and mobilising opinion. As parties of mass organisation with local branches have declined, voter attention has shifted from the local to the national stage, with parties shifting their emphasis from local to national leaders in parallel. There is less focus on policy, and more on the personality of the leader. Leadership effects on voting outcomes are now widely recognised.

In government, the complexity of modern decision making has shifted the emphasis towards charisma, authority and decision, and away from collegial consensus: the Prime Minister has thus become far more than the 'first among equals' (see Weller 1985). With the declining influence of party structures, the Prime Minister's power over political careers (and hence as the driver of party discipline and object of loyalty) has been much enhanced. The Prime Minister has become 'central in how responsible government operates; he or she may choose to include or exclude particular actions under the doctrine, thereby determining [a] minister's fate . . . [T]he prime minister, rather than the parliament . . . determines how the doctrine is implemented' (McAllister 2004: 5). Arguably, globalisation plays a part: 'parliamentary systems are becoming more presidential in character, style and operation, as the environments in which they operate become more uniform' (McAllister 2004: 8; see also Marsh 2003).

There is little doubt that the public service within Westminster-type political systems has become more compliant of late, and in the Australian case, more politicised. (For more discussion of this proposition, see Chapter 6 in this book.) Reforms to the Australian public service, intended to make it more responsive to the government of the day, began under Labor governments in the 1970s and 1980s. Labor Prime Minister Gough Whitlam (1972–1975) introduced expanded ministerial staff (Walter 1986). Under the Hawke Labor government (1983–1991), a key measure was the shift of career public servants at the top levels to contract appointments (Keating 2003). The government under Coalition Prime Minister John Howard has simply continued since 1996 where Labor governments began. But that Departmental Secretaries (Departmental chief executive officers) now serve at their Minister's pleasure was signalled by the sacking of a number immediately upon Howard's assumption of office, and a later controversial dismissal of (and unsuccessful legal appeal by) a well-regarded career officer who was effective, but not to his Minister's liking. (The case in question was that of the dismissal of, and appeal by, Paul Barratt, Secretary of the Department of Defence: see Weller 1999; Richardson 2000.) The perception that public-spirited career civil servants have been replaced by political appointees is inevitable.

The picture is further clouded by the increasing augmentation of public servants by partisan ministerial staff (see also Chapter 6 in the book). Originally introduced to maximise sources of advice, to provide alternative options and critical dissent rather than to impose concurrence-seeking behaviour (see Walter 1986), ministerial staff have arguably come to have the opposite effect (see Keating 2003; Weller 2002). Their ability to intervene in departmental processes; to mediate between the political and administrative domains; to drive, sieve and skew advice; to insist upon what the Minister wants (as opposed to the public interest or the integrity of government) has amplified concern about public sector reform.

What have been the effects on leadership behaviour? One indicator, in relation to the Howard Coalition government, is the prevalence of commentary on the fraught issue of truth in government.

Most such commentary is provoked by incidents that call to mind the way that Prime Minister Howard and his Ministers handled the so-called 'children overboard' affair (2001), the use of intelligence in the presentation of the case for war in Iraq (2002/3), instances of adverse and peremptory confrontation of dissenting public servants (for instance, the pressure for Federal Police Commissioner, Mick Keelty, to rectify his comments on terrorism in 2003 and the attack on the credibility of former public servant Mike Scrafton in 2004) and denial of timely knowledge about the abuse of Iraqi detainees (2004). Some of these issues have been analysed in detail—see for instance Patrick Weller's book on the 'children overboard' affair (Weller 2002), or the Parliamentary Joint Committee report (2004) and the Flood report (2004) on intelligence in relation to the case for war in Iraq. In most cases only disclosures by the press and in Senate committees brought the truth to light: doyenne of the Canberra press gallery Michelle Grattan remarked, 'If it had been left to the PM, we'd never have found out' (Grattan 2004).

All these cases raise the issues of information, communication and truth, and the proper role of the executive. Even if one accepts that the government whole-heartedly believed in what it was doing, it is clear in such instances that it was economical in what it would divulge, chose evidence that suited a preordained purpose rather than heeding more cautious advice, used ministerial staff to filter information and to police the party line, refused to hear evidence that would contradict its stance (thus being able to claim it 'didn't know' when evidence ran against it—the tactic of 'plausible deniability') and expected concurrence from its public servants rather than frank and fearless advice. Notice how closely such tactics parallel the behaviour described earlier as groupthink—indeed inquiries into similar patterns in the UK and the USA described it thus.

Whether the case for groupthink is persuasive or not, such propensities subvert due process; in challenging the division between politics and administration they erode the integrity of the system; they deny accountability; they evade transparency and so impede the capacity for citizen judgment. Such practices have emerged from institutional transitions that have undermined the entities and conventions that served to constrain leadership.

Formerly, the conventions of political practice—in the traditional party democracy—facilitated reasonably robust policy decisions. While no government would perfectly have met the pattern of broad expectations, these expectations pushed behaviour in certain ways. The need to connect a personal agenda with a broad philosophy, to carry party followers with you by negotiated support (through, for instance, party forums) and by showing how current action connects with common goals was one form of check on leadership caprice. The tradition of collective authority and ministerial responsibility ensured debate, consensus and accountability. The separation of politics and administration and the belief in the function of the public service to deliver disinterested advice with a degree of independence expanded options (there were always partisan sources whose inputs could be weighed alongside those of the public service). All of the above imposed threshold requirements—winning the party, gaining Cabinet support, acknowledging responsibility for decisions, balancing competing options from partisan and public service advice—that were an incentive for periodic reality checks and a restraint on leaders.

Arguably, those requirements also limited the more adverse proclivities of particular power-oriented leadership types, such as those identified by, for instance, Lasswell, Barber and Little (as discussed earlier). The changes reviewed here have weakened such threshold requirements. They have given greater momentum to personalised leadership, allowing leadership tendencies relatively free rein while diminishing the incentive for reality checks. In short, as institutions become less effective, leaders may tip the balance within what I earlier called the leadership quandary, pursuing what they regard as imperative at the expense of their group's objectives and needs. This may, as suggested above, foster actions that recklessly engender cynicism (and undermine confidence in democratic institutions); tactics that create a vacuum where accountability should be; and practices that deny transparency.

It may well be that there is a confluence between contemporary circumstances and Prime Minister Howard's leadership style. He is a fighter who thrives on crisis and transforms policy problems 'from a matter of calculation of results to a matter of emotional loyalty to ideals . . . [whose] view of reality must be accepted else the cause fall apart' (Barber 1972, describing one of the traits of the active–negative leader). But Howard is not the catalyst for the institutional changes observed; they have been evolving since the 1970s. Public sector reform began then, and party change even earlier. The tenor of what was to come (leader-dominated hard-ball politics) was most clearly signalled in the memoir of Hawke government Minister Graham Richardson, *Whatever It Takes* (Richardson 1994). The sheer aggression of Labor Prime Minister Paul Keating's attempts to box-in the Coalition Opposition by defining issues in ways it could not accommodate was a prelude to the ruthlessness with which Howard would later, as Prime Minister, reverse the valencies of political discourse to disable the ALP (Brett 2003; 2005).

It will not have escaped the reader that, though leadership styles differ (as, say, between US President George W. Bush, British Prime Minister Tony Blair and Australian Prime Minister John Howard), the pattern of a manipulative leadership politics and its outcome in different countries is remarkably similar (on the UK, for instance, see Foley 2000; Sampson 2004). The idiosyncrasies of our leaders and their inner circles have determined the vicissitudes of the war on terror. The strength of leader conviction has driven the misuse of intelligence. The urgency of their self-belief has dictated obedience rather than initiative (or dissent) among their advisers. The certainty of being right has fuelled manipulation and, when challenged, deception. And all of these traits have provoked cynicism and distrust within the polity.

The challenge today is not only to understand leadership, but also to insist upon the renovation of institutions that will serve as a hedge against leadership dominance.

REFERENCES

Aitkin, D. 1977, *Stability and Change in Australian Politics*, ANU Press, Canberra.
Aldag, R.J. & Fuller, S.R. 1993, 'Beyond Fiasco: A Reappraisal of the Groupthink Phenomenon and a New Model of Group Decision Processes', *Psychological Bulletin*, vol. 113, no. 3, pp. 533–52.
Barber, J.D. 1972, *The Presidential Character: Predicting Performance in the Whitehouse*, Prentice-Hall, Englewood Cliffs, N.J.
Bion, W.R. 1961, *Experience in Groups*, Tavistock, London.
Brett, J. 1992, *Robert Menzies' Forgotten People*, Pan Macmillan, Sydney.
Brett, J. 2003, *Australian Liberals and the Moral Middle Class*, Cambridge University Press, Melbourne.
Brett, J. 2005, *Relaxed and Comfortable: The Liberal Party's Australia*, Quarterly Essay no. 19, Black Inc., Melbourne.
Burns, J.M. 1978, *Leadership*, Harper and Row, New York.

Davies, A.F. 1980, *Skills, Outlooks and Passions*, Cambridge University Press, Melbourne.

Elcock, H. 2001, *Political Leadership*, Edward Elgar, Cheltenham.

Encel, S. 1974, *Cabinet Government in Australia*, 2nd edn, Melbourne University Press, Melbourne.

Flood, P. 2004, *Report of the Inquiry into Australian Intelligence Agencies*, Australian Government, Canberra.

Foley, M. 2000, *The British Presidency: Tony Blair and the Politics of Public Leadership*, Manchester University Press, Manchester.

Glad, B. 2002, 'Why Tyrants Go Too Far: Malignant Narcissism and Absolute Power', *Political Psychology*, vol. 23, no. 1, pp. 1–20.

Goot, M. 2003, 'Helped or Hindered? Pauline Hanson's One Nation Party and the Cartelisation Thesis', Australasian Political Studies Association Conference, Hobart, refereed paper, at <http://www.utas.edu.au/government/APSA/MGootfinal.pdf>, accessed April 14, 2005.

Grattan, M. 2004, 'The White Gloves of Ignorance', *The Age*, 2 June.

Greenstein, F. 1982, *The Hidden Hand Presidency*, Basic, New York.

Greenstein, F. 2000, *The Presidential Difference: Leadership Style From FDR to Clinton*, Free Press, New York.

Hook, S. 1943/1955, *The Hero in History*, Beacon, Boston.

Jaensch, D. 1994, *Power Politics: Australia's Party System*, Allen & Unwin, Sydney.

Janis, I. L. 1972, *Victims of Groupthink*, Houghton Mifflin, Boston.

Kaarbo, J. 1997, 'Prime Minister Leadership Styles in Foreign Policy Decision-Making: A Framework for Research', *Political Psychology*, vol. 18, no. 3, pp. 553–81.

Kane, J. 2001, *The Politics of Moral Capital*, Cambridge University Press, Cambridge.

Katz, R. & Mair, P. 1995, 'Changing Models of Party Organization and Party Democracy: The Emergence of the Cartel Party', *Party Politics*, vol. 1, no. 1, pp. 5–28.

Keating, M. 2003, 'The Public Service and the Management of the Public Sector', in *The Hawke Government: A Critical Retrospective*, eds S. Ryan & T. Bramston, Pluto Press, North Melbourne, pp. 367–80.

Kemp, D. 1978, *Society and Electoral Behaviour in Australia*, University of Queensland Press, St Lucia.

Latham, M. 1998, *Civilising Global Capital: New Thinking for Australian Labor*, Allen & Unwin, St Leonards.

Latham, M. 2001, *What Did You Learn Today?: Creating an Education Revolution*, Allen & Unwin, Crows Nest.

Latham, M. 2003, *From the Suburbs: Building a Nation from our Neighbourhoods*, Pluto Press, Annandale.

Lasswell, H.D. 1930/1977, *Psychopathology and Politics*, University of Chicago Press, Chicago and London.

Lasswell, H.D. 1936/1950, *Politics: Who Gets What, When, How*, Peter Smith, New York.

Lasswell, H.D. 1948/1976, *Power and Personality*, Greenwood Press, Westport, Conn.

Little, G. 1985, *Political Ensembles: A Psychosocial Approach to Politics and Leadership*, Oxford University Press, Melbourne.

Little, G. 1988, *Strong Leadership: Thatcher, Reagan and an Eminent Person*, Oxford University Press, Melbourne.

Maddox, G. 2000, *Australian Democracy in Theory and Practice*, 4th edn, Longman, Frenchs Forest.

Marsh, I. 1995, *Beyond the Two Party System*, Cambridge University Press, Melbourne.

Marsh, I. 2003, 'Consensus in Australian Politics', in *Australia's Choices: Options for a Fair and Prosperous Society*, ed. I Marsh, UNSW Press, Sydney.

Marsh I. & Yencken, D. 2004, *Into the Future: The Neglect of the Long Term in Australian Politics*, Australian Collaboration/Black Inc., Melbourne.

McAllister, I. 2004, 'Political Leaders in Westminster Systems', in Technical Report Seminars, Political Science Program, RSSS, ANU at <http://eprints.anu.edu.au/archive/00002580/>, Canberra.

Neustadt, R. E. 1990, *Presidential Power and the Modern Presidents*, Free Press, New York.

Papadakis, E. 1999, 'Constituents of Confidence and Mistrust in Australian Institutions', *Australian Journal of Political Science*, vol. 34, no. 1, pp. 75–94.

Parliamentary Joint Committee on ASIO, ASIS and DSD 2004, *Intelligence on Iraq's Weapons of Mass Destruction*, Parliament of the Commonwealth of Australia, Canberra.

Pusey, M. 2003, *The Experience of Middle Australia*, Cambridge University Press, Melbourne.

Richardson, G. 1994, *Whatever It Takes*, Bantam, Sydney.

Richardson, J. 2000, 'Defenceless Secretaries—A Commentary on the Barratt Case', *Canberra Bulletin of Public Administration*, no. 97, pp. 5–6.

Sampson, A. 2004, *Who Runs this Place? The Anatomy of Britain in the 21st Century*, John Murray, London.

Saunders, P. 2002, *The Ends and Means of Welfare: Coping with Economic and Social Change in Australia*, Cambridge University Press, New York.

Stogdill, R. 1974, *Handbook of Leadership*, Free Press, New York.

Turner, M.E. & Pratkanis, A.R. 1998, 'Twenty-Five Years of Groupthink Theory and Research: Lessons from the Evaluation of a Theory', *Organizational Behavior and Human Decision Processes*, vol. 73, no. 2/3, pp. 105–15.

Uhr, J. 2002, 'Political Leadership and Rhetoric', in *Australia Reshaped: 200 Years of Institutional Transformation*, eds G. Brennan & F.G. Castles, Cambridge University Press, Melbourne, pp. 261–94.

Uhr, J. 2003, 'Just Rhetoric? Exploring the Language of Leadership', in *Management, Organisation and Ethics in the Public Sector*, eds P. Bishop, C. Connors, C.J.G. Sampford, & C. Sampford, Ashgate, Aldershot, ch. 7.

Walter, J. 1980, *The Leader: A Political Biography of Gough Whitlam*, University of Queensland Press, St. Lucia.

Walter, J. 1986, *The Ministers' Minders: Personal Advisers in National Government*, Oxford University Press, Melbourne.

Walter, J. 2004, 'Why Howard Goes too Far: Institutional Change and the Renaissance of Groupthink', Australasian Political Studies Association Conference, Adelaide, refereed paper, at <http://www.adelaide.edu.au/apsa/docs_papers/Aust%20Pol/Walter.pdf>, accessed May 19, 2005.

Ward, I. 1991, 'The Changing Organisational Nature of Australia's Political Parties', *Journal of Commonwealth and Comparative Politics*, vol. 24, no. 2, pp. 153–74.

Watson, D. 2002, *Recollections of a Bleeding Heart: A Portrait of Paul Keating PM*, Knopf, Milsons Point, NSW.

Weber, M. 1922/1957, *The Theory of Social and Economic Organization*, ed. T. Parsons, Free Press, New York.

Weller, P. 1985, *First Among Equals: Prime Ministers in Westminster Systems*, Allen & Unwin, Sydney.

Weller, P. 1999, 'In Hot Pursuit of a Departmental Secretary: The Barratt Case', *Canberra Bulletin of Public Administration*, no. 93, pp. 4–8.

Weller, P. 2002, *Don't Tell the Prime Minister*, Scribe Publications, Carlton North.

Winter, D.G. 1973, *The Power Motive*, Free Press, New York.

Wolfenstein, E.V. 1967, *The Revolutionary Personality*, Princeton University Press, Princeton, N.J.

Interest groups and political lobbying

Introduction

An *interest group* is an association of individuals or organisations which attempts to influence government and public policy without seriously seeking election to Parliament. Interest groups are sometimes called other names such as *pressure group* or *lobby group* or *NGO* (non-government organisation). Their attempts to influence public policy occur in a variety of ways and are called *lobbying*. An individual *lobbyist* is a person who represents an interest to government in order to exert influence in that group's favour. Lobbyists can be interest-group employees or they can be paid intermediaries or volunteers.

A well-functioning liberal democracy accommodates interest groups and lobbying because these activities facilitate and encourage citizen participation and help to maintain genuine and democratic competition between interests. While citizens can always participate as individuals in the democratic process, they can also choose for reasons of greater effectiveness to participate via group membership.

Participation via interest groups may involve fewer individuals than does compulsory voting in elections, but it certainly involves more than those who participate through membership of political parties, the other medium of collective action in a liberal democracy. Moreover, interest-group participation is generally deeper and more frequent than voting. This extra dimension of participation within a liberal-democratic system arguably helps to compensate for some of the limitations of the parliamentary system of representative government, which some critics claim includes undesirable levels of apathy, cynicism and feelings of disconnection from the system. Many of the interest groups, from the labour movements in the 19th century through to the new social movements in the 20th and 21st centuries, arguably also provide a more expressive and attractive type of participation for motivated citizens through public activism such as media-oriented public protests.

Interest-group politics is pervasive. Turn on the television for a debate about a public issue like skill shortages in industry or the benefits of a minimum wage. Follow an election campaign, especially after the major parties' policy launches. Observe a protest march through the city streets. Sit in on a parliamentary committee public hearing or a government community consultation. In all these cases, public participation will be dominated or organised by interest-group staff or office-bearers. They are the obvious point of contact when government or Parliament or the media are seeking input or a reaction from a representative, rather than a random, citizen.

Interest groups

Interest groups form and grow naturally, and to some extent independently, to represent community interests. But they can only be understood in the context of government. Government action, itself often stimulated by organised public interests, often generates the formation or growth of interest groups. This has been the case throughout the modern history of Australia. For instance, elements of the so-called 'Australian settlement' following federation, such as the creation of the arbitration system, the Tariff Board and the rural marketing boards, generated the need for various organisations to represent the needs of those affected (Matthews 1994b; Kelly 1992). More recently, some decisions of the Family Court encouraged by the women's movement have generated the growth of countervailing men's groups (Sawer 2000).

Ian Marsh (1995) argues that such government-induced 'top down' formation of interest groups explains the longstanding pattern of groups operating in the labour, business and farm sectors. In many cases, governments have favoured and encouraged interest groups as the most efficient means to discuss policy with a representative sample of a key interests. Where encouragement was not enough, such as with the representation of consumer interests, governments have actually set up and funded representative groups. Such government support and funding is surprisingly common. For instance, a recent survey reported that 29 per cent of NGOs in the welfare sector had full government funding and only 24 per cent had no government funding at all (Maddison, Dennis & Hamilton 2004).

Interest groups can be categorised in several ways. Given the dominance of political parties in Australian politics, one useful categorisation distinguishes between those which are close to one or other of the political parties (Matthews & Warhurst 1993). The structures for group–government interaction, such as departmental consultative mechanisms, tend to incorporate the favoured groups much more than others. Changes of government between Labor and the Coalition can dramatically influence the fortunes of an interest group tradition-ally allied to one party or another.

An alternative classification of groups might recognise that they form and operate at different levels: some are local, others State, national or international. Some groups prominent in Australian politics, like Amnesty International and Greenpeace, are branches of international organisations. In Australia's federal system, many groups active at the national level are federations of State-based groups. Groups relate to governments at their respective levels. While there are connections between levels, this distinction has a great deal of practical significance.

Another way to categorise interest groups is to look at the nature of the interests that they claim to represent. A distinction is commonly made between *sectional groups* and *promotional groups*. Sectional groups claim to represent the interests of particular sections of society, while promotional groups claim to promote particular ideas and values.

Among sectional groups, three long-established groupings—those represent-ing business, labour and farmers—are sometimes highlighted as *producer groups* because of their integration into the production side of the economy. They tend to be powerful, well-resourced, and generally very experienced and comfortable in dealing as insiders with government. Over the years, their ambit of represen-tation has expanded to give, for example, greater representation to sub-interests, such as white-collar unionism within the labour movement and small business within the business sector.

Other sectional groups may be based on occupations, such as groups representing particular professions like doctors or lawyers. Some groups repre-sent interests like the ex-service community (e.g. the Returned and Services League) and welfare clients and providers (e.g. the Australian Council for Social Service).

The groups classified as promotional groups exist to promote such ideas and causes as women's rights, protection of animals and the temperance movement. Some specific organisations (such as the RSPCA, the Royal Society for the Prevention of Cruelty to Animals) have been in existence for a long time. But many new groups emerged out of the so-called 'new social movements' from the 1960s onwards. Marsh (1995) identifies nine such movements. Two of them—the environmental and women's movements—have probably had the most influence on Australian politics. The others in Marsh's list are the peace, consumers, gay rights, animal liberation, ethnic, Aboriginal rights and New Right movements.

There is a danger of over-categorisation, which can oversimplify and mislead. Groups representing women's interests, for example, could possibly be understood as sectional as well as promotional. Groups in different categories may have much in common and may have learnt a great deal from each other in the style in which they go about their lobbying. Some sectional or producer groups have learned to harness popular strategies like the more successful promotional groups, while some of the promotional groups have become more institutionalised and professional like the more successful sectional groups. Furthermore, coalitions and alliances between producer and issue groups can be very important, such as cooperation between union, business and environmental groups in lobbying for so-called green jobs.

Many issues feature opposing groups in a symbiotic relationships with each other. Historically this has been the case of the relationship between unions and employer organisations. Other more recent examples include pro-choice and anti-abortion groups, and republican and monarchist groups. In the latter case, the formation of the Australian Republican Movement in 1991 was followed quickly by the emergence of Australians for Constitutional Monarchy in 1992. There are other examples of so-called counter-groups (Vromen & Gelber 2005: 370–4).

While each political issue has a different pattern of group politics, some groups stand out for the regularity and force of their interventions. Those with most leverage on economic questions at the national level lead the way. The most prominent groups in contemporary national politics would include the Australian Council of Trade Unions (ACTU), the National Farmers' Federation (NFF), the Business Council of Australia (BCA), the Australian Chamber of Commerce and Industry (ACCI), the Australian Industry Group (AIG), the Australian Council of Social Service (ACOSS), the Australian Medical Association (AMA), the Catholic Church and the Returned and Services League (RSL). Equivalent groups loom large at the State level. Some interests, including Aboriginal and Torres Strait Islanders, the churches and women, have more fragmented patterns of group representation.

A number of trends and tendencies have characterised interest-group dynamics over the past 30 or 40 years.

The more successful groups have become bigger, richer and with better resources. This is because of the tendency, encouraged by governments, for major interests to achieve greater unity through the formation of representative peak organisations at the national level. For instance, the ACTU has widened its support base considerably by incorporating the peak organisations that once represented white-collar unions, as well as bringing the last of the big formerly independent unions like the Australian Workers Union into the fold. Beneath the ACTU's umbrella, 25 'mega-unions' were formed during the 1980s out of hundreds of smaller unions (Peetz 1998). The National Farmers' Federation was formed via several amalgamations in 1979 (Connors 1996). The BCA was formed in 1983 after business interests were dissatisfied with the way that they were represented at the National Economic Summit convened by the Hawke Labor government. But growth can cause problems, because maintaining unity while representing a larger and more diverse range of interests can be difficult. For example, the pork producers decided to split off from the NFF.

Associated with this trend towards greater size and scale has been the corresponding tendency for interest-group leaders to be increasingly removed from their own grassroots members. Most attention has been focused on the travails of trade unions in this regard, and it has been put forward as one of the reasons for union membership falling substantially. But it is a frequent complaint within many groups that the grassroots members are not taken seriously enough.

Centralisation of interest groups in Canberra, the national capital, has steadily grown. More organisations have responded to the growth of Commonwealth government power by moving their headquarters to Canberra because of the personal contact and time saving that close proximity to public servants and Ministers brings. There are still, however, cogent reasons for maintaining close proximity to State governments and with the centres of population and economic activity in the two big State capitals, Sydney and Melbourne. Melbourne hosts the ACTU, the BCA and the Australian Conservation Foundation (ACF), for instance. Many groups remain federated rather than truly national, with the consequence that many State branches of groups, including the RSL and ACOSS, remain very strong and well staffed to deliver services to members within each of the States.

Successful interest groups have long recognised that interaction with modern government requires that they employ professionally trained and politically experienced senior staff. Such staff have often formerly been senior public servants who bring to their positions not only specialist knowledge but also an appreciation of the processes by which policy is made within government. Other sources of recruits include former politicians, political advisers and political journalists. Within the new social movements, some have experience working for international interest groups.

The incorporation of interest-group representatives into official advisory positions with the potential to influence government policies has grown steadily from the mid-1950s (Matthews 1976). Well established by the 1970s, this reached new heights under the so-called corporatist style of governance identified particularly with the Hawke Labor government (Moore 2003). The Hawke government formally consulted with major interest groups not just through its Economic Planning Advisory Council but also in a wide range of social fields, to the extent that Labor's own traditional supporters began to complain that they were being squeezed out (Burchell & Matthews 1991).

The Howard Coalition government may have reversed this trend somewhat; certainly some groups accustomed to easier access to government have discovered that they are apparently out of favour (Maddison, Dennis & Hamilton 2004). Some groups dependent upon government funding have been asked to sign contracts that, in return for the continuation of government funding, limited their freedom to criticise the government. The privatisation of some public services under the Howard government has enabled some charity groups and churches to successfully tender to participate in the delivery of government programs. This development, which has made some previously staunchly independent groups in effect the deliverers of government services, has been particularly controversial in relation to the delivery by so-called faith-based groups of services to the unemployed (e.g. the Salvation Army's 'Employment Plus' job network program).

Since the early 1970s, a pattern of interest-group disaffection with the major political parties has grown. Beginning with the Women's Electoral Lobby at the 1972 federal election, a new style of so-called *single-issue politics* has emerged in which groups have challenged voters to cast off their traditional allegiances to political parties which, by their nature, necessarily encompass a package of positions across a range of issues. Voters have been asked by these groups to vote for favoured candidates regardless of their party. The anti-abortion Right to Life Association adopted this tactic with some success. Even the NFF experimented with this approach, supporting candidates from various parties to signal its disaffection with the Coalition government, its traditional partner. This kind of single-issue activity has been common ever since the 1970s and indeed continues, though it now seems to have a lower profile as a possible avenue to influence election results.

Lobbying and lobbyists

Lobbying is the process by which groups and other political actors attempt to influence policies. It can be done directly, that is by a group's own personnel (the larger groups employing specialised government liaison officers), or through an intermediary such as one of many professional lobbying companies. Either way, the person involved is called a *lobbyist* (Cullen 1991; Sekuless 1984).

Pressure groups have been lobbying governments and legislatures since the beginnings of modern government. The largest groups, such as Associated Chambers of Manufactures of Australia, followed the Commonwealth government to Canberra when it shifted there from Melbourne in 1927. By the 1940s, one observer could paint the following picture: 'Governments come and go but the lobbyists continue to flutter around power, wherever it lies' (Crisp 1949: 59).

Given the highly protected nature of Australian industry, specialist trade and tariff consultants had set up businesses in Canberra from the late 1940s onwards. While the decline of protectionism has now meant less business for these lobbyists, a number of firms specialising in trade issues remain. They produce detailed submissions and make representations to government departments and agencies on behalf of individual firms and industry associations, seeking the best deal possible within the general rules. In the past, their business often meant dealing on behalf of clients with the Tariff Board or its successor the Industries Assistance Commission.

By the late 1960s a different type of lobbyist had emerged: a 'jack-of-all trades' operator dealing with a wider variety of issues. The first was Peter Cullen, whose background was as a political staffer. The number of such lobbyists mushroomed from then onwards. This is the type of lobbyist closest to the popular notion of freelance undercover agents. Labor Minister Mick Young was referring to them when he declared in 1983: 'Virtually unheard of at the beginning of the 1970s, lobbying has become a major profession in the national capital' (quoted in Warhurst 1987).

Such was the scope of the development that it attracted allied professions, such as lawyers and accountants as well as public relations and political communication specialists. More recent specialisations include media monitoring and events management. The big national law firms entered the field too from the 1970s onwards (Darke 1997). They can all be found in the telephone directory under a variety of headings, including Lobbyist, Government Relations, and Public Relations. Each of these names gives a clue to the type of activities involved.

By the early 21st century, lobbying has become increasingly specialised with some large firms offering a variety of services and smaller firms specialising in one aspect or the other, such as media or dealings with the public service.

Much of the work of lobbyists is beneath the surface, like an iceberg. The starting point for a lobbying campaign on behalf of a client may be a watching brief that defines the issue and guides further research. Then may follow advice to a client on how to proceed, such as setting up meetings with ministers and public servants and perhaps accompanying clients to such meetings. According to Cullen (1991), only in rare cases would the lobbyist actually personally represent the client.

The types of lobbying may be categorised usefully to distinguish between what Lloyd (1991) describes as 'political pressure' and 'rational persuasion'. The former can be characterised as 'outside or political work' and the latter as 'inside or administrative work'. Often the two types of lobbying will proceed side by side in the one cause. One will complement the other.

Political/outside work involves putting pressure on governments through influencing and mobilising public opinion. At election time, it may involve making threats to persuade voters to vote against the government. Invariably this involves the use of the mass media. Using the media is an art form in itself and can involve attempting to secure favourable reporting, organising letters to the editors of newspapers in the hope that they will be published, attempting to influence editorial comment or paid advertising.

Persuasive/inside work involves putting arguments to politicians and public servants. This can involve taking part in formal hearings by committees or tribunals through public submissions or speaking to potentially influential groups like party committees. It can also involve arranging private meetings where possible to explain the case to decision makers and to pass on relevant information.

The combination of skills necessary to engage successfully in such work is relatively uncommon. That is why effective lobbyists are in demand. The skills are learnt more on the job than from taking any particular university degree or professional training course.

The targets of lobbying vary according to the situation (Matthews & Warhurst 1993). But in general lobbying is directed towards those decision makers, officials and advisers who can influence the desired outcome. Determining just who that is in particular situations is part of the skill of a lobbyist. Within the Australian system, people with potential influence are normally part of the executive government, Ministers first and foremost and as well as those who advise them—public servants and ministerial advisers. Within executive government, considerable specialist knowledge is needed to be sure of the dynamics on any issue at any time. Whether or not the issue is a matter for an individual Minister or for the whole Cabinet, for instance, is just one of the possible questions. Another might be just which adviser or public servant is advising the Minister on this question.

Members of Parliament may be targeted at election time when they are particularly vulnerable, and especially in a close contest when the government needs every one of them to be re-elected. Once a government is re-elected, then Parliament is only influential if it has a means of holding the government accountable. While party discipline means this is unlikely within the governing party or coalition itself, opportunities can arise elsewhere in the case of a minority government dependent on Independents or in the case of a government that does not control its upper house. There have been many such cases in Australia in recent years. In the Australian Senate, for instance, for more than 20 years until July 2005 minor party and Independent Senators were particularly influential. But they lost that influence once circumstances changed with the Howard government securing a Senate majority, and so attention turned quickly to lobbying backbench government Senators instead.

Occasionally the courts are in a position to influence policy directly, but access is difficult and appearing before a court usually involves a client in considerable expense. In recent years, however, native title and anti-discrimination cases have seen status granted in the courts to submissions by Indigenous bodies, farmers' groups, the Catholic Church and the Women's Electoral Lobby to name just a few.

There are a number of other avenues, including the Opposition parties and State governments. The Opposition comes into its own when it has serious claims to winning the next election. State governments not only control their own jurisdictions but have leverage on issues, like the environment or industrial relations, where intergovernmental agreement is necessary.

Institutions: corporations and churches

The political lobbying world does not divide easily just into pressure groups and individuals. Another obvious group of lobbyists has an institutional basis. In contemporary Australian politics the two most prominent types of institutions are the large firms and the churches.

The business community is distinctive among interest groups in that it is composed of corporations and business associations working side by side. Where the firms are small, the associations have no competition. But where the firms are large, they will do much of their lobbying themselves directly. The Business Council of Australia (BCA) is a case in point. It is made up of the CEOs of the 100 largest companies, each of which would have its own extensive lobbying capacity which it would use for its own individual interests through its own in-house government relations departments, through its upper management and even through the members of its board of directors (Bell & Warhurst 1993). These large firms will only use the collective capacity of the BCA when they need extra support on an individual issue or with an issue, like tax reform, that clearly applies to all companies and that needs a broad representative voice. On tax reform, the BCA set up a special lobbying organisation, the Business Coalition for Tax Reform, in an alliance with 37 industry associations (Warhurst, Brown & Higgins 2000).

The other set of institutions that play a large political role are the churches, especially the Christian churches. Strictly speaking the umbrella pressure group representing these churches is the National Council of Churches. But most of the lobbying is not done collectively but by individual church leaders and church agencies. These churches are extremely complex organisations with many voices. Perhaps the most complex of all is the Catholic Church which has no agreed national voice (notwithstanding the existence of the Australian Catholic Bishops Conference) and which tends to be divided according to region and issue (Warhurst 2004) in a way that even the media find impossible to comprehend. So whichever Catholic agency or individual makes a statement is typically (and misleadingly) reported by the media as just 'the Catholic Church says'.

There are other institutions that do not fit comfortably into the pressure group schema. Some, like the Australian Vice-Chancellors Committee, represent semi-autonomous public-sector interests, or government business enterprises like the Australian Broadcasting Corporation. Each will frequently set out to 'lobby Canberra' (in the case of the AVCC from its own offices in Canberra).

Think tanks and the battle of ideas

An important element of all group lobbying has always been the battle of ideas. Groups rely on as deep an understanding and sympathy as possible prevailing in the wider community for the values for which they stand and represent, whether they be free enterprise, trade unionism, ecological values or religious faith. For this reason, many groups devote some of their time and resources to research, public education and ideological debate. The Minerals Council of Australia (MCA), for instance, produces curriculum materials for schools that explain the contribution of the mining industry in a favourable way. Explicitly and implicitly MCA sets out to counter the 'propaganda' of the environmental lobby in schools by providing its own 'propaganda' materials that assist teachers to take into account a pro-mining perspective.

There is a constellation of private research institutes that advocate public policies and, in effect, lobby government according to particular ideological principles. The most longstanding example is the Institute of Public Affairs (IPA), a Melbourne-based pro-business organisation active since the early 1940s and predating the Liberal Party with which its ideas tend to be most closely aligned. In the 1980s IPA was revitalised as part of the neoliberal intellectual and political movement (also known—to its critics at least—as the New Right). A more recent research institute also associated with neoliberal ideas is the Centre for Independent Studies, based in Sydney, and there are several others.

There are now a number of 'think tanks', including some, such as the Liberal Party's Menzies Foundation, sponsored by the political parties. The best known of the Left-inclined think tanks is the Australia Institute, based in Canberra. All such think tanks influence policy indirectly by shaping public attitudes, making them receptive to certain types of policies. At times they can also exercise a more direct influence by allying themselves on an issue with governments or political parties.

Governments and groups

Pressure groups are a constant irritant to governments. They can be as much the opposition as the Opposition party. They can bring to public debate a depth of expertise and experience that is often unmatched. At key points in the parliamentary year, such as at the time of the annual budget presentation, they are the sources to whom the media turn for expert critical commentary. Should they oppose a government action, they can add to the discomfort of governments and individual Ministers. Pressure groups concentrate on issues even when they are not in the limelight. Pressure groups have a long-term agenda that they attempt to feed into policy deliberations. When angered they can bring to any political fight considerable resources. The more powerful ones can run long-term campaigns on a general principle (such as the BCA on taxation reform), while at the same time they can marshal the facts for a debate about the detail of proposed legislation.

For these reasons governments do their best to keep pressure groups on their side by building a two-way relationship (Sawer & Jupp 1996). This may involve inviting group representatives on to government committees and giving groups advance warning of forthcoming legislation. Governments can try to avoid negative publicity by coopting groups on to the side of the government. If governments are wise, they try out new ideas on the major pressure groups before they seek to implement them.

There are, however, many other reasons for governments to be favourable towards groups. Groups offer an easily accessible representative view of a section of the community. That is why it is so important to governments that groups actually are reasonably representative of their claimed constituents. Their very existence makes the daily life of government easier because governments dislike having to deal with a fragmented, unrepresented sector. Umbrella interest groups make consultation practicable even at short notice. They make filling a representative position on a committee easier. They make 'selling' a policy to the community easier. Groups can provide information on request about their sector that is not available anywhere else. Whether it is the likely response to the privatisation of Telstra among farmers or the extent of sex education in Catholic schools, it is the relevant interest group that is typically the most reliable and authoritative source. Its support or acquiescence can be valuable to government in warding off other critics.

In certain circumstances, governments delegate to groups the right to administer government policies, such as the role of the Country Women's Association in drought relief funding. In some fields such as the media, and in some professions such as law and medicine, governments allow a degree of self-regulation by representative groups.

Faced with a situation in which a pressure group is either weak or non-existent, the government may move to rectify that situation by encouraging the formation or strengthening of groups, or even actually setting up and funding groups. This was how the Hawke government moved, for instance, in setting up both the Australian Federation of AIDS Organisations and the Consumers Health Forum (Altman 2001; Short 1998). Such groups run the risk of being incapacitated should a change of government bring a change of funding policy.

The Australia Institute has documented such a consequence for NGOs after the Howard government came to office in 1996 (Maddison, Dennis & Hamilton 2004).

The regulatory framework

The regulatory framework within which pressure group lobbying occurs is generally loose. There are few regulatory limitations on how groups go about their business, though trade unions are an important exception. Recent years have brought increasing demands elsewhere in the political system for greater transparency. Much of the attention has been directed at other participants in politics and policy making, such as Ministers, public servants and political parties. There are rules about ministerial codes of conduct, post-separation employment for public servants and public disclosure of donations to political parties. But these regulations, whatever their impact on political life, have virtually no impact on pressure group campaigns. On the other hand, it must be conceded that there have been no glaring examples of corruption to force greater regulation of groups and lobbying.

One occasion on which a government was forced to act was in 1983. And even then the outcome was inconsequential to most pressure groups and hardly threatening even to the intended target, lobbyists. The occasion was the so-called Ivanov Affair in which a lobbyist, former Labor Party National Secretary David Combe, became so entangled with the affairs of a Soviet diplomat that he was declared to be a security risk by the Australian Security Intelligence Organisation (Marr 1984). Not only was Combe declared *persona non grata* by the Hawke government, but the government took the opportunity to introduce a scheme to register lobbyists. Under the scheme, registration was limited just to intermediaries (i.e. paid lobbyists like Combe) who dealt with Ministers and public servants. Lobbying Members of Parliament could continue without registration, the two registers (domestic and foreign) were not open to public scrutiny, and only the actual contact meeting between the lobbyist and the target had to be registered. Any preliminary research and advice, the most common form of lobbyist work, was not covered by the legislation, and in any case the sanctions for noncompliance with the regulations were weak. Over time the limitations of this scheme became obvious to all involved (Warhurst 1987). When the Howard government took office in 1996 it was able to abolish the scheme with hardly any complaint from the Opposition (Warhurst 1998).

Limitations as representatives

If interest groups are to play a legitimate representative function in liberal-democratic politics, then they need to be reasonably representative of the interest for which they claim to speak. The community therefore has a legitimate interest not only in knowing the size of a group's membership but also in the degree of internal democracy which it practices. Historically trade unions have been the focus of this concern, while the business community has generally escaped it. Current Australian practice of trade union elections being conducted by the Australian Electoral Commission to ensure their integrity owes its genesis to past disputes over malpractice in union elections.

But some groups active in politics, such as some of the big Christian churches, make no claims to be democratic. They are unapologetically hierarchical organisations. Others, like Greenpeace, are organised in such a way that almost all of their so-called members are legally defined as merely 'supporters' and can take no part in voting within the organisation.

Even if they intend otherwise, it is common for the leaders of groups to become detached from their grassroots members. There is typically closer contact between interest-group leaders and government than between the leaders and their members, and leaders can be co-opted into a government-centric policy-making 'club'. For example, the Accord between the Hawke Labor government and the ACTU during the 1980s and early 1990s has been identified as a possible contributor to the decline in trade union membership because the Accord did not sufficiently value consultation within the union movement. The location of the federal government in Canberra, with interest group headquarters in the vicinity, may also contribute to this tendency, as may the gap in experience and expertise that often emerges between a professional class of group bureaucrat/leader and the ordinary group member.

Conclusion: interest groups and democracy

Critics of pressure-group politics draw attention to some important issues arising from their role within a liberal-democratic system. Two broad issues are particularly critical: the significance of inter-group inequality (especially the allegedly privileged position of business interests) and the dangers to broader community or majority interests of pressure groups promoting minority interests.

The American critic Charles Lindblom (1977) has described what he portrays as the privileged position that business pressure groups occupy. Because all group activity is embedded within a market economy, Lindblom argues that business groups enjoy unparalleled structural power in the sense that governments cannot afford to neglect their interests. Yet actual examples of the exercise of this postulated structural power are scarce, and there are counter-examples, such as the campaign for a consumption tax, of a relatively united business community struggling for 15 years to convince government of the merits of its case. Even after the Howard government decided to proceed, the terms of its

Goods and Services Tax legislation were altered due to the necessity for compromise with several Australian Democrat Senators to ensure its passage through the Senate.

Furthermore, a great deal of business lobbying involves competition between business firms rather than competition between business and the remainder of the community. The issue of structural power is irrelevant if the issue at stake involves firm versus firm competition for a government contract (Nicholas 2005) or competition between different business sectors such as the exporting and importing sectors fighting over protection for local industry.

Inequality of resources available to competing pressure groups undoubtedly makes for an unequal contest, and business as a sector can command great financial resources that can be committed to any political contest. Money buys professional staff, including lobbyists if need be. Even if devoted followers of social movements work for lower rates of pay, and even if government funds are used to try to even out the inequalities by giving financial resources for administrative expenses to underprivileged groups such as pensioners' organisations, this does little to correct the inherent inequalities. Likewise, the occasional *pro bono* work undertaken by lobbyists for good causes (such as Cullen's work almost 40 years ago on behalf of the Council for the Single Mother and Her Child), does not detract from this point (Cullen 1991).

Some critics have also claimed that there is a danger of so-called special interests unfairly outweighing broader interests within the political process. A frank expression of this view came in 1992 when then Liberal Party leader, John Hewson, railed against all special interest groups in his Alfred Deakin Lecture: 'The contemporary political debate does not pit pragmatists against ideologists—rather, it pits advocates for the national interest against captives of vested interest' (*Australian* 15 October 1992). In the same spirit, the Treasurer Peter Costello told an audience in 2005:

> Adam Smith famously said in *The Wealth of Nations* [that] people of the same trade seldom meet together even for merriment and diversion, but the conversation ends in a conspiracy against the public . . . Every time I see a lobbyist walking the halls of Parliament House I think of that quote. (*Australian* 23 June 2005; see Smith 1776/1976: vol. 1, bk. 1, ch. 10)

There is a possible danger of minority interests using pressure group politics to subvert majority opinion. This was a common criticism of anti-abortion and pro-environment groups at their peak in the 1980s. Pressure group politics reward intensity and energy rather than majority opinion. Marginal seat campaigning, for instance, can use the threat of a small number of voters changing their vote to extract concessions from a candidate or even a government.

Determining the overall impact of pressure groups and lobbyists can be quite difficult (Matthews 1994a). There is a good deal of self-promotion by pressure groups and lobbyists who are inclined to claim success even when their contribution to the outcome is probably quite small. What can be said with confidence is that governments continue to utilise groups, the lobbying industry continues to grow, and the number of active groups shows no signs of slackening off. Citizens continue to put their trust in groups as the most practical way to try to exert an influence beyond either periodic voting in elections, individual effort, or joining a political party. Yet it must be acknowledged that organisations do not speak with equal voices and that some parts of society are not effectively represented by organisations at all. This unevenness is both a cause and a reflection of the unequal distribution of power within Australian society.

REFERENCES

Altman, D. 2001, 'Representation, Public Policy and AIDS', in eds M. Sawer & G. Zappala, *Speaking for the People: Representation in Australian Politics*, Melbourne University Press, Carlton South, ch. 9.

Bell, S. & Warhurst, J. 1993, 'Business Political Activism and Government Relations in Large Companies in Australia', *Australian Journal of Political Science*, vol. 28, no. 2, July, pp. 201–20.

Burchell, D. & Mathews, R. 1991, *Labor's Troubled Times*, Pluto Press, Sydney.

Connors, T. 1996, *To Speak with One Voice*, National Farmers' Federation, Barton.

Crisp, L.F. 1949, *The Parliamentary Government of the Commonwealth of Australia*, Longmans Green, London.

Cullen, P. 1991, *No is Not an Answer: Lobbying for Success*, Allen & Unwin, North Sydney.

Darke, M. 1997, 'Lobbying by Law Firms: A Study of National Law Firms in Canberra', *Australian Journal of Public Administration*, vol. 56, no. 4, December, pp. 32–46.

Kelly, P. 1992, *The End of Certainty*, Allen & Unwin, St. Leonards.

Lindblom, C. 1977, *Politics and Markets*, Basic Books, New York.

Lloyd, C. 1991, in P. Cullen, *No is Not an Answer: Lobbying for Success*, Allen & Unwin, North Sydney, pp. 1–44.

Maddison, S., Dennis, R. & Hamilton, C. 2004, *Silencing Dissent: Non-Government Organisations and Australian Democracy*, The Australia Institute, Discussion Paper 65, June.

Marr, D. 1984, *The Ivanov Trail*, Nelson, Melbourne.

Marsh, I. 1995, *Beyond the Two Party System*, Cambridge University Press, Melbourne.

Matthews, T. 1976, 'Interest Group Access to the Australian Government Bureaucracy', in Royal Commission on Australian Government Administration, *Appendixes to the Report: Volume Two*, Australian Government Publishing Service, Canberra, pp. 332–65.

Matthews, T. 1994a, 'Interest Groups', in R. Smith ed. *Politics in Australia*, Allen & Unwin, St. Leonards, 3rd edn.

Matthews, T. 1994b, 'Employers' Associations, Corporatism and the Accord: The Politics of Industrial Relations', in eds S. Bell & B. Head, *State, Economy and Public Policy in Australia*, Oxford University Press, South Melbourne.

Matthews, T. & Warhurst, J. 1993, 'Australia: Interest Groups in the Shadow of Strong Parties', in C. Thomas ed. *First World Interest Groups*, Greenwood Press, Westport, Connecticut, pp. 81–95.

Moore, T. 2003, 'Hawke's Big Tent: Elite Pluralism and the Politics of Inclusion', in eds

S. Ryan & T. Bramston, *The Hawke Government*, Pluto Press, North Melbourne, pp. 112–27.

Nicholas, K. 2005, 'Frantic Jockeying for the Telstra Tart', *The Australian Financial Review*, January 22–3.

Peetz, D. 1998, *Unions in a Contrary World*, Cambridge University Press, Melbourne.

Sawer, M. 2000, 'Women: Gender Wars in the Nineties', in eds M. Simms & J. Warhurst, *Howard's Agenda*, University of Queensland Press, St. Lucia.

Sawer, M. & Jupp, J. 1996, 'The Two-Way Street: Government Shaping of Community Based Advocacy', *Australian Journal of Public Administration*, vol. 55 no. 4, December, pp. 82–99.

Sekuless, P. 1984, *The Lobbyists*, Allen & Unwin, North Sydney.

Short, S. 1998, 'Community Activism in the Health Process: The Case of the Consumers Health Forum of Australia, 1987–96', in A. Yeatman ed. *Activism and the Policy Process*, Allen & Unwin, St. Leonards, ch. 6.

Smith, A. 1776/1976, *An Inquiry into the Nature and Causes of the Wealth of Nations*, Clarendon Press, Oxford.

Vromen, A. & Gelber, K. 2005, *Powerscape: Contemporary Australian Political Practice*, Allen & Unwin, Sydney.

Warhurst, J. 1987 'Lobbyists and Policy Making in Canberra', *Current Affairs Bulletin*, vol. 64, no. 3, August, pp. 13–19.

Warhurst, J. 1998, 'Locating the Target: Regulating Lobbying in Australia', *Parliamentary Affairs*, vol. 51, no. 4, October, pp. 538–50.

Warhurst, J. 2004, *The Catholic Church and Public Debate*, Catholic Social Justice Series 50, Australian Catholic Social Justice Council, North Sydney.

Warhurst, J., Brown, J. & Higgins, R. 2000, 'Tax Groupings: The Group Politics of Taxation Reform', in eds M. Simms & J. Warhurst, *Howard's Agenda*, University of Queensland Press, St. Lucia.

Government– business relations

ANDREW PARKIN AND LEONIE HARDCASTLE

CHAPTER 18

One of the most significant, and one of the most potentially troubling, dimensions of public life within liberal-democratic political systems is the relationship between government and the business sector. That key relationship is the subject of this chapter.

The chapter contemplates the capacity of the government-controlled public sector—and of the democratic politics that legitimises it—to exercise influence over the private business sector. The discussion needs to take into account the reverse direction of influence: how the business sector can shape, and potentially dominate, aspects of government. The chapter concludes with an assessment of debates about the overall balance: to what extent are government–business relations essentially antagonistic and to what extent can they be cooperative or complementary?

It is no accident that a liberal-democratic political system coexists with a strong private business sector. This is because respect for private enterprise and for the freedom of people to engage in profitable lawful business activities, without undue governmental constraint, is a key feature of liberal thinking. Indeed modern liberalism emerged in Western societies as the ideological voice of an entrepreneurial business class keen to shake off the shackles of traditional authoritarian governments. The liberty that is a core liberal principle is inextricably linked to a liberty to own private property, to conduct private business, and to accumulate private wealth in the process. This is a form of 'negative freedom' (see Chapter 2 of this book) that presupposes limitations on the reach of government.

But the evolution of liberal-democratic politics has seen this liberal respect for private liberty and business enterprise counterbalanced by a democratic insistence on a legitimate government sector accountable to citizens and sensitive to their welfare. Democratic politics encourages citizens to act collectively — not least to constitute the majority support for an election-winning party or coalition — and to demand that the government sector provides tax-funded public services and collective policy solutions.

How government affects business

In practice, the government and business sectors interact dynamically. It is helpful to disentangle some of the elements of this interaction, beginning in this section of the chapter with some of the key ways that government policies and actions affect business.

LEGAL INFRASTRUCTURE

Even a classical liberal of the most zealous pro-market persuasion needs to concede a defining role for government in providing a *legal infrastructure*. It is the government sector that enacts (through its legislative institutions), administers (through its executive institutions) and where necessary enforces (through its policing and judicial institutions) the legal basis for business activity and interaction. A robustly private-enterprise-based market sector needs a complex legal apparatus — ranging from commercial law to criminal law — that recognises and enforces contracts, maintains a viable system of currency, ensures that business transactions are based on genuine agreement rather than coercion, specifies the obligations of employers and employees, recognises the ownership of property and validates its trade, and so on. While some elements of this activity might conceivably be privatised — for example, in some countries (though not Australia) the money used in everyday transactions can consist of currency issued by private banks — the legal authority under which this happens seems to be irreducibly governmental.

It has become more widely accepted in recent years, even by the strongest defenders of private enterprise, that governments can have a further, somewhat paradoxical role, in establishing the legal infrastructure necessary to ensure *competitive* private markets. When liberal ideologists extol the 'public interest' merits of private markets, their case rests on the claimed virtues of competitive markets in determining what products need producing, and what their price should be, by calibrating supply and demand. But if there is an *un*competitive market — if, for example, a monopolistic or oligopolistic set of private suppliers dominates some essential industry like telecommunications or food retailing or electricity supply — then the supposed competitive check on prices and products is weakened.

In Australia, the governmental regime that tries to ensure competitive private markets is called 'national competition policy' (Hollander 2004: 197–202). Some businesses — such as those prevented from winning a bigger market share in some sector by taking over a rival company — do not like the 'national competition policy' framework implemented through such laws as the *Trade Practices Act* and through such institutions as the Australian Competition and Consumer Commission. But this framework, while it might impinge on the freedom that some particular companies may want to enjoy, is not in itself anti-business. On the contrary, it attempts to set arrangements in place that allow the business sector to claim that it can serve the public interest and not just the private interests of particular companies or their shareholders.

Consumer protection law has been enacted primarily in response to democratically expressed demands to protect consumers against unfair business practices. But, like competition law, it can also be justified as necessary for a well-functioning and legitimate business sector. Private markets do not operate in the 'public interest' if key participants — such as consumers — are hampered by inadequate product disclosure, by faulty manufacturing, by high-pressure sales techniques or by the myriad other doubtful business practices that consumer protection law seeks to combat. Again, some individual business people may rail against how such laws 'interfere' with their business freedom, but prudent business leaders surely know otherwise: that the claim made by the business sector that it serves defensible societal goals needs business customers to be well informed and empowered.

ECONOMIC POLICY

It is now commonly accepted that governments should bear a major responsibility for ensuring the overall health of the nation's economy. Voters are liable to punish a government at the next election if it presides over a significant economic downturn, and governments seem quick to claim credit if they preside over a period of economic prosperity.

There remains some doubt about the extent to which a national economy can reliably be micromanaged by governments using various metaphorical levers. This may especially apply to a national economy like Australia's which is integrated via trade and a floating currency into the international economic apparatus. There are nonetheless a range of such levers — such as settings within fiscal policy (the degree to which the government sector operates a budget deficit or surplus) and monetary policy (the setting of base-level interest rates, now handled in Australia via the autonomous Reserve Bank). These and other aspects of economic policy are discussed further by Woodward in Chapter 22 of this book.

The business sector can be deeply affected by economic policy decisions reached within the public sector. In late 1989, for example, businesses faced interest rates exceeding 20 per cent on borrowed funds, as a consequence of monetary policy settings intended to rein in an economy thought to be over-heating (RBA 2005). That these policy settings were intended to work in the longer-term interests of a healthy Australian economy, and hence in the longer-term interests of Australian business, was unlikely to have been much comfort to the many thousands of business operations struggling to survive or crippled into closure by the cost of borrowed funds.

PHYSICAL INFRASTRUCTURE

It was once well accepted that the government sector had a responsibility for ensuring the adequate provision—not least to the business sector—of key infrastructural services such as telecommunications, transportation, roadways and railways, energy, water supply and drainage. These physical infrastructural networks were mostly thought to be unsuited to private-sector provision. Due to economies of scale, monopoly rather than competitive provision was regarded as sensible, and unfettered private-sector monopolies were, for good reason, regarded as inappropriate. Physical infrastructure was thought to involve 'community service obligations' to serve or cross-subsidise more disadvantaged customers or regions, a process difficult to reconcile with a profit-maximising business orientation. In some cases, infrastructure was regarded as an essential community-wide asset best shared in common ownership via the public sector. In developing economies (such as Australia's in the past), only the public sector seemed to have the capacity to tackle various nationwide infrastructure tasks. Such reasoning explains why public-sector provision used to predominate. It means that, for business customers, the ease and profitability of their operations depended in part on the availability and cost of these public-sector services.

There has been a substantial change in fashion and orientation over the past 15 years in regard to the delivery and management of physical infrastructure (EIT 2005: 19). The notion that this was not an area suited to private-sector provision has been radically reassessed, much of it under the rubric of 'micro-economic reform'—reforms intended mainly to reduce business input costs. It is now quite common for private companies—some of them the privatised successors of former government-owned corporations—to be involved in many of these tasks. This has weakened the government sector's role and has ceded capacity and autonomy to the business sector.

The effect of the shift should not be exaggerated. Governments still tend to be held responsible for the overall adequacy of physical infrastructural pro-vision. It is just that their means of trying to manage this increasingly involves the *regulation* (see below) of private-sector operators, and/or the oversight of various outsourced contracts with private providers and managers. The business sector generally still needs reliable electricity, highway access, port facilities and the like, and any frustrations about their inadequacy are likely still to be directed at the overall government-set regulatory framework.

And, interestingly, there seems to have been a recent renewal of government-level interest in remedying a perceived under-investment in physical infrastructure (e.g. EIT 2005). The Howard government's Auslink program, intended to be a major investment in highway and railway provision, is a good example (Auslink 2005).

SOCIAL INFRASTRUCTURE

The social services needed by citizens — in education, health, welfare, and so on — are delivered by a mix of public and private providers, as other chapters in this book explain. This affects the business sector most directly when governments compete with private-sector operators in providing similar services. Consider, for example, the potential competition between the government school system and the private school sector, and between the public hospital system and privately owned hospitals. In practice, these relationships can be quite convoluted (there are, for example, common public-sector-regulated Year 12 assessment systems for students from government and private schools).

There is another, less obvious but crucially important, way that governments' social infrastructure spending affects business. A productive business sector needs healthy and well-educated employees, and businesses depend on the wellbeing of customers willing and able to purchase business products. While conceivably employee health care and employee training, for example, could be funded or provided directly by employers (and on-the-job training is indeed quite common), it is in the interests of the business sector if the cost and burden of health care, education and other such services are mainly borne elsewhere.

This is indeed what happens in Australia. In relation to education and training, for example, the school, university and TAFE systems are in effect funded by the community (via taxes and/or enrolment fees) rather than directly by the businesses which benefit from the availability of well-educated job seekers. This is a situation that leads to important debates about the fundamental purposes of education: how schools should balance preparation for the future job market against more intrinsic educational aspirations, and to what extent educational institutions should regard the business sector as a legitimate 'stakeholder' to be consulted about curriculum and funding.

A key area of social infrastructure with important implications for business and the economy, and unambiguously under government control in Australia, is the shaping of Australia's population size and composition via immigration (see Parkin & Hardcastle 1997). The Australian government each year announces an immigration intake target that is an aggregation of three broad categories of immigrants: a 'family' category (those with family links to existing Australian residents), a 'humanitarian' category (those seeking asylum from political persecution elsewhere or with some other humanitarian case for seeking admission) and a 'skills' category (those with occupational, educational and financial credentials assessed as likely to contribute to the Australian economy).

Much of the controversy about immigration policy in recent years has related to its humanitarian (and especially its asylum-seeker) component. But, for the business sector, a more important aspect is the announced target for the 'skills' category of immigrants (Birrell *et al.* 2004). Some of the immigrants admitted via the 'skills' category are directly nominated by employers who can demonstrate difficulty in finding equivalent staff in Australia. Some are granted a residency visa on condition that they invest in some Australian-based business enterprise. The others in the 'skills' category have been favourably assessed as likely to contribute to the employee skill base needed by the Australian business sector. The business sector has also been active in lobbying for an increase in the number of 'skilled' applicants permitted to enter Australia as temporary rather than permanent residents (Khoo *et al.* 2004).

REGULATION

The public sector engages in regulation when it establishes and enforces, under the authority of law, rules governing how people and organisations in the private sector are supposed to operate. Regulation is arguably becoming the most significant arena of government–business interaction. Governments are today less involved than in the past in direct service provision, as a result of a sustained period of privatising public corporations and outsourcing services to contracted private providers. But counterbalancing this is a much more prominent, even if less direct, role for the government sector in regulatory activity.

Some of the most prominent public-sector bodies today are regulatory authorities. Australian governments no longer own an airline, but the government-sector regulators—the (Commonwealth) Department of Transport and Regional Services, Airservices Australia and the Civil Aviation Safety Authority—have regulatory responsibility for the airline industry. Australian governments mostly no longer own financial institutions like savings banks or insurance companies, but the financial sector is regulated by government-sector institutions like the Australian Prudential Regulation Authority, the Australian Securities and Investments Commission, and the Reserve Bank. The powerful private media companies are subject to the oversight of the Australian Communications and Media Authority. The Australian Competition and Consumer Commission regulates company takeovers, acquisitions and product pricing to ensure the maintenance of competitive markets and to prosecute businesses alleged to have engaged in price collusion. Most States have created regulatory authorities of various kinds to oversee privatised or outsourced service provision of electricity, gas and water supply.

There are many other examples of government-sector regulators, at the national and State levels, whose job it is to regulate the business sector across practically the whole gamut of business activities. There is typically a regulator that specifies the allowable number of licenced taxis and a regulator that enforces the number of hours per week that shops are allowed to trade. A regulator checks on required standards in the trucking industry and another regulator checks on required standards in the childcare industry. Various regulators oversee product safety; others oversee occupational safety. The allowable content of manufactured food products is subject to regulation; so is the allowable content of children's television programs.

There are numerous regulatory devices employed by these various government-sector regulators. Certain business types may be required to obtain a *licence* to operate, on conditions intended to ensure competence or minimum training qualifications; this can apply in enterprises as diverse as nightclub crowd control and brain surgery. A limitation on the number of licences technically creates a government-mandated *franchise*; an example is the fixed number of licences available to commercial free-to-air television stations. Regulation may involve public officials engaging in *inspection*—of mines, of restaurant kitchens, of kindergarten playgrounds, of boarding houses, of waste disposal procedures, and so on. It may specify minimum *standards*—of product labelling, of the number of children per qualified worker in a childcare centre, of the number of hours between roadside breaks for interstate truck drivers, of the chemical content of petrol, etc. Some industries, such as electricity generation and distribution, feature regulated *price control*: the approval of the regulatory authority is needed before a private operator can increase charges for customers. And regulatory *enforcement* can likewise cover a whole range of strategies from voluntary industry self-regulation through to prosecution in the courts for serious regulatory infractions (Ayres & Braithwaite 1992).

INDUSTRY PLANS AND SUBSIDIES

A characteristic of some state-dominated governmental systems—such as the pre-1990s Soviet bloc and some developing countries today—is the promulgation of ambitious society-wide economic plans that seek to guide the direction of investment and the distribution of some of its rewards. National 'five-year plans' seem to be particularly prevalent in such systems; Malaysia, for example, adopted its eighth successive five-year plan in 2001. But it is a defining characteristic of liberal-democratic societies like Australia that they eschew such grand plans. Liberal democracies allow more space for relatively unplanned market forces, they are more reluctant to concede to government the kind of all-encompassing power that grand plans assume, and they are more sceptical about the ability of public officials to 'pick winners' (to use a phrase commonly adopted by critics of government intervention).

The closest that Western liberal democracies have come to serious government-led national planning was in the late 1940s, when a combination of factors—recent memories of the Great Depression, the experience of war and the advent of social-democratic governments (such as the Chifley Labor government in Australia)—produced ambitious government-led postwar reconstruction plans. But this phase did not last long, with conservative governments back in office in most Western countries by the early 1950s.

A more common device, though still more characteristic of governments of the Left rather than the Right, is the construction of specific industry plans of various kinds. A government may decide to engage with a particular industry sector by bundling together a package of regulatory and incentive elements. For example, the Australian car manufacturing and steel industries used to enjoy significant tariff protection via an impost added to the cost of imported cars and steel. This helped to protect employees and companies engaged in these industries but, according to critics, imposed significant costs on Australian consumers and reduced incentives for product innovation and quality. Under negotiated 'industry plans' beginning in the 1980s, the Australian government agreed to a protracted phasing down of tariff levels in return for company investment in new plant and equipment. This kind of joint government–industry planning remains controversial, because in effect it imposes an authoritative top-down plan rather than allowing market forces to determine the trajectory and survival of firms and industries.

Even more common are *ad hoc* firm-specific 'plans'. Governments seeking to induce particular firms to invest, or seeking to retain a business considering relocating elsewhere, sometimes offer 'packages' of incentives such as tax concessions, start-up seeding grants, guaranteed government contracts and/or fast-tracked approvals. This kind of activity has been sufficiently prevalent among Australian State governments—competing with each other for investments—that the Industry Commission warned in 1996 that its net effect was to weaken the government sector as a whole and to penalise other businesses not given the same kind of subsidies (Industry Commission 1996).

GOVERNMENT BUSINESS ENTERPRISES

Governments can impact on the business sector by operating major business enterprises in their own right (Hughes 2003: ch. 5). These are businesses that, much like their private-sector counterparts, produce a product or service that is sold to customers, are expected to generate an overall surplus of revenue over costs, and typically pay a 'dividend' to the owners (in this case, the government rather than private shareholders). Some of them have been legally protected monopolies, others have competed against private companies selling the same kind of product or service. Government business enterprises of this kind were used in the past for the provision of most key utilities. Governments in Australia owned savings banks, airlines and insurance companies. Today, Australia Post (for example) remains a huge government-owned business enterprise.

Defenders of 'public enterprise' regard government-sector authorities as an appropriate way to ensure well-coordinated services, to facilitate a more equitable distribution, to generate revenue for the government sector, and/or to remove some kinds of 'essential' services and products from the domain of private profit-seeking. But this view has diminishing support. Many government business enterprises around the Western world have been privatised over the past few decades (Hodge 2002). In Australia, iconic public corporations like Qantas, the Commonwealth Bank and Telstra have been notable privatisation targets. State governments have likewise jettisoned banks, electricity authorities, port management and myriad other enterprises.

TAXATION

Government affects business through its taxation regime. The business sector faces the same kind of contradictory incentives as individual taxpayers: on the one hand, each firm has an interest in minimising tax liabilities while, on the other hand, each firm needs a functioning government sector supported by enough tax-derived funding to allow it to do its job (much of it, as we have seen, supportive of business activity). Governments likewise need to set and adjust business taxes (such as the corporate income tax imposed by the Commonwealth and the payroll taxes imposed by the States) with a view to achieving a balance between, on the one hand, their revenue needs and citizen demands for better services and, on the other hand, their recognition that taxes are a business cost that can affect profitability, investment and private-sector job creation. The fact that some business conglomerates are multinational, potentially able to shift some transactions across national borders, is a further complication. Fenna discusses some of these tax-related issues in Chapter 23 of this book.

How business affects government

The previous section identified the key ways in which the activities and policies of government affected the business sector. Reversing the perspective, what are the ways in which the business sector shapes and constrains the activities of governments?

BUSINESS AS INVESTOR

Democratic governments are liable to be judged by voters on the state of the economy. They therefore depend on a healthy level of private-sector business investment, in terms of both established business investment (in property, equipment, manufacturing processes and the like) and new investment.

Some types of business investment are relatively long term and stable — investment in agricultural production or real estate, or big retail establishments like major shopping malls are examples — and not likely to change quickly in response to some governmental policy reorientation. Other types of investment are notoriously short term and unstable — e.g. the overnight money market, where investment is likely to shift electronically across jurisdictional borders in an instant if there is a hint of some announcement or policy shift that might make a marginal difference to the return on the investment. Most types of business investment fall somewhere between these two extremes, relatively stable in the short term but in principle capable of shifting in the long term in response to changing business conditions.

The direction, scale and scope of business investment depend on many factors, many of them (such as access to raw materials or consumer markets) beyond the immediate control of governments. But some factors may be more directly influenced by government policies, decisions or services: a firm contemplating where to locate a new factory might consider the impact of government taxes, the ease of obtaining development permits, the cost of utilities, the adequacy of roadways and transport infrastructure, and so on.

BUSINESS AS EMPLOYER

The business sector is the major source of employment within liberal-democratic countries. In Australia, it accounts for about 85 per cent of employees (ABS 2002). Firms within the business sector range widely in terms of the size of their workforce. Some large corporations employ many tens of thousands of workers (the biggest private-sector employer being the retail conglomerate Coles Myer, with more than 165 000 staff (Coles Myer 2005)). At the other end of the scale, there are many micro-businesses with just a few employees, each individually making only a tiny contribution to the overall employment rate but collectively adding up to a major source of jobs. The Australian Bureau of Statistics (ABS) reports that 'small businesses' — defined for ABS purposes as firms with fewer than 20 employees — together account for nearly half of all private-sector employment (ABS 2002).

Overseeing the creation of new jobs and lowering the unemployment rate are key governmental objectives. Presiding over good outcomes on employment is politically positive for incumbent governments, and hence the regular ABS monthly announcements are pored over by journalists and party officials for their political significance. But it is clear that the outcomes at stake here are overwhelmingly business-generated; the political fate of democratic governments is bound up with business-sector decisions about labour hiring.

Because most Australians work in the private business sector, the laws and regulations that frame their rights and rewards as employees are potentially of great significance. This can elevate *industrial relations policies* to prominence within the political system. The Howard Coalition government has decided to make industrial relations reform a major focus of its fourth term. It has proposed a substantial further deregulation of employer–employee relations away from the traditional framework of trade union-negotiated occupational awards overseen by the Industrial Relations Commission. It wants to encourage individual workers to sign more flexible Australian Workplace Agreements, and to exempt smaller businesses from some of the current restrictions on their capacity to dismiss employees. The Howard government is motivated by a conviction that this kind of labour-market deregulation is good for business, which should make it good for stimulating business-generated employment and hence (in the government's view) good for employees. Critics are concerned that it tilts the balance of power in employer–employee relations too much towards employers, leaving many employees potentially open to exploitation.

BUSINESS AS TAXPAYER

This chapter noted above that government affects business through its taxation regime. But this relationship can also be expressed from the reverse perspective: that business affects government by comprising its prime source of taxation revenue. Some tax revenue comes directly from business, such as in the form of (Commonwealth-levied) corporate income tax and (State-levied) payroll taxes. But most of the rest of the taxation regime is also business-derived in effect. The personal income tax is, for most ordinary individual taxpayers, a tax on the wage or salary paid to them by a business employer. Likewise, the Goods and Services Tax is paid by consumers as an impost on a retail business transaction. This means that among the factors at stake for governments is the role of the business sector as a tax base.

BUSINESS AS LOBBYIST

The interdependency of the government and business sectors means that business has an interest in the policy-making process within the governmental and political systems. Liberal democracies allow for the open expression of different interests and, in addition to the regular elections that determine the party or coalition that wins office, they provide avenues for interests to be communicated to governments on an ongoing basis. This leads to the kind of lobbying activity that Warhurst describes in Chapter 17 of this book.

It is not just the business sector that engages in lobbying, but there are few parallels to the kind of influence and access that business interests tend to enjoy. It would not be much of a distortion to suggest that there are just two kinds of lobby groups: those representing direct business interests and those urging government to eschew an immediate business perspective in favour of some broader interest—such as environmental sustainability or employee rights or welfare entitlements or gender equity or humanitarian assistance.

Lobbying may be undertaken on behalf of individual firms seeking some specific preferment or contract. Alternatively, it may be undertaken by sectoral associations (like the Minerals Council of Australia, the National Association of Forest Industries or the Australian Retailers Association) or by pan-business cross-sectoral organisations (like the Business Council of Australia and the Australian Chamber of Commerce and Industry). Particular issues may see lobbying configurations waxing and waning at different stages: for example, the sectoral and pan-business associations may be active in attempting to influence broad policy parameters, and then individual firms enter the scene in pursuit of particular deals.

As Warhurst makes clear in Chapter 17, the government–lobbyist exchange is two-way. It is often very useful for the government sector to have access to a viewpoint that claims to represent a consolidated business-wide or sector-wide perspective. For this reason, business groups can be asked to nominate representatives to serve on government advisory boards and consultative committees.

Political parties may provide a key conduit for business input into the policy-making process. Some business firms make donations to political parties, which the parties must in turn disclose to the Australian Electoral Commission (AEC). The 2003–04 AEC report, for example, reveals that Croissy Pty Ltd (a company associated with the Westfield corporate group which owns and manages major shopping malls) donated $300 000 to the Labor Party and $200 000 to the Liberal Party, and that the ANZ Bank donated $75 000 to Labor and $150 000 to the Liberals (AEC 2005; see also Priest & Fabro 2005). All sides to these transactions would deny that any untoward influence is being 'bought', yet such donations must be regarded by the donors as making good business sense.

Five perspectives on business–government relations

Overall, how can government–business relations best be characterised in terms of the balance of influence between them and the nature of their interaction? Because this question brings into focus the two dominant power centres of modern societies, it should not be surprising that it has been a matter of contention, and the stimulus to much academic theorising and research, for a long time.

At the risk of caricature, it is useful to simplify and consolidate some of the seminal answers to this question to produce five distinct interpretations on the balance of power between the government and business sectors within liberal-democratic societies. We will call these five the 'crowding-out/contradiction' perspective, the 'complementary coexistence' perspective, the 'corporatist collusion' perspective, the 'capitalist control' perspective and the 'circumvention' perspective.

CROWDING-OUT/CONTRADICTION

This perspective perceives a basic conflict and a degree of incompatibility between the government and business sectors. Neoliberal economists describe this in terms of 'crowding out', while neo-Marxist analysts on the Left refer to 'contradiction', but for our purposes here they are making similar points.

Among economists, the technical meaning of 'crowding out' is that excess government spending inhibits ('crowds out') business investment because it tends to lead to higher interest rates (by increasing competition for the remaining supply of money). More loosely, the idea can be generalised to the claim (which lies at the heart of a classical liberal perspective, as rehearsed by neo-liberals and 'economic rationalists' in recent decades) that, regretfully, the less efficient government sector can 'crowd out' the more efficient business sector by occupying, through its use of superior legal authority, too much of its space. This perspective is confident that the private business sector tends to be more efficient, in the sense of expending fewer resources to achieve a given output, than the government sector. But a government business enterprise might, for example, muscle out a private business competitor because it enjoys favourable access to government contracts, or is not liable for taxation, or some such other advantage. According to this perspective, society as a whole tends to be disadvantaged.

Whereas 'crowding out' is an argument associated with the neoliberal ideological Right, 'contradiction' is an argument associated with the neo-Marxist ideological Left. Yet the two arguments occupy some significant common ground in perceiving a fundamental conflict between government and business. A noted formulation of a government–business 'contradiction' is put forward by James O'Connor (1971) in his book *The Fiscal Crisis of the State*. According to O'Connor, liberal-democratic governments need to achieve two contradictory goals—*accumulation* (achieved by economic prosperity via a profitable private sector) and *legitimisation* (achieved by a harmonious society that is supportive enough of the system to ensure its stability and continuation). The problem—the alleged 'contradiction'—is that governments pursue legitimisation by taxing the private sector to fund public-sector benefits and services, but this tends to undermine the viability of the private sector which is necessary for sustained accumulation. In the end, predicted O'Connor, this would lead to a 'fiscal crisis' as the government sector extracted more revenue than a viable private sector would be able sustainably to yield.

COMPLEMENTARY COEXISTENCE

Some interpreters strongly contest the bleak and inherent tension claimed by the crowding-out/contradiction perspective. They argue that the realm of government and the realm of business can be mutually supportive within a so-called 'mixed economy'. Some social and economic functions, according to this 'complementary coexistence' viewpoint, necessarily require governmental authority or coordination (including functions necessary for secure and stable business operations). Other functions benefit from public-sector-led management that takes into account equity issues rather than being focused principally on profit maximisation. Other social and economic functions, they contend, are best left to the incentive and reward system embodied in the market. Defenders of the 'mixed economy' regard such a mixture as providing a safe balance of interests and values.

The Australian social scientist Hugh Stretton (1987: chs 1–2) is an analyst who adopts something like this 'complementary coexistence' perspective (see also Stretton & Orchard 1994: ch. 7; Quiggin 1999). And much of the description earlier in this chapter of the governmental functions necessary for a productive and legitimate business sector can likewise be categorised as promoting a 'complementary coexistence' interpretation.

This is not an anti-business perspective; rather, it insists on a proper sphere for business and a proper sphere for government, to their mutual benefit, and an area of overlap. The 'mixed economy' defenders are confident that the sections of the economy where private business interests and values appropriately hold sway benefit from the stability, legitimacy, legal infrastructure, social trust and social harmony facilitated by also having a strong governmental sector.

But advocacy of a 'mixed economy' may also require political action to defend the legitimate sphere of governmental authority against too much power being ceded to the private sector. In an enduring phrase, the American economist John Kenneth Galbraith (1958: 257)—a strong defender of the 'mixed economy'—wrote of the dangers of 'private opulence and public squalor' in a society which undervalued its public sphere, a situation not in the best long-term interests of business.

A government–business power balance within the 'mixed economy' is facilitated not just by the governmental sector having its own sphere of genuine authority, at the apex of a democratic political system, but also by competitive forces within the business sector itself. Provided that markets are reasonably competitive, the biggest immediate conflict that a business is likely to face is not from the government but rather from a rival firm producing a similar product or service. And there are other tensions and strains within the business sector. Import businesses compete against the domestic manufacturers or agricultural growers of the same product. Finance-related businesses like banks lend money to other businesses at a profitable interest rate, and can be quite ruthless in how they treat business borrowers unable to keep up their repayments. Many businesses have other businesses as their customers or suppliers, so they have directly competing interests in relation to the price of the product or service. Bigger businesses, like supermarket chains and discount stores, are a constant threat to smaller businesses, like neighbourhood groceries. These internal business-sector competitive pressures help to check the overall power of business vis-à-vis government within the 'mixed economy'.

CORPORATIST COLLUSION

The 'corporatist collusion' perspective highlights the benefits and dangers of close collaboration between government leaders and 'big business'.

In much of Western Europe, formalised collaboration between governments and the leaders of major representative organisations in the business sector (along with the leaders of some other key sectors like peak trade union organisations) has been a feature for many decades. It is an arrangement described by analysts as *corporatist* in the sense defined by Cawson as a process by which 'a limited number of monopolistic organisations representing functional interests engage in bargaining with state agencies over public policy outputs [and] in exchange for favourable policies, the leaders of the interest organisations undertake the implementation of policy through delivering the co-operation of their members' (Cawson 1987: 38, as cited in Head 1997: 335).

In the Western European case, corporatist-style collaboration and bargaining has been practiced in the past in relation to key economic decisions such as major business or government investments, tax reform, adjustments to wage levels, national health and pension schemes, and so on. The Hawke Labor government in Australia during the 1980s attempted to create what were, in effect, corporatist-style arrangements along these lines, through such devices as its Economic Planning Advisory Council (Head 1997).

Provided that such arrangements can be held democratically accountable (via the periodic elections to which governments are subjected), then—according to its advocates—corporatist-style arrangements of this kind are claimed to facilitate greater social harmony and better economic coordination than can be achieved via more adversarial political arrangements or via private market outcomes.

But critics worry about how accountable a collusion between 'big government' and 'big business' can really be to the rest of society. Some critics point to the corporatist tendencies evident within the authoritarian Fascist regimes in parts of Western Europe in the period leading up to the Second World War. In more recent times, there have been suggestions that close corporatist-style government–business relationships in some East Asian states are problematic in the way that they may insulate the top levels of both sectors from scrutiny by, and accountability to, the rest of society, in some cases descending into alleged 'crony capitalism' (Hewison, Robison & Rodan 1993; Hughes 1999).

CAPITALIST CONTROL

The overwhelmingly significant feature of liberal-democratic societies, according to this perspective, is the domination of the interests of the business sector. While not all individual business enterprises prosper and while sometimes public policies with which the business sector may not be happy are promulgated, in the end, governments—however responsive they try to be, via democratic mechanisms, to the broader interests encompassed within society—are forced by necessity to support a kind of pro-business regime. A business sector that is more productive and profitable is likely to employ more people, pay better wages, contribute more tax revenue, and reward governments with greater electoral popularity. It is therefore unsurprising that governments of all partisan persuasions seem so mindful of the needs of the business sector.

Adherents to a 'capitalist control' perspective come from a variety of interpretive traditions. For Marxists, the notion that capitalist systems are governed in the interests of private capital accumulation is a defining insight (see Gilding in Chapter 20 of this book). But an interpreter does not need to subscribe to all the theoretical accoutrements of Marxism to reach a similar conclusion. The American political scientist Charles Lindblom, noted for his benign 'muddling through' interpretation of how everyday political decisions tend to be made by bargaining and compromise (Lindblom 1959), has argued that the 'privileged position of business' is an entrenched structural feature of liberal-democratic systems (Lindblom 1977: 170–8; see also Lindblom 2001).

CIRCUMVENTION

A final interpretive perspective that can usefully be identified is of a somewhat different character to the others. It is a perspective that focuses on the possibilities for *circumventing* both the sphere of government and the sphere of business. It is a perspective that is mindful of the criticisms which business advocates often direct at government (e.g. that it can be too inefficient, bureaucratic, remote, inflexible or impersonal, or induce too much dependency). Hence it tends to support the shift of governmental activity away from direct public enterprise towards a regulatory oversight of a market-based private-sector economy. But it is also mindful of the criticisms that public-sector advocates often direct at business (e.g. that it can be too exploitative, uncoordinated or ruthless or likewise too impersonal or generate too much inequality).

Analysts and practitioners who see merit in both sets of criticisms have contemplated whether there is a viable 'Third Way' (their own self-adopted term) that can meld together some aspects of the market and the public sphere while circumventing the problems thought to be caused by both 'big government' and 'big business' (Giddens 1998 & 2000; Orchard 2005). The 'Third Way' came into prominence in Britain by being associated with some of the policies of the Blair Labour government, and in Australia through its advocacy by the (short-duration) Labor Opposition Leader, Mark Latham (e.g. Latham 2001).

For 'Third Way' advocates, the 'community' is typically envisaged as the sphere within which goods and services can be provided in response to human needs without risking the exploitative dangers of the business sector or the dependency dangers of the traditional government sector. Some of the 'Third Way' advocates focus in particular on the value of organisations in what they call the 'third sector'. The 'third sector' encompasses community-based groups, nonprofit organisations, voluntary associations and other organisations capable of delivering services and yet overlapping neither with the conventional government sector nor with the conventional business sector.

Its advocates propose that the 'Third Way' can offer the basis for circumventing or transcending the unattractive features of both big business and big government, and restoring a community-level focus that can reflect the authentic values and aspirations of communities of people. But critics are sceptical. The 'Third Way', they imply, may be a recipe not just for circumventing the perceived disadvantages of government and business but also for circumventing their strengths. The 'third sector' may have its merits, they suggest, but it does not yet seem to offer the kind of scale, dynamism or avenues for genuine accountability that, in very different ways, governments and markets can claim to provide. And the idea that the 'Third Way' promotes more personalised, community-derived processes and values may not impress those for whom the less intrusive impersonality of bureaucratic government and business is among their positive features.

Government, business and levels of analysis

These different interpretations are not necessarily mutually exclusive. Each offers some insights into the dynamics at work in government–business relations. They differ in their understanding of the overall balance of power, and this may be in part because they focus on different aspects or levels of analysis.

A useful way to understand power relations as operating at different levels of analysis is through an enduring three-dimensional interpretive model of the exercise of power constructed by Steven Lukes (1974). Lukes notes that analyses of the exercise of power typically begin by focusing on the everyday politics of lobbying, decision making, governmental policy formulation, political debate and party competition. This is an important focus, and for Lukes constitutes his first dimension of power.

At this level, we can observe business lobby groups operating, sometimes competitively and sometimes with a common voice, with varying degrees of influence over government. Political decisions are made that sometimes favour business interests while other decisions might upset business organisations.

But Lukes argues that this level of analysis, focusing on overt governmental decision making and lobbying, is best understood as simply one dimension of a multi-dimensional framework. How, he next asks, is the *agenda* for this realm of everyday politics constructed? What issues are at stake in this public arena of politics, what issues are somehow kept off the public agenda, and in whose interests does the agenda-shaping process operate? Understanding *agenda-shaping* involves, for Lukes, a second dimension of power.

At this second level, an analyst might be able to infer a strong influence for business interests. Consider, for example, how the 'public agenda' about media policy in Australia focuses mainly on technical issues such as digital broadcasting and focuses little on structural business-related issues like the appropriate role for privately owned media conglomerates.

Finally, Lukes draws attention to an overarching, more structurally entrenched third dimension of power. This third dimension, for Lukes, encompasses the way in which certain interests are promoted by the structured patterns of advantage *embedded within* a system. Particular interests can be powerful without necessarily involving overt lobbying (as recognised within the first dimension) or even behind-the-scenes agenda setting (as recognised within the second dimension). Interests can be powerful simply because of systemic structures and assumptions deeply entrenched within the political and economic systems, and normally regarded as uncontroversial 'given' facts about how the systems operate.

Lindblom's observation, noted above, about the 'privileged position of business' in liberal-democratic societies, fits within Lukes' third analytical dimension. This *structural* power of the business sector is not necessarily based on the enduring power of any particular company nor of any particular business leader. Rather, it is a systemic bias within a system that seems to need to operate—if it is to be sustainable—in the overall interests of a favourable business climate.

For analysts of the role of business in Australian politics, a nuanced multi-levelled approach along the lines sketched by Lukes is sensible. At times the focus of analysis, for good reason, needs to be on the cut and thrust of everyday politics—the lobby groups that are mobilising to contest the issues of the moment, the electoral conflict between the political parties, the various claims and counterclaims made in political debate. A more forensic analysis might want to step back a little from this contestation in order to deconstruct the agenda-setting process and to infer from the kinds of issues seemingly kept off the agenda which interests are predominant in shaping the limits and the trajectory of everyday politics. And sometimes it is valuable to contemplate an even more abstract and systematic explanation for the deeper structures of the political system.

We can be confident that, in a liberal-democratic society like Australia, business interests are a key element at every level of this analytical story.

REFERENCES

ABS [Australian Bureau of Statistics] 2002, 'Small Business in Australia', ABS Catalogue no 1321.0, Canberra, 23 October.

AEC [Australian Electoral Commission] 2005, 'Annual Returns Locator Service', <http://fadar.aec.gov.au/arwdefault.asp?submissionid=6>.

Auslink 2005, 'Auslink: Building our National Transport Future', Website, Department of Transport and Regional Services, Canberra, <http://www.auslink.gov.au/>.

Ayres, I. & Braithwaite, J. 1992, Responsive Regulation, Oxford University Press, New York.

Birrell, B., Rapson, V., Dobson, I. & Smith, T.F. 2004, 'Skilled Movement in the New Century: Outcomes for Australia', Centre for Population and Urban Research, Monash University, Melbourne, <http://www.immi.gov.au/research/publications/skilled_movement.pdf>.

Cawson, A. 1987, 'Corporatism', in The Blackwell Encyclopaedia of Political Thought, ed. D. Miller, Blackwell, Oxford.

Coles Myer 2005, 'About Coles Myer', Website, Melbourne, <http://corporate.colesmyer.com/>.

EIT [Exports and Infrastructure Taskforce] 2005, Australia's Export Infrastructure: Report to the Prime Minister, Canberra, <http://www.infrastructure.gov.au/pdf/Report.pdf>.

Galbraith, J.K. 1958, The Affluent Society, Penguin, Harmondsworth.

Giddens, A. 1998, Third Way: The Renewal of Social Democracy, Polity Press, Cambridge.

Giddens, A. 2000, The Third Way and its Critics, Polity Press, Malden MA.

Head, B. 1997, 'Corporatism', in Government, Politics, Power and Policy in Australia, 6th edn eds D. Woodward, A. Parkin & J. Summers, Longman, Frenchs Forest, pp. 333–55.

Hewison, K., Robison, R. & Rodan, G. eds 1993, Southeast Asia in the 1990s: Authoritarianism, Democracy and Capitalism, Allen & Unwin, St Leonards.

Hodge, G. 2002, 'Privatisation: Lessons from the War', Alternative Law Journal, vol. 27, no. 4, pp. 177–83.

Hollander, R. 2004, 'Reforming Business Regulation', in Governing Business and Globalisation, eds E. van Acker & G. Curran, Pearson Longman, Frenchs Forest.

Hughes, H. 1999, 'Crony Capitalism and the East Asian currency and Financial "Crises"', Policy, vol. 15, no. 3, pp. 3–9.

Hughes, O. 2003, *Public Management and Administration*, 3rd edn, Palgrave Macmillan, Houndmills.

Industry Commission 1996, *State, Territory and Local Government Assistance to Industry*, Report 55, October, Canberra.

Khoo, S., Voigt-Graf, C., McDonald, P. & Hugo, G. 2004, 'A Global Market: The Recruitment of Temporary Skilled Labour from Overseas', Report prepared for the Department of Immigration and Multicultural and Indigenous Affairs, Canberra, <http://www.immi.gov.au/research/publications/employers_report_internet.pdf>.

Latham, M. 2001, 'In Defence of the Third Way', in *Left Directions: Is There a Third Way?*, eds P. Nursey-Bray & C. Bacchi, University of Western Australia Press, Crawley, pp. 12–31.

Lindblom, C. 1959, 'The Science of Muddling Through', *Public Administration Review*, vol. 19, no. 2, pp. 70–88.

Lindblom, C. 1977, *Politics and Markets*, Basic Books, New York.

Lindblom, C. 2001, *The Market System: What It Is, How It Works, and What To Make of It*, Yale University Press, New Haven.

Lukes, S. 1974, *Power: A Radical View*, Macmillan, London.

O'Connor, J. 1971, *The Fiscal Crisis of the State*, St Martin's Press, New York.

Orchard, L. 2005, 'Third Way', in M. Griffiths ed. *Routledge Encyclopaedia of International Relations and Global Politics*, Routledge, London.

Parkin, A. & Hardcastle, L. 1997, 'Immigration and Ethnic Affairs Policy', in *Government, Politics, Power and Policy in Australia*, 6th edn, eds D. Woodward, A. Parkin & J. Summers, Longman, Frenchs Forest, pp. 486–509.

Priest, M. & Fabro, A. 2005, 'Lost Cause: How Business Backed Labor', *Australian Financial Review*, 2 February.

Quiggin, J. 1999, 'The Future of Government: Mixed Economy or Minimal State?', *Australian Journal of Public Administration*, vol. 58, no. 4, pp. 39–53.

RBA [Reserve Bank of Australia] 2005, 'F05 Indicator Lending Rates', Excel file of Historical Statistics, Sydney, <http://www.rba.gov.au/Statistics/Bulletin/F05hist.xls>.

Stretton, H. 1987, *Political Essays*, Georgian House, Melbourne.

Stretton, H. & Orchard, L. 1994, *Public Goods, Public Enterprise, Public Choice*, Macmillan, Houndmills.

CHAPTER 19

The media, power and politics

IAN WARD

The mass media are crucial institutions within liberal democracies like Australia, but the role and influence of the media within the political system are problematic and contentious. Media outlets are indispensable information sources: Australia's democratic political life would be almost inconceivable without the news and interpretation provided by the media. But at the same time, the media are themselves potential sources of, and conduits for, influence and power; hence they might arguably threaten the kind of openness and transparency that liberal-democratic politics requires. This chapter critically examines problems and issues arising in the interaction between the media, power and politics.

Parliamentary elections, which are the hallmark of representative democracy, predate television and the broadcast news media. In an earlier age, candidates relied substantially on word of mouth, public meetings and face-to-face canvassing to communicate with voters. But it is difficult now to imagine how an election campaign might be successfully conducted without news media coverage. Present day democratic political life is 'mediated'. People 'generally do not directly encounter politicians' and are exposed to politics only through 'media images, representations and stories' (Craig 2004: 4). In this sense, the media have become a vital part of Australian democracy. However the news media exist for a very different purpose. With the exception of the Commonwealth government-funded ABC network, Australia's mainstream news media are privately owned and commercial organisations whose chief goal is to return a profit for their shareholders. Their principal business is advertising.

News and current affairs in which political events are described and analysed comprise only a small part of media content. Commercial media generate profits for their shareholders by gathering audiences or readers and selling access to these to advertisers. Even newspapers, which are purchased by readers, are heavily reliant on advertising revenue. Free-to-air commercial radio and television broadcasters are entirely dependent on advertising sales. Not surprisingly, the greater part of their content consists of sport, drama, soap opera, quiz, 'reality' and other entertainment programs intended to attract the largest possible audiences. Even newspapers ostensibly devoted to reporting 'hard' news now also carry an extensive magazine and 'soft news' content. The Australian news media may have a significant role in sustaining a democratic politics, but their *raison d'être* is commercial rather than political.

The important role that news media have in Australian political life can be simply explained. Australia has a form of representative parliamentary government. Elections are regularly held in which voters must choose which party or parties in Parliament will form the Ministry and thus govern. In a complex, diverse and geographically dispersed society, the mainstream news media are the chief means of political communication, and the only substantial arena (or public sphere) in which public debate of political issues is possible. If, individually and collectively, voters are to make wise, informed choices at the ballot box, the news media must provide them with access to a diverse range of views as well as information about rival parties and their policies.

Unlike comparable democracies such as Canada and the USA, Australia does not have a Charter or Bill of Rights which provides an express constitutional guarantee of 'press freedom'. However, arguing that free media are a necessary precondition for democratic elections, in 1992 the High Court of Australia found an implied (rather than expressly written) constitutional guarantee of free and open political debate. In the *Political Broadcasting* case,[1] it offered this as its reason for overturning legislation which the Labor government had introduced to prevent parties from purchasing broadcast advertising air time during election campaigns.

Journalists and the news media proclaiming 'freedom of the press' have used the same argument to claim a special right to pursue the collection and publication of news in the public interest. For example, the preamble to the code of ethics of the professional association covering Australian journalists (the Media, Entertainment and Arts Alliance) suggests that journalists and, by implication, the news media must 'inform citizens and animate democracy'. A variation of the argument that the media play an essential role in a democracy, grounded in traditional liberal thinking, casts journalists and the news media in the role of 'a "public watchdog" over the state' (Wheeler 1997: 6). Here the idea is that news media serve as the fourth estate,[2] ensuring accountability and transparency by closely scrutinising the government. They have a role in identifying issues of public concern, as well as providing a necessary check on the misuse and abuse of political power (Schultz 1998).

In essence, any claim that news media can animate democracy or serve as a fourth estate by scrutinising, holding accountable and checking executive government, also makes the case that the news media can exercise significant political power. The basis of this power lies in their ability to inform and mobilise public opinion. It flows from the capacity that radio, newspapers and, above all, television have to reach very large, albeit different, audiences. As the leading Australian commercial network reminds its viewers, 'more Australians get their news from Channel Nine than any other source'. Insofar as news media do wield power, it is because they provide a means for a few to transmit simultaneously the same message to a large, diverse and geographically dispersed audience. Thus, to understand how power flows through and is wielded by mass media, we can ask some quite simple questions. Who prepares and controls the preparation of news 'messages'? Who controls the media through which news is transmitted? And what impact or effect do messages have on audiences? The last of these is the most obvious starting point.

Do media have the power to mould public opinion?

The suggestion that the news media wield or channel great power is predicated on the assumption that newspapers, radio and especially television have a marked effect on the thinking of their audiences—that they are persuasive and able to shape audience behaviour. This assumption is often made. For instance, it underpins the concern that led to the formation in 1996 of a Ministerial Committee on violence in the media and to the Australian government's 1996 endorsement of its advice to secure the installation of 'V-chips' in all new television sets in order that parents might block programs seen to be encouraging violent behaviour among children. The media have also been variously blamed for carrying ads that 'brainwash' children; for fostering eating disorders among women driven to imitate unnaturally thin television models and actresses; for dwelling on and encouraging an unwarranted public apprehension about levels of crime; even for focusing on political squabbles and thus fuelling an increasing antipathy towards politicians and cynicism about public affairs (Ward 1995: 20–2). All of these arguments attribute to the media a power to exert a substantial influence on the thinking of their audiences. The existence of a very large advertising industry surrounding the commercial media, and the willingness of large corporations such as Nike and Toyota to spend very large sums to advertise their products, are factors that also point to power of the media to shape the opinions and preferences of audiences.

However, the belief that persuasive mass communication has the power to sway audience opinion is more problematic than it might initially seem.

Advertising campaigns do not always have the desired effect on their audience, as the losing party in any federal election campaign will testify. Voting behaviour is now more fluid and less predictable than it was for much of last century. However it is still the case that a majority of Australians habitually vote for the same party at election after election, and are seemingly immune to the influence of news media. Media scholars have long understood that mass communication campaigns will not shift entrenched political opinion—that propaganda will have minimal effect where, as is commonly the case, individuals hold strong political attitudes or an attachment to one or another political party (see McQuail 1994: 353ff). However, even if people have their own fixed ideas and there are few empty heads for the media to fill with propaganda, those few voters whose views will be shaped by the news or talkback radio coverage to which they are exposed may well determine the outcome of elections in key marginal seats. In such circumstances, Windschuttle (1988: 311) suggests that the media can be 'politically powerful', even though 'most people vote the same way most of their lives' and are shielded from the influence of news media by a party allegiance that actually 'influences how they interpret media reporting'.

Recent evidence which suggests that the number of Australians without a firm partisan allegiance is now growing (see Chapter 15 of this book) adds some force to Windschuttle's argument that the media are indeed powerful, even though they have a limited effect on the thinking of much of their audience. However, the news media may exert a more subtle influence on public opinion than Windschuttle allows, and thereby wield a power that extends well beyond influencing a few swinging voters. Perloff (1998: 338) makes this point. He concedes that 'classic and contemporary studies in political communication leave little doubt that news does not change people's basic political attitudes', but adds 'having said this, there is also little doubt that news *does influence* some types of belief and attitudes'. For example, the particular way in which news media focus on some stories rather than others can exert a powerful influence on 'people's priorities—or upon what they perceive to be salient problems for the country or community' (Perloff 1998: 338, 209).

In other words, the power of the media may reside in *agenda setting*. There is now an extensive academic literature on agenda setting which explains how news media can shape the thinking of an audience, many of whom will have entrenched political views and partisan attachments and who therefore routinely filter or selectively read or watch news stories. Agenda-setting theory advances the hypothesis that the media may not be able to tell people what to think but that they are remarkably successful in telling audiences what issues to think about (Cohen 1963: 13). It rests on the accumulated findings of several hundred, mostly supportive (and mostly American) studies conducted since McCombs and Shaw's (1972) original Chapel Hill study, which combined content analysis and survey methods and recorded a strong correlation between the list of issues identified as important by undecided voters and the priority accorded them by news media.

Agenda *setting* is a macro-level theory which suggests that audiences will collectively see as more important those particular issues given prominent coverage by news media—that news media can transfer to audiences a sense of what issues are important. Agenda-*priming* theory provides an individual-level explanation grounded in cognitive psychology, which explains how this process might work (Willnat 1997). Simply put, it claims that individuals make judgments about issues based on information immediately to hand and from easily retrieved memories. Experimental research (e.g. Iyengar 1990) shows that television and other news media do provide individuals with information that is accessible and readily recalled. Such studies appear to confirm that people's sense of which political issues are important is coloured by news broadcasts and stories to which they have recently been exposed. More recent agenda-setting research (e.g. Ghanem 1997; McCombs *et al.* 2000) has identified a 'second-level' agenda-setting effect, and a capacity for news not only to signal the importance of issues, but to influence the judgments voters make of political leaders. This evidence suggests that, by emphasising certain issues rather than others, the news media can alter the criteria people use to evaluate political leaders. For example, in circumstances where the media focus on issues such as terrorism voters may look favourably upon leaders who appear resolute and strong. If indeed, as a considerable body of empirical investigation now suggests, the way in which news media select, prioritise and report political events does shape the public agenda, then we need look very carefully at who shapes the media agenda—at who decides which issues will be covered and which will not.

Who owns and controls the media agenda?

In the 18th and 19th centuries, liberal theory painted state censorship and regulation as the chief threat to press freedom. However the progressive concentration of media into a very few private hands now suggests a new danger. Media ownership in Australia is now highly concentrated. The controlling ownership of Australia's commercial media rests in very few hands: companies associated with the Packer family own the Nine television network and a great many magazines, while News Ltd, which forms part of Rupert Murdoch's vast global media empire, controls two-thirds of Australian newspapers. Both are very large corporate concerns with interests spreading beyond the media and well able to command the attention of Cabinet and Prime Ministers (as any large business has the power to do). Both the Packer and Murdoch groups have the additional political weight that comes from owning news media in a position to boost or damage any party's electoral prospects through the way in which the news is reported.

Not surprisingly, then, one common suggested answer to the question 'Who controls the news agenda?' is that the media owners must. Mayer ([1983] 1994: 20), sceptical of this answer, observed that media critics are 'obsessed with the goings on of press barons, with bias in the news, and with oligopolistic control by three major groups'. A variation on this obsession has been speculation about the favours given to and received by the 'media mates' of Labor and Liberal federal governments (see Tiffen 1995).

Like any other business organisations, news media must comply with an array of legislation regulating corporate activity 'ranging from the taxation system to copyright law'. However the media are also subject to laws which specifically regulate their activities and which cover 'such matters as ownership structures and content provisions' and reflect their special place in Australia's democracy. 'Important democratic principles' inform Australia's 'media regulatory framework', which is intended to ensure a plurality of voices and that broadcasters meet their responsibility to provide Australian content and 'adequate levels of news and information' (Craig 2004: 37, 39).

These laws may well curtail the business plans of major media companies. For example, both the Packer and Murdoch groups have expressed interest in acquiring the profitable Fairfax-owned newspapers (*Sydney Morning Herald*, *The Age* and *Australian Financial Review*). However legislation put in place by the Hawke government in 1986 restricted the extent of foreign ownership of media companies and hence blocked the foreign-owned News Ltd from buying Australian newspapers. This legislation also prohibited cross-media ownership (that is, the same person or corporation owning both a television licence and a major newspaper covering the same geographical market) and blocked the Packer group from bidding for Fairfax newspapers because it owns the Nine Network. For all the power they possess and for all their sophisticated lobbying capacity, neither Packer nor Murdoch was able to engineer a swift change in the laws that stood in their way. They did persuade the Howard government of the need to ditch legislation regulating the media introduced by the previous Labor government, but until July 2005 the Coalition has not been in a position to get such legislative changes through the Senate.

As Craig (2004: 38) points out, 'media policy is not simply implemented by government'. It is not just a technical matter. Policy is shaped by a highly political process involving debate between, and lobbying by, 'corporations, trade unions, think tanks, [and] public-interest advocacy groups'. In this contest, the major media corporations carry a substantial political weight. Since the broadcast media operate with licences issued by the Commonwealth government and in a regulatory environment established by Commonwealth legislation, it is inevitable that media owners will seek to exert political influence in defence of their commercial interests.

Whether media owners seek to influence the ebb and flow of politics on an ongoing basis is a rather different question. Australia does have a long history of 'press barons' playing political favourites and even intervening in party affairs. While newspaper owners have never overtly declared their papers to be partisan organs, there is evidence that on many occasions they have been more than willing to campaign for one or another party. For example, at its proprietor's direction, newspapers owned by Murdoch's News Ltd group actively supported the election of the Whitlam Labor government in 1972. However, in 1975 Murdoch marshalled his newspapers in a campaign to oust Labor which was so blatantly and enthusiastically fought in the pages of his *Australian* newspaper that it triggered an unprecedented strike by journalists, who resented their work being edited in such a partisan way. Against this long history of political intervention, mostly in favour of anti-Labor parties, it would be foolish to imagine that present-day media proprietors might not seek to exert a behind-the-scenes political influence on governments by threatening to use (or using) their news outlets to sway public opinion.

However the corporations that control the news media in Australia are very large. Clearly, the era in which Rupert Murdoch could wander downstairs from his office to lend a hand with, and watch over, the preparation and printing of the *Australian* has long passed. While he does retain the power to intervene, Murdoch's global media empire is so vast that he can no longer take a close interest in how individual newspapers cover and report politics. Proprietors may well have their own ideological and political preferences. Yet we need to be cautious of a stereotypical caricature that portrays powerful barons directing their staff to run this or that political line.

The power that media owners have to influence the way news is gathered and reported is more subtly exercised. They will be centrally involved in decisions affecting the profitability of media as business—for example decisions about marketing strategy, about corporate budgets, investment in new technologies, or the appointment of editors and other key staff. But day-to-day decisions routinely fall to managers and editors who will have a large degree of autonomy.

A number of studies have now reported that journalists do enjoy a considerable freedom in identifying and reporting news stories. Because they operate within editorial policies and staffing and other resource limitations imposed by owners and their managers, and because owners retain the prerogative to intervene, it may well be that journalists have what Curran (1990: 133) terms a 'revocable and conditional' autonomy. But it is a significant degree of autonomy nonetheless. The day-to-day news coverage generated by television and newspapers is typically decided by journalists and editors, not by owners. In Australia the major political parties, pressure groups, and governments too, have long recognised this and developed sophisticated strategies aimed at securing favourable news coverage.

The Canberra Press Gallery

News as a published or broadcast product is generated in large organisations. It is generated by journalists, camera operators, editors, subeditors, producers and other newsworkers who must constantly make judgments about what to report and what to omit. Journalists typically work in newsrooms that are highly organised and hierarchical in nature. News by its nature consists of stories about novel, unpredictable events. What will make news may be unpredictable but, in sharp contrast, newswork is governed by routine practices intended to ensure that newsrooms meet their production deadlines and make the best economic use of their capital and human resources. For example, journalists are often assigned to 'rounds' and to locations where news stories are known to break on a regular basis. Typically, a newsroom will have journalists assigned to a police round, to cover local government, sport, business, and perhaps policy areas such as the environment.

News rounds bring journalists regularly into contact with sources on whom they may come to rely for information. Often these sources are spokespersons for large and important institutions—for corporations, police, hospitals, universities, government departments and regulatory agencies. Many of these spokespeople are employed as media advisers (more recently dubbed 'spin doctors') to manage relations with the media. They and their employing institutions are well prepared to deal with journalists and are accustomed to providing the press releases, news conferences, doorstop interviews and background briefings that meet the journalists' needs. Prime Ministers, Ministers, Opposition leaders and political parties all have media advisers, and, in Canberra, the journalists with whom they most often come into contact are members of the press gallery, itself essentially a news round.

The Press Gallery comprises approximately 180 journalists, plus editors, producers, camera crew and others, assigned by rival news organisations from around Australia and officially accredited to work within Parliament House. There are some influential media commentators who are based in Sydney and Melbourne—including talkback radio hosts who have a sizeable audience. However gallery journalists are collectively responsible for the great majority of news stories about federal politics that appear in Australian print and broadcast media.

The Gallery is an archetypal case illustrating Nimmo's (1978: 194–6) argument that 'in the everyday world of government–press relations' journalists and officials have negotiated 'profitable ways of doing business' which have, over time, solidified into news-gathering conventions. The Gallery is also clearly a target for all those interest groups who wish to shape the reporting and public debate of issues and is, in its own right, a potentially powerful institution. Press galleries are the descendents 'of the [centuries] long struggle of the British press to report the debates at Westminster' (Lloyd 1988: 7) and are found in all other parliamentary systems (including those of the Australian States).

Gallery journalists work in Canberra and therefore, for the vast majority, at a distance from their employing news organisations. They have an unusual independence from their editors and a considerable discretion to judge what political events are—and are not—newsworthy. However, as Franklin (1998)—with the UK in mind—has observed, 'politician–journalist relations are inherently collusive. Each needs the other to achieve their objectives'. To cover politics, reporters need at least 'minimal co-operation' from politicians, and to reach voters with their message politicians need to 'establish productive working relationships with journalists'. The result, Franklin argues, is a symbiotic relationship not wholly precluded from 'becoming adversarial' but which is, on a day-to-day basis, 'essentially co-operative, even if it oscillates "between trust and suspicion"' (Franklin 1998). His thesis holds especially for Australia, where the national Press Gallery uniquely occupies a physical location within Parliament House, which, in a wing immediately above the Senate chamber, supplies news media with TV studios, radio booths, and all the office space necessary to generate a continuous news coverage. Journalists literally share the same 'kennel' (Steketee 1996) and work at close quarters with the politicians and their minders whose activities they report.

Spin doctors and media units

Not all news is good news. In an effort to ensure they are reported favourably, governments have developed ploys for influencing how the Gallery interprets and reports politics. Some are overt, others covert (see Tiffen 1989). Overt management of the media includes arranging media conferences and 'doorstop' interviews, and providing media releases in print and via the Internet. Covert methods of news management used by governments are less easily observed. They include the Prime Minister's habit of inviting selected journalists to dine privately at Kirribilli House; 'punishing' journalists for critical stories by withholding access and information; providing 'off-the-record' background briefings to favoured journalists in order to ensure that events are reported with the preferred 'spin'; 'leaking' confidential information when there is an advantage to doing so; even monitoring the public statements of political opponents and releasing details of gaffes they may make to selected journalists.

Governments have increasingly entrusted management of the media to professional advisers. Their media 'minders' are often former journalists with an intimate knowledge of how the gallery thinks and functions. As of 2001, the Howard government had almost three dozen media advisers working for Ministers. The Prime Minister's own staff of 18 included a Senior Communications Adviser, a Senior Media Adviser and a Press Secretary.

As well as employing media advisers attached to ministerial offices, governments have established specialised media units. From 1983 to 1996 the Hawke and Keating governments were served by the National Media Liaison Service (dubbed 'the aNiMaLS' by the gallery). It comprised 23 journalists based in Canberra and the various capital cities. Its ostensible task was to coordinate the government's relationship with the media. In fact, it played a more extensive and political role, monitoring statements made in the media by members of the government with a view to gauging its public image and, increasingly, statements by the members of the Opposition with a view to identifying politically embarrassing utterances. The aNiMaLS systematically fed the Press Gallery with transcripts and stories which fuelled the leadership instability that the Liberal Party suffered during the 1980s. Thus they earned the animosity of the Coalition parties, which promptly closed the unit on winning office in 1996. In its place the Howard Coalition government outsourced its media monitoring work to private sector providers; created a covert media unit (from its pool of ministerial press secretaries) which the gallery promptly dubbed 'the baby aNiMaLS'; and created the Government Members' Secretariat to assist with media liaison. Governments have also been increasingly willing to turn the advantages of incumbency into political advantage by hiring private sector public relations consultants to manage particular policy issues or to assist with the managing of the news media.

The background against which media units have become an institutionalised feature of modern government is worth noting. Prior to the 1998 federal election, the Howard government authorised the expenditure of $16 million on a campaign promoting the introduction of the Goods and Services Tax. The Liberals' election advertising seamlessly adopted this same theme when the election writs were issued. In all, according to Young's calculation, 'the Howard government spent $29.5 million in the three months before the 1998 election' on promotional advertising. She adds that it spent 'another $78 million in the four months before the 2001 election'; and—ahead of the 2004 election—broadcast television ads 'on everything from Medicare to superannuation' in a 'frenzied attempt to influence voters' perceptions' (Young 2004: 127). Her wider point is that governments can use departmental publicity programs to secure a political advantage. These 'community information' campaigns are overseen and coordinated by the Ministerial Committee on Government Communications, which is responsible for the Coalition government's overall media strategy and which receives strategic-level advice from, and is supported by, the Government Communications Unit within the Department of the Prime Minister and Cabinet. Furthermore, most public service departments and agencies now have public affairs or information units whose activities, ostensibly non-partisan, are surprisingly difficult to investigate (Terrill 2000: 127) but whose publicity programs are nonetheless likely to indirectly benefit the governing party. These are all indications that Australia is developing into what Deacon and Golding (1994: 4–7) have described as a 'public relations state' (Ward 2003).

The press gallery and other newsworkers who cover national politics face a small well-drilled and skilled 'army of . . . "media advisers" ' pressing the government's case (Grattan 1998: 35). It is ironic then that, as Prime Minister, John Howard has been one of the Gallery's most trenchant critics. On numerous occasions he has accused it of being out of touch with ordinary Australians and having a Canberra-centric bias. Howard's own preference as Prime Minister has been to circumvent the Gallery and to appear regularly on talk-radio programs. This strategy has offered two clear advantages. First, it has allowed him to address an older, more conservative audience which he regards as his natural constituency. Second, it has allowed Howard to evade questioning by specialist political journalists and to put his case direct to voters in his own words.

Howard's sustained suspicion of the Press Gallery points to the difficulty that any government will have in exerting a complete control over the news agenda. Governments may routinely engage in 'the highly professional selling of a political message that involves maximum management and manipulation of the media' (Grattan 1998: 34). However, journalists are not entirely reliant on government sources and information handouts. There are rivals for their attention. The Opposition may have fewer media advisers and a lesser capacity to generate news, but it will happily provide journalists with an alternative source of news and provide them with a different 'spin' on events. There are minor party leaders and interest groups to whom journalists can also turn. This serves as a small check on the power of governments to manipulate the news media.

The spread of PR politics

A great many pressure groups are now media-savvy and well able to utilise highly professional methods to sell their political messages. They too target the Canberra Press Gallery. This development points to the importance of the news media as an arena in which to lobby for particular policy outcomes, and, more importantly, to the pervasive influence that public relations (PR) has had on Australian politics generally. As Schudson (2003: 29) observes, the news is an 'amplifier'. 'When the media offer the public an item of news, they confer on it public legitimacy. They bring it into a common public forum where it can be known to and discussed by a general audience.' Lobbying has acquired a new public, mediated dimension. Competing interest groups seek to use the news media to establish the legitimacy of their cause and to bring pressure on governments to accommodate their demands. Sometimes the goal is to mobilise public opinion but often 'elites are simultaneously the main sources, main targets and some of the most influenced recipients of news' (Davis 2003: 673).

Hence the ability to 'package' stories for the news media has become the new currency of political influence (Franklin 1994). Not surprisingly, this development is often argued to have entrenched the power wielded by governments, corporations and the large established interest groups. Such groups are able to afford to employ PR professionals, either as hired consultants or on a continuing 'in-house' basis, and hence to engage in the sophisticated politics of 'issue management'. Thus the emergence of the news media as an important arena in which to press political interests has been seen as ushering in a new era of 'capital-intensive' politics and as replacing an earlier period of 'labour-intensive' politics, which favoured trade unions and other organisations with limited finances but with the capacity to mobilise large numbers of members in support of a particular cause.

The thesis that news media are now a central focus for a capital-intensive politics is largely consistent with the argument that journalists tend to routinely rely on government and other established, authoritative sources for certain types of news; that media which are themselves large organisations are drawn to similar powerful business and government institutions with whom they have a bureaucratic affinity; and that those groups best placed to gain access to the news media and to serve as the primary definers of news 'are likely to be powerful, well resourced and well organised' (McQuail 1994: 225). In short, these arguments suggest that the increasing political importance of the media has enhanced the power of government and business and other well-financed interests at the expense of other resource-poor groups, whose voices will go unreported.

There is, however, a contrary view. It sees public relations not as consolidating the control that powerful interests exercise but as enabling a more dynamic contest and thus creating opportunities for resource-poor groups to access news media normally dominated by official sources (Davis 2000: 50). During the 1980s, environmental activists discovered that political protests and stunts that generated dramatic TV news footage invariably received wide coverage, and that this developed public awareness of, and forced policy makers to address, environmental and conservation issues. Indeed, groups such as Greenpeace were so successful that PR companies working for miners and foresters imitated their methods in an attempt to counter them (by creating 'astroturf' or synthetic grassroots organisations to mount similar pro-development campaigns). The hiring of PR professionals to press a political campaign in the media may be costly and beyond the resources of many groups. However a great many are able to stage demonstrations or organise stunts which will attract news coverage and thus use the methods of PR to advantage. Davis (2000: 52) says 'the principal point to make is that effective public relations is aided by economic resources but need not be especially dependent upon them'.

The suggestion that otherwise resource-poor organisations have been able to defy the logic of a capital-intensive politics by utilising their knowledge of the routine ways news is gathered to engineer favourable news coverage of issues of concern to them needs be carefully considered. Even Davis (2000: 54), who is sympathetic to this view, concedes that possessing 'economic resources and institutional advantages' does matter, and that groups and organisations with the advantage of political and economic resources are much better placed to exploit public relations and to capture the media agenda. However, it does serve to remind us that news media are sites of political conflict. News media are magnets for governments, Opposition parties and a host of large and small interest groups, all seeking to influence the ways news is reported. The nature of the ongoing contest between them to influence the news may well favour institutionally powerful and well-financed groups. But the media door remains open to others who manage to frame their message in ways that pique the interest of news media.

Talkback radio

One method which interest groups such as the Australian Bankers' Association and the Australian Trucking Association found to get their message across was to privately 'sponsor' prominent talk-radio hosts to spruik their cause on air. A 1999 inquiry by the regulatory body charged with oversight of broadcast media, the Australian Broadcasting Authority, uncovered and then prohibited this covert practice. The advantage that the sponsors of talkback hosts had sought was to harness the influence that an Alan Jones or John Laws wields. In Sydney, Jones commands a large and loyal local audience, while Laws' program is relayed to more than 60 stations across Australia. Both regularly interview political leaders and even break news stories. However commercial talk radio operates outside of the conventions of balance and objectivity which govern news journalism. Many talkback hosts offer a mix of news and forthright conservative political commentary. They may well drive public opinion. In the USA, Lee and Cappella (2001: 389) have shown that 'when an audience is exposed to an intense, one-sided message, their agreement with the positions advocated increases as exposure and reception increase'. In 1997 John Howard remarked that he thought 'people on talkback radio have more influence now than many print journalists' (cited in Hall 2001).

Some critics have dubbed talkback radio as the 'new news media' and complain about its non-traditional news format, partisan content and propensity to trivialise and reduce politics to a form of 'infotainment' and hence encourage its audience to think poorly of politicians and public life (Taylor 1992). However, there is a contrary view which emphasises that this style of radio program nonetheless contributes to a democratic politics. For example, Herbst argues that talkback 'programs provide an excellent, unstructured outlet for public discourse. Unlike voting and participation in opinion polls, call-in programs let callers (those who can get through) express themselves in their own words—sometimes at great length'. She concedes that it does not provide an 'unlimited discursive space' and that hosts do 'cut off callers, and it is sometimes nearly impossible . . . to reach the program'. Nonetheless she considers that talkback has the potential for free, unstructured public debate: 'only call-in programs give citizens—who have no particular expertise or educational training—the opportunity to engage in mass dialogue about public affairs. Apart from the inchoate internet system, there are few such opportunities in our highly rationalised political sphere' (Herbst 1995: 270–1).

Politicians clearly believe that news-talk radio is an important public forum (Ward 2002). As Prime Minister, John Howard installed a radio studio in his Sydney offices and developed a comunication strategy that relied heavily on news-talk radio and allowed him to 'talk to Australians over the heads of the press gallery'. Acknowledging 'the political influence of the shock-jocks and the need to engage with them', Howard's media advisers 'set up a schedule of regular radio interviews' on better-rating stations in major cities across Australia (Steketee 2001). Clearly lobby and activist groups also seek to exploit talkback radio programs to promote their own political interests. Equally, aggrieved individuals will often call in to complain about their treatment by government agencies or about issues which concern them. During election campaigns, political parties frequently flood programs with callers seeking to promote their candidates and cause. Furthermore, talkback hosts will often seize upon and 'beat up' political issues, stirring public interest and drawing politicians into public debate. A few individual talkback hosts are themselves significant political actors well able to command the attention of Ministers and governments. All of this points to the political importance of talkback radio.

However there is a caveat. It is important to recognise that news-talk radio is a commercial format which targets a niche rather than mass audience. The Rehame (2002) company, which monitors talkback radio for its corporate and government clients, does claim that 'careful analysis reveals that the views of talkback callers generally match the results of opinion polls' and that the views of callers are 'the best daily barometer of public opinion'. Yet the results of the 2001 Australian Election Study survey suggests that talkback has a relatively small audience share: just 5.9 per cent of respondents listened every day with another 9 per cent listening most days. Moreover its audience is rather older and not representative of the wider population. Although it is well entrenched in Sydney, which is Australia's largest market (and a significant political battleground), commercial talkback radio is essentially a local medium. Its popularity and style—and therefore its political influence—varies between capital cities. A wider point to note here is that media are in fact quite diverse. They have different formats, different approaches to reporting political news, and different audiences.

'New' media

As Deacon and Golding (1994: 8, 4) observe, news media are far more than witnesses to, and recorders of, policy debates in the public arena. Rather, they are 'inherently part of the modern policy processes'. The ways in which issues and events are framed and reported can determine their eventual outcomes. Amid the confusion arising as parties and pressure groups and others clamour for the attention of decision makers in government, 'the media have a strategic role' in 'labelling and evaluating' the merits of policy claims and of their promoters. Thus journalists, editors, producers and the newsworkers who generate the mixture of fact and opinion that is news have a considerable power to shape public opinion, and even the determination of policy. However, it is a power checked by the constraints imposed by their employing organisations; by the particular commercial and political interests of their employers; by the dependency of journalists on sources and their 'collusion' with politicians; by an expanding 'PR state'; and by an increasingly pervasive public relations industry ever ready to assist journalists in deciding what is and what is not news.

We have seen that, at its core, the power that is channelled through and wielded by news media stems from their capacity to quickly and efficiently disseminate information to large audiences. It may well be a power that is beginning to leach away. During the 2004 federal election, 1.4 million viewers watched the debate between the leaders televised by Nine as a *Sixty Minutes* episode. But a further 2.3 million viewers tuned instead to *Australian Idol* on a rival channel. While free-to-air television still retains a sizeable audience, many viewers are uninterested in political news. Furthermore the television audience is fragmenting as pay TV multiplies the available viewing choices. The Internet is also emerging as a rival and more chaotic source of information. The technological division between traditional broadcasting and the Internet is dissolving (as the latter resolves bandwidth obstacles to 'video streaming'). Digital television and the flexible viewing that personal digital recorders allow is likely to further diminish the audience for free-to-air television news. Mainstream TV news and newspapers alike are finding it more difficult to command the attention and time of audiences.

There is a final lesson here. Australia's news media may be conceived of as comprising large and powerful organisations like the Nine Network or News Ltd which are in the news business. Or, more narrowly, we can think of the media as those journalists, editors, producers and newsworkers employed in newsrooms (and in the Press Gallery) who act as gatekeepers and each day decide on the content of newspapers and news broadcasts. However, the news media are also technologies for the collation and distribution of information. Since the arrival of television half a century ago, broadcasting technology has evolved and changed, in ways that have substantially reshaped the conduct of politics. The much more recent digital marriage of computer and telecommunications technologies has greatly accelerated this change. One result is the Internet. Its champions see the Internet as a user-driven, empowering and more democratic communication technology, with the potential to reverse the trend towards a capital-intensive politics and to erode the political power which the 'old' media currently enjoy. This may be an overly optimistic view, as the established broadcast media are mounting a determined bid to absorb the changes which the new technology is bringing. However, the pace of change is such that we will probably shortly need to revisit the question of media power and the place of news media in Australia's democracy.

NOTES

1   *Australian Capital Television Pty Ltd* v *The Commonwealth of Australia*, 1992, 177 CLR 106.
2   Today the media are often ideally seen as 'a fourth estate' watching over and holding accountable the legislative, executive and judicial branches of government. This implies that the media are an important part of the political system. The idea of a 'fourth estate' can be traced to the 18th century. In 1789, Louis XVI summoned to Versailles a full meeting of the 'Estates General'. The First Estate consisted of three hundred nobles. The Second Estate, three hundred clergy. The Third Estate, six hundred commoners. Several years later, after the French Revolution, Edmund Burke, looking up at the press gallery of the House of Commons, said, 'Yonder sits the Fourth Estate, and they are more important than them all'. Since then the term has been used to suggest that the media are an important check upon the misuse of political power.

REFERENCES

Cohen, B. 1963, *The Press and Foreign Policy*, Princeton University Press, Princeton, NJ.

Craig, G. 2004, *The Media, Politics and Public Life*, Allen & Unwin, Crows Nest.

Curran, J. 1990, 'Cultural Perspectives of News Organisations: A Reappraisal and a Case Study', in *Public Communication: the New Imperatives*, ed. M. Ferguson, Sage, London.

Davis, A. 2000, 'Public Relations, News Production and Changing Patterns of Source Access in the British National Media', *Media, Culture & Society*, vol. 22, no. 1.

Davis, A. 2003, 'Whither Mass Media and Power?', *Media Culture & Society*, vol. 25, no. 5, pp. 669–90.

Deacon, D. & Golding, P. 1994, *Taxation and Representation: The Media, Political Communication and the Poll Tax*, John Libbey, London.

Franklin, B. 1994, *Packaging Politics: Political Communications in Britain's Media Democracy*, Edward Arnold, London.

Franklin, B. 1998, 'Tough on Soundbites, Tough on the Causes of Soundbite', *Catalyst Pamphlet*, no. 3, <http://www.catalyst-trust.co.uk/pub3.html>, accessed 21 April 2003.

Ghanem, S. 1997, 'Filling in the Tapestry: The Second Level of Agenda-Setting', in *Communication and Democracy*, eds M. McCombs, D.L. Shaw & D. Weaver, Lawrence Erlbaum Associates, Mahwah, NJ.

Grattan, M. 1998, 'The Politics of Spin', *Australian Studies in Journalism*, no. 7.

Hall, J. 2001,'The Public View of Private Health Insurance', <http://www.usyd.edu.au/chs/ahpi/publications/hall/carterchapman commentary.pdf>, accessed 2 October 2003.

Herbst, S. 1995, 'On Electronic Public Space. Talk shows in theoretical perspective', *Political Communication*, vol. 18, no. 3, pp. 263–74.

Iyengar, S. 1990, 'The Accessibility Bias in Politics: Television News and Public Opinion', in *International Journal of Public Opinion Research*, vol. 2, no. 1.

Lloyd, C. 1988, *Parliament and the Press: The Federal Parliamentary Press Gallery*, Melbourne University Press, Melbourne.

Lee, G. & Cappella, J.N. 2001, 'The Effects of Political Talk Radio on Political Attitude Formation', *Political Communication*, vol. 18, no. 4, pp. 369–94.

Mayer, H. 1983/1994, *Mayer on the Media*, ed. R. Tiffen, Allen & Unwin, Sydney.

McCombs, M. & Shaw, D. 1972, 'The Agenda-Setting Function of the Mass Media', *Public Opinion Quarterly*, vol. 36, pp. 176–87.

McCombs, M., Lopez-Escobar, E. & Llamas, P. 2000, 'Setting the Agenda of Attributes in the 1996 Spanish General Election', *Journal of Communication*, vol. 50, no. 2.

McQuail, D. 1994, *Mass Communication Theory*, 3rd edn, Sage, London.

Nimmo, D. 1978, *Political Communication and Public Opinion in America*, Goodyear, Santa Monica, CA.

Perloff, R.M. 1998, *Political Communication*, Lawrence Erlbaum, Mahwah, NJ.

Rehame 2002, [Rehame Homepage] <http://www.rehame.com.au/default.cfm>, accessed 3 March 2003.

Schudson, M. 2003, *The Sociology of News*, W.W. Norton, New York.

Schultz, J. 1998, *Reviving the Fourth Estate: Democracy, Accountability and the Media*, Cambridge University Press, Melbourne.

Steketee, M. 1996, 'The Press Gallery at Work', in *The House on Capital Hill*, eds J. Disney & J. Nethercote, Federation Press, Sydney.

Steketee, M. 2001, 'Minder over Media—How the Flacks Control the Political Message, Canberra in Control', *Australian* [Media supplement], 8 March.

Taylor, P. 1992, 'Political Coverage in the 1990s: Teaching the Old News New Tricks', in *The New News v the Old News*, eds J. Rosen & P. Taylor, Twentieth Century Fund Press, New York.

Terrill, G. 2000, *Secrecy and Openness*, Melbourne University Press, Melbourne.

Tiffen, R. 1989, *News and Power*, Allen & Unwin, Sydney.

Tiffen, R. 1995, 'The Packer–Labor Alliance, 1978–95: RIP', *Media International Australia*, no. 77.

Ward, I. 1995, *Politics of the Media*, Macmillan, Melbourne.

Ward, I. 2002, 'Talkback Radio, Political Communication and Australian Politics', *Australian Journal of Communication*, vol. 29, no. 1, pp. 21–38.

Ward, I. 2003, 'An Australian PR State?', *Australian Journal of Communication*, vol. 30, no. 1, pp. 25–42.

Wheeler, M. 1997, *Politics and the Mass Media*, Blackwell, Oxford.

Willnat, L. 1997, 'Agenda-Setting and Priming: Conceptual Links and Differences', in *Communication and Democracy*, eds M. McCombs, D. Shaw & D. Weaver, Lawrence Erlbaum Associates, Mahwah, NJ.

Windschuttle, K. 1988, *The Media*, 3rd edn, Penguin, Ringwood.

Young, S. 2004, *The Persuaders*, Pluto Press, North Melbourne.

Class and elite analysis

The liberal and democratic traditions have long provided the dominant accounts of social order and government in Western capitalist societies. Together, they provide a consensual liberal-democratic account of Australian society, portraying its citizens as consenting to the overall social order on the basis of liberal and democratic principles.

Yet there are other longstanding critical traditions, presenting very different accounts of social order and government in Western societies. The most influential tradition in this respect is socialism, especially Marxism. This tradition underpins what is often described as class analysis, focusing on the powerful effects of ownership and economic power in capitalist societies. Another tradition is elitism, grounded in the work of central- and southern-European thinkers in the early 20th century. This tradition focuses less on economic power, and more on political and military power.

Marxist and elitist perspectives are in many respects different. The elitist perspective emerged as a critique of Marxism. In turn, Marxists have been deeply critical of elitist perspectives. Notwithstanding their differences, both perspectives share a view that government in Western capitalist societies is not grounded in consent. On the contrary, they emphasise the importance of power and division in understanding so-called liberal democracies. Put bluntly, they argue that liberal democracies are a sham. A relatively small 'class' of people, or an 'elite', govern the population through a combination of force and ideology, notwithstanding so-called free elections and representative political institutions.

This chapter is about the Marxist and elitist traditions, applied to Australian society. It begins with brief accounts of the origins of these traditions. It then discusses their early application and elaboration in the Australian context during the 1970s and 1980s; their application in relation to neoliberal economic reform during the 1980s and 1990s; and their application in relation to wealthy Australians in the late 1990s and the 2000s. It argues that class and elite analysis provide crucial conceptual tools for understanding contemporary Australian politics and society.

The Marxist tradition

Karl Marx (1818–1883), a German political exile who spent most of his adult life in England, developed his ideas in the mid-19th century, at a time when industrial capitalism was growing rapidly. The first sentence of his most famous book, *The Communist Manifesto* (co-written with Friedrich Engels and first published in 1848), declared: 'The history of all hitherto existing society is the history of class struggles' (Marx & Engels 1967: 79). In earlier times, Marx explained, societies were divided into complicated gradations of social rank. The new modern capitalist era had 'established new classes' and 'simplified the class antagonisms'. Capitalist societies were 'more and more splitting up into two great hostile camps, into two great classes directly facing each other: Bourgeoisie and Proletariat' (Marx & Engels 1967: 80).

Adopting the Marxist terminology, the *bourgeoisie* were the capitalists ('the owners of the means of production') who owned the factories of the new industrial age. The *proletariat* were the wage labourers who sold their labour power and worked in the factories. There were other social classes: the aristocracy (the ruling class of the feudal age), the lower middle class ('the small manufacturer, the shopkeeper, the artisan, the peasant') and the *lumpen proletariat* ('the social scum, that passively rotting mass thrown off by the lowest layers of the old society'). But these other classes, according to Marx, were destined to 'decay and finally disappear in the face of modern industry' (Marx & Engels 1967: 90–2). The conflict between the *bourgeoisie* and the *proletariat* was the fundamental enduring division in capitalist society, driving economic, political and social change.

The *bourgeoisie* had been an 'oppressed class' in the previous feudal era, but it had now 'conquered for itself, in the modern representative state, exclusive political sway'. In Marx and Engels' blunt and sloganeering words: 'The executive of the modern state is but a committee for managing the common affairs of the whole bourgeoisie' (Marx & Engels 1967: 82). Marx's own account of contemporary political events presented a more nuanced account than this of the 19th-century state, recognising that the state constrained the power of the *bourgeoisie*. Even so, his account presumed that the state ultimately acted on behalf of those who owned and controlled the means of production. More than this: the coercive power of the state (through the army and police) ultimately underpinned the power of the *bourgeoisie.*

From the late 19th century, Marx's ideas—denouncing the privileged *bourgeoisie* and championing the oppressed and exploited *proletariat*—became the inspiration of revolutionary movements around the world. Ironically, the Communist Parties that stood for these ideas successfully seized power in feudal societies such as Russia and China, but not in the capitalist societies such as the United Kingdom and Australia which were Marx's focus. In the 1930s, Antonio Gramsci (1891–1937), an Italian Communist, reflected upon the failure of Communism in capitalist societies. Gramsci used the concept of *hegemony* to describe the way in which class domination was based not just upon coercion, but also upon the 'manufactured consent' of subordinate classes. In turn, according to Gramsci, the state consisted of the 'entire complex of political and theoretical activities with which the ruling class not only justifies and maintains its dominance, but manages to win the active consent of those over whom it rules' (cited in Taylor 1995: 254).

The elitist tradition

As Marx's theories became the inspiration of revolutionary movements, they also became a point of departure for intellectual debates. In English-speaking societies, the critique of Marxism was largely grounded in the liberal tradition. In central- and southern-European societies, on the other hand, there arose alternative critiques. Vilfredo Pareto (1848–1923), Gaetano Mosca (1858–1941), Max Weber (1864–1920) and Robert Michels (1876–1936) were prominent European intellectuals who took issue with both the liberal and democratic traditions in the early 20th century.

Pareto, Mosca and Michels argued that the concentration of power in small elites was inevitable in all societies. Liberal democracy was a sham, they maintained, but so was democratic socialism. Pareto, for example, was an early-20th-century Italian political sociologist who analysed the different strategies of ruling elites, distinguishing between those who ruled by force as 'lions' and those who ruled by guile as 'foxes'. He argued that elites typically came to rule through natural ability, but then tried to pass on their privileges to their children. Elites thus invariably lost their vitality and were overthrown by the leadership of previously subordinate groups, who then repeated the process (Evans 1995: 229).

Weber, a German social theorist, also believed in the inevitability of hierarchy. In 1908 he wrote to Michels: 'All ideas aiming at abolishing the dominance of men over men are illusory' (cited in Evans 1995: 232). By the same token, Weber's account of domination in liberal democracies was more historically informed and more nuanced, and he is accordingly sometimes described as a 'democratic elitist' (Evans 1995: 232). Above all, Weber drew attention to the advance of bureaucratic organisation, characterised by principles of technical rationality. Bureaucracy involved a hierarchy of domination, whereby specialised officials administered rationally consistent rules in an impersonal way. It did so across all aspects of society. In his own words:

> Already now, rational calculation is manifested at every stage. By it, the performance of each individual worker is mathematically measured, each man becomes a little cog in the machine and aware of this, his one preoccupation is whether he can become a bigger cog. (Cited in Clegg 1990: 30)

Elites, integrated to greater or lesser degree

In the wake of World War Two, liberal-democratic regimes were ascendant throughout Western capitalist societies. The prevailing interpretation of these regimes was described as *pluralism*, portraying a plurality of interests (business groups, unions, churches, returned soldiers and so on) competing for influence on governments. In the mid-1950s, the American sociologist C. Wright Mills' *The Power Elite* (1956) challenged the pluralist orthodoxy in the United States (and, by implication, in other liberal democracies like Australia). Mills was a democrat, closer to Marx than Pareto. Nonetheless he framed his analysis of social order and governance in terms of a 'power elite' grounded in the economy, government and the military. In his own words:

> At the top of the economy, among the corporate rich, there are the chief executives; at the top of the political order, the members of the political directorate; at the top of the military establishment, the elite of soldier-statesmen clustered in and around the Joint Chiefs of Staff and the upper echelon. As each of these domains has coincided with the others, as decisions tend to become total in their consequence, the leading men in each of the three domains of power—the warlords, the corporation chief-tains, the political directorate—tend to come together, to form the power elite of America. (Mills 1956: 9)

Mills' analysis inspired a resurgence of research on elites in Western capitalist societies, including Australia. Sol Encel's pioneering study of hierarchy and power in Australia, *Equality and Authority* (1970), arose from his attempt to answer the question 'Is there an Australian power elite?' But Encel (1970: 3) rejected Mills' concept of the power elite, at least in the Australian context. Instead, he identified a variety of elite groups, arising from a distinction (drawing upon Weber) between 'three dimensions of social inequality': class, status and power. In particular, he identified a business elite (at the top of the class dimen-sion of inequality) and a bureaucratic elite (at the top of the power dimension).

There were instances where, according to Encel, the elite structures over-lapped. For example, he described the premier families of Australian business, and how they were interconnected through directorships of public companies, schools, clubs and intermarriage. In these circumstances he referred to an 'estab-lishment', or alternatively, an 'upper class'. For example:

> The Adelaide Club, centre of what is frequently described as the South Australian 'establishment', reflects a remarkably close-knit, complacent and old-fashioned upper class whose ramifications include the land, politics, one or two private schools, commerce and industry; whose solidarity is buttressed by a high degree of endogamy among the 'forty famous families'; and whose values remain strongly coloured by an atavistic attachment to Edwardian England. (Encel 1970: 135)

Encel drew particular attention to the links between the economic and polit-ical elites. Quoting Mills, he observed how the bureaucracies of business and government faced one another 'across the bargaining tables of power', while 'underneath the tables their myriad feet are interlocked in wonderfully complex ways' (cited in Encel 1970: 355). A wide range of advisory boards and commit-tees provided regular opportunity for 'feet under the table'. There was also steady traffic of personnel between the top levels of government and industry, with 'recurrent changes of status from gamekeeper to poacher' (Encel 1970: 361, 370). In Encel's words:

> Leaving the rural sector aside, the Australian economy might be accurately described as a system of monopoly capitalism, operating through a highly regulated structure of output, prices and wages, which is interlocked with and maintained by an exten-sive system of government activity. (Encel 1970: 322)

In other words, business was no ordinary interest group counterbalanced by others as portrayed in the pluralist interpretation. Instead, it had privileged access to government, with a power and privilege that compromised liberal-democratic principles. While this interpretation is consistent with a Marxist class interpretation, Encel nonetheless concluded that the effects of class on 'daily social life' in Australia were 'less obtrusive' than in other industrial societies. More generally, the dimensions of class, status and power were 'not closely articulated' in Australia because they were constrained by geographical dispersion and the 'prevailing ideology of egalitarianism' (Encel 1970: 101–2). There was, Encel argued, 'neither a ruling class . . . nor a power elite . . ., but a loose collection of elite groups linked together by what may be called a *govern-ing consensus*' (Encel 1970: 4).

Almost a decade later, John Higley, Desley Deacon and Don Smart's *Elites in Australia* (1979) also drew its inspiration from US research on elites. Unlike Encel, Higley and his colleagues understood elites in terms of complex organi-sations. More specifically, elites were 'persons with power to affect organizational outcomes individually, regularly and seriously' (Higley, Deacon & Smart 1979: 3). 'Non-elites', in their analysis, were everybody else. Adopting this framework, Higley and his colleagues interviewed 370 individuals from the business elite, the trade union elite, the political elite, the public service elite, the media elite, the voluntary association elite and the academic elite.

Higley and his collaborators found diverse views among these elite personnel as to whether there was 'a ruling group' in Australia. For example, a Labor Party cabinet minister (a member of what these analysts identified as the political elite) said that the financial institutions and the media ran the country; while the Chairman of the Stock Exchange (a member of the business elite) said that the trade unions were dominant, because business and the conservative opposition were too fragmented (Higley, Deacon & Smart 1979: 225–6). The researchers argued that this diversity of views supported a 'pluralist model' of power characterised by multiple elites, rather than a 'power elite model' along the lines earlier applied to the USA by Mills.

Higley and his collaborators also mapped the interpersonal relationships among elite personnel, finding that 'personal familiarity' and 'issues-based interpersonal links' were 'consistently more pronounced within elite categories and sectors than between them' (Higley, Deacon & Smart 1979: 262). In other words, business leaders knew other business leaders, trade unionists knew other trade unionists; bishops knew other bishops, and so on. This finding further supported the pluralist model. By the same token, 'there was a great deal more elite contact' between different categories 'than the pluralist model's emphasis on separate institutional elites' would suggest. In particular, the researchers observed strong links between politicians, businesspeople and public servants. 'If there is a power elite in Australia', they concluded without conviction, 'then it rather clearly consisted of these three groups' (Higley, Deacon & Smart 1979: 263).

In summary, the concept of elites was elaborated and applied in the Australian context during the 1970s. Researchers used the concept of elites to make the point—contra C. Wright Mills—that there was *not* a power elite (nor a ruling class) in Australia. Rather, there were a variety of elites, integrated to greater or lesser degree.

The ruling class, divided to greater or lesser degree

The critical outlook of C. Wright Mills flourished in the 1960s and 1970s in the wake of the radicalisation of political interpretation inspired by opposition to the Vietnam War. Australian 'New Left' academics cited Mills as one of their points of departure for the analysis of power and inequality in the Australian context (e.g. Playford 1970: 38). By the same token, they largely rejected the concept of the power elite, preferring instead to address these issues in the

Marxist terms of the 'ruling class'. The sociologist R.W. Connell was the outstanding exponent of class analysis in Australia. From the 1970s he wrote—often with collaborators—a steady stream of books and articles grounded in class analysis.

Connell's landmark book *Ruling Class, Ruling Culture* (1977) argued that the ruling class in Australia—as in all capitalist societies—was defined by 'the institution of private property itself' (Connell 1977: 131); not by close overlapping of class, status and power hierarchies (as per Encel), or by overlapping interpersonal networks (as per Higley, Deacon & Smart). The ruling class, argued Connell, was Marx's *bourgeoisie*, the owners and managers of capitalist enterprises—or, in a word, business. Connell elaborated: 'The main form of ruling-class organization in Australia is the company; a fact so familiar, so mundane, that it is often overlooked'. It was in companies that the 'daily life of capitalism occurs—power exercised, profit extracted, accumulation made possible' (Connell 1977: 60). The biggest companies operated on a scale far greater than was the case in Marx's time, and exercised enormous power:

> They control key technologies—mechanized mining, oil refining, steel making, motor manufacturing, air transport, and so on—and often have flocks of smaller companies closely tied to their operations. The oil and motor industries, for example, both have a few very large producers and then a wide spread of agents, distributors, parts suppliers, etc., in various relations of dependence. (Connell 1977: 61)

The ruling class, argued Connell, did not just exercise economic power. It also exercised political power. In Marx's time this power was exercised directly through parliaments dominated by capitalists, who were elected on the basis of restricted suffrage (only property owners could vote). Universal suffrage, the rise of organised labour and the growing scale of capital now meant that this arrangement no longer worked. A new strategy was in order.

> Top political management was now moved decisively into the hands of specialists who ceased to have any significant personal connection with business . . . and increasingly the senior civil servants through whom they governed. This progressive bifurcation of political and business leadership in the ruling class created problems of co-ordination that at times became open conflict . . . but it was essential in establishing the flexibility that allowed ruling-class control of the process of industrialisation. (Connell & Irving 1980: 289–90)

The ruling class also exercised cultural power: hence the title of Connell's book *Ruling Class, Ruling Culture*. Here class analysis built on Gramsci's concept of hegemony to explain the relative quiescence of the Australian working class. Business now directed the 'stimulation of wants and tastes through advertising and fashion' (Connell & Irving 1976: 33). Suburbanisation committed families 'to a pattern of life that absorbed an increasing share of their energies in private activities and bound them economically to the system' (Connell 1977: 216). Men and women were bound to the system through their mortgages, hire purchase and debt. Families became more home-centred, and less likely to mobilise around class-based industrial and political causes.

Although the ruling class was united around the institution of private property, Connell argued that there were divisions and conflicts at every other level. There were divisions between managers (who operated businesses) and *rentiers* (who lived off their wealth); between different industrial sectors, such as pastoralists, miners, manufacturers and bankers; between the managers of international businesses and local businesses; between old money and new money; and so on. 'Internal conflicts of interest, ideology, and outlook' were a 'permanent, necessary feature of the ruling class' (Connell *et al.* 1982: 152). The leadership of the ruling class—both in business and in politics—had to work hard to overcome the effects of these conflicts. They did so through 'unifying institutions', such as business lobby groups (e.g. the Chambers of Commerce), political parties (notably the Liberal Party), kinship (intermarriage among wealthy families) and cultural organisations (such as private schools and exclusive clubs).

An example of class analysis can be found in *Class Structure in Australian History* in which Connell and Irving (1980) described the 'political crisis of the ruling class' in the 1940s. The strains of depression and war, they explained, tore apart the 'ramshackle structure' of conservative political parties. Labor came to power at the national level, while 'the upsurge of socialism promised even worse to come'. In response, 'a major ruling-class political mobilisation occurred, consciously planned and directed by a revived leadership and supplied with a new ideology' (Connell & Irving 1980: 289). Business groups came together in the formation of the Liberal Party under the leadership of R.G. Menzies in 1944. The 'offensive broke' over the Labor government's attempt to nationalise the private banks:

> The mobilisation extended far beyond the Liberal Party, with business publicity and financial resources being co-ordinated by the banks—the chief manager of the National Bank, L.J. McConnan, working practically full-time on the campaign. The Liberal president R.G. Casey, a scion of Mt Morgan [mining] money, raised large campaign funds from English capitalists; Menzies built the issue into a general campaign against rationing and government control as a foretaste of socialist leadership; and the Labor cabinet went down to defeat in 1949, hardly knowing what had hit it. (Connell & Irving 1980: 291)

Similarly, in *Making the Difference: Schools, Families and Social Division*, Connell and his collaborators explored how private schools served to '*create a unity*' among capitalists 'where only narrow common ground and a fragile common interest was before' (Connell *et al.* 1982: 151–2, emphasis in original).

More specifically, they established contacts and built networks. They also defined 'Us' and 'Them'; that is, who belonged to the ruling class and who did not belong. The following interview with a private school girl exemplified these themes:

What about the boys around your way, what schools do they go to?

Well most of the boys go to St Peter's and a couple go to Milton or Scotch or Churchill or Loyola, you know just these sort of schools, private schools. Some used to go to high school in Smith Street.

Any of the kids stay there?

I don't really have any friends going to high school. Just a bit slack and horrible.

What type of people are they?

Oh, they don't care about anything, you know. They don't know what they are going to do when they get older, and they're terribly slack . . .

Do you have much contact with the boys in the private schools?

Yes, because they travel from Jones Street Wharf on the ferry, and they sort of all catch the bus. Like the whole ferry knows, each kid knows the other one . . . All the kids just get on one ferry, scream and yell around together. I think most of the kids that go to a private school, go to parties together, but they don't really invite any outsiders. They don't invite kids from public schools all that much, because I think you know each other better. (Connell *et al.* 1982: 150)

In summary, the concept of the ruling class was elaborated in the Australian context during the 1970s and early 1980s. Researchers, led by R.W. Connell, drew upon the socialist tradition to make the point that there *was* a ruling class in Australia, divided to greater or lesser degree.

A class analysis of neoliberal economic reform

The 1970s and 1980s were a high-water mark for class and elite analysis in Australia (Gilding 2004: 141–2). These decades were also a time of instability at the top levels of Australian society. In 1986 *Business Review Weekly (BRW)* declared—on the basis of the 'Rich 200', its list of the richest 200 individuals and families in Australia—that a 'new Australian establishment is in the making'. Entrepreneurs were 'breaking down the boardroom doors, sending "old" establishment chairmen off to illustrious retirement and encouraging salaried managing directors to try their hands at ventures of their own' (Uren 1986: 47). A year later *BRW* elaborated:

A new order of power and influence is emerging. The old alliances and certainties are breaking down. The new order of financial power has less to do with the Western Districts of Victoria, or Geelong Grammar, or the Liberal Party. It is essentially fast money, hard-working money, clever money, one or two-generation money. (Carlyon 1987: 47)

Some social scientists made the same point in more measured terms. In 1992, for example, Connell and Irving issued a revised edition of *Class Structure in Australian History* with a new chapter entitled 'Class restructured 1975–1990'. Here they described 'the eclipse of manufacturing capital as the key group in the ruling class'. They were not so sure about what was replacing it. In the mid-1980s—as *BRW* had observed—'a new form of finance capital seemed ascendant', exemplified by corporate raiders such as Robert Holmes à Court, Alan Bond and Christopher Skase. By the end of the decade the raiders' corporate empires were in ruins. The relations between government and business were continually being renegotiated, 'with the long-term outcome unsettled' (Connell & Irving 1992: 247).

A decade later—and 25 years after the publication of *Ruling Class, Ruling Culture*—Connell (2004) was surer of what had happened. There had been an international 'shift in hegemony from industrial capital to finance capital'. Bankers and financiers had taken the lead from steel producers and car makers. This shift had been lubricated through the ideology of neoliberalism. In the Australian context, neoliberalism had become progressively more influential, supporting 'the expansion of markets and the spread of the commodity form' at the expense of government (Connell 2004: 2, 7). The earlier model of Australian capitalism—what Encel had described as 'monopoly capitalism . . . maintained by an extensive system of government activity' (Encel 1970: 322)—was dismantled.

More specifically, protective tariffs were progressively cut, notably for cars, and textiles, clothing and footwear. Government enterprises were sold; for example, banks, utilities, serum laboratories, telecommunications, airlines and public transport. Government activities—for example, prisons, employment services and information technology—were outsourced to private companies. 'User pays' became pervasive; for example, in higher education, water and toll-ways. Government regulation was cut back; first in the financial system, then in the labour market. In Connell's words:

> More and more of the goods and services formerly provided by the public sector, voluntary agencies, and even families, have been turned into commodities sold for profit by entrepreneurs. We not only have fast food sold by franchises. Increasingly we have fast education, fast health, fast welfare, fast prisons, not to mention private freeways, private railways, private electricity, and private water supply. (Connell 2004: 6)

The triumph of neoliberalism occurred in spite of the balance of public opinion being opposed to its prescriptions. In the 1970s Connell had emphasised the cultural power of the ruling class and 'manufactured consent' among the working class. In the wake of neoliberal economic reform, consent was precarious. 'There is a great secret about neoliberalism,' Connell observed, 'which can only be whispered, but which at some level everyone knows: neoliberalism does not have popular support' (Connell 2004: 4).

> New Right leaders, from Thatcher and Reagan to Howard, Kennett and Bush, have come to power because they seemed strong, or tapped into nationalism and racism, or because previous governments imploded and became vulnerable to electoral manipulation. But in power, these leaders have had to introduce neo-liberal policies without popular backing, as have Labor neo-liberals. (Connell 2004: 16–17)

Neoliberal economic reform was the 'ruling-class agenda', implemented in spite of the balance of popular opinion being in the contrary direction. But, according to Connell, it was *not* a result of 'straightforward ruling-class mobilisation', unlike the conservative revival of the late 1940s. In particular, sections of the Australian Labor Party and trade union leadership supported and facilitated economic reform. In this context, Connell observed that there were two conditions for reform. First, it was accomplished by 'essentially administrative means, or by controllable mechanisms of assent'. Most obviously, governments never campaigned on a platform of privatisation. Second, reform depended upon 'the absence of an alternative' (Connell 2004: 17). In particular, the influence of neoliberalism within the Labor Party eliminated the local political alternative.

The neoliberal victory was vulnerable. The political leadership had reduced its own capacity to influence the course of events by handing over its powers to the market. It was also vulnerable to electoral backlash, highlighted by the collapse of the Kennett Liberal–Country Coalition government in Victoria. More generally, there was, according to Connell, 'almost universal contempt for politicians', fuelled by unpopular reforms; 'helpless bitterness against the most visible part of finance capital, the banks'; and 'deepening alienation' as social life took the 'alienated form of commodity exchange, governed by a calculus of self-interest' (Connell 2004: 18–19).

Even so, there was no vehicle for a meaningful challenge to neoliberalism. Once the Labor Party would have provided such a vehicle. This was no longer the case. The working class was 'still there'—'double the size' of what it had been 25 years earlier, 'ethnically diverse, changed in gender relations and industrial composition'—but 'now without a political voice'. In this context, Connell observed, 'strange things' were happening. It was John Howard who 'presented himself as the friend of the "battlers" against the "elites" ', while Pauline Hanson 'gained some urban working-class support, as well as rural support' (Connell 2004: 21).

Connell's class analysis highlighted the powerful effects of ownership and economic power in neoliberal economic reform. Business-funded 'think tanks' most actively advanced the neoliberal cause. Their backers included mining companies, farmers' organisations, business associations and financial companies (Kelly 1992: 47; Teicher & Van Gramberg 1999: 161–2; Cahill 2004: 92–3). Peak business organisations such as the Business Council of Australia consistently pressed for economic reform in the wake of the think tanks (Pusey 2003: 11; Sklair 1996: 11–12). The big corporations, such as BHP, the National Australia Bank (NAB) and Publishing and Broadcasting Limited (PBL), were also active (Sklair 1996: 7–12; Lavelle 2000: 76).

Connell's analysis also highlighted the extent to which neoliberal reform was imposed by governments irrespective of the balance of popular opinion. In this context, the National Social Science Survey found that between 1984 and 1996 the mean rating of confidence in banks and government plummeted (from 82.6 per cent to 53.5 per cent for the banks, and from 73.4 per cent to 54.3 per cent for the federal government); while it rose for trade unions (from 60.8 per cent to 63.3 per cent) (Reed & Blunsdon 2002). In turn, the electorate was volatile, notwithstanding the bipartisan backing of the neoliberal agenda. In 1996 the conservative parties swept to power at the federal level, attracting more working-class voters—manual workers and people in routine clerical jobs— than Labor (Betts 1996a: 38); hence the epithet 'Howard's battlers'. Pauline Hanson's One Nation party—hostile to the dismantling of protectionism—also attracted a rising tide of blue-collar support (Betts 1999: 320–1), and in 1999 Kennett's neoliberal government in Victoria was swept from power.

An elite analysis of neoliberal economic reform

As Connell observed, the rise of neoliberalism is 'a global event' (Connell 2004: 2). But—in the words of the American sociologist Neil Fligstein (2001: 200)—it is an 'American project' in particular. Moreover, he argues, it is steadily resisted by 'the rest of the world', on account of the fact that 'nation-states and local elites' often have much to lose by its implementation (Fligstein 2001: 189). Nation states and local elites have *not* been compelled to adopt neoliberalism in order to become more competitive on the global market. This is because most trade is between developed countries, where technological innovation is critical and wage competition is unimportant. After all, the countries that trade most successfully on the global market often have interventionist governments (notably Japan) and big-spending welfare states (say, Germany and Sweden). In other words, the comprehensive neoliberal victory in Australia was distinctive. As the British sociologist Leslie Sklair (1996: 3) observed, in the 1980s and 1990s 'Australia made a rapid and deep-reaching transition from a high tariff, ultra-protectionist inward-looking economy' to 'one of the most open economies in the world'. In this context, the neoliberal victory in Australia begs closer inquiry, paying attention to the structure of 'local elites'.

Three points about the neoliberal victory in Australia warrant particular attention. First, senior government officials strongly supported economic reform. In the mid-1980s, the sociologist Michael Pusey interviewed 215 such officials from the Senior Executive Service (SES) in Canberra. His respondents came disproportionately from managerial and professional backgrounds; a disproportionate number had attended the elite Protestant private schools; and 58 per cent of them had trained in economics or business. Pusey emphasised the influence of their training in economics especially. In earlier times the study of economics had occurred within a liberal educational curriculum, but during the postwar era it became (in the words of one prominent Australian economist) 'much more technical and specialised—one might say, summarily, American-ised' (cited in Pusey 1992: 40). In turn, 'a new elite of narrow neo-classical economists, business-oriented economists, accountants, and people with degrees or experience in business administration and corporate management' (Pusey 2003: 10) took over the Senior Executive Service. The new elite had an over-whelmingly 'economic rationalist orientation to policy and government'. SES officers with 'economics cum commerce and business training' were eight times more likely to score 'high' on a scale of economic rationality than those with other social science degrees (Pusey 1991: 63).

Second, in the 1980s and early 1990s the federal Labor Party leadership drove economic reform. For his part, Pusey described 'an increasingly stable and symbiotic relationship' between the top cabinet ministers of the Hawke Labor government and senior public servants. The ministers came from the Right faction of the Labor Party and controlled the key departments, notably Prime Minister and Cabinet, Treasury and Finance (Pusey 1991: 7). On the same tack, Leslie Sklair's 1995 survey of corporate and political leaders found that then Prime Minister (and former Treasurer) Paul Keating was by far the individual most commonly described as responsible for the globalisation of Australian business. Some corporate respondents described Keating as *the* key individual, pointing out the irony that the 'Labor Party should have emerged in the 1980s and 1990s as the party of modernization and, latterly, globalisation' (Sklair 1996: 18). In 1989 the Labor Minister of Finance Senator Peter Walsh had made the same point:

> Few, if any, people would have believed that any Australian government would have engineered these changes. Most would have thought it even less likely that a Labor government would do so. (cited in Pusey 1991: 4)

Third, business leaders in Australia were divided on economic reform. There were strong advocates of reform from industries and businesses with a global orientation, notably mining (due to export) and finance (due to international investment). There were also strong advocates from the beneficiaries of privatisation, notably finance and infrastructure firms. But there were also opponents, especially among established business elites and domestic manufacturers (Emy 1993: 22–5). Indeed, there is a good case that it was precisely Labor's social distance from the established business leadership that allowed it to push through its reforms. Paul Kelly's landmark study, *The End of Certainty: The Story of the 1980s*, observed that Bob Hawke and Paul Keating were 'Labor leaders sympathetic to the ideology of the market but, unlike the Liberals, devoid of vested interests and associations within the old business or corporate establishment' (Kelly 1992: 56). In turn, they operated with 'a ruthlessness and freedom which the Liberals had never displayed in power':

> They supported a series of revolutions within capitalism—the float [of the dollar]; the new breed of entrepreneurs of whom Alan Bond was the most spectacular; the BHP takeover bid by Robert Holmes à Court; media changes which saw the older companies, the Herald and Weekly Times and John Fairfax and Sons, either fall or falter; and the most sweeping reductions of industry protection in Australia's history. If this was the path to efficiency, then Hawke and Keating saw no obstacle in its pursuit. It had the added plus of destroying the old anti-Labor establishment. (Kelly 1992: 56)

In other words, the local elites that drove neoliberal economic reform included senior government officials, the Labor leadership and some (but not all) business leaders. As already described, Connell's analysis emphasised the influence of business. Similarly, Sklair argued that 'there is little evidence that the administrative elite (or, for that matter, the political elite) could ever carry such an agenda to a successful conclusion without the support of the corporate elite' (Sklair 1996: 27). For his part, Pusey maintained that 'no single fraction of the elite can for long drive economic reform on its own', and that 'flexible but loose and effective coordination is everything'. More specifically, coordination between 'the commanding heights of both Canberra and the big business sector' had 'all but drowned the interests of domestic manufacturing' (Pusey 2003: 11).

But the problem with all of these accounts is that they assume the neoliberal victory too readily. As Connell observed, a 'straightforward ruling-class mobilisation' did not occur. Perhaps it was not possible. After all, what Connell (1977: 131) described as the basic level of collective interest among the ruling class—'the institution of private property itself'—was not at stake in neoliberal economic reform. What was at stake was the way in which local capitalism articulated with global capitalism. Business was divided on this issue. In turn, the conservative parties—in Connell's terms, a key unifying institution of the ruling class—played a relatively limited role in neoliberal economic reform. By implication, other pathways were possible in Australia, for better or for worse. It was precisely the distinctive interplay of elites—notably the role of the Labor leadership and the government bureaucracy—that caused the neoliberal victory in Australia to be so comprehensive.

Middle Australians and neoliberal economic reform

Both class and elite analysis of neoliberal economic reform emphasise the fact that it occurred notwithstanding significant popular opposition. Connell (2004: 4), for example, described popular opposition as a 'great secret about neoliberalism', framing his account in terms of the 'working class'. Pusey (2003: 1) observed that economic reform came 'from the top down', although he framed his account of the opposition in terms of 'middle Australians'. Yet the evidence about popular opinion—whether framed in terms of 'working class' or 'middle class'—is more complicated than this. There were not just differences and divisions among most Australians about economic reform. There were differences and divisions among those Australians who opposed economic reform.

Pusey's own research is revealing on this point. In the late 1990s, Pusey conducted a survey of 400 'middle Australians'—'the broad urban middle class, that is just about all of us who live between the rich and the poor' (Pusey 2003: 3)—about their experience of economic reform. To be sure, there was widespread anger and disillusion. In 1996, for example, 65 per cent of his respondents believed that incomes and job prospects for middle Australians were falling; 59 per cent believed that wage and salary earners were the losers from economic change during the past 15 years; and 76 per cent thought that there was more insecurity than 20 years before. Four years later these views had hardened: 70 per cent of respondents now believed that wage and salary earners were the losers from economic change, and 81 per cent thought there was more insecurity (Pusey 2003: 53).

By the same token, Pusey acknowledged a variety of responses among middle Australians to economic reform. Two groups among his respondents were angry about reform. The first group Pusey described as the 'Battlers and Hansonites'. In the wake of retrenchments, they were 'reeling from permanent insecurity'. Often they did the same work as they had before, but now as subcontractors. They complained 'of stress, of irregular and long working hours, and of tasks that outstrip either their willingness or capacity to undertake them, or both'. In turn, they detested politicians, big business, 'free-loaders' and 'elites'. The second group Pusey called the 'Improvers'. They were 'proactive achievers' with university degrees, full-time professional and managerial work (often in the public sector), and large mortgages. They were angry about economic reform in general, and the 'mounting pressures of flexible, rationalised, and demanding workplaces' in particular (Pusey 2003: 59–60).

On the other hand, there were another two groups of respondents who were not angry. One group had done well out of economic reform. Pusey called them

'North Shore People', in reference to the comfortable suburbs north of Sydney Harbour where he did his research. They included IT specialists, human resource personnel, financial services professionals, accountants and market researchers. Notwithstanding job insecurity, they had good work prospects and felt optimistic about the 'challenges' and 'opportunities' of the new era. The other group were the 'Survivors'. They had survived the huge shakeout in manufacturing. In turn, they seemed to say, 'Hold tight and you can still get through', or even 'You don't have to worry if you knuckle down and work hard' (Pusey 2003: 58–9).

In this context, Pusey found that just over one-quarter (29 per cent) of his respondents rated themselves 'warm' towards neoliberal economic reform; slightly less (26 per cent) gave a 'cold' rating; and 45 per cent were 'neutral' (Pusey 2003: 139). In other words, there was a hard core of Australians—blue collar and white collar—who were angry about economic reform; but a much greater number were either uncertain or cautiously reconciled. The big picture was not so much one of popular opposition, but rather uncertainty and diversity. This explains both the volatility and ambiguity of electoral behaviour—or, in Connell's words, the fact that 'strange things' were happening.

Middle Australians were not only divided in relation to neoliberal economic reform. Those who opposed economic reform were themselves divided in significant ways, notably around immigration. The issue of immigration was related to neoliberal economic reform, both in terms of its impact on the labour market and the role of government. On this account Sklair bracketed the issues when he described the transition in the 1980s and 1990s 'from a high tariff, ultra-protectionist inward-looking economy and society to one of the most open economies in the world and, through deliberate policies of multiculturalism, one of the most ethnically mixed societies' (Sklair 1996: 3). Immigration was also related—but not reducible—to the issue of racial discrimination, making it politically sensitive.

The major parties were mostly bipartisan in support of high immigration in the 1980s and early 1990s, just as they were bipartisan in relation to economic reform. More than this: most Australians opposed high immigration in the 1980s and 1990s, just as they opposed neoliberal economic reform. For example, a 1984 opinion poll found that 62 per cent of respondents thought that there were too many migrants, 27 per cent thought the numbers were about right, and 4 per cent thought there were too few. Similarly, the figures in 1996 were 63 per cent, 31 per cent and 6 per cent respectively (Betts 1999: 122–4). Yet the breakdown of this opposition was not the same as for economic reform. In particular, tertiary-educated Australians strongly supported high immigration. In 1996, for example, 50 per cent of graduates thought that the number of migrants was 'about right', compared with 25 per cent of respondents with no qualifications and 23 per cent of those with trade qualifications (Betts 1999: 123–4). In other words, there was a sharp difference on immigration between those whom Pusey would describe as the 'Battlers' and 'Hansonites' (as well as the 'Survivors') on the one hand, and the 'Achievers' (as well as the 'North Shore People') on the other.

Katharine Betts has observed that the different outlooks of tertiary-educated and non tertiary-educated Australians were at least partly grounded in economic security. Betts described the latter group—including Pusey's 'Battlers' and 'Hansonites'—as 'Parochials'. They feared competition for jobs and wanted government protection across the board, through 'immigration control, labour-market regulation and industrial protection' (Betts 1999: 322). On the other hand, Betts described the graduates—including Pusey's 'Achievers'—as 'Cosmopolitans'. Their job market was often international, and they did not fear competition for their jobs from migrants (Betts 1999: 10–16). The agenda of the Labor Party was once driven by its blue-collar 'Parochials'. The new breed of 'Cosmopolitan' Labor leaders—including Hawke and Keating—not only supported neoliberal economic reform, but more immigration (Betts 1999: 16–17). In this context, Pusey's 'Battlers' and 'Hansonites' turned to One Nation and the Liberals (who broke with bipartisanship on immigration in the 1990s), while his 'Achievers' stuck with Labor or turned to the Greens (Betts 1996b: 27–37).

In other words, elites did not create 'manufactured consent' in relation to economic reform, but nor did they face broad opposition. Just as there was 'no straightforward ruling-class mobilisation' in support of neoliberal economic reform, there was no straightforward working-class—or middle-class—defence of the old order. Popular opposition was compromised by widespread uncertainty, divisions around the impact of economic reform, and divisions around immigration. In this context, economic growth, consumer confidence and employment growth meant that many voters gave economic reform the benefit of the doubt in the 1990s and early 2000s (Bramble 2005: 7–10).

Unifying institutions among wealthy Australians

During the late 1990s and early 2000s, in the wake of economic reform, I interviewed 43 wealthy Australians, drawn from the 1999 *BRW* Rich 200. Some participants had made their fortunes in recent decades across a variety of industries, including property development, financial services and retailing. Others had family fortunes dating back three or more generations. In terms of class analysis, they were part of the ruling class; in the language of elite analysis, they were the members of business elites. Whatever the case, it was difficult to identify unifying institutions that drew the participants together. There were three ways in which this was so.

First, ethnic and religious diversity fuelled institutional diversity. The unifying institutions of earlier times—such as private schools, inter-marriage, exclusive clubs and the British honours system—were partly grounded in British Protestantism. In contrast, the new wave of entrepreneurs included individuals from Irish Catholic, Jewish and Mediterranean backgrounds. Participants from such backgrounds described instances of social exclusion from exclusive clubs and the boards of public companies. For example, one informant put forward the example of Solomon Lew, the wealthy Melbourne businessman who once chaired but then departed from the board of the retail conglomerate Coles Myer:

> Why was Solomon Lew never accepted at Coles Myer? Because it's not just a question of money to be establishment: it's a question of breeding. It's a question of being around at the right time, going to the right school, having the right friends. Establishment doesn't mean rich. If you're rich and established—great! (Gilding 2004: 138)

Second, participants emphasised their ability to work with whatever party was in power, irrespective of their personal preferences. There was little evidence of the Liberal Party as a unifying institution. For example, one man reflected:

> Politicians are in business to be elected and stay in power. We're in business to be in business. If you've got a major issue, you've got to try and solve it. Working with government is part and parcel of being in business. (Gilding 2004: 140)

Finally, globalisation fuelled international networks at the expense of unifying institutions at the regional and national level. Entrepreneurs regularly described gruelling itineraries, demanded by the nature of their businesses. For example:

> It's a world market as far as we are concerned. So we purchase on a worldwide basis. We sell on a worldwide basis. We just happen to manufacture in Australia, but we run numerous other businesses around the world. We're not an Australian company from that point of view. We are an international company. ... The year before last, I was 140-odd days away. This year it's going to be more like 190, 200 days away. (Gilding 2004: 141)

In this context, one participant spoke with regret about the decline of 'traditional families', and the emergence of 'these other people': 'some of them get there by all sorts of devious means and haven't really been taught to eat with a knife and fork properly' (Gilding 2004: 137). Similarly, another participant described how in the 'Scottish, Protestant, capitalist world of Melbourne' where he grew up, there were 'unwritten sanctions' that guided behaviour among the 'very powerful'. Shaming and shunning were effective instruments of control. Nowadays there was 'a much more diverse community'. This meant more reliance upon legal sanction: 'Everything is lawyers and contracts, and so on.' It also meant that trust was 'channelled in a different way': 'It's not necessarily coming through some sort of wider association, it's much more through individuals' (Gilding 2004: 138).

The interviews suggested that if there was not a tightly integrated 'power elite' or 'ruling class' in the 1970s and 1980s, there was even less integration in the 1990s and early 2000s. Perhaps the decline of organised labour and international socialism meant that there was less call for unifying institutions than in earlier times. After all, 'the institution of private property itself' (Connell 1977: 131) was more secure than it had been for a long time. In turn, elites were more able to pursue separate agendas, giving rise to looser networks and neoliberalism.

Conclusion

The liberal-democratic account is the dominant account of social order and government in Australia, but it is not the only account. Marxist and elitist traditions provide alternative frames of reference, drawing attention to power, division and conflict.

The high-water mark of Marxist and elite analysis in Australia was in the 1970s and 1980s. Researchers who framed their analysis in terms of elites mapped the structure of those elites and the ways in which they connected with each other. Researchers who framed their analysis in terms of class mapped the structure of what they identified as the ruling class, the ways in which it was divided, and the scope of its power. Both accounts agreed that there were concentrations of power, centred on business and government.

But they also agreed that there was not a tightly integrated 'power elite' or 'ruling class' in Australian society. Integration between elite groups depended upon institutional structures—or, as Connell put it, unifying institutions—such as exclusive clubs, inter-marriage, political parties and private schools. At some points of time (say, the mobilisation against the Labor government in the 1940s) and in some places (say, 'the Adelaide establishment') the integration of elites was tight. At other times and places it was not.

The 1970s and 1980s were not only a high-water mark for class and elite analysis in Australia. These decades were a time of instability at the top levels of Australian society. The rising tide of neoliberal economic reform—tariff cuts, privatisation, outsourcing, user pays and deregulation—exemplified this instability. The Hawke–Keating Labor governments of the 1980s and early 1990s led the way with economic reform. Economic reform prevailed notwithstanding public opposition. The liberal-democratic account struggles to make sense of these dynamics. In turn, researchers have applied class and elite analysis to neoliberal economic reform more than any other issue. Class analysis has emphasised the pivotal role of business in economic reform. Elite analysis has emphasised the important role of political and bureaucratic elites, and divisions among business elites.

There is a good case for the pivotal role of business in neoliberal economic reform. Yet this argument should not be pressed too far. Established business elites (such as the so-called 'Adelaide establishment') and domestic manufacturers lost heavily in the 1980s. The fact that Labor leaders were often antagonistic to established elites gave them more freedom of action in their reforms. They were strongly supported by the public service elite, increasingly schooled in US-based neoliberal economic theory. Many Australians were uncertain or divided about the reforms. Economic and employment growth in the 1990s and early 2000s further muted popular opposition. Alignments of local elites and the limits of popular opposition explain the comprehensiveness of the neoliberal victory in Australia.

In the wake of economic reform, the unifying institutions that once bound elites together—and made them into a class—are less important. Perhaps there is less call for unifying institutions than was once the case, given the ascendancy of international capitalism and neoliberalism. In turn, there is more scope for different elites pursuing their own agendas. Then again, there is also more scope for instability, in the absence of unifying institutions and manufactured consent. Class and elite analysis provide valuable conceptual tools for understanding these dynamics.

REFERENCES

Betts, K. 1996a, 'Class and the 1996 Australian Election', *People and Place*, vol. 4, no. 4, pp. 38–45.

Betts, K. 1996b, 'Patriotism, Immigration and the 1996 Australian Election', *People and Place*, vol. 4, no. 4, pp. 27–37.

Betts, K. 1999, *The Great Divide: Immigration Politics in Australia*, Duffy & Snellgrove, Melbourne.

Bramble, T. 2005, 'Contradictions in Australia's "Miracle Economy"', *Journal of Australian Political Economy*, no. 54, pp. 5–31.

Cahill, D. 2004, 'Contesting Hegemony: The Radical Neo-liberal Movement and the Ruling Class in Australia', in *Ruling Australia: The Power, Privilege & Politics of the New Ruling Class*, ed. N. Hollier, Australian Scholarly Publishing, Melbourne.

Carlyon, L. 1987, 'Rich 200', *Business Review Weekly*, August 14, pp. 42–7.

Clegg, S.R. 1990, *Modern Organizations: Organization Studies in the Postmodern World*, Sage, London.

Connell, R.W. 1977, *Ruling Class, Ruling Culture: Studies of Conflict, Power and Hegemony in Australian Life*, Cambridge University Press, Cambridge.

Connell, R.W. 2004, 'Moloch Mutates: Global Capitalism and the Evolution of the Australian Ruling Class', in *Ruling Australia: The Power, Privilege & Politics of the New Ruling Class*, ed. N. Hollier, Australian Scholarly Publishing, Melbourne.

Connell, R.W., Ashenden, D.J., Kessler, S. & Dowsett, G. 1982, *Making the Difference: Schools, Families and Social Division*, Allen & Unwin, Sydney, <http://www.allenandunwin.com.au>.

Connell, R.W. & Irving, T.H. 1976, 'Yes Virginia, There is a Ruling Class', in *Australian Politics: A Fourth Reader*, eds H. Mayer & H. Nelson, Longman Cheshire, Melbourne.

Connell, R.W. & Irving, T.H. 1980, *Class Structure in Australian History: Documents, Narrative and Argument*, Longman Cheshire, Melbourne.

Connell, R.W. & Irving, T.H. 1992, *Class Structure in Australian History: Poverty and Progress*, 2nd edn, Longman Cheshire, Melbourne.

Emy, H.V. 1993, *Remaking Australia: The State, the Market and Australia's Future*, Allen & Unwin, Sydney.

Encel, S. 1970, *Equality and Authority: A Study of Class, Status and Power in Australia*, Cheshire, Melbourne.

Evans, M. 1995, 'Elitism', in *Theory and Methods in Political Science*, eds D. Marsh & G. Stoker, Macmillan, Houndmills.

Fligstein, N. 2001, *The Architecture of Markets: An Economic Sociology of Twenty-First Century Capitalist Societies*, Princeton University Press, Princeton.

Gilding, M. 2004, 'Entrepreneurs, Elites and the Ruling Class: The Changing Structure of Power and Wealth in Australian Society', *Australian Journal of Political Science*, vol. 39, no. 1, pp. 127–43 <http://www.tandf.co.uk>.

Higley, J., Deacon, D. & Smart D. 1979, *Elites in Australia*, Routledge & Kegan Paul, London.

Kelly, P. 1992, *The End of Certainty: The Story of the 1980s*, Allen & Unwin, Sydney.

Lavelle, K. 2000, 'Victoria's Paradox. A Popular Government with Unpopular Policies: The Kennett Government 1992–1996', MA Thesis, Swinburne University of Technology.

Marx, K. & Engels, F. 1848/1967, *The Communist Manifesto*, Penguin, Harmondsworth.

Mills, C.W. 1956, *The Power Elite*, OUP, Oxford.

Playford, J. 1970, 'Myth of the Sixty Families', *Arena*, no. 23, pp. 26–42.

Pusey, M. 1991, *Economic Rationalism in Canberra: A Nation Building State Changes its Mind*, Cambridge University Press, Cambridge.

Pusey, M. 1992, 'The New Mandarins', in *Shutdown: The Failure of Economic Rationalism and How to Rescue Australia*, eds J. Carroll & R. Manne, Text, Melbourne.

Pusey, M. 2003, *The Experience of Middle Australia: The Dark Side of Economic Reform*, Cambridge University Press, Cambridge.

Reed, K. & Blunsdon, B. 2002, 'Declining Trust in Australian Companies', Refereed Proceedings of ANZAM, Victoria, December.

Sklair, L. 1996, 'Who are the Globalisers? A Study of Key Globalisers in Australia', *Australian Journal of Political Economy*, vol. 38, no. 1, pp. 1–30.

Taylor, G. 1995, 'Marxism', in *Theory and Methods in Political Science*, eds D. Marsh & G. Stoker, Macmillan, Houndmills.

Teicher, J. & Van Gramberg, B. 1999, '"Economic Freedom": Industrial Relations Policy Under the Kennett Government', in *The Kennett Revolution: Victorian Politics in the 1990s*, eds B. Costar & N. Economou, UNSW Press, Sydney.

Uren, D. 1986, 'Rich 200', *Business Review Weekly*, 15 August, pp. 47–50.

ACKNOWLEDGMENTS

Extracts from Connell 2004 on pages 389 and 390 reproduced with kind permission of Australian Scholarly Publishing.

Extracts from Connell *et al.* 1982 on pages 387 and 388 reproduced with permission of the authors.

Extracts from Connell & Irving 1980 on pages 386 and 387 reproduced with kind permission of the authors.

Extracts from Gilding 2004 on pages 397–8 reproduced with permission of the publisher.

CHAPTER 21

Feminism, power and the representation of women

JENNIFER CURTIN

In March 2005, an Australian women's magazine published an article headed with the question 'Will Australia ever have a female Prime Minister?' (Loane 2005). The context was the recent leadership contest that had been prompted by Mark Latham's resignation from the leadership of the federal Labor Party. Much of the media frenzy focused on whether Julia Gillard, a prominent member of Labor's Shadow Cabinet, would put herself forward for the position.

What is it about politics in Australia that makes such a question newsworthy? While women are more visible in the world of politics than they were 50 years ago, they are still enough of a novelty to attract attention when they aspire to political leadership. Joan Kirner (Victoria), Carmen Lawrence (Western Australia), Kate Carnell (ACT) and Clare Martin (Northern Territory) have headed governments at the State and territory level over the past 15 years, but the top leadership jobs of Prime Minister or even Leader of the Federal Opposition remain elusive. This is despite the fact that Australia once led the world on women's political rights, giving (non-Indigenous) women the right to vote and stand for the national Parliament in 1902, with two of the States—South Australia and Western Australia—having enacted women's suffrage even earlier.

This chapter examines a significant but insufficiently appreciated aspect of Australia's liberal-democratic political system: the under-representation of women. While the chapter's primary focus is on parliamentary and party politics, it also reviews feminist critiques of traditional understandings of what constitutes the 'political', challenging the notion that politics should be understood as limited to the parliamentary and party arenas. The chapter analyses various claims about women's political representation in Australia, including whether attaining an equal number of women in Parliament would be a sufficient achievement or whether additional measures are needed to provide women with substantive representation of their interests.

Studying politics: a feminist perspective

In recent years, women's contributions have been recognised as integral to extending our understandings of Australian politics and government (Sawer 2004a). But prior to this, academic studies of politics had a long history of presenting their subject matter as universal when in fact it had been partial, neglecting issues of gender. As Canadian political scientist Jill Vickers (1997: 11) noted, 'like race, disability and sexual orientation, sex and gender were considered irrelevant to the study of politics and government', a trend similarly evident in Australian political science.

For example, sophisticated studies of women's voting behaviour were largely non-existent until recent decades, though a confident view that women were more likely than men to be conservative voters nonetheless came to predominate both here and overseas. Goot and Reid (1975) noted that the research questionnaires used to study samples of voters up until that time were often only administered to male respondents on an assumption that women would vote the same way as their husbands or fathers. Even when these early studies included women in their samples, women's behaviour was typically not analysed since it was thought that interest in politics was largely concentrated among men—although Goot and Reid (1975) themselves estimated on the basis of a survey that 43 per cent of women did have an interest in politics. Due to this sort of inadequacy in older studies, we have no real understanding of, for example, the gendered impact of the introduction of compulsory voting in the 1920s.

Until feminists entered the discipline of political studies, there was much about women's activism and participation in politics that went unnoticed. Until then, the study of politics tended to be based on a traditional view of what constitutes the 'political'. Politics, according to this traditional view, meant the ideas, institutions and processes constituting the official political process. This orientation largely ignored gender inequality in the distribution of political power.

For centuries it had been assumed that only men would inhabit the public arena, where 'politics' was performed. Thus it should come as no surprise then that the establishment of Australia as a nation, and the drafting of its Constitution, was undertaken by founding fathers. All delegates to the constitutional conventions in the 1890s were men (although Catherine Spence from South Australia stood unsuccessfully for election as a convention delegate). While some women and Indigenous people in a few States could take part in voting to select delegates, ultimately no women or Aboriginal people were elected. As a result, the full range of citizens of the soon-to-be Commonwealth of Australia was not involved in the federation process. This has led to criticism that Australia's political institutions were designed in a way that reflected ethno-centric and patriarchal views about who could participate and what constituted legitimate politics (Irving 1996).

Campaigns in the 19th century for expanding the right to vote in parliamen-tary elections were pitched first at enfranchising men, and the extension of similar rights to Australian women in the 19th and early 20th centuries was strongly resisted by much of the male elite. Anti-suffragists argued that provid-ing women with political rights as citizens would undermine the established moral order. Questions were raised as to who would undertake housework and other supposed feminine responsibilities if women were to aspire to a political career. Suffragists countered these claims by arguing the traditional roles of women were not being displaced, but rather were being complemented:

> There is no reason why women's sphere should be circumscribed. Her duty begins in the home but it does not end there. . . . No woman could be so much interested in a budget speech or an electoral Bill to forget to the put the chops on. (*Southern Mail* 7 November 1904, quoted in Sawer & Simms 1993: 30)

While women activists at this time were content to claim a dual identity as 'citizen-mothers', arguing that their qualities as mothers and carers would enhance the practice of politics, the public–private divide that such a dual identity implies was challenged by later feminists in the 1960s and 1970s. This challenge involved a strategy of redefining the 'political'. The catchcry of the 'personal is political' became entrenched as one of the most famous feminist slogans.

The aim was a positive one: to 'reveal and valorise women's participation' outside formal politics (Squires 1999: 195). It also drew attention to the way in which a liberal perspective, so influential in shaping a liberal democracy like Australia, imagined public and private realms as separate rather than as inher-ently interconnected. Liberals defend the primacy of the 'private' sphere (comprising civil society and the family) where individuals are free to pursue their interests without interference from the state. But feminists contested this claimed public/private separation, arguing that such a dichotomy undermined any possibility of substantive equality for women. Their critiques highlighted the way in which women were relegated or confined to the private sphere by patriarchal views that saw women as less capable of reason and logic (virtues thought to be necessary for participation in public life) (Pateman 1989; Young 1998; Porter 1991).

Feminist analyses also revealed how much of what actually happens within the domestic realm is inherently political because it reflects the distribution and exercise of power and requires state intervention if women's equality is to become a reality. As a result of the later acceptance of this feminist perspective, issues such as sexual and domestic violence, prostitution and pornography have now become matters of public policy concern and regulation (van Acker 1999).

However, this broadening by feminist analysts of what constitutes the 'political' also brought with it a danger: that feminist engagement with formal politics (within the so-called 'public' sphere) could become 'delegitimised' as a practical strategy and as a field of academic study (Vickers 2006). Institutions of government were labelled in these feminist analyses as inherently male and impenetrable and as sites where the interests of men would ultimately dominate. If women participated at all, it was interpreted in these analyses as either tokenism or cooption.

More recently, however, some feminist political scientists have argued that dissolving the meaning of 'politics' to the point where formal institutional politics is not recognised as a site of power requiring feminist critique is not in the interests of women.

It is widely acknowledged by feminist thinkers and activists that, because of the diversity among women, it is neither true nor desirable to claim that there exists an objective set of identical interests common to all women. But Anne Phillips (1995) nonetheless maintains that one specific interest common to all women is having a strong women's political presence. Phillips argues that increasing the presence of women in legislatures, for example, is important, not only because political participation in a democracy should be equally open to all citizens—women and men—but also because women may bring new perspectives to bear on existing ways of interpreting politics and operating in the legislative environment. Moreover, given that women's experiences and claims are indeed multiple and diverse, the more women there are elected, the more likely that the diversity among women will be reflected in formal politics and, as a consequence, in the definition and construction of policies concerning the lives of women (Phillips 1995).

The issue of women's under-representation in legislatures regained momentum in the 1990s, with many national and international women's organisations identifying it as warranting immediate attention by governments and political parties. With this has come an increase in research focusing on the factors that either inhibit or enhance women's participation in electoral politics.

At the systemic level, an electoral system featuring proportional representation has been identified, both within particular countries and in cross-national analyses, as a key factor in promoting women's representation (Castles 1981; Curtin 2003b; Rule 1994). The political culture of particular countries—particularly when measured in terms of the strength of the women's movement—also appears to matter (Grey & Sawer 2005; Sawer 1991; Chappell 2002). Political parties have been identified consistently as the primary gatekeepers that regulate the opportunities for women's election to Parliament (Curtin & Sexton 2004; Simms 1993).

This chapter now turns to an examination of two interconnected aspects of women's representation within formal institutional politics in Australia. First, it addresses the issue of *descriptive representation*—the number of women pre-selected and elected to Australian parliaments, with a focus on the federal Parliament, and the number of women prominent elsewhere in the formal political system. Second, it also addresses the notion of *substantive representation*, examining whether elected representatives who happen to be women necessarily really represent the interests of women.

Women, politics and parties

VOTING RIGHTS

In 1902, non-Indigenous women were successful in obtaining not only the right to vote in federal elections but also the right to stand for election. While the Women's Christian Temperance Union had been an active campaigner for women's voting rights, the eventual success of suffragists owed much to the political opportunity provided by the process of federation.

Several (male) South Australian delegates to the 1897 Constitutional Convention had been strong advocates of female suffrage. Frederick Holder made the threat that South Australian voters could thwart the federation process if it was proposed that South Australian women's voting rights, which had been conferred in 1894, were to be forfeited. Holder argued that 'women as well as men should be recognised as electors of this great commonwealth' (Fitzherbert 2004: 7). Because the federation process required all colonies to support it via referendum endorsement, the Convention was in a sense forced to pacify the South Australians. In the end, the Convention agreed—by a margin of just three votes—that women could have the right to vote and stand for election to the proposed new Commonwealth Parliament. An additional clause which protected the voting rights of women in States where they had won that right was inserted into the draft Constitution to become what is now section 41. It provides that no person who had already been enfranchised in a State could be denied the right to vote (Grey & Sawer 2005).

There had been some anticipation internationally and in Australia that when women first got the vote they would then create a unified political force. However, this was not to be. As Catherine Spence wrote in 1903, 'women do not vote as women for women[;] . . . if the South Australian women had done so I should have been elected to the Federal Convention' (cited in Daniels &

Murnane 1989: 280). Thus, while women in many countries had organised *en masse* around issues of suffrage and temperance, there was no translation of this into female solidarity as voters. On the other hand, neither should it be assumed that married women necessarily voted the same way as their husbands (Curtin 2003a; Leithner 1997).

PARTY POLITICS

While the Australian party system was not fully developed prior to 1910, it was strong enough for an anti-party or anti-establishment sentiment to be felt amongst early women political activists. Many regarded the party system as being designed by men to support men's interests, leaving little room for women's interests to be adequately represented within party platforms. Victorian suffragist Vida Goldstein, who stood as an Independent candidate for the Senate in 1903 and on four subsequent occasions, argued:

> We have all got very decided views as to the merits of the various political parties . . . But we differ from those organized along party lines in one important particular. We believe that questions affecting honour, private and public integrity and principle, the stability of the home, the welfare of children, the present salvation of the criminal and the depraved, the moral, social and economic injustice imposed on women — we believe that all these questions are greater than party. (Goldstein cited in Summers 1994: 412)

This feminist non-party ideal was strong in all States. Organisations were established by women to educate women on how to use their vote in a discriminating manner, and Goldstein herself launched a newspaper called the *Woman Voter*. However, most of these women eventually realised the futility of a non-party stance. The *Woman Voter* ceased publication in 1919 although the Australian Federation of Women Voters remained viable for several more decades.

While party politics may have come to usurp the ability of women to remain separate or independent, this did not mean that the major parties could rely on consistent support from women voters. Indeed women regularly demonstrated their anti-party sentiments by standing as Independent candidates and/or by voting independently (Curtin 2003a).

Parties on the conservative Right of the political spectrum recognised early on that accessing the women's vote was important for electoral success, and they decided that separate women's political organisations were the best means for mobilising women. For example, the Queensland Women's Electoral League was decidedly partisan in its electoral advice in 1910 despite also emphasising the right of women to vote without coercion from any party: 'in the hands of women lies the tremendous power of making Queensland either a progressive liberal State or a retrogressive socialist one . . . Help Queensland . . . by voting for the Liberal Policy' (cited in Daniels & Murnane 1989: 283).

The most famous Liberal women's organisation in Australia's history is undoubtedly the Australian Women's National League (AWNL) established in Victoria in 1903. The League, declaring that its members wanted to do more than provide tea and scones for their male counterparts, focused instead on the preselection of candidates for the Liberal Party (or its equivalent at various stages in the evolution of the Australian party system), participating in election campaigns and ensuring women's social and political rights were addressed by Liberal Party policy (Fitzherbert 2004). When Robert Menzies formed the modern Liberal Party in 1944, the AWNL negotiated itself permanent representation on the Federal Executive of the party, guaranteed positions on State Executives and State Councils, and the creation of Women's Sections in the party (Fitzherbert 2004; Sawer & Simms 1993).

Since then, there have been a number of other initiatives to promote women's presence within the ranks of Liberal Party parliamentarians. In 1981, Australian Business Woman of the Year Eve Mahlab and Julie McPhee helped to establish the Liberal Feminist Network. The Network stood outside the Liberal Party, but was concerned with supporting Liberal women who wanted to enter politics. In 1982 it published a *Guide for women seeking preselection in the Liberal Party*. While the Network itself did not last beyond the 1980s, Liberal women continued to promote the need to increase women's parliamentary representation (Whip 2003). An updated *Guide* was released in 1990, and a National Women's Candidate Forum, headed by Dame Margaret Guilfoyle, led to the establishment in 1993 of the Liberal Women's Forum Program. Unlike its predecessor, this Program has not been avowedly feminist in inspiration and nor does it deal with issues of policy. Rather its main purpose is to identify and encourage individual women to stand for election and assist them in the campaign to do so (Brennan 2002; van Acker 1999).

The Liberal Party has the strongest record on being an attractive party to women, if measured in terms of party membership, voting support and promoting women's parliamentary presence (Brennan 2002). Liberal Party women are vehemently against the provision of quotas guaranteeing a minimum level of places for women in the preselection of parliamentary candidates, believing that preselection should be based solely on merit (Henderson 1999). However, these women also believe that the merit principle needs to be applied fairly, and in practice that belief has led to considerable activism on the part of Liberal women to attract good women candidates.

By contrast, Labor Party women were only partially successful prior to the 1980s in maintaining women's networks and national women's conferences within the party (Sawer 2002). Indeed, it is widely acknowledged that the ALP considered itself a party for working men, with women being seen as peripheral, if not as damaging, to the electoral aspirations of the party (ALP 1978; Sawer 2000a). While Labor Prime Minister Gough Whitlam was praised for initiating during his term (1972–1975) a range of progressive policy measures on behalf of women, including the establishment of an Office of the Status of Women located within the Department of the Prime Minister and Cabinet, this did little to ensure that a significant proportion of the women's vote shifted from Liberal to Labor (Aitkin 1982).

By the late 1970s, some within the Labor Party had recognised the need to make their party appear more inclusive of women. A Committee of Inquiry Discussion Paper canvassed a number of affirmative action strategies (ALP 1978). For example, it suggested that each State branch 'might be required to endorse a woman candidate for one safe seat at each federal election until women are represented in the federal Parliament in proportion to their membership of the party in that State' (ALP 1978: 36). It went on to suggest the possibility of women-only short-lists: 'a mechanism by which this recommendation could be implemented is to declare that nominations for a specified safe seat will be accepted only from women' (ALP 1978: 36). Interestingly, women-only short-lists were later used for a short period by the British Labour Party before the policy was ruled illegal in 1996 (Studlar & McAllister 1998).

The 1981 ALP National Conference endorsed affirmative action principles under which women were to be represented across all party structures in proportion to their overall membership. However, the Conference decision requested rather than required State branches to implement the strategy and it did not explicitly refer to candidate selection for winnable seats. This inadequacy led to a second affirmative action strategy—a gender quota—adopted at the 1994 National Conference. What became known as Rule 12 in the ALP Constitution stated that, by 2002, 35 per cent of the parliamentary party, members of party committees and conference delegates at both federal and State levels were to be women. The target of 35 per cent corresponded to women's proportion of Labor's party membership at the time, but it was also recognised by women party activists as the proportion of party positions at which women were likely to achieve a critical mass and be able then to overcome the structural and cultural obstacles that remained (Sawer 2002). The eight-year time schedule encompassed three electoral terms, in recognition that an extended time frame was necessary for implementation through natural replacement rather than through deposing sitting members (Dahlerup 1988; Hughes 1983; Zetlin 1996). A number of studies have detailed the battles that women in the ALP fought in order to achieve this success: the difficulties and tensions associated with the institutionalisation of factions which began to divide women within the party; the difficulties with bringing recalcitrant trade unions into line given their influence at party conferences; and forcing the party hierarchy to recognise the value of attracting more women voters to the party (Gillard 2000; Hennessy 2000; Lawrence 2000; Sawer 2000a, 2002; Summers 1983; Zetlin 1996).

Because the ALP's State branches are responsible for parliamentary candidate preselection, they were delegated responsibility for ensuring that the gender quota was met. Progress reports were required to be delivered to the National Conference to ensure a satisfactory degree of accountability. The National Executive was empowered to intervene in the preselection process if the quota was not being met; it could declare candidature for all parliamentary seats open, potentially threatening incumbent male Labor Members of Parliament with the possibility of being disendorsed. This would have acted as a significant punitive incentive within State branches.

In 2002, a Special Rules Conference extended the quota target to 40 per cent as a minimum proportion of positions (including among trade union delegations to party conferences) to be held by either gender by 2012. This quota increase had been recommended by the Hawke–Wran report (2002) on the ALP's organisational processes, described in more detail in Chapter 12 of this book. The recommendation appeared to be influenced by motions carried at an earlier National Labor Women's Conference and by submissions from two groups—EMILY's List and the Labor Women's Network.

EMILY's List was founded in 1996 and led by former Victorian Labor Premier Joan Kirner. Formally independent of the Labor Party, EMILY's List supports Labor women preselected for winnable seats who demonstrate a commitment to a number of women's rights, providing them with a range of resources and support during their campaign (Sawer 2004b). The Labor Women's Network was established in 1997 within the Labor Party following the creation of the EMILY's List group. It also aims to promote women's political participation in the party but, as an internal party body, remains accountable to the National Executive. It is worth noting that in 1981, when the first affirmative action measure was adopted, neither EMILY's List nor the Labor Women's Network existed to support or promote the issue of women's selection.

Thus the Labor Party has, in recent decades, accelerated and institutionalised its commitment to the representation of women in parliaments across Australia.

PARLIAMENTARY REPRESENTATION

Although women gained the right to vote and stand for election comparatively early in Australia, it was a long time before a woman was elected. Australia's first female parliamentarian was Edith Cowan, elected to the Western Australian Legislative Assembly in 1921. This was only one year after Western Australian women were granted the right to stand for election at the State level. But the lag in all other States between gaining the formal right and the actual election of a woman was considerable. In South Australia, for example, Joyce Steele was elected as the first woman in the SA Parliament in 1959 fully 65 years after women gained the right to stand for Parliament (Wilson & Lamour 1997; Sawer & Simms, 1993; McAllister, 2006).

At the Commonwealth level, women did not gain a parliamentary presence until 1943, with the election of Enid Lyons (United Australia Party) to the House of Representatives and Dorothy Tangney (Australian Labor Party) to the Senate. Between 1943 and 1980, women's representation in the federal Parliament was sporadic. Liberal women were more successful than Labor women, Joan Child in 1974 becoming the first ALP woman elected to the House of Representatives (and later to become the House's first female Speaker).

Since the 1980s, there has been a fairly continuous upward trend in the levels of female representation in the Commonwealth Parliament, with a significant increase evident after 1996. This trend is evident in Figure 21.1. Also evident is the extent to which women are more likely to be elected to the Senate than to

| FIGURE 21.1 | Proportion of women among federal parliamentarians 1943–2004 |

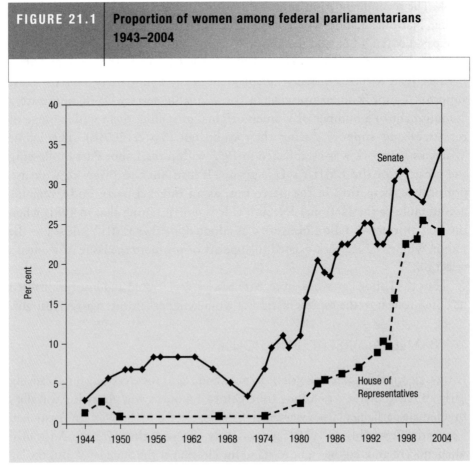

Sources: Parliament of Australia (2005), Electoral Commission cited in McAllister (2006).

the House of Representatives. Indeed, the proportion of women in the House of Representatives has never exceeded the proportion of women in the Senate. There are several possible explanations for this.

The first possible explanation is that the proportional representation electoral system used in the Senate favours the preselection and election of women. Each State acts as a single district with six Senators up for election or 12 if there is a double dissolution (Curtin 2003b). Such large multi-member districts substantially increase women's chances of election because there is less intra-party competition for selection and, as a result, parties are more likely to recruit women (Rule 1994). Historically, political parties have been averse to selecting women in single-member or small districts because party officials perceived (incorrectly) that women were vote-losers (Mackerras 1977).

Women's election is also more likely in the Senate because of the increased chances of minor party representation in that chamber. Minor parties are more successful in winning Senate seats because the threshold quota needed for election is relatively low (around 14.3 per cent of the total vote for a normal half-Senate election and just 7.7 per cent for a full-Senate double-dissolution election). Women's representation benefits because Australia's established minor parties, the Australian Democrats and Greens, have a much better record than the major parties on pre-selecting women candidates.

There may be a third reason, relating to arguments about gender and power, why women are better represented in the Senate. Scandinavian feminist scholars have argued that women enter an arena of power *en masse* only when that arena is no longer considered powerful (Bergqvist 1995). This Scandinavian literature focuses primarily on trade unions and the business sector, but a similar argument could be made about the Australian Senate. While the Senate can be powerful as a 'house of review' when not controlled by the government, it is in the House of Representatives that the government is formed and where the Prime Minister sits. In addition, about three-quarters of Cabinet is usually drawn from the House of Representatives. As a result, various women Senators who have had leadership aspirations have had to relinquish their Senate position and seek election to the lower house. Bronwyn Bishop (a Liberal Senator from 1987 to 1994), Cheryl Kernot (a Democrats Senator from 1990, and party leader from 1993, until she defected to the Labor Party in 1997) and Janine Haines (a Democrats Senator from 1977 to 1978 and from 1981 to 1990, and party leader from 1986) all attempted to take this route, with varying degrees of success.

As Table 21.1 reports, the proportion of women in all Australian parliaments has now reached nearly 30 per cent. The Greens and the Democrats are the parties with the highest levels of female representation. Their success in recruiting women candidates appears to be partly attributable to their emergence since the rise of so-called new social movements, including the women's liberation movement. Viewed as 'new politics' parties informed by ideas of gender

TABLE 21.1	Composition of Australian Parliaments by party and gender as at 1 July 2005		
	Male	Female	% Female
Labor	274	154	36.0
Liberal	196	53	21.3
Nationals	56	10	15.2
Country Liberal	9	3	25.0
Democrats	4	4	50.0
Greens	7	8	53.3
One Nation	0	1	100.0
Independent	25	12	32.4
Other	8	0	0.0
TOTAL	579	245	29.7

Source: Updated from Wilson (2005).

equality and participatory democracy, they contrast with the major parties' traditional image of being male-dominated. The Democrats in particular have had an inspiring record of female involvement since their inception in 1977, with over 50 per cent of their membership and six of their national parliamentary leaders being female. The democratic nature of both the Democrats and the Greens has meant that they appear more open and less intimidating to women seeking a political career or to have a say in the drafting of policy platforms (van Acker 1999; Brennan 2002).

By contrast, the National Party has only recently begun to address the need to become more inclusive of women. The Nationals are Australia's most conservative established party and this, in combination with their rural focus, has meant they have largely ignored women's role in politics. Moreover, the fact that the Nationals tend to win only safe seats, the number of which is in decline, also means that incumbency has protected sitting (male) members and provides women with fewer opportunities to obtain preselection.

Federally the National Party's history begins in 1920, and since then there have only been two National Party women Senators elected—Agnes Robertson (1955–62) and Flo Bjelke-Petersen (1981–1993). It took until 1996 for the first Nationals woman (De-Anne Kelly) to be elected to the House of Representatives. Since then Kelly has been joined by Kay Hull in 1998 and Senator Fiona Nash in 2005.

The traditional 'male' image associated with the Nationals was encapsulated in the 2001 federal election when the party contested three-cornered contests (i.e. competing against a candidate endorsed by their Liberal Coalition partner as well as against a Labor candidate) in the House of Representatives seats of Farrer (New South Wales, a seat formerly held by the retiring National Party leader Tim Fischer) and Indi (Victoria) . The contrast in candidates—with the Liberals preselecting younger women compared to the Nationals older male candidates—was highlighted in media coverage. Ultimately, the Nationals lost Farrer to the Liberals' Sussan Ley (now a Parliamentary Secretary in the Howard government) and failed to win Indi (held by the Liberals' Sophie Panopoulos). In the election post-mortem, then National Party leader John Anderson suggested a review would be needed of the National's preselection process (Curtin & Woodward 2002).

This gloomy portrayal needs to be moderated by an acknowledgment that women have been active as ordinary and executive members within the National Party over a number of decades. The Party first adopted a comprehensive women's policy platform in 1992, it has produced a manual for women recruits similar to that of the Liberals and it has sought to create stronger women's networks and recruitment strategies. The Nationals were the first party to appoint women to the positions of Federal President, State Director and Federal Director (Gardiner & Ferguson 1996). International research indicates that having women as party officials promotes women's parliamentary presence and, in the case of the Nationals, clearly the activism of women in the party has contributed to the increase, albeit small, in women's preselection and election (Gardiner & Ferguson 1996).

While the Liberal Party once surpassed the Labor Party in its proportion of women elected, Table 21.1 reveals that this is no longer the case. Labor has reached its initial target of 35 per cent, no doubt a result of the adoption in 1994 of its gender quota. Prior to this, Labor women were seldom endorsed in winnable seats. Since 1994, the number of female Labor candidates nominated has more than doubled, while the number of those selected for winnable seats has almost quadrupled from four to 15. As of 2005, all of Labor's women federal members in the House of Representatives hold safe seats. Fourteen of the 15 elected in 2004 were re-elected incumbents.

Between 1984 and 1996, the Liberals were competitive with, if not surpassing, the Labor Party in terms of the number of women preselected. Moreover, the number of Coalition women preselected for safe seats rose from three in 1996 to 14 in 1998, and all of these were re-elected in 2004. This significant increase can be partly explained by the large number of women who won marginal seats in the 1996 election and then went on in the 1998 election to turn these into fairly safe Coalition seats. However, it has also been argued that the Labor Party's quota approach has had a contagion effect on the Liberal Party, provoking it into promoting the preselection of women to safe seats in order to neutralise an initiative which might attract voters to their opponents (Curtin & Sexton 2004).

Outcomes for women

This chapter concludes by briefly examining the *substantive representation* issue of whether we should expect women, once elected, to act on behalf of women.

There is clearly a range of compelling reasons why women's parliamentary presence should be encouraged, not least because it is important for the Parliament to reflect the diversity of Australian society (for others, see Trimble 2006; Sawer 2002; Phillips 1995). A proper consideration of women's perspectives and experiences would be unlikely without the presence of women (Phillips 1995). Rather, 'deliberations and outcomes [would] most likely reflect the goals of the dominant groups' (Young 1990: 184).

However, to suggest that we should have more women in Parliament because it will make a substantive difference to the representation of women's interests is problematic for at least two reasons. First, outcomes favouring women constituents may not result irrespective of the number of women elected. Second, we cannot assume that women's interests are homogenous and therefore easily identifiable.

One way to measure the degree of substantive representation of women by women might be to examine the actions of women in Parliament. How do women Members of Parliament vote on bills that might directly impact on women? To what extent do they cross party lines and work together as women around issues perceived to be of immediate concern to women? This is a research approach commonly adopted in the United States but it is less applicable in Australia because party discipline here is much stronger and this makes it extremely unlikely that women can work across party lines. When a conscience vote is allowed, for example on the issue of abortion, an alliance between women parliamentarians could in principle occur but it is still unlikely due to the considerable disagreement amongst women parliamentarians on this issue even within the same political party.

Within the ALP, a Status of Women Committee which cuts across factional lines is credited with ensuring the Labor Caucus is cognisant of the way in which particular policies are likely to impact on women constituents. Labor women elected with the support of the EMILY's List group are expected to represent women's interests in Parliament, and there is evidence—based not on parliamentary votes but rather on the extent to which these women raise certain issues on the floor of the Parliament—to suggest that this is indeed happening (Sawer 2004).

Some feminist scholars have argued that, because of the presence of strict party discipline, it is meaningless to examine the parliamentary voting record of women politicians. Instead, they argue, the focus should be on recognising the complexities associated with expecting a particular social perspective (in this case gender identity) to inform the process of representation (Trimble 2006; Cramer Walsh 2002). A more nuanced analysis which focuses on such a broader understanding reveals that the representation of women by women does indeed matter.

For example, an examination of Australian women parliamentarians indicates that they do in fact see themselves as having a role in representing women as citizens with particular interests (Sawer 2001; Tremblay 2003). Over the years many women parliamentarians, from all sides of politics, have referred in their maiden speeches to their experiences as women and/or feminists and how this has informed their positions and opinions on particular issues. In addition, women politicians are more likely than their male colleagues to raise issues of concern to women, such as domestic violence and child care, during parliamentary debates (Williamson 2000; Sawer 2004a).

There is also much networking and lobbying around such issues that go on behind closed doors, invisible to those on the outside. For example, in the lead-up to the 1998 election, Senator Helen Coonan and others in the Liberal parliamentary party raised concerns about the extent to which childcare funding had been cut (Sawer 2000b: 152). More recently, a number of Liberal Party women politicians and party members have expressed public concern over the Howard government contemplating cuts to publicly funded access to *in vitro* fertilisation procedures for women. Liberal Senator Marise Payne has been active in her committee work to protect the *Sex Discrimination Act* from being watered down. (But it is also revealing that, partly as a result of such an 'independent' stand, Senator Payne was relegated to the vulnerable third place on the NSW Coalition Senate ticket in the 2001 election. In the end, the total vote for the Liberal Party ticket was sufficient to ensure she was re-elected.)

If the aim is to ensure that gender equity considerations are integrated into the policy-making process, then this requires more than a parliamentary presence. It requires, as Sawer (2002: 17) argues, an institutionalisation of a range of measures throughout the policy-making process. It is particularly important to recognise that much of what becomes policy is decided by Cabinet. If we assume that the presence of women matters, if only to provide a diverse range of opinion and experience in the process of deliberation, then the representation of women in Parliament needs to be complemented by an increased representation of women in Cabinet.

For a long time, the Liberals were the only party which, when in government, provided women with Cabinet positions. In late 1949, under the incoming Menzies Coalition government, Dame Enid Lyons became the first woman to hold Cabinet rank when she was named Vice-President of the Federal Executive Council. In 1966, Senator Annabelle Rankin became the first woman to be Minister responsible for a government department (Housing) but this was not a Cabinet position. It was not until late 1975, under the incoming Fraser

Coalition government when Senator Margaret Guilfoyle entered Cabinet as Minister for Education, that a woman held a portfolio inside Cabinet. In 1976, Guilfoyle became Minister for Social Security and remained in Cabinet for more than seven years, still the record as Australia's longest-serving woman Cabinet Minister. In 1983, Senator Susan Ryan became Labor's first woman Cabinet Minister as part of the incoming Hawke Labor government's first Cabinet.

Between 1975 and 1996 there was only one woman in Cabinet at any time (Curtin 1997). With the arrival of the Howard Coalition government in 1996, this number increased to two, and as of 2005 it stands at three: Senator Amanda Vanstone (Immigration, Multicultural and Indigenous Affairs), Senator Helen Coonan (Communications, Information Technology and Arts) and Senator Kay Patterson (Family and Community Services).

In 1994, Margaret Guilfoyle noted that unless women were positioned in the Cabinet then the effect of more women in Parliament would not be felt in the arena where the decisions are taken and the policy directions are set (Guilfoyle 1995). The under-representation of women in Cabinet thus remains a critical weakness. Addressing it probably requires increasing the number of women in the House of Representatives (particularly in safe seats to allow longevity of service) and including more women in the outer Ministry as the pathway into Cabinet.

Yet despite the prominence of women in the Howard Coalition government's Cabinet and the relatively large influx of Liberal women into the federal Parliament at and since the 1996 election, the Howard government's record on women's issues is dismal. There have been significant cuts in budget and resources for the Office of the Status of Women (now the Office for Women) and it has been relocated from the central and powerful Department of the Prime Minister and Cabinet to the Department of Family and Community Services. Many of the women's groups and non-government organisations which represent a wide range of women's interests have had their government funding cut, undermining their capacity to research and contest government policies considered to be detrimental to women. The *Affirmative Action Act* has been abolished, replaced with legislation that is significantly less stringent in its requirements for businesses to demonstrate that they are implementing equal opportunity for women (Whip 2003; Chappell 2002). Proposed new industrial relations laws would further diminish equity for women in the labour market. In addition, there has been only cosmetic attention to issues of child care and domestic violence, while demands for paid maternity leave have been displaced by the introduction of a baby bonus. Conservatives within the Howard government continually call for a tightening of access to abortion, while 'feminists' are regularly referred to by prominent government spokespersons as representing only the special interests of a few women (Curtin 2003c; Sawer 1997).

These shortcomings in relation to the substantive representation of women, as measured by government outcomes, do not weaken the case for continuing to tackle the issue of descriptive representation by seeking gender parity in Australian parliaments. While it is arguably the role of all politicians—male and female—to promote improvements in gender equity if they are truly representing the interests of their constituents, descriptive representation remains 'a marker of justice, political equality, and the democratic legitimacy of electoral and deliberative political institutions' (Trimble 2006). If we want our parliaments to reflect a diverse range of views and experiences, then the idea and practice of representation needs to be extended to become more inclusive of women.

REFERENCES

Aitkin, D. 1982, *Stability and Change in Australian Politics*, 2nd edn, Australian National University Press, Canberra.

ALP, 1978, Australian Labor Party National Committee of Inquiry: Discussion Papers, *APSA Monograph*, No. 23, Flinders University, Adelaide.

Bergqvist, C. 1995, 'The Declining Corporatist State and the Political Gender Dimension', in *Women in Nordic Politics. Closing the Gap*, eds L. Karvonen & P. Selle, Dartmouth, Aldershot.

Brennan, D. 2002, 'Women and Political Representation', in *Government, Politics, Power and Policy in Australia*, eds J. Summers, D. Woodward & A. Parkin, Pearson Education, Sydney.

Castles, F. 1981, 'Female Legislative Representation and the Electoral System', *Politics*, vol. 1, no. 1, pp. 21–6.

Chappell, L. 2002, *Gendering Government. Feminist Engagement with the State in Australia and Canada*, UBC Press, Vancouver.

Cramer Walsh, K. 2002, 'Enlarging Representation. Women Bringing Marginalized Perspectives to Floor Debate in the House of Representatives', in *Women Transforming Congress*, ed. C.S. Rosenthal, University of Oklahoma Press, Norman.

Curtin, J. 1997, *Women in Australian Federal Cabinet*, Research Note 40, Department of the Parliamentary Library, Canberra.

Curtin, J. 2003a, 'White Women and the Federal Vote, 1902–1949: Challenging the Idea of Women's Conservatism', in *Selective Democracy. Race, Gender and the Australian Vote*, eds J. Chesterman & D. Philips, Circa, Melbourne.

Curtin, J. 2003b, 'Women and Proportional Representation in Australia and New Zealand', *Policy, Organisation and Society*, vol. 22, no. 1, pp. 48–68.

Curtin, J. 2003c, 'Representing the "interests" of Women in the Paid Maternity Leave Debate', Paper presented to Australasian Political Studies Association Conference, University of Tasmania, Hobart.

Curtin, J. & Sexton, K. 2004, 'Selecting and Electing Women to the House of Representatives: Progress at last?', Refereed Conference Paper, Australasian Political Studies Association Conference, University of Adelaide, Adelaide, <http://www.adelaide.edu.au/apsa/docs papers/Aust%20Pol/Curtin.pdf>.

Curtin, J. & Woodward, D. 2002, 'Rural and Regional Interests: the Demise of the Rural Revolt', in *2001: The Centenary Election*, eds J. Warhurst & M. Simms, University of Queensland Press, St Lucia.

Dahlerup, D. 1988, 'From a Small to a Large Minority. Women in Scandinavian Politics', *Scandinavian Political Studies*, vol. 11, no. 4, pp. 275–99.

Daniels, K. & Murnane, M. 1989, *Australia's Women. A Documentary History*, University of Queensland Press, St Lucia.

Fitzherbert, M. 2004, *Liberal Women. Federation to 1949*, Federation Press, Sydney.

Gardiner, J. & Ferguson, C. 1996, 'Women and the National Party of Australia', in *The Paradox of Parties*, ed. M. Simms, Allen & Unwin, Sydney.

Gillard, J. 2000, 'The Future is Female: Pursuing Change in the Labor Party', in *Party Girls: Labor Women Now*, eds K. Deverall, R. Huntley, P. Sharpe, & J. Tilly, Pluto Press, Sydney.

Goot, M. & Reid, E. 1975, *Women and Voting Studies: Mindless Matrons or Sexist Scientism?*, Sage, London.

Grey, S. & Sawer, M. 2005, 'Under the Southern Cross: Women's Political Representation in Australia and New Zealand', in *Sharing Power: Women, Parliament, Democracy*, eds Y. Galligan & M. Tremblay, Ashgate, Aldershot.

Guilfoyle, M. 1995, 'Women, Parliament and Cabinet', *Canberra Bulletin of Public Administration*, no. 78, p. 22.

Hawke, R. & Wran, N. 2002, *National Committee of Review*, ALP, Canberra.

Henderson, A. 1999, *Getting Even: Women MPs on Life, Power and Politics*, Harper Collins, Sydney.

Hennessy, J. 2000, 'Natural Selection and the Political Animal', in *Party Girls: Labor Women Now*, eds K. Deverall, R. Huntley, P. Sharpe, & J. Tilly, Pluto Press, Sydney.

Hughes, C. 1983, 'An Election about Perceptions', in *Australia at the Polls. The National Elections of 1980 and 1983*, ed. H.R. Penniman, Allen & Unwin, Sydney.

Irving, H. 1996, 'Equal Opportunity, Equal Representation and Equal Rights?: What Republicanism Offers to Australian Women', *Australian Journal of Political Science*, vol. 31, no. 1, pp. 37–50.

Lawrence, C. 2000, 'The Gender Gap in Political Behaviour', in *Party Girls: Labor Women Now*, eds K. Deverall, R. Huntley, P. Sharpe & J. Tilly, Pluto Press, Sydney.

Leithner, C. 1997, 'A Gender Gap in Australia? Commonwealth Elections 1910–1996', *Australian Journal of Political Science*, vol. 32, no. 1, pp. 29–37.

Loane, S. 2005, 'Will Australia ever have a Female PM?', *Madison*, March, pp. 92–94.

Mackerras, M. 1977, 'Do Women Candidates Lose Votes?', *Australian Quarterly*, vol. 49, no. 3, pp. 6–11.

McAllister, I. 2006, 'Women's Electoral Representation in Australia', in *Representing Women in Parliament: A Comparative Study*, eds M. Sawer, M. Tremblay & L. Trimble, Routledge, London (forthcoming).

Parliament of Australia 2005, 'Number of women in Parliament', Parliamentary Handbook of the Commonwealth of Australia, Canberra, <http://www.aph.gov.au/library/handbook/historical/women_number.htm>.

Pateman, C. 1989, *The Disorder of Women: Democracy, Feminism and Political Theory*, Polity Press, Cambridge.

Phillips, A. 1995, *The Politics of Presence*, Clarendon Press, Oxford.

Porter, E. 1991, Women and Moral Identity, Allen & Unwin, Sydney.

Rule, W. 1994, 'Parliaments of, by, and for the People: Except for Women?', in *Electoral Systems in Comparative Perspective*, eds W. Rule & J.F. Zimmerman, Greenwood Press, Westport.

Sawer, M. 1991, 'Why has the Women's Movement had more Influence on Government in Australia than Elsewhere?', in *Australia Compared. People, Policies, Politics*, ed. F.G. Castles, Allen & Unwin, Sydney.

Sawer, M. 1997, 'A Defeat for Political Correctness?', in *The Politics of Retribution: The 1996 Federal Election*, eds C. Bean, M. Simms, S. Bennett & J. Warhurst, Allen & Unwin, Sydney.

Sawer, M. 2000a, 'Women and Labor: a Question of Heartland?', in *The Machine. Labor Confronts the Future*, eds J. Warhurst & A. Parkin, Allen & Unwin, Sydney.

Sawer, M. 2000b, 'Women: Gender Wars in the Nineties', in *Howards Agenda: The 1998 Australia Election*, eds M. Simms & J. Warhurst, University of Queensland Press, St Lucia.

Sawer, M. 2001, 'A Matter of Simple Justice? Women and Parliamentary Representation', in *Speaking for the People. Representation in Australian Politics*, eds M. Sawer & G. Zappala, Melbourne University Press, Melbourne.

Sawer, M. 2002, 'The Representation of Women in Australia: Meaning and Make Believe', *Parliamentary Affairs*, vol. 55, no. 1: pp. 5–18.

Sawer, M. 2004a, 'The Impact of Feminist Scholarship on Australian Political Science', *Australian Journal of Political Science*, vol. 39, no. 3, pp. 553–66.

Sawer, M. 2004b, 'When Women Support Women: EMILY's List and the Representation of Women in Australia', *Australasian Political Studies Association Conference*, University of Adelaide, <http://polsc.anu.edu.au/Sawer.pdf>.

Sawer, M. & Simms, M. 1993, *A Woman's Place. Women and Politics in Australia*, 2nd edn, Allen & Unwin, Sydney.

Simms, M. 1993, 'Two steps Forward, One Step Back: Women and the Australian Party System', in *Gender and Party Politics*, eds J. Lovenduski & P. Norris, Sage, London.

Squires, J. 1999, *Gender in Political Theory*, Polity Press, Malden, Mass.

Studlar, D.T. & McAllister, I. 1998, 'Candidate Gender and Voting in the 1997 British General Election: Did Labour Quotas Matter?', *Journal of Legislative Studies*, vol. 4, no. 3, pp. 72–91.

Summers, A. 1983, 'Holding the Balance of Power? Women in Australian Electoral Politics', in *Australia at the Polls. The National Elections of 1980 and 1983*, ed. H.R. Penniman, Allen & Unwin, Sydney.

Summers, A. 1994, *Damned Whores and Gods Police*, Penguin Books, Ringwood.

Tremblay, M. 2003, 'Women's Representational Role in Australia and Canada: The Impact of Political Context', *Australian Journal of Political Science*, vol. 38, no. 2, pp. 215–38.

Trimble, L. 2006, 'When do Women Count? Substantive Representative of Women in Canadian Legislatures', in *Representing Women in Parliament: A Comparative Study*, eds M. Sawer, M. Tremblay & L. Trimble, Routledge, London (forthcoming).

van Acker, E. 1999, *Different Voices. Gender and Politics in Australia*, Macmillan, Melbourne.

Vickers, J. 1997, *Reinventing Political Science. A Feminist Approach*, Fernwood Publishing, Halifax.

Vickers, J. 2006, 'The Problem with Interests: Making Political Claims for 'Women', in *The Politics of Women's Interests*, eds L. Chappell & L. Hill, Routledge, London.

Whip, R. 2003, 'The 1996 Australian Federal Election and its Aftermath: a Case for Equal Gender Representation', *Australian Feminist Studies*, vol. 18, no. 40, pp. 73–97.

Williamson, M. 2000, 'Do Women Make a Difference? Testing for a Critical Mass in the Australian Senate and New Zealand Parliament', Unpublished paper, Political Science Program, Australian National University, Canberra.

Wilson, J. 2005, 'Composition of Australian Parliaments by Party and Gender, as at 23 March 2005', Politics and Public Administration Group, Parliamentary Library, Commonwealth Parliamentary Library, Canberra, <http://www.aph.gov.au/library/intguide/pol/currentwomen.pdf>, accessed April 2005.

Wilson, J. & Lamour, C. 1997, *First Women in Australian Parliaments—A Historical Note*, Research Note 55, Dept of Parliamentary Library, Canberra.

Young, I.M. 1998, 'Polity and Group Difference: A Critique of Universal Citizenship', in *Feminism and Politics*, ed. A. Phillips, Oxford University Press, Oxford.

Young, I. M. 1990, *Justice and the Politics of Difference*, Oxford University Press, Oxford.

Zetlin, D. 1996, 'We're Here Because We're Here: Women and the ALP Quota', in *Gender Politics and Citizenship in the 1990s*, eds B. Sullivan & G. Whitehouse, University of New South Wales Press, Sydney.

Policy

PART 5

Introduction

Previous parts of this book examine the institutions, processes and structures which shape government, politics and power in Australia. This fifth part draws on all of these elements to discuss the impact of governmental systems on Australian society within a number of key policy areas.

The expression *public policy* is a general term denoting the *purpose, substance* and *effect of governmental action.* Each of these elements is important. The notion of *purpose* indicates that government actions can be assessed in terms of the goals which they are designed to achieve, leading frequently to political debates about what the appropriate purpose should be. The notion of *substance* refers to the actual content of the governmental action: the rules it sets in place, the administrative apparatus for the implementation of programs and the enforcement of regulations, the actions of government officials in providing services, and so on. The notion of *effect* looks at the impact of government policies on society.

It should not be assumed that the three elements are necessarily consistent even within a particular policy area: purposes are sometimes hard to translate into substantive programs, while substantive programs can likewise produce unintended effects. Analysts of public policy try to disentangle these elements of the process, in order to obtain a better understanding of how the whole governmental system operates and sometimes to provide insights into how the process might be improved.

Six policy areas—chosen because of their significance for the system of government and politics, for their potential insights into the nature of liberal-democratic politics in particular, for their prominence in recent debates and for their pervasive impact on the Australian people—have been selected for intensive analysis in this section.

In Chapter 22, Dennis Woodward examines policy with respect to the economy. He places recent economic problems in their historical context by discussing the so-called 'Australian settlement' which, for most of the 20th century, entailed a significant role for government involvement in, and regulation of, economic activity. Woodward argues that global changes in the last decades of the 20th century resulted in the adoption of neoliberal policies and greater reliance on market forces in the belief that this was necessary to make Australia more internationally competitive. Australian economic policy at the beginning of the 21st century remains deeply affected by these great changes.

Tax policy is the focus in Chapter 23. Alan Fenna provides an account of the structure of the Australian tax system and the recent debates in Australia about tax 'reform'. He discusses tax policy in terms of the variety of economic and social purposes (often conflicting) for which taxation is levied, and he examines the debate about various measures (again often conflicting) against which the appropriateness and effectiveness of a tax system could be assessed.

In Chapter 24, Jane Robbins analyses welfare policy. This is another area where previously well-established policies are being challenged by new political, social and economic forces. Robbins examines the recent debates about the extent to which the government sector should be responsible for addressing social disadvantage, and the extent to which—alternatively—individuals should take greater responsibility for their own welfare and the community rather than the government for the provision of social support.

The focus shifts in Chapter 25 to health policy. Gwen Gray notes that the major political parties in Australia have had held strongly opposed policy positions on health policy. The Coalition parties have supported an approach which relies primarily on private health insurance while the Labor Party has favoured a government-controlled nationally administered system. Gray examines the making of health policy in Australia as the interplay of interests and arguments about the appropriate respective roles of private-sector and public-sector actors, and provides in this way an insight into how liberal-democratic politics often operates.

In Chapter 26, Jane Robbins and John Summers explore Indigenous affairs policy. They outline past policies towards Australia's Indigenous population to provide the historical background against which current debates need to be understood. For the last three decades or so, all Commonwealth governments have espoused policies involving a substantial level of Indigenous self-determination or self-management. Robbins and Summers argue that initiatives by the Howard government that reject the notion of self-determination and place much greater emphasis on the importance of economic advancement for Indigenous people, represent an important turning point.

Finally, Chapter 27 examines the interestingly contested arena of environmental policy. Jenny Stewart explains how environmentalism challenges aspects of how liberal-democratic politics normally operate. She traces the emergence of environmental issues on to the Australian political agenda, the response that Australian governments have made in terms of environmental policies and programs, and the range of policy instruments that governments can call upon to promote sustainable environmental management. She concludes with some thoughts on the possibilities for genuine future progress.

Economic policy

DENNIS WOODWARD

The liberal elements of Australia's liberal-democratic system feature prominently in aspects of economic policy in Australia, but the extent to which the supposed democratic elements impinge on economic policy is more problematic.

Liberal ideas have underpinned and justified a range of economic policies that, beginning in the early 1980s, have marked a change from previous practice. These policies, and the ideology that has inspired them—variously called 'neoliberalism', 'economic rationalism' and 'economic liberalism' (see also Fenna in Chapter 2 of this book)—are examined in this chapter.

By contrast, the degree to which economic policy has been democratically shaped is a moot point. Certainly, claims of sound economic management and scare campaigns centring on particular economic policies or outcomes have come to be central features of election campaigns in Australia. Yet the often bipartisan acceptance of specific economic policies limits the democratic choice facing electors. This arguably, according to some critics, undermines democracy itself (e.g. Maddox 1989: 14). Similarly, the rather closed nature of the 'economic policy community' that determines economic policy casts doubt on its democratic credentials, as does the fact that specific economic policies are often implemented despite their being opposed, to the extent that this can be measured via opinion polls, by a majority of the electorate. In addition, a number of statutory bodies, such as the Reserve Bank of Australia and the Australian Competition and Consumer Commission, make decisions that affect the general public but are not directly democratically accountable. These questions over the democratic character of public policy in the economic field need also to be seen in a context where major economic decisions are made by *private* economic actors—and their role appears to be increasing as that of the public sector diminishes.

The extent to which economic policy is democratically determined is a matter of some consequence, since economic policy has considerable impact on the lives of citizens that extends beyond the usual preoccupation with taxation levels and mortgage interest rates. The actions of governments (or their inaction) can affect the level of economic growth, the levels of employment and unemployment, and conditions of work. Governments set the 'ground rules' for economic activity: they regulate the financial system, sign trade treaties and regulate trade. They directly or indirectly provide the transportation infrastructure needed for economic growth, and they regulate the power and communications industries. Governments can encourage or block foreign investment and their policies can support or undermine domestic industries. Governments in Australia have historically shaped the country's developmental path and they continue to do so.

This chapter focuses on the changed economic policy direction that Australian governments have pursued since the early 1980s. It argues that this has represented a sharp departure from earlier economic policy and, in particular, from the types of policies followed in the immediate post-World War Two period. It further argues that this changed policy direction has been adopted in response to the changed nature of the global economy and has been inspired by the acceptance of neoliberal views. As this economic policy shift began under the Hawke and Keating Labor governments, this chapter scrutinises particular policy areas beginning with those administrations but devotes more attention to the more recent period of the Howard Coalition government.

Historical background

In order to understand why a neoliberal-inspired change in Australia's economic policy took hold in the 1980s, it is necessary to trace both the long-term and more immediate historical background that shaped the Australian economy. White settlement in Australia was brought about by Britain establishing penal colonies. From the outset, therefore, there emerged a reliance on government for not only the provision of infrastructure and services but also the welfare of the (convict) inhabitants. This high dependence on the state continued as the various Australian colonies became self-governing and pursued policies dedicated to economic development—a process that has been called 'colonial socialism' (Butlin 1983: 82).

At the same time, the colonial links to Britain influenced the developmental trajectory undertaken in Australia. Australia came to be reliant on its export of farm and mineral commodities to Britain whence it derived its capital inflow and manufactured imports. This heavy reliance on commodity exports, which has continued to the present, is a root cause of the economic problems that have confronted Australia since the mid-1970s. However, it (and the British connection) delivered considerable benefits from the latter half of the 19th century and through most of the 20th century. For example, Australia is reputed to have had the highest Gross Domestic Product (GDP)[1] per capita in the world in the 1880s (Kelly 1992) and its commodity exports underpinned the post-World War Two 'long boom' (1949–1970) which saw continuous high economic growth (6 per cent annual growth rates in the 1960s) and virtually full employment (Boehm 1993).

These (and other) legacies from the colonial era formed the basis for the adoption (by all the parties) of a group of interconnected policies in the first decade after federation that remained largely in place ('settled') until the new policy direction of the 1980s. Paul Kelly (1992) has popularised a particular conceptualisation of these policies as the 'Australian Settlement'.[2] His portrayal of the 'settlement' comprises five key features: industry protection, wage arbitration, white Australia, state paternalism and imperial benevolence.

'State paternalism' and 'imperial benevolence' are the somewhat pejorative terms used by Kelly to describe the tradition of reliance on the state and dependence on Britain that have been discussed earlier. 'Industry protection' refers to the use of tariffs to protect Australia's emerging manufacturing industry from overseas competition. Its adoption resolved the dispute between the 'free traders' and 'protectionists' that had proved the most divisive issue of the early Commonwealth Parliament.[3]

'Wage arbitration' refers to the national arbitration system, established to resolve industrial relations conflict, that came to rule on wage levels. It represented a compromise between capital and labour with an 'independent' (government-appointed) arbitrator who would mediate in disputes and make binding rulings on the parties concerned. It gave legal recognition to trade unions; helped to lessen the impact of strikes and lockouts; and (following the High Court's 1907 *Harvester* judgment) set a minimum (male) wage that was designed to allow workers and their families to live in 'frugal comfort' (McCarthy 1976: 41).

'White Australia' refers to the enactment of Commonwealth legislation designed to prevent non-white immigration into Australia. While this policy was clearly based on racist views about preserving 'racial purity' in Australia, it was strongly supported by the labour movement as a measure to protect wage levels.

Together, Kelly argues, these five aspects of the 'Australian Settlement' set the pattern for Australia's economic and social development for most of the 20th century. They reinforced each other. The British relationship guaranteed defence security and markets for Australian commodities. Protectionism ensured a domestic market for manufacturers. White Australia, protectionism and wage arbitration gave workers a reasonable standard of living. The state supported economic development and a 'wage-earners' welfare state' (Castles 1994). The settlement muted class struggle, led to a more egalitarian distribution of wealth, and underpinned a high degree of social cohesion.

While the notion that Australia had settled its basic policies by the end of the first decade after federation is an attractive one and Kelly's exposition of it does highlight some core elements of Australia's political economy, both the broad argument and Kelly's version of it are open to challenge. For example, Stokes (2004) has criticised both Kelly's selective choice of policies to be recognised in the 'settlement' and his terminology. In particular, Stokes argues that other aspects that could equally lay claim to being part of a 'settlement' include *terra nullius*,[4] 'state secularism', masculinism, democracy and 'welfare minimalism' (Stokes 2004). Brett (2004) has argued that the 'settlement' between the 'city and country' should also be included.

The 'settlement' was not monolithic and there were alternative dissenting views. Moreover, the 'settlement' was not frozen in time or uncontested. In a sense, it needed to be constantly renegotiated. It changed. Some elements disappeared long before the 1980s and other elements were added. In particular, the adoption of Keynesian economic policies, the expansion of the welfare state, and the commitment to full employment created a qualitatively different post-World War Two 'settlement' that underpinned the 'long boom' experienced in Australia and other advanced industrial nations (Smyth 1994).

Essentially, this prolonged period of economic growth and prosperity was based on government acceptance of the economic views of Keynes and the architecture for the international economy (known as the Bretton Woods system)[5] that was established at the end of the Second World War. Keynesian economics (and the Bretton Woods system) were inspired by the failure of the previously dominant economic paradigm, *laissez faire*, in the Great Depression. Unlike *laissez faire*, which advocated a minimal role for governments in economic matters (believing that the 'free market' if left unhindered would correct itself and return to prosperity), Keynesian economics provided a theoretical justification for government involvement in the economy. Keynes argued that economic recessions (leading to unemployment) were caused by insufficient demand for goods. They could, however, be overcome by governments increasing their spending to stimulate economic activity (even if that meant presiding over budget deficits). In times of boom, governments could act to dampen economic activity. In this way, the fluctuations of the 'business cycle' could be smoothed. Keynes also provided an economic rationale for the redistribution of wealth and income and for the development of the welfare state.

At the same time, the Bretton Woods system saw the establishment of a system of fixed exchange rates between national economies that were relatively autonomous and in which financial capital was largely constrained within national boundaries. The International Monetary Fund was established to finance short-term trade and payments imbalances and the World Bank was formed to lend capital on a long-term basis to assist countries in their economic development.

The Bretton Woods system of fixed exchange rates collapsed in 1971 when the United States no longer backed its currency with gold reserves and moved to a system of 'floating' exchange rates (Schwartz 2000: 205). Its collapse can be understood (in part) as the result of financial capital having managed to break free from its national constraints with the result that central banks were unable to resist the currency speculation of financial markets. This, in turn, is an aspect of a larger process of 'globalisation' (Schwartz 2000; Woods 2000; Capling, Considine & Crozier 1998).

Globalisation refers to the phenomenon that has seen national barriers to trade, investment, culture and (even) labour reduced (or removed) to create global markets. It has been enabled by technological change and faster and cheaper transportation and communications. It has seen a dramatic increase in global trade since the end of the Second World War, particularly in manufactured goods. More particularly, it has seen a massive increase in the global movement of financial capital and a delinking of foreign exchange and foreign trade. That is, the trade in foreign currencies (and other financial products) now bears no relationship to the trade in goods, with a few days' trade on global financial markets representing more than a full year's trade in actual goods.

Globalisation undermined the efficacy of Keynesian economic policies that were predicated on a system of largely self-contained national economies. When Keynesian policies were ineffective in the face of the 1970s recession (triggered by the first OPEC-induced oil crisis),[6] there were forces eager to see their abandonment. This was because the prolonged period of full employment and the introduction of relatively comprehensive welfare states in advanced industrial countries had somewhat shifted the balance of power between capital and labour in favour of labour (Bell 1997: 89). Without the threat of unemployment, capital was less able to discipline labour with the result that the share of national product going to labour (as wages) had increased at the expense of profits going to capital. Business interests therefore had good reason to fund (if not lead) a conservative backlash against Keynesianism and the ever-expanding welfare state. The widespread dissemination of these New Right views (Sawer 1982; Coghill 1987) saw Keynesianism discredited and ultimately replaced by neo-liberal economics. This process occurred initially in Britain under the Thatcher government and in the United States under President Ronald Reagan, before spreading to other western countries and thereafter more globally.

In Australia's case, however, the adoption of neoliberal economic policies was a response to a sense of 'crisis' that emerged from Australia's failure to fully recover from the recession of the mid-1970s before succumbing to another recession in the early 1980s and then facing 'balance of payments' problems in the mid-1980s. At the heart of this 'crisis' was the realisation that Australia's economic problems were not simply the result of temporary falls in demand for its commodity exports but were the product of major structural problems with the economy. The traditional reliance on commodity exports could no longer guarantee Australia's prosperity in the new global economy. Essentially, this resulted from the fact that commodities (agricultural products and mining output) represented a declining share of global trade and the prices that they commanded had fallen relative to manufactured goods. Australia could no longer 'ride on the sheep's back'.

NEOLIBERALISM

The ideology of *liberalism* has been linked with the rise of capitalism (Macpherson 1977: 2; see also Fenna in Chapter 2 of this book). Its emphases on the right to property ownership, individual rights and freedoms, and limitations on the actions of the state, paved the way for 'free markets' and 'free trade'. Intertwined with this ideology was the body of writings extolling *laissez faire* economics that can be traced back to the publication in 1776 of Adam Smith's *Wealth of Nations* (Smith 1995). Smith's insights into the operations of markets, whereby the self-interested behaviour of individuals operating through the 'invisible hand' of the market were argued to produce the 'public interest' in the form of the most efficient allocation of goods and services, became a central axiom of the discipline of classical economics. Since the market, if left 'free' from government interference, would—according to this perspective—produce optimum outcomes, limiting the role of government to maintaining law and order and defending the nation was argued to be essential.

As noted earlier, this dominant economic paradigm was discredited by the Great Depression in the 1930s and replaced by Keynesianism as the accepted guide to economic policy. Ironically, it was to be largely revived under the labels of 'neoliberalism', 'economic rationalism' and 'economic liberalism' in the wake of the perceived failure of Keynesianism in the 1970s. In the neoliberal view, bloated welfare states were taking away individual initiative, and the high taxes extracted to fund welfare states were reducing the incentives for wealth generation. The neoliberals argued that entrepreneurs needed to be given more freedom (by removing burdensome government regulations) to take the risks essential for a dynamic economy. Government intervention in the economy had restricted economic growth by curbing the activities of the 'free market'.

In broad terms, therefore, neoliberalism advocated a reduction in the size and role of 'big government'; a paring back of the welfare state; and giving greater scope to the unhindered operation of market forces. It tended to place economic considerations above all other values. The policies that followed the adoption of the neoliberal paradigm included:

- deregulation: the removal or reduction of government regulations that impeded business
- the privatisation of government-owned businesses
- the 'contracting out' to the private sector of many tasks previously performed by government
- tax cuts for high-income earners
- the reduction of taxes on business and a shift to taxes on consumption
- the reduction of government expenditure
- a move to greater use of 'user pays' principles
- an emphasis on balanced or surplus budgets
- the removal (or reduction) of interference (by government and unions) in the workings of the labour market
- the removal (or drastic reduction) of tariffs and other obstacles to international 'free trade'.

It was these neoliberal-inspired policies that began to be adopted in the early 1980s and have been progressively implemented since. Their dominance of economic policy has marked a break with previously accepted practice and seen the virtual demise both of what remained of the post-federation 'Australian Settlement' and the post-World War Two 'Keynesian settlement'. It is to an examination of these policies that this chapter now turns.

Economic policies under the Hawke, Keating and Howard governments

Elements of the neoliberal resurgence were first detectable in Australia during the Whitlam Labor government's final year (1975) and during the Fraser Coalition government (1975–1983) that replaced it. The last budget under the Whitlam government cut expenditure and attempted to achieve a budget balance. The Fraser government abandoned the goal of full employment as the first priority in favour of a strategy of 'fighting inflation first'. However, these were piecemeal changes made as governments grappled in the changed environment, rather than part of any coherent plan to pursue neoliberalism. Indeed, the latter was more characteristic of the Liberal Party while in Opposition (from the mid-1980s, once the 'dries' had triumphed over the 'wets')[7] than of the Hawke Labor government that was elected in 1983.

Yet it was to be the Hawke Labor government that first embarked down the neoliberal road and increasingly came to adopt such policies. This policy direction has been further continued with greater fervour by the Howard Coalition government since it came to power in 1996.

The fact that it was a Labor government that ultimately set Australia firmly in the neoliberal economic direction seems anomalous given the Labor Party's previous ('democratic socialist') adherence to government enterprises, to full employment, and to a generous welfare state, and given its previous ambiguous attitude towards capitalism. Indeed, this policy shift sparked a debate over whether it represented a betrayal of 'Labor tradition' (Maddox 1989; Johnson 1989; Jaensch 1989; Beilharz 1994). The Labor Party did not come to national office with a neoliberal agenda. If anything, it initially believed that economic recovery could be achieved by means of a Keynesian type of stimulus with inflation kept in check through an 'Accord' with the trade unions. This was part of a wider attempt to pursue a consensual 'corporatist' strategy (Boreham 1990; Gerritsen 1986). The Hawke Labor government seems almost to have accidentally stumbled onto the neoliberal path with the decision to 'float' the Australian dollar in December 1983. This action was to have repercussions that set the stage for further neoliberal measures.

FLOATING THE DOLLAR AND FINANCIAL DEREGULATION

Allowing the value of the Australian currency to fluctuate according to the decisions of traders on international foreign exchange markets—'floating the dollar'—instead of it being set by government was a decision largely forced upon the Hawke Labor government. While it was a response to speculative money market pressure to force a devaluation of the Australian dollar, it was also a logical outcome of the emerging globalised financial system. Not only had most of Australia's trading partners already floated their currencies, but the Reserve Bank of Australia simply did not have the resources to resist market forces, given the scale of global money flows (Emy & Hughes 1991: 25).[8]

The upshot of floating the dollar was to see it become one of the most traded currencies in the world (sixth) despite Australia not being in the top 20 exporting nations (Ravenhill 1994: 90). Its value (against the US dollar) has fluctuated through a range from its initial US 91 cents, to below US 60 cents in 1986, back to close to US 90 cents in 1988, to below US 50 cents in 2001 and back to a general level of between US 70 and 80 cents since then. Importantly, since floating the dollar, Australian governments have felt constrained in framing their budgets because of fears of adverse reaction by money markets (Gruen & Grattan 1993: 104).

The Hawke Labor government undertook further financial deregulation in 1984 when the distinction between trading and savings banks was abolished; non-bank financial institutions were licensed to trade in foreign exchange, interest rate ceilings on deposits and loans were removed, and certain government controls over bank lending and liquidity levels were lifted. This was followed in 1985 with allowing the entry of foreign banks into Australia and, from 1992, permitting them to establish full branch operations.

The Howard Coalition government inherited a substantially deregulated financial system. It commissioned an inquiry in 1996 to evaluate the impact of financial deregulation and to recommend any necessary further changes. The inquiry report (Wallis 1997) made 115 recommendations that were a mixture of further deregulation combined with a strengthening and slight streamlining of the regulatory bodies that governed the various financial institutions.

The only recommendation of the inquiry that the Howard government did not fully accept was that concerning mergers. The existing regulations regarding mergers of major financial institutions (put in place in 1990) were known as the 'six pillars policy'. This prevented mergers between Australia's 'big four' banks—the National Australia Bank, the Commonwealth Bank, the ANZ Bank and Westpac—and two largest insurance companies—Australian Mutual Provident and National Mutual. The Howard government refused to lift the restrictions preventing foreign takeovers of Australian banks and stopping mergers and takeovers of the 'big four' banks, but opted to allow mergers of insurance companies. The 'six pillars policy' had become a 'four pillars' policy.

The major change implemented by the Howard government from this inquiry saw the establishment of a new financial regulatory regime based on type of activity performed rather than type of institution. The Reserve Bank of Australia lost its regulatory powers over banks; its role was to control monetary policy, the payments system and 'system stability'. The three other financial regulators were merged into two new bodies, the Australian Prudential Regulation Authority (APRA) and the Australian Securities and Investments Commission (ASIC). APRA was to regulate deposit taking, life and general insurance and superannuation, while ASIC was charged with overseeing consumer protection, market integrity and corporations. These changes recognised and further encouraged the blurring of distinctions between different types of financial institutions. Indeed, one result of accepting the inquiry's recommendations was the removal of existing distinctions between banks and building societies that led to virtually all building societies becoming banks.

Financial deregulation in Australia (and elsewhere) has reflected the triumph of neoliberal economics. Much of the initial impetus came from the financial sector itself and, in particular, from the banks seeking the removal of restrictions that placed them at a competitive disadvantage compared with non-banking financial institutions. The impact of financial deregulation has been the subject of debate. Critics argue that it facilitated speculative booms that led to spectacular and economically damaging corporate collapses in the late 1980s and early 1990s, and again in 2001. It increased the level of foreign ownership of Australian assets and led to a massive increase in foreign debt (discussed further below). It has also seen a greater concentration of the financial sector in fewer hands as a result of mergers and takeovers.

Supporters of financial deregulation, by contrast, argue that its benefits have outweighed any drawbacks. The stock and property market collapses of the late 1980s and early 1990s are seen more as 'teething troubles' as players learnt how to operate in the new environment. The development of a world-class financial industry in Australia is regarded by deregulation supporters as a clear benefit of the changes, and the fact that Australia was spared involvement in the 'Asian financial crisis' of 1997–8 (Pempel 1999) is seen as a testament to the fundamental soundness of Australia's economic arrangements. Efficiency in the banking and finance sector has greatly increased; new financial products are available; and both consumers and businesses have benefited from the expanded credit and investment opportunities.

PRIVATISATION

Privatisation is the process of placing in private ownership or control something that was previously in public-sector ownership or control. It encompasses the sale of government assets (particularly government business enterprises), contracting out government services to the private sector, increased liberalisation or competition within a sector previously dominated by the public sector, the shift to the 'user pays' principle in the provision of public services, and the use of 'public–private partnerships' for infrastructure development (Wiltshire 1994: 203; Greve & Hodge 2005).

The trend towards privatisation is inextricably linked with the rise to dominance of neoliberal views. Privatisation reduces the size of government and expands the scope of the market sector. One of its main justifications is the claim that it increases *efficiency*, a characteristic associated by its advocates with the private rather than the public sector. It also challenges the tradition of reliance on government ('state paternalism') embodied in the 'Australian Settlement' and the mixed economy that was a feature of the Keynesian settlement.

Again, there was considerable irony in the fact that it was a Labor government that first moved to privatise public enterprises. The Labor Party had in the past advocated its opposite—the public takeover (nationalisation) of key privately owned industries (O'Meagher 1983)—and Labor Prime Minister Hawke had forcefully argued against privatisation in 1985 when it was being put forward by the Opposition Liberal Party. The decision of senior members of Labor's parliamentary party to support privatisation initiatives apparently resulted less from a wholehearted acceptance of privatisation *per se* than from the indirect influence of neoliberalism. That is, the growing pervasiveness of neoliberal views among the economic policy community, including public servants in the central ministries (Pusey 1991), had led Labor leaders to accept the necessity of balanced or surplus budgets. This is evident from the Hawke government's commitment in the 1984 election to a so-called 'trilogy' of undertakings—

to keep taxes (relative to GDP) at their existing level, to ensure that government expenditure (relative to GDP) likewise did not increase and to reduce the budget deficit (Gruen & Grattan 1993: 100). When the need for expensive purchases of new aircraft by the government-owned international airline, Qantas, threatened to drive the budget into deficit, privatisation became an appealing option. Not only would the government be relieved of the budget-draining costs of capital expenditure for Qantas, but its sale would provide the government with extra revenue.

While the policy shift had to overcome some opposition within the Labor Party, by the time that the Labor government lost office in 1996, it had overseen the privatisation of a merged Qantas and Australian Airlines, the Commonwealth Bank, the Commonwealth Serum Laboratories, the Snowy Mountains Engineering Corporation, the Moomba-to-Sydney gas pipeline, and Aerospace Technologies of Australia (Walker & Walker 2000: 20–1).

The Howard Coalition government, elected in March 1996, has also pursued a privatisation agenda in line with its commitment to neoliberal views. It has sold the national transmission network of the ABC and SBS. It has sold all the airports in the various capital cities as well as numerous regional airports. It has privatised the national shipping line, Australian Defence Industries, the National Railways Commission, the National Rail Corporation and the Housing Loans Insurance Corporation (Walker & Walker 2000: 20–1). Critics argue that its sale of government buildings and their subsequent leasing back, and its sale of the government car fleet (Dasfleet) and its leasing back, have actually cost taxpayers more than if the assets had remained in government ownership (*The Age* 30 June 2002). The Howard government has also outsourced many activities previously undertaken by the Commonwealth public service and allowed the private sector to compete against government agencies for contracts in service delivery such as job placement.

The Howard government's privatisation vision for the telecommunications company Telstra has been its most significant initiative, although the process has been far from smooth. It managed to enlist the support of two Independent Senators in order to legislate for the initial privatisation of one-third of Telstra, but it failed to gain Senate approval for the sale of the remainder in 1998 and was forced to compromise and accept the sale of only a further 16 per cent, leaving Telstra in majority government ownership. Opposition to the sale of the remaining government share of Telstra from National Party members and rural constituents saw the government postpone further privatisation until telecommunication services in rural areas had attained a desired level. After winning the 2001 election, the Howard government again found its legislation to sell the rest of Telstra blocked by the Senate. Winning the 2004 election and especially gaining control of the Senate from mid-2005 has greatly increased the prospect for a full sale of Telstra. Even before the completion of Telstra's privatisation, the Howard government had raised in excess of $56 billion through its privatisation program (*The Age* 30 June 2002). Most of this revenue was used to reduce government debt.

Despite the widespread privatisations undertaken by Australian governments and despite what the neoliberals claim to be its benefits, studies of the actual outcomes have revealed minimal economic gains. Critics argue that investors who bought shares in privatised companies have benefited while other citizens have at best gained nothing or at worst have been clear losers (Hodge 2002: 57). The 'decision to privatise', according to one group of critics, 'has cost the citizen and the state dearly' (Collyer, Wettenhall & McMaster 2003: 21–2).

TARIFF REDUCTION AND MICROECONOMIC REFORM

A key economic reform consistent with a neoliberal outlook is the reduction, and ideally the removal, of tariff protection (another aspect of the 'Australian Settlement') in the belief that it would force manufacturing industry to become globally competitive. The Hawke government announced in 1988 that tariff cuts would be phased in so that the effective rate of protection for manufacturing would be reduced to 12 per cent by July 1992. In March 1991 this was further revised with the goal becoming an average effective rate of protection of only 5 per cent by 2000, the only exceptions being for the textiles, clothing and footwear (TCF) industry (25 per cent by 2000) and for cars (15 per cent by 2000) (Quiggin 1996: 127).

The Howard government initially continued the tariff-cutting schedule that it had inherited from its predecessors. However, it later bowed to industry pressure and extended the period over which tariffs will be phased down. But it still envisages a reduction—tariffs for the car industry will be cut to 5 per cent after 2005 and for the TCF industry to 5 per cent after 2015—confirming the ultimate victory of Australia's 'free traders' over its 'protectionists'.

The term 'microeconomic reform' came into vogue after the 1987 election to cover the reform agenda upon which the re-elected Hawke Labor government embarked. Microeconomic reform refers to structural economic changes designed to reduce business enterprise input costs, especially in terms of transportation, telecommunications and utilities, arising from what were argued to be uncompetitive and hence unnecessarily costly government monopoly provision or restrictive labour practices. Thus microeconomic reform encompassed a drive to create greater efficiency in the transportation sector by means of deregulation, ending (State) government monopolies and promoting competition. This was initiated under the Hawke and Keating Labor governments and continued under the Howard government. It has included Labor government measures such as eliminating the requirement that grain had to be transported on State railways (Emy & Hughes 1991: 165), waterfront reform that involved shedding labour and increasing productivity, and reform of coastal shipping that involved a reduction of average crew size (Kelly 1992: 396–7). The Howard government took more drastic action with respect to reform of the waterfront and coastal shipping by seeking, during the waterfront dispute of 1998, to remove union labour from the docks (discussed further below) and by phasing out the system of 'cabotage',[9] opening coastal shipping to competition and privatising the Australian National Line.

The Hawke Labor government deregulated the airlines, ending the long-standing 'two airline agreement'[10] in October 1990, and opening domestic air travel to new competitors. This resulted in the entry (and subsequent commercial failure) of a third airline company, Compass. In 1999, the Howard government attempted to revive competition in the domestic air industry by removing limitations on foreign ownership of domestic airlines with the result that a new (foreign) entrant, Virgin Airlines, prospered and Ansett Airlines collapsed in 2001. The Hawke and Keating Labor governments also carried out reforms to interstate road freight, established a joint Commonwealth–State National Rail Corporation, and sought improved productivity of Australian National Rail.

Telecommunications has been another major area of microeconomic reform. Under the Hawke government in 1989, Telecom, the statutory authority that held a monopoly over domestic telecommunications services, was corporatised in 1989. In 1991, Telecom was merged with the Overseas Telecommunications Corporation (another statutory body) to form Telstra. Private companies were invited to tender to purchase the government-owned domestic communications satellite, Aussat, and to share the domestic landline phone network in competition with Telstra. The winning bidder, Optus, became part of a duopoly, with Telstra, that was to last until 1997. Open competition was allowed in the mobile phone market. The Howard government's major move in the telecommunications field has focused on the privatisation of Telstra.

Another major aspect of microeconomic reform resulted from the 'Hilmer Report' (Hilmer 1993) whose recommendations to foster competition in the public as well as the private sector, especially by privatising and then regulating public monopolies, was a key driver in this area. It led to the Commonwealth, State and Territory governments jointly forming a National Competition Council to oversee needed changes (for example, in the power industry) and to the establishment of the Australian Competition and Consumer Commission (ACCC), replacing the Trade Practices Commission and the Prices Surveillance Authority, as a 'watchdog' to guard against collusive behaviour by business (Hughes 1998: 91). The ACCC has, at times, blocked mergers and takeovers of companies if it felt that it would result in a diminution of competition within the Australian domestic market.

The Howard government established an institutional base for further microeconomic reform by forming the Productivity Commission in place of the

Economic Planning Advisory Council, the Bureau of Industry Economics and the Industry Commission. The Productivity Commission has ever since been a staunch proponent of neoliberal views, invariably recommending further tariff cuts, more privatisation and further cost cutting. The Howard government also conducted a review of the *Trade Practices Act* (and the operations of the ACCC) in response to business complaints. The review's report rejected calls for fundamental changes but did suggest a less aggressive ('anti-business') role for the ACCC (*The Age* 17 April 2003).

INDUSTRIAL RELATIONS

The Hawke Labor government came to office in 1983 after Labor had negotiated, while in Opposition but in anticipation of winning back government, an 'Accord' with the Australian Council of Trade Unions (ACTU). The original compact entailed the ACTU undertaking that unions would maintain industrial peace and not to seek wage rises in excess of the agreed limits, in return for the government agreeing to restore the centralised wage-fixing of the arbitration system, to ensure that real wages were maintained via 'wage indexation' (whereby wage rises in line with price rises would be granted through the arbitration system), to facilitate the creation of more jobs, and to increase welfare benefits (the 'social wage') for low-income earners (Stilwell 1986; Carney 1988). Over time, the Accord was renegotiated and renewed on seven successive occasions, and in the process changed its character, as the Hawke and Keating Labor governments insisted upon more labour market reform as part of their microeconomic reform agenda.

Full wage indexation was the first casualty of the renegotiations. It was superseded by the government and the unions agreeing that partial wage discounting would be acceptable if compensated by tax cuts so that workers in effect maintained their take-home pay. Later the introduction of mandatory occupational superannuation, as well as increases in the 'social wage', were likewise used to recompense workers for accepting wage restraint. A two-tier wage system was introduced, comprising centrally awarded (discounted) flat pay rises coupled with bargaining for additional wage increases that needed to be justified on the basis of improved productivity (Gardner 1990). By the time the Keating Labor government lost office in 1996, enterprise bargaining had been introduced and the basis for wage rises had largely shifted from being linked to increases in the cost of living to being based on achieving workplace reforms and productivity increases.

The various Accords played an important role in changing the culture of industrial relations in Australia. They delivered wage restraint and facilitated economic growth and employment growth without significant inflation. They ushered in an era of low levels of strike activity and a shift to productivity-based pay rises. They also paved the way for a reduction in the role of the arbitration system, a shift to enterprise bargaining and greater workforce flexibility.

The Howard Coalition government, rather than seeking to work collaboratively with the ACTU, has adopted a more confrontational approach to industrial relations. It has pressed forward with neoliberal-inspired plans designed to further curtail the role of the arbitration system, minimise the role of unions, and give greater scope to market forces.

Soon after coming to power, the Howard government introduced the legislative basis for its 'first wave' of industrial relations reforms that eventually (with considerable amendments) was passed by the Senate with support from the Australian Democrats (Singleton 2000: 140). This legislation banned 'secondary boycotts' by unions, made strikes illegal except during a period of enterprise bargaining, and placed restrictions on permissible strikes. It allowed the formation of enterprise-based unions, prevented the entry of union organisers to a workplace unless there was a written request from the workers, and stipulated that workers could not be discriminated against for not belonging to a union. It encouraged direct negotiations (without union involvement) between employers and employees to establish individual employment contracts—Australian Workplace Agreements. In addition, industrial awards were 'streamlined' so that they covered only a core minimum number of conditions. The Australian Industrial Relations Commission's (AIRC) role was restricted to maintaining these minimum award conditions, dealing with (less strict) 'unfair dismissal' claims in the federal jurisdiction and managing intra-union competition in a site dispute (Wooden 2000: 30).

Controversially, the Howard government became involved in plans to have the entire unionised workforce on the Australian waterfront, where the dominant union was the Maritime Union of Australia (MUA), dismissed and replaced by a non-union workforce. Among other things, this involved assisting in an abortive scheme to have a non-union workforce trained offshore and providing financial assistance for redundancy payments. Only one of the two main Australian stevedoring companies (Patrick Stevedores), however, took action against its unionised workforce. In April 1998 Patrick effectively dismissed all its MUA-associated employees, and replaced them with non-union workers. This led to unionists and their supporters picketing Patrick wharves while the real battle moved to the courts where the union claimed that a 'criminal conspiracy' existed between Patrick and the government against the MUA (Trinca & Davies 2000).

Successive Federal Court and High Court rulings provided some solace to the MUA, but the final High Court ruling was not totally clear-cut. The dispute was ultimately resolved through a compromise agreement whereby the MUA dropped its criminal conspiracy case against Patrick and government members, MUA members were rehired as Patrick employees, but the enterprise bargaining agreement reached saw a reduction in staffing levels on the docks (Singleton 2000: 147–8). Productivity on the waterfront also improved in the wake of the waterfront dispute (Trinca & Davies 2000: 281; Anderson 2002).

In mid-1999, the Howard government introduced a planned 'second wave' of industrial relations reforms to Parliament. It proposed changing the AIRC into the Australian Workplace Relations Commission, reducing the lifetime tenure of Commissioners to seven-year contracts, cutting Commission powers over compulsory conciliation, introducing private 'mediation agents', stripping awards of various conditions,[11] forcing trade unions to hold secret ballots before striking, and requiring the Commission to make orders against illegal strikes within 48 hours of being notified (*The Age* 1 July 1999). This legislation was shelved after it was rejected by the Senate, but much of it can be expected to be put in place in the wake of the Howard government gaining control of the Senate from mid-2005.

UNEMPLOYMENT

Labor gained office in 1983 partly as a result of the Fraser Coalition government having presided over a recession. Unemployment was a key election issue in 1983, and Labor made a commitment to give lowering unemployment a greater priority than had its predecessor, which had tended to focus more on lowering inflation. The Accord was central to Labor's plan to expand economic growth and employment without corresponding wage rises leading to increased inflation.

The Hawke Labor government initially more than delivered on its promise to create half a million jobs within three years (Gruen & Grattan 1993: 100). The number of people employed grew by 1.45 million between 1983 and 1989, with unemployment falling from 9 per cent in early 1983 to around 6 per cent by 1990 (Stewart & Jennett 1990: 6). Much of this growth, however, was in part-time rather than full-time employment. And the recession of the early 1990s then saw the unemployment rate escalate to a post-World War Two record of 11.2 per cent in December 1992 (*The Age* 14 July 2000).

The Labor government responded to this setback by adopting two stimulatory packages ('One Nation' and 'Working Nation'), in 1992 and 1994 respectively, that aimed in Keynesian fashion to boost demand. It also initiated a series of labour-market programs with a particular focus on finding employment for the long-term unemployed.[12] While these specific programs appear to have had only a marginal impact on redressing unemployment problems, unemployment fell in any case to around 8 per cent, as the Australian economy recovered from recession, by the time Labor lost office in 1996.

The Howard government's approach to unemployment has been informed by its neoliberal predilections and its greater concern to keep more electorally sensitive inflation and interest rates low. Its unemployment policy has been closely linked to its industrial relations policy; for example, relaxing unfair dismissal laws has been presented as a necessary move to promote more employment. It has also tended to see unemployment as significantly caused by minimum wages being too high for job creation to be attractive to employers, and it has acted on the assumption that greater reliance on market forces would significantly reduce unemployment.

In this vein, the Howard government abolished the labour-market programs of the previous government and effectively privatised the operations of the former monopoly government employment agency, the Commonwealth Employment Service (CES) (Aulich 2000: 169). The CES was abolished in 1998 and its role as a provider of employment services was transferred to a new Job Network made up of more than 300 organisations (private, community and government) that successfully tendered to provide such services (Webster 2000: 238). Eligibility for unemployment benefits has been tightened with the introduction of a 'jobs diary' that the unemployed need to keep to demonstrate their efforts to obtain work, and a 'work for the dole' scheme[13] has been established.

The Howard government policies on unemployment appear to have been quite successful. Although the national unemployment rate initially increased a little after its assumption of office and then remained around the 8 per cent mark for several years, the rate then began to fall substantially. It moved below 6 per cent during 2004 and kept falling further. The June 2005 unemployment rate of 5.0 per cent was the lowest for 29 years (*The Age* 8 July 2005).

This is a noteworthy achievement, but these figures also need to be seen in perspective. While the number of short-term unemployed has fallen dramatically, the scrapping of schemes designed to get the long-term unemployed back to work appears to have led to their numbers slightly increasing (e.g. *The Age* 7 August 2000). More than 70 per cent of the new job growth since 1994 has been in part-time or casual employment (Hywood 2004), giving Australia the second highest proportion of its workers (27 per cent) in part-time employment among developed (OECD)[14] countries, and a level of part-time employment nearly twice the OECD average of 15 per cent (*The Age* 23 July 2002). The Australian Bureau of Statistics found that 578 000 workers in part-time employment want more work and up to 2 million Australians who are willing and able to work are unemployed, underemployed or discouraged from seeking work (*The Age* 16 March 2005). Moreover, despite Australia having enjoyed more than a decade of continuous high economic growth, its unemployment rate remained one of the highest within the 19 richest OECD members for a considerable time (*The Age* 23 July 2002). By 2004, however, Australia's unemployment rate had both moved from the bottom half of the richest 25 OECD countries (*The Age* 30 June 2005) and, as it approached 5 per cent, it was significantly below the OECD average of 6.7 per cent (OECD 2005: 1, 73).

FREE TRADE AGREEMENT WITH THE US

The Labor governments of the 1980s and early 1990s tended to pursue multilateralism in trade negotiations, believing that Australia's interests would be best served by multi-country agreements. It was instrumental in forming the Cairns Group of agricultural-exporting countries, in placing the issue of agricultural protectionism on the negotiating agenda with respect to a revised General Agreement on Tariffs and Trade (GATT),[15] and in the formation of the Asia-Pacific Economic Cooperation (APEC) grouping of countries in our region.

The Howard government, by contrast, has tended to adopt a more bilateral approach to its trade negotiations, exemplified by its Free Trade Agreement (FTA) with the United States (signed in May 2004) and by the pursuit of bilateral FTAs with other countries such as Thailand (signed in July 2004) and, probably most ambitiously of all, China (currently under discussion).

Previous overtures by the US government proposing a FTA with Australia had been rejected by both the Keating Labor government and the Howard Coalition government, but the idea was put back on the agenda in 2001 (*The Age* 1 August 2001). When a final agreement was reached in February 2004, it appeared that most of the concessions had been made by Australia and that very little further access to the US market for Australian agricultural produce had been granted. This became more obvious when the full details of the agreement were released a month later and it became evident that Chile had been able to get more favourable terms in its bilateral FTA with the US than had Australia (*The Age* 9 March 2004). Critics argued that the US government negotiators seemed to be more concerned with gaining greater access for investment, tendering for government contracts and dealing with issues of intellectual property rights, than with 'free trade' (Weiss, Thurbon & Mathews 2004; Capling 2005).

The main features of the US–Australia FTA include the immediate removal of most tariffs on manufactured goods in 2005 and the removal of all such tariffs by 2015 (although Australian fast ferries are excluded). Australia has agreed to remove all its tariffs on farm exports from the US and, in return, the US has agreed to reduce its tariffs on and give greater access to Australian rural produce. US concessions, however, were limited. There is no increase in the quota imposed on Australian sugar exports to the US, the beef quota is to be phased out over 18 years (and even then the US can reimpose tariffs if Australian imports became too competitive). Australian dairy farmers get immediate access to the US market for previously excluded cheeses, milk, ice-cream and cream (although quotas would still apply). Businesses from both countries are now allowed to tender for government contracts in both jurisdictions (although Australian firms are excluded from smaller contracts) and the threshold for automatic approval of foreign investment in each country has been raised to $A800 million. US manufacturers of pharmaceuticals are allowed to appeal against any decisions excluding their products from Australia's Pharmaceutical Benefits Scheme (PBS), copyright protection has been extended to 70 years after the author's death (a provision of most benefit to the US given its domination of English-language publishing and broadcasting), and local content rules currently requiring at least minimum levels of Australian content on Australian television and radio will not henceforth apply to new forms of media (*The Age* 10 February 2004).

Predictions about the impact of the FTA have varied. A government-commissioned report claimed that Australia would benefit by $52.5 billion over the next 20 years (*The Age* 22 June 2004). A report commissioned by the Australian Manufacturing Workers Union claimed, to the contrary, that the agreement would *cost* Australia $46.9 billion (and more than 50 000 jobs per year) over the same period (*The Age* 8 June 2004).

Despite some disquiet within the Labor Opposition over the pact, the enabling legislation for the FTA was passed by the Australian Parliament in December 2004, after the government accepted Opposition amendments designed to strengthen Australian control over its media content and to prevent the PBS being undermined by US drug companies.

FOREIGN DEBT

Australia has a large foreign debt that can be traced back to its persistent trade and current account deficits.[16] Prior to financial deregulation, net foreign debt (like the current account deficit) was restricted, but it accelerated rapidly thereafter in both dollar terms and as a percentage of GDP. For example, it stood at around $7 billion dollars prior to deregulation in 1980 (5.5 per cent of GDP) but had grown to over $123 billion (nearly 34 per cent of GDP) after deregulation by 1990. This was close to the level that had led then Treasurer Paul Keating in 1986 to warn that Australia faced becoming a 'banana republic' (Emy & Hughes 1991: 64). This level of foreign debt prompted the Business Council of Australia to hold a 'debt summit' in 1990 and led the Coalition parties, then in Opposition, to highlight foreign debt (by means of a 'debt truck' that toured electorates) as an issue in the 1996 election.

Foreign debt stood at around $193 billion (39 per cent of GDP) when the Howard government came to office (ABS 1998: 762). By 2005, it had increased to $421.9 billion (around 51 per cent of GDP) (*The Age* 2 March 2005). But despite this level of foreign debt (and record current account deficits), foreign debt has slipped from the political agenda. Once again, this can be seen as resulting from the dominance of neoliberal views. For neoliberals, foreign debt is only a problem when it is *government* debt which is argued to 'crowd out' the private sector and increase interest rates. Private debt, they contend, is only a problem for the private creditors and debtors involved (Pitchford 1990). Since the overwhelming majority (96 per cent in 2002) of Australia's foreign debt is private (ABS 2003: 906), neoliberals can argued that it can be safely ignored.

But a close examination suggests otherwise. Over 75 per cent of Australia's foreign debt has resulted from borrowings by banks and other financial institutions and most of this has been on-lent to Australian households. Australian household debt has now risen from the equivalent of 80 per cent of household income in 1996 to 140 per cent in 2004 (*The Age* 8 July 2004). This suggests that like many Australians the Australian economy is now particularly vulnerable to any economic recession or major fall in the value of the Australian dollar.

Conclusion

Australia's economic policies have been shaped by its historical development. But neither the 'Australian Settlement' achieved in the first decade after federation nor the post-World War Two 'Keynesian settlement' survived the changes to the global economy in the last third of the 20th century. Beginning under the Hawke and Keating Labor governments, economic policy in Australia departed from previous practice and has been increasingly influenced by neoliberal views. Greater scope has been given to the play of market forces in the belief that fostering competition within Australia will enable its economy to become internationally competitive.

These neoliberal-inspired policies, such as privatisation and tariff reduction, may have achieved a degree of bipartisan support but, on the evidence of opinion polls, they have consistently not been supported by a majority of the general public (Manne 1994). Indeed, the electoral backlash that saw Labor lose office in 1996, and that saw a burst of support for Pauline Hanson's One Nation party in the late 1990s, can be seen as (at least in part) resulting from public disquiet over the direction of economic policy.

It is interesting that the Howard government has been so electorally successful while further pursuing neoliberal policies. It has evidently reaped the reward of presiding over a prolonged period of (almost continuous) high economic growth, low inflation, low interest rates, and a lowering of official unemployment rates. The only apparent challenge to its credentials as a sound economic manager is its failure to bring the trade and current account deficits into balance and to halt the burgeoning of foreign debt. This failure may ultimately prove to be the biggest indictment against it and against neoliberal economic policies more generally.

NOTES

1 GDP is a monetary measure of all the goods and services produced within an economy.

2 Frank Castles (1998) had earlier used the term 'domestic defence' to describe the linked policies of protectionism and wage arbitration and Gerard Henderson (1990) had similarly discussed what he called the 'Australian Trifecta' of white Australia, trade protection, and wage arbitration.

3 In fact, it was the issue on which the two largest political parties were based—Deakin's Radical Liberals/Protectionists and Reid's 'Free Traders'. The (initially) smaller Labor Party supported Deakin (and protection). Once the issue had been resolved and Labor had increased its support sufficiently to form government in its own right, the two non-Labor parties merged.

4 This refers to the legal assertion that Australia constituted an 'empty land' that was therefore legitimately open to settlement, effectively denying Aboriginals any claims of prior ownership.

5 Bretton Woods was the location in the United States where the meetings were held to establish institutions and procedures to promote freer trade and to stabilise exchange rates for currencies to avoid crises (Gilpin 2001).

6 OPEC is the Organisation of Petroleum Exporting Countries. Created in 1960, OPEC began operating as a cartel in the 1970s to restrict the output of oil. This helped to engineer a dramatic jump in its price virtually overnight. This was to trigger not only a global recession but also a decade of 'stagflation'—a stagnant economy combined with inflation (Gilpin 2001: 58–60, 234).

7 These terms were derived from the Conservative Party in Britain during the period of Margaret Thatcher's leadership. Essentially, the 'dries' believed in minimal government while the 'wets' (the original pejorative term applied by the Thatcherites to critics within their own party) believed that government had an important ameliorative role to play.

8 Australia was not alone in this. The daily transactions on foreign exchange markets exceed the total foreign currency reserves of all the world's central banks (Gray 1998: 62).

9 This excluded foreign vessels from coastal trade, thus protecting the government-owned Australian National Line as well as the wages and conditions of Australian crews.

10 This agreement dated back to 1957. Under its regulations, the government-owned Trans-Australia Airlines (later called Australian Airlines before its merger into Qantas) and the privately owned Ansett Airlines enjoyed a government-enforced duopoly that ensured almost identical fleets of planes, flight schedules and fares (Quiggin 1996: 103).

11 For example, skill-based classifications, tallies and bonuses, public holidays not declared by governments, termination notices, accident pay, training and education provisions, long-service leave, paid jury leave and superannuation were to be pared from awards.

12 These included Jobtrain, Skillshare, Jobskills and Jobstart. They involved training programs, work experience and subsidies to employers designed to get the long-term unemployed back in the workforce. See Langmore and Quiggin (1994, ch. 10) for a good analysis of these programs.

13 This has involved certain categories of the unemployed being required to undertake community work in return for their unemployment benefits.

14 The Organisation for Economic Cooperation and Development (OECD) is composed of 30 (predominantly European and North American) countries with free markets and a commitment to democracy. It includes the most advanced, wealthy, industrial countries.

15 The original GATT was signed by 23 governments in 1947 as a 'temporary' measure to

promote freer world trade. It was intended to be replaced by an International Trade Organisation (ITO) as part of the Bretton Woods settlement, but the US Congress refused to support the ITO. As a result, the GATT continued its existence through various rounds of negotiations. It was eventually succeeded by the creation of the World Trade Organisation (WTO) in January 1995 (Cohn 2005: 29–31).

16 The current account is a measure of Australia's net financial relationship with the rest of the world. It includes the balance of trade in goods and services and the net effects of income transfers (net repatriated profits from foreign investments in Australia and from Australian investments abroad, and net interest payments on foreign loans to Australia and Australian loans abroad). By far the largest part of the current account (and what causes it to be in deficit) is the interest paid on foreign loans to Australian borrowers. Australia last ran a current account surplus in 1973. Indeed, Kryger has noted, 'Since 1959-60 Australia has had only one surplus on its current account and that was in 1972-73' (Kryger 2001).

REFERENCES

ABS [Australian Bureau of Statistics] 1998, *Year Book Australia: 1998*, no. 71, Canberra.

ABS [Australian Bureau of Statistics] 2003, *2003: Year Book Australia*, no. 85, Canberra.

Anderson, J. 2002, 'Waterfront Productivity Reaches New Record Levels', Media Release by Deputy Prime Minister, 26 September, Canberra, <http://www.ministers.dotars.gov.au/ja/releases/2002/september/A123_2002.htm>, accessed 2/08/05.

Aulich, C. 2000, 'Privatisation and Contracting Out', in *The Howard Government: Australian Commonwealth Administration 1996–1998*, ed. G. Singleton, University of New South Wales Press, Sydney.

Beilharz, P. 1994, *Transforming Labor: Labour Tradition and the Labor Decade in Australia*, Cambridge University Press, Cambridge.

Bell, S. 1997, *Ungoverning the Economy: The Political Economy of Australian Economic Policy*, Oxford University Press, Melbourne.

Boehm, E. 1993, *Twentieth Century Economic Development in Australia*, 3rd edn, Longman Cheshire, Melbourne.

Boreham, P. 1990, 'Corporatism', in *Hawke and Australian Public Policy: Consensus and Restructuring*, eds C. Jennett & R. Stewart, Macmillan, Melbourne.

Brett, J. 2004, 'Comment: The Country and the City', *Australian Journal of Political Science*, vol. 39, no. 1, pp. 27–9.

Butlin, N. 1983, 'Trends in Public/Private Relations, 1901–75', in B. Head ed. *State and Economy in Australia*, Oxford University Press, Melbourne.

Capling, A. 2005, *All the Way with the USA: Australia, the US and Free Trade*, University of New South Wales Press, Sydney.

Capling, A., Considine, M. & Crozier, M. 1998, *Australian Politics in the Global Era*, Longman, Melbourne.

Carney, S. 1988, *Australia in Accord: Politics and Industrial Relations Under the Hawke Government*, Sun Macmillan, Melbourne.

Castles, F. 1994, 'The Wage Earners' Welfare State Revisited: Refurbishing the Established Model of Australian Social Protection 1983–93', *Australian Journal of Social Issues*, vol. 29, no. 2, pp. 120–145.

Coghill, K. ed. 1987, *The New Right's Australian Fantasy*, Penguin, Melbourne.

Cohn, T. 2005, *Global Political Economy: Theory and Practice*, 3rd edn, Pearson Longman, New York.

Collyer, F., Wettenhall, R. & McMaster, J. 2003, 'The Privatisation of Public Enterprises: Australian Research Findings', *Just Policy*, no. 31.

Emy, H. & Hughes, O. 1991, *Australian Politics: Realities in Conflict*, 2nd edn, Macmillan, Melbourne.

Gardner, M. 1990, 'Wages Policy', in C. Jennett & R. Stewart eds *Hawke and Australian Public Policy; Consensus and Restructuring*, Macmillan, South Melbourne.

Gerritsen, R. 1986, 'The Necessity of "Corporatism": The Case of the Hawke Labor Government', *Politics*, vol. 21, no. 1, pp. 45–54.

Gilpin, R. 2001, *Global Political Economy: Understanding the International Economic Order*, Princeton University Press, Princeton.

Gray, J. 1998, *False Dawn: The Delusions of Global Capitalism*, Granta, London.

Greve, C. & Hodge, G. 2005, 'Introduction', in C. Greve & G. Hodge eds *The Challenge of Public-private Partnerships: Learning from International Experience*, Edward Elgar, Cheltenham.

Gruen, F. & Grattan, M. 1993, *Managing Government: Labor's Achievements and Failures*, Longman Cheshire, Melbourne.

Henderson, G. 1990, *Australian Answers*, Random House Australia, Sydney.

Hilmer, F. 1993, *National Competition Policy: Report by the Independent Committee of Inquiry*, Canberra.

Hodge, G. 2002, 'Good Governance and the Privatising State: Some International Lessons (One Cheer for Victoria's Privatisations, Now What Have we Learned?)', *Journal of Economic and Social Policy*, vol. 6, no. 2.

Hughes, O. 1998, *Australian Politics: Third Edition*, Macmillan, South Melbourne.

Hywood, G. 2004, 'Election 2004: It's About the Economy *and* Values, Stupid', *The Age* 5 August.

Jaensch, D. 1989, *The Hawke-Keating Hijack: The ALP in Transition*, Allen & Unwin, Sydney.

Johnson, C. 1989, *The Labor Legacy: Curtin, Chifley, Whitlam, Hawke*, Allen & Unwin, Sydney.

Kelly, P. 1992, *The End of Certainty: The Story of the 1980s*, Allen & Unwin, Sydney.

Kryger, T. 2001, *Monthly Economic & Social Indicators: Balance of Payments*, Parliamentary Library, Canberra, <http://www.aph.gov.au/library/pubs/mesi/features/bop.htm>.

Langmore, J. & Quiggin, J. 1994, *Work for all: Full Employment in the Nineties*, Melbourne University Press, Carlton.

Macpherson, C. 1977, *The Life and Times of Liberal Democracy*, Oxford University Press, Oxford.

Maddox, G. 1989, *The Hawke Government and Labor Tradition*, Penguin, Melbourne.

Manne, R. 1994, 'Has the Liberal Party Lost "Middle Australia"?', in *For Better or Worse: The Federal Coalition*, ed. B. Costar, Melbourne University Press, Melbourne.

McCarthy, P. 1976, 'Justice Higgins and the Harvester Judgement', in J. Roe ed. *Social Policy in Australia: Some Perspectives 1901–1975*, Cassell, Stanmore.

OECD 2005, *Economic Outlook no. 77*, vol. 2005, issue 1.

O'Meagher, B. ed. 1983, *The Socialist Objective: Labor and Socialism*, Hale & Iremonger, Sydney.

Pempel, T. ed. 1999, *The Politics of the Asian Economic Crisis*, Cornell University Press, Ithaca.

Pitchford, J. 1990, *Australia's Foreign Debt: Myths and Realities*, Allen & Unwin, Sydney.

Pusey, M. 1991, *Economic Rationalism in Canberra: A Nation Building State Changes its Mind*, Cambridge University Press, Cambridge.

Quiggin, J. 1996, *Great Expectations: Microeconomic Reform in Australia*, Allen & Unwin, St Leonards.

Ravenhill, J. 1994, 'Australia and the Global Economy', in S. Bell & B. Head eds *State, Economy and Public Policy in Australia*, Oxford University Press, Melbourne.

Sawer, M. ed. 1982, *Australia and the New Right*, George Allen & Unwin, Sydney.

Schwartz, H. 2000, *States Versus Markets: The Emergence of a Global Economy*, 2nd edn, Macmillan, London.

Singleton, G. 2000, 'On the Waterfront: The Howard Government's Approach to Industrial Relations', in *The Howard Government: Australian Commonwealth Administration 1996–1998*, ed. G. Singleton, University of New South Wales Press, Sydney.

Smith, A. 1995, *An Inquiry into the Nature and Causes of the Wealth of Nations*, 11th edn, ed. W. Playfair, W. Pickering, London.

Smyth, P. 1994, *Australian Social Policy: The Keynesian Chapter*, University of New South Wales Press, Sydney.

Stewart, R. & Jennett, C. 1990, 'Introduction', in C. Jennett & R. Stewart eds *Hawke and Australian Public Policy; Consensus and Restructuring*, Macmillan, South Melbourne.

Stilwell, F. 1986, *The Accord and Beyond: The Political Economy of the Labor Government*, Pluto Press, Sydney.

Stokes, G. 2004, 'The "Australian Settlement" in Australian Political Thought', *Australian Journal of Political Science*, vol. 39, no. 1, pp. 5–22.

Trinca, H. & Davies, A. 2000, *Waterfront: The Battle that Changed Australia*, Doubleday, Milsons Point.

Walker, B. & Walker, B. 2000, *Privatisation: Sell off or Sell out?: The Australian Experience*, ABC Books, Sydney.

Wallis, S. 1997, *Financial System Inquiry: Final Report*, AGPS, Canberra, <http://fsi.treasury.gov.au/content/FinalReport.asp>.

Webster, E. 2000, 'What Role for Labour-market Programs?', in S. Bell ed. *The Unemployment Crisis in Australia: Which Way Out?*, Cambridge University Press, Cambridge.

Weiss, L., Thurbon, E. & Mathews, J. 2004, *How to Kill a Country: Australia's Devastating Trade Deal with the United States*, Allen & Unwin, Crows Nest.

Wiltshire, K. 1994, 'Privatisation and Corporatisation', in R. Stewart ed. *Government and Business Relations in Australia*, Allen & Unwin, St Leonards.

Wooden, M. 2000, *The Transformation of Australian Industrial Relations*, Federation Press, Leichhardt.

Woods, N. ed. 2000, *The Political Economy of Globalization*, Macmillan, Basingstoke.

Tax policy

ALAN FENNA

Taxation may not be one of the most popular activities of government, but it is one of the most important—if only for the simple reason that, without revenue, government cannot function. In that sense, tax is quite different from the more typical policy areas examined in this book. Taxation is primarily a servant of the other functions of government. We nonetheless treat tax as a policy area in its own right because the way governments choose to raise their revenue has a significant policy impact on society. Deciding who will bear the cost of government shapes the distribution of income in society. Deciding what activities to tax and what not to may shape the choice people make about those activities. Any tax system, then, expresses a broad policy about the type of society we want.

Because there are few areas where the immediate impact of policy decisions on different sections and interests in society is so starkly visible, tax policy provides an excellent insight into the relationship between the individualistic/liberal and the collectivist/democratic conceptions about the role of governments, as described in Chapter 1 of this book, and more specifically the competing ideological perspectives on politics described in Chapter 2. From the extreme classical or market liberal point of view, taxation is expropriation; it deprives individuals of their legitimate property in a way that is both morally wrong and economically harmful. From a more democratic perspective, taxation is merely the individual's proper contribution to the maintenance of the community and the provision of public services and is an acknowledgment that without that community the individual would not be in a position to enjoy that wealth. Of course the typical taxpayer is torn between both these positions, understandably resistant to paying more tax, but recognising that education systems, health systems, national defence, transportation infrastructure, and countless other valued services of government require funding.

The reality is that liberal democracy is about arriving at a balance between these two sets of considerations. But it is not simply a question of how much tax, it is also a question of what kind of tax is imposed on which people—the 'tax mix' as it is called. There are many different ways to tax and there are various opinions about what might be 'good taxes' and 'bad taxes'—or perhaps bad taxes and not-so-bad taxes.

Support for specific taxes or for taxation in general is influenced by judgments about whether:

- others are paying their share
- the burden is being apportioned fairly
- the level of tax seems proportional to the range and quality of service government delivers
- the tax is easily borne by the economy.

Debates about the virtues and vices of different taxes and about the nature of the optimal tax regime revolve around considerations of equity and efficiency. How is revenue to be raised with the least economic cost and the greatest fairness? The past 20 years in Australia have seen an ongoing process of tax policy debate and adjustment revolving around these considerations, much of which came to a head with the introduction of the GST (Goods and Services Tax) in 2000.

Tax principles, tax practices

TYPES OF TAX

Taxes have traditionally been divided into two main categories: those levied on money one *receives* and those levied on money one *spends*. The former are called 'direct' taxes because the person from whom they are collected is the person who pays them. The latter are called 'indirect' taxes since they are typically collected from the vendor but borne by the purchaser. Income taxes, which are usually applied to both corporate and individual earnings (profits, salaries and wages), are direct taxes. Sales or consumption taxes are indirect taxes; they can be applied to any range of goods and services that one purchases.

Historically Australia relied heavily on one specific type of indirect or consumption tax; the customs tariff levied since federation by the Commonwealth government on goods imported into the country. Now that Australia has abandoned the policy of tariff protectionism, that source of revenue has largely dried up. A more contemporary consumption tax is the petrol excise duty that makes up a good part of the pump price motorists pay when they fill up their vehicles. The introduction of the GST in 2000 gave Australia its first 'broad-based consumption tax'—that is, a sales tax on virtually all goods and services across the economy.

Direct taxation can also apply to wealth as distinct from income. Taxing wealth is not as straightforward as taxing income since much of the time wealth accumulates with no transaction taking place. A property could stay in the hands of one family for generations without ever changing hands commercially. Thus governments sometimes tax wealth by imputing a value—as local governments do when they levy their annual property rates. The transfer of property through inheritance provides another opportunity for taxing wealth ('death duties'); however, Australia has abandoned this form of taxation. In 1985, the Hawke Labor government introduced capital gains taxation as another component of the wealth tax system. Capital gains tax (CGT) does not attempt to tax wealth as it is being accumulated, but only if and when the owner sells or cashes out to realise the gains from the appreciation in the value of the asset. Such taxation becomes particularly important when large numbers of individuals exploit capital gains as their main income source—thereby, under the old (pre-1985) regime, avoiding the income tax that their fellow citizens were paying.

Thus, there is a wide range of ways in which governments can tax, though not all of them have always been feasible. While taxation is very old indeed, the ability to tax effectively is a relatively new phenomenon in world history. Effective taxation requires effective surveillance and control, and only in the 20th century did the administrative and technical capacity for such surveillance and control develop. Prior to that, governments often settled for easily targetable commodities (e.g. salt tax, tea tax), proxies for wealth (e.g. window tax, chimney tax), or easily monitored transactions (e.g. customs tariffs at ports) and even farmed out their taxing powers to private agents and enterprises.

THE PURPOSES AND USE OF TAX

The overriding purpose of tax is to supply government with the revenue it needs to fund its operations and deliver its services. However, in the process of raising those funds, governments also have the opportunity both to redistribute wealth between different groups in society and to influence the behaviour of individuals (Pender 1997: 22).

Tax systems inevitably have a redistributive effect of some kind. Depending on who or what is taxed, at what rates, a tax system may redistribute income in at least three distinctly different ways. First, it may redistribute income *vertically*, that is between different income groups—from the poor to the rich or vice versa. Second, it may redistribute income *horizontally*, that is between individuals of similar income or from one sector of the economy to another.

Third, it may redistribute income *intergenerationally*, that is from people in one period of time to people in another.

A large part of the GST debate was about the 'vertical' dimension in relation to the allegedly 'regressive' nature (explained further below) of consumption taxes—the suggestion being that, in essence, consumption taxes redistribute income from poorer to wealthier people. Few people argue—at least publicly— that tax systems should redistribute money from the poor to the rich. That the reverse should occur is much more widely accepted.

Tax systems can burden some types of economic activity with greater costs while penalising others less. Thus they are always in danger, as the economists like to say, of 'distorting' economic behaviour—of causing individuals to deviate from what would be the most economically rational allocation of investment and effort if there were no tax system. For instance, a system that taxes earnings much more than it taxes consumption discourages work and savings; a system that taxes capital gains discourages some types of investment.

Both the redistribution of income and the influencing of behaviour may (and do) happen inadvertently. Presumably, the GST was not introduced for the purpose of redistributing wealth from the poor to the wealthy. Insofar as it has that effect, it does so incidentally. However, deliberate efforts are often made to use the 'distorting' effect of taxes in a positive way to achieve public policy goals. Individually or socially damaging activities such as smoking and drinking may be discouraged through especially high taxes (sometimes called 'sin taxes'), while socially beneficial activities such as having children, saving for your retire- ment, or undertaking research and development, may be encouraged through tax concessions. Such concessions are known as 'tax expenditures' in reference to the way that governments (in effect) 'spend' money simply by giving some categories of people preferential tax treatment. Commonwealth government 'tax expenditures' in 2003–04 were $31 billion, of which by far the largest component was accounted for by the preferential tax rate applied to superannu- ation (Treasury 2005). Steering Australians toward funding their own retire- ment has long been a policy objective of the both major parties, reflecting the classical liberal emphasis on self-sufficiency, and these subsidies through the tax system have been one of the primary instruments for achieving that goal. A major criticism of such uses of 'tax expenditure' is that they constitute an 'upside down subsidy' with disproportionate benefit to people with higher incomes since the higher your income, the more you stand to benefit from such 'loopholes' in the tax system (Peters 1991: 196).

PRINCIPLES OF TAXATION

Economists typically nominate a list of principles that should be applied to designing a tax system. These can be summed up in the suggestion that the costs of levying the tax should be kept to a minimum. Tax costs include the burden such imposts place on economic growth and the administrative effort required for collection.

Certain recommendations follow from these principles. One is that governments should tax as many revenue sources as possible, in order to spread the tax burden as evenly and thinly as possible across the economy. Another is that governments should tax savings and investment earnings relatively lightly so as not to discourage activities seen as the drivers of economic growth. Consumption should be taxed more heavily (such as through a GST) than earnings to reduce the penalty for working hard and creating wealth.

However, these economists' injunctions are not necessarily compatible with other considerations regarded as equally important by many. In particular, they are not necessarily compatible with concerns for equity and fairness. There is a wide expectation that governments should moderate the inequality of wealth that is an inherent feature of a private enterprise market economy. Such a focus on the fair treatment of people at different income levels is referred to as 'vertical equity'. Vertical equity needs to be distinguished from 'horizontal equity', the principle that likes should be treated alike—individuals in the same income stratum should be taxed the same regardless of the source of their earnings.

In focusing on vertical equity, it is useful to distinguish between regressive, proportional and progressive taxes.

- A tax is *regressive* if it has a lower impact per dollar of income for those on higher incomes.
- A tax is *proportional* if has the same impact per dollar of income on all incomes. A proportional tax is sometimes also referred to as a *flat* tax.
- A tax is *progressive* if its impact per dollar of income rises as one goes up the income scale.

Regressive taxes thus exacerbate existing income inequalities; proportional taxes leave them untouched; progressive taxes moderate them.

Consumption taxes such as the GST are regressive in their impact. Such taxes cost a poor person and a rich person the same amount of money in dollar terms for any particular purchase. This is regressive in impact because the same amount of money is a much greater proportion of a poor person's income than it is of a rich person's. Australian Bureau of Statistics (ABS) data confirm the highly regressive impact of Australia's consumption taxes at the aggregate level as well. While receiving 50 times the income of the bottom 20 per cent of households, the top 20 per cent pay only 3.5 times as much indirect tax (Warren 2004: 48).

The Australian personal income tax system, by contrast, has a progressive structure built into it. The rate structure is graduated or stepped by having periodic increases in the 'marginal rate' as income rises (see Figures 23.1 and 23.2). The first $6000 one earns are not taxed at all (the 'tax-free threshold'); every dollar one earns over $6000 a year is taxed at 15 per cent until one's earn-

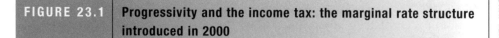

FIGURE 23.1 | **Progressivity and the income tax: the marginal rate structure introduced in 2000**

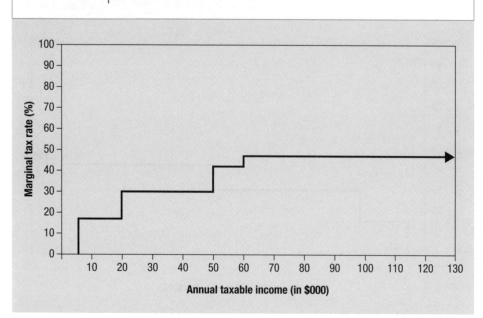

Following the adjustments introduced by the Howard government's GST tax reform package on 1 July 2000, the personal income tax was graduated in the steps you see here. It began with a rate of zero for the first $6000 of earnings, and peaked at a rate of 47 per cent (plus the 1.5 per cent Medicare levy) for every dollar of earnings above $60 000. Each successive step is known as the 'marginal rate'.
Source: Treasury (2000).

Actual data:

0–6,000	0%
6,001–20,000	17%
20,001–50,000	30%
50,001–60,000	42%
60,001+	47%

ings exceed $21 600 a year at which point the next tax bracket cuts in and every subsequent dollar is taxed at 30 per cent, and so on. In the current arrangement there are five such brackets in total. ABS data indicate that this progressive income tax structure, by sharp contrast with the flat-rate indirect tax system, is highly progressive in its impact. The top 20 per cent of households pay 300 times as much income tax as the bottom 20 per cent (Warren 2004: 48).

What is the overall impact of Australia's tax system, taking into account all of the taxes paid? Judged by the results, it would appear that the system is, in aggregate, highly progressive—effecting a substantial redistribution of income from the rich to the poor. The evidence for this is in ABS figures showing that while the ratio of *before-tax* income between the top 10 per cent of earners and the bottom 10 per cent is 9 to 1, the ratio in *after-tax* income is only 4.5 to 1 (Warren 2004: 45).

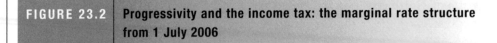

FIGURE 23.2 | **Progressivity and the income tax: the marginal rate structure from 1 July 2006**

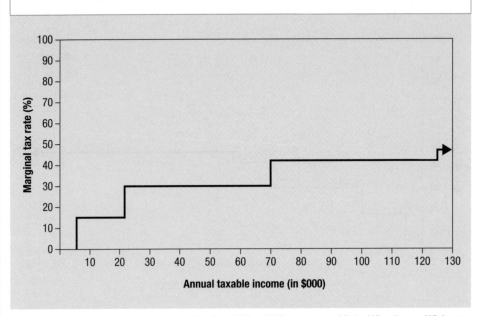

Significant lifting of the upper two thresholds legislated to take effect in 2005 and 2006 restores progressivity to middle and upper middle income levels by lifting the top marginal rate to over twice average earnings and protecting average earners from being dragged by continuing bracket creep into the 42 per cent bracket. Note, however, that the thresholds at the bottom of the scale remain unchanged.
Source: Costello (2005).

Actual data:

0–6,000	0%
6,001–21,600	15%
21,601–70,000	30%
70,001–125,000	42%
125,001+	47%

Some important taxes are proportional rather than progressive, including the corporate income tax and the Medicare levy. 'Flat tax' proponents argue that progressivity in the income tax should be abandoned altogether and replaced with a proportional income-tax system—that is, a single rate of income tax for all income earners. Justifications for this vary from the economic argument that progressivity represents a disincentive to initiative and effort, to the practical argument that the flat tax would abolish a complexity that is said to characterise existing multi-rate income tax systems, to the ethical argument that progressivity is unjust (Mitchell 1998; Chipman 2004). These proponents tend to be associated with the free-market Right, their argument being consistent with a view that market inequalities are the natural rewards for effort, initiative and merit, while government-executed redistribution (in the name of 'vertical equity') is unjust. The flat-tax movement has not won wide support in Australia but has done so in parts of North America and is causing concern among defenders of progressive tax systems in the European Union because of its spread among EU member and non-member states in Eastern Europe (*Economist* 2005). While the flat tax is often promoted on the basis that it will bring about an enormous simplification of individual income tax returns, it is only a related but separate reform—the elimination of deductions—that would really achieve that goal. The main effect of the flat tax would be to shift the emphasis in the tax system away from prevailing conceptions of vertical equity (Fougere & Ruggeri 1998).

All this said, it must be remembered that the ultimate effect a tax system will have on inequality cannot be determined without taking into account the way the resulting government revenue is spent. If revenue from a progressive tax is spent on services primarily enjoyed by the affluent, for instance, then the element of vertical redistribution will be reduced or negated.

WHO'S PAYING THEIR TAX?

Principles are one thing, practice another. What happens if a tax system—designed to spread the costs of government fairly across the community, to reward the right types of behaviour while discouraging the wrong, and to promote economic growth—is widely rorted? Individuals know that they stand to gain very tangible and direct benefits from cheating the tax system. They figure that the little bit that they are thereby stealing from the rest of the community is far too small to cause a measurable reduction in the services that government provides to them personally. They may also think that many others in the rest of the community are cheating anyway.

Tax *minimisation* strategies are a fact of life. However, the practice of tax minimisation varies significantly in its degree and its corrosiveness. Tax systems are generally designed on the assumption that individuals and companies will try to minimise paying tax where and when they can. There are numerous legitimate ways in which they may do this and, insofar as they exploit those opportunities honestly, individuals and companies are legitimately minimising tax. Assisted by tax accountants, higher-income Australians commonly minimise their tax by such devices as channelling income into tax-sheltered family trusts and tax deductible investments. Tax deductible investments—most notoriously the deductibility of interest payments on money borrowed for investment rental property—allow those on higher incomes to deduct net annual losses of maintaining and operating the property against their personal income tax bill (negative gearing) while eventually either reaping a capital gain profit down the track or simply becoming more wealthy due to owning an asset that is appreciating in value.

The temptation always exists to cross the line and practise tax *evasion*. Companies may fraudulently claim losses or channel earnings offshore to associated companies located in foreign low-taxing 'tax havens'; individuals may fraudulently claim that their investment property costs are much bigger than they really are or they may fraudulently abuse tax-sheltered family trusts; small businesses may operate outside the tax system in the so-called 'black economy', able to offer customers reduced prices for 'cash jobs' because the business does not intend to disclose the transaction in its tax return; and so on.

The perception that these practices are particularly iniquitous arises from the fact that such opportunities to cheat the system tend to increase with wealth. The greater the wealth one has, the greater the resources one has to hire cunning tax accountants and the greater opportunities one has to shift wealth within and between business entities and across jurisdictions.

At various times in Australian tax history, the line between (legitimate) minimisation and (illegitimate) evasion has become blurred. The most notorious of these periods was in the 1970s, when the High Court applied a radically permissive interpretation of the tax code which had the effect of permitting as legitimate 'minimisation' what the prosecuting taxation authorities (and much of the community) had regarded as inappropriate 'evasion'. Today, there are suggestions that there should be a reform of the tax advantages enjoyed by family trusts, generated by controversy about the degree to which these tax-minimisation instruments are being exploited for tax-evasion purposes.

The Australian Taxation Office (ATO) invests a considerable part of its resources in seeking to ensure compliance with the law and identifying what it describes as 'aggressive arrangements' that push the boundary of minimisation towards evasion. A spate of mass-marketed tax minimisation schemes attracted ATO attention in the late 1990s for the way they promised high-earning workers tax relief through alleged tax-deductible investments. This time the courts sided with the ATO's claim that the schemes involved illegal tax evasion, with the unprecedented conviction and jailing in 2004 of a number of accountants for 'conspiracy to defraud the Commonwealth' (DPP 2004: 82).

Tax reform

Tax reform has been a ubiquitous feature of politics and policy across the Western liberal-democratic world and a major ingredient in policy debates for nearly three decades now. By 'reform' is almost always meant a simplification and 'flattening' of the progressive income tax structure, a reduction in corporate and personal income tax rates, and a shift away from income to consumption taxes. The deliberate use of the word 'reform' is intended by its proponents to convey the impression that these are changes necessary to make the tax system work better rather than changes to serve any particular set of interests.

This sort of 'reform' was made famous by the radical flattening of British and US personal income tax scales implemented under the free-market conservative governments of Prime Minister Thatcher and President Reagan in the 1980s. The main proposition justifying those reductions was the argument that increasing incentives to effort and enterprise would pull those economies out of the economic stagnation in which they seemed to be mired—a so-called 'supply-side economics' argument. But wouldn't radical tax cuts lose governments too much revenue, requiring either savage expenditure cuts or much larger budget deficits to compensate for this? The answer, according to supply-side economists, was no. They argued that, first of all, rate cuts would be partially funded by closing some of the many loopholes that had allowed some higher-income earners to avoid paying anything like what they might have been expected to pay. Second, they argued that the tax cuts would partially fund themselves—a reduction in tax rates should produce more, not less, revenue for government because, the proponents claimed, it would increase the incentive for individuals and businesses to work and trade and then pay tax on their increased earnings.[1]

In Australia, the focal point of tax reform for two decades was the claimed need to introduce a broad-based consumption tax, a process that culminated in the Howard government's introduction of the GST on 1 July 2000. Advocates for the GST argued that it would rationalise the indirect tax system and take some of the burden off the direct tax system, contributing, they argued, to economic efficiency and to the increased wealth of society as a whole.

The Australian tax system

Taxation in Australia is overwhelmingly dominated by the Commonwealth government (see Table 23.1). As is discussed in Chapter 7, control of the main revenue sources has been both a symptom and a source of Commonwealth predominance in Australia's federal system. With its appropriation of corporate and personal income tax from the States in 1942, the Commonwealth took a stranglehold over revenue raising and today controls 75 to 80 per cent of all the tax raised. The result is acute 'vertical fiscal imbalance', with the States heavily reliant on financial transfers from the Commonwealth to fund their many spending responsibilities from infrastructure to schools to hospitals. The States raise own-source revenue from a motley collection of sources but their options are very limited and tax policy is overwhelmingly a Commonwealth matter, with its income tax (and particularly the personal income tax) being the main feature of the system.

Within the Commonwealth government, tax policy is the responsibility of the Department of the Treasury. Treasurer Peter Costello has been the long-standing face of the Howard government's tax policy and the Treasurer's annual May budget speech typically features tax as one of its highlights. Tax administration, meanwhile, is the responsibility of the Australian Taxation Office (ATO), an autonomous agency within the Treasury portfolio whose 21 000

TABLE 23.1	Taxes levied by level of government (with estimated receipts 2004–05)				
Commonwealth government		**State governments**		**Local governments**	
Personal income tax	$109.0 bn	Payroll tax	$10.0 bn	Property taxes	$7.0 bn
Corporate income tax	$40.0 bn	Stamp duties	$11.0 bn		
Goods and Services Tax *	$35.5 bn	Gambling taxes	$3.8 bn		
Capital gains tax	**	Motor vehicle fees	$4.7 bn		
Petrol excise duty	$13.6 bn	Insurance taxes	$3.1 bn		
Tobacco and alcohol excise	$7.9 bn	Land taxes	$2.5 bn		
Customs duty	$5.7 bn				
Fringe benefits tax	$3.0 bn				
Total	$214.7 bn		$35.1 bn		$7.0 bn

* all granted to States

** Capital Gains Tax included in personal income tax figure

employees advise the public on tax matters, process tax returns and carry out various audit and investigative work to ensure compliance. In 2002 the office of Inspector-General of Taxation, analogous to the Ombudsman and the Auditor-General, was created to provide enhanced monitoring and accountability of the ATO and tax administration.

Decay of progressivity in income tax

The uniform national income tax introduced by the Curtin Labor government in 1942 (replacing the previous mixture of a uniform Commonwealth tax and different levels of State-levied income taxes) was a highly progressive tax (Smith 1993: 45). It brought low-income working-class Australians into the income tax net for the first time, but it did so at lower rates of taxation than applied to middle-income Australians and much lower than those applying to very high-income earners.

Over the subsequent decades, this progressivity was steadily, and at times rapidly, eroded by a phenomenon called 'bracket creep' (Krever 1991). Bracket creep arises when, over time, the apparent or 'nominal' level of wages and salaries rises but, because that rise is merely part of a general inflation in the price of goods and services, the *real* value of these wages and salaries grows by nothing like the same amount or indeed does not grow at all. In these circumstances, a substantial part of most people's wage increases are illusory—merely keeping up with inflation. But if the income tax brackets, meanwhile, remain unchanged, income earners whose *nominal* incomes have increased can find themselves paying tax rates at a higher rate because their income now places them in a higher tax bracket, even though their *real* income has not changed. The only way to avoid this is for the income tax brackets to be 'indexed' to inflation, so that the tax brackets move upwards to keep pace with inflation.

Bracket creep, however, has proven very attractive to governments — having the double bonus that it silently brings about a steady rise in tax revenue while also allowing the government to get credit for periodic tax 'cuts'. With a short-lived exception in the late 1970s, indexation has not been applied in relation to the Australian income tax system. Combined with the availability of tax deductions and loopholes for upper-income earners, this has greatly diminished the personal income tax as an agent for pursuing vertical equity.

Until very recently, Australian governments whether Labor or Liberal made only the occasional gesture towards restoring progressivity. Rather than making the necessary upward adjustment of thresholds, governments around the world have chosen the path of reducing tax rates at the top of the scale, flattening the personal income tax scale.

Since the mid-1970s crisis of Keynesian economics, the politics of tax have been dominated by pressure to shift revenue-raising away from income taxes in general and towards consumption taxes. Two decades of inflation exposed increasing numbers of ordinary income earners to high levels of taxation, at the same time that Western economies were suffering economic stagnation and persistent inflation ('stagflation'). Political pressure to unfetter business and restore economic incentives by reducing government spending and taxing exposed the tax system to the criticism that high marginal rates on higher incomes were an obstacle to renewed economic growth. Not only should taxes in general be cut, it was argued, but the tax burden should be shifted from earnings to expenditure.

The GST—fourth time lucky

Australia resisted these pressures longer than many countries. Proposals for a general goods and services tax (GST) were blocked three times before achieving success in 1999. The idea first made it on to the political agenda in the late 1970s but the proposal by then Treasurer John Howard was rejected in Cabinet by the Fraser government. The idea returned in 1985, when a version was proposed by the Labor Treasurer, Paul Keating, at the Hawke Labor government's 'National Tax Summit'. To Keating's frustration, the proposal had to be withdrawn in the face of opposition from within his own Labor Party and from across the interest-group spectrum. Then in the 1993 federal election, Liberal leader John Hewson made a GST the centrepiece of the Coalition's *Fightback!* election platform (LNP 1991), but Labor Prime Minister Paul Keating seized upon the complexities of the scheme — and the strongly pro-market policies with which it was linked—to turn the campaign around and win for Labor the 'unwinnable' election.

Following that electoral defeat in 1993, business organisations—who had until to that point taken a back seat on proposed reforms or even opposed them—mobilised to promote tax reform. Under the leadership of the Business Council of Australia, a lobby group calling itself the Business Coalition for Tax Reform (BCTR) was created. Importantly, the Business Coalition succeeded in getting qualified support from major welfare organisations—notably the Australian Council of Social Service (ACOSS), the peak body for the social welfare sector—thereby reducing potential opposition from those concerned about a more regressive taxation structure (Mendes 1997). Organisations such as ACOSS were prepared to consider the GST because it promised sufficient revenue to fund the costly social programs that were being jeopardised by budget deficits. This ACOSS involvement was later to help undermine the Labor Opposition's efforts to mount a persuasive social equity campaign against the Howard government's GST proposals.

When the Howard government announced its intention to introduce a GST, it cleverly won support from the State Premiers by undertaking to tie the proposed revenue to reform of Commonwealth–State financial relations. Allocation of all the GST revenues to the States would liberate the States from the vagaries of Commonwealth financial assistance grants and give them a potentially very lucrative 'growth tax'—that is, a tax whose revenues would steadily increase as economic activity increased. Re-elected at the 1998 federal election with a pro-GST platform, the Howard government then introduced its tax reform package to Parliament.

The 'new tax system' and its politics

The core of the package was legislation replacing the Commonwealth government's existing wholesale sales tax (WST) with the much more comprehensive value-added tax (see below) to be called the GST. The WST had applied to various goods at different rates (e.g. 12 per cent on household goods versus 22 per cent on motor vehicles) and did not apply to services at all. The proposed across-the-board GST levied at a flat rate of 10 per cent would simultaneously reduce the taxation of most manufactured goods and raise more revenue by taxing services as well. The extra revenue, in turn, was proposed to fund major cuts to the income tax, with the end result being 'revenue neutrality'—that is, the same aggregate amount of tax being raised as before, just raised differently (Treasury 1998).

For the entire 20th century, manufactured goods had borne the brunt of the consumption tax burden and services had escaped altogether. The proposed GST would bring them into the 'tax net' for the first time. This was particularly significant because services — everything from takeaway food and haircuts to insurance and consulting — had come to make up by far the largest component of economic activity (75 per cent of Gross Domestic Product). Replacing the WST with the GST would remove an economic distortion that previously favoured services over goods, and in the process take some pressure off the manufacturing sector of the economy.

A major selling point for the Howard government was that the introduction of this powerful new consumption tax would be accompanied by a reduced dependence on income tax. This goal was embodied in companion legislation primarily directed to reducing personal income tax rates. Most notably, average income earners had their marginal tax rate reduced from 43 per cent to 30 per cent. A promised $12 billion in tax would thereby be shifted from the personal income tax to consumption tax.

A major factor in the defeat of previous attempts to introduce a GST was opposition to its implications for distributional fairness ('vertical equity'). The progressive income tax had been a major element in the postwar social consensus, promising some compensatory fairness for inequalities in income and wealth. Proposals for a quantum shift to much more regressive consumption taxes signalled an abandonment of that approach.

To assuage concerns about the GST's regressive impact, the government included compensatory measures as part of its reform package. When the Canadian government introduced its GST in the late 1980s, it had introduced a GST tax rebate that provided cash payments for all low-income earners. The Howard government's proposal likewise offered compensation for lower-income earners, in this case through such measures as increased social security pension payments and reduced income tax rates at the low- and middle-income levels. Opponents of the GST proposal argued that these income tax reductions for low-to-middle income earners were insufficient, merely restoring an element of what had been lost over the years to bracket creep.

Using their balance-of-power position in the Senate, the Australian Democrats declared that they would not support the legislation unless greater compensation was made for the regressive nature of consumption taxes. With the Labor Opposition pledged to vote against the proposal, this stance by the Democrats would have blocked the reform in the Senate and quite possibly killed off the GST for a fourth time. Intense negotiations between Prime Minister Howard and Democrats' leader Senator Meg Lees then ensued.

The government had sought a single tax to apply at the same rate across the full range of goods and services. This had the double benefit of reducing administrative complexity (by removing the need to differentiate between taxable and nontaxable items) and reducing the rate at which the tax would have to be applied to generate the same amount of revenue. But the Democrats argued that one major sector — food — should be exempted. As food is a non-discretionary purchase that makes up a much larger proportion of low-income than high-income household budgets, a GST on food would have had a particularly regressive effect. Reducing income taxes while introducing a tax on food had been described by ACOSS (1999: 8) as a 'diabolical trade-off', as it was the wealthy who stood to benefit in both instances.

The result of the negotiations was a compromise that dismayed the economic purists but promised to reduce the adverse impact of the new tax. The agreement between the Howard government and the Democrats exempted from the GST almost all food other than prepared or convenience food (i.e. food typically sold either for consumption on the premises, such as restaurant meals, or for immediate consumption, such as takeaways). This increased the system's complexity somewhat (for example, a bottled drink that is 85 per cent fruit juice attracts the GST, but one that is 90 per cent fruit juice does not) and it diminished revenues somewhat. It also opened the door to other special requests. If food was to be exempt, why not (for example) books: how could the government justify a 'tax on learning'?

Out of parliamentary necessity, the Howard government reached this compromise with the Democrats, with the final package settling for a lower total revenue take from a slightly narrower base than had been planned. By contrast with its counterparts in both New Zealand and Canada, the Australian government was forced to make popular concessions by the fact of a strong upper house that it did not control.

The GST as implemented is a 'value-added' tax, a sophisticated form of sales tax that is now used in all but one of the 30 advanced countries that comprise the OECD.[2] It is levied on the increased value of goods or services at every transaction point in the process, from (for example) the sale of raw materials from a supplier to a manufacturer to the retail sale of a product by a shop to a consumer. Under the GST arrangement, this is calculated in practice by a system of levies and rebates. For example, a retail business is required to add a 10 per cent tax to the price of the goods or services that it sells to consumers, but the amount that it then forwards to the Australian Taxation Office is this tax minus the 10 per cent tax that it has already paid for any 'input' goods or services (such as when buying goods from a supplier). A consequence of this sophisticated system is complexity: small business in particular has often objected to the additional bookkeeping burden that the GST entails.

Reforming the personal income tax

Within only a couple of years, the GST had clearly demonstrated that it could live up to some of its expectations. Most importantly, it quickly proved itself a handsome earner ($35.5 bn in 2004–05), exceeding revenue expectations and rapidly confirming for the States the superiority of access to a growth tax over reliance on financial assistance grants from the Commonwealth. One promise it conspicuously failed to live up to, though, was the promise to solve deep problems in the personal income tax system. Any progress it made in that regard was modest and temporary, quickly eaten away by bracket creep. The GST's 'New Tax System' as the government had promoted it, soon began to look merely like one more instalment in an ongoing process of making tax policy.

BRACKET REFORM AT THE TOP

Some sort of ongoing adjustment to address this problem was implicit in the Coalition government's boast that, with the GST-funded changes to the income tax system, at least 80 per cent of taxpayers would be paying no more than the 30 per cent rate. It was not long before bracket creep was threatening to make a mockery of that assurance. Many average earners were being pushed increasingly close to the 42 per cent threshold, while large numbers of those who hardly qualified as rich were already paying the top marginal rate of 47 per cent.

The Howard government was faced with two main alternatives for further adjustment and reform. One choice was to counteract bracket creep by continuing with the incremental policy of periodically reducing top rates and flattening the income tax scale so that less of a burden would be placed on those middle-income earners who were being ratcheted into high income tax brackets. This choice, however, would reward all higher income earners, including the truly rich—indeed, it would reward the truly rich the most. The other alternative was to counteract bracket creep by maintaining the top rates as they were but lift the thresholds at which they cut in.

In 2002 and 2003 the government made minor upward adjustments that were too small to do anything but draw attention to the problem, and that were quickly ridiculed for their triviality. Pressure was mounting for the government to demonstrate its tax reform *bona fides* and introduce more substantial reforms.

The Business Coalition for Tax Reform, which had scored a resounding success with its campaign for introduction of the GST, put the government on notice that reforms to the personal income tax system were now overdue. In the Business Coalition's analysis, there were two interrelated problems: the income level at which the top rates took effect was too low, and the rates at which they were levied were too high (BCTR 2004: 6). In the BCTR's view, there was no need to make a choice between which of these should be fixed: the two were complementary. Lifting the thresholds would make it easy to reduce the rates since it would greatly reduce the number of taxpayers in that top bracket and thus there would be relatively little revenue to lose (BCTR 2004: 9).

Some economists and business commentators argued that the top tax rate should be reduced to something much closer to the corporate income tax rate of

30 per cent. Such a radical reduction was promoted in part on the grounds that it would remove the incentive to evade personal income tax by disguising individual earnings as business earnings. Meanwhile, a group of Coalition back-benchers went public with demands that the government introduce a range of reforms to cut income tax. The group called for indexation to end bracket creep, lifting of the tax-free threshold, lifting of the top threshold, and reduction in the top rate. Then in March 2005, an OECD report revealed that Australia was one of the only two OECD countries where the total tax burden had increased rather than decreased since the mid-1990s (Uren 2005; OECD 2005).

The Howard government's response was embodied in the Treasurer's 2005 budget announcements. Rather than cutting income tax rates, it elected to under-take a radical attack on the effects of decades of bracket creep by substantially lifting the tax thresholds. The Treasurer announced that as of 1 July 2006, the top threshold would be lifted to $125 000 annual income (see Figure 23.2) — double what it had been after the GST had supposedly given Australia 'not a new tax, but a new tax system'. Against the predominant advice from its own side of politics, and contrary to the direction reform had taken in other English-speaking democracies, the Coalition opted to restore progressivity rather than reduce the rates and flatten the scale. The top rate was left at the comparatively high level of 48.5 per cent (including the Medicare levy) but it would no longer loom on the horizon for those on middle incomes.

BRACKET REFORM AT THE BOTTOM?

This is not to say that the dramatic lifting of the top two thresholds was greeted with universal acclaim. Aside from the very modest reduction of the bottom rate from 17 to 15 per cent, no alleviation was offered for all those earning under $50 000 a year. Thus the Labor Opposition and the Australian Council of Social Service could claim that the reforms did little or nothing for those on the lower end of the income scale whose incomes were never in any danger of being pushed into the top tax brackets.[3]

As can be clearly seen from Figures 23.1 and 23.2, Australia's tax system has been and remains steeply progressive at the bottom end. Only the first $6000 is earned tax free; at $6001 the tax rate of 15 per cent cuts in; then at $20 000 the next rate of twice that, 30 per cent, cuts in. Thus, by 1 July 2006 someone earning only $25 000 per annum is paying the same marginal rate of tax as someone earning $65 000.

One partial solution that would help those on low incomes would be to lift the tax-free threshold. This would provide a major benefit to those on lower incomes, restoring some of what they have lost to bracket creep just as those on higher incomes have had some of their losses restored. As McDonald and Kippen (2005: 2) explain:

In 1983/84, the tax-free threshold was 20 per cent above the single adult rate of unemployment benefit. Now, it is 40 per cent below, effectively halving its value relative to the unemployment benefit . . . In the past 20 years, the average tax rate on an income of one quarter of average weekly earnings has increased from around one per cent to around nine per cent . . . No higher multiple of average weekly earnings has experienced a rise in taxation anything like this much. (McDonald and Kippen 2005: 2)

RATE REFORM?

While, analytically, it is easy to see the problem of marginal rates being too high at the bottom of the income scale, politically it is not clear that there is a strong constituency lobbying for such reforms. Things are different at the other end of the income scale. If the BCTR is correct, the path is now clear for the rates themselves to be cut since the revenue losses will be now be considerably lower. It was anticipated that there will be less political pressure on the government to implement such cuts since so many fewer voters are now affected by that top rate. However, political pressure from business and some media outlets has continued. The Prime Minister himself floated the idea of the BCTR's second component as a prospect for 2006, and it was also strongly pushed by such high-profile Liberals as the prominent backbencher Malcolm Turnbull. Turnbull's commissioned research argued that cutting the top rate from 47 to 40 per cent would indeed be inexpensive now that the threshold had been raised (Turnbull & Temple 2005: 20).

Remaining issues

There remains ample room for improvement in Australia's tax system. However, judgments about the kind of improvements that should be made inevitably reflect the political values brought to the discussion.

OVERTAXED?

The introduction of the GST temporarily reduced the aggregate amount of personal income tax that Australians pay but it did not reduce the aggregate amount of tax that Australians pay in total. And indeed, contrary to what one might expect from a decade of government by parties strongly influenced by the 'small government' ideologies of classical liberalism and social conservatism, total tax take in Australia is at historically high levels. According to OECD (2004: 68) figures, it rose from 29.6 per cent of GDP in the year the Howard government came to office to 31.5 per cent in fiscal year 2002–03. As we have seen, the GST and subsequent reforms have also left unchanged the top marginal rate at which the personal income tax is levied on the highest income. This raises the question whether Australians are overtaxed, or at least whether a reduced tax burden would help make the Australian economy more internationally competitive.

In the classical or market liberal view of the world, any amount of tax is a burden on the economy and as the tax level increases so the burden increases. By contrast, some reformers, inspired perhaps by a reform liberal or collectivist/democratic perspective, see taxation playing an essential role in funding a range of important social benefits such as public health care and public education.

The classical liberal attack on 'big government' is based on the proposition that taxes inflict two sets of costs on the economy. According to the theory of 'deadweight costs', individuals reduce their level of economically productive activity in response to the disincentives of taxation and a large and wasteful 'army' of tax bureaucrats, tax lawyers and tax accountants are paid to administer the tax system, ensure compliance, and assist individuals in minimising their tax. Thus, according to the market liberals, every dollar the government raises in taxation actually costs the economy more like a dollar and a half (Robson 2005: ix). As a result, high-taxing countries, they claim, do not perform as well economically as low-taxing ones. For these reasons, peak business organisations such as the Australian Chamber of Commerce and Industry press the government to cut spending and taxes, preferably to the point where the top marginal rate on the personal income tax scale is 30 per cent (e.g. Moore 2005).

But how highly is Australia taxed? According to both the Australian Council of Social Service and the Howard government the answer is: not very. ACOSS (2005: 13) argues that 'Australia is the seventh lowest taxing country out of the 30 OECD countries, ahead of only the US, Mexico, South Korea, Ireland, Turkey and Japan'. Hence, according to ACOSS, there is no need to make tax reduction a priority. A very similar comparison is highlighted in the Howard government's 2005 budget papers (Treasurer 2005).

But this sort of comparison is triply misleading, according to the market liberals (e.g. Burn 2004). First, it grants each OECD country an equal weight even though Japan and the US are massively larger than such European OECD minnows as Luxembourg and Iceland. Weighting the average according to economic significance immediately puts Australia in the middle rank of taxers rather than near the bottom. Second, it ignores the fact that so much of Australia's OECD-related trade is with non-European OECD countries, who cluster in the bottom half of the tax ranking. Third, it ignores the fact that so much of Australia's trade and economic competition is with non-OECD countries, such as China, which have very low effective tax rates.

None of this matters, however, unless it can be convincingly demonstrated that higher levels of taxation and larger government actually do harm economic performance, and so far the evidence on that is inconclusive (Lindert 2004). But even if it could be demonstrated that current levels of taxation compromise economic growth, voters would have to be persuaded that this was a matter of overriding concern. The democratic ingredient of our liberal-democratic system ensures that we make a collective choice (through our votes at elections) about what trade-offs to make between individual and public provision and between economic growth and other considerations. Interestingly, opinion poll data indicate that while voters in the mid-1990s were strongly inclined to favour tax reduction over increased government service provision, the pendulum has swung back quite measurably since, with the tax-reduction option appealing to only a slightly larger share of voters (Grant 2004: 2; Wilson, Meagher & Breusch 2005).

FAMILY BURDENS

The personal income tax treats taxpayers as individuals, but one of the most important economic and social entities in society is the family. How should the tax system treat the relationship between income-earners within a family? To what extent should the tax system reward the effort and cost invested in raising children? After some decades of neglect, public policy has renewed its focus on the family in recent years, responding to the decline of the traditional family as a core social institution and evidence that the weakened position of the family is linked to other social ills.

Conservatives contend that it is not just 'the family' that is important but, more specifically, the traditional single-income nuclear family where a male breadwinner supports a dependent wife and children. A double-income family, with two adults in the paid workforce, enjoys a slight advantage under the current tax system compared with a single-income family earning the same total amount, as the two earners can each take advantage of the tax-free threshold and the lower tax rates on the lower portions of their respective incomes. The single-income household thus takes home less money. Some conservatives have argued that this should be corrected through permitting 'income splitting' (i.e. notionally dividing between the two spouses, for tax calculation purposes, the income earned by the single breadwinner) so that the tax system does not penalise what they see as the cornerstone of a sound society. Income splitting, though, has had to contend with the objection that it is essentially a subsidy to the wealthy, since it only offers significant benefits to those in top tax brackets.

More importantly, it is also several decades since tax policy made any real concession to the cost of raising children. The result is a reduction in horizontal equity since 'taxation today disregards differences in ability to pay determined by the number of persons an income supports' (Sullivan 1998/99: 62). Individuals are taxed essentially the same regardless of whether they are supporting only themselves or paying the costs of supporting several children. Implicitly or explicitly, this reflects an assumption that children are a mere 'consumption choice' (Smith 1999: 119). In a period when the national birthrate has retreated to well below the population replacement rate, there are reasons to think that policy might return to a more 'human capital' view supporting the investment in reproduction.

Making 'the family' a concern of public policy has been more consistent with the ideological orientation of the Coalition parties than of the Labor Party. Arguably, the Labor Party's concern with buttressing the position of those at the bottom end of the income scale has come at the expense of middle-income earners with children (Smith 1999: 119). Consistent with their ideological leanings, the Coalition parties have moved since coming to power in 1996 to address concerns about the tax treatment both of single-income couples and of dependent children. Beginning with its Family Tax Initiative, the Howard government has introduced measures that increase the tax deductions for dependent children and do so with particular advantage to single-income families.

TAXING WEALTH

The progressive income tax system ostensibly does something to tackle concern about inequality of *income* in society. It does less, though, to tackle concern about inequalities of *wealth* in society. There is a strong tendency to tax what people earn and what they buy, but there is a far weaker effort to tax what they have. Australia does levy some taxes on wealth, notably local government rates and State government land taxes of various kinds (Warren 2004: 236), while the Commonwealth government's capital gains tax (though it is levied in practice as part of the income tax system) is in effect a tax on a realised increase in wealth.

Many commentators suggest that this is all insufficient and that the tax system is biased in favour of passive wealth, with this bias placing a greater burden on productive economic activities. So, for instance, it is argued that business taxes are heavier than necessary due to the failure to tax wealth sufficiently, and this provides a disincentive to investment, job creation, growth and exports. Shifting the tax burden away from business towards accumulated private wealth would be both more efficient and more equitable (Pender 1997: 55).

Some aspects of wealth enjoy privileged tax status thanks to such features of the Australian tax system as capital gains tax exemption on the sale of the family home and the absence of any inheritance tax. Neither exemption is easy to justify on either efficiency or equity grounds (Haslett 1986; Allen 1997; Warren 2004: 236–52; O'Dwyer 2000).

'SIN TAXES'

Earlier in this chapter we noted the phenomenon of 'sin taxes' — taxes levied, often at very high levels, on commodities or activities officially regarded as undesirable. Typical sin taxes are those on cigarettes and alcohol. Governments persist with sin taxes for two rather incompatible reasons. On the one hand, the tax is applied as a policy instrument: to act as a deterrent. Were the deterrent to work perfectly, then governments would raise no revenue from the tax as people would cease consuming the product. On the other hand, sin taxes are also popular with governments precisely because they fail as deterrents: no matter how much tax is added to some products, it seems that people will go on buying them (a phenomenon described in the jargon as 'inelasticity of demand') and the government reaps the tax revenue generated in this way.

Leaving aside moral judgments, there is a justification in economic theory for imposing a tax where people enjoying an activity manage to displace on to others ('externalise') some or all of the costs associated with that activity. Because, for example, smoking creates the 'negative externality' of polluting the air breathed by others and creating a higher burden on the health system that will be borne by the community as a whole, government policy can legitimately force smokers to take responsibility for those externalised costs by imposing a commensurate extra tax on smoking.

A 'glaring omission' in the Australian tax system, according to Pender (1997: 132), is 'the lack of taxes on the negative externalities generated, firstly, by urban vehicle use and secondly by carbon emissions from fossil fuel combustion'. With the issue of global warming at the forefront of international concern, a 'carbon tax' has been advocated as a way of forcing users to pay something closer to the full social cost of their utilisation of non-renewable energy sources. A 'carbon tax' could be calculated according to the amount of CO_2 emitted in combustion. The challenge in the Australian context is to reconcile such a tax with the requirements of an economy heavily dependent on fossil fuels (Hamilton, Hundloe & Quiggin 1997).

Conclusion

Australian tax policy raises fascinating and important questions about the relationship between a range of often conflicting forces, values and considerations. How pressing are the imperatives of economic management in an age of globalisation? How should we define fairness and equity in the context of distributional conflicts within a capitalist society? To what extent should the tax system be used to influence individual behaviour and in what areas? These questions are entangled in the debate about the appropriate design and necessary 'reform' of the tax system.

Economists promote a set of design criteria for tax systems that seek to minimise the adverse impact on the operation of the market economy. These efficiency considerations favour a widely dispersed tax regime that touches all activities relatively lightly and does as little as possible to distort the reward structure of capitalism. An emphasis on taxing consumption rather than income and having flatter rather than progressive scales is consistent with these principles.

Equity considerations give rise to a rather different set of design criteria. From this perspective, the hallmark of a good tax system is the contribution it makes to ameliorating the inequalities of income and wealth characteristic of a capitalist society. These equity considerations favour a regime of progressive taxes that increase their impact as incomes rise, along with taxes on accumulations of wealth. Progressivity is regarded by reform liberals and social democrats as the cornerstone of a system of public policy that gives individuals born into lower income families a fair go in life. Classical liberal thinking, by contrast, has little time for such truncation of the reward structure of a market economy.

Emphasis shifted between these two poles over the course of the 20th century. Equity considerations got the upper hand for the first time with the postwar Keynesian tax regime based on a steeply progressive personal income tax that applied much lower marginal rates to low- and middle-income earners than to high-income earners. 'Bracket creep', proliferating deductions, and the backlash against the Keynesian welfare state allowed efficiency considerations to reassert themselves in the 1970s. Since then, the argument for tax reform has revolved around the need to reduce income tax rates and shift the tax burden from income to consumption. Because of the increased mobility of investment capital and knowledge workers, globalisation has placed downward competitive pressure on national tax regimes and reinforced this argument in recent times.

The Howard government's introduction of the GST in July 2000 seemed to mark Australia's acceptance of this logic. However, the restoration of progressivity to the upper levels of the personal income tax system and the retention of relatively high top marginal tax rates in the reforms of 2005 indicated that Australia has deviated, in this respect at least, from the neoliberal path followed in other English-speaking democracies.

NOTES

1   This second argument draws on the so-called 'Laffer curve'. The Laffer curve is a graph purporting to show the relationship between the rate of taxation and the revenue yield to government. It reports that increasing the rate of taxation initially delivers proportionally more revenue to government. But beyond a certain point that proportion diminishes as the disincentive effects of taking people's earnings away begin to reveal themselves. Finally it reaches a point where a further increase in taxation actually reduces the amount of revenue the government receives (because people would rather earn less money than pay even higher rates of tax). Thus, if tax rates at any particular time have moved beyond the peak of the curve, then tax reductions can be expected—so the theory says—to increase revenue.

2   The Organisation for Economic Co-operation and Development (OECD) is an association between the leading advanced industrial democracies, most notably those of Western Europe, North America and Australasia, now with 30 member states. The organisation's

main service is the provision of high quality research on policy issues relevant to its members.

3   The reforms also failed to address another longstanding feature arising from the inter-action of the tax system with Australia's targeted, means-tested social security and welfare system: the problem of so-called 'poverty traps'. Recipients of welfare payments tend to have those payments reduced if their incomes rise (through, for example, entering the workforce or working more hours). But, once above the tax-free threshold, these recipi-ents also pay tax on their increased income. Adding the income tax to the reduction of welfare payments creates what can be a surprisingly high 'effective marginal tax rate' (much higher than for those just paying income tax on high incomes) for those seeking to work their way out of poverty. This can discourage people from moving out of 'welfare dependency' into self-supporting employment, hence the notion of a 'poverty trap'.

REFERENCES

ACOSS [Australian Council of Social Service] 1999, 'Making the Tax Package Fairer', *Impact*, March.

ACOSS [Australian Council of Social Service] 2005, *ACOSS Federal Budget Priorities State-ment 2005–2006*, Strawberry Hills, NSW.

Allen, R. 1997, 'The Question of Inheritance: Why Shouldn't the Undeserving Rich Be Tapped to Help the Deserving Poor?', *Res Publica*, vol. 6, no. 1.

BCTR [Business Coalition for Tax Reform] 2004, *Federal Budget Submission*, Melbourne.

Burn, P. 2004, *How Highly Taxed Are We? The Level and Composition of Taxation in Australia and the OECD*, Centre for Independent Studies, Sydney.

Chipman, L. 2004, *The Very Idea of a Flat Tax*, Centre for Independent Studies, Sydney.

Costello, P. 2005, *Budget Speech 2005–06*, Australian Government, Canberra.

DPP [Department of Public Prosecutions] 2004, *Annual Report 2003–04*, Canberra.

Economist 2005, 'The Spread of Flat Taxes in Europe', 3 May.

Fougere, M. & Ruggeri, G.E. 1998, 'Flat Taxes and Distributional Justice', *Review of Social Economy*, vol. 61, no. 3.

Grant, R. 2004, 'Less Tax or More Social Spending: Twenty Years of Opinion Polling', *Research Note*, no. 57 2003–04, Parliament of Australia Parliamentary Library, <http://www.aph.gov.au/library/pubs/rn/2003-04/04rn57.htm>.

Hamilton, C., Hundloe, T. & Quiggin, J. 1997, *Ecological Tax Reform in Australia: Using Taxes, Charges and Public Spending to Protect the Environment Without Hurting the Economy*, Australia Institute, Lyneham, ACT.

Haslett, D. 1986, 'Is Inheritance Justified?', *Philosophy and Public Affairs*, vol. 15, no. 2.

Krever, R. 1991, 'The Slow Demise of Progressive Income Tax', in *Inequality in Australia: Slicing the Cake*, eds J. O'Leary & R. Sharp, Heinemann, Melbourne.

Lindert, P.H. 2004, *Growing Public: Social Spending and Economic Growth Since the Eighteenth Century. Volume 1: The Story*, Cambridge University Press, Cambridge.

LNP [Liberal and National Parties] 1991, *Fightback! The Liberal and National Parties Plan to Reward and Rebuild Australia*, Canberra.

McDonald, P. & Kippen, R. 2005, 'Reform of Income Tax in Australia: a Long-term Agenda', *Working Papers in Demography*, no. 95, Demography and Sociology Program, Research School of Social Sciences, Australian National University.

Mendes, P. 1997, 'The Welfare Lobby, Tax Reform and a GST: High Risk Politicking', *Current Affairs Bulletin*, vol. 74, no. 1.

Mitchell, D. 1998, 'Why Not a Flat Tax?', *IPA Review*, vol. 50, no. 4.

Moore, D. 2005, *Commonwealth Spending (and Taxes) Can Be Cut—and Should Be*, Australian Chamber of Commerce and Industry, Melbourne.

O'Dwyer, L. 2000, 'Bequeathing and Inheriting Housing Wealth', in *Home Truths: Property Ownership and Housing Wealth in Australia*, eds B. Badcock & A. Beer, Melbourne University Press, Melbourne.

OECD [Organisation for Economic Co-operation and Development] 2005, *Taxing Wages 2003–2004*, OECD, Paris.

OECD 2004, *Revenue Statistics, 1965–2003*, OECD, Paris.

Pender, H. 1997, *The Joy of Tax: Australian Tax Design—Directions for Long Term Reform*, Australian Tax Research Foundation, Sydney.

Peters, B.G. 1991, *The Politics of Taxation: A Comparative Perspective*, Blackwell, Oxford.

Robson, A. 2005, *The Costs of Taxation*, Centre for Independent Studies, Sydney.

Smith, J. 1993, *Taxing Popularity: The Story of Taxation in Australia*, Federalism Research Centre, Australian National University, Canberra.

Smith, J. 1999, 'Progressing Tax Reform', in *Out of the Rut: Making Labor a Genuine Alternative*, eds M. Carman & I. Rogers, Allen & Unwin, Sydney.

Sullivan, L. 1998/99, 'Taxation of Family Income: The Lost Concept of Horizontal Equity', *Policy*, vol. 14, no. 4.

Treasury 2005, 'Statement 5: Revenue', *2005–06 Budget Paper No. 1: Budget Strategy and Outlook 2005–06*, Australian Government, Canberra, <http://www.budget.gov.au/2005-06/bp1/download/bp1.pdf>.

Treasury 2000, 'Statement 3: Maintaining Low Inflation and Strong Growth', *2000–01 Budget Paper No. 1: Budget Strategy and Outlook 2000–01*, Commonwealth of Australia, Canberra.

Treasury 1998, *Tax Reform: Not a New Tax, a New Tax System*, Commonwealth of Australia, Canberra.

Turnbull, M. & Temple, J. 2005, *Taxation Reform in Australia: Some Alternatives and Indicative Costings*, Sydney.

Uren, D. 2005, 'PM Bucks World with Tax Hikes', *The Australian*, 10 March.

Warren, N. 2004, *Tax: Facts Fiction and Reform*, Australian Tax Research Foundation, Sydney.

Wilson, S., Meagher, G. & Breusch, T. 2005, 'Where to for the Welfare State?', in *Australian Social Attitudes: The First Report*, eds S. Wilson, G. Meagher, R. Gibson, D. Denemark & M. Western, UNSW Press, Sydney.

Welfare policy

CHAPTER 24

JANE ROBBINS

The Howard Coalition government has nominated welfare as one of its priority areas of reform in Australia. Over the last few years important changes have been introduced that have changed the basis of individual entitlement to social security benefits. On the whole, these changes have been received with popular support. Among academic commentators, however, there has been considerable debate about the impact of welfare reform. Some commentators have concluded that the relationship between the individual and the state has been transformed via changes in welfare policy, in ways that require the fundamental nature of citizenship in Australia to be reassessed.

The debates about welfare policy are interesting and deeply significant in their own right. They also illuminate aspects of the political and policymaking process that are characteristic, as sketched in Chapter 1 of this book, of liberal democracies. As elaborated further below, a classical liberal perspective engenders a scepticism about the extent to which self-reliant individuals should be taxed in order for governments to provide welfare support for other individuals deemed to be disadvantaged. But a democratic perspective is quite comfortable with this being discussed and resolved by political debate and decision, and with considerable weight being given to community norms, mutual assistance and some sense of a collective social responsibility for all citizens. Liberal democracies are responsive to both sets of ideas—and hence welfare policy debates are typically lively and likely to remain so.

Welfare as a concept

It is difficult to be precise in defining the concept of 'welfare' as it can be given a number of different meanings. In a policy sense, it is used to denote a range of government programs delivered to people in need. In its narrowest use, it means 'social security' or income support. More broadly, the term is also often used to describe a number of 'human services' such as health, housing, aged care and community services.

The term 'welfare state' is used to describe a country in which government has embraced the role of ameliorating social inequalities arising from the operation of the market or private sector, either by compensating individuals or by intervention in the activities of markets. The task for government in a welfare state is not merely the alleviation of individual need or short-term incapacity, but a larger one that also addresses issues of social justice and equal opportunity.

In Western political tradition, the ideological 'Right' is often identified with a minimalist or 'residual' position on welfare. According to this classical liberal position, state intervention should be minimised to avoid any distortion of the competitive 'supply and demand' dynamics of the market. Only the 'deserving poor' and those with acceptable reasons for requiring assistance should, as a last resort, be given help by the state. This is welfare as a 'social safety net', constructed to preserve the incentives for individuals to take responsibility for their own needs. Welfare initiatives formulated from this value base typically limit access to benefits by tightly defining eligibility, requiring income or assets tests and offering minimal levels of support.

The 'Left', on the other hand, is associated with the more collective approach of the social-democratic tradition. Here, welfare policy is seen in the context of the development of more democratic and equitable social institutions, and embodies the expanding entitlements of citizenship. This view was expressed strongly in the work of sociologist T.H. Marshall, who described the evolving acquisition of civil, political and social rights as fundamental to the historical process of modernisation of society (Marshall 1963; Pierson 1998: 21–2). In the postwar era the British scholar Titmuss (1958, 1970) was influential in promoting the idea that a strong welfare system strengthened social cohesion and harmony, 'civilising' the forces of capitalism.

In this paradigm, welfare is not intended only for those in crisis but is a dimension of citizenship in a just and benevolent society. It is the responsibility of governments to provide fair and equitable access to a range of social benefits in order to promote equal opportunity for all. 'Universal' benefits (i.e. benefits available to all irrespective of immediate need) and significant levels of income support are typical of this approach, which also incorporates a very broad conception of the scope of welfare policy. National universal-membership health schemes, widely accessible public housing schemes, publicly provided aged care and education are policies that are characteristic of the development of welfare states in this broad sense.

Trends in welfare policy

While these ideological differences between Right and Left are widely recognised, in practice a considerable degree of consensus emerged in the postwar period from governments on both sides of the political spectrum, that government should play a role in social protection. The postwar period of relative economic prosperity, which lasted until the late 1960s, was an era of unprecedented expansion of welfare systems around the world. This said, there were important differences in scale and style that distinguished the welfare strategies implemented within different countries. The distinctive characteristics of Australia's welfare system are considered below.

In recent years, many countries have reassessed their approach to welfare policy in the face of growing claims that the welfare state is in crisis. From the Left, feminists, Greens and others concerned with minority rights have criticised welfare systems for their failure to tackle social exclusion and cultural difference and for perpetuating patriarchal social relations and unsustainable growth (Pierson 1998; Williams 1989). For many of these critics, social welfare would be better managed on a participative, locally based community development model (Ife 1995). For critics on the Right, escalating rates of expenditure on welfare programs, ageing populations and the development of long-term social dependency in a significant proportion of the population are confirmation that social expenditure at this level is unsustainable and damaging to economic growth (Saunders 2004).

Such concerns stimulated an interest in welfare reform, although there is ongoing debate about the direction this should appropriately take. In many countries, including Australia, there has been a trend of 'rolling back the state'— reducing the size of government by privatising, outsourcing or contracting out public sector activities. This has included changes to many traditional practices of 'public administration', which have been reformed to mirror the management ethos of the private sector (as elaborated by Stewart in Chapter 6 of this book). Government agencies, including human service providers, are now typically required to have mission statements, to define their activities on a program basis and measure achievements against performance indicators. Government departments have become 'purchasers' of services while private and community-based 'providers' compete for publicly funded contracts through tendering processes. Some would say this has led to an improved focus on effectiveness and efficiency in service delivery, but not all agree. In Australia such changes have been slightingly termed 'economic rationalism' by scholars who interpret these trends as an attack on citizenship and social justice. Dalton and colleagues (1996: 17) comment that these practices 'have been legitimated by rational and techno-cratic values and a focus on technique, with less emphasis on social values, priorities, philosophical questions and principles as a starting point for policy development'.

An interesting recent ideological development is the concept of a 'Third Way', a departure from the traditional position of the Left that has adopted some of the language and methods associated with the Right. In his books *Beyond Left and Right* and *The Third Way*, Giddens (1994, 1998) argues that the challenges now facing social-democratic nations cannot be met by the outdated and simplistic ideas of the past. In the face of the complex dynamics of globalisation, ecological stresses, changing social order and identities, a new politics is required. He argues that the welfare policies of the past have been passive, producing high levels of social dependency and exclusion that have demoralised and disadvantaged many recipients. The 'Third Way' replaces old forms of government paternalism while eschewing the more radically parsimo-nious or market solutions advocated by the Right. It emphasises individual empowerment, choice and responsibility, but endorses a supportive role for government in facilitating and resourcing this objective. Orchard (1999: 21) summarises the Giddens vision as 'a *positive welfare* agenda' that emphasises the development of human capital rather than income support.

The role for government under this 'Third Way' vision is to make it possible for individuals to address their own social problems and become self-reliant— that is, to develop social capacity.[1]

The idea of *mutual obligation*, which echoes some of the 'Third Way' rheto-ric, has attracted support in countries like Australia, Britain, New Zealand and the United States. A key aspect of mutual obligation is the expectation that welfare recipients must undertake approved activities, such as looking for work, volunteer work, education or training in return for benefits. In this respect, mutual obligation emphasises the reciprocal rights and responsibilities theme of the 'Third Way' theorists. In practice, its ideological underpinnings are less clear and there is ongoing debate about whether it serves a right-wing agenda to limit access to welfare or an innovative left-wing agenda to promote social inclusion.

In Australia, one of the most important concerns about the introduction into government policy of mutual obligation as an approach to welfare is the rate of 'breaching', that is, the penalties applied for failure to meet requirements. Bene-fits can be reduced or discontinued for significant periods, leaving individuals without any income support. For this reason some have argued that mutual obligation introduces a stigmatised and punitive form of welfare and amounts to a reduction of citizenship. In Australia, Michael Raper (2000: 265), past President of the Australian Council of Social Service (ACOSS), commented: 'Under this approach, a government takes a very direct role in the lives of poor people who depend on public support and actively seeks to change their behaviour by using sticks rather than carrots'.

The development of Australia's welfare system

Australia differs from many other Western countries, particularly those in Northern Europe, in the degree of centralisation of its social security (income support) system and in the design of welfare benefits (OECD 1998: 19). Income support in Australia is a responsibility of the national government, rather than State or local governments. This was formalised by a Constitutional referendum in 1946, which gave the Commonwealth Parliament responsibility for a range of welfare entitlements (s. 51 xxiiiA).

Australian welfare benefits are funded out of general government revenue. There is no dedicated 'social insurance' scheme into which individuals or employers pay contributions, unlike the British and Northern European systems. The significant exceptions to this pattern are the Medicare levy, which partially funds the public health system,[2] and the compulsory employer superannuation contribution scheme.[3]

Most Australian social security benefits are means tested and narrowly targeted to ensure restricted eligibility. The level of benefit paid is not linked to prior contributions made by the individual, but is paid at a flat rate to all eligible recipients.[4] Monetary benefits tend to be set at low levels by Western international standards, and since the mid-1960s have been linked to the concept of a 'poverty line' (Jones 1996: 2).

While spending on welfare payments has risen in Australia over the past 30 years, it is low by international standards. As Figure 24.1 reports, on the basis of 1998 data, the OECD lists rank Australia (which spent 10 per cent of GDP on social security) above only the US, Ireland and Japan for social security spending (ACOSS 2004: 1). On the other hand, the number of working-age Australians receiving income support has increased dramatically from 5% in 1974 to 20%, that is, approximately 2.6 million people of working age (ATO 2005: 2).

Figure 24.2 shows the relative cost of types of welfare payments in 2003–04.

Table 24.1 summarises the significant social benefit initiatives introduced by the Commonwealth government. The earliest national benefits were introduced shortly after federation: the age pension in 1909 and the invalid pension in 1910. Jones (1996: 20) suggests that benefits were limited to the 'deserving' and excluded 'Aborigines, ex-prisoners, Asiatics, and others declared undesirable'. A male applicant for the age pension was required "to be 'of good character', having not deserted his wife without just cause, or neglecting to maintain his children" (Jones 1996: 20).

Jones' detailed analysis of Australian welfare is critical of the 'reactive ad hoc' approach adopted by governments, which he believes has resulted in a

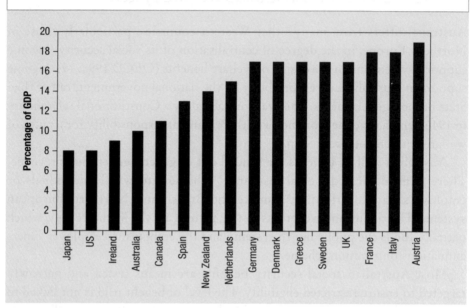

FIGURE 24.1 | OECD countries' social security expenditure as a proportion of GDP (1998)

Source: OECD 2002 Social Expenditure data base as reported in ACOSS (2004).

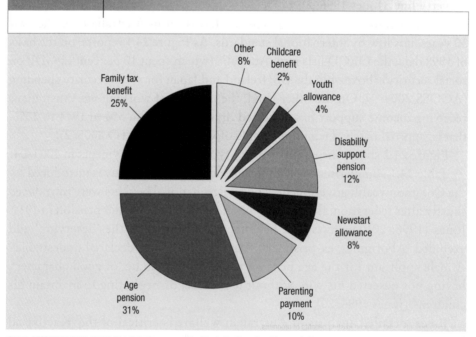

FIGURE 24.2 | Major income support and family assistance payments, 2003–4

Source: DFCS (2004: Vol 1, Part 1). Copyright Commonwealth of Australia. Reproduced by permission.

TABLE 24.1	Commonwealth social benefits, 1901–2005

Year	Benefit introduced
1909	Age pension
1910	Invalid pension
1912	Maternity allowance (abolished 1978)
1914	War pensions
1935	Service pensions for ex-servicemen
1941	Child endowment (later Family Allowance Supplement)
1942	Widow's pension (later widowed person's allowance/bereavement allowance)
1943	**Dependent spouse/child pension (later wife pension/carer payment/family allowance)**
1945	Funeral benefit
1945	Unemployment & sickness benefit
1951	**Commonwealth scholarships for tertiary education (later TEAS 1973 & Austudy 1986)**
1967	Sheltered Employment Allowance
1973	Supporting mother's benefit (later sole parent/parenting payment)
1973	Double orphan's pension
1974	Handicapped child's allowance
1976	Community Development Employment Projects (for Indigenous unemployed)
1983	Family income supplement
1985	Carer's pension (later carer's payment)
1985	Home & Community Care Program
1987	Family Allowance Supplement
1988	Child support scheme
1988	Job Search Allowance (replaced unemployment benefits for recipients under 21)
1991	**Newstart Allowance (replaced unemployment benefit, & Job Search Allowance from 1996)**
1991	**Disability support (formerly Invalid pension & Sheltered Employment Allowance)**
1992	Compulsory superannuation payments
1995	Youth Training Allowance
1996	Maternity allowance (new basis)
1998	**Youth Allowance (replaced Youth Training Allowance, Newstart & sickness allowance recipients under 21 & Austudy recipients under 25)**
2000	**Family tax benefit A & B (replaced family allowance plus a number of tax rebates)**
2005	**Maternity payment**

Note: some benefits listed replaced existing benefits or programs.

Source: Compiled from Jones (1996: 8–29); Parliamentary Library (2000a); DFCS (2001); DFCS (2003).

piecemeal, poorly rationalised welfare system (Jones 1996: 1). He argues that the selective, means-tested approach is a historical anachronism that may have been suitable for a protected economy with the high levels of employment enjoyed by Australia in the first half of the 20th century. Now circumstances have changed considerably, especially in the number of people reliant on welfare, creating problems for the system as a whole. This 'patchwork system', he argues, 'contains internal contradictions and system flaws that make it far from satisfactory as a long-term strategy for dealing with poverty, inequality, or achieving "social justice" ' (Jones 1996: 1).

Looking beyond income support, the most important welfare initiative of the postwar period was the introduction of Medibank—a public health service available to all—by the Whitlam Labor government in the 1970s. Despite some cutbacks by the Fraser Coalition government which followed, the concept survived and was reinstated as Medicare by the Hawke Labor government in the 1980s. While Medicare has never been as extensive as some of the European national health schemes and coexists with a significant private health system, it represents a substantial expansion of the Australian welfare state. It is one of the few measures funded (partially) by a specified levy, rather than through the general tax revenue system. These health policy matters are fully discussed by Gray in Chapter 25 of this book.

The historic compromise

Esping-Andersen (1990: 26–30) identifies three sorts of 'welfare capitalist' systems among Western countries. He describes Australia (along with Britain, the United States, Canada and New Zealand) as one of the *liberal* welfare states because its benefit structure is residual and modest, expenditure on income support is relatively low as a proportion of GDP, and there is strong emphasis on private insurance and self-help. This contrasts it with the *corporatist* and *social-democratic* welfare states more common in Western Europe.

Castles and Mitchell (1992) dispute Esping-Andersen's classification of Australia, arguing that his analysis is too narrowly focused and has missed some important features of the welfare system. Castles (1985, 1994) has written extensively on what he argues to be the unique qualities in the development of social protection in Australia. He places significance on what he calls the 'historic compromise' put in place by government to balance the interests of industrialists and workers after federation in 1901. The key features of this arrangement, according to Castles, were:

- strict controls over immigration to protect wages (the White Australia Policy)
- tariffs to protect developing industries from international competition
- a system of arbitration and conciliation of wages and industrial conditions enshrined in legislation and determined by a court.

Policies such as these are not conventionally considered to be relevant indicators of the level of social protection in place in a country, but Castles argues that, in practice, these were measures that delivered significant social benefits. It could be said that in actively averting social distress by the pursuit of full employment and good working conditions, Australia was closer to a true strategy of social *protection*—Castles (1998: 97–104) himself uses the term 'domestic defence'—than the benefit-based social *compensation* schemes that were typical elsewhere. What flowed from this strategy in Australia was a society in which 'wages policy was *the* substitute for social policy' (Pixley 1996: 43) or, as Castles puts it, 'a wage-earners' welfare state':

> Arbitration delivered welfare 'by other means' because, in principle, and later in fact, it meant that those who were waged were able to maintain a decent life for themselves and their dependants without further intervention by the state. Because of arbitration, Australia's wage dispersion was, right through until the 1980s, more equal than in most other countries. Because of arbitration, waged poverty was far rarer in Australia than in other comparable nations and, because of arbitration, Australian workers enjoyed a variety of benefits from their employers, such as sickness leave, which in other countries are counted as part of the welfare state. (Castles 2001: 30)

Other analysts have been less positive about the social impact of the 'historic compromise', stressing the significant exclusion of women, Indigenous people, ethnic and cultural minorities and others unable to access the benefits associated with the workplace (Pixley 1996; Cass 1998: 42). The racist implications of the White Australia Policy have created a social and international relations legacy that Australia has yet to resolve completely (McDougall 1998: 157–63). The Arbitration Court's so-called 'Harvester judgment' of 1907, which laid down a basis for the concept of a minimum Australian wage, has been disparaged by feminist analysts as the beginnings of structural wage inequality for women which was to last for many years (van Acker 1999: 172; Thomson 2000: 82). Pixley writes that these early employment and wages policies all arose:

> from value commitments that more or less excluded the needs and rights of women, children and non-Anglo-Irish populations in Australia and, until recently, accepted that the welfare of Aboriginal populations should be systematically destroyed. These various forms of welfare state circumscribed the nature of social and economic participation, explicitly defined who were the citizens in the process and, particularly with the arbitration system, supported a long-lasting, distinctive form of white male domination. (Pixley 1996: 39)

This disagreement about the character of Australia's early social achievements is an interesting historical debate in its own right, but it has also been projected into analyses of more recent social policies. Contemporary social commentators argue about the appropriate way to interpret the modern Australian approach to welfare. Are traditional indicators—such as the proportion of expenditure directed to social programs—the most important measures of government's commitment to welfare and social justice, or is there still a broader agenda (an 'alternative to welfare') that is uniquely Australian? Should Australia be seen as a second-class welfare state or as a radical social experiment?

Social policy after the 'historic compromise'

By the 1980s, the 'historic compromise' had been more or less dismantled. Restrictions on immigration had been progressively reduced in the face of a postwar demand for labour and the racially biased application process had been moderated. The Whitlam Labor government officially abandoned the White Australia Policy in 1972 (building on reforms to racially discriminatory immigration practices earlier initiated under the Holt Coalition government), adopting a non-discriminatory immigration policy and a domestic policy of 'multiculturalism' (McDougall 1998: 157–63). The extensive system of tariffs that had protected Australian industry and jobs was recognised as unsustainable in a changing and increasingly competitive international market (Bell 1998: 158–9). Tariff levels were reduced under the Labor government in the early 1970s and were further reduced in the 1980s (Green 1998: 181). Centralised wage fixing through the arbitration system gave way to the concept of 'enterprise bargaining'—the workplace-based negotiation of working conditions and remuneration between employers and union representatives of workers. This was an era in which Australian policy makers confronted what Kelly (1992) has called 'the end of certainty'.

With the removal of these traditional social defences, the effectiveness of the welfare system, particularly income support, became a crucial question for the Labor federal governments that held power from 1983 to 1996. While the Whitlam Labor government had implemented several new initiatives in the early 1970s, the welfare system as a whole was badly in need of review. Many of the existing schemes had been in operation for decades, virtually unchanged. In 1986 the Hawke Labor government established a major review to evaluate social security programs. The outcomes of this review were (Parliamentary Library 2000a: 8):

- an increased emphasis on linking income support to training and job placement
- the indexation of most payments to cost of living (CPI) increases
- a recognition of the need for monitoring and evaluation of programs.

While there was no systematic reworking of the benefit system, under both the Hawke and Keating Labor governments there was a shift from 'passive' to 'active' assistance. In essence, this placed greater obligation on welfare recipients to help themselves, tightened the targeting of benefits and more frequently withdrew benefits when clients 'breached' strict eligibility requirements. For example, unemployment benefit recipients were required to register with an employment service and to record their attempts to find work—the 'activity test' (Parliamentary Library 2000a: 9–10). This approach was later reaffirmed in the Keating government's *Working Nation* 'White Paper' (Keating 1994). Assistance for the unemployed was integrated with a rigorous program of training, reskilling and job placements.

In 1991 the unemployment benefit was replaced by two schemes. The JobSearch allowance, incorporating an activity test, was created for those unemployed for up to 12 months (Parliamentary Library 2000a: 9). The Newstart allowance was paid to people unemployed for over 12 months; recipients were 'required to enter into an individual Newstart Activity Agreement, outlining an agreed course of action aimed at maintaining their job search efforts and/or improving labour market competitiveness' (Raper 2000: 262).

A Jobs, Education and Training (JET) program was introduced in 1989 to improve the opportunities for sole parents to enter the workforce. It was later extended to widows and carers. Likewise, a Disability Reform package was established in 1991, which replaced the invalid pension with a number of measures that placed 'more emphasis on work capacity rather than impairment or disability' (Parliamentary Library 2000a: 10).

Each of these changes conformed to a pattern: an emphasis on directed self-help, and an assumption that employment was the solution to social disadvantage.

While some critics have argued that the emphasis in this era on improving the skills of the individual obscures the underlying problem of long-term structural levels of unemployment, which is beyond the control of any individual (Stilwell 1996: 17), others are more positive. Michael Raper (2000: 263) argues that—compared to programs introduced by later governments—these changes expanded choice and opportunity, although, especially in the case of the unemployed, they were combined with tighter, more punitive and, in Raper's view, less desirable penalties for non-compliance.

In a different vein, Prime Minister Hawke's well-publicised commitment in the 1987 federal election campaign to eradicate child poverty by 1990 led to the introduction of a means test on one of the few universal benefits in Australia—payments to families for children. The new Family Allowance Supplement was targeted specifically at low-income families and was financed by imposing a means test on child endowments and child rebates in the tax system (Manning 1998: 24; Sullivan 2000). A more radical initiative—the Child Support Agency—was established to enforce financial contributions towards child-rearing by non-custodial parents (Jones 1996: 28). This was achieved by using the tax office to enforce compliance—a controversial use of government powers.

Other aspects of Labor's policy agenda provoked debate among social commentators and revived speculation about Australia's record as a social laboratory. The 1983 'Accord' (and its successors) was an agreement between the Labor government and trade unions (through the peak Australian Council of Trade Unions) to moderate wage demands in return for improvements in the government-provided 'social wage'—that is, public spending on health, social security, housing, education and so on. This was linked to a broader agenda of economic reforms intended to reduce unemployment and restructure the economy. Judgments vary about the level of success achieved by the Accord. With the exception of the reinvigoration of the health service as 'Medicare', the social outcomes were disappointing to many Left-oriented analysts. Stilwell wrote of the Accord era:

> It is also significant to note the effects of 'economic rationalist' policies in undermining the regulatory model on which the welfare state had hitherto been based. Such policies included deregulation of financial institutions, partial privatisation of public enterprises, cuts in tariffs on imported goods, relaxation of controls on capital movements and the push for more labour market flexibility through encouraging 'enterprise bargaining'. In practice the effects of these 'economic rationalist' policies, with their reliance on the role of 'free market forces', swamped the more regulatory aspects of the Accord. The combination was particularly effective in redistributing income from labour to capital. (Stilwell 2000: 30–1. Copyright of this material remains with the editors; see also Stilwell 1986)

What is noteworthy here is that, whether or not the Accord achieved the goals to which it aspired, social objectives were once again being explicitly linked to economic strategies in a way that evoked the 'historic compromise' policies of the beginning of the century.

Contemporary social policy and 'mutual obligation'

The Howard Coalition won power in 1996 with a pledge that the social security system would remain intact (Sullivan 2000: 179). Despite this, important changes have taken place under the direction of this government.

Many of the labour market programs set up by the Labor government under its *Working Nation* policy were withdrawn by the Howard government as part of a cost-cutting exercise which saw government spending (as a proportion of national income) reduced to its second-lowest level since the 1970s (Stilwell 2000: 33). In 1998, the Youth Allowance was introduced, replacing Austudy for under 25-year-olds and replacing unemployment benefits for 18–20-year-olds. According to the then Minister for Family and Community Services, Senator Newman (1999b: 8), this was intended to end a situation where 'unemployment was a more attractive option than staying on in education'. The program was controversial for its use of a means test based on parents' income, which effectively restricted access by many individuals (Stilwell 2000: 34). It reinforced a message that families, rather than government, were expected to support their children into young adulthood.

In 1996 the Howard government announced the establishment of Centrelink as a 'one-stop shop' for most welfare benefits. Since 1998 Centrelink has been responsible for managing the payments coming from 10 different government departments, including the former Department of Social Security, which was restructured and renamed. Centrelink also performs a central role in a new approach to employment services. It is responsible for registration, assessment and referral of job seekers to a range of contracted non-government employment service agencies known as Job Network (Webster 1999; Centrelink 2005). This privatisation of the former Commonwealth Employment Service was seen by many as symbolic of the Howard government's desire to 'roll back the state', the antithesis of a 'state-centred model of regulation, redistribution and welfare provision' (Stilwell 2000: 36. Copyright of this material remains with the editors). Funding for employment services overall was reduced by 50 per cent (Webster 1999: 34).

In 1997 the 'Work for the Dole' program was set up as part of the implementation of a mutual obligation regime. The measure has been seen as a radical change in Australian welfare philosophy. Under the program young unemployed people are required to work in supervised community-based projects as a condition for receipt of benefits. The principle of mutual obligation is explicitly referred to in the *Social Security Legislation Amendment (Work for the Dole) Act 1997*:

> The object of this Act is to reinforce the principle of mutual obligations applying to payments under the Social Security Act 1991 in respect of unemployment by recognising that it is fair and reasonable that persons in receipt of such payments participate in approved programs of work in return for such payments and to set out the means by which they may be enabled, or required, to undertake such work. (Cited in McMahon 2000: 47)

While relatively few people were required to engage in the Work for the Dole scheme originally, it has since been considerably expanded. The policy is controversial because it is seen by some as an attack on the accepted ethos of the welfare state. The compulsory nature of the directed work program is disturbing to those who see such measures as authoritarian, punitive and stigmatising to the participant (Raper 2000).

Welfare reform: 'social coalition' and 'welfare to work'

The Howard government has identified welfare as one of its key areas of reform. In January 2000, Prime Minister Howard elaborated his notion of a 'social coalition' which, together with the principle of mutual obligation, has been the keystone of the government's social policy. The concept of social coalition, Mr Howard explained, describes 'a partnership of individuals, families, business, government, welfare and charitable organisations, each contributing their unique resources and expertise to tackle disadvantage at its source'. Mr Howard went on to explain his ideas:

> I have remained true to a modern conservative approach to social policy that supports the bedrock social institutions such as the family and promotes enduring values such as personal responsibility, a fair go and the promotion of individual potential.
>
> Australians are decent and fair-minded. Decent communities find within them-selves ways to mutually support each element of their societies.
>
> Working in partnership this way has the potential to enrich people's lives and deliver tangible benefits to all Australians. It can do so by harnessing the energy and sensitivity of community organisations, the drive and innovation of local businesses and the ambitions of parents to make a better life for themselves and their families. (Howard 2000a)

This announcement was assessed with some cynicism by Left social commentators wary of attacks on the traditional welfare responsibilities of government. Eva Cox, for example, argued that the so-called social coalition 'is not the basis on which to develop a new social compact or contract, because its central message is that the faults are not social but individual and we therefore can solve them with goodwill and charity'. In her view, the real problems that policy should address are structural economic and demographic changes that require public services (*Australian* 19 January 2000).

In September 1999, the Minister for Family and Community Services, Senator Newman, announced a major review of welfare, which she described as part of a reform agenda intended to address the challenges facing Australia in a globalised world economy:

> Modernising the welfare system is an important part of our wider reform process. It is a first order issue. A strong, modern welfare system is integral to both a globalised economy and a cohesive society. It should complement other policies that promote a skilled, adaptable and productive workforce. Appropriately designed, the welfare system is part of the solution, not just residual support for those out of work or in need. (Newman 1999a)

Patrick McClure (CEO of the non-government charity Mission Australia) was appointed by the Minister to chair a Reference Group. Its primary objective was to address the problem of welfare dependency among people of working age (Newman 1999b: 3). The Reference Group's report, *Participation Support for a More Equitable Society* (known informally as the McClure Report), was released in August 2000 (McClure 2000). It emphasised the need for measures that 'optimise [individuals'] capacity for participation' (McClure 2000: 4).

The McClure Report put forward five principles to improve participation:

- individualised service delivery
- a simpler income support structure
- incentives and financial assistance to encourage and enable participation
- mutual obligations underpinned by the concept of social obligations
- social partnerships to build community capacity and increase opportunities for social and economic participation.

The issue of most concern to the defenders of the traditional welfare state was whether the McClure Report would recommend a withdrawal of entitlements in favour of the 'reward for participation' model. The Report gave mixed messages. While it acknowledged the necessity of poverty alleviation through adequate income support, it also recommended the expansion of the mutual obligation regime to other categories of welfare recipients, including those on Disability Allowance and Sole Parent Benefits. It argued that voluntary compliance should be encouraged and that financial penalties should be a last resort. The government formally adopted the recommendations of the McClure Report in December 2000, taking its five principles as the blueprint for future strategy (Howard & Newman 2000).

A further driver of the Howard government's commitment to reform in welfare has been a concern about the predicted 'ageing' of the Australian population and the impact it could have on social expenditure. The Treasurer, Peter Costello, released the *Intergeneration Report* (Commonwealth of Australia 2002) alongside the 2002 Budget. A key point (illustrated by Figure 24.3) is the claim that, if current policy commitments remained stable, by 2041 the Commonwealth government will face an overall shortfall of revenue compared with its expenditure of 5% of GDP due to falling fertility rates and more people in older age cohorts (Commonwealth of Australia 2002). This assumes that there will be fewer taxpayers and more people requiring high cost age and health care services. While some experts disagree with the government's analysis of the impact of population ageing (see Healy 2004), the *Intergenerational Report* continues to shape the government's social policy perspective, especially its prioritisation of workforce participation as an over-riding policy objective.

The government's attempts to implement its welfare reform agenda have not gone unopposed. The 2001 *Australians Working Together* reform package was held up for some time in the Senate, where the concerns of the Labor Party and the Australian Democrats centred on the extension of mutual obligation to additional categories of welfare beneficiaries. This proposal imposed participation requirements on older unemployed and sole parents whose youngest child was in high school. A Senate inquiry raised questions about the impact of such measures on the most vulnerable members of these groups and also discussed the application of penalties for failure to meet mutual obligation requirements (SCARC 2002). This echoed the concerns of an independent review set up by

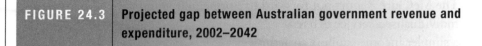

FIGURE 24.3 | Projected gap between Australian government revenue and expenditure, 2002–2042

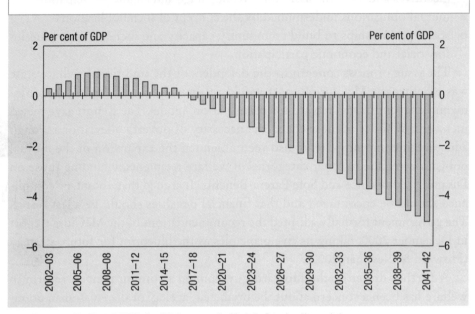

Source: Commonwealth of Australia (2002). Copyright Commonwealth of Australia. Reproduced by permission.

nine charities in 2001 (the Pearce Review) which found that 'the income support system has concentrated excessively on achieving high breach rates and penalties rather than on encouraging active efforts to find work' (SCARC 2002: 5).

After considerable negotiation in the Senate the measures were introduced in 2003, together with a *Working Credit* scheme designed to ease the transition from welfare to work by allowing people to build up credits and keep some of their benefits as they start to earn. This addresses the problem of poverty traps — the phenomenon where earning more income disadvantages welfare recipients as they lose entitlements as well as paying additional income tax which together can be worth more than their increased wages.

In the 2002 Budget, the Treasurer announced that the Disability Support Pension would be restricted to those capable of working less than 15 hours a week, a reduction from the existing 30-hour test. In the Senate, Labor and the Democrats opposed the measure because of the difficulty people with disability would experience in finding work and the lower benefits they would receive on the unemployment scheme.

With its re-election in October 2004, the Howard government claimed a mandate had been won for its welfare agenda. From July 2005 its majority in the Senate removes the capacity of the Opposition and minor parties to block reform. The government has introduced a new welfare policy package *Welfare to Work*. From July 2006 a sole parent whose youngest child is over six years of age will be included in the mutual obligation expectations of the Newstart unemployment benefit, rather than the more generous parenting benefit. The proposed changes to the Disability Support Pension will also be implemented, although in both cases existing beneficiaries' entitlements will be preserved. At the same time, many of the specialist services that help the disabled to find work will be withdrawn. With its political control of the Parliament assured, it is certain that further reforms will be proposed by the Howard government.

Which way forward?

The direction of future reform is likely to see mutual obligation extended to new categories of welfare. An objective that has been flagged by government is the creation of a simpler benefit system that removes the current distinctions between 'pensioners' and the unemployed. As one journalist put it: 'The system treats unemployed people as the undeserving poor, and pensioners as the deserving poor, and pays them accordingly' (Horin 2005). The dilemma here is whether uniformity should be achieved by pushing more people into the lower paid categories, or by raising unemployment benefits to the same levels as pensions. The Labour government in New Zealand recently adopted the latter strategy (*The Age* 24 May 2005).

In general, the key principles of the Howard government's welfare agenda appear to have been accepted. Both Labor and the Australian Democrats endorsed the general concept of mutual obligation, and gave cautious approval to the McClure Report's recommendations (*Australian* 17 August 2000). However, there continues to be disagreement about the interpretation of these principles in practical application.

Amongst social policy analysts, there is less consensus about the desirable way forward. Frank Castles, whose interpretation of Australia's distinctive welfare history was outlined earlier in this chapter, argues that a change in fundamental values has taken place. He thinks it is for the worse:

> It seems to me that, together with the industrial reforms of the 1990s, the adoption of the kind of welfare reforms visualised in the McClure report will complete the process of tearing down the edifice of Australia's distinctive welfare state. What will remain will be a system of mean, discretionary and moralistically charged benefits, wholly inappropriate to an advanced, democratic, nation. (Castles 2001: 29)

Arguing from the Right, there are also commentators who believe that the reform agenda has not yet gone far enough. For example, Peter Saunders from the Centre for Independent Studies refers to welfare as 'an addiction' which is not only bad for the self-esteem of recipients and damaging to their dependents, it also imposes a heavy tax burden on others. He comments:

This trend is clearly unsustainable . . . We have locked ourselves into a vicious spiral. This cannot go on indefinitely; we are chasing our tails . . . All that is needed is a government prepared to get on with the task. (Saunders 2004: 5)

A gendered welfare state?

Feminist analyses of welfare systems have challenged the very conception of citizenship: has it been constructed around the male experience and an assumption of women as wives and mothers (Weeks 2000: 57)? Many aspects of the Australian 'historic compromise' discussed above are now argued to have severely disadvantaged women, especially in respect of wages and participation in the workforce. With most of the formal barriers to gender equality now removed, how well has recent Australian welfare policy addressed the needs of women?

In some ways, the traditional Australian approach to social security promotes gender equality, once men and women have the same entitlements to benefits. As income support benefits are paid at a flat rate rather than being linked to income-based contributions, it prevents the lower average wages of women being translated into lower average welfare entitlements. On the other hand, because women have been the main recipients of welfare services,[6] the Australian practice of tying benefits to the poverty line at a low rate has meant that many women live in poverty. Van Acker (1999: 134) comments:

> The shift to gender equality in social security puts a greater emphasis on changing gender relations in domestic life and paid employment. For many women the private sphere and the workplace remain the source of unequal opportunity, but this has not been a priority for federal governments.

The Howard government has attracted criticism for some of its policies affecting women. It has adopted a general approach of 'mainstreaming' women's issues—that is, devolving responsibility for monitoring and promoting equal opportunity measures back into ordinary government departments, rather than having separate agencies specifically responsible for such issues. The Office of the Status of Women has had its budget cut, as have both the Human Rights and Equal Opportunity Commission (HREOC) (responsible for administering the *Sex Discrimination Act*) and the Affirmative Action Agency. Similarly, the national women's health program is no longer funded separately for services such as women's refuges. The government claimed this was 'a message of self-reliance to women' (van Acker 1999: 134–6). In 2004 the Office of the Status of Women was relocated from the Department of the Prime Minister and Cabinet to the Department of Family and Community Services, indicating a 'down-grade' of its importance, according to some feminists (Cox 2004).

Childcare policies have been particularly controversial, as these are programs with obvious implications for women's capacity to participate in the workforce. While the government has claimed that accessible, affordable child care is an 'essential element' of its assistance to families, critics have pointed out that 'an increased demand that the user should pay means that, in effect, access to child care has become more difficult' (Thomson 2000: 87. Copyright of this material remains with the editors.).

As part of its *Stronger Families and Communities* policy, the Howard government committed an additional $240 million over four years (Parliamentary Library 2000b). Some of this money ($65 million over four years) was directed to improving 'families' ability to access and choose child care that meets their needs' (Newman 2000: 4). In announcing this measure, the Prime Minister described its purpose as improving parental choice in that the new arrangements would 'allow the child carers to go to the home rather than insisting on every occasion that the children should be taken to an institution' (Howard 2000b: 3). The changes were intended particularly to help those in rural areas and shift-workers. The plausibility of this objective has been challenged on the grounds that private provision of child care may not be viable in many circumstances. There has also been concern that the government has ceased to provide capital funding for child care (Parliamentary Library 2000b: 4). In the 2004 election campaign a notable difference between the major parties was that the Coalition promised a 30% rebate on child care, while Labor promised an extra 14 500 childcare places (*West Australian* 29 September 2004).

In a related policy area, a discussion paper released by Pru Goward, the HREOC Sex Discrimination Commissioner, provoked much debate about the issue of paid maternity leave (HREOC 2002). The government, however, has not been prepared to commit funds for a government-funded scheme, despite its concerns about falling fertility rates and the predicted long-term impact of population ageing. It is of some concern to many women that the government insists on a 'family policy' perspective at the expense of a policy focus on women as individuals:

> In spite of women's efforts to assert themselves as citizens, the Howard government has firmly kept a focus on families, rather than citizenship. It is an odd contradiction in many ways as the government strongly supports individualism—yet what is presented is possessive individualism and the related classic image of the male citizen and his family. Single women, never married women, lesbian women, poor older women, the over-representation of women with disabilities living alone and outside the paid labour force are all invisible within the nostalgic image of 'family'. (Weeks 2000: 68. Copyright of this material remains with the editors.)

In general, the Howard Coalition government has not been seen as sympathetic to women's issues in its policy formulation both at home and abroad. Its refusal to ratify the Optional Protocol of the Convention on the Elimination of

All Forms of Discrimination Against Women (CEDAW) is regarded by many feminists as symbolic of a strong conservatism in its attitude to gender equality.

Indigenous welfare: a racist welfare state?

It is widely acknowledged that, as a group, Indigenous people are the most disadvantaged and marginalised in Australian society (see Chapter 26 of this book). For much of Australia's history, Indigenous people were excluded from the ordinary legal, political and civil rights extended to other citizens (Chesterman & Galligan 1997). This included the right to vote, freedom of association and equal pay, as well as everyday freedoms such as the right to buy alcohol. Their life choices were restricted and controlled by authoritarian legislation, which, in many States, made welfare authorities the key agents of state intervention in Indigenous families.

In recent years the legacy of these policies is starting to be recognised. Indigenous Australians rate poorly on almost every relevant health and socio-economic indicator. They are significantly over-represented in prisons and in the criminal justice system (HREOC 2000). The *National Inquiry into the Separation of Aboriginal and Torres Strait Islander Children from their Families*, while causing some controversy in relation to its methodology, has raised public awareness of the devastating impact of past policies of separating children from their families and institutionalising them (HREOC 1997; Haebich 2000).

Historically, Indigenous people were not automatically eligible for welfare payments such as unemployment benefits or maternity allowances. Access to welfare on an equal legislative basis was confirmed only in 1966 (Sanders 1994; Shaw 1999: 20). More recently, there has been a simmering controversy, fuelled partly by the One Nation party's platform in the late 1990s, over claims that Indigenous people are entitled to 'special benefits' that are unavailable to other people. While it is true that there are some special Indigenous programs for health, housing, education and employment, these are probably far less extensive than the public imagination would have it, and few of them are 'cash-in-hand' benefits. What is more important is that studies have consistently shown that Indigenous people benefit substantially less than other Australians from other major general programs (Neutze, Sanders & Jones 1999).

Noel Pearson, a high-profile Aboriginal leader from Queensland's Cape York Peninsula, has recently stimulated considerable discussion by his attack on what he calls the 'passive welfare' approach of the past, which he argues is destroying the culture of Indigenous people. In language drawing much from the 'mutual obligation' and 'Third Way' rhetoric, he has argued that communities such as his own in the Cape York region need to 'get rid of the passive welfare mentality that has taken over our people'. There is, he says, a right to 'take responsibility' (Pearson 2000). This is a complex issue in the context of severe Indigenous disadvantage and economic exclusion. As the Aboriginal and Torres Strait Islander Commission (ATSIC) pointed out in its submission to the McClure review, the importance of welfare as a safety net is paramount for those with no realistic alternative (ATSIC 2000a). In a further submission, ATSIC Commissioner Brian Butler addressed the particular difficulties of 'mutual obligation' in a post-colonial relationship:

> The principle issue in any mutual obligation scheme must be the obligation on the government to act in an empowering way towards benefit recipients. Given the experience of Aboriginal people and Torres Strait Islanders, who have been disempowered historically through process of colonisation, this matter is particularly acute. The structural relationship between Aboriginal people and Torres Strait Islanders and the wider community has not been resolved by a settlement process as has occurred to varying degrees with the Indigenous people of New Zealand and Canada. Many Aboriginal people and Torres Strait Islanders assert that empowerment can only flow from the recognition and redress of past wrongs. (ATSIC 2000b: 24–5)

Despite such views the government has implemented new policies that emphasise mutual obligations for Indigenous communities. Shared Responsibility Agreements (SRAs) are negotiated agreements in which Indigenous groups or communities 'offer commitments and undertake changes that benefit the community in return for government funding' (DIMIA 2004: 18). Reported examples of SRAs included a community agreement to wash children's faces in return for a petrol pump. Concerns have been voiced that this does not make a sensible link between the desired outcome and the reward and also that those people who live in less enterprising communities will miss out on essential services and funding.

The government has, in addition, made a dramatic change to the administration of Indigenous programs by abolishing the elected body ATSIC and transferring service delivery and funding to mainstream government agencies. This raises many questions about the right of Indigenous people to participate in the decisions that shape their future development.

The stark disadvantage of Indigenous people presents a challenge for policy makers, especially in the welfare area. The issues are complicated, but need to be addressed as a national social justice priority.

Conclusions

Australia's welfare system has evolved with many unique features, but the system is now being challenged. The historical reliance on 'wage earners' welfare' through the workplace is inappropriate for a society in which unemployment has become systemic. In designing a new system for new conditions, there are many choices to be made and they are choices about the fundamental values of Australian society. The current policy debate is couched in terms of 'mutual obligation' and 'social coalition', but behind these popular slogans there are some familiar issues. The basic arguments are still about the role that government should play in achieving equal opportunity and addressing disadvantage. 'Mutual obligation' and 'Third Way' ideas have expanded the traditional debate by encouraging a rethinking of the means used to achieve social objectives, but the important issue remains the same: should governments take responsibility for the development of citizenship and social justice, or should this be left to the efforts of individuals and the community? It appears that in recent times both major Australian political parties are moving towards the latter position.

NOTES

1 In Australia, Mark Latham (1998) and Lindsay Tanner (1999) are perhaps the best-known advocates of 'Third Way' policies.

2 The Medicare levy is currently 1.5 per cent of taxable income, phased in over a minimum income threshold. There is a further surcharge paid by those on higher incomes who do not have private health insurance (ATO 2000). Despite the income-related nature of contributions, Medicare entitlements are universal and not linked to contribution levels. It should be noted, however, that this public health system exists alongside a significant private health system. The Howard Coalition government recently introduced a penalty for those above a certain income who choose not to subscribe to private health insurance and rely solely on the public health system.

3 Employer superannuation contributions were made compulsory for all employees in 1992 and were set at 7 per cent of income in 2000 financial year, increasing to 8 per cent in 2001 and 9 per cent in 2003. This initiative was designed to reduce dependency on government-provided age pensions. Although contributions are required by law, the superannuation schemes are privately operated rather than administered by government.

4 Most benefits are structured to phase out at a determined level of income, with reduced payments across bands of income levels and phasing out completely at the set eligibility point.

5 Pensioners currently include the aged, the disabled and those on parenting payments. The government has indicated it wishes to introduce a single payment for all 'working-age people', presumably excluding the aged.

6 As of the early 1990s, approximately 96 per cent of sole parents were women, and 98 per cent of family allowance payments went to women (van Acker 1999: 133).

REFERENCES

ACOSS [Australian Council of Social Service] 2004, *Australia's Social Security System: International Comparisons of Welfare Payments*, ACOSS Info 360, August, <http://www.acoss.org.au/upload/publications/papers/info%20360_social%20spending.pdf>.

ATO [Australian Taxation Office] 2000, *Tax Pack 2000*, Canberra.

ATO [Australian Taxation Office] 2005, *Welfare to Work, Budget Overview Paper 2005–6*, Canberra, <http://www.budget.gov.au/2005-6/overview2/download/overview_welfare.pdf>.

ATSIC [Aboriginal and Torres Strait Islander Commission] 2000a, *Social Welfare Reform: ATSIC Submission*, first submission, January, <http://www.atsic.gov.au/default ns.asp>.

ATSIC 2000b, *Response to Participation Support for a More Equitable Society*, second submission, May, Commissioner B. Butler, Canberra, <http://www.atsic.gov.au/default ns.asp>.

Bell, S. 1998, 'Economic Restructuring in Australia', in *Contesting the Australian Way: States, Markets and Civil Society*, eds P. Smyth & B. Cass, Cambridge University Press, Melbourne, pp. 157–68.

Cass, B. 1998, 'The Social Policy Context', in *Contesting the Australian Way: States, Markets and Civil Society*, eds P. Smyth & B. Cass, Cambridge University Press, Melbourne, pp. 38–54.

Castles, F. 1985, *The Working Class and Welfare*, Allen & Unwin, Wellington.

Castles, F. 1994, 'The Wage Earners' Welfare State Revisited', *Australian Journal of Social Issues*, vol. 29, no. 2, pp. 120–45.

Castles, F. 1998, *Australian Public Policy and Economic Vulnerability*, Allen & Unwin, Sydney.

Castles, F. 2001, 'A Farewell to the Australian Welfare State', *Eureka Street*, vol. 11, no. 1, pp. 29–31.

Castles, F. & Mitchell D. 1992, 'Identifying Welfare State Regimes: The Links between Politics, Instruments and Outcomes', *Governance*, vol. 5, no. 1, pp. 1–26.

Centrelink 2005, Website, Canberra, <http://www.workplace.gov.au/workplace/Individual/Jobseeker/JobSeeking/JobNetwork>

Chesterman, J. & Galligan, B. 1997, *Citizens Without Rights: Aborigines and Australian Citizenship*, Cambridge University Press, Melbourne.

Commonwealth of Australia 2002, *2002–3 Budget Paper No. 5: Intergenerational Report 2002-3*, Canberra, <http://www.budget.gov.au/2002-03/bp5/html/index.html>.

Cox, E. 2004, 'Reframing the Issues of Unfairness', *New Matilda*, 3 November, <http://www.newmatilda.com/policytoolkit/printpolicy.asp?PolicyToolkitID=39>.

Dalton, T., Draper, M., Weeks, W. & Wiseman, J. 1996, *Making Social Policy in Australia*, Allen & Unwin, Sydney.

DFCS [Department of Family & Community Services] 2001, *A Short Genealogy of Income Support Payments*, Research FaCS Sheet No. 11, <http://www.facs.gov.au/internet/facsinternet.nsf/research/researchfacssheets.htm>.

DFCS [Department of Family & Community Services] 2003, *Income Support Customers: A Statistical Overview 2001*, Occasional Paper Number 7, Department of Family & Community Services, Canberra.

DFCS [Department of Family & Community Services] 2004, *Annual Report 2003–4*, vol. 1, part 1, Canberra, <http://www.facs.gov.au/annualreport/2004/index.htm>.

DIMIA [Department of Immigration and Multicultural and Indigenous Affairs] 2004, *New Arrangements in Indigenous Affairs*, Office of Indigenous Policy Coordination, Canberra.

Esping-Andersen, G. 1990, *The Three Worlds of Welfare Capitalism*, Polity Press, Cambridge.

Giddens, A. 1994, *Beyond Left and Right*, Polity Press, Cambridge.

Giddens, A. 1998, *The Third Way: The Renewal of Social Democracy*, Polity Press, Cambridge.

Green, R. 1998, 'The Accord and Industrial Relations', in *Contesting the Australian Way: States, Markets and Civil Society*, eds P. Smyth & B. Cass, Cambridge University Press, Melbourne, pp. 38–54.

Haebich, A. 2000, *Broken Circles: Fragmenting Indigenous Families 1800–2000*, Fremantle Arts Centre Press, Fremantle.

Healy, J. 2004, *The Benefits of an Ageing Population*, Discussion Paper no. 63, March, The Australia Institute, Australian National University, Canberra.

Horin, A. 2005, 'Too Much Gap Between the Have-nots', *Sydney Morning Herald*, 5 March.

Howard, J. 2000a, 'Quest for a Decent Society', *The Australian*, 12 January.

Howard, J. 2000b, Address to the Liberal National Convention, 16 April, Melbourne, <http://www.pm.gov.au/news/speeches/2000/convention1504.htm>.

Howard, J. & Newman, J. 2000, *Welfare Reform: A Stronger, Fairer Australia, The Government's Statement on Welfare Reform*, 14 December, Canberra.

HREOC [Human Rights and Equal Opportunity Commission] 1997, *National Inquiry into the Separation of Aboriginal and Torres Strait Islander Children from their Families*, Commonwealth of Australia, Canberra.

HREOC [Human Rights and Equal Opportunity Commission] 2000, *Statistics: Aboriginal and Torres Strait Islander Peoples*, Aboriginal and Torres Strait Islander Social Justice, Canberra, <http://www.hreoc.gov.au/social_justice/statistics/index.htm>.

HREOC [Human Rights and Equal Opportunity Commission] 2002, *A Time to Value: Proposal for a National Paid Maternity Leave Scheme*, Sex Discrimination Unit, HREOC, Canberra.

Ife, J. 1995, *Community Development: Creating Community Alternatives—Vision, Analysis and Practice*, Addison Wesley Longman, Melbourne.

Jones, M. 1996, *The Australian Welfare State: Evaluating Social Policy*, 4th edn, Allen & Unwin, Sydney.

Keating, P. 1994, *Working Nation: The White Paper on Employment and Growth*, AGPS, Canberra.

Kelly, P. 1992, *The End of Certainty: The Story of the 1980s*, Allen & Unwin, Sydney.

Latham, M. 1998, *Civilizing Global Capital: New Thinking for Australian Labor*, Allen & Unwin, Sydney.

Manning, I. 1998, 'Policies: Past & Present', in *Australian Poverty: Then and Now*, eds R. Fincher & J. Nieuwenhuysen, Melbourne University Press, Melbourne.

Marshall, T.H. 1963, *Sociology at the Crossroads*, Heinemann, London.

McClure, P. 2000, *Participation Support for a More Equal Society. Final Report of the Reference Group on Welfare Reform*, Reference Group on Welfare Reform, Department of Family and Community Services, Canberra.

McDougall, D. 1998, *Australian Foreign Relations: Contemporary Perspectives*, Addison Wesley Longman, Melbourne.

McMahon, A. 2000, 'Understanding the Welfare State', in *Understanding the Australian Welfare State*, eds A. McMahon, J. Thomson & C. Williams, Tertiary Press, Melbourne, pp. 6–16.

Neutze, M., Sanders, W. & Jones, G. 1999, *Public Expenditure on Services for Indigenous People*, Australia Institute Discussion Paper no. 24, September, University House Australian National University, Canberra.

Newman, J. 1999a, *Discussion Paper: The Challenge of Welfare Dependency in the 21st Century*, Department of Family & Community Services, Canberra.

Newman, J. 1999b, 'The Future of Welfare in the 21st Century', Speech to National Press Club, Canberra.

Newman, J. 2000, *Strengthening Our Commitment to Women: Statement by the Minister for Family and Community Services & Minister Assisting the Prime Minister for the Status of Women*, Canberra, 9 May, <http://www.budget.gov.au/minst/women.htm>.

OECD [Organisation for Economic Cooperation & Development] 1998, *The Battle Against Exclusion: Social Assistance in Australia, Finland and the United Kingdom*, OECD, Paris.

Orchard, L. 1999, 'Which Way Third Way', *AQ*, vol. 71, no. 3, pp. 18–24.

Parliamentary Library 2000a, *Welfare Review*, Current Issues E-Brief, Parliamentary Library, Social Policy Group, Canberra, <http://www.aph.gov.au/library/intguide/SP/welfarebody.htm>.

Parliamentary Library 2000b, *Bills Digest No. 16 2000–01: Family and Community Services (2000 Budget and Related Measures) Bill 2000*, Parliamentary Library, Canberra, <http://www.aph.gov.au/library/pubs/bd/2000-0101BD016.htm>.

Pearson, N. 2000, *Our Right to Take Responsibility*, Noel Pearson & Associates, Cairns.

Pierson, C. 1998, *Beyond the Welfare State? The New Political Economy of Welfare*, 2nd edn, Polity Press, Cambridge.

Pixley, J. 1996, 'Economic Democracy: Beyond Wage Earners' Welfare?', in *The Australian Welfare State: Key Documents and Themes*, eds J. Wilson, J. Thomson & A. McMahon, Macmillan Education, Melbourne, pp. 38–62.

Raper, M. 2000, 'Examining the Assumptions behind the Welfare Review', in *Reforming the Australian Welfare State*, ed. P. Saunders, Australian Institute of Family Studies, Melbourne, pp. 250–70.

Sanders, W. 1994, 'Social Security', in *Encyclopaedia of Aboriginal Australia*, ed. D. Horton, vol. 2, Aboriginal Studies Press, Canberra, pp. 1002–3.

Saunders, P. 2004, *Australia's Welfare Habit and How to Kick It*, Duffy & Snellgrove & the Centre for Independent Studies, St. Leonards.

SCARC [Senate Community Affairs References Committee] 2002, *Report on Participation Requirements and Penalties in the Social Security System*, Australian Parliament, Canberra.

Shaw, D. 1999, 'Myths and Facts about Aborigines and Social Security', *Indigenous Law Bulletin*, vol. 4, no. 19, pp. 20–1.

Stilwell, F. 1986, *The Accord and Beyond: The Political Economy of the Hawke Labor Government*, Pluto Press, Sydney.

Stilwell, F. 1996, 'Fraught with Contradictions: Work, Wages, Welfare', in *The Australian Welfare State: Key Documents and Themes*, eds J. Wilson, J. Thomson & A. McMahon, Macmillan Education, Melbourne, pp. 9–20.

Stilwell, F. 2000, 'Work, Wages, Welfare', in *Understanding the Australian Welfare State*, eds J. Wilson, J. Thomson & A. McMahon, Tertiary Press, Melbourne, pp. 23–38.

Sullivan, L. 2000, 'A Sorry Tale: Welfare Against the Family', in *Reforming the Australian Welfare State*, ed. P. Saunders, Australian Institute of Family Studies, Melbourne, pp. 177–205.

Tanner, L. 1999, *Open Australia*, Pluto Press, Sydney.

Thomson, J. 2000 'One Size Fits All?: Gender and the Capitalist Welfare State in Australia', in *Understanding the Australian Welfare State*, eds J. Wilson, J. Thomson & A. McMahon, Tertiary Press, Melbourne, pp. 82–90.

Titmuss, R. 1958, *Essays on the Welfare State*, Allen & Unwin, London.

Titmuss, R. 1970, *The Gift Relationship*, Allen & Unwin, London.

van Acker, E. 1999, *Different Voices: Gender & Politics in Australia*, Macmillan Education, Melbourne.

Webster, E. 1999, 'Job Network: What Can it Offer?', *Just Policy*, no. 17, pp. 32–42.

Weeks, W. 2000, 'Women's Citizenship: Back into the Family?', in *Understanding the Australian Welfare State*, eds A. McMahon, J. Thomson & C. Williams, Tertiary Press, Melbourne, pp. 55–69.

Williams, F. 1989, *Social policy: A Critical Introduction*, Polity Press, Cambridge.

Health policy

Australian health policy is unique. No other country has introduced major national health programs then abolished them when the sponsoring government lost office. But this is the pattern that has persisted in Australia since the 1940s. The main reason for chopping and changing from one system to another is that, historically, the two major political parties have taken strongly opposed policy positions. The Liberal Party of Australia and its coalition partner, the National Party, favour a predominantly private health insurance scheme (publicly subsidised to expand membership, if necessary), whereas the Australian Labor Party has supported a national publicly administered system.

These party differences largely prevail to the present day. The Howard Coalition government, like the Fraser Coalition government before it, was elected on a promise to maintain Labor's national insurance scheme, Medicare, 'in its entirety' (DHA 1999a: 2). It has not kept that commitment and, instead, has steadily introduced a series of privatisation measures, diminishing Medicare's importance and coverage.

Nonetheless, the polarised party positions of previous decades appear to have been replaced recently by some measure of cross-party accommodation. Although Medicare has been downgraded, elements of the system have survived the arrival of a Coalition government, which was not the case with previous Labor schemes. At the same time, the Labor Party has come around to supporting the public subsidisation of private insurance and, with it, a two-tier (i.e. a public tier and a private tier) health system. Thus, in the last nine years, the gap between the parties appears to have narrowed and both parties support a large—but unspecified—role for a private sector, operating alongside a national health insurance system, Medicare.

The intended role of private hospitals and private insurance under Medicare has never been openly clarified by either political party. Public and private services operate side-by-side. Public hospitals have been the backbone of the Australian health system from the earliest days, even when so-called voluntary (private) health insurance operated. Conversely, a large sector of private hospital and medical services operates alongside Medicare. Therefore, precisely what retaining Medicare 'in its entirety' would mean in practice is unclear. What is clear, however, is that Medicare was originally set up as a national health insurance scheme, intended to cover everyone and to eventually replace private health insurance (PHI) for most citizens. Policies that reduce its coverage and transfer funding away from the public hospital system seriously undermine its role and function.

The layout of this chapter is as follows. First, the main structural features of the health system are outlined. Second, the chapter reviews the longstanding conflict about the best methods of paying for hospital and medical services. It then describes the various competing interests that inhabit the health policy arena. A survey of the health policy changes during the period of the Howard Coalition government is followed by an evaluation of the system as it now operates in terms of access, equity, cost control, stability and the appropriateness of services. The chapter concludes with a discussion of what we can learn about Australian politics from an understanding of the health sector.

A NOTE ON 'HEALTH'

The term *health policy* is widely used to describe arrangements that focus predominantly on hospital and medical services. However, these services are not strictly health services at all. They are *sickness* services used, almost exclusively, as curative measures *after* people become ill. While they are important and in practice are the major focus of what we must reluctantly call health policy for the purposes of this chapter, health experts—especially women's health groups—argue that they are only a small proportion of the services that a good system should provide. Very little money is spent on 'public health' programs such as preventive services and health promotion initiatives. The Australian Institute of Health and Welfare (AIHW 2002) has pointed out that public health spending is a good investment because 'there is a double pay off—people enjoy better health . . . and the spending actually leads to reduced need in the future for the more costly treatment services'. The women's health movement, along with community health and public health advocacy groups, has been highly critical of the over-emphasis on curative medicine and has argued for delivery system reorientation to provide comprehensive and diverse prevention- and wellness-focused services.

The structure of the Australian health system

Public and private providers, public and private funders and all levels of government are involved in Australia's complex system of producing and paying for hospital and medical services. Figure 25.1 charts the main elements of the complicated interrelationships within this system.

GOVERNMENT SECTOR

At federation, under the constitutional division of powers between the Commonwealth and the States, health was one of the residual powers left with the States. But constitutional responsibility for health became divided when section 51(xxiiiA), which gives the Commonwealth power to provide hospital, medical and pharmaceutical benefits, among other payments, was added to the Constitution in 1946, after one of Australia's few successful referendums. Australians may generally be reluctant to vote for increased central government power but they were evidently not about to deny the Commonwealth the capacity to pay social benefits after it had, just a few years earlier, successfully taken over the income tax system.

Under the system of divided responsibility, the Commonwealth's role is concerned primarily with funding, whereas the States and Territories are responsible for the administration, and some of the funding, of publicly provided services, including hospitals. This division of responsibility gives rise to intergovernmental conflict and to frequent attempts by each level of government to shift costs on to the other, in what may be a characteristic feature of a federal form of government. At the direction of their State masters, local governments also provide and fund a small number of services, which are financed from grants made by both the Commonwealth and the respective States.

The Commonwealth accounts for over 60 per cent of total government health expenditure (AIHW 2004a: 26). It finances services through five main channels:

- It partly funds medical services through the national health insurance scheme, Medicare. All Australians are entitled to some level of reimbursement for the cost of visiting a doctor. The size of the reimbursement depends on the price the doctor chooses to charge unless the doctor chooses to bulk-bill the Commonwealth directly. In practice, the Commonwealth meets about 80 per cent of the total cost of medical services (AIHW 2004a: 49).
- Under Medicare funding arrangements, the Commonwealth provides approximately 50 per cent of hospital funding. Australian Health Care Agreements are negotiated every five years between the Commonwealth and the States and Territories. The Commonwealth money is paid to the States on a per capita basis, adjusted for age and sex profiles to account for different

FIGURE 25.1 The financing and administration of the Australian health system

Financing ------- Administration ——

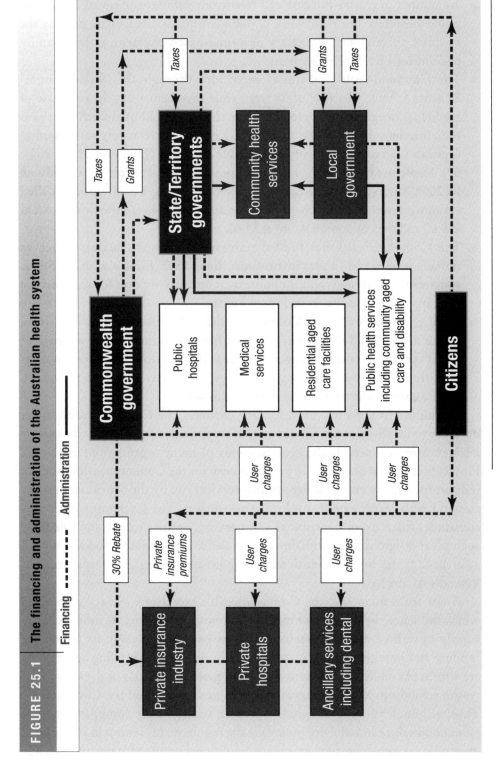

utilisation patterns between jurisdictions. Under Medicare, all Australians are insured to receive full care and treatment, without additional charges, in public hospitals. For their work in public hospitals, doctors are paid by the hospital, through either a salary or a time-based payment, rather than by patients on a fee-for-service basis.

● The Commonwealth subsidises medicines through the Pharmaceutical Benefits Scheme. Because of its large-scale involvement in the purchase of medicinal drugs, it is able to influence their cost and quality. Australians therefore have better access to relatively cheap and relatively safe pharmaceuticals than people in many comparable countries (Hilless & Healy 2001: 69). Medicines listed on the pharmaceutical benefits schedule are subsidised. In 2005, for example, the cost to citizens of filling a prescription (called variously a user charge, a co-payment or an out of pocket expense) was set at $28.60 and the concessional rate at $4.60.

● The Commonwealth has funded residential aged-care facilities, such as nursing homes and similar institutions, since 1962. Jointly with the States and Territories, it funds and administers community services for older people who are still able to live in their own homes.

● More controversially, the Commonwealth subsidises the cost of private health insurance. Since January 1999, it has undertaken to pay a rebate of 30 per cent of the cost of premiums to those able to afford to insure privately. No other country uses taxpayer's money to directly subsidise the health service costs of the relatively well off in this way.

In addition to these five main funding channels, the Commonwealth has at different times also directly funded certain service agencies, such as community health centres, women's health centres, family planning organisations and so on. However, the trend of the last 10 years has been for the Commonwealth to adopt indirect funding by contributing towards services run by the States and Territories and, to a lesser extent, by local government. The Commonwealth also sometimes finances, or contributes to financing, health promotion campaigns such as campaigns dealing with domestic violence and with AIDS education and awareness. It also finances health services indirectly through the Department of Veterans Affairs.

Apart from financing, the Commonwealth exercises a variety of powers which influence the delivery of medical and hospital services. It influences the supply of trained medical practitioners, for example, through its university funding and immigration policies. The Medicare hospital funding agreements are a form of conditional grant to the States, paid on the basis of the Commonwealth's conditional grants power specified in section 96 of the Constitution. Thus, although running hospitals is a state and territory responsibility, the Commonwealth can influence policy via the requirements set out in conditional grants. For example, hospital grants are conditional upon the States and Territories not charging individual patients for public hospital services, which is how the Medicare system ensures universal access to public hospitals.

The States and Territories are responsible for the provision and administration of direct health services, as well as being partly responsible for their funding. Hospitals are by far the biggest expenditure item, consuming approximately one-third of entire State and Territory budgets. Other services include community health and women's health centres, mental health, child, adolescent, family, rehabilitation and dental health services. Health promotion and public health regulation and inspection are also State responsibilities. Home and community care and disability services are shared Commonwealth and State responsibilities, funded jointly by both levels of government.

Local governments provide a range of health services, although their extent varies enormously from State to State. Funding is derived partly from local property taxes and partly from State and Commonwealth grants. A number of public health surveillance functions, such as monitoring food standards, have been devolved to the local level. Maternal and child health, including immunisation, has been a local responsibility for more than a century and some local areas provide a range of other services, including mental health, aged care, youth and children's programs and health promotion.

PRIVATE SECTOR

The private sector provides a range of services and a range of contributions to funding within the health system. To begin with, private citizens contribute through the tax system, through the Medicare levy (1.5 per cent of taxable income), through the 1 per cent levy surcharge paid by middle- and high-income earners without PHI, through private hospital and 'extras' insurance, and through uninsured user charges.

Most medical services are provided by doctors in private practice. These doctors have fought successfully to retain their status as independent business operators with the right to set their own fees, despite the fact that nearly 80 per cent of medical incomes are paid directly from taxation (AIHW 2004a: 49). The Commonwealth has stipulated by law that PHI cannot be offered for medical services outside hospitals, because policy makers fear that it would lead to excessive increases in medical fees: once people have high levels of insurance, the danger is that there would be little constraint on private doctors to limit either the price or the volume of services.

Sixty-six per cent of Australian hospital beds are in public hospitals but private hospitals play a significant role, providing the remaining 34 per cent of beds (AIHW 2004b: 9). Private hospitals may be either for-profit or not-for-profit, the proportion with a for-profit mission having increased in recent years. Ownership is concentrated: as of 2001, just five interests—four large for-profit chains plus the Roman Catholic Church—owned hospitals accounting for two-thirds of all private hospital beds (Hilless & Healey 2001: 25). Diagnostic services, such as pathology and radiology, are also supplied primarily by the private sector.

Clashes, campaigns, contestants

Health policy making in Australia has been described by a former senior policy maker as 'a strife of interests' (Sax 1984). Conflict between competing interests has not been directly about health or health objectives but rather has hinged almost entirely on how services should be paid for. In particular, there has been contention about whether arrangements should be left to a private market, in which people pay from their own pockets, or whether governments should institute a collective, tax-financed, publicly administered payment system such as Medicare. The rationale for government intervention is that health services are what economists describe as 'merit' goods. Access can determine life and death. Citizens should therefore not be prohibited from using services because of insufficient money. Public financing and administration means that the principle of financial contribution according to ability to pay can operate while ensuring that everybody has access to service.

PROVIDER INTERESTS

For more than a century, the Australian medical profession has vehemently resisted any policy or institution with the potential to reduce the size of the private medical market (Pensabene 1980; Gray 1991: 53–103). In a private medical market, citizens pay the doctor directly, seeking reimbursement from their insurer if they hold PHI. Doctors therefore enjoy economic autonomy as independent business operators. While Australian medical unions have always supported government subsidies for low-income earners who cannot afford to pay private fees, they otherwise regard government interference as an intrusion to be minimised.

Medical union activity began in earnest in the late 19th century in campaigns against what the profession then called 'hospital abuse': the admission to public hospitals of people who could afford to pay private fees. Doctors wanted admission to public hospitals restricted to the very poor. At that time, the well off were usually treated in their own homes. The profession also opposed any form of remuneration from government, including the capitation system (a government payment to a doctor for each person registered as that doctor's patient) introduced in Britain in 1911, and any form of publicly managed health insurance. The British Medical Association in Australia, which is what today's Australian Medical Association (AMA) was called before 1962, told the Royal

Commission on National Insurance in 1923 that 'no existing form of national health insurance would be acceptable' (Gray 1991: 84–5).

Conflict erupted every time governments (predominantly Labor governments) tried to take control of public hospitals away from voluntary boards, in order to open them to all citizens. The organised medical profession also opposed the introduction of publicly financed services, such as baby health centres, school health services, tuberculosis dispensaries, sexual health clinics and nursing services. Such programs reduced the numbers of people seeking services from private practitioners (Gray 1991: 60–2).

Conflict also erupted when non-Labor governments at the Commonwealth level proposed to introduce national insurance on a contributory basis in the 1920s and 1930s. Non-Labor governments were of the view that it had been a mistake to finance social programs, especially age pensions, from general revenue (Watts 1983: 93–120). R.G. Casey, the Treasurer in the Lyons government, told the national Parliament in 1935 that, unless people were required to contribute directly rather than indirectly through the tax system, 'the whole financial fabric of the Commonwealth' would be threatened (Kewley 1973: 159). Unfortunately for the Commonwealth government's aims in the 1930s, the expert brought from England to design a national scheme insisted that pensions and health 'be treated as one organic whole' (Gray 1991: 88). The inclusion of health in the proposed national insurance system provoked the opposition of the medical profession, which was the main reason that the legislation, which was passed in both houses of Parliament in 1938, was finally abandoned (Watts 1983: 161–219; Sax 1984: 41–2).

Originally, the most important provider interest in health was the medical profession but, as the industry expanded, other stakeholders emerged. These included insurance interests and for-profit providers of hospital services, pharmaceuticals and various advanced technologies. PHI interests have been strongly active for decades, typically supporting Coalition policies and vehemently opposing those of Labor. The Australian Health Insurance Association (AHIA) runs an ongoing campaign in support of PHI and regularly challenges the Labor Party to commit itself unambiguously to public subsidisation of private insurance (AHIA 2005). The Australian Private Hospitals Association (APHA) is also highly active and one of its main objectives is to 'champion the cause of private hospitals in delivering the very best in hospital care to patients' (APHA 2005). Both organisations react immediately and publicly to any perceived political threat. Producers of new technologies, such as manufacturers of pharmaceuticals and radiological equipment, are also important interest groups but much less is known about their activities and their interactions with governments. One of the reasons may be that their negotiations with government bodies usually take place in private.

HEALTH CONSUMER INTERESTS

Compared with provider groups, consumer groups are poorly organised, poorly resourced and, even when they have resources, they find it harder to attract media attention. They correspond to what Alford (1975) calls 'repressed' interests, whereas provider groups are what he labels 'dominant' interests. Consumer groups often have little or no money and are usually run by busy people who volunteer their labour. Australian trade unions and nursing groups, which often advocate on behalf of consumer interests, have access to a reasonable level of resources but other groups do not. Unions, public health associations, welfare and health coalitions at the national and State and Territory levels organise and campaign whenever they perceive public health and public health financing systems to be threatened but they have been unable to prevent privatisation.

POLITICAL PARTIES

Differences between the major parties were apparent from the beginning but it was in the 1940s that their policy positions polarised dramatically (Gray 1991: 50–79; 87–9). While it is common for parties to try to distinguish their policies from those of their competitors, it is not so common for mainstream parties to vehemently and enduringly disagree about fundamental principles. Yet that is exactly the Australian experience since the 1940s.

In keeping with collectivist values, Labor has sought to provide universal access to services, has been willing to arrange for government to assume primary responsibility for funding, and has sought to provide a range of services, such as community health and women's health centres, financed through the public sector. In contrast, the Coalition has tried to keep government intervention to a minimum, whether in financing or in direct service provision, a position which accords with a neoliberal point of view.

A national health service, comprising a national medical service, a pharmaceutical benefits scheme and a prepaid hospitals scheme, was proposed by a Labor government in the 1940s. The opposition of medical interests scuttled most proposals but a national, tax-financed hospital scheme was introduced successfully.

After Labor lost office in 1949, the Menzies Coalition government introduced its own 'national' health system, a publicly subsidised private health insurance scheme. This policy had been developed in the late 1940s, not by the government but by the medical profession, with the aim of retaining private medical practice and fee-for-service (Gray 1991: 89–94). Labor's national hospital system was abolished, to force people who could afford it to buy 'voluntary' health insurance or face the risk of heavy expenses. The new scheme was, despite its name, not truly national because approximately 20 per cent of people had no insurance and many more had inadequate cover. Moreover, those without insurance, generally poor people who experience more sickness, received no public subsidy, which was available only to the privately insured. By the 1960s, the scheme was highly unpopular and it became a political liability for the Coalition.

After Labor returned to national government in 1972, a universal health insurance scheme was put in place, amid a storm of protest from the Coalition and private-sector interests. Included in this scheme was a new version of the prepaid hospital scheme of the 1940s. Medibank, as this program was known, was in turn abolished (in stages) by the Fraser Coalition government after 1975, and the 'voluntary' health insurance system of the 1950s and 1960s was reinstated in 1981.

On Labor's return to power in 1983, national health insurance—this time called Medicare—was introduced again. Like previous Labor policies, it met with strong opposition from the Coalition and from private-sector interests, giving rise to an 18-month strike by specialist doctors in New South Wales. However, as Medicare became established, support for it grew. Despite this, the Coalition maintained its opposition. At the 1987 federal election, it campaigned on a policy favouring a predominantly private system. 'The Medicare system is a total disaster', John Howard, then Leader of the Opposition, declared in June 1987: 'We'll pull it right apart . . . the second thing we will do is get rid of bulk billing' (Bevis 2004). But the Howard-led Coalition failed to displace the Hawke Labor government at the 1987 election.

Detailed privatisation proposals were later outlined as an element in the Coalition's controversial *Fightback!* policy package, prepared for the 1993 election to be fought against the Keating Labor government:

> Over time the Coalition will reduce the dominance of government in the nation's health . . . the experience of recent years has shown that the dead hand of public sector management leads in the end to deterioration of service to the public and to the demoralisation of the professionals and other workers in the system. (Liberal and National Parties 1991: 9)

The *Fightback!* document set out the way that the role of the private sector would be progressively expanded to 'restore the viability of private medical practice and private health insurance' (Liberal and National Parties 1991: 1). In the event, the *Fightback!* proposals became a major election liability. The Coalition's Shadow Health Minister, Dr Bob Woods, lost his seat. Later research revealed that, had the parties attracted equal support for their health proposals, the Coalition would have won the 1993 election (Bean 1994: 154–5).

By the mid-1990s, popular support for Medicare as measured in opinion polls had reached 93 per cent (HIC 1997: 42). The former AMA President,

Dr Brendan Nelson, now a Minister in the Howard government, acknowledged in 1997 that 'market solutions' for health had been rejected by the electorate:

> Opinion polls conducted prior to the last federal election indicated overwhelming support by Australians for Medicare and the universal access to public health services that this entails. And if you want to touch a broad nerve in public opinion polling then any politician just has to suggest some sort of change to universal and/or so-called free access to health care. (Nelson 1997: 52)

And so it was that John Howard, reinstated as Leader of the Opposition, promised during the 1996 election campaign that the Coalition would maintain Medicare. The promise did not mean, however, that the Coalition now supported the public financing and administration of hospital and medical services. Once in office, Dr Nelson explained how the Howard government's approach differed from that of Labor:

> The previous government's policy position was mostly to say that private health insurance and the private health sector was supplementary to Medicare. Labor thought it had a role but in their view a relatively minor role compared with Medicare—and a role which would phase out over time. This government, however, holds a view that we need a robust and healthy private health financing sector . . . the government's message is loud and clear: that the private sector is a vital component of the long-term viability of Medicare and the public hospital system. (Nelson 1997: 54)

Privatising Medicare

In office, the Howard government has pursued a policy of steadily restoring 'the viability of private medical practice and private health insurance', just as *Fightback!* had previously promised. It has not, however, achieved 'a robust and healthy private health financing sector' because restoring viability has required a large injection of taxation-derived public money. In the course of propping up the private sector with public money, the contribution of private insurance to health financing has actually fallen since 1996.

THE FIRST HOWARD GOVERNMENT 1996–1998

The first move in the Howard government's program to reduce the size of the publicly financed health sector was the abolition of the Commonwealth Dental Program, effective from 1 January 1997. This was a scheme that had improved dental health of 500 000 low-income people per year (Gray 2004: 34). Family planning funding was cut by 10 per cent. Other 1996 budget changes were a reduction of $80 million for disability accommodation, increased user charges for hearing services and home and community care (HACC) services and a

20 per cent increase in charges for medicines. Family Allowance Supplement recipients lost entitlement to Health Care Cards, unless they received the full Supplement.

The 1997 Budget announced further changes that restricted the medications available at a concessional rate to low-income earners, increased the waiting time for a Health Care Card from four to eight weeks and closed 43 Medicare offices (HIC 1998: 19; Frank Small and Associates 1998: 53–5). All of these policy changes fell most heavily on low-income earners, a majority of whom were women. Women, for example, comprise 65 per cent of age pensioners and 93 per cent of sole parent beneficiaries. Several of the changes disproportionately affected older women, including increased user charges for hearing and HACC services, the abolition of the Commonwealth dental program and increases in charges for medicines. These changes also broke the Coalition's election promise that all Commonwealth pensioner concessions would be preserved.

At the same time that selected services were being wound back and user charges increased, new expenditures were initiated to underpin the private sector. A \$2 million publicity campaign promoting PHI was launched in 1996. This was followed by the reintroduction of public subsidisation for PHI. The Private Health Insurance Incentives Scheme, introduced in July 1997, incorporated a 'carrot and stick' approach. Under the 'carrot' part of the scheme, low- and middle-income singles and families became eligible for subsidies if they bought PHI. The 'stick' part of the scheme required uninsured middle- and high-income earners to pay a Medicare levy surcharge of 1 per cent (HIC 1998: 73). These measures were intended to stop the rate of decline in PHI and 'hopefully achieve some increase' (Nelson 1997: 54–7).

The intended effect was not achieved. Most high-income people already had PHI and, for those on low incomes, the financial incentive to join PHI was weak. The cost of PHI premiums continued to rise and the proportion of people privately insured continued to fall. By June 1998, only 30.6 per cent of the population was privately insured (PHIAC 2005).

As it became clear that the incentives scheme was not working, the AMA called for further action. In February 1998, the AMA's Federal President, Dr. Keith Woollard, said that means testing for access to public hospitals should be reintroduced (repeating the demand first made in the 1890s). The Prime Minister is reported to have agreed that further reforms were needed (*Canberra Times* 26 February 1998). In May, the AMA branded the incentives scheme a 'disaster' and said that its relations with Health Minister Michael Wooldridge were 'absolutely appalling'. With an election in the offing, the AMA announced that henceforth it would deal directly only with the Prime Minister. Needless to say, consumer groups had no comparable access (*Canberra Times* 23 May 1998).

THE SECOND HOWARD GOVERNMENT 1998–2001

The Coalition policy that emerged for the 1998 election was announced as part of its proposed Goods and Services Tax (GST) package. The proposal was for a large increase in the public subsidisation of PHI, to take the form of an across-the-board 30 per cent rebate on the cost of PHI premiums (Costello 1998). Introduced on 1 January 1999 after the Howard government had been returned to office, the cost to taxpayers was initially estimated to be $1.6 billion per annum but this sum rose quickly as further incentives were put in place to promote private coverage. Significantly, the rebate was not means tested. But this measure brought about an increase in PHI coverage of less than 1 per cent in the first nine months of operation. Almost all of the new expenditure of public funds represented a windfall gain to the mostly well-off people who already held private insurance, reducing their contribution to total health financing.

If large taxpayer subsidies would not pull people away from Medicare, then further measures were clearly needed to advance the government's goals. In the May 1999 Budget, the government announced that the principle of community rating within PHI—the principle that insurers must not refuse to insure people or vary the price of premiums on grounds such as age, sex, health status, service use, employment or occupation—would be modified. Since the first subsidisation of PHI in the early 1950s, pure community rating had been mandatory (Willcox 2001: 157). Lifetime Health Cover (LHC), as the Howard government initiative has been called, required private insurers to set different premium rates for different people, depending on age: all persons over 30 years of age pay an additional 2 per cent for each year of non-membership, up to a maximum of 70 per cent. The government described LHC as 'part of a comprehensive strategy' to arrest the decline in PHI, 'to strike a better balance between public and private sectors' and to ensure that citizens have a 'level of choice as well as universal access to excellent health care' (DHA 1999b: 1). In addition, the scheme was designed to militate against 'adverse election', the situation where young, healthy people do not buy PHI or drop their private cover when premiums rise, leaving a greater proportion of older, less healthy people (who incur more health service costs) in the insurance pool.

Arrangements for LHC were phased in over 12 months. The government launched an $8.7 million media campaign to induce people to 'Run for Cover'. In response, nearly 2.1 million new members, 11 per cent of the Australian population, bought PHI in the three-month period before the deadline. The government then extended the deadline by two weeks, during which time another 550 000 people joined up (Willcox 2001: 158). By September 2000, 45.8 per cent of the population were covered by PHI, an increase of more than 50 per cent from the previous level of coverage over 21 months. Most of the increase was due to people indeed 'running for cover', fearing that they might not be able to access public hospital services (Deeble 2003a: 6).

The final policy element intended to bolster private insurance was to allow the insurers to reintroduce an option for 'gap insurance'—covering the 'gap' between the insurance rebate and the fee charged by a doctor, an out-of-pocket expense or user charge borne by a patient—for in-hospital medical services. This was introduced in August 2000. These 'gap' charges were regarded as a serious deterrent to the take up of PHI (Gray 1999: 23).

Controversy over the 'gaps' is as old as the public subsidisation of PHI. The medical profession has always insisted that insurance and tax benefits together should not cover the full fee, realising that this would invite pressure for government-mandated fee standardisation. When Medicare was introduced in the 1980s, medical gap insurance was initially prohibited for all services, in the belief that lack of full insurance coverage would militate against steep rises in medical fees. Lifting this prohibition became one of the key demands of the AMA and of organisations representing medical specialists. As part of the settlement of the 1984–85 NSW doctors' strike, modified gap insurance was permitted: insurance was allowed to cover the gap for the difference between the Medicare benefit and the government-determined schedule fee for medical services provided in hospitals (Gray 1999: 22). Throughout the 1990s, controversy raged over the size of gaps, with private sector interests arguing for the reintroduction of full gap insurance. What the August 2000 changes permitted was full gap insurance for in-hospital medical services. While the Minister must formally approve all schemes before they begin operation, the medical profession has succeeded in preserving its financial and clinical autonomy. This change underpinned later steep rises in medical fees (Deeble 2003b).

THE THIRD HOWARD GOVERNMENT 2001–2004

Controversy over a decline in the proportion of private doctors who were choosing to bulk bill the Commonwealth, rather than individually bill their patients, engulfed the Howard government in its third term of office. The level of bulk billing had increased steadily after the introduction of Medicare in 1984, reaching a peak of 72.3 per cent of services in 1999–2000. But by December 2003, the level had fallen back to 66.5 per cent. Given that direct user charges severely inhibit low- to middle-income earners from using services, concern was expressed by unions, welfare and consumer groups that the breadth of coverage—the 'universality'—of Medicare was being eroded (Gray 2004: 42–3). Their anxiety intensified in March 2003, when the Prime Minister claimed that bulk billing had never been intended to be universal, instead being a 'safety net' for lower-income patients (*Australian* 4 March 2003).

This anxiety was exacerbated by the announcement of the government's

'A Fairer Medicare' reform package in April. The complex package was criticised by almost all affected interest groups, including the medical profession. Critics argued that it would not stem the decline of bulk billing, that it could not even guarantee prepaid services for concession cardholders and that it would institutionalise user charges as an integral part of Medicare. It contained a proposal, viewed with alarm by pro-Medicare groups, to reintroduce private insurance for out-of-hospital medical services. Private medical insurance is exactly what Medicare was introduced to replace.

In the event, the government's legislation failed to pass the Senate, which instead voted to set up a Select Committee of Inquiry (Gray 2004: 44–47). This Senate committee heard evidence in public hearings across the country and received a hundred submissions over several months. It reported in October 2003, finding that user charges for health services had risen 'quite markedly' and that the government's package would do little to relieve the situation. It recommended 'a reorientation towards the role of Medicare as a universal insurer, with equal benefits for everyone' and that grants be made available to set up community health centres in areas where bulk billing was low (SSCM 2003).

In what was interpreted by observers as an attempt for more effective political management of the health portfolio, Prime Minister Howard replaced his Health Minister, the unassuming Senator Kay Patterson, with the robust and prominent Tony Abbott in October 2003. But 'A Fairer Medicare' continued to be blocked in the Senate. Health remained highly controversial and an election was looming in 2004. A modified policy package—'Medicare Plus'—was therefore devised and announced in November 2003. The proposal to reintroduce private insurance for out-of-hospital services was abandoned and the dollar incentive to doctors for bulk billing concession cardholders and children was increased. Additional resources were earmarked to expand the numbers of trained doctors and nurses, and a new set of 'safety net' arrangements (capping the overall annual out-of-pocket cost to be borne by any individual) was proposed.

While Medicare Plus met with a more positive reception than the previous package, it was criticised because it did little to restore bulk billing. Indeed, the safety net was only necessary because user charges had increased and were expected to remain high. It was predicted, correctly, that the safety net would be very expensive and would lead to large increases in doctors' fees. After another Senate inquiry and months of negotiations with independent Senators, the necessary legislation was finally passed in March 2004 (Gray 2004: 48–51). Medicare Plus had the desired effect of partly defusing health as an issue for the 2004 election campaign, during which Minister Abbott gave 'an absolutely rock-solid, ironclad commitment' that the new safety net thresholds would be maintained (Metherell 2005: 35).

THE FOURTH HOWARD GOVERNMENT 2004–

The Howard Coalition government was returned to office for a fourth term in the election of October 2004. Six months later, in response to the predictable cost blowout, Minister Abbott's 'absolutely rock-solid, ironclad commitment' with respect to the safety net was abandoned by the Prime Minister. The thresholds at which the safety net comes into operation were raised—from $300 to $500 for low-income earners and from $700 to $1000 for everyone else.

Since 1996, the Howard government has succeeded in privatising key elements of the national health insurance system. The importance of Medicare as the national insurer has been downgraded and PHI has been acclaimed as a vital part of the system. Ironically, despite its population coverage having expanded by 50 per cent, PHI now actually contributes less than it used to towards total health financing because the 30 per cent tax rebate has largely replaced what was previously private spending. At the same time, privatisation through increased user charges and longer public hospital waiting times, partly a consequence of diverting resources to the private sector, has weakened access for Medicare-only citizens.

Evaluation

The policies pursued by the Howard government run counter to international evidence about the best ways of providing accessible services at an affordable price. They also run counter to evidence about the value of strong primary health care systems and they weaken the conditions necessary for moving to a genuine health focus.

The principal reason that Western governments intervened strongly in health financing after the Second World War was to remove financial barriers faced by lower-income citizens seeking access to health services. However, hospital and medical costs rapidly increased, primarily because (costly) technologies advanced rapidly. Cost control soon became a major objective for national health systems. Effective mechanisms were gradually developed but they met with strong opposition from health providers, who called for increased private funding to offset reluctance by cost-conscious governments to provide the 'necessary' money. As Canadian health economist R.G. Evans points out, 'all [health] expenditure is, by accounting definition, income for someone—cost control is income control' (Evans 2002a: vi). However, privatisation reintroduces the very market forces that government intervention originally aimed to supplant: it undermines the reform objectives of access, equity and cost control.

ACCESS

Public financing is critically important to facilitate access by all citizens. Financial barriers to access are broken down when services are prepaid through tax systems. Further, public financing is necessary to remove the geographical barriers between metropolitan and rural and regional Australia (Lokuge, Denniss & Faunce 2005).

In systems which are predominantly publicly funded, hospital and medical costs can be completely prepaid from taxation if that is the public policy goal, as happens in Canada. In predominantly privately financed or mixed systems, costs can also be fully prepaid but the result is a high cost system with prohibitively expensive insurance premiums. In addition, user charges are typically employed as a cost control mechanism. The problem is that, as international experience shows, user charges strongly discourage people, especially lower-income earners, from accessing services (which is primarily how user charges operate to control costs). And because low socioeconomic status is associated with poor health, the people most likely to have difficulty with user charges are also likely to be the sickest (Richardson 1991; Newhouse 1993; Evans, Stoddart, Barer & Bhatia 1994; Rice & Morrison 1994; Gray 1998, 2004). As Evans (2002a: 39) argues, user charges 'selectively deter access by those with lower incomes, thereby improving access for those with greater ability to pay'.

While all Western health systems have some level of private financing, including user charges, particularly for services other than hospital and medical care, Australian user charges are among the highest (OECD 2004). The increasing user charges of the Howard years have had a serious impact on access (Gray 2004: 65–77). For example, a 2002 study estimated that 20 per cent of survey respondents thought the overall cost of medical care, including services to cope with chronic illness, was a major burden. Sixteen per cent of respondents reported that they did not seek services when they needed them, 23 per cent that they did not fill a prescription, 16 per cent that they did not get a test, treatment or follow up, and 44 per cent that they did not get dental care because of cost. In relation to specialist care, 41 per cent of respondents were experiencing obstacles to access, and 17 per cent reported that they could not afford to pay (Blendon *et al.* 2003). Studies in New South Wales show that private patients account for the vast bulk of non-emergency surgery (Tridgell 2003). And as conditions and remuneration in the private sector become more attractive, medical professionals are drawn away from employment in the public sector.

EQUITY

There are different views on what is equitable. On the one hand, there are those who favour universal access to services funded from a progressive tax system.

This we can call the social- democratic or social-liberal perspective (Sawer 2003). It envisages the community, through its government, providing a set of services for itself which would otherwise be accessible only to the well off. On the other hand, there are those who believe that choice and economic freedom are paramount goals: those who can afford it should be able to spend their money as they please on the health services of their choice. To the extent that tax-funding of services is acceptable, according to this perspective, access to such services should be limited to the very poor. The well off in society should not be expected to contribute towards health care for the less well off; private financing rather than tax funding is preferred. Lower-income people should either save hard or go without services.

Opinion surveys indicate that most Australians agree with the social-democratic/social-liberal perspective. Medicare was supported by 93 per cent of survey respondents in 1996–97 (HIC 1997: 42). A market research report, undertaken for the Health Insurance Commission in 1998, found that the two strongest reasons for supporting Medicare were that 'everybody is covered by it' and that it 'helps low-income earners'. The report argued that:

> support for Medicare was driven by an overriding sense of the equality it delivers. It ensures that everybody gets the same minimum level of access to health care and because it invokes a sense of security of assured treatment for those who cannot afford alternative sources of health care. (Frank Small & Associates 1998: 30–1)

Further evidence of support is that, again according to opinion surveys, most Australians wanted 2004 budget tax cuts to be redirected to health and education, the two top policy areas reported to be at stake in the 2004 election (Gray 2004: 12; 73–6).

Public financing of health services is more equitable because it is funded from general taxation, which—in terms of income tax at least—is levied on a progressive scale in relation to income. Private financing, on the other hand, is not related to income: user charges and PHI premiums are levied at a flat rate. Any shift, therefore, from public to private financing involves a reduced overall contribution from the well off and a higher overall contribution from those further down the income scale. As leading Canadian health economist Robert Evans has argued, 'the more heavily a national system relies on private financing, the larger the proportion of overall health costs that will be borne by those with lower incomes' (Evans 2002a: 37). And because myriad international studies show a very strong relationship between low income and poorer health status, private financing means not only increased contribution by those on lower incomes but increased contribution by those with the worst health status because the two are correlated (Evans 2002b: 40–1). In Australia, this general situation is exacerbated by the 30 per cent rebate for PHI costs, through which public money is expressly directed towards the better-off members of society.

A related issue is queue-jumping. Those with private insurance are able to avoid the queues of people waiting for elective surgery in the public hospital system and they are subsidised by taxpayers to do so. As Roos and Frohlich have put it, 'The more private funding we have, the more those with high incomes can assure themselves of first-class care without having to pay taxes to help support a similar standard of care for everyone else' (quoted in Evans 2002a: 42).

Thus the Howard government's policies run counter to the view of equity held by a majority of Australians.

COST CONTROL

Privatisation undermines a community's capacity to manage health care costs. The United States' system is both the world's most expensive and the most reliant on private financing. In 2003, its total health spending reached 15.3 per cent of GDP, approximately 4 percentage points higher than any other nation (Smith *et al.* 2005; OECD 2004). Such high spending does not, however, necessarily result in better health: US health outcomes do not rate well when compared with similar countries. Switzerland has the world's second most expensive health system, with the second highest proportion of private financing (Gray 2004: 53). High health expenditures and health inflation are not necessarily concerns in themselves: rich countries might simply choose to spend more of their national incomes on health. However, when money is consumed unnecessarily by high administrative expenses, exceedingly large profits, high incomes for medical professionals and less than effective or even dangerous therapies, heavy opportunity costs are incurred.

Australia has a mixed financing system. Medicare is predominantly tax-funded but also includes a significant private component in the form of user charges. It operates alongside a large, multi-payer private health insurance sector, funded through tax subsidies, user charges for the uninsured gap, and PHI premiums.

If Australia featured a fully tax-based funding system, such a 'single payer' approach would provide levers with which governments could monitor and control expenditures, as demonstrated in cross-national studies of health costs (Hussey & Anderson 2003). But in privately funded or mixed financing systems like Australia's—so-called 'multi-payer systems'—an array of institutions and individuals pay for health services through multiple channels. The opportunities for coordination and oversight are weakened. No single agency has the capacity to steer the system or to control total expenditure and no-one is responsible for the direction of policy. Typically, individuals and agencies have difficulty controlling even their own costs. A recent World Health Organisation study of 12 countries found that private insurance systems cost between 5 and 27 per cent more in administrative expenses (WHO 2004). As Evans (2000: 18–19) explains:

> Private insurers, and all who make their living from the multitude of administrative functions that this requires, are the most obvious beneficiaries from increases in private financing. The high administrative overheads associated with private coverage are the sales revenue of this industry, and the sources of its wages and profits. In [tax-funded] systems, more administratively efficient, these costs and corresponding income opportunities do not exist.

A recent OECD review of PHI in Australia concluded that cost control mechanisms are weak and ineffective. Private funds, it found, were 'not effectively engaged' in controlling costs and had limited tools and few incentives to do so (OECD 2003: 39).

Together, these factors explain why, under the Howard government's policy changes, Australian health expenditures have increased faster than before, faster than those in other countries and faster than other Australian prices. Whereas Australia's health spending represented 8.2 per cent of GDP in 1992–93, it had grown to 9.5 per cent by 2002–03. The OECD average remained at 8.4 per cent of GDP (AIHW 2004a: 8, 60).

STABILITY

The Howard government's public/private split is unsustainable except at the cost of large increases in public subsidies. Australian experience shows that it is difficult, if not impossible, to maintain a stable balance between public and private sectors in a two-tier system. The reasons are straightforward. First, as long as Medicare provides reasonable access and a decent standard of services, there is a strong tendency for the extent of private insurance coverage across the community to decline. Second, as costs escalate in the private sector, large numbers of people choose to either drop private insurance, particularly during periods of economic downturn, or not to buy it in the first place. Something like this dynamic is now under way in Australia. The cost of PHI is rising steadily, and PHI coverage is slowly declining.

Moving to a real health system?

Public financing and public-sector leadership are essential to any move away from a narrow focus on hospital and medical services towards a system focusing on health. Since the 1960s, women's health movements and community health advocates have urged that delivery systems be reformed to provide a comprehensive range of preventive, educational, rehabilitative and caring services, as well as hospital and medical services. In this perspective, primary health care should be strengthened. Multidisciplinary teams of professionals should replace solo and small group medical practices, and citizens should participate in decision making so that services can be tailored to their needs and the needs of local areas. These ideas were expressed at the Fourth World Congress on Women in Beijing in 1995 and form a central part of the health *Platform for Action* (United Nations 1995).

Privatisation diminishes a nation's chances of moving to a real health system because, just as no single authority is able to oversee and manage costs, no single authority is in charge of system-wide policy making. In private systems, entrepreneurialism and profit motives are the operative dynamics and there are few institutional mechanisms through which change can be effected.

Conclusion

The politics of health offers insights into the way in which the Australian political system operates. It illuminates the role of political parties, the relative influence of various interest groups, the effect of different ideological approaches, and the kind of democracy we live in.

Health policy clearly demonstrates party competition in action. Unlike the situation in most Western countries, bipartisanship over health policy has never developed in Australia. Although the distance between the parties now appears to be narrower than in the past, a gulf still exists. The Labor Party does support the Coalition's 30 per cent PHI rebate, but its other policies aim to strengthen Medicare where those of the Coalition do not. Health policy thus clearly remains an area where significant policy convergence between the major parties, otherwise claimed by some observers to have characterised many policy areas (Davies 1964: 124–6; Aitkin 1977: 1–2), has not occurred. This helps to account for why Australia, alone amongst Western countries, has ricocheted backwards and forwards between predominantly public and predominantly private health financing systems.

International studies of interest group activity in the health sector consistently show an imbalance of power between producer and consumer groups (see e.g. Blanpain 1978; Alford 1975; Hunter 1980; Gray 1987). Producer groups wishing to influence policy generally enjoy good access to Ministers and senior public servants, and are markedly over-represented on government advisory committees and in decision-making processes (Matthews 1997: 278–86). Unlike consumer groups, health producer groups are well resourced and are able to work steadily and successfully to promote the values of private medicine. More than 20 years ago, Opit (1983) argued that the shape of the Australian health system had been determined by professional and commercial interests. Although pro-Medicare groups have mobilised in opposition to the Howard government's policies, they have had few resources and have not been able to get their views onto the political agenda or to attract significant media attention. The Howard government's capacity to proceed with privatisation and to successfully steer its policies through the 2004 election, despite evidently widespread public support for Medicare, demonstrates the weakness of the health consumer lobby.

Ideas, values and ideologies have also been important in shaping health policy. The major political parties can be seen as representing contrasting ideological perspectives which have their roots in Australian political culture. The Coalition expresses views, on health and social policy issues at least, that fit within a liberal individualist or neoliberal framework. The Labor Party, on the other hand, has generally espoused social-liberal or social-democratic views. The oscillation between systems of public and private health insurance in Australia can thus be seen as the manifestation of a perpetual struggle between liberal individualist and social-liberal perspectives about what constitutes good public policy and a good society.

As discussed, the Howard government's policies fly in the face of international and Australian evidence about health system sustainability and the achievement of goals such as access and equity. Given this evidence, the Howard government's policy choices must be motivated by ideological preference for goals other than sustainability, access and equity. Prime Minister Howard is on record as having been highly critical of Medibank and Medicare throughout his career (Schrader 2003a and 2003b) and he has taken the lead in championing his government's changes since 1996 (Gray 2004: 90). Ignoring or oblivious to serious problems with privately financed systems such as that of the United States, he told journalists prior to the 2001 election, that the introduction of Medibank had been a 'cardinal mistake'. This overlooks Australian evidence from the 1960s, when problems, well known enough to be noted by a Canadian Royal Commission (Hall 1964: 743), prompted widespread demands for change (Kewley 1973: 385). Mr Howard told the press that PHI had worked well for 90 per cent of the population and special arrangements should have been made for the other 10 per cent. Instead, 'we turned the whole thing on its head . . . In the process we dismantled a perfectly functioning health system' (*Sydney Morning Herald* 27 October 2001).

Finally, health policy decision making tells us something about the kind of democracy we live in. Australia has a long tradition of health policy making behind closed doors among medical and political elites. Between 1949 and 1972, health was managed through what the 1950s' Health Minister, Sir Earle Page, called 'a cooperative partnership'. The partnership consisted of the government, the private health insurance agencies and the medical profession (Kewley 1973: 391).

As we have seen, Australia is without robust agreement on the appropriate role of government in health care. However, the struggle between competing views does not mean that Australians as a whole are significantly divided on the health question. Citizen support for a national health system or national health insurance has been strong for decades. Opinion polls consistently show that a large majority of people support Medicare and increased public spending on health (Gray 2004: 73–6). Views do divide somewhat along party lines. A large minority of Coalition voters has always supported a predominantly private system but this is still a minority, even of Coalition voters. Among Labor voters, a large majority has supported public financing and control for decades (Gray 1991: 195–8). The Howard government's policies, like those of the Fraser government before it (Duckett 1979 and 1980), were introduced in the absence of any widespread public call for reform and, indeed, are the selfsame policies that were resoundingly rejected at the 1993 election. For all that is written about democracy and majority rule, the Coalition's health policies have arguably never enjoyed the support of more than a minority of Australians.

REFERENCES

Aitkin, D. 1977, *Stability and Change in Australian Politics*, Australian National University Press, Canberra.

Alford, R.R. 1975, *Health Care Politics*, University of Chicago Press, Chicago.

AHIA [Australian Health Insurance Association] 2005 Website, Deakin ACT, <http://www.ahia.org.au/>.

AIHW [Australian Institute of Health & Welfare], 2002, Public Health Less than 2 per cent of Health Expenditure, *Media Release*, 13 December, <http://www.aihw.gov.au/mediacentre/2002/mr20021217a.cfm>.

AIHW [Australian Institute of Health & Welfare], 2004a, *Health Expenditure Australia, 2002–03*, catalogue number HWE 27, Canberra, <http://www.aihw.gov.au/publications/index.cfm/title/10043>.

AIHW [Australian Institute of Health & Welfare], 2004b, *Australian Hospital Statistics, 2002–03*, catalogue number HSE 22, Canberra, <http://www.aihw.gov.au/publications/index.cfm/title/10015>.

APHA, [Australian Private Hospitals Association], 2005, Website, Barton ACT, <http://www.apha.org.au/index.html>.

Bean, C. 1994, 'Issues in the 1993 Election', *Australian Journal of Political Science*, vol. 29, pp. 134–57.

Bevis, A. 2004, 'Is There a Doctor in the House?', Website of Hon. Arch Bevis MHR, Brisbane, <http://www.archbevis.com/35.html#>.

Blanpain, J. 1978, *National Health Insurance and Health Resources: The European Experience*, Harvard University Press, Cambridge.

Blendon, R., Schoen, C., DesRoches, C., Osborn, R., Scoles, K., Zapert, K. 2003, 'Inequities in Health Care: A Five Country Survey', *Health Affairs*, volume 21, issue 3, pp. 182–6.

Costello, P. 1998, 'How the Government is Making Private Health Insurance More Affordable', Tax Reform Fact Sheet no. 16, Australian Government, Canberra.

Davies, A.F. 1964, *Australian Democracy*, 2nd edn, Longmans Green, London.

Deeble, J. 2003a, 'The Private Health Insurance Rebate', Report to State and Territory Health Ministers, January 2003. Typescript.

Deeble, J. 2003b, Presentation to the inaugural Whitlam Institute Forum on Health, 15 July.

Whitlam Institute, University of Western Sydney, Penrith South NSW, <http://www.whitlam.org/html/2003/deeble_0703.html>.

DHA [Department of Health and Ageing] (1999a) *Budget 1999-2000—The Government's Private Health Insurance Plan*, Canberra, <http://www.health.gov.au/internet/wcms/publishing.nsf/Content/health-pubs-budget99-fact-phi.htm>.

DHA [Department of Health and Ageing] 1999b, *Why Is Lifetime Health Cover Necessary?*, Canberra, <http://www.health.gov.au/internet/wcms/publishing.nsf/Content/health-privatehealth-lhc-consumers-whynec.htm>.

Duckett, S.J. 1979, 'Chopping and Changing Medibank, Part 1', *Australian Journal of Social Issues*, vol. 14, no. 3, pp. 230–43.

Duckett, S.J. 1980, 'Chopping and Changing Medibank, Part 2', *Australian Journal of Social Issues*, vol. 15, no. 2, pp. 79–91.

Evans, R.G. 2000, 'Financing Health Care: Taxation and the Alternatives', Health Policy Research Unit, Discussion Paper Series, Centre for Health Services Policy Research, University of British Columbia, Vancouver, October.

Evans, R.G. 2002a, *Raising the Money: Options, Consequences, and Objectives for Financing Health Care in Canada*, Discussion Paper no. 27, Commission on the Future of Health Care in Canada, Ottawa, catalogue no. CP 32-79/27-2002E-IN.

Evans, R.G. 2002b, 'Health for all or Wealth for Some? Conflicting Goals in Health Care Reform', in A. Mills, ed. *Reforming Health Sectors*, Kegan Paul International, London.

Evans, R. Stoddart, G. Barer, M. & Bhatia, V. 1994, *It's Not the Money, It's the Principle: Why User Charges for Some Services and Not Others?*, Premier's Council on Health, Well-being and Social Justice, Toronto.

Frank Small & Associates, 1998, *Exceeding the Service Expectations of the Australian Community for HIC Programs*, A Marketing Research Report prepared for the Health Insurance Commission, Canberra, August.

Gray, G. 1987, 'Privatisation: An Attempt that Failed', *Politics*, vol. 22, no. 2, pp. 15–28.

Gray, G. 1991, *Federalism and Health Policy*, University of Toronto Press, Toronto.

Gray, G. 1998, 'Access to Medical Care under Strain: New Pressures in Canada and Australia', *Journal of Health Politics, Policy and Law*, vol. 23, no. 6, pp. 905–48.

Gray, G. 1999, 'No Gaps Health Insurance: A Gain for Consumers or a Windfall for Specialists?', *Australian Health Review*, vol. 22, no. 3, pp. 18–26.

Gray, G. 2004, *The Politics of Medicare: Who Gets What, When and How*, University of New South Wales Press, Sydney.

Hall, E.M. 1964, *Royal Commission on Health Services*, Queen's Printer, Ottawa.

HIC [Health Insurance Commission], 1997, *Annual Report 1996–97*, Greenway ACT, <http://www.hic.gov.au/>.

HIC [Health Insurance Commission], 1998, *Annual Report 1997–98*, Greenway ACT, <http://www.hic.gov.au/>.

Hilless, M. & Healy, J. 2001, *Health Care Systems in Transition: Australia*, European Observatory on Health Care Systems, Copenhagen.

Hunter, T. 1980, 'Pressure Groups and the Australian Political Process: The Case of the Australian Medical Association', *Journal of Commonwealth and Comparative Politics*, vol. 18, no. 2, pp. 190–206.

Hussey, P. & Anderson, G. 2003, 'A Comparison of Single- and Multi-Payer Health Insurance Systems and Options for Reform', *Health Policy*, vol. 66, issue 3, December.

Kewley, T. 1973, *Social Security in Australia 1900–72*, 2nd edn, Sydney University Press, Sydney.

Liberal and National Parties 1991, *Fightback!* Supplementary Paper no. 3, 21 November, Panther Publishing and Printing, Fyshwick ACT.

Lokuge, B. Denniss, R. & Faunce, T. A. 2005, 'Private Health Insurance and Regional Australia', *Medical Journal of Australia*, vol. 182, no. 6, pp. 290–3.

Matthews, T. 1997, 'Interest Groups', in R. Smith, ed. *Politics in Australia*, 3rd edn, Allen & Unwin, St Leonards.

Metherell, M. 2005, 'Net Loss for the Sick', *Sydney Morning Herald*, 16–17 April.

Nelson, B. 1997, 'Private Insurance Sensible and Vital Protection Against the Unknown', *Healthcover*, October–November, pp. 52–7.

Newhouse, J.P. 1993, *Free for All? Lessons from the RAND Health Insurance Experiment*, Harvard University Press, Cambridge MA.

OECD [Organisation for Economic Cooperation and Development] 2003, *Private Health Insurance in Australia: A Case Study*, OECD Health Working Papers, no. 8, October.

OECD [Organisation for Economic Cooperation and Development] 2004 *OECD Health Data 2004*, 3rd edn, Paris <www.irdes.fr/ecosante/OCDE/510050.html>.

Opit, L. J. 1983, 'Wheeling, Healing and Dealing: The Political Economy of Health Care in Australia', *Community Health Studies*, vol. 7, no. 3, pp. 238–46.

Pensabene, T.S. 1980, *The Rise of the Medical Profession in Victoria*, Research Monograph 2, Health Research Project, Australian National University, Canberra.

PHIAC [Private Health Insurance Administration Council], 2005, Industry Statistics, Website, Deakin ACT, <http://www.phiac.gov.au/statistics/membershipcoverage/hosyear.htm>.

Rice, T. & Morrison, K. 1994, 'Patient Cost Sharing for Medical Services: A Review of the Literature and Implications for Health Care Reform', *Medical Care Review*, vol. 51, no. 3, pp. 235–87.

Richardson, J. 1991, *The Effects of Consumer Copayments in Medical Care*, National Health Strategy, Background Paper no. 5, June, AGPS, Canberra.

Sawer, M. 2003, *The Ethical State?*, Melbourne University Press, Melbourne.

Sax, S. 1984, *A Strife of Interests*, George Allen & Unwin, Sydney.

Schrader, T. 2003a, 'Down the Gurgler? Howard Dangles Medicare Overboard, Part 1', *New Doctor*, no. 78, Autumn, <http://www.drs.org.au/new_doctor/78/Schrader78.htm>.

Schrader, T. 2003b, 'Down the Gurgler? Howard Dangles Medicare Overboard, Part 2', *New Doctor*, no. 79, Winter, <http://www.drs.org.au/new_doctor/79/Gurgler.htm>.

Smith, C., Cowan, C., Sensenig, A., Catlin, A. 2005, 'Health Spending Growth Slows in 2003', *Health Affairs*, vol. 24, issue 1, pp. 185–94.

SSCM [Senate Select Committee on Medicare] (2003) *Medicare—HealthCare or Welfare?* Report, Parliament of Australia: Senate, Canberra, <http://www.aph.gov.au/Senate/committee/medicare_ctte/fairer_medicare/report/index.htm>.

Tridgell, P. 2003, 'Public/Private Separation Rates: The Evidence for Inequity and Private Health Insurance Policy Failure', Paper delivered to the Australian Health Care Summit, Canberra, 17 August, <http://www.healthsummit.org.au/program.htm>.

United Nations 1995, *Declaration and Platform for Action*, Report of the Fourth World Conference on Women, Section C, Women and Health, October, <http://www.un.org/womenwatch/daw/beijing/platform/>.

Watts, R. 1983, 'The Light on the Hill: The Origins of the Australian Welfare State, 1935–45', PhD Thesis, University of Melbourne, Melbourne.

WHO [World Health Organisation] 2004, *What are the Equity, Efficiency, Cost Containment and Choice Implications of Private Healthcare Funding in Western Europe?* Health Evidence Network, Geneva, July, <http://www.euro.who.int/eprise/main/WHO/Progs/HEN/Syntheses/hcfunding/20040629_3>.

Willcox, S. 2001, 'Promoting Private Health Insurance in Australia', *Health Affairs*, vol. 20, no. 3, pp. 152–61.

CHAPTER 26

Indigenous affairs policy

JANE ROBBINS AND JOHN SUMMERS

On the first of July 2005 the Aboriginal and Torres Strait Islander Commission (ATSIC) ceased to exist. This marked a turning point in Indigenous affairs administration. ATSIC had been established in 1989 by the Hawke Labor government as a means of implementing a policy of Indigenous self-determination. It was both an elected Indigenous body to advise the Commonwealth on Indigenous issues and, more controversially, an administrative body to manage the Commonwealth's Indigenous affairs programs. It had controlled a budget of over $1 billion and, through its Regional Councils, had developed a process of locally based regional Indigenous development. It had been in many ways a bold experiment in Indigenous self-management. This approach to Indigenous affairs had always been contentious, and ATSIC had numerous critics, but many people were still surprised when the Howard Coalition government made the watershed decision that ATSIC would be dismissed and would not to be replaced with any other elected Indigenous body.

The demise of ATSIC is symbolic of a fundamental shift in values that has taken place under the Howard government. The government has formally abandoned the concept of self-determination, which it argues was a form of separatism and a threat to national unity. Instead the government has coined the phrase 'practical reconciliation' to indicate a policy which addresses the everyday disadvantage of Indigenous people, such as health, housing, employment and so on. These policy objectives, it maintains, should be pursued through mainstream government agencies. Most emphatically, the Howard government has moved away from any agenda of Indigenous rights. The Prime Minister has made it clear that, in his view, Indigenous people are to be seen as one disadvantaged group amongst many. Campaigns for a treaty, a national apology for past injustice, or indeed any acknowledgment of special status for Indigenous people, are perceived by the Prime Minister and his government as a distraction from the priority goal of improving social and economic participation in Australian society.

These developments raise many questions about the appropriate objectives for Indigenous policy. This chapter examines the background to these questions and documents the key events that have shaped the administration of Indigenous affairs policy in recent times.

The historical assault on Aboriginal society

At the census of 2001, the number of Indigenous people in Australia was estimated at approximately 458 520, or 2.4 per cent of the total population (ABS 2003). The greatest *numbers* of Indigenous people live in New South Wales (home to 29 per cent of the Indigenous population) and Queensland (27 per cent), but the greatest *concentration* is in the Northern Territory (26.5 per cent of the Territory's population) and the northern areas of Queensland and Western Australia. Although increasingly moving to the cities, many Aborigines live outside the capital cities in rural towns and outback areas, often in extremely deprived circumstances.

Twenty-five per cent of the Indigenous population live in very remote areas. Many live in poor housing in communities without reticulated water, electricity or adequate sanitation. In these areas, there are few employment opportunities and the average income is extremely low. These factors, combined with poor nutrition, result in extremely poor standards of health.

The Aboriginal society that the European colonists first confronted in the late 18th century was based on hunting and gathering, and thus on extensive use of the land. Land was not only an economic asset but also a religious phenomenon, owned not by individuals but rather a collective possession. British law, however, did not recognise any Indigenous title to the land. Australia was said to be 'waste and unoccupied' and all land became the property of the Crown. Aborigines were declared to be British subjects, entitled to full and equal protection under British law. In each of the colonies, it was anticipated that they would be assimilated into white society.

Within a short time, however, the Indigenous population was in rapid decline, and the surviving Aborigines and part-Aborigines had become subject to protectionist and segregationist laws. The disruption to Aboriginal habit and economy, the depletion of food supplies, the introduction of new diseases and physical violence by white settlers left tens of thousands of Aborigines dead. In parts of south-eastern Australia, whole Aboriginal groups disappeared within several decades of white settlement. In the areas of white settlement, the surviving remnants of tribes and part-Aborigines became fringe dwellers, living on the edges of towns and surviving on seasonal work at low wages or minimal rations. In many areas, the remnant groups were relegated to reserves and missions, which often did little more than (in a commonly used phrase) 'smooth the dying pillow'.

The role of State governments

With the creation of the Commonwealth of Australia in 1901, it might have been expected that the new national government would be granted jurisdiction over Indigenous affairs. The Constitution, however, did not make any grant of power to the Commonwealth government in relation to Aborigines. Section 51(xxvi) stated that Commonwealth Parliament had power to make laws with respect to the 'peoples of any race, *other than the aboriginal race in any State*' (emphasis added). Aboriginal affairs thus remained within the jurisdiction of the States. The Commonwealth did become involved in Aboriginal affairs when, in 1911, it took over the administration of the Northern Territory from South Australia, but it played no direct *national* role in relation to Aborigines.

Although each State passed its own laws on Aborigines, government policy on Indigenous matters became surprisingly uniform across Australia. In all States, and in the Northern Territory, Aborigines were subject to segregationist laws that took away their legal rights. Aborigines became 'wards of the state' or 'protected persons'. Guardianship of Aboriginal children was appropriated by government and all aspects of the lives of Indigenous people—their movements, place of residence, employment, sexual relations, access to alcohol— were regulated and became subject to the whim of the officials who administered them.

Separation of Aboriginal children (particularly paler-skinned children of mixed descent) from their families was common practice in each of the mainland States, especially after World War I. The effect of these policies on the family life of a great number of Indigenous people was devastating. Children who were forcibly taken from their parents were subject to arbitrary direction by government officials and without warning or consultation, children could be shifted from one family or institution to another and from one town to another. Some children lost all contact with their families and, for many the only knowledge of their family is the memory of the extreme anguish of being seized from their parents by government officials. These children have now become known as 'the stolen generations'.

Assimilation and its abandonment

In the 1940s, State and the Commonwealth governments formally adopted a policy of *assimilation*. The aim, it was said, was to absorb all Aborigines into the white society to form a single Australian community. The repeal of the previous discriminatory and segregationist laws in favour of new nondiscriminatory laws that made no special provisions for Aborigines took place very slowly, especially in Queensland. However, as the policy of assimilation became the new official orthodoxy, it was, itself, increasingly criticised.

Most obviously, critics argued that the assimilation policy was a failure in its own terms. Despite the repeal of much of the discriminatory legislation, most Aborigines remained socially and economically excluded and continued to be severely disadvantaged.

More fundamentally, the very idea of the assimilation of Aborigines into the majority white society was criticised. The policy objective of assimilation that was adopted by the State and Commonwealth governments through the 1950s was expressed in emphatic terms. In 1961 State and federal Ministers of Aboriginal Affairs agreed that:

> The policy of assimilation means in the view of all Australian governments that all Aborigines and part-Aborigines are expected eventually to attain the same manner of living as other Australians and to live as members of a single Australian community enjoying the same rights and privileges, accepting the same responsibilities, observing the same customs and influenced by the same beliefs, hopes and loyalties as other Australians. (Quoted in Gale & Brookman 1975: 72)

Such rigid statements of the goal of assimilation were criticised because they were seen to involve forced social change that aimed to obliterate any Indigenous culture. The white culture was presented as being superior in all ways, and Aboriginal culture as having nothing of value worth preserving. Indigenous communities were expected to disappear as Aborigines were absorbed, as individuals, into the dominant culture. The policy of assimilation, critics argued, was in reality a policy of 'cultural genocide'. To obtain equality and be assimilated, Aborigines would have to change.

Opponents of the policy observed that the one-sidedness of the assimilation policy—requiring change by Aborigines but not by members of the majority culture—overlooked the reality that Aboriginal disadvantage was the product of prejudice and of the excluding nature of white society.

One feature of Indigenous policy at this time was that Aborigines themselves had largely been denied any opportunity to participate in policy decisions about their own future. In this sense Aborigines remained an administered people. Reformers called for Aborigines to be given greater scope to manage their own affairs, and for recognition of their distinctive culture and traditions.

The Commonwealth enters the field of Aboriginal affairs

Many of those committed to reforming Aboriginal conditions believed that it was necessary to give the Commonwealth government a greater role in Indigenous policy. For the Commonwealth to become fully involved, a Constitutional amendment was necessary to change section 51(xxvi) which, as noted above, prohibited the Commonwealth from making laws with respect to peoples of 'the aboriginal race in any State'.

Concern about Australia's international reputation persuaded some members of the Commonwealth Parliament that the Commonwealth should take a more forceful role to advance Indigenous rights. One Opposition member described the Constitutional limitation on the national government as a 'liability on Australian diplomacy' and claimed:

> At international conferences the Commonwealth bears the odium of any discrimination against aborigines. Absence of any discrimination would be a significant part of the defence of the nation. (CPDHR 30 August 1962: 877)

A referendum question was put to the voters in 1967 proposing to amend the Constitution to remove the words 'other than the aboriginal race in any State' from section 51 (xxvi) and, at the same time, to delete section 127, which prevented Aborigines from being counted in the census. The referendum was overwhelmingly passed in all States with an overall 'yes' vote of 91 per cent, the largest ever obtained by a constitutional referendum proposal.

This amendment to section 51(xxvi) gave the Commonwealth government significant new powers to enter the field of Aboriginal affairs. While the change was generally seen as a positive development, there was little public reflection at the time on the deeper aspects of the purposes to which the new power might be put. Complex questions about the nature of Indigenous rights were not aired, let alone any discussion of what 'equality' might mean in the context of a culturally distinct and dispossessed Indigenous minority.

The passing of the referendum is often presented in the media and elsewhere as having given Aborigines 'citizenship', or some other enhanced rights, or 'better opportunities' (Bennett 1988: 18). This is misleading. By itself, the referendum did not change the legal status of Aborigines. Apart from providing for Aborigines to be counted in the census, the change made to the Constitution simply gave the Commonwealth power to legislate with respect to Aboriginal people.

Despite the apparent widespread support for the Commonwealth becoming involved in Aboriginal affairs, the Commonwealth government was slow to take up its new mandate. It was not until Australia Day in January 1972, when the Coalition government led by Prime Minister McMahon was under pressure from well-publicised and sympathetically reported Aboriginal protests, that McMahon announced a significant Commonwealth commitment to Aboriginal welfare.

The Commonwealth was also slow to abandon its assimilationist approach. Again, it was not until Prime Minister McMahon's statement in 1972 that it was announced that assimilation would be replaced by the goal of 'integration' which, it was claimed, would allow Aborigines some choice about 'the degree to which, and the pace at which they [would come] to identify themselves with [white] society'. Aborigines, it was said, would no longer be required to abandon all their traditional 'beliefs, hopes and loyalties' (McMahon 1972: 3–4).

The initiatives of the McMahon government did not include any concessions on the matter of 'land rights'. In the 1960s, the matter of Aboriginal land rights had been politicised by the widely publicised activities of several Indigenous communities. In 1963, the Yirrkala people of Arnhem Land protested against the Nabalco mining company being granted a lease over land at Gove which was part of an Aboriginal Reserve. The cause of the Yirrkala people obtained widespread publicity when they presented a petition, written on bark in their own language, to the House of Representatives. The issue of land rights was forced on to the national political agenda again in 1966 when Gurindji stockmen employed at Wave Hill cattle station in the Northern Territory went on strike. The Gurindji strike was in part a protest against a decision of the Arbitration Commission, to defer for 30 months the implementation of equal wages for Aborigines, and against appalling working and living conditions, but it also entailed a demand for the 'return' of 'their land'. Over the next five years, the Coalition government in office at the Commonwealth level consistently refused to make any concessions to the Gurindji but their battle attracted support from a wide range of community groups and became a rallying point for a strengthening campaign for Aboriginal land rights.

The campaign to force the Commonwealth government to make some concession on land rights intensified when, in 1971, the Yirrkala people lost a case in the Supreme Court of the Northern Territory in which they had sought to obtain legal recognition of traditional title to their land. In his judgment in this case, *Milirrpum v Nabalco*, Justice Blackburn held that communal title was not part of Australian law. The loss of this legal battle for recognition of title to land left Indigenous people with the sole alternative of a political campaign to win land rights through legislative change.

In 1972, Aboriginal disappointment with the McMahon government's failure to make any concessions on land rights was publicised in an inspired political gesture, which not only attracted the attention of the Australian press, but was also reported around the world. A tent, erected on the lawns outside Parliament

House in Canberra, was named the 'Aboriginal Embassy' and became both a symbol of Indigenous dispossession within their own country and a focus for political lobbying for land rights legislation. The contrast between the canvas tents of the protesters and the grand architectural backdrop of Parliament House provided a dramatic visual image that the media fully appreciated. Extensive coverage of the protesters' arguments raised the profile of Aboriginal policy issues to a new level, especially when the Leader of the Opposition, Gough Whitlam, made land rights one of the priorities of the Labor Party. The 'tent embassy' marked a new level of Aboriginal activism and demonstrated the significance of land rights as a unifying and mobilising political cause for Indigenous people.

The Whitlam government 1972–75

It was not until the Whitlam Labor government came to office at the end of 1972, having promised to make Aboriginal affairs a national issue and to commit more Commonwealth resources to Aboriginal programs, that there was decisive change. Labor had come to office after an electoral campaign which gave unprecedented attention to Aboriginal issues. Labor's policy was ambitious and the Whitlam government marks a turning point in Indigenous affairs in a number of respects.

First, the scale of Commonwealth activity expanded enormously and brought the Commonwealth government into areas of Aboriginal welfare that overlapped with State responsibilities. In three years under the Whitlam government, Commonwealth spending on Aboriginal affairs increased over sevenfold. Ever since, despite some fluctuations and some attempts by different governments to wind back the amount of Commonwealth expenditure devoted to Aboriginal affairs, Commonwealth funds have remained a large part of total government spending on Aboriginal welfare, and Indigenous affairs has become one of the most complex areas of intergovernmental relations within the federal system.

Second, the Whitlam government adopted a policy of 'self-determination' for Indigenous people. From that time until the Howard government came to office in 1996, all Commonwealth governments espoused, in general terms, a commitment to some form of Indigenous autonomy—variously called 'self-determination' or 'self-management'—and some recognition of Indigenous rights.

Third, the Whitlam government initiated moves to legislate for Aboriginal land rights in the Northern Territory and, ever since, land rights have been a political issue that has troubled Commonwealth governments. These three issues—Commonwealth Aboriginal programs, Commonwealth policy and land rights—need further elaboration.

Commonwealth programs and intergovernmental relations

Given the rhetoric of the Whitlam government, and the constitutional powers which the Commonwealth had obtained in the 1967 referendum, it might have appeared that the Commonwealth would take over all Aboriginal matters from the States. The division of responsibility between the Commonwealth and the States, however, has been much less clear than this. The nature of Aboriginal programs is such that it is almost impossible to draw an unambiguous line between what should be Commonwealth responsibilities and what should be State responsibilities.

The Whitlam government created a full Commonwealth Department of Aboriginal Affairs and dramatically increased spending on a wide range of new national Aboriginal programs. However, many of these programs involved such matters as health, hospitals, housing, education, training, law enforcement and correctional services, and these are all areas of State responsibility. The Commonwealth government itself did not have service-delivery agencies in these areas and, in order to implement Aboriginal programs, the Commonwealth made grants to State governments or directly to Aboriginal organisations.

In funding Aboriginal programs, successive Commonwealth governments have maintained that the Commonwealth should not provide funds for ordinary State services which a State government ought to be providing for *all* residents in the State, whether Aboriginal or non-Aboriginal. In 1982, the Fraser Coalition government tried to establish principles to delineate the funding responsibilities of the two tiers of government: the Commonwealth would provide funds for programs aimed at combating what was termed the 'double disadvantage' suffered by Aboriginal Australians—'the particular or severe disadvantage due to Aboriginality'—but would not provide funds for ordinary State services for Aborigines (Robbins & Summers 1996: 180). All Commonwealth governments since then have maintained this general approach.

However, drawing definite lines of accountability and responsibility has proven to be an intractable problem. Notwithstanding the apparent shift in power to the Commonwealth at the 1967 referendum, there is no clear jurisdictional division in Indigenous affairs between the powers, or the responsibilities of the two tiers of government. The Commonwealth and States have each, on the one hand, attempted to shift funding responsibilities and other problems on to the other tier of government and, on the other hand, attempted to maintain control of programs. The effect is that Indigenous affairs is an area that is affected by overlap and blurred accountability, and by political, financial and administrative disputes between the Commonwealth and the States.

Related to the problems of jurisdiction have been complaints about overlap, duplication and lack of coordination in Aboriginal programs. This has been seen to be due in part to the federal division of power and the overlap of responsibility, but also in part to the fact that Aboriginal affairs involves such a wide range of other policy areas. Numerous reports have identified the difficulties of sharing power in Aboriginal affairs. In 1988, for example, the Bonner Review of the communities in South Australia's north-west reported that an 'impossibly high' number of government agencies were involved, and that problems of coordination were exacerbated by, amongst other things, 'policy inconsistencies between some agencies and bureaucratic rivalries' (Bonner 1988: 13–4). The House of Representatives Standing Committee on Aboriginal Affairs likewise concluded in 1990 that there were problems of coordination in Aboriginal programs throughout Australia (HRSCAA 1990: 68).

Both State and Commonwealth governments have acknowledged the problems of achieving coordination and the pernicious effect it has on the delivery of effective services to Indigenous communities. There have been a number of attempts to improve intergovernmental cooperation, the most recent being a November 2000 Council of Australian Governments (COAG) decision to adopt a coordinated partnership approach to improve the economic and social well-being of Indigenous people and to advance reconciliation (HREOC 2005: 149). In 2002 this led on to the implementation of COAG 'trial sites' in Indigenous communities across Australia, to demonstrate what coordinated action can achieve. Each trial site is under the responsibility of a Commonwealth and a State minister. The outcome of these trials are still to be evaluated.

A further initiative of COAG led to the establishment of a national reporting framework for Indigenous disadvantage. The Productivity Commission has been instructed to report regularly on key indicators of Indigenous disadvantage, such as life expectancy and employment rates. This provides a basis for assessment of the effectiveness of strategies put in place to address Indigenous needs. In 2005, the second *Overcoming Indigenous Disadvantage Report* was released. It indicated that while there had been some improvement in some areas such as employment, home ownership and education, there were also significant areas where outcomes had got worse, notably in child protection notifications and imprisonment rates (SCRGSP 2005). While this is a disappointing development, the reporting framework provides an important new tool for governments to use in designing joint activities to confront the unacceptable dimensions of Indigenous inequality.

Commonwealth policy: 'self-determination'

In 1972 Whitlam government adopted a policy of 'self-determination' for Aboriginal Australians. Whitlam spoke of the reversal of 'two hundred years of despoliation, injustice and discrimination' and declared that the objective of government policy was to 'restore to the Aboriginal people their lost power of self-determination in economic, social and political affairs' (Whitlam 1973: 697). Unfortunately, a clear definition of self-determination was not elaborated nor were the principles upon which it was to be based made plain. On the one hand, the policy appeared to be directed at recognition of cultural *difference* and at facilitating the maintenance of a *separate* group identity. On the other hand, it appeared to be aimed at achieving improved opportunity and greater social and economic equality for a demonstrably disadvantaged group *within* the larger Australian society. The concept of self-determination was allowed to remain essentially vague despite political speeches which alluded to Aboriginal 'independence' and to Aborigines 'making their own decisions' and so on. What this was supposed to mean in terms of real political power was not addressed. With such uncertainty about the parameters of the policy, it is not surprising that there were discrepancies between the expectations of some Aboriginal groups and the intentions of the government.

The establishment of a representative Aboriginal body, the National Aboriginal Consultative Committee (NACC), was a key plank of the Whitlam government's policy. It was described by the then Minister as the 'Aboriginal Peoples' voice at national level' (Bryant 1973: 904, 910). But the NACC was not a success. It was a casualty partly of policy makers' problems in grappling with the complexity of Indigenous political demands—a failing that was to afflict successive governments—and of a government having promised to Aboriginal groups much more than it was actually prepared to deliver. Aboriginal representatives elected to the NACC body believed that they had been elected to a 'Black Parliament' and that they could assume an executive role appropriate to that position, with control over policy and finances in the portfolio (DAA 1976). To the government, which wanted only an advisory body, this was quite unacceptable. The failure of the NACC was indicative of the gap between the intentions of the government of the day and the expectations of some Indigenous activists. It also demonstrated the inadequacy of ambiguous policy statements. Subsequent governments had similar problems with ambiguity and apparent contradictions in their policy objectives.

The Fraser Coalition government that came to office in 1975 preferred the term 'self-management' rather than 'self-determination'. The 'self-management' policy claimed to provide for a significant degree of participation by Aboriginal people in decision making (Viner 1976: 2–4), but was no less ambiguous than the previous policy. It replaced the NACC with the National Aboriginal Conference, a representative body with a firm role as an advisory body to government.

In the 1980s and 1990s, the Hawke and Keating Labor governments returned to the notion of 'self-determination' but, once again, gave a mixed set of signals about what the policy might mean.

COUNCIL FOR ABORIGINAL RECONCILIATION

In 1991 the Hawke Labor government set up the Council for Aboriginal Recon-ciliation (CAR), to focus on the broader relationship between Indigenous people and other Australians. In particular, its purpose was to identify ways to 'construct meaningful and worthwhile race relations' in Australia and to suggest whether there would be 'any merit or advantages in formalising our relationship in some meaningful way' (CAR 1994: vii). The most important activities of the CAR were aimed to raise the Australian public's awareness of Indigenous issues. The CAR distributed an enormous amount of information, held conferences and encouraged local study groups to consider options for reconciliation. Before it disbanded in 2000, the CAR organised a number of bridge walks to symbolise support for reconciliation. These events were highly popular, with up to 300 000 people walking across the Sydney Harbour Bridge on one occasion (CAR 2000a: 3). Its final report, *Roadmap for Reconciliation* (CAR 2000b), outlined a range of strategies designed to sustain the reconciliation process and to promote the recognition of Aboriginal and Torres Strait Islander rights, to overcome Indige-nous disadvantage and advance economic independence.

ABORIGINAL AND TORRES STRAIT ISLANDER COMMISSION (ATSIC)

Another initiative of the Hawke government, the establishment of the Aborigi-nal and Torres Strait Islander Commission (ATSIC), was of particular signifi-cance. ATSIC was an elected Indigenous body, comprising a national Board of Commissioners as well as Regional Councils, which exercised devolved respon-sibility for the Commonwealth's Aboriginal Affairs budget. Announcing the measure in 1987, the Minister for Aboriginal Affairs spoke of the importance of involving Aboriginal and Torres Strait Islander people in the decision-making processes of government 'in order that the right decisions are taken about their lives'. He said that 'Aboriginal people need to decide for themselves what should be done—not just take whatever governments think or say is best for them' (Hand 1987: 1–2). ATSIC came into existence in March 1990 and the first elections took place in November of the same year.

Responses to ATSIC varied. From one point of view, it was argued that ATSIC was too firmly bound into mainstream government processes to be a vehicle for any real form of self-determination, and that the Commissioners and regional councillors had little autonomy (see Rowse 1992a and 1992b). On the other hand, Lowitja O'Donoghue, the first Chairperson of ATSIC, believed ATSIC empow-ered Indigenous people and that it 'signalled an end of domination, even the benevolent domination of distant administrators' (O'Donoghue 1992: 221).

Beyond such differing views, including among Indigenous people them-selves, are the unresolved dilemmas of the broader objective of Aboriginal policy. What level of political independence is appropriate and just? Who should decide what policies best meet Indigenous peoples' needs? It is not surprising that, without definitive answers to these important questions, ATSIC's operational history proved controversial, particularly in relation to its political and financial accountability.

The Howard government: a retreat from self-determination

The Howard Coalition government that came to office in March 1996 has retreated from the use of the term 'self-determination', preferring the phrase 'self-empowerment' and an emphasis on economic independence.

The first Minister for Aboriginal Affairs in the Howard government, Senator John Herron, indicated three objectives for government policy: improvements in Indigenous health, housing and other socioeconomic outcomes; ensuring that State and local governments meet their responsibilities; and shifting resources towards remote communities (ATSIC 1997: 7). This agenda became known as 'practical reconciliation'. It sought to focus on program delivery and services rather than on structural or conceptual issues such as political rights or independence (OATSIA 2003a). It also suggested that the incoming Howard government regarded remoteness and social disadvantage as the most important aspects of Aboriginal and Islander policy, rather than any concept of cultural difference or entitlement to compensation for dispossession. Given these views, it is not surprising that the Howard government refused to endorse the CAR's final recommendations, especially its proposal for the negotiation of a treaty between Indigenous and non-Indigenous Australians.

The Howard government has been explicit that its objection to the concept of self-determination is because 'it has implications of separate nations or governments' (OATSIA 2003b). It was inevitable, therefore, that the Howard government would have difficulty accepting the role of ATSIC.

In 2002, after expressing serious dissatisfaction with ATSIC's performance, the government established an inquiry to consider ATSIC's future role. The inquiry reported the following year and recommended changes to ATSIC's structures to give greater responsibilities to the regional councils (ATSIC Review 2003). In the meantime, however, several ATSIC leaders, including its chairperson Geoff Clark, had become embroiled in personal controversies which attracted considerable media attention. The government announced what it called a 'separation of powers', removing control of budget allocations from ATSIC's elected arm and transferring financial responsibilities to a separate body called ATSIS—Aboriginal and Torres Strait Islander Services—which was formerly the ATSIC administrative arm. In a further major move, in July 2004, ATSIC program responsibilities and ATSIS staff were allocated to a range of other government departments, effectively 'mainstreaming' the delivery of services to Indigenous people.

In a development that surprised many people, Labor Opposition leader, Mark Latham, announced his view that ATSIC had lost community support and was 'no longer capable of addressing endemic problems in Indigenous communities' (*Australian* 31 March 2004). He indicated that, were his party to win government, it would introduce significant reforms to ATSIC. Prime Minister Howard seized the opportunity created by this apparently bipartisan dissatisfaction with ATSIC and, in April 2004, declared his government's intention to abolish ATSIC completely, declaring it a 'failure' (Robbins 2004). Implementation of this decision was delayed by the ensuing dissolution of Parliament in the lead up to the 2004 election, but the re-election of the Howard government with a majority in the Senate was the death knell for ATSIC. The final stage of its abolition was completed in June 2005 when its regional councils were disbanded.

There is now no longer a representative Indigenous body at national level, although the government has appointed an Indigenous advisory body (the National Indigenous Council) which consists of people with 'expertise and experience in particular policy areas . . . not representing particular regions' (OIPC 2005).

The Howard government has embraced a strong retreat from any concept of self-determination. It has explicitly rejected the concept of Indigenous rights and prefers to define the problems that Indigenous people face as stemming from their position as a disadvantaged minority within Australian society. The Howard government emphasises the need to address the social and economic marginalisation of Indigenous communities through 'practical reconciliation' and sees the pursuit of a 'rights' agenda as a distraction from this priority and a threat to national unity.

THE 'RIGHT TO TAKE RESPONSIBILITY'

Many analysts disagree with the Howard government's focus on 'practical reconciliation'. Behrendt, for example, argues that '[p]ractical reconciliation does not attack the systemic and institutionalised aspects of the impediments to socio-economic development' (Behrendt 2003: 11). But support for one aspect of the Howard government's approach has come from an unexpected quarter. Aboriginal leader Noel Pearson has attacked the orthodox welfare approach to Indigenous disadvantage, arguing that the policies of the last several decades, which have claimed to be based on a goal of self-determination, have not achieved real self-determination for Aboriginal communities. Rather, they have produced 'passive welfare dependency'. Writing of Queensland's Cape York Peninsula in particular, but with relevance to most parts of Australia, Pearson argues that, under the welfare system which has been in place for several decades, Aboriginal communities have become 'severely dysfunctional'. The symptoms, he says, are clear:

- [Aboriginal] people die more than 20 years earlier, on average, than other Australians
- [Aboriginal] health is by far the worst of any group in the Australian community
- [Aboriginal] people suffer from diseases that other Australians simply do not have
- [they] are vulnerable to new health threats, like HIV
- [their] children do not participate in the education system anywhere near as successfully as other Australian children
- [they] are over-represented in the juvenile justice system, in the criminal justice system and the jails
- there is more violence among [Aboriginal] people than in other communities in Australia. (Pearson 2000: 15)

The biggest problem for Aboriginal communities, Pearson argues, is what he calls 'passive welfare'. Unlike the welfare support paid to most other needy Australians to alleviate short-term problems, the welfare payments made to Aboriginal communities, year after year, are typically their only source of income. The welfare payments do not depend on any effort or reciprocity from the recipients. The ubiquitous presence of welfare payments and the absence of the kind of paid employment typical elsewhere means that Aboriginal communities, according to Pearson, are removed from the 'real economy'. 'Passive welfare', he argues, 'kills initiative and breeds dependency', 'pacifies recipients' and creates welfare and victim mentalities. Far from the communities being self-determining, Aboriginal recipients of 'passive welfare expect others to solve their problems' and '[fail] to take responsibility for [themselves] or their families or communities' (Pearson 2000: 21–2; see also Attorney-General's Department 2001). Pearson argues for the establishment of a more appropriate economic dynamic, allegedly even proposing that welfare should be withheld from parents who fail to send their children to school (*Australian* 22 July 2005).

In what might be seen as a similar perspective, the Howard government has recently introduced the concept of Shared Responsibility Agreements (SRAs), which are negotiated with Indigenous family or community groups. SRAs embody the concept of 'mutual obligation', which has become the guiding principle of welfare policy in Australia (see Chapter 24 in this book). Mutual obligation requires the recipient of welfare to 'do something in return'. In the government's words: 'Under the new approach, groups will need to offer commitments and undertake changes that benefit the community in return for government funding' (OIPC 2005: 18). An example of a SRA is an agreement between the Mulan community and the government in which the community agreed to wash its children's faces daily in return for the provision of a petrol pump (*Sydney Morning Herald* 11 December 2004). Despite the apparent convergence of ideas between himself and the Prime Minister, Pearson has criticised this development, arguing that the Mulan SRA is in danger of undermining the goal of 'normalis[ing] obligations between Aboriginal parents and their children' (Dodson & Pearson 2004). In his 2004 Social Justice Report, Tom Calma, the Aboriginal and Torres Strait Islander Social Justice Commissioner, raises concerns that SRAs may, in some circumstances, be contrary to the provisions of the *Racial Discrimination Act* if they breach basic human rights (HREOC 2005: 191–3).

Land rights

Another perennial controversy in Indigenous policy since the 1970s has been the way in which the Commonwealth government has responded to demands for the recognition of Aboriginal land rights.

The South Australian Parliament in 1966 created an Aboriginal Lands Trust which established a precedent for the recognition of Aboriginal land rights. In the early 1970s, at the national level, the Whitlam government undertook to legislate for Aboriginal land rights in the Northern Territory but its *Aboriginal Land Rights (NT) Bill* was still being considered by Parliament when the Whitlam government was dismissed. A modified version was subsequently passed in 1976 under the Fraser Coalition government. The Act transferred all Aboriginal reserves in the Northern Territory to Aboriginal ownership, established a process for Aboriginal groups to claim Crown land that was their traditional territory, and provided that royalties from mining on Aboriginal land would be paid to Aboriginal Land Councils and to traditional owners (Maddox 1983: 60–82).

This Act was passed by the Commonwealth Parliament against what was almost certainly the wish of a majority of voters in the Northern Territory. Dealing with States, however, is a different matter. The approach to land rights has been quite different in the different States, and the Commonwealth has tended to respond accordingly. South Australia has had the most advanced legislation of any State, with its *Pitjantjatjara Land Rights Act 1981* being 'the first negotiated land rights settlement in Australia' (Peterson 1981: 121). Opposition to land rights has been greatest in Western Australia and Queensland. Both Labor and Coalition governments in Canberra have backed away from disputes about land rights with those States (see Libby 1989; Bennett 1989: 36).

MABO AND WIK

A decision in 1992 by the High Court imposed upon the Australian legal system a radical new interpretation of Aboriginal entitlements to land and forced governments to consider the appropriate legislative response. The legal case was brought by a group of Torres Strait Islanders who sought to establish that they held title to land that their families had occupied for many generations. In the *Mabo* case, the High Court held that previous legal decisions which had found that at the time of European colonisation Australia was *terra nullius*, or 'land belonging to no-one', were wrong (see Bartlett 1993). The Court found that native title to land had existed prior to white settlement, that it had survived the acquisition of sovereignty by the Crown, that it potentially still existed and that it is claimable under certain circumstances, summarised by the Attorney-General's Department (1994: 7) as

- where Aboriginal and Torres Strait Islander people have maintained their connection with the land through the years of European settlement; and
- where their title has not been extinguished by valid acts of Imperial, Colonial, State, Territory or Commonwealth Governments.

In other words, while the sovereignty of the Crown and the right of governments to sell or give leases to land was not brought into question by the *Mabo* decision, where land had *not* been 'alienated' in this way then certain Aboriginal people might be able to claim native title.

In response to this new legal finding, and after protracted negotiations with Aboriginal and other groups (as described below), the Keating Labor government proposed a *Native Title Bill*, which was enacted in December 1993 after being heavily amended by the Senate. This Act set up a National Native Title Tribunal (NNTT) and laid down the procedures for application for native title claims and compensation. Under the Act, the NNTT can mediate between parties to a claim, and if this is successful, its determination is lodged in the Federal Court for registration. If there are unresolved disputes, the Federal Court hears the case (Brennan 1995: 97).

Later, in the *Wik* case of 1996, the High Court further extended its definition of native title. The Wik and Thayorre peoples of Queensland asked the Court to determine whether pastoral leases inevitably extinguished native title or, alternatively, whether they could co-exist. Even if pastoral leases did extinguish native title, they wished to determine whether, at the end of a lease, native title rights could be resumed by traditional owners (Willheim 1997: 20–6).

The decision of the Court was that these matters could only be determined on a case-by-case basis, taking into consideration the relevant State legislation and patterns of land usage by the traditional owners. In some circumstances, according to the Court majority, it was possible for native title in some form to co-exist with a continuing pastoral lease. However, in the event of a conflict between the terms of a lease and native title, the Court ruled that the terms of the pastoral leases take precedence.

This *Wik* decision caused considerable controversy. Aboriginal leaders welcomed the decision and argued that, while it potentially recognised Aboriginal claims in appropriate cases, it also gave adequate protection to pastoralists and miners. Some State governments and pastoral and mining lobby groups, however, argued that the lack of 'certainty' created profound economic disruption and disadvantaged many existing leaseholders. This argument was influential with the Coalition government that won the election of 1996.

Prime Minister Howard responded to the *Wik* decision in May 1997 with a proposal for amendments to the *Native Title Act 1993* based on a 'Ten Point Plan' which he said would both give the pastoralists certainty in relation to 'primary production' and at the same time preserve Indigenous rights. The plan, however, was bitterly attacked by both pastoral and Aboriginal interests. The Queensland government and pastoral lobby groups argued that the plan did not provide the uniform and full extinguishment of native title on pastoral leases which they sought. On the other hand, Indigenous leaders argued that implementation of the plan would see the loss of some existing native title rights and would potentially make it harder to establish claims in the future.

One of the key issues was the question of the 'right to negotiate'—the entitlement of native-title holders to negotiate in the event of the grant of mining rights or compulsory acquisition of land over which they have rights. After considerable political manoeuvring in the Senate an amended version of the Ten Point Plan was adopted which, due to the intervention of Senator Harradine, retained some rights for native-title holders to negotiate, albeit in diminished form. The outcome was still a disappointment to many Indigenous leaders, who felt that the certainty required by the pastoral lobby had been achieved at the expense of Indigenous rights.

REGIONAL AGREEMENTS

The use of negotiated regional agreements—agreed between Indigenous native-title holders and other interested parties such as mining companies or pastoralists—is one which has considerable advantages over the legalistic, adversarial approach of the courts. The amendments to the *Native Title Act* in 1998 encouraged the use of Indigenous Land Use Agreements by providing a process of formal registration. This means that native-title claimants and holders can enter into voluntary negotiations with mining companies or pastoralists about the use or development of their land and have legal protection for the terms and conditions of the agreement. This avoids the need to engage in the onerous requirements of a full native title claim and removes many of the lengthy delays which have frustrated mining companies.

The 'stolen generations'

As discussed above, numbers of part-Aboriginal children were separated from their parents under laws and policies in effect in the States and the Northern Territory until the 1960s. Concerns expressed in recent years about the ongoing impact of these past polices resulted in the Human Rights and Equal Opportunity Commission establishing an inquiry into the 'stolen generations'. A particular concern was the link, suggested by the report of the Royal Commission into Aboriginal Deaths in Custody, between the separation of Aboriginal children from their families and their over-representation in the criminal justice system (RCADC 1991: 253–96). The *Report of the National Inquiry into the Separation of Aboriginal and Torres Strait Islander Children from their Families*, released in April 1997, caused considerable controversy (HREOC 1997). An enormous amount of public debate was stimulated by the Inquiry's findings that the forcible removal of Indigenous children was a gross violation of their human rights and amounted to an act of genocide contrary to the international Convention on Genocide ratified by Australia in 1949. The Convention defined genocide not just in terms of murder, but also in terms of intention to destroy a group. The *Report* argued that the policy of removing children was intended to culturally absorb them so that Aborigines would disappear as a distinct group in Australian society.

The *Report* of the Inquiry made a number of recommendations about reparation for the historical and contemporary impact of these policies. One of these was that all Australian parliaments and police forces should apologise and acknowledge the responsibility of their predecessors for past practices of removal. This became a highly political issue when Prime Minister John Howard refused to make a formal apology on behalf of the government, stating that he did not believe in a 'black armband' version of history. While making a personal statement of regret, he said he did not feel that it was appropriate to say 'sorry' for actions for which current generations were not responsible (see CPDHR 26 August 1999: 9205–22). This continues to be a very divisive and strongly contested issue in Australian politics.

Aborigines and politics

Aborigines are a small proportion of the Australian population, which makes it very difficult for them to make a direct impact on the electoral process. A possible exception might be those parts of northern Australia where Aborigines comprise a significant proportion of the population. In the Northern Territory, where Aboriginal Australians comprise 27 per cent of the population, the June 2005 election saw a record five Aboriginal MPs win seats in the 25-member Northern Territory Parliament.

Historically, most Aboriginal political activity has been concerned not with mainstream electoral politics but rather with pressure-group activity over land rights and with other bodies such as Land Councils, Aboriginal Legal Aid Services and Aboriginal Health Services. Indigenous policy issues have at times been of deeply symbolic importance within the Australian political system. One matter that has changed in recent years is the impact of Indigenous leaders and spokespersons on Australian public life. Leaders from ATSIC, from the various Land Councils and from other Aboriginal bodies have come to play a prominent role in the public debate about Indigenous issues. Aboriginal groups—Land Councils, Legal Services and other Aboriginal associations—have become better organised and are in a better position to inject their views into the public debate. They have grown adept at reaching global audiences through the media and international forums such as the UN. It has become difficult for the Commonwealth government to completely ignore a concerted and unified push by a wide range of representative Aboriginal groups.

With the abolition of ATSIC, Indigenous leaders can be expected to use public forums to raise public awareness of their concerns and aspirations. The Howard government's current agenda will no doubt attract resistance from Indigenous leaders who reject the direction policy is taking, especially in respect of the recognition of Indigenous rights. The political dynamics of that conflict are likely to be sophisticated and high profile.

A 'Fourth World' people

The position of the majority of Aborigines continues to be unacceptable, being hugely disadvantaged on a wide range of socioeconomic indicators (SCRGSP 2005). Aborigines are now sometimes described as being part of the 'Fourth World'—a sub-group with Third-World living standards living within a dominant and prosperous First World nation (Dyck 1985). Although some Aborigines have gained advancement in governmental employment through secondary and tertiary education and although the proportion of Aborigines continuing in tertiary education is increasing, the educational and employment status of the majority remains low. In employment, health and housing, Aborigines remain severely disadvantaged.

One measure of the deprived circumstances of Aborigines' lives is provided by health statistics, particularly the infant mortality rate. Although there has been some improvement in recent years, the Aboriginal infant mortality rate remains much higher than for non-Aborigines (SCRGSP 2005: 16). Recent statistics indicate that the life expectancy at birth of Aboriginal males is 18 years less than that for non-Aboriginal males, and for Aboriginal females 17 years less than for non-Aboriginal females (SCRGSP 2005: 5).

There is overwhelming evidence that Indigenous people of low socio-economic status continue to be disadvantaged in the legal system. Relative to their numbers in the total population, Aborigines are very significantly over-represented amongst the prison population and, in a number of cases, the Aborigines are being detained on quite minor charges. Indigenous people are 11 times more likely to be imprisoned than other Australians (SCRGSP 2005: 13). The deprived circumstances in which many Aborigines live has left them completely alienated from the institutions of the majority culture. White attitudes, particularly among white Australians living in proximity to Aborigines, are an important factor in maintaining this situation, and recent policies have done little to change the reality of Aborigines' lives in outback areas and rural towns (Cowlishaw 1988: 151–283).

In the last two or three decades the legal framework which formerly prescribed Indigenous inequality has been dismantled. Indigenous people are now formally equal citizens but, in many parts of Australia, white attitudes have changed little. Indeed, there is some evidence that there has been a backlash within white public opinion against Aborigines. In those outback areas and country towns where many Aborigines live, the opportunities to gain even low-paid employment are minimal and the impediments to economic advancement and social acceptance appear insurmountable. While this situation continues, there is a risk that many Aborigines will continue to be 'Fourth World' people, pauperised and with little or no capacity to determine their own future.

REFERENCES

ABS 2003, *The Health and Welfare of Australia's Aboriginal and Torres Strait Islander Peoples*, cat. no. 4704.0, ABS, Canberra.

ATSIC [Aboriginal and Torres Strait Islander Commission] 1997, *ATSIC News*, vol. 6, no. 2.

ATSIC Review 2003, *In the Hands of the Regions—A New ATSIC. Report of the Review of the Aboriginal & Torres Strait Islander Commission*, (J. Hannaford, J. Huggins & B. Collins) Commonwealth of Australia, Canberra.

Attorney-General's Department 1994, 'Commentary on the *Native Title Act 1993*', in *Native Title*, AGPS, Canberra.

Attorney-General's Department, 2001, *Violence in Indigenous Communities: Report to Crime Prevention Branch of Attorney General's Department*, by P. Memmott *et al.* in association with Aboriginal Environments Research Centre, University of Queensland, Attorney-Generals Department, Canberra.

Bartlett, R. 1993, *The Mabo Decision: Commentary and Full Text*, Butterworths, Sydney.

Bennett, S. 1988, 'Federalism and Aboriginal Affairs', *Australian Aboriginal Studies*, no. 1.

Bennett, S. 1989, *Aborigines and Political Power*, Allen & Unwin, Sydney.

Behrendt, L. 2003, *Achieving Social Justice: Indigenous Rights and Australia's Future*, The Federation Press, Sydney.

Bonner, N. 1988, *Always Anangu: A Review of the Pitjantjatjara and Yunkunytjatjara Aboriginal Communities of Central Australia*, Department of Aboriginal Affairs, Canberra.

Brennan, F. 1995, *One Land One Nation. Mabo—Towards 2001*, University of Queensland Press, St. Lucia.

Bryant, G. 1973, 'Aboriginal Policy Outlined', *Australian Government Digest*, vol. 1, no. 3, speech, 15 July.

CAR [Council for Aboriginal Reconciliation] 1994, *Walking Together: The First Steps. Report of the Council for Aboriginal Reconciliation to Federal Parliament*, AGPS, Canberra.

CAR [Council for Aboriginal Reconciliation] 2000a, *Walking Together*, no. 29, Canberra.

CAR [Council for Aboriginal Reconciliation] 2000b, *Roadmap for Reconciliation*, Council for Aboriginal Reconciliation, Canberra.

Cowlishaw, G. 1988, *Black, White or Brindle: Race in Rural Australia*, Cambridge University Press, Melbourne.

CPDHR *Commonwealth Parliamentary Debates, House of Representatives*, Canberra.

DAA [Department of Aboriginal Affairs] 1975a, *Report for Period December 1972 to June 1974*, Government Printer, Canberra.

DAA [Department of Aboriginal Affairs] 1975b, *Report for the Year 1974–75*, Government Printer, Canberra.

DAA [Department of Aboriginal Affairs] 1976, *The Role of the National Aboriginal Consultative Committee. Report of the Committee of Inquiry*, the 'Hiatt Report', AGPS, Canberra.

Dodson, P. & Pearson, N. 2004, 'The Dangers of Mutual Obligation', *The Age*, 15 December.

Dyck, N. 1985, *Indigenous People and the Nation State: Fourth World Politics in Canada, Australia and Norway*, Institute of Social and Economic Research, Memorial University of Newfoundland, St. Johns.

Gale, F. & Brookman, A. 1975, *Race Relations in Australia: The Aborigines*, McGraw-Hill, Sydney.

Hand, G. 1987, *Foundations for the Future*, Policy Statement to the House of Representatives, 10 December, AGPS, Canberra.

HREOC [Human Rights & Equal Opportunity Commission] 1997, *Bringing Them Home: Report of the National Inquiry into the Separation of Aboriginal and Torres Strait Islander Children from their Families*, Sydney.

HREOC 2005, *Social Justice Report 2004*, Tom Calma, Aboriginal and Torres Strait Islander Social Justice Commissioner, Human Rights & Equal Opportunity Commission, Sydney.

HRSCAA [House of Representatives Standing Committee on Aboriginal Affairs] 1990, *Our Future Ourselves. Aboriginal and Torres Strait Islander Community Control, Management and Resources*, AGPS, Canberra.

Libby, R. 1989, *Hawke's Law. The Politics of Mining and Aboriginal Land Rights in Australia*, Pennsylvania State University Press, Pennsylvania.

Maddox, K. 1983, *Your Land Is Our Land*, Penguin, Melbourne.

McMahon, W. 1972, *Australian Aborigines: Commonwealth Policies and Achievements*, Government Printer, Canberra.

OATSIA [Office of Aboriginal & Torres Strait Islander Affairs] 2003a, *Reconciliation: Indigenous Issues Fact Sheet No. 3*, Department of Immigration and Multicultural Affairs, Canberra.

OATSIA 2003b, *Indigenous Self-Management: Indigenous Fact Sheet No. 12*, Department of Immigration and Multicultural Affairs, Canberra.

OIPC [Office of Indigenous Policy Co-ordination] 2005, *New Arrangements in Indigenous Affairs*, Updated edition February 2005, Department of Immigration and Multicultural and Indigenous Affairs, Canberra.

O'Donoghue, L. 1992, 'Ending the Despair', *Australian Journal of Public Administration*, vol. 51, no. 2, pp. 214–22.

Pearson, N. 2000, *Our Right to Take Responsibility*, Noel Pearson & Associates Pty. Ltd., Cairns.

Peterson, N. 1981, 'South Australia', in *Aboriginal Land Rights: A Handbook*, ed. N Peterson, Australian Institute of Aboriginal Studies, Canberra.

RCADC [Royal Commission into Aboriginal Deaths in Custody] 1991, *National Report*, vol. 2, AGPS, Canberra.

Robbins, J. 2004, 'The Failure of ATSIC and the Recognition of Indigenous Rights', *Journal of Australian Indigenous Issues*, vol. 7, no. 4, December 2004.

Robbins, J. & Summers, J. 1996, 'Aboriginal Affairs', in *South Australia, Federalism and Public Policy*, ed. A. Parkin, Federalism Research Centre, Australian National University, Canberra.

Rowse, T. 1992a, 'Top-Down Tensions: Can ATSIC Really Contribute to Aboriginal Self-Determination?', *Modern Times*, no. 4, June, pp. 22–3.

Rowse, T. 1992b, *Vision and Pragmatism*, Kaurna Public Lecture Series, Kaurna Higher Education Centre, University of South Australia, 28 September.

SCRGSP [Steering Committee for the Review of Government Service Provision] 2005 *Overcoming Indigenous Disadvantage: Key Indicators 2005 Overview*, Productivity Commission, Canberra.

Viner, I. 1976, 'The New Policy', *Aboriginal News*, vol. 3, no. 1, pp. 2–4.

Viner, I. 1977, *Commonwealth Record*, vol. 2, no. 10.

Whitlam, E.G. 1973, 'Aborigines and Society', press statement, 6 April, *Australian Government Digest*, vol. 1, p. 697.

Willheim, E. 1997, 'Casenote: Queensland Pastoral Leases and Native Title: Wik Peoples v Queensland', *Aboriginal Law Bulletin*, vol. 3, no. 89, pp. 20–6.

LEGAL CASES

Mabo v Queensland (1992) 107 CLR 1
Milirrpum v Nabalco Pty Ltd (1971) FLR 141
Wik Peoples v Queensland & Others (1996) 187 CLR 1

CLR = Commonwealth Law Reports
FLR = Federal Law Reports

Environmental policy

CHAPTER 27

JENNY STEWART

Without doubt, the environment represents a most demanding group of political and policy challenges. Environmental problems are demanding because of their complexity and interconnectedness, and because dealing with them, even in a palliative sense, means confronting the basic process upon which all growth-led economies are built—the expansion of production in the pursuit of rising material standards of living.

This basic process has worked spectacularly well for the advanced liberal democracies of the West through their capitalist economies, and it is one that is now eagerly embraced (although with varying degrees of success) by many developing countries in Asia, Africa and Latin America. Unfortunately, no-one has yet found a way of inducing economic growth which does not also involve substantial environmental change and degradation. *Ecologically sustainable development*, which aims to harmonise growth with the needs of the environment, remains mostly an aspiration rather than a reality.

At an international level, the world economy is caught between two powerful tensions: the understandable wish for poorer countries to become richer (which will mean, even with the most energy-efficient technologies, considerable environmental damage) and the need to stabilise the intricate ecological systems upon which all life on planet earth depends. Of these, none is more delicately poised than the atmosphere itself, with evidence mounting steadily that human-caused global warming (itself a consequence of the burning of fossil fuels) is a reality.

At the national level, there is a further dilemma which goes to the heart of politics in a democratic country such as Australia. To what extent does fixing up the environment justify the unilateral use of public power (legitimised, within liberal democracies at least, as the exercise of democratically endorsed authority) when such action can directly and negatively affect particular individuals and groups who, consistent with liberal principles, can resent and resist such interference and intrusion into their everyday freedoms, expectations and living standards? For example, should we legislate to stop farmers from engaging in further land clearing? If we do, should we negotiate some form of compensation with them? If all logging in old-growth eucalypt forests is to cease, what happens to timber workers and their families who depend upon logging those forests for their livelihood? Conversely, what if public power (however democratically endorsed) is used for purposes that seem to threaten rather than protect the environment? If, for example, a roads department wants to blast a new motorway through bushland near where you live, what rights should you have to oppose such a move?

Making progress with many environmental problems requires not only a good understanding of how to translate ecological values into practical management strategies, but also an appreciation of the human consequences of change. On whom should the costs of environmental amelioration fall?

These are huge questions. Inevitably and appropriately, liberal democracies will need to devise solutions that embrace both private and public action. This chapter argues that, while private initiatives will continue to grow in importance, it is public policies (that is, collective, democratically endorsed decision making using the powers of the state) operating at local, regional, national and international levels that will be needed to set the new frameworks in place.

What do we mean by 'the environment'?

The environment is not one problem, or even one kind of problem, but many. One way of classifying environmental issues is to think of them as *green* or *brown*. *Green* environmental issues are those that involve the preservation of pristine (unaltered) or almost-pristine areas of natural beauty and/or ecological significance. In the Australian context, think of the long drawn-out battle to protect the Great Barrier Reef or, in the international arena, the fight to prevent wholesale destruction of the Amazonian rainforest. In political terms, the *green* agenda emphasises the importance of lifestyles and attitudes that embody principles of sustainability; renewable sources of power (solar, wind, hydro) as distinct from non-renewable sources (coal, gas, nuclear).

Brown environmental issues involve efforts to manage a range of human impacts: to halt or even reverse the consequences of past industrial activity, as well as to manage new initiatives. Think of pollution control, sewage treatment, rehabilitation of mine sites or degraded industrial land, the regulation of pesticide use, the disposal of toxic wastes, minimising urban waste, improving energy conservation in cities. The regulation of new technologies, such as the production and marketing of genetically modified food, might also be included in this category.

Many issues do not fit readily into the green or brown categories: for example, cultural heritage protection (keeping buildings, artefacts and landscapes that embody cultural values). Others, such as Aboriginal land rights, while not strictly environmental in themselves, have attracted strong support from green groups because of the special affinity that Indigenous peoples have for their traditional lands.

The types of problems that nations will experience depend very much on their environmental history—where they started from, the types of industries they have developed, and the density of the populations their landmass must support. The environmental problems faced by the Dutch (for example) differ in kind from those faced by Australians. The Netherlands has very little of its original vegetation left; indeed much of its landmass has been artificially reclaimed from the sea. At the same time, it has intensive agriculture in a small, highly fertile area—the disposal of manure from intensive farming is one of the Netherlands' most pressing and difficult issues (de Graaf, Musters & ter Keurs 1999). By contrast, Australia, with a very large, dry, thinly populated landmass, retains parts of its original forest cover, some of it in pristine or 'wilderness' condition. Australian soils lack nutrients and are easily eroded; rainfall is very variable across much of the continent and most forms of intensive agriculture require irrigation, which in turn raises soil salinity (Yencken & Wilkinson 2000).

Australia's environmental problems show a range of characteristics. Many of our industries and activities impact directly on areas of significant environmental value (think of the impact of woodchipping on forests, the constant pressure on coastal estuaries caused by new housing and tourist developments, and the proposals that have been made over the years to drill the Barrier Reef for oil, to mine the sands of Fraser Island, to build a marina near Ningaloo Reef off the coast of Western Australia, and so on). In addition to these specific 'environment versus development' problems, there are pressing needs to address environmental degradation caused by past development (particularly agriculture), as well as safeguarding animal and plant species that are unique to Australia.

At the international level, if human-caused global warming is accepted as a reality, then Australia may well be forced to rethink its opposition to ratifying the Kyoto Protocol on Climate Change; to develop greater energy-efficiency domestically; and, if it wishes to safeguard its export industries, to play a proactive role in relation to new energy-related technologies, such as carbon sequestration, cleaner-burning fossil fuels, and the safer use of nuclear power.

Environmental values

All public policy is values based, because it expresses preferences about desirable states of the world. As Davis and colleagues formulate it: 'Public policy is the interaction of values, interests and resources, guided through institutions and mediated by politics' (Davis *et al.* 1993: 15). Our values, to use Berlin's words, are 'what we think good and bad, important and trivial, right and wrong, noble and contemptible' (Berlin 1998: 127). In a liberal democracy like Australia, broad liberal and democratic values help to shape more specific value judgments. These in turn shape the goals that are embodied in, and implemented through, the collective choices we make through policy processes. Environmental values are these value judgments as applied to the environment.

Are environmental objectives a new kind of phenomenon on the public policy scene, or can we regard them as being no different from other 'valued ends', such as improved health care or better roads? There is a widely shared view among scholars that environmentalism represents a distinctive shift in values from *materialist* to *post-materialist* (Papadakis 1996: 65). *Materialist* in this context refers to economic values, the belief that personal happiness is best served through the pursuit of money, wealth and possessions. *Post-materialist*, most extensively researched by the American sociologist Ronald Inglehart (e.g. 1990), describes a set of animating political values that are based on different principles, largely the need for self-fulfilment in personal life. Post-materialist social movements have championed the rights of oppressed or overlooked groups (such as women or gays) or (in this case) the need to preserve, and indeed to celebrate, the non-human world.

Within the environmental movement, it is possible to discern two distinct value positions, reflecting different perspectives on the relationship between humanity and the natural world. The first, the *deep green* position, argues that harmony between human society and nature requires the overthrow (or at least replacement) of our 'polluting, plundering and materialistic industrial society' and its replacement by a 'new economic and social order'. The second, *light green* position, is satisfied that a managerial approach to the environment, within the context of present political and economic practices, is sufficient (Dobson 1995: 35).

As Australian environmentalism began to gather political momentum in the 1960s and 1970s, it developed a much stronger, radical, 'deep green' edge (Hutton & Connors 1999). In the early 1970s, a number of 'green bans' (imposed by trade unions refusing to permit work on particular developments) cemented alliances between urban residents' action groups and the Builders Labourers Federation. Certain student groups identified themselves with the so-called 'New Left', which (in contrast with the Old Left) preached values of individual creativity and a simpler more fulfilling lifestyle. Some Australian 'baby boomers' (i.e. the generation born in the decade or so after the Second World War) pursued this dream by moving from cities and suburbs to idyllic rural retreats (such as the beautiful countryside around Byron Bay in northern New South Wales) to follow an environmentally committed communal lifestyle, changing forever the politics of these areas and figuring strongly in local environmental campaigns (such as the ultimately successful campaign near Byron Bay to save rainforest at Terania Creek that was due to be logged).

The values of the Australian Greens (the political party that grew out of the environmental activism of the 1970s) remain strongly identified with the agenda of that era: a commitment to local activism and a deep suspicion of the motives and practices of big business, while embracing a raft of other related issues such as Aboriginal reconciliation and opposition to nuclear power and uranium mining.

In the 21st century, the Australian environmental movement, considered as a whole, is extremely diverse, with groups occupying the entire spectrum from palest to deepest green. While the Wilderness Society and Greenpeace continue to advocate radical change, other groups (such as the Australian Conservation Foundation, the National Parks Association and many smaller regional groups) remain dedicated to conservation objectives, working largely within the framework of conventional politics (lobbying governments over specific issues and working where necessary with public bureaucracies to establish new management regimes). In addition to groups that aim to influence public opinion and public policy, important work is being done through private, often not-for-profit bodies that carry out conservation initiatives directly. An example of this type of activism is the Australian Nature Conservancy, a not-for-profit entity that buys land with donated funds, fences it (to keep feral animals out) and uses it to conserve endangered species such as desert mammals in their native habitat.

Membership of environmental groups (at least as reported by those groups) is widespread in Australia, with one 2004 survey estimating that 7 per cent of Australians were members (Australian Election Study 2004) and an earlier 1995 survey putting the figure at 10 per cent (National Social Science Survey as reported in Papadakis & Young 2000: 167), though such estimates may be inflated by respondents identifying themselves as members simply because they had made a donation to an environmental group.

Green politics in Australia

Australia has a long history of environmental concern. The Royal National Park, south of Sydney, was created in 1879 and was one of the first national parks anywhere in the world. In the years before the Second World War, bushwalker and conservationist Miles Dunphy led the way in helping Australians to

understand the beauty of the bush and the need to preserve it for future generations. In the 1930s, Sydney solicitor Marie Byles began the fight to protect bushland at Pittwater near Sydney (later to become Bouddi National Park). By the
1950s, conservationists in NSW, Victoria, South Australia and Queensland had
led campaigns to save significant areas of bushland from development (Hutton
& Connors 1999: ch. 2). It was not until the 1970s, however, that environmental
concern became part of the political agenda at both the State and national levels.

It is not possible to understand Australian environmental politics without
appreciating its federal dimension. Under the Australian Constitution, most
powers that impact directly on the environment (such as land use and planning,
pollution control, and the regulation of industry) belong to the States. Hence
responsibility for the basic environmental resources of land, air and water
remains with the States. The States came under increasing pressure, from the
1970s onwards, to address air and water pollution caused by industry and by
motor vehicle exhausts, leading to the establishment of a range of public agencies
to implement legislation designed to curb the problem.

But environmental concern has also been projected into the national policy
arena, largely because the States, which tend to be dependent on resource-based
industries such as mining and agriculture, often would not (or indeed could not)
readily respond to the new values. The federal government can constitutionally
exercise power over environmental issues that have an international, foreign
policy or trade dimension, and (as Chapter 7 in this book explains) its overwhelming fiscal power may enable it to influence policy in any field that it
wishes via conditional grants to the States. Hence environmental issues have
become a prominent feature of Australian intergovernmental relations and
indeed from time to time provoke significant intergovernmental conflict.

To understand this interplay, we can do no better than to turn to Tasmania.
This is the Australian State with the richest recent history of environmental
politics and policy making and it figures strongly in many excellent accounts
(e.g. Hutton & Connors 1999; Papadakis 1996; Doyle & Kellow 1995; Stewart
& Jones 2003; Dargavel 1995). It is not just that Tasmania's environmental
problems have at times assumed national (and indeed international) significance, or that Tasmania's activists represent the 'deep green' edge of Australian
environmentalism. It is also that the Tasmanian dilemma—how to retain
natural beauty while building a modern economy—is the world's dilemma in
a nutshell.

The Tasmanian environmental story

From the early days of white settlement, and well into the 20th century,
Tasmania subscribed enthusiastically to the developmentalist philosophy that
drove Australian State politics (Bell & Head 1994). Tasmanian industry was

based on hydro-electric power (ironically a form of power now considered clean and green). Hydro-electric power was planned, developed and sold by a public authority, the Hydro-Electric Commission (known locally as 'the Hydro'). But generating power meant damming rivers and creating artificial lakes.

LAKE PEDDER

The Lake Pedder controversy marked the beginning of environmental consciousness for many Australians. Lake Pedder was a natural wonder, an inland lake with a beach of startling beauty. Tasmanian conservationists had been instrumental in pressuring the State government to create the Lake Pedder National Park in 1955. The Hydro's plan to create a larger, artificial lake in order to expand its hydro-electric generating capacity envisaged the end of Lake Pedder in its pristine form. Beginning in the 1960s, Tasmanian conservationists mounted a determined effort to save the lake, but to no avail. The old lake disappeared under the waters of the new, artificial Lake Pedder in 1973.

THE FRANKLIN

The next major issue, the Franklin River, arose when the Hydro planned to dam one of the last 'wild rivers' in Tasmania. The Tasmanian government of the day, reflecting the strong balance of popular opinion in the State at the time, was determined to support the Hydro's plan. The Tasmanian Wilderness Society, of which Bob Brown (much later to be elected as a Tasmanian Senator in the national Parliament) became Director in 1977, was at the forefront of the battle to bring the river's future to the attention of the federal government. The Coalition government in Canberra, led by Prime Minister Fraser, was sympathetic to the goal of saving the Franklin but, in accordance with the Liberal Party's (then) philosophy, held that the river's fate was properly a decision for Tasmania. Thus it decided that it would not intervene, although in 1982 the Fraser government did place Tasmania's south-west wilderness (encompassing the river) on the World Heritage List to which Australia had subscribed by international treaty.

In the end, the Franklin was saved when Bob Hawke, newly installed as Labor leader in 1982 and responding to the immense public concern that the activists had aroused across the nation, placed the issue of stopping the Franklin Dam in the Labor Opposition's policy platform for the 1983 federal election. Labor won that election, and the Hawke government's subsequent legislation to protect the Franklin was upheld by the High Court (on the grounds of the Federal government's international treaty and corporations powers) and the river was saved.

LOGGING OF OLD-GROWTH FORESTS

The preservation of Tasmania's forests was the next major issue, one which pitted environmentalists against the State government, the timber industry, timber workers and the Tasmanian Forestry Commission. While Tasmania's south-west wilderness covered an immense area, much of it was not sought after by the timber industry either because the land did not support trees or because the terrain was too inaccessible and remote to log economically. But the tall, wet forests of the north-east and south-east contained stands of forest giants, trees of immense age and presence. These were the same areas which were most valuable from the point of view of the timber industry.

The battle to save these forests was a different type of campaign from the one that had saved the Franklin, because action was required in a number of localities. It focused in the mid-1980s on the Lemonthyme and southern forests which were adjacent to the south-west World Heritage area. An inquiry headed by Justice Helsham proposed that the two forests be incorporated into the nearby World Heritage wilderness. This would have meant that the forests involved could be protected under Commonwealth legislation. But the Helsham Inquiry, far from defusing the forests issue, simply inflamed it further.

So successful were the Greens in raising environmental concern among Tasmanians that in 1989 five Green candidates were elected to the Tasmanian Parliament. This meant that the Greens held the balance of power. But it was a position which had to be used adroitly because neither of the two major parties had much sympathy with the environmentalist position. Eventually the Greens were able to bring down the Liberal government and forge an Accord with a new Labor government headed by Michael Field. However, the Accord proved short lived, largely because the ideological distance between the Greens and Labor was too great for an enduring compromise to be forged.

DEFUSING CONFLICT: REGIONAL FOREST AGREEMENTS

The next stage in the forests policy story, the formation of a Regional Forest Agreement (RFA) for the whole of Tasmania, resulted from the entry of the Commonwealth government into the process. RFAs—originating from a 1992 intergovernmental National Forests Policy Statement—are formal agreements between Commonwealth and State governments which aim to balance the conflicting claims of conservation and development in Australia's native forests. The agreements provide for the setting up of a 'reserve system that preserves from logging representative examples of every forest ecosystem type, and to establish management plans for the conservation of rare and endangered species. The agreements also set out, for a period of 20 years, the basis on which forest industries, on both public and private land, are to be managed and developed.

Separate RFAs have been negotiated for each State with substantial native forests and, in some cases, for areas within States. While each agreement reflects the particular situation of the area to which it applies, the underlying structure of all RFAs is similar. They rely essentially on a form of land-use planning in which certain areas of forest are allocated to timber production, while others are placed in conservation reserves. Each agreement requires the State government in each case to legislate to give effect to the resulting reserve system. There was provision for annual monitoring of implementation, and for a five-yearly review of outcomes. Once each RFA was signed, the Commonwealth exercised no further direct influence on the timber industry in that area—an important consequence in a policy arena in which Commonwealth–State relations had been difficult.

The Commonwealth played a major role in steering the process in each case, seeking to ensure that the resulting agreement met its own criteria, while confronting a different political scenario in each State. In NSW, an environmentally minded Premier, Bob Carr, created a number of new national parks upon coming to office in 1995, and in that State, conservationists had a stronger say in the trade-offs that occurred with the timber industry, than they did elsewhere. In Tasmania, however, the Greens were effectively shut out of the process, and the RFA represented a decisive industry 'win'. In Western Australia, the RFA effectively collapsed when it was repudiated by the Richard Court government in the lead-up to the 2001 State election, and was superseded when the incoming Labor government led by Geoff Gallop succeeded in placing a moratorium on logging of old-growth forests. In Queensland, a stakeholder-led process that involved a staged transition towards plantation-based forestry was rejected by the Commonwealth on the somewhat surprising grounds that it did not deal with old-growth forests in the prescribed way (Brown 2001).

The RFAs describe and give effect to a number of balances and compromises: between the Commonwealth and the States, and between conservationists and economic interests (miners, loggers and processors). For the Commonwealth, weary of forest disputes, retirement from the fray was undoubtedly a welcome relief. The States were happy to resume unimpeded control of their forest assets. But many conservationists were apprehensive about the withdrawal of Commonwealth government power in from such a vital area.

It has been argued by some critics that the RFAs represent an old approach in which trade-offs based on compromises between interests are orchestrated 'top-down' by governments, rather than via a more appropriate 'new politics' of sustainability (which would fit industry to the environment, rather than the other way around) or even of adaptive management. But the RFAs do represent a start and, in any case, as the agreements unfold on the ground (and in some cases at least, it appears as though the timber supply targets cannot be met in the longer run), further changes will be required. Environmental governance is never over, but must of necessity evolve and adapt.

Institutions for the earth

A key question in environmental policy analysis is the extent to which environmental renovation requires institutional change—that is, a change in the kinds of organisations, processes and rules that constitute our approach to environmental governance. There is certainly a good deal of evidence to suggest that 'institutions for the earth', to use a phrase coined by Haas, Keohane & Levy (1993), can be constructed out of the raw materials of conventional politics. For example, an analysis by Levy (1993) of the European response to acid rain (the product of sulphur dioxide produced by power stations burning 'dirty' coal) shows that effective regulation of polluting activities can be achieved provided that the problem is seen as significant enough by a sufficiently large political constituency to have it placed on the political agenda.

'Institutions for the earth' in the international arena are characterised by concerted processes of international bargaining and, as with institutions at the national level, are easier to construct when there is a clearly defined problem, a good scientific understanding of the processes involved, and a technical solution that can be implemented without undue disruption to business, industry or consumers. The Montreal Protocol, which was established in 1992 in response to the hole in the ozone layer, is an example of this kind of problem and response.

Environmentalism and the policy agenda

Despite the importance and centrality of environmental questions, the environment waxes and wanes as a political issue (Downs 1972). The 1980s have been described as the 'green decade' of Australian federal politics, culminating in the 1990 election win for Labor in which Green preferences were decisive (Warhurst 1990). But the 1990s were much quieter. The RFAs, begun by a federal Labor government in the early 1990s, were arguably as much an attempt to get forests off the national political agenda as they were motivated by any environmental concern (Dargavel 1998).

The Howard Coalition government, in office since 1996, has applied its own particular brand of anaesthetic to the issue by enacting (in 1999) the *Environment Protection and Biodiversity Conservation Act*. This Act more tightly circumscribes the Commonwealth's involvement in environmental matters (Mercer 2000: 95–6; Crowley 2004). While not a particularly federalist government in other areas, the Howard government evidently concluded that the environment could be safely depoliticised by passing it back to the States. The Howard government has refused to ratify the Kyoto Protocol on Climate Change. But this was not a significant election issue in 2004, while Labor leader

Mark Latham's clumsy attempt to favour the conservationists' side in Tasmania's continuing forest battles backfired badly.

But environmental questions have not so much gone away as become institutionalised within the Australian governmental system itself (Howlett & Ramesh 1995: 112–3). In addition to agencies with specific environmental functions, there are now mandated processes for evaluating environmental risks when new developments are proposed. An Environmental Impact Assessment (EIA) requires proponents to address not only ecological consequences but also a range of social and economic impacts. Legislation to mandate EIAs was initially enacted by the Commonwealth in 1974, and had been introduced in all Australian States by the mid-1980s (Gilpin 1995). A set of principles governing EIAs was agreed to by Commonwealth and State Environment Ministers in 1992, and includes principles for proponents to observe as well as guidance for authorities (including the promotion of public participation throughout the process). More generally, the principles of ecologically sustainable development, while they continue to be difficult to put into practice, are now expressed as statutory objectives in more than 120 Australian laws (Dovers 2003: 144).

The characteristics of environmental problems and the implications for policy making

This chapter has argued that environmental problems pose particular challenges to policy-making systems. Understanding the nature of these challenges helps us to appreciate just why solutions are so difficult, and why it will be necessary to develop new forms of governance to connect the policy-making and policy-implementation apparatus of the state with stakeholder views and interests, and the needs of the ecosystem.

COMPLEXITY

Environmental problems require two very different sorts of systems—ecological systems and economic systems—to be linked. Environmental science can describe the processes that lead to degradation of natural systems: for example, scientists have shown how removal of vegetation cover in the Western Australian wheatbelt causes salt present in groundwater to be drawn up to the surface, resulting in the land becoming salted and hence unproductive. But doing anything about salinity means changing the agricultural practices that produced the problem, which means intervening in the human economic systems that shape and reflect behaviour. Effective policy interventions, therefore, require some understanding of the complexity of the systems involved.

RISK, UNCERTAINTY AND THE PRECAUTIONARY PRINCIPLE

Our understanding of the working of ecological systems is improving, but ecologists are the first to concede that there is much that is not known. Indeed, in many cases, we do not even know the right questions to ask. In these circumstances, it has been argued that policy makers should observe the 'precautionary principle'—that is, where there are threats of serious or irreversible environmental damage, lack of full scientific certainty should not be used as a reason for postponing measures to prevent environmental degradation (Intergovernmental Agreement on the Environment 1992, s. 3.5.1). The precautionary principle is, however, difficult to apply in practice, when decisions must be made in response to urgent proposals for new developments and changing circumstances in existing management regimes. While environmental impact assessments attempt to identify and quantify the environmental 'bads' that may flow from new developments, and so assist in the process of risk assessment, the process often underestimates adverse consequences.

SCALE

So-called 'point-source' pollution (such as when a paper mill deposits toxic waste in a river) is relatively easy to identify. But most environmental problems have much more diffuse sources (for example, photochemical smog caused by car exhausts, and the over-loading of rubbish tips caused by exuberant consumerism, planned obsolescence and the over-packaging of goods). The behaviour of many people must change if there is to be any real improvement in these areas: ways must be found (for example) to encourage public transport use, and to promote recycling. But success in these areas requires complex strategies to change the systems that produce the behaviour in the first place. For example, more Australians will not use public transport unless it is more convenient and accessible, yet most Australian cities were built around the motor vehicle, with public transport either non-existent or operating on only a limited number of routes. 'Sustainable cities' must somehow address the dominance of the private motor vehicle (Newman, Kenworthy & Vintila 1992).

IRREVERSIBILITY

Species extinction is the most obvious example of environmental irreversibility, because it truly is forever. Most people feel the world is the poorer when we lose fascinating and unique species such as the Tasmanian tiger, although the loss of less-heralded animals (such as species of ants) may have far greater ecological implications. Species loss from particular geographical areas can be reversed, but only if the habitat can be restored to some semblance of its pristine condition, so that re-introduced animals do not suffer the fate of their predecessors. While some degraded environments can be repaired, reducing the pressures that caused the degradation takes immense effort. Australia's Snowy River, diverted since the early 1950s to furnish the Snowy Mountains hydro-electricity scheme with water, received an environmental flow for the first time in 50 years in 2002. But this was only after years of concerted lobbying by environmentalists, extensive work by public agencies to establish a scientific basis for environmental flows, legislative opportunities provided by the corporatisation of the Snowy Mountains Hydro-Electric Authority, and a favourable alignment of political forces in the Victorian Parliament resulting from the election of an Independent member for Gippsland East (White 2004).

EXTERNALITIES

The discipline of economics can assist policy makers to give quantitative form to environmental issues and to structure problems in ways that give a clearer perspective on economic costs and benefits (Common 1995). The economic concept of 'externalities' (sometimes called 'spillovers') is particularly important. It provides a rationale for government to get involved in environmental regulation by demonstrating the limits of unregulated markets. It also enables analysts to come to grips with the way in which environmental problems and solutions can displace costs from one group to another and hence create high levels of conflict.

'Externalities' simply refer to instances where the costs (or benefits) of an action are not reflected in the system of market prices. For example, consider two neighbours. Neighbour 1 lives in a nice, quiet street. But this suburban tranquility is shattered when the house next door is occupied by a noisy newcomer (Neighbour 2) who is in the habit of playing very loud music at all hours of the day and night. This is a *negative externality*, imposing costs on Neighbour 1 (lost sleep, nervous stress) that Neighbour 1 cannot recoup from Neighbour 2 through the normal private economic market. Public policy intervention is thus required, e.g. to establish enforceable legal rights to quiet enjoyment or more specifically in the form of anti-noise laws setting limits on the amount and timing of noise that people may emit.

But developing these kinds of regulatory regimes and then implementing them is not a simple task. Where the externality caused by the actions of individuals is small in relation to the overall environmental resource, we have what Hardin (1968) has famously described as 'the tragedy of the commons'. The phrase describes the situation where a natural resource (such as a fishery or a forest) tends to be over-used, because each person has an incentive to utilise the resource to satisfy his or her own wants and to reap the full benefit of doing so, while only incurring a small fraction of the resultant costs which are shared among all users. Strict regulation, usually in the form of quotas, is required to limit exploitation to sustainable levels, but new technologies often outpace the regulators. In extreme cases (as in the cod fishing industry off Atlantic Canada in 1992), over-exploitation can lead to the collapse of the resource and permanent closure of the industry (Grafton, Steinshamn & Sandal 2000).

EQUITY

Politics is often characterised by short-term thinking. In Australia, federal governments are elected for a maximum period of three years, and this can lead to short time-horizons. Environmental sustainability, however, means taking the needs of future generations into account—i.e. considering 'intergenerational equity'—when making decisions today. While public policy is capable of responding to longer-term as well as to immediate issues (e.g. consider the changes to superannuation policy designed to lessen Australia's future dependence upon the publicly funded old-age pension system), the environmental needs of future generations are more difficult define, and much more difficult to 'sell' to voters.

Equity issues also arise when industries are restructured in response to new environmental policy priorities. Environmentalists need to be particularly sensitive to this. They tend to be urban and middle class, with jobs in the knowledge economy (teaching or professional work of various kinds). But many communities dependent in a direct way on natural resources (for example, timber towns or small-scale irrigation settlements) are less well off and often less well educated. Contraction of their industries will impose a higher relative cost on these communities than on those urging change. When the rules change in this sort of way, equitable treatment requires that some form of compensation should be directed to those negatively affected.

CONFLICT

Many environmental issues generate high levels of conflict (Mercer 2000; Stewart & Jones 2003). These conflicts arise from a complex interplay of values and interests. Some conflicts are sudden and colourful, with the media especially likely to be interested when there are physical confrontations. Other disputes, however, simmer over many years. For example, some landowners whose properties adjoin national parks in the Australian Alps have been highly critical of what they see as the failure of public authorities managing the parks to reduce fuel loads by regular burning, but the public authorities themselves see this practice as being overly interventionist. Legal remedies, while they may give a short-term victory to one side or the other, do very little to address the underlying differences in values and outlooks, which often require more consultative processes to identify and resolve. Conflict is not necessarily bad in itself, because it provides political energy for the resolution of complex problems, but the skills and time for dealing with it are often not available when politicians demand 'quick-fix' solutions.

THE ENVIRONMENT AND PUBLIC BUREAUCRACIES

Public bureaucracies are often described as 'silos'—their work takes place via organised hierarchies dedicated to particular functions. Thus there tend to be separate State government departments for lands, for water, for roads, for mines, for forests, and so on. Such functional separation has its merits when there is a clear, narrowly circumscribed job to be done but it has many deficiencies when it comes to addressing problems of policy and management that cross functional boundaries.

Attempts have been made to introduce new kinds of whole-of-government networked management, or horizontal governance, to overcome the effects of the silos (Edwards & Longford 2002). When environmental issues began to require new institutions in the 1970s, Environmental Protection Agencies and Departments of the Environment were created. But it is impossible to make meaningful policy for the environment without changing the policies and practices of the industry-based departments at the same time. State governments have made a number of attempts to rebalance their agencies by splitting regulatory from production activities (for example in relation to forestry) and by creating agencies with integrated resource management functions. In addition, new kinds of governance have been established away from the capital cities. Catchment management authorities, for example, bring together community, government and industry representatives to give advice to Ministers about the management of specific river catchments (Stewart 1997).

BOUNDARY-CROSSING

Political and ecological boundaries rarely coincide. The most prominent Australian example of this is the Murray–Darling Basin, a river catchment that occupies most of south-eastern Australia and which includes parts of four States—Queensland, New South Wales, Victoria and South Australia—as well as the Australian Capital Territory. For most of the 20th century, these State governments, along with the Commonwealth, searched for ways to reconcile their constituents' competing claims to the water. A Ministerial Council comprising Ministers from each participating State and from the Commonwealth responsible for land, water and environmental management constitutes the key intergovernmental negotiating forum for the river system. The executive arm of the Council, the River Murray Commission, was established in 1916, and became the Murray–Darling Basin Commission in 1987. From 1995, the Ministerial Council agreed to impose 'caps' on water extraction from the river, with each state required to observe its component of the overall cap (Independent Audit Group 2004).

Other intergovernmental institutions have also evolved. Examples include groundwater management (e.g. a cross-border management agreement between Victoria and South Australia), arrangements to improve consultation in relation to national parks in the Australian Alps (encompassing Victoria, the ACT and NSW), and the coordination of decision making for the Lake Eyre Basin (Crabb 2003).

Policy instruments

Governments possess a range of tools they can use to influence individual behaviour, to resolve conflict and to bring new technologies to bear on environmental problems.

INCENTIVES

According to economists, one of the reasons we gobble up environmental resources is because they are part of the 'commons' (not owned by individuals), they are under-priced and they are therefore under-valued. As a result, the incentives are perverse. If water, for example, is underpriced or is sold as a 'block' entitlement (that is, a fixed charge with little or no consumption-related component), then there is no incentive to use less. Yet until the National Competition Policy reforms of 1994 mandated a consumption-based component for water-charging, most Australian households paid for water, to varying degrees, via fixed charges (Australian Department of Environment and Heritage 2001). Where price reform is not possible, governments can reshape incentives by taxing goods or services that create environmental costs. Carbon taxes have been proposed as one solution to the problem of excessive fossil fuel use (Common 1995). By the same token, environmentally friendly technologies can be encouraged through the price system—rebates for the installation of rainwater tanks, or solar heaters, for example.

REGULATION

Regulation involves setting rules for conduct, and can range from precisely specified legal requirements to more flexible guidelines. Specific enforceable emissions standards, for example, have the advantage of being clear, they can be monitored by inspectors, and offenders prosecuted or fined. But there is evidence that more flexible regulatory approaches, in which regulators act as educators rather than enforcers (while still retaining their capacity to use their powers under the law where necessary) can work better (Ayres & Braithwaite 1992).

MARKET-BASED INSTRUMENTS

Many environmentalists are wary of market-based instruments because they are convinced that it is marked-based capitalist production, and the political forces that accompany it, that has been a major factor in causing environmental degradation (Crowley 2004). They look to the legislative power of the state to prevent further despoliation, and are suspicious of attempts to use market-based mechanisms to bring about improvements. Creating markets in environmental resources (such as air and water) is particularly controversial because, in order for markets to work, ownership rights in the particular resource to be traded must first be established.

It is now possible in parts of the Murray–Darling Basin for water to be bought and sold via tradeable water rights. For example, a licence to extract a certain quantity of water from the Murray River at a downstream point might be sold to an upstream producer who is able to make more money than the original owner from using the water (and hence is prepared to pay a higher price for the entitlement). Tradeable water rights are seen as a good way of implementing extraction caps, because the available water goes to higher-valued uses, thereby improving the efficiency of the system as a whole. Emissions trading, in which firms that meet emissions targets can on-sell their entitlement, is another example of an environmental market.

While they may be a good idea in theory, markets in environmental 'goods' and 'bads' need considerable nurturing to make them work effectively. Water markets, in particular, are problematic, as 'sleeper' licences (held by licence holders who do not make use of them) may be reactivated (because they now have a market value) and sold, with the effect of increasing rather than reducing demand pressures. And redistributing water use does not necessarily improve the environment unless, over time, extraction targets are reduced (McKay 2003: 379).

ACTION STRATEGIES

There is a growing understanding that the next stage of environmental modernisation in Australia will require coordinated action across a number of fronts. Action plans or strategies provide ways of drawing resources together to combat problems with complex causes and many interests to consider. A good example is the National Salinity Action Plan, which mandates a range of actions to address the problem, involving public agencies, farmers and the community.

Action strategies represent collaborative rather than authoritative policy values as governments, both State and federal, have opted for policy instruments that rely on persuasion to change behaviour, rather than legislating for it.

PARTNERSHIPS

If the environment challenges governments, it has also produced considerable policy creativity. An example is Landcare, a program to restore mainly rural environments based on partnerships between governments, landowners and community groups. Beginning in Victoria in the 1980s, Landcare was adopted nationally later in the decade, and now involves over 4000 Landcare groups with around 120 000 volunteer members (Curtis 2003). A number of programs for community-based environmental monitoring (such as Waterwatch) have also been implemented (Harding & Trainor 2003).

Environmentalism and the liberal-democratic state

The array of policy instruments that can be deployed by governments show the potential and the limitations of the liberal-democratic state in responding to environmental challenges. New technologies of governing have shown that the state may work, not only as a commander, but also as a facilitator and broker, producing practical compromises and encouraging policy learning (Eckersley 1995).

Some scholars have argued that this is about as good as it gets, and that the political economy of advanced capitalism, with its globalisation of production and consumption and its all-pervasive media, precludes more radical institutional change (Walker 1994). The type of radical change required is much debated. John Dryzek (among others) has proposed that standard forms of representative democracy, in which voters lose direct control over their elected representatives, should give way to forms of 'discursive democracy', in which political meaning is created through devolved forms of discussion and debate, from which he is apparently confident that environmentally wise decisions will emerge (Dryzek 1990).

A test of political and policy capacity is the degree of environmental improvement that results. So, how well are we doing in relation to the environment?

Despite a well-developed scientific infrastructure, we do not know what the specific trends are for a number of key variables, because systematic measurement and monitoring have not yet been done in Australia. But the *State of the Environment* report (issued every five years) does record legislated and strategy-based conservation activity across a wide range of habitats (Australian Department of Environment and Heritage 2001). Where there has been concerted action over a number of years, there have been some notable successes: for example, the clean-up of Sydney's beaches; and the successful conservation of humpback whales. Overall, however, the story is one of continuing pressures and inadequate responses. The 2001 *State of the Environment* report concluded that 'the state of the Australian natural environment has improved very little since 1996, and in some critical respects, has worsened' (Australian Department of Environment and Heritage 2001: 8). Water quality in inland rivers and in many estuaries continues to deteriorate; dryland salinity affects 5 per cent of the land area in cultivation, with the same area again considered to be at risk; native vegetation continues to be cleared at an accelerating pace, particularly in Queensland; biodiversity (the range of plants and animals in particular areas) is on the decline (Australian Department of Environment and Heritage 2001).

Internationally, particularly in the less developed world, pressures on remaining pristine environments are relentless. Not surprisingly, developing countries wish to exploit their resources as their richer exemplars have done. Even if the Kyoto Protocol is fully implemented, it will make little difference to global warming because of the exclusion of the developing world from emission-reduction targets (Lomborg 1998: 302)

Public policy in the developed world remains dominated, at a fundamental level, by the imperatives of growth. More growth is accepted as good, and less growth is regarded as bad. Governments that do not deliver low interest rates and a buoyant economy are punished at the polls. Australia is no exception. While this situation continues, it is difficult to see how decisive progress towards the goal of ecological sustainability can be achieved.

REFERENCES

Australian Department of Environment and Heritage, 2001, *Australia State of the Environment 2001*, <http://www.deh.gov.au/soe>, accessed 26/3/05.

Australian Election Study 2004, <http://www.assda.anu.edu.au>.

Ayres, I. & Braithwaite, J. 1992, *Responsive Regulation*, Oxford University Press, New York.

Bell, S. & Head, B. 1994, *State, Economy and Public Policy in Australia*, Oxford University Press, Melbourne.

Berlin, I. 1998, *The Proper Study of Mankind: An Anthology of Essays*, Pimlico, London.

Brown, A. 2001, 'Beyond Public Native Forest Logging: National Forest Policy and Regional Forest Agreements after South East Queensland', *Environmental and Planning Law Journal*, vol. 18, no. 2, April, 189–208.

Common, M. 1995, *Sustainability and Public Policy: Limits to Economics*, Cambridge University Press, Cambridge.

Crabb, C. 2003, 'Straddling Boundaries: Intergovernmental Arrangements in Managing Human Resources', in eds S. Dovers & S. Wild River, *Managing Australia's Environment*, Federation Press, Sydney.

Crowley, K. 2004, 'Environmental Policy and Politics in Australia', in A. Fenna, *Australian Public Policy*, 2nd edn, Pearson Education Australia, Frenchs Forest, NSW.

Curtis, A. 2003, 'The Landcare Experience', in eds S. Dovers & S. Wild River, *Managing Australia's Environment*, Federation Press, Sydney.

Dargavel, J. 1995, *FashioningAustralia's Forests*, Oxford University Press, Melbourne.

Dargavel, J. 1998, 'Politics, Policy and Process in the Forests', *Australian Journal of Environmental Management*, vol 5, no. 1, March, pp. 25–37.

Davis, G., Wanna, J., Warhurst, J. & Weller, P. 1993, *Public Policy in Australia*, 2nd edn, Allen & Unwin, Sydney.

de Graaf, H. Musters, C. & ter Keurs, W. 1999, *Regional Opportunities for Sustainable Development: Theory, Methods, and Applications*, Kluwer, Dordrecht.

Dobson, A. 1995, *Green Political Thought*, Routledge, London.

Dovers, S. 2003, 'Discrete, Consultative Policy Processes: Lessons from the National Conservation Strategy for Australia and National Strategy for Ecologically Sustainable Development', in eds S. Dovers & S. Wild River, *Managing Australia's Environment*, Federation Press, Sydney.

Downs, A. 1972, 'Up and Down with Ecology: The "Issue-Attention" Cycle', *The Public Interest*, vol. 28, pp. 38–50.

Doyle T. & Kellow A. 1995, *Environmental Politics and Policy Making in Australia*, Macmillan Education, South Melbourne.

Dryzek, J. 1990, *Discursive Democracy—Politics, Policy and Political Science*, Cambridge University Press, Melbourne.

Eckersley, R. ed. 1995, *Markets, the State and the Environment: Towards Integration*, Macmillan, Melbourne.

Edwards, M. & Longford, J. eds 2002, *New Players, Partners and Processes: A Public Sector Without Boundaries*, National Institute for Governance, Canberra.

Gilpin, A. 1995, *Environmental Impact Assessment: Cutting Edge for the Twenty First Century*, Cambridge University Press, Cambridge.

Grafton, R., Steinshamn, S. & Sandal, L. 2000, 'How to Improve the Management of Renewable Resources: The Case of Canada's Cod Fishery', *American Journal of Agricultural Economics*, vol. 82, pp. 570–80, August 2000.

Haas P., Keohane, R. & Levy M. 1993, *Institutions for the Earth: Sources of Effective International Environmental Protection*, MIT Press, Cambridge, Mass.

Hardin, G. 1968, 'The Tragedy of the Commons', *Science*, vol. 162 pp. 1243–8.

Harding, A. & Trainor, D. 2003, 'Informing ESD: State of Environment Reporting', in eds S. Dovers & S. Wild River, *Managing Australia's Environment*, Federation Press, Sydney.

Howlett, M. & Ramesh, M. 1995, *Studying Public Policy: Policy Cycles and Policy Subsystems*, Oxford University Press, Don Mills, Ontario.

Hutton, D. & Connors, L. 1999, *A History of the Australian Environmental Movement*, Cambridge University Press, Melbourne.

Independent Audit Group 2004, *Review of Cap Implementation 2002/03*, <http://www.mdbc.gov.au>, accessed 28/3/05.

Inglehart, R. 1990, *Culture Shift in Advanced Industrial Society*, Princeton University Press, Princeton.

Intergovernmental Agreement on the Environment 1992, Canberra, <http://www.deh.gov.au>.

Levy, M. 1993, 'European Acid-Rain: The Power of Tote-Board Diplomacy', in P. Haas, R. Keohane & M. Levy, 1993, *Institutions for the Earth: Sources of Effective International Environmental Protection*, MIT Press, Cambridge, Mass.

Lomborg, B. 1998, *The Skeptical Environmentalist: Measuring the Real State of the World*, Cambridge University Press, Cambridge.

McKay, J. 2003, 'Marketisation in Australian Freshwater and Fisheries Management Regimes', in eds S. Dovers & S. Wild River, *Managing Australia's Environment*, Federation Press, Sydney.

Mercer, D. 2000, *A Question of Balance: Natural resource Conflict Issues in Australia*, 3rd edn, Federation Press, Leichhardt NSW.

Newman, P., Kenworthy, J. & Vintila, P. 1992, *Housing, Transport and Urban Form*, Australian Government Publishing Service, Canberra.

Papadakis, E. 1996, *Environmental Politics and Institutional Change*, Cambridge University Press, Melbourne.

Papadakis, E. & Young, L. 2000, 'Mediating Clashing Values: Environmental Policy', in eds G. Davis & M. Keating, *The Future of Governance: Policy Choices*, Allen & Unwin, Sydney.

Stewart, J. 1997, 'Australian Water Management: Towards the Ecological Bureaucracy?', *Environmental and Planning Law Journal*, vol. 14, no. 4, August, pp. 259–67.

Stewart, J. & Jones, G. 2003, *Renegotiating the Environment: The Power of Politics*, Federation Press, Sydney.

Walker, K. 1994, *The Political Economy of Environmental Policy: An Australian Introduction*, University of NSW Press, Sydney.

Warhurst, J. 1990, 'The National Campaign', in eds C. Bean, I. McAllister & J. Warhurst, *The Greening of Australian Politics: The 1990 Federal Election*, Longman Cheshire, Melbourne.

White, G. 2004, 'The Snowy River Alliance Story', <http://www.snowyriveralliance.com.au>, accessed 28/3/05.

Yencken, D. & Wilkinson, D. 2000, *Resetting the Compass: Australia's Journey Towards Sustainability*, CSIRO Publishing, Melbourne.

Index